D0612405

fodor's

# OREGON
## 4TH EDITION

Where to Stay and Eat
for All Budgets

Must-See Sights
and Local Secrets

Ratings You Can Trust

Fodor's Travel Publications   New York, Toronto, London, Sydney, Auckland
www.fodors.com

**FODOR'S OREGON**

**Editor:** Paul Eisenberg

**Editorial Contributors:** Zach Dundas, Susan Honthumb, Satu Hummasti, Sarah Kennedy, Janna Mock-Lopez, Lori Tobias

**Maps:** David Lindroth, *cartographer*; Bob Blake and Rebecca Baer, *map editors*

**Design:** Fabrizio La Rocca, *creative director* ; Guido Caroti, *art director*; Melanie Marin, *senior picture editor*

**Production/Manufacturing:** Angela L. McLean

**Cover Photo:** (Hood River Valley): Craig Tuttle/Corbis

Fourth Edition

ISBN 1-4000-1314-3

ISSN 1523-8776

**SPECIAL SALES**

This book is available for special discounts for bulk purchases for sales promotions or premiums. Special editions, including personalized covers, excerpts of existing books, and corporate imprints, can be created in large quantities for special needs. For more information, write to Special Markets/Premium Sales, 1745 Broadway, MD 6-2, New York, NY 10019 or e-mail specialmarkets@randomhouse.com. Inquiries from Canada should be directed to your local Canadian bookseller or sent to Random House of Canada, Ltd., Marketing Department, 2775 Matheson Boulevard East, Mississauga, Ontario L4W 4P7. Inquiries from the United Kingdom should be sent to Fodor's Travel Publications, 20 Vauxhall Bridge Road, London SW1V 2SA, England.

**AN IMPORTANT TIP & AN INVITATION**

Although all prices, opening times, and other details in this book are based on information supplied to us at press time, changes occur all the time in the travel world, and Fodor's cannot accept responsibility for facts that become outdated or for inadvertent errors or omissions. So **always confirm information when it matters,** especially if you're making a detour to visit a specific place. Your experiences—positive and negative—matter to us. If we have missed or misstated something, **please write to us.** We follow up on all suggestions. Contact the Oregon editor at editors@fodors.com or c/o Fodor's at 1745 Broadway, New York, NY 10019.

PRINTED IN THE UNITED STATES OF AMERICA

10 9 8 7 6 5 4 3 2 1

# DESTINATION OREGON

High in the Oregon Cascades near a tiny isolated lake, peaks wrapped in autumn snow are blurred by the dusk. As the sun sinks in the west, darkness falls over the dense forest. A wispy fog from the upper basin slips over the lake; the tall firs creak in the wind, and to the east, barely visible, three rugged peaks shrug in the distance. Hundreds more tableaux, similar in composition and serenity, recur throughout the state. The sensation of being alone with nature, of being in the very cup of her hands, is familiar to those who live in Oregon. Within a 90-minute drive from Portland or Eugene, you can lose yourself on uncrowded ocean beaches, in a snow-silvered mountain wilderness, or in a monolith-studded desert. On your first full day, mingle with the glorious chill and light of daybreak and you'll discover morning the way it was meant to be. This is not tourism gimmickry: these are the same treasures and moments that so thrill Oregonians themselves. Welcome. Or—and this is often more accurate for those who come to the state—welcome back.

*Karen Cure, Editorial Director*

# CONTENTS

About This Book *F6*
On the Road with Fodor's *F12*
What's Where *F13*
Great Itineraries *F16*
When to Go *F18*
On the Calendar *F19*
Pleasures & Pastimes *F24*
Fodor's Choice *F26*
Smart Travel Tips *F32*

**1    The Oregon Coast**                                                  *1*

The Oregon Coast A to Z *55*

**2    Portland**                                                          *59*

Exploring Portland *63*          Sports & the Outdoors *117*
Where to Eat *83*                Shopping *121*
Where to Stay *99*               Portland A to Z *126*
Nightlife & the Arts *111*

**3    The Columbia River Gorge & the Oregon Cascades**                    *133*

The Oregon Cascades *158*        The Columbia River Gorge
Side Trip to Washington *165*       & the Oregon Cascades
                                    A to Z *166*

**4    Central Oregon**                                                    *170*

Central Oregon A to Z *195*

**5    The Willamette Valley & the Wine Country**                          *199*

The Willamette Valley & the
   Wine Country A to Z *244*

**6    Southern Oregon**                                                   *248*

Southern Oregon A to Z *281*

**7    Eastern Oregon**                                                    *285*

Eastern Oregon A to Z *326*

**Understanding Oregon**                                                   *330*

Oregon Country *331*             Books & Movies *337*
Pacific Northwest Field
   Guide *333*

**Index**                                                                  *339*

## Maps

The Pacific Northwest *F8–F9*
Oregon *F10–F11*
**The Oregon Coast** *8*
**Downtown, the Pearl District &
  Old Town & Chinatown** *66*
Nob Hill & Vicinity *76*
Washington Park & Forest
  Park *78*
East of the Willamette
  River *81*
Where to Eat in Portland *84–85*
Where to Stay in
  Portland *100–101*

**Columbia River Gorge &
  the Cascades** *142*
**Central Oregon** *176*
Bend *185*
**Willamette Valley & Wine
  Country** *204*
Salem *224*
Eugene *235*
**Southern Oregon** *256*
Crater Lake National
  Park *257*
**Eastern Oregon** *294*

## CloseUps

Astoria's Colorful Past *11*
Beloved Lousy Weather *17*
Lighthouse Lore *36*
Coming Up Roses *68*
Microbrews of the Pacific
  Northwest *91*
The Shanghai Tunnels *110*
Great River of the West *144*
Breitenbush: A Spa with a
  Conscience *161*

Three Nations, One
  Landscape *177*
Lava Jive *188*
Oregon's Covered Bridges *237*
The Play's the Thing *269*
Ghost Towns of Eastern
  Oregon *311*
The Lesser-Known Gold
  Rush *315*
Oregon Trail, 1853 *320*

# ABOUT THIS BOOK

There's no doubt that the best source for travel advice is a like-minded friend who's just been where you're headed. But with or without that friend, you'll have a better trip with a Fodor's guide in hand. Once you've learned to find your way around its pages, you'll be in great shape to find your way around your destination.

**SELECTION**

Our goal is to cover the best properties, sights, and activities in their category, as well as the most interesting communities to visit. We make a point of including local food lovers' hot spots as well as neighborhood options, and we avoid all that's touristy unless it's really worth your time. You can go on the assumption that everything you read about in this book is recommended wholeheartedly by our writers and editors. Flip to On the Road with Fodor's to learn more about who they are. It goes without saying that no property mentioned in the book has paid to be included.

**RATINGS**

Orange stars ☆ denote sights and properties that our editors and writers consider the very best in the area covered by the entire book. These, the best of the best, are listed in the Fodor's Choice section in the front of the book. Black stars ★ highlight the sights and properties we deem Highly Recommended, the don't-miss sights within any region. Fodor's Choice and Highly Recommended options in each region are usually listed on the title page of the chapter covering that region. Use the index to find complete descriptions. In cities, sights pinpointed with numbered map bullets ❶ in the margins tend to be more important than those without bullets.

**SPECIAL SPOTS**

Pleasures & Pastimes focuses on types of experiences that reveal the spirit of the destination. Watch for Off the Beaten Path sights. Some are out of the way, some are quirky, and all are worth your while. If the munchies hit while you're exploring, look for Need a Break? suggestions.

**TIME IT RIGHT**

Wondering when to go? Check On the Calendar up front and chapters' Timing sections for weather and crowd overviews and best days and times to visit.

**SEE IT ALL**

Use Fodor's exclusive Great Itineraries as a model for your trip. (For a good overview of the entire destination, follow those that begin the book, or mix regional itineraries from several chapters.) In cities, Good Walks guide you to important sights in each neighborhood; ⌐ indicates the starting points of walks and itineraries in the text and on the map.

**BUDGET WELL**

Hotel and restaurant price categories from ¢ to $$$$ are defined in the opening pages of each chapter; expect to find a balanced selection for every budget. For attractions, we always give standard adult admission fees; reductions are usually available for children, students, and senior citizens. Look in Discounts & Deals in Smart Travel Tips for information on destination-wide ticket schemes.

**BASIC INFO**

Smart Travel Tips lists travel essentials for the entire area covered by the book; city- and region-specific basics end each chapter. To find the best way to get around, see the transportation section; see individual modes of travel ("By Car," "By Train") for details. We assume you'll check Web sites or call for particulars.

| | |
|---|---|
| **ON THE MAPS** | Maps throughout the book show you what's where and help you find your way around. Black and orange numbered bullets ❶❶ in the text correlate to bullets on maps. |
| **BACKGROUND** | In general, we give background information within the chapters in the course of explaining sights as well as in CloseUp boxes and in Understanding Oregon at the end of the book. To get in the mood, review the suggestions in Books & Movies. |
| **FIND IT FAST** | Within the book, chapters are arranged regionally. Chapters are divided into smaller regions, within which towns are covered in logical geographical order; attractive routes and interesting places between towns are flagged as En Route. Heads at the top of each page help you find what you need within a chapter. |
| **DON'T FORGET** | Restaurants are open for lunch and dinner daily unless we state otherwise; we mention dress only when there's a specific requirement and reservations only when they're essential or not accepted—it's always best to book ahead. Hotels have private baths, phone, TVs, and air-conditioning and operate on the European Plan (a.k.a. EP, meaning without meals). We always list facilities but not whether you'll be charged extra to use them, so when pricing accommodations, find out what's included. |
| **SYMBOLS** | |

**Many Listings**

- ★ Fodor's Choice
- ★ Highly recommended
- ⊠ Physical address
- ⊹ Directions
- 🕮 Mailing address
- ☎ Telephone
- 🖷 Fax
- ⊕ On the Web
- ✉ E-mail
- 🎫 Admission fee
- ☉ Open/closed times
- ► Start of walk/itinerary
- Ⓜ Metro stations
- ⊟ Credit cards

**Outdoors**

- 🏌 Golf
- ⛺ Camping

**Hotels & Restaurants**

- 🏨 Hotel
- 🛏 Number of rooms
- ⚲ Facilities
- 🍽 Meal plans
- ✕ Restaurant
- ⟁ Reservations
- 🏛 Dress code
- ↘ Smoking
- 🍸 BYOB
- ✕🏨 Hotel with restaurant that warrants a visit

**Other**

- ⚄ Family-friendly
- 🛈 Contact information
- ⇨ See also
- ⊠ Branch address
- ☞ Take note

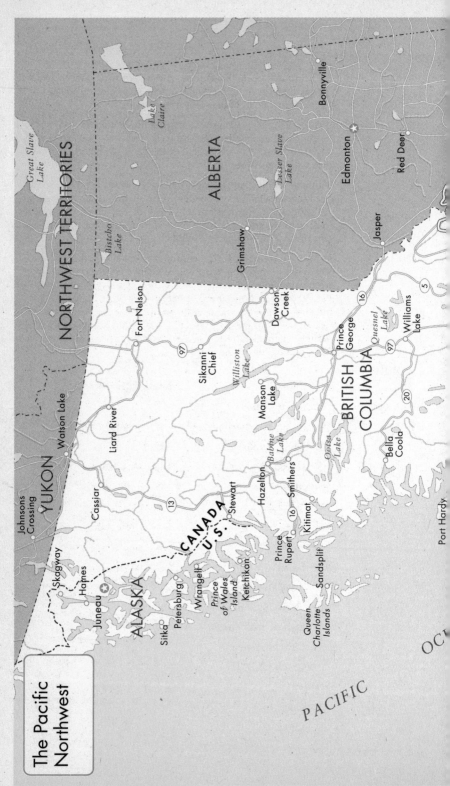

The Pacific Northwest

NORTHWEST TERRITORIES

Great Slave Lake

Lake Claire

Bistcho Lake

ALBERTA

Lesser Slave Lake

Bonnyville

Edmonton

Red Deer

Jasper

Grimshaw

Fort Nelson

Dawson Creek

Prince George

Quesnel Lake

Williams Lake

Sikanni Chief

Williston Lake

Manson Lake

Babine Lake

Ootsa Lake

BRITISH COLUMBIA

Bella Coola

Watson Lake

Liard River

Hazelton

Smithers

Kitimat

Prince Rupert

Sandspit

Port Hardy

Cassiar

Johnsons Crossing

YUKON

Skagway

Haines

Juneau

Sitka

Petersburg

Wrangell

Prince of Wales Island

Ketchikan

Stewart

CANADA

U.S.

ALASKA

Queen Charlotte Islands

PACIFIC

OCE

97

16

5

20

97

13

16

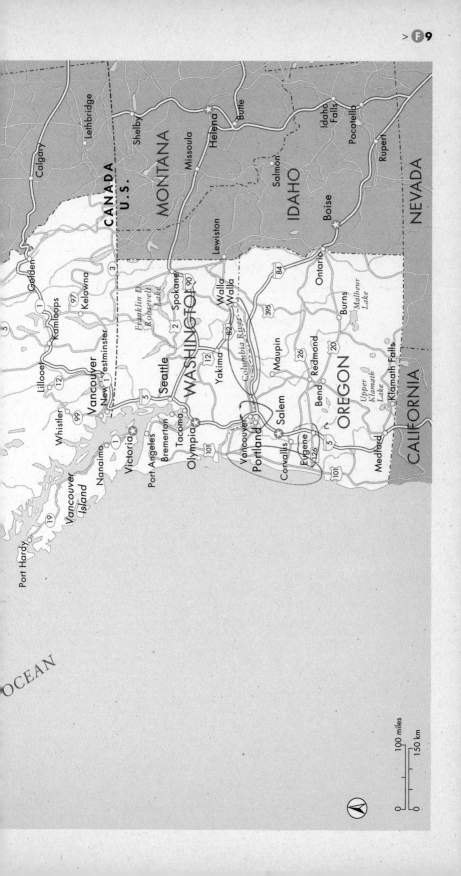

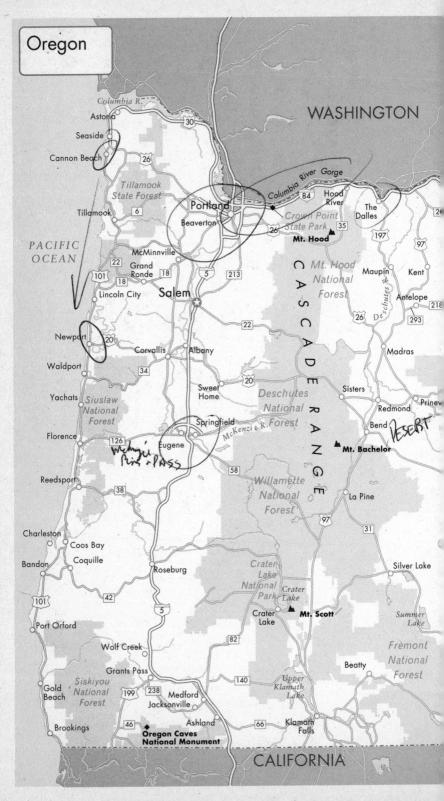

Oregon

WASHINGTON

Columbia R.

Astoria

Seaside

Cannon Beach

Tillamook
State Forest

30

26

6

Columbia River Gorge

Portland

Beaverton

Crown Point
State Park

84

Hood
River

The Dalles

26

35

Mt. Hood

197

24

PACIFIC
OCEAN

Tillamook

McMinnville

Grand
Ronde

22

18

101

18

Lincoln City

Salem

5

213

Maupin

Kent

Antelope

26

293

22

C
A
S
C
A
D
E

Mt. Hood
National
Forest

Deschutes R.

Newport

20

Corvallis

Albany

20

Madras

Waldport

34

Yachats

Siuslaw
National
Forest

Sweet
Home

Deschutes
National
Forest

Sisters

Redmond

Prinev

Bend

DESERT

Florence

126

Springfield

McKenzie R.

Eugene

McKenzie
Pass+PASS

58

R
A
N
G
E

Mt. Bachelor

Reedsport

38

Willamette
National
Forest

97

31

La Pine

Charleston

Coos Bay

Coquille

Bandon

42

Roseburg

5

Crater
Lake
National
Park

Crater
Lake

Silver Lake

Mt. Scott

Summer
Lake

Port Orford

101

Wolf Creek

Crater
Lake

82

Fremont
National
Forest

Beatty

Grants Pass

140

Upper
Klamath
Lake

Gold
Beach

Siskiyou
National
Forest

199

238

Medford

Jacksonville

Brookings

46

Ashland

66

Klamath
Falls

Oregon Caves
National Monument

CALIFORNIA

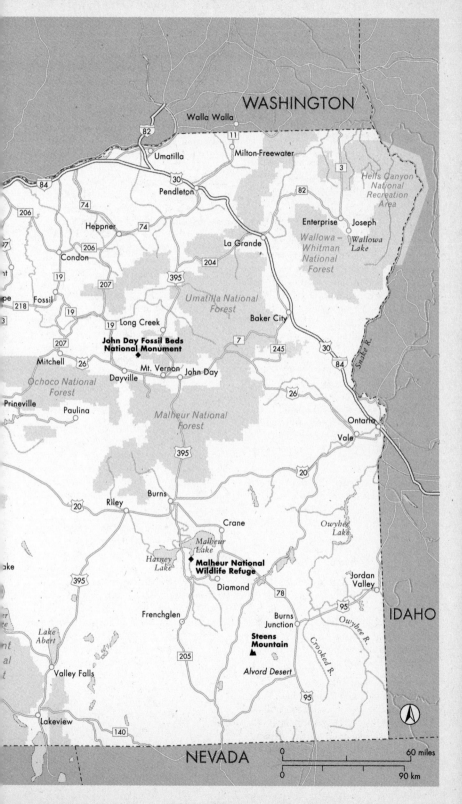

WASHINGTON

Walla Walla

82

Milton-Freewater

11

Umatilla

30

3

Hells Canyon
National
Recreation
Area

Pendleton

82

84

Enterprise   Joseph

206

74

Heppner    74

Wallowa –
Whitman
National
Forest

Wallowa
Lake

La Grande

206

204

Condon

207

395

19

Fossil

19

207

Umatilla National
Forest

Baker City

218

19   Long Creek

3

John Day Fossil Beds
National Monument ◆

7

245

30

Mitchell

26

Mt. Vernon

Dayville    John Day

84

Ochoco National
Forest

26

Snake R.

Prineville

Paulina

Malheur National
Forest

Ontario

395

Vale

20

Riley

20

Burns

Crane

Owyhee
Lake

Malheur
Lake

Harney
Lake

ake

◆ Malheur National
Wildlife Refuge

Diamond

395

78

Jordan
Valley

Frenchglen

Burns
Junction

95

IDAHO

Lake
Abert

205

Steens
Mountain ▲

Owyhee R.

Crooked R.

Valley Falls

Alvord Desert

95

Lakeview    140

NEVADA

0                    60 miles

0                    90 km

# ON THE ROAD WITH FODOR'S

A trip takes you out of yourself. Concerns of life at home completely disappear, driven away by more immediate thoughts—about, say, what marvels will beguile the next day or where you'll have dinner. That's where Fodor's comes in. We make sure that you know all your options, so that you don't miss something that's around the next bend just because you didn't know it was there. Because the best memories of your trip might well have nothing to do with what you came to Oregon to see, we guide you to sights large and small all over the region. You might set out to tackle Mt. Hood or Crater Lake National Park, but back at home you find yourself unable to forget your moments of reflection while ambling through the vineyards of Yamhill County or hearing the silence during a moonlight canoe ride in central Oregon. With Fodor's at your side, serendipitous discoveries are never far away.

Our success in showing you every corner of Oregon is a credit to our extraordinary writers. Although there's no substitute for travel advice from a good friend who knows your style, our contributors are the next best thing—the kind of people you would poll for travel advice if you knew them.

Zach Dundas has worked as a writer and editor in Montana and Oregon for seven years, and he has lived in the Pacific Northwest all his life. Since 1999, he's written for *Willamette Week,* the award-winning weekly newspaper in Portland, Oregon. He lives in North Portland.

Born and raised in Boston, Yankee Susan Honthumb found her way to Eugene 20 years ago. For the last nine years, she has spent her weekdays at Eugene's daily newspaper, the *Register-Guard,* while on weekends she travels around the Northwest bowling competitively.

A native of upstate New York and a former Bostonian, Sarah Kennedy lives in the Alberta Arts District of Northeast Portland. A former Harvard student, she has dabbled in the sundry working worlds of retail, restaurants, libraries, and amusement parks

and has edited a guidebook of the American Southwest. She currently divides her time between writing, bicycling, waitressing, playing the oboe, and exploring the Northwest.

Janna Mock-Lopez is a freelance writer and public relations consultant residing in Beaverton. Born and raised in Los Angeles, she has lived in Oregon for seven years. Her writing has appeared in numerous publications, including Portland's daily paper, the *Oregonian.* She writes a regular column based upon parenthood paradoxes called "In Mother Words," which appears in local newspapers throughout the state, and also covers arts and entertainment for *Portland Magazine.*

A journalist of 18 years, Lori Tobias was born and raised in central Pennsylvania. At 18, she went to Alaska for a three-week visit and stayed eight years. She's been traveling ever since, logging time in Connecticut, Colorado, Seattle, and southern Oregon. When she happened upon the small town of Newport on the central Oregon coast, she knew she'd found home. When she's not on the beach walking her dogs, she writes for Alaska Airlines in-flight magazine, *Ladies' Home Journal, Oregon Home, Oregon Coast Magazine,* the *Oregonian,* and the *Seattle Times,* among other publications. She is a 2002 recipient of the Oregon Literary Art Fellowships.

For their assistance during the research and reporting of this guide the editor gratefully acknowledges Todd Davidson and Natalie S. Barnes, Oregon Tourism Commission; Gretchen Heilshorn, Portland Oregon Visitors Association; Jackie French and Sam Handelman, Bend Visitor & Convention Bureau; Pam Duncan, Central Oregon Visitors Association; Genevieve Scholl-Erdman, Hood River County Chamber of Commerce; Marilyn Dell Worrix, McMinnville Downtown Association; John G. Miller, Yamhill Valley Visitors Association; Donald S. Olson; Brian Mock; and the many other citizens of Oregon for their kindness and unfailingly accurate driving directions.

These thumbnail sketches of various regions and metro areas should help you find your place in the Beaver State:

## ① The Oregon Coast

Immaculate beaches, old-growth forests, rocky sea stacks, and vast stretches of rippled dunes await you on the Oregon coast. Numerous capes afford prime spots to watch sea lions and migrating whales. If the wind or rain drives you inside, head for the Oregon Coast Aquarium in Newport. And don't miss a chance to sample fresh salmon, crab, and other seafood specialties from bay-front shops or fresh from boats docked at port. One Clatsop Indian legend has it that the rough-hewn Oregon coastline was created by Coyote, the trickster god who stood at the top of Neahkahnie Mountain on the north coast and hurled chunks of molten rock into the water below. Waters continue to boil at Devil's Punch Bowl, Cape Perpetua, Cape Foulweather, and Deception Bay. More than 200 shipwrecks near the mouth of the Columbia River between 1725 and 1961 are testament to the churning waters, although there are ample shelters on the Oregon coast as well. Along the 296 mi of coastline that stretch from California to Washington are 14 major bays with direct access to the Pacific Ocean. Among them on the north coast is Depoe Bay, with the world's smallest harbor, only 50 feet wide at its mouth.

## ② Portland

Oregon's largest city, Portland, in the northwest part of the state, is among the nation's most livable—not surprising given its unspoiled setting and host of urban amenities. To find out the secret to Portland's allure, stroll through the city's parks and gardens, explore the intriguing neighborhoods and lively downtown, peruse the galleries and museums, or just sit back and enjoy the buzz at any of the dozens of coffeehouses, cafés, and microbreweries. The city is divided in half by the Willamette River, which runs north–south through the center of Portland. West of the river is Downtown, as well as the trendy neighborhoods of Nob Hill and the Pearl District, and the city's largest parks, Washington Park and Forest Park. On the east side, a different city presents itself. Several popular neighborhoods, including the Hawthorne District, the Alberta Art District, and Sellwood's antique district, are in the middle of large residential neighborhoods. Some of these areas on the east side feel like small towns in and of themselves, with a main street of shopping and restaurants surrounded by quiet residential areas. On the east side there are also many small neighborhood parks that provide a respite from sightseeing.

## ③ The Columbia River Gorge & the Oregon Cascades

The Columbia River Gorge is defined by basaltic cliffs that rise 1,500 to 3,000 feet above the Columbia River, while 77 waterfalls tumble from the glaciers and snowfields of Mt. Hood, including the 620-foot Multnomah Falls, one of the highest in the United States. You can speed through the gorge on I-84, but an especially scenic alternative, offering a glimpse of the region's rugged origins, is accessible on the historic Columbia River Highway. The contrast in scenery, plant life, wildlife, and climate is stark between the east and western slopes of the Cascades. Travelers exploring the Cascade range slightly south of Mt. Hood delight in the infinite yet-to-be-snapped photos of old growth cedar and Ponderosa pine, sapphire lakes, blackened lava fields, and snow-capped peaks. Many highlights from this region are those that remain untouched. You'll witness nature's gifts just as they were granted thousands of years ago.

**4** **Central Oregon**

Central Oregon's dramatic high desert can feel like the end of the earth; in fact, the region centered on the resort playground of Bend is smack in the middle of the state, hundreds of miles from eastern communities like John Day and Ontario. The region's heart lies almost exactly due south of The Dalles, due east of Eugene, and due north of Klamath Falls on the inland side of the Cascade Range. If you're traveling by road from Portland, you'll traverse Mt. Hood on U.S. 26, headed more or less southeast. Central Oregon's prime attraction is its untamed landscape, which is never wilder than it is on the Warm Springs Reservation at the region's northern edge. World-class skiing at Mt. Bachelor, the surreal volcanic environment of Newberry National Monument, and the wealth of outdoor recreation available in Sisters and Prineville add to the allure. With all that natural beauty, Bend's considerable urban charm is icing on the cake.

**5** **The Willamette Valley & the Wine Country**

The Willamette Valley extends more than 100 mi in length, from south of Eugene north to the Portland area, and in width about 20 to 30 mi, from the Coast Range to the Cascades. It is essentially a flat green prairie, the watershed of the circuitous, 187-mi north-flowing Willamette River; buttes, hills, lush vegetation, streams, waterfalls, and springs give dimension to the area. Sometimes called the breadbasket of the West, the valley produces much of the nation's food as well as grass seed and sod, Christmas trees, and flower bulbs. Driving along I–5 or many of the meandering side routes, one finds fields of irises, dahlias, tulips, and daffodils that give way to acres of mint, corn, hops, vegetables, berries, wheat, hazelnut groves, orchards, and nurseries. A temperate climate, a long growing season, and clay-based soil have also given birth to the state's burgeoning wine industry. Within minutes of I–5 are many wineries that grow numerous varieties of grapes but have become internationally known for their superior pinot gris and pinot noir. Among the most compelling of the out-of-the-way destinations are Oregon's covered bridges, most of which are in the valley: Originally built to keep ice from forming on the wooden roadways that cross rivers and streams, Oregon's collection is the largest west of the Mississippi. Each has its own architectural style, from Gothic shingle roofs to exposed trusses.

**6** **Southern Oregon**

Southern Oregon, as defined by the chapter, begins where the Willamette Valley ends south of Eugene, immediately to the east of Oregon's southern coastal region. The confluence of the North and South Umpqua rivers, and the surrounding complex of valleys around Roseburg, marks the area's northern tier. Grants Pass, Medford, Ashland, and Jacksonville are on or near I–5, along the edge of the Siskiyou Mountains and very near the 42nd Parallel—that invisible but psychologically very real line between Oregon and California. Klamath Falls and Crater Lake lie considerably inland, Crater Lake to the northeast of Medford and Ashland, K-Falls almost exactly due east.

## (7) Eastern Oregon

East of the Cascades, Oregon is a land of dry, sweeping plains; wild horses; volcanic rock pillars and plateaus; and historic Oregon trail markers. Attend a rodeo, take a self-guided tour through the John Day fossil beds, or take a raft ride down the Snake River Corridor. Wherever you go, take time to breathe deeply the clean air and to appreciate the vastness of the land. Bordering Washington, Idaho, and Nevada, the region is at once the largest and the least populated expanse of Oregon. It extends from the Columbia River and the cities of Pendleton and La Grande in the north to the sparse Harney and Malheur counties in the south, where you will not find a town with more than a few thousand people. In the northeast corner, Hells Canyon National Recreation Area is North America's deepest gorge, forged by the Snake River. A huge swath of national forest and mountain range passes through the central part of the region and includes the Wallowa-Whitman National Forest, the Umatilla National Forest, the Eagle Cap Wilderness, and the Blue Mountains. All of these areas yield chances for rugged adventures, including fishing, hiking, river rafting, mountain biking, and llama trekking.

Much of Oregon's distinctiveness is rooted in its abundance of natural resources, its many topographies, and its history, as illustrated by this tour.

## Beaches, Wineries & the Gorge
### 3 to 4 days

**CANNON BEACH AND NEWPORT 1 day.** Cruise U.S. 101 to the coastal resort town of Cannon Beach, named for a cannon that washed ashore from a schooner in 1846. There's plenty of shopping here—one of the more upscale resort towns on the Oregon coast—but the real glory of the place is its broad, sand beach, great for walking and kite flying and presided over by a formidable offshore monolith known as Haystack Rock. Continue south to Newport, with an old bay-front area where you'll find galleries, stores selling fresh crab and fish, and good seafood restaurants. A colorful fleet of fishing boats is docked in Yaquina Bay. As you leave Newport, signs on the south side of Yaquina Bay Bridge will direct you to the famous Oregon Coast Aquarium, a 4½-acre complex that provides a wonderful introduction to the various marine habitats found along the Oregon coast. ⇨ Cannon Beach & Newport *in* Chapter 1.

**WILLAMETTE VALLEY & WINE COUNTRY 1 day.** Drive east on U.S. 20, stopping briefly in Corvallis, with plenty of outdoor activities as well as scenic attractions, from covered bridges to local wineries and gardens. Continue east on U.S. 20 and north on I–5 to Salem, the state capital. Its farmlands are devoted to the cultivation of vegetables, berries, hops, and flowers, and more than a dozen wineries are in and near Salem. Numerous gardens around the city are likewise indicative of the moderate climate and lush growing conditions. After touring Salem, visit one or more of the Willamette Valley vineyards around Forest Grove, Newberg, and Dundee before stopping in McMinnville for the night. ⇨ The Willamette Valley & the Wine Country *in* Chapter 5.

**THE COLUMBIA RIVER GORGE 1 day.** Take Highway 99 W north toward Portland and connect with I–5 heading north to I–84. The interstate winds eastward to the Columbia River Gorge. At Troutdale, get on the Historic Columbia River Highway, which passes Multnomah Falls before rejoining I–84. Continue east to the Bonneville Dam and The Dalles. If you'll be staying in the area for four days, spend night three in Hood River and swing down to Mt. Hood the next morning. ⇨ The Columbia River Gorge & the Oregon Cascades *in* Chapter 3.

## Cities & Landmarks
### 7 to 8 days

This tour covers more of the coast and touches the central, southern, and eastern parts of the state, giving you tastes of many cities and towns and some national landmarks along the way.

**ASTORIA & CANNON BEACH 1 day.** Begin in Oregon's northwest, in Astoria, where the Columbia River meets the Pacific Ocean. Maritime history buffs should stop in at the Columbia River Maritime Museum to see memorabilia salvaged from the almost 2,000 ships that have foundered in the treacherous waters; you can also explore a fully operational U.S. Coast Guard ship. The observation platform atop the 125-foot Astoria Column overlooks Astoria, the Columbia River, and the Coast Range. From there, continue south on U.S. 101 to Cannon Beach. ⇨ Astoria & Cannon Beach *in* Chapter 1.

**TILLAMOOK TO FLORENCE** **1 day.** On day two head south from Cannon Beach to Tillamook, which is surrounded by lush green fields and is long known for its dairy industry. Stop in at the Tillamook County Creamery to sample the cheese and ice cream that have made this town famous. From Tillamook, take the Three Capes Loop (marked turnoff in town), a 35-mi scenic byway that passes three magnificent headlands—Cape Meares, Cape Lookout, and Cape Kiwanda—as it winds along the coast. Continue south to Newport. Spend the night south of Newport in the Florence area, where you'll find good seafood restaurants. ⇨ Tillamook, Three Capes Loop, Newport, and Florence *in* Chapter 1.

**SOUTHERN OREGON** **2 days.** Drive south to Coos Bay, a former lumber town with beautiful oceanfront parks in its environs, and Bandon, famous for its cranberry products and its cheese factory, as well as its artists' colony. Then head east on Highway 42 over the Coast Range to pick up I–5 heading south to Ashland, home of the world-renowned Oregon Shakespeare Festival. The town has become a center for contemporary theater as well as for music and dance. Overnight in Ashland and the next day backtrack north on I–5 to Medford, where you can pick up Highway 62 heading north and then east to Crater Lake National Park. Spend the night at the park. ⇨ Coos Bay and Bandon *in* Chapter 1 and Southern Oregon *in* Chapter 6.

**BEND AREA** **1 day.** Take Highway 138 east from the north end of Crater Lake National Park to U.S. 97, which travels north past the Newberry Volcanic National Monument to Bend. Once a timber-oriented mill town, Bend is now a popular year-round vacation destination. Shops, galleries, and restaurants abound in the downtown area, bordered by Drake Park and the river. Music festivals, arts-and-crafts shows, and markets keep visitors outdoors during the summer. ⇨ Bend *in* Chapter 4.

**EASTERN OREGON** **1 day.** On day six head north on U.S. 97 and east on Highway 126 and U.S. 26 past the Ochoco National Forest and the John Day Fossil Beds National Monument. The beds, which were designated a National Monument in 1974, contain bones, leaves, wood, nuts, and seeds from the Age of Mammals, between the time when the dinosaurs become extinct and the beginning of the Ice Age. You have three options for lodging, depending on how much time you spend at the fossil beds: Mitchell and John Day are both on U.S. 26; farther east on Highway 7 is Baker City, originally a mining town and now the site of the National Historic Oregon Trail Interpretive Center. ⇨ Eastern Oregon *in* Chapter 7.

**WEST TO THE GORGE** **1 or 2 days.** Take scenic U.S. 30 north from Baker City to North Powder, and then continue north on I–84 to La Grande, an attractive venue for hikers, skiers, riders, anglers, and rock climbers. Continue north to Pendleton, where the world-famous Pendleton Round-Up takes place in September. The town also has an intriguing Old Town area and the Pendleton Woolen Mills, which offers a close-up look at the production of the robes and shawls for which it earned its reputation. If you have the time, spend the night in Pendleton, and the next day drive west on I–84 to the Columbia River Gorge, stopping at the Bonneville Dam and Multnomah Falls. ⇨ Eastern Oregon *in* Chapter 7 and The Columbia River Gorge & the Oregon Cascades *in* Chapter 3.

# WHEN TO GO

June–September are your best bets for clear days along the coast and in the mountains; these are also the best months to visit the many wineries in the Willamette Valley. July and August are the prime months for visiting Crater Lake National Park, which is often snowed in for the rest of the year. Portland, Jacksonville, and Eugene host world-class summer music festivals, and the theater season in Ashland lasts from mid-February to early November. December–April are the best months for whale-watching along the coast, and February–May are best for bird-watching at the Malheur National Wildlife Refuge. Spring weather is changeable on both sides of the Cascades, but the landscape is a Technicolor wonder of wildflowers, flowering fruit trees (in the Hood River valley), and gardens bursting with rhododendrons and azaleas. Fall is spectacular throughout the state, with leaves at their colorful peak in late October. The prices for accommodations, transportation, and tours can be lower, and the crowds much smaller, in spring and fall.

## Climate

Average daytime summer highs are in the 70s; winter temperatures are generally in the 40s. Rainfall varies greatly from one locale to another. In the coastal mountains, for example, 160 inches of rain fall annually, creating temperate rain forests. In eastern Oregon near-desert conditions prevail, with rainfall as low as 6 inches per year. Throughout the Pacific Northwest, however, most rain falls during the winter months, when cloudy skies and drizzly weather persist. More than 75% of Seattle's annual precipitation occurs October–March.

What follows are average daily maximum and minimum temperatures for Portland.

 Forecasts **Weather Channel Connection** ☎ 900/932-8437 95¢ per minute from a Touch-Tone phone ⊕ www.weather.com.

## PORTLAND

| Jan. | 44F | 7C | May | 67F | 19C | Sept. | 74F | 23C |
|---|---|---|---|---|---|---|---|---|
| | 33 | 1 | | 46 | 8 | | 5↑ | 10 |
| Feb. | 50F | 10C | June | 72F | 22C | Oct. | 63F | 17C |
| | 36 | 2 | | 52 | 11 | | 45 | 7 |
| Mar. | 54F | 12C | July | 79F | 26C | Nov. | 52F | 11C |
| | 37 | 3 | | 55 | 13 | | 39 | 4 |
| Apr. | 60F | 15C | Aug. | 78F | 25C | Dec. | 46F | 8C |
| | 41 | 5 | | 55 | 13 | | 35 | 2 |

# ON THE CALENDAR

Whether Oregonians are celebrating a regional crop, taking pride in their community, or just blowing off steam, know that you're more than welcome to join them. If you want your visit to coincide with one of these occasions, be sure to plan well in advance.

## ONGOING

**Jan. and Mar.**
In Newport plant yourself someplace north of Yaquina Bay and south of Yaquina Head Lighthouse for Whale Watching Week (☎ 800/262–7844, Newport Chamber of Commerce) during the last weeks of December and March.

**Mid-Feb.– early Nov.**
The Oregon Shakespeare Festival (☎ 541/482–4331 ⊕ www.orshakes.org) in Ashland spotlights contemporary playwrights as well as the Bard.

**Mid-June– early Sept.**
The open-air Britt Festivals (☎ 541/773–6077 or 800/882–7488 ⊕ www.brittfest.org) present classical, pop, and jazz concerts at an outdoor amphitheater in historic Jacksonville.

## WINTER

**Dec.**
The Oregon Coast Aquarium becomes a Sea of Lights (☎ 800/262–7844, Newport Chamber of Commerce) during the first weekend of December. That same weekend, fishing and pleasure boats strewn with Christmas lights partake in the Lighted Boat Parade in Yaquina Bay.

**Feb.**
The non-competitive Portland International Film Festival (☎ 503/221–1156 ⊕ www.nwfilm.org) typically focuses on non-U.S. films.

At the Charleston Marina in Coos Bay is the Charleston Seafood Festival (☎ 800/824–8486, Bay Area Chamber of Commerce), during the first weekend in February.

Live reggae tunes and a "Jamaican Jam" superpipe contest keep Jamaican Days (☎ 503/337–2222 ⊕ www.skihood.com) hopping at the Mt. Hood Meadows Ski Resort during the third weekend of the month.

Within walking distance of the Oregon Coast Aquarium is the Newport Seafood and Wine Festival (☎ 800/262–7844, Newport Chamber of Commerce) during the last weekend of February.

## SPRING

**Mar.**
Bands, dancing, and, of course, clams figure into the South Coast Dixieland Clambake Jazz Festival (☎ 800/824–8486, Bay Area Chamber of Commerce) during the second weekend of March in Coos Bay.

McMenamins Edgefield Manor in Troutdale throws a popular St. Patrick's Day Celebration (☎ 800/669–8610 ⊕ www.mcmenamins.com).

**Apr.**
Mid month, the Hood River Valley Blossom Festival (☎ 800/366–3530) is a springtime floral spectacle.

The Dalles is the site of the Northwest Cherry Festival (☎ 800/255–3385 or 541/296–2231), with a parade and a Cherry Stomp Dance, during the third weekend of April.

Crab races and a petting zoo are among the attractions at the Astoria-Warrenton Crab & Seafood Festival (☎ 800/875–6807, Astoria-Warrenton Area Chamber of Commerce) during the last weekend in April.

| May | The Cinco de Mayo Festival (☎ 503/222–9807) in Portland is one of the largest such celebrations this side of Guadalajara. |

Bed races are among the events at Newport's Loyalty Day and Seafair Festival (☎ 800/262–7844, Newport Chamber of Commerce) during the first weekend in May.

A parade and discussions of alien sightings are among the highlights of UFO Fest (☎ 503/472–8427 or 888/472–8427 ⊕ www.ufofest.com) hosted by McMenamins Hotel Oregon, in mid-May in McMinnville.

In Bend, mid-month brings the U.S. Bank Pole Pedal Paddle (⊕ ppp.bendnet.com), a popular team relay race that incorporates downhill and cross-country skiing, kayaking, biking, and running. The event benefits the Mt. Bachelor Ski Education Foundation.

A modest entry fee and less-modest prize money make the Detroit Lake Fishing Derby (☎ 503/854–3496 ⊕ www.detroitlakeoregon.org) a popular annual event. It's during the third weekend in May.

Windsurfers gather on the Hood River to compete in the Gorge Cup race series (☎ 541/386–9225 ⊕ www.cgwa.net) during the third weekend of the month.

Celtic music, Irish derbies, and local wines are on hand at Bandon's Irish Fest (☎ 541/347–9616, Bandon Chamber of Commerce) on Memorial Day weekend. The event was formerly known as the Wine and Food Festival.

Memorial Day weekend also brings the Brookings Azalea Festival (☎ 800/535–9469, Brookings Chamber of Commerce), which shows off the azaleas of Oregon's southern coast and includes a parade and street fair.

**SUMMER**

| June | Chamber Music Northwest (☎ 503/223–3202 or 503/294–6400 ⊕ www.cmnw.com) holds a summer festival including classical and contemporary pieces. |

If you think strawberry shortcake is worth waiting for, the Strawberry Festival (☎ 541/258–4444) in Lebanon in early June yields the largest such cake in the world. About 17,000 people line up after the festival's parade for a complimentary slice.

The first 700 runners to register are eligible for the Newport Marathon (☎ 800/262–7844, Newport Chamber of Commerce ⊕ www.newportmarathon.org), the first Saturday after Memorial Day.

The Cannon Beach Sand Castle Contest (☎ 503/436–0434, Cannon Beach Chamber of Commerce) is the oldest such competition in the United States.

The Portland Rose Festival (☎ 503/227–2681), beginning in early June, packs diverse events—an air show, three parades, auto racing, and a riverside carnival among them—into 25 days.

The Warm Springs Reservation has three tribes with distinct histories and traditions, all of which are on display during June's Pi-Ume-Sha Pow Wow (☎ 541/553–3333), commemorating the treaty that created the reservation. Native American dancers, drummers, and singers from across western North America head for Warm Springs to showcase traditional and modern pow-wow dances, costumes, and drum-chants. If you've never been to a pow-wow before, you're in for a spine-tingling and highly enjoyable experience.

In mid-June the Sisters Rodeo (☎ 800/827–7522 ⊕ www.sistersrodeo.com), "the Biggest Little Show in the World," comes to town for several days of performances.

The Wallowa Valley Festival of the Arts (☎ 541/432–3031), mid-June in Joseph, showcases local artists during a juried art show.

| | |
|---|---|
| Late June–mid-July | The Oregon Bach Festival (☎ 800/457–1486) in Eugene celebrates the works of the great composer. |
| July | The Oregon Coast Music Festival (☎ 541/267–0938) in Coos Bay, North Bend, and Charleston presents classical bluegrass, jazz, and other concerts. |
| | The Oregon Brewer's Festival (☎ 503/295–1862), a beer lover's delight, is held in Portland. |
| | A popular Saturday activity on Independence Day weekend is Fireworks Over the Lake (☎ 503/854–3496 ⊕ www.detroitlakeoregon.org). |
| | Lakeview, known in sports circles as the hang-gliding capital of the West, hosts the National Hang Gliding and Para Sailing Championships (☎ 541/947–6040) on Independence Day weekend. |
| | In early July the Scandinavian Midsummer Festival (☎ 800/875–6807, Astoria-Warrenton Area Chamber of Commerce) celebrates Scandinavian culture with dancing, food, and crafts. |
| | In mid-July, the Salem Art Fair and Festival (☎ 503/581–2228), Oregon's biggest art fair, includes exhibits, food, entertainment, and tours of historic mansions. |
| | Sculpture vehicle races and a theatrical performance are among the events celebrating Leonardo during da Vinci Days (☎ 541/757–6363 ⊕ www.davinci-days.org), mid-month in Corvallis. |
| | The population of Yamhill County swells for several days in late July during the International Pinot Noir Celebration (☎ 503/472–8964 or 800/775–IPNC), when McMinnville's Linfield College and area vineyards draw wine lovers to the area. |
| Aug. | The Mt. Hood Jazz Festival (☎ 503/224–4400) early in the month brings nationally acclaimed jazz musicians to Gresham for outdoor performances. |

Country headliners perform at the Oregon Jamboree (☏ 541/367–8800 or 888/613–6812 ⊕ www.oregonjamboree.com) in Sweet Home, where attendees can camp in tents and RVs during the three-day event at the beginning of the month.

The couch racing is enough of a draw for most attendees of the Homer Davenport Days (☏ 503/573–5615 ⊕ www.silvertonchamber. org) in early August, a three-day celebration of the late 1800s and early 1900s political cartoonist and Silverton native.

During the second weekend in August, the Seaside Beach Volleyball Tournament (☏ 800/444–6740, Seaside Chamber of Commerce) draws more than 80,000 spectators for three days of pro and semi-pro play during the largest beach volleyball tourney worldwide.

With the motto "Fun stinks!" and the promise of garlic ice cream, it's difficult not to toy with the idea of attending the Elephant Garlic Festival (☏ 503/647–2207 ⊕ www.funstinks.com) in mid-August.

The Mt. Hood Bluegrass Festival (☏ 541/354–2865 ⊕ www. mthoodbluegrassfestival.com) draws many acts to Hood River during the third weekend of the month.

The last weekend of the month brings the Annual Hood to Coast Run (☏ 800/444–6740, Seaside Chamber of Commerce) to Seaside.

The Oregon State Fair (☏ 503/378–3247) takes place in Salem the 11 days before Labor Day.

**FALL**

Sept.

Beer, bratwurst, and a parade figure into the Huckleberry Festival (☏ 509/493–3630 ⊕ www.mtadamschamber.com) the weekend after Labor Day.

The North by Northwest Music Festival (☏ 512/467–7979 ⊕ www. nxnw.com) is a music showcase for acts worldwide as well as a major networking scene for the music industry.

Celebrate the harvest at the Bandon Cranberry Festival (☏ 541/347–9616, Bandon Chamber of Commerce) during the second weekend of September.

In mid-September, the Pendleton Round-Up (☏ 541/276–7411) draws thousands to Pendleton for a world-renowned rodeo and related events.

Oktoberfest (☏ no phone) brings half a million people to Mt. Angel mid-month for an extravaganza of Bavarian food, beer, wine, and cabaret.

Since 1974, Wallowa Lake has hosted a popular Swiss-Bavarian festival called Alpenfest (☏ 541/426–4622) in late September.

Oct.

Two Pacific Northwest favorites are feted early in the month at the Mt. Hood Salmon and Mushroom Festival (☏ 503/622–4798 ⊕ www. mthood.org).

The second weekend of the month, the Silver Salmon Celebration (☎ 800/875–6807, Astoria-Warrenton Area Chamber of Commerce) yields crafts, music, and food, including fresh-caught salmon for purchase.

Fruit, food, and fun commingle at the Hood River Valley Harvest Fest (☎ 541/386–2000 ⊕ www.hoodriver.org), a celebration of the fall harvest during the third weekend in October.

Nov.

You'll find a mix of art, poetry, and music at the Stormy Weather Arts Festival (☎ 503/436–0434, Cannon Beach Chamber of Commerce) during the first weekend in November.

# PLEASURES & PASTIMES

**Beaches** Oregon has the most accessible shoreline in the Pacific Northwest. The long, sandy beaches run for miles at a stretch. But the waters are generally too cold or treacherous for swimming. Even in summertime, beachgoers must be prepared to dress warmly.

**Biking & Hiking** For the past 20 years, Oregon has set aside 1% of its highway funds for the development and maintenance of bikeways throughout the state, resulting in one of the most extensive networks of bicycle trails in the country. The system of hiking trails through state-park and national-forest lands is equally comprehensive.

**Boating, Canoeing & Rafting** Oregon's swift rivers provide challenges to boaters, canoeists, kayakers, and rafters. Many of these rivers should be attempted only by experienced boaters. Many companies operate boating and white-water rafting tours, or you can rent equipment and head out on your own. The Deschutes River north of Bend is a popular white-water rafting destination. Boating and rafting permits are required for the Rogue and lower Deschutes rivers. Recreational access to the Rogue is limited; a lottery for permits is held each February. For more information, contact the Rand Visitors Center in Galice. Permits for the Deschutes can be obtained at the Bureau of Land Management office in Prineville. June through September are prime months for white-water rafting.

**Driving** While bicycling has a special place in the hearts of many Oregonians, motoring can be transformed from a utilitarian chore into a simple pleasure if you slow it down, drink in the scenery, and make liberal use of the state's many turnouts and overlooks. Driving along the coast is a singular pleasure, while taking the Columbia River Highway through the Columbia River Gorge is a historical and leisurely delight. McKenzie Pass, a scenic route in the Cascade Range that winds through the Mt. Washington Wilderness Area, is a challenging and indelible driving experience with its tight turns and birdseye views. Hitting any road in Oregon at daybreak may heighten your driving experiences; you'll seemingly have the byways and pink and orange morning skies to yourself, at least for a while.

**Fishing** The coastal regions and inland lakes and rivers of Oregon are known for excellent fishing. Depoe Bay is a leading port for cruising and deep-sea-fishing charters. Visiting anglers must possess a nonresident license for the state or province in which they plan to fish. Licenses are easily obtainable at sporting-goods stores, bait shops, and other outlets in fishing areas.

**Golf** The Northwest has many excellent golf courses, but not all of them are open to the public. Consequently, visitors may find it difficult to arrange a tee time at a popular course. If you are a member of a golf club at home, check to see if your club has a reciprocal playing arrangement with private clubs in the areas that you will be visiting.

**Hot-Air Ballooning** If you've ever wanted to float over a verdant landscape in the basket of a hot-air balloon, come to the Willamette Valley in the warmer months for an aerial view of Oregon's wine country.

# Rockhounding

Rockhounding—searching for semiprecious or unusual rocks—is very popular in the Ochocos in central Oregon and Harney County and the Stinkingwater Mountains in eastern Oregon. Agate, obsidian, jasper, and thunder eggs are among the sought-after stones.

# Sailboarding

The Columbia River, particularly at Hood River, is one of the world's premier locations for windsurfing. Sailboard rentals and lessons are available from local specialty shops.

# Skiing

Most Oregon downhillers congregate around Mt. Hood and Mt. Bachelor, but there is also skiing to the south, at Willamette Pass and Mt. Ashland. The temperate Willamette Valley generally receives only a few inches of snow a year, but the Coast Range, the Cascade Range, and the Siskiyou Mountains are all Nordic skiers' paradises, crisscrossed by hundreds of miles of trails. Every major downhill ski resort in the state also has Nordic skiing, but don't rule out the many Forest Service trails and logging roads. Resort and lift-ticket prices tend to be less expensive in Oregon than at the internationally known ski destinations, but the slopes, especially on weekends, can be crowded.

# Wildlife Viewing

Sea lions, seals, dolphins, and whales are a few of the marine mammals that can be observed in bays, near headlands, and along the coast. In the spring and summer thousands of gray whales pass by the Oregon coast on their seasonal migration from Alaska to Baja California in Mexico. One of the easiest and most exciting ways to see them is by taking a whale-watching boat excursion. In the forests and along coastal rivers and estuaries deer, bald eagles, herons, and egrets are commonly seen. The dedicated birders who annually trek to the Northwest find that their efforts are amply rewarded.

# Wine Tasting

The Willamette Valley is Oregon's main region for viticulture—many area wineries are open for tours, tastings, or both. Wineries near Forest Grove can be toured in an afternoon outing from Portland. South of the Willamette Valley are the Umpqua Valley and Rogue River wine-growing regions. The free Oregon winery guide published by the Oregon Wine Advisory Board (☎ 503/228–8336) provides profiles, detailed maps, and service information about most Oregon wineries that welcome visitors. It's available at many wine shops and visitor centers in the state.

# FODOR'S CHOICE

The sights, restaurants, hotels, and other travel experiences on these pages are our editors' top picks—our Fodor's Choices. They're the best of their type in the area covered by the book—not to be missed and always worth your time. In the destination chapters that follow, you will find all the details.

## LODGING

| | |
|---|---|
| $$$$ | **Metolius River Resort, Camp Sherman.** Flawless comfort and rustic elegance permeate the entire cabin experience. The sun on your face warms the soul while sounds of the gentle river gliding by soothe the senses. |
| $$$$ | **Sunriver Resort, Sunriver.** A former military base near Bend has transformed into an almost self-contained resort village. Golf, great food, luxury rooms, and, above all, the high desert's sweeping sense of splendid isolation are the main draws here. |
| $$$–$$$$ | **Dolce Skamania Lodge, Stevenson, Washington.** A premier forested perch overlooking the Columbia River, outstanding recreational facilities, and terrific service make this a worthy resort experience. |
| $$$–$$$$ | **Tu Tu' Tun Lodge, near Gold Beach.** Tucked just far enough away from U.S. 101 to feel like a secret retreat, the Tu Tu' Tun Lodge on the banks of the Rogue River is pure class. Bed linens and room furnishings are designer quality, complementing (not competing with) the natural rustic mood. The spirit is relaxed and friendly. |
| $$$–$$$$ | **Valley River Inn, Eugene.** The southern Willamette Valley's premier hotel is pleasantly set on the banks of the Willamette River and near numerous restaurants as well as the Valley River Center mall. |
| $–$$$$ | **Flying M Ranch, Yamhill.** "Daniel Boone eclectic" might be the best description of the furnishings at this great log lodge, the centerpiece of a 625-acre complex of cabins and riverside hotel units. |
| $–$$$$ | **Timberline Lodge, Mt. Hood.** A National Historic Landmark that is as much a quintessential sight as it is a place to stay, the lodge has withstood howling winter storms for more than six decades and warms its guests with hospitality, hearty food, and rustic rooms. |
| $$$ | **Heathman Hotel, Portland.** Elegant rooms, beautifully restored public spaces, an exceptional restaurant, and superior service have earned this downtown hotel a reputation as one of the finest establishments in the city. |
| $$–$$$ | **Crater Lake Lodge.** A king among America's national park lodges, this spot provides an express ticket to a quieter and more rustic bygone era. The view of the lake's searing blue expanse is singular. |
| $$–$$$ | **Newport Belle B&B, Newport.** With first-class views of the arcing Yaquina Bay Bridge and front seats to the bustling bay front, the triple-decker *Newport Belle* stern-wheeler, with staterooms and a woodstove-warmed salon, is one of the most unusual places on the coast to settle in for the night. |

| $$-$$$ | **Under the Greenwood Tree, Medford.** Luxurious rooms, stunning 10-acre gardens, and breakfasts cooked by the owner, a Cordon Bleu–trained chef, make a visit here memorable. |
|---|---|
| $-$$$ | **Lara House Bed & Breakfast Inn, Bend.** Across from Bend's Drake Park, the Deschutes River, and Mirror Pond, this brawny 1910 boarding house has become a stylish B&B; each room has its own bath, there's a hot tub, and breakfasts are dynamite. Downtown Bend is just a few blocks away. |
| $-$$$ | **Out N' About, near Oregon Caves.** Sleep in a tree house 37 feet above terra firma at this unusual but affordable resort. |
| $-$$$ | **Pine Valley Lodge, Halfway.** Pick a room in one of three rustic buildings at this eccentric lodge, which occupies much of tiny Halfway's Main Street, and look forward to a delectable breakfast before heading into Hells Canyon. |
| $-$$$ | **The Steamboat Inn, Steamboat.** A veritable Who's Who of the world's top fly fishermen have visited Oregon's most famous fishing lodge; others come simply to relax in the reading nooks or on the broad decks of the riverside cabins. |
| $$ | **Lion and the Rose, Portland.** In a restored Victorian home in the city's Irvington neighborhood, this bed-and-breakfast, with friendly owners and fine food, is a luxurious historic inn. |
| $-$$ | **Mattey House Bed & Breakfast, McMinnville.** Whether you're a wine aficionado or just looking for a pleasurable stay in Yamhill County, this Victorian home is an immersion in comfort and the area's wine culture, thanks largely to the knowledgeable and welcoming owners. |
| $-$$ | **McMenamins Edgefield, Troutdale.** A McMenamins outpost just east of Portland, Edgefield combines a fabulously renovated lodge, several tiny bars, a vineyard, two restaurants, and a golf course, creating a fun, laid-back version of a resort at reasonable prices. |

## BUDGET LODGING

| ¢–$$ | **Bend Riverside Motel.** This clean and comfortable budget accommodation puts all the perks of downtown Bend at your doorstep. |
|---|---|
| ¢–$ | **Union Hotel, Union.** Just outside La Grande, this historic inn has restored a feeling of age-old elegance to an Old West town, with unique and beautifully furnished rooms. |
| $ | **Parker House, Pendleton.** This beautiful B&B on a hill just north of downtown Pendleton has been preserved with the same French neoclassical and Italianate styles that it has had since 1917. |

## RESTAURANTS

| $$$ | **Tina's, Dundee.** With fish, game, and desserts every bit as strong as the exemplary wine list, and service that can only come from people who love what they do, it's all good. |
|---|---|

| | |
|---|---|
| $$–$$$ | **Cork, Bend.** This romantic candle-lit restaurant and wine bar in downtown Bend infuses its Continental cuisine with Northwest freshness and bursts of Latin heat. |
| $$–$$$ | **Merenda, Bend.** The cooking at this swaggering and confident spot backs up the large, loud room's verve, with hardy French and Italian influences brought to bear on Northwest ingredients. |
| $$–$$$ | **Higgins, Portland.** Pacific Northwest ingredients augment traditional French dishes with international flair at this sophisticated and popular spot near Portland's Art Museum and the Arlene Schnitzer Concert Hall. |
| $$–$$$ | **Paley's Place, Portland.** French cuisine is served Pacific Northwest style at this charming Nob Hill bistro with porch seating. |
| $–$$$ | **Black Sheep, Ashland.** Have a high-quality bite with a pint of Tetley's at this pub, what many quasi-British bars want to be but aren't. A raucous music selection and general feeling of rowdy bonhomie provide an antidote to a sometimes overly sedate theater town. |
| $–$$$ | **The Cascade Room at Dolce Skamania Lodge, Stevenson, Washington.** Fresh Pacific Northwest ingredients tantalize taste buds while views delight diners marveling at the Columbia Gorge's dramatic scenery. |
| $–$$$ | **La Serre, Yachats.** The chef at what many consider to be the best restaurant on the Oregon coast has a deft touch with seafood, which is always impeccably fresh and never deep-fried. |
| $–$$$ | **Raphael's, Pendleton.** Fine and adventurous dining in this favorite might include alligator or Indian salmon with huckleberries, and you can always count on excellent steak. |
| $–$$$ | **Red Agave, Eugene.** What inauspiciously used to be the site of a refuse dump couldn't distance itself further from its history; Mexican and Latino flavors inspire the menu, which includes a different flan according to the season. |
| $–$$ | **Multnomah Falls Lodge.** Wonderful service and zesty food combine under vaulted ceilings at this spot on the National Register of Historic Places. |
| ¢–$$$ | **Foley Station, La Grande.** An open kitchen in a comfortable, laid-back dining space prepares some of the best food in town, with fresh Pacific Northwest ingredients. |
| ¢–$$ | **Turtles Bar & Grill, Eugene.** Great food and friendly service compensate for the meager parking around this spot, where the inevitable wait for a table yields tasty barbecue. |

## BUDGET RESTAURANTS

| | |
|---|---|
| ¢–$ | **Montage, Portland.** Jambalaya, catfish, and Cajun mac and cheese are just a few of the specialties at this loud, festive, and sassy bistro on the east side. |
| ¢ | **The Depot Deli & Cafe, Sisters.** An anomaly on Sisters' kitschy Wild West–style main street has a train theme, quality jazz on the stereo, |

and inexpensive sandwiches and burgers several cuts above tourist-trap fare.

¢ **Panini Bakery, Nye Beach.** At this little shop, which doesn't skimp on butter and eggs, "fresh" takes on a whole new meaning: breads are made from home-grown starter, croissants take four days to rise, coffee is organic and fresh roasted, and the orange juice and lemonade are hand-squeezed.

¢ **Summit Grill and Alpine Patio, Joseph.** What more could you want after ascending the steepest gondola in North America than to enjoy a simple sandwich, burger, or cup of soup amid the peaks of the Wallowa Mountains?

## HISTORY

**Fort Clatsop National Memorial, Astoria.** Lewis and Clark's humble winter fort, a log stockade built in 1805 at the conclusion of their trailblazing journey across North America, has been faithfully reconstructed on what is believed to be its original site.

**Jacksonville Cemetery, Jacksonville.** With orange madrona branches tangling over tombstones dating back to the 1850s, this resting place provides a glimpse into this gold-rush town's frontier mores and culture.

**Underground, Pendleton.** Explore the scandalous and fascinating history of Pendleton on this guided tour of its brothels, saloons, and opium dens, as well as the living quarters of its Chinese laborers.

## MUSEUMS

**Columbia River Maritime Museum, Astoria.** The observation tower of a World War II submarine and the personal belongings of the passengers of area shipwrecks are among the exhibits here.

**Evergreen Aviation Museum, McMinnville.** Engrossing facts about aviation complement an awesome assortment of flying machines at this expansive repository best known as the address of Howard Hughes's "flying boat," the *Spruce Goose,* which has the wingspan of a football field and its end zones.

**High Desert Museum, Bend.** Evocative and intricate walk-through dioramas and an indoor-outdoor zoo with creatures great and tiny convey the High Desert's past and present in a delightfully airy and family-friendly space.

**Museum at Warm Springs.** Get a one-of-a-kind introduction to the culture and history of the three tribes that call the surrounding reservation home. The thoughtfully curated, beautifully designed museum is regarded as a national model for other tribes.

## NATURE

**Crater Lake National Park, eastern Oregon off Rte. 62.** Rain and snowmelt have filled the caldera left by the eruption of Mt. Mazama, creating a sapphire-blue lake—at a depth of 1,900 feet the nation's deepest—so clear that sunlight penetrates 400 feet. The park is dazzling and draws crowds, but its pristine backcountry awaits for more adventurous souls.

**Hells Canyon, northeast of Joseph.** The deepest river-carved gorge in North America makes for an awe-inspiring visit, whether you experience it via a three-day backpacking trip or by a fleeting peek over the edge at one of the lookout points.

**John Day Fossil Beds.** Who knew that 40 million years of fossil formation could make for such an unusually beautiful landscape? Be sure to check out all three units to see the blue-green spires of Sheep Rock, the deep red and brown hills of Painted Hills, and the rough cliffs and and outcroppings of Clarno.

**Metolius Recreation Area, northwest of Sisters.** Witness a billowing river bubble to life and gently cascade through grassy fields lined by pine forests, turquoise skies, and the snow-capped peak of Mt. Jefferson.

**Siltcoos River Canoe Trail, Florence.** Every second on this blissful stretch of water offers something new to see: one moment, towering sand dunes, spotted with sea grass and lone islands of trees; the next, dense rain forest, where evergreens grow thick and tall and wild azaleas dot the brush in bursts of pink; and finally, the rolling Pacific and endless blue sky.

**Valley of the Rogue State Park, Grants Pass.** If you're not quite intrepid enough to book a trip into the legendary river's wilderness heartland, you can wander its untamed banks on your own.

## PARKS & GARDENS

**Classical Chinese Garden, Portland.** A team of 60 artisans and designers from China literally left no stone unturned—500 tons of stone were brought here from Suzhou—in their efforts to create this walled Suzhou-style garden, the largest outside China. It occupies one city block in the Old Town/Chinatown area.

**Japanese Garden, Portland.** Considered the most authentic Japanese garden outside Japan, this serene spot provides a peaceful retreat only minutes from city traffic, and a glimpse at an ever-changing landscape with plants and flowers blooming at all times of year.

## SHOPPING EXPERIENCES

**Portland Saturday Market.** North America's largest open-air handicraft market transforms the area under and around the Burnside Bridge into a festive celebration of craft, food, and music every weekend.

**Powell's City of Books, Portland.** The largest independent bookstore in the world, with more than 1.5 million new and used books, is a delightful place to spend a few minutes or several hours.

**VIEWS**

**Beacon Rock, Stevenson, Washington.** Breathtaking views of the Columbia River and the gorge await you atop the 800-foot lava flows of this volcanic remnant.

**Cape Perpetua, south of Yachats.** The highest lookout point on the Oregon coast is part of a 2,700-acre scenic area with a visitor center and several hiking trails, including one that winds through a rain forest to an enormous 500-year-old Sitka spruce.

**Cove Palisades State Park, Madras.** Arid red-rock cliffs and the confluence of the Metolius, Deschutes, and Crooked rivers combine for a gleaming, refreshing destination, a favorite among boaters and anglers.

**Smith Rock State Park, Redmond.** Rock climbers from all over the world visit this vivid red-orange 550-foot slab of compressed volcanic ash. Even if you have no desire to assault Monkey Face, the Pleasure Palace, or any other piece of the Rock, the surrounding state park offers miles of horizontal hiking opportunities.

**Yaquina Head Natural Outstanding Area, Newport.** From miles away the Yaquina Head Lighthouse beckons with its stately white tower and flashing beacon, a favorite landmark up and down the coast. But don't miss the exceptional beauty that surrounds it—acres of meadow, nature trails, cobblestone beaches and tidal pools, and rocky headlands.

# SMART TRAVEL TIPS

Air Travel
Airports
Bike Travel
Bus Travel
Cameras & Photography
Car Rental
Car Travel
Children in Oregon
Consumer Protection
Cruise Travel
Customs & Duties
Disabilities & Accessibility
Discounts & Deals
Eating & Drinking
Ecotourism
Emergencies
Gay & Lesbian Travel
Holidays
Insurance
For International Travelers
Lodging
Media
Money Matters
National Parks
Packing
Senior-Citizen Travel
Shopping
Sports & the Outdoors
Students in the Pacific Northwest
Tax
Time
Tipping
Tours & Packages
Train Travel
Travel Agencies
Visitor Information
Web Sites

*Finding out about your destination before you leave home means you won't squander time organizing everyday minutiae once you've arrived. You'll be more streetwise when you hit the ground as well, better prepared to explore the aspects of Oregon that drew you here in the first place. The organizations in this section can provide information to supplement this guide; contact them for up-to-the-minute details, and consult the A to Z sections that end each chapter for facts on the various topics as they relate to the state's many regions. Happy landings!*

## AIR TRAVEL

### BOOKING

When you book, look for nonstop flights and remember that "direct" flights stop at least once. Try to avoid connecting flights, which require a change of plane. Two airlines may operate a connecting flight jointly, so ask whether your airline operates every segment of the trip; you may find that the carrier you prefer flies you only part of the way. To find more booking tips and to check prices and make on-line flight reservations, log on to www.fodors.com.

### CARRIERS

Leading regional carriers in Oregon are Horizon Air and United Express. The two airlines provide frequent service between cities in Washington and Oregon. Air B.C. also has daily flights from Vancouver to Portland.

🛪 Major Airlines **Air B.C.** ☎ 888/247-2262 ⊕ www.aircanada.ca. **Air Canada** ☎ 888/247-2262 ⊕ www.aircanada.ca. **Air North Ltd.** ☎ 800/661-0407 in Canada, 800/764-0407 in the U.S. ⊕ www.flyairnorth.com. **Alaska** ☎ 800/252-7522 ⊕ www.alaskaairlines.com. **American** ☎ 800/433-7300 ⊕ www.aa.com. **British Airways** ☎ 800/247-9297 ⊕ www.britishairways.com. **Continental** ☎ 800/523-3273 ⊕ www.continental.com. **Delta** ☎ 800/221-1212 ⊕ www.delta.com. **EVA Airways** ☎ 800/695-1188 ⊕ www.evaair.com. **Hawaiian** ☎ 800/367-5320 ⊕ www.hawaiianair.com. **Japan** ☎ 800/525-3663 ⊕ www.japanair.com. **Lufthansa** ☎ 800/645-3880 ⊕ www.lufthansa-usa.com. **Mexicana** ☎ 800/531-7921 ⊕ www.mexicana.com. **Northwest** ☎ 800/225-2525 ⊕ www.nwa.com. **United/United Express** ☎ 800/241-6522 ⊕ www.ual.com. **US Airways/US Airways Express** ☎ 800/428-4322 ⊕ www.usair.com.
🛪 Smaller Airlines **Air B.C.** ☎ 800/776-3000. **America West** ☎ 800/235-9292 ⊕ www.

americawest.com. **Frontier** ☎ 800/432-1359 ⊕ www.frontierairlines.com. **Harbor Airlines** ☎ 800/359-3220. **Helijet** ☎ 800/665-4354 or 604/273-1414 in Vancouver ⊕ www.helijet.com. **Horizon Air** ☎ 800/547-9308 ⊕ horizonair.alaskaair.com. **Kenmore Air** ☎ 800/543-9595 ⊕ www.kenmoreair.com. **Skywest** ☎ 800/453-9417 ⊕ www.skywest.com. **Southwest** ☎ 800/435-9792 ⊕ www.southwest.com. **United/United Express** ☎ 800/241-6522 ⊕ www.ual.com. **Westjet** ☎ 800/538-5696 ⊕ www.westjet.com.

## CHECK-IN & BOARDING

Always **find out your carrier's check-in policy.** Plan to arrive at the airport about 2 hours before your scheduled departure time for domestic flights and 2½ to 3 hours before international flights. You may need to arrive earlier if you're flying from one of the busier airports or during peak air-traffic times.

To avoid delays at airport-security checkpoints, try not to wear any metal. Jewelry, belt and other buckles, steel-toe shoes, barrettes, and underwire bras are among the items that can set off detectors.

Assuming that not everyone with a ticket will show up, airlines routinely overbook planes. When everyone does, airlines ask for volunteers to give up their seats. In return, these volunteers usually get a several-hundred-dollar flight voucher, which can be used toward the purchase of another ticket, and are rebooked on the next flight out. If there are not enough volunteers, the airline must choose who will be denied boarding. The first to get bumped are passengers who checked in late and those flying on discounted tickets, so get to the gate and check in as early as possible, especially during peak periods.

Always **bring a government-issued photo ID** to the airport; even when it's not required, a passport is best.

## CUTTING COSTS

The least expensive airfares to Oregon are priced for round-trip travel and must usually be purchased in advance. Airlines generally allow you to change your return date for a fee; most low-fare tickets, however, are nonrefundable. It's smart to call a number of airlines and check the Internet; when you are quoted a good price, book it on the spot—the same fare may not be available the next day, or even the next

hour. Always check different routings and look into using alternate airports. Also, price off-peak flights, which may be significantly less expensive than others. Travel agents, especially low-fare specialists (⇨ Discounts and Deals), are helpful.

Consolidators are another good source. They buy tickets for scheduled flights at reduced rates from the airlines, then sell them at prices that beat the best fare available directly from the airlines. Sometimes you can even get your money back if you need to return the ticket. Carefully read the fine print detailing penalties for changes and cancellations, purchase the ticket with a credit card, and confirm your consolidator reservation with the airline.

When you fly as a courier, you trade your checked-luggage space for a ticket deeply subsidized by a courier service. There are restrictions on when you can book and how long you can stay. Some courier companies list with membership organizations, such as the Air Courier Association and the International Association of Air Travel Couriers; these require you to become a member before you can book a flight.

◪ Consolidators **AirlineConsolidator.com** ☎ 888/468-5385 ⊕ www.airlineconsolidator.com; for international tickets. **Best Fares** ☎ 800/576-8255 or 800/576-1600 ⊕ www.bestfares.com; $59.90 annual membership. **Cheap Tickets** ☎ 800/377-1000 or 888/922-8849 ⊕ www.cheaptickets.com. **Expedia** ☎ 800/397-3342 or 404/728-8787 ⊕ www.expedia.com. **Hotwire** ☎ 866/468-9473 or 920/330-9418 ⊕ www.hotwire.com. **Now Voyager Travel** ⊠ 45 W. 21st St., 5th floor, New York, NY 10010 ☎ 212/459-1616 ☐ 212/243-2711 ⊕ www.nowvoyagertravel.com. **Onetravel.com** ⊕ www.onetravel.com. **Orbitz** ☎ 888/656-4546 ⊕ www.orbitz.com. **Priceline.com** ⊕ www.priceline.com. **Travelocity** ☎ 888/709-5983, 877/282-2925 in Canada, 0870/111-7060 in the U.K. ⊕ www.travelocity.com.

◪ Courier Resources **Air Courier Association/Cheaptrips.com** ☎ 800/282-1202 ⊕ www.aircourier.org or www.cheaptrips.com; $29 annual membership. **International Association of Air Travel Couriers** ☎ 308/632-3273 ⊕ www.courier.org; $45 annual membership.

## ENJOYING THE FLIGHT

State your seat preference when purchasing your ticket, and then repeat it when you confirm and when you check in. For more legroom, you can request one of the few emergency-aisle seats at check-in, if you are capable of lifting at least 50 pounds—a Federal Aviation Administration requirement of passengers in these seats. Seats behind a bulkhead also offer more legroom, but they don't have under-seat storage. Don't sit in the row in front of the emergency aisle or in front of a bulkhead, where seats may not recline.

Ask the airline whether a snack or meal is served on the flight. If you have dietary concerns, request special meals when booking. These can be vegetarian, low-cholesterol, or kosher, for example. It's a good idea to pack some healthful snacks and a small (plastic) bottle of water in your carry-on bag. On long flights, try to maintain a normal routine, to help fight jet lag. At night, get some sleep. By day, eat light meals, drink water (not alcohol), and **move around the cabin** to stretch your legs. For additional jet-lag tips consult *Fodor's FYI: Travel Fit & Healthy* (available at bookstores everywhere).

Smoking policies vary from carrier to carrier. Many airlines prohibit smoking on all of their flights; others allow smoking only on certain routes or certain departures. Ask your carrier about its policy.

### FLYING TIMES

It takes about 5 hours to fly nonstop to Portland from New York, about 4 hours from Chicago, and 2½ hours from Los Angeles.

### HOW TO COMPLAIN

If your baggage goes astray or your flight goes awry, complain right away. Most carriers require that you **file a claim immediately.** The Aviation Consumer Protection Division of the Department of Transportation publishes *Fly-Rights*, which discusses airlines and consumer issues and is available on-line. You can also find articles and information on mytravelrights.com, the Web site of the nonprofit Consumer Travel Rights Center.

🛪 Airline Complaints **Aviation Consumer Protection Division** ✉ U.S. Department of Transportation, C-75, Room 4107, 400 7th St. SW, Washington, DC 20590 ☎ 202/366-2220 ⊕ airconsumer.ost.dot.gov. **Federal Aviation Administration Consumer Hotline** ✉ for inquiries: FAA, 800 Independence Ave. SW, Washington, DC 20591 ☎ 800/322-7873 ⊕ www.faa.gov.

### RECONFIRMING

Check the status of your flight before you leave for the airport. You can do this on your carrier's Web site, by linking to a flight-status checker (many Web booking services offer these), or by calling your carrier or travel agent.

## AIRPORTS

The major airports in Oregon are Portland International Airport and Eugene Airport, also known as Mahlon Sweet Field. See the A to Z sections of the individual chapters for details about other airports.

🛪 Airport Information **Eugene Airport (EUG) (Mahlon Sweet Field)** ✉ 28855 Lockheed Dr. ☎ 541/682-5430 ⊕ www.eugeneairport.com. **Portland International Airport (PDX)** ✉ N.E. Airport Way at I-205 ☎ 877/739-4636 ⊕ www. portlandairportpdx.com or flypdx.com.

## BIKE TRAVEL

According to the Oregon Department of Transportation, Oregon ranks first in the country for bikeability due in part to an act of the legislature in 1971 that decreed that 1% of Oregon's gasoline tax would be spent the construction of bike paths and on-street bike lanes. That plan has blossomed. Portland is ranked number one in the big-city category for providing safe venues for cyclists. Eugene's bikeway master plan has put the smaller community in the number one position for its size. There are also bike paths along the Willamette River and other areas throughout the state for commuters as well as recreational users. Buses have bike racks for easy transport.

### BIKES IN FLIGHT

Most airlines accommodate bikes as luggage, provided they are dismantled and boxed; check with individual airlines about packing requirements. Some airlines sell bike boxes, which are often free at bike shops, for about $15 (bike bags can be considerably more expensive). International travelers often can substitute a bike for a piece of checked luggage at no charge; otherwise, the cost is about $100. U.S. and Canadian airlines charge $40–$80 each way.

Many bike shops will dismantle and box your bike for about $20 and will ship it for additional costs.

## BUS TRAVEL

Experience Oregon in Eugene and Gray Line in Portland operate charter bus services and scheduled sightseeing tours that last from a few hours to several days. Greyhound Lines services Oregon with routes from elsewhere on the West Coast and from points east. People Mover travels on U.S. 26 between Bend and John Day.
🚍 Bus Companies **Experience Oregon** ✉ 1574 Coburg Rd., No. 123, Eugene ☎ 541/342-2662 or 800/342-2662 ⊕ www.experience.oregon.com. **Gray Line** ☎ 503/285-9845 or 800/422-7042 in Portland ⊕ www.grayline.com. **Greyhound** ☎ 800/231-2222 ⊕ www.greyhound.com. **People Mover** ✉ 229 N.E. Dayton St., John Day ☎ 541/575-2370 or 800/527-2370.

## DISCOUNT PASSES

Greyhound's Ameripass, valid on all U.S. routes, allows unlimited bus travel within a 7-, 15-, 30-, or 60-day period. Greyhound also offers a **Western CanAm Pass** that's good for travel in British Columbia, Alberta, California, Arizona, New Mexico, Nevada, Utah, Oregon, Idaho, Washington, and Tijuana, Mexico.
🚍 Passes **Greyhound Ameripass** ☎ 800/231-2222 or 888/454-7277.

## CAMERAS & PHOTOGRAPHY

Whether you're snapping a gently reddening sunrise sky or bikers streaming through the streets of Portland, the light in Oregon lends itself to sharp outdoor photography. Many of the best photo ops are serendipitous, particularly when you're on the road or in between destinations; even a light, disposable camera, stowed in the glove compartment or your pocket, will do a more-than-serviceable job during your outdoor pursuits.

The *Kodak Guide to Shooting Great Travel Pictures* (available at bookstores everywhere) is loaded with tips.
🚍 Photo Help **Kodak Information Center** ☎ 800/242-2424 ⊕ www.kodak.com.

## EQUIPMENT PRECAUTIONS

**Don't pack film or equipment in checked luggage,** where it is much more susceptible to damage. X-ray machines used to view checked luggage are extremely powerful and therefore are likely to ruin your film. Try to ask for hand inspection of film, which becomes clouded after repeated exposure to airport X-ray machines, and keep videotapes and computer disks away from metal detectors. Always keep film, tape, and computer disks out of the sun. Carry an extra supply of batteries, and be prepared to turn on your camera, camcorder, or laptop to prove to airport security personnel that the device is real.

## CAR RENTAL

Rates in Portland begin at $35 a day and $145 a week, not including the 12.5% tax. Rates in Eugene begin at $19.95 a day and $125 a week, not including the 10% tax.
🚗 Major Agencies **Alamo** ☎ 800/327-9633, PDX: 503/249-4907 ⊕ www.alamo.com. **Avis** ☎ 800/331-1212, PDX: 503/249-4953, 800/879-2847 or 800/272-5871 in Canada, 0870/606-0100 in the U.K., 02/9353-9000 in Australia, 09/526-2847 in New Zealand ⊕ www.avis.com. **Budget** ☎ 800/527-0700, PDX: 503/249-4556, 0870/156-5656 in the U.K. ⊕ www.budget.com. **Dollar** ☎ 800/800-4000, PDX: 503/249-4792, 0124/622-0111 in the U.K., where it's affiliated with Sixt, 02/9223-1444 in Australia ⊕ www.dollar.com. **Hertz** ☎ 800/654-3131, PDX: 503/249-8216, 800/263-0600 in Canada, 0870/844-8844 in the U.K., 02/9669-2444 in Australia, 09/256-8690 in New Zealand ⊕ www.hertz.com. **National Car Rental** ☎ 800/227-7368, PDX: 503/249-4907, 0870/600-6666 in the U.K. ⊕ www.nationalcar.com. **Thrifty** ☎ 503/254-6563.

## CUTTING COSTS

For a good deal, book through a travel agent who will shop around. Also, price local car-rental companies—whose prices may be lower still, although their service and maintenance may not be as good as those of major rental agencies—and research rates on the Internet. Remember to ask about required deposits, cancellation penalties, and drop-off charges if you're planning to pick up the car in one city and leave it in another. If you're traveling during a holiday period, also make sure that a confirmed reservation guarantees you a car.
🚗 Local Agencies **Crown Auto Rental** ✉ 1315 N.E. Sandy, Portland ☎ 503/230-1103 ⊕ www.crownautorental.com. **Kendall Rent A Car** ✉ 10 Coburg Rd., Eugene ☎ 541/242-5820. **Rent-A-Wreck** ☎ 541/242-5820 or 800/327-0116 ⊕ www.rentawreck.com.

## INSURANCE

When driving a rented car, you are generally responsible for any damage to or loss of the vehicle. You also may be liable for any property damage or personal injury that you may cause while driving. Before you rent, see what coverage you already have under the terms of your personal auto-insurance policy and credit cards.

For about $9 to $25 a day, rental companies sell protection, known as a collision- or loss-damage waiver (CDW or LDW), that eliminates your liability for damage to the car; it's always optional and should never be automatically added to your bill. In most states you don't need a CDW if you have personal auto insurance or other liability insurance. However, **make sure you have enough coverage to pay for the car.** If you do not have auto insurance or an umbrella policy that covers damage to third parties, purchasing liability insurance and a CDW or LDW is highly recommended.

### REQUIREMENTS & RESTRICTIONS

In Oregon you must be 21 to rent a car. Non-U.S. residents will need a reservation voucher, a passport, a driver's license, and a travel policy that covers each driver, in order to pick up a car.

### SURCHARGES

Before you pick up a car in one city and leave it in another, ask about drop-off charges or one-way service fees, which can be substantial. Note, too, that some rental agencies charge extra if you return the car before the time specified in your contract. To avoid a hefty refueling fee, fill the tank just before you turn in the car, but be aware that gas stations near the rental outlet may overcharge. It's almost never a deal to buy the tank of gas that's in the car when you rent it; the understanding is that you'll return it empty, but some fuel usually remains.Surcharges may apply if you're under 25 or if you take the car outside the area approved by the rental agency. You'll pay extra for child seats (about $6 a day), which are compulsory for children under six, and usually for additional drivers (about $10 per day).

### CAR TRAVEL

I–5 and U.S. 101 enter Oregon heading north from California and south from Washington. I–84 and U.S. 26 head west from the Idaho border to Portland.

### ROAD CONDITIONS

Winter driving in Oregon can sometimes present some real challenges. In coastal areas the mild, damp climate contributes to frequently wet roadways. Snowfalls generally occur only once or twice a year, but when they do, traffic grinds to a halt and the roadways become treacherous and stay that way until the snow melts.

Tire chains, studs, or snow tires are essential equipment for winter travel in mountain areas. If you're planning to drive into high elevations, be sure to check the weather forecast beforehand. Even the main-highway mountain passes can be forced to close because of snow conditions. During the winter months state and provincial highway departments operate snow-advisory telephone lines that give pass conditions.

**Road Conditions hotline** ☎ 503/588–2941, 800/977–6368 in Oregon.

### ROAD MAPS

Road maps and atlases can be purchased at major bookstores and pharmacies. Many service stations with convenience stores also sell maps. Free maps can be obtained from state and province tourism offices ( ⇨ Visitor Information).

### RULES OF THE ROAD

The use of seat belts and child safety seats is mandatory for drivers and passengers in Oregon. The speed limit in Oregon on rural interstate highways is 65 mph. In urban areas the speed limit is 55 mph unless otherwise posted. Right turns, and left turns on adjoining one-way streets, are permitted at red lights after stopping. You must carry proof of liability auto insurance. It is a criminal offense to drive a vehicle with a blood alcohol content of 0.08 or more in Oregon.

Always strap children under age four or children 40 pounds or less into approved child-safety seats. Children who are at least four years old and under six years old or those who weigh between 40 and 60 pounds must be strapped into a seat that elevates the child so that a safety belt or harness properly fits the child. Children at least six years old who weigh 60 pounds or more must be strapped in with a safety belt or safety harness.

## CHILDREN IN OREGON

Children in Oregon will have plenty to do. Portland has a zoo and many parks with playgrounds. Indoor ice-skating rinks, ocean beaches, and aquatic centers are other child-friendly possibilities.

Be sure to plan ahead and involve your children as you outline your trip. When packing, include things to keep them busy en route. On sightseeing days try to schedule activities of special interest to your children. If you are renting a car, don't forget to arrange for a car seat when you reserve. For general advice about traveling with children, consult *Fodor's FYI: Travel with Your Baby* (available in bookstores everywhere).

### FLYING

If your children are two or older, ask about children's airfares. As a general rule, infants under two not occupying a seat fly at greatly reduced fares or even for free. But if you want to guarantee a seat for an infant, you have to pay full fare. Consider flying during off-peak days and times; most airlines will grant an infant a seat without a ticket if there are available seats.

Airlines set their own policies about safety seats: if you use one, U.S. carriers usually require that the child be ticketed, even if he or she is young enough to ride free, because the seats must be strapped into regular seats. And even if you pay the full adult fare for the seat, it may be worth it, especially on longer trips. Do **check your airline's policy about using safety seats during takeoff and landing.** Safety seats are not allowed everywhere in the plane, so get your seat assignments as early as possible.

When reserving, request children's meals or a freestanding bassinet (not available at all airlines) if you need them. But note that bulkhead seats, where you must sit to use the bassinet, may lack an overhead bin or storage space on the floor.

### LODGING

Most hotels in Oregon allow children under a certain age to stay in their parents' room at no extra charge, but others charge for them as extra adults; be sure to find out the cutoff age for children's discounts.

## SIGHTS & ATTRACTIONS

Places that are especially appealing to children are indicated by a rubber-duckie icon (☺) in the margin.

## CONSUMER PROTECTION

Whether you're shopping for gifts or purchasing travel services, **pay with a major credit card** whenever possible, so you can cancel payment or get reimbursed if there's a problem (and you can provide documentation). If you're doing business with a particular company for the first time, contact your local Better Business Bureau and the attorney general's offices in your state and (for U.S. businesses) the company's home state as well. Have any complaints been filed? Finally, if you're buying a package or tour, always consider travel insurance that includes default coverage (⇨ Insurance).

🏢 BBBs **Council of Better Business Bureaus** ✉ 4200 Wilson Blvd., Suite 800, Arlington, VA 22203 ☎ 703/276-0100 🖷 703/525-8277 ⊕ www. bbb.org.

## CRUISE TRAVEL

American West Steamboat Company runs stern-wheeler trips on the Columbia, Snake, and Willamette rivers. Portland Spirit has dining cruises on the Columbia and Willamette.

To learn how to plan, choose, and book a cruise-ship voyage, consult *Fodor's FYI: Plan & Enjoy Your Cruise* (available in bookstores everywhere).

🏢 Cruise Lines **American West Steamboat Company** ✉ 1200 N.W. Naito Pkwy., Suite 500, Portland 97209 ☎ 503/227-8047 ⊕ www. columbiarivercruise.com. **Portland Spirit** ✉ 110 S.E. Caruthers St., Portland 97214 ☎ 503/224-3900 or 800/224-3901 ⊕ www.portlandspirit.com.

## CUSTOMS & DUTIES

When shopping abroad, keep receipts for all purchases. Upon reentering the country, **be ready to show customs officials what you've bought.** Pack purchases together in an easily accessible place. If you think a duty is incorrect, appeal the assessment. If you object to the way your clearance was handled, note the inspector's badge number. In either case, first ask to see a supervisor. If the problem isn't resolved, write to the appropriate authorities, beginning with the port director at your point of entry.

## IN AUSTRALIA

Australian residents who are 18 or older may bring home A$400 worth of souvenirs and gifts (including jewelry), 250 cigarettes or 250 grams of cigars or other tobacco products, and 1,125 ml of alcohol (including wine, beer, and spirits). Residents under 18 may bring back A$200 worth of goods. Members of the same family traveling together may pool their allowances. Prohibited items include meat products. Seeds, plants, and fruits need to be declared upon arrival.

**Australian Customs Service** ☐ Regional Director, Box 8, Sydney, NSW 2001 ☎ 02/9213-2000 or 1300/363263, 02/9364-7222 or 1800/803-006 quarantine-inquiry line 🖷 02/9213-4043 ⊕ www.customs.gov.au.

## IN CANADA

Canadian residents who have been out of Canada for at least seven days may bring in C$750 worth of goods duty-free. If you've been away fewer than seven days but more than 48 hours, the duty-free allowance drops to C$200. If your trip lasts 24 to 48 hours, the allowance is C$50. You may not pool allowances with family members. Goods claimed under the C$750 exemption may follow you by mail; those claimed under the lesser exemptions must accompany you. Alcohol and tobacco products may be included in the seven-day and 48-hour exemptions but not in the 24-hour exemption. If you meet the age requirements of the province or territory through which you reenter Canada, you may bring in, duty-free, 1.5 liters of wine *or* 1.14 liters (40 imperial ounces) of liquor *or* 24 12-ounce cans or bottles of beer or ale. Also, if you meet the local age requirement for tobacco products, you may bring in, duty-free, 200 cigarettes and 50 cigars. Check ahead of time with the Canada Customs and Revenue Agency or the Department of Agriculture for policies regarding meat products, seeds, plants, and fruits.

You may send an unlimited number of gifts (only one gift per recipient, however) worth up to C$60 each duty-free to Canada. Label the package UNSOLICITED GIFT—VALUE UNDER $60. Alcohol and tobacco are excluded.

**Canada Customs and Revenue Agency** ☐ 2265 St. Laurent Blvd., Ottawa, Ontario K1G 4K3 ☎ 800/461-9999, 204/983-3500, 506/636-5064 ⊕ www.ccra.gc.ca.

## IN NEW ZEALAND

All homeward-bound residents may bring back NZ$700 worth of souvenirs and gifts; passengers may not pool their allowances, and children can claim only the concession on goods intended for their own use. For those 17 or older, the duty-free allowance also includes 4.5 liters of wine or beer; one 1,125-ml bottle of spirits; and either 200 cigarettes, 250 grams of tobacco, 50 cigars, *or* a combination of the three up to 250 grams. Meat products, seeds, plants, and fruits must be declared upon arrival to the Agricultural Services Department.

**New Zealand Customs** ☐ Head office: The Customhouse, 17–21 Whitmore St., Box 2218, Wellington ☎ 09/300-5399 or 0800/428-786 ⊕ www.customs.govt.nz.

## IN THE U.K.

If you are a U.K. resident and your journey was wholly within the European Union, you probably won't have to pass through customs when you return to the United Kingdom. If you plan to bring back large quantities of alcohol or tobacco, check EU limits beforehand. In most cases, if you bring back more than 200 cigars, 3,200 cigarettes, 10 liters of spirits, 110 liters of beer, and/or 90 liters of wine, you have to declare the goods upon return.

From countries outside the European Union, including the United States, you may bring home, duty-free, 200 cigarettes or 50 cigars; 1 liter of spirits or 2 liters of fortified or sparkling wine or liqueurs; 2 liters of still table wine; 60 ml of perfume; 250 ml of toilet water; plus £145 worth of other goods, including gifts and souvenirs. Prohibited items include meat products, seeds, plants, and fruits.

**HM Customs and Excise** ☐ Portcullis House, 21 Cowbridge Rd. E, Cardiff CF11 9SS ☎ 0845/010-9000 or 0208/929-0152, 0208/929-6731 or 0208/910-3602 complaints ⊕ www.hmce.gov.uk.

## DISABILITIES & ACCESSIBILITY

Travelers with disabilities will find Oregon well equipped to handle their needs, especially in Portland, Eugene, and Salem. City buses have lifts. Most buildings have ramps or elevators. Based in Eugene, Mobility International runs exchange and development programs for people with disabilities worldwide. Adventures Without Limits and Big Bear Countree offer trips to people of all abilities.

**🛈 Local Resources Adventures Without Limits** ✉ 1341 Pacific Ave., Forest Grove 97116 ☎ 503/359-2568. **Big Bear Countree** ✉ 17415 Panther Creek Rd., Carlton 97111 ☎ 503/852-7926 ⊕ www.bigbearcountree.com. **Mobility International** ✉ 45 W. Broadway Eugene 97401 ☎ 541/343-1284 [tel./TTY] ⊕ www.miusa.org.

## LODGING

Despite the Americans with Disabilities Act, the definition of accessibility seems to differ from hotel to hotel. Some properties may be accessible by ADA standards for people with mobility problems but not for people with hearing or vision impairments, for example.

If you have mobility problems, ask for the lowest floor on which accessible services are offered. If you have a hearing impairment, check whether the hotel has devices to alert you visually to the ring of the telephone, a knock at the door, and a fire/emergency alarm. Some hotels provide these devices without charge. Discuss your needs with hotel personnel if this equipment isn't available, so that a staff member can personally alert you in the event of an emergency.

If you're bringing a guide dog, get authorization ahead of time and write down the name of the person with whom you spoke.

## RESERVATIONS

When discussing accessibility with an operator or reservations agent, ask hard questions. Are there any stairs, inside *or* out? Are there grab bars next to the toilet *and* in the shower/tub? How wide is the doorway to the room? To the bathroom? For the most extensive facilities meeting the latest legal specifications, opt for newer accommodations. If you reserve through a toll-free number, consider also calling the hotel's local number to confirm the information from the central reservations office. Get confirmation in writing when you can.

## SIGHTS & ATTRACTIONS

In compliance with the Americans with Disabilities Act, major attractions and zoos in Oregon are accessible to persons with disabilities via wheelchair ramps, elevators, and automatic doors.

## TRANSPORTATION

Portland's Tri-Met buses, streetcars, and MAX light-rail trains operate accessible public transit vehicles for persons with physical disabilities.

**🛈 Complaints Aviation Consumer Protection Division** (⇨ Air Travel) for airline-related problems. **Departmental Office of Civil Rights** ✉ for general inquiries, U.S. Department of Transportation, S-30, 400 7th St. SW, Room 10215, Washington, DC 20590 ☎ 202/366-4648 ᴁ 202/366-9371 ⊕ www.dot.gov/ost/docr/index.htm. **Disability Rights Section** ✉ NYAV, U.S. Department of Justice, Civil Rights Division, 950 Pennsylvania Ave. NW, Washington, DC 20530 ᴁ ADA information line 202/514-0301, 800/514-0301, 202/514-0383 TTY, 800/514-0383 TTY ⊕ www.ada.gov. **U.S. Department of Transportation Hotline** ᴁ for disability-related air-travel problems, 800/778-4838 or 800/455-9880 TTY.

## TRAVEL AGENCIES

In the United States, the Americans with Disabilities Act requires that travel firms serve the needs of all travelers. Some agencies specialize in working with people with disabilities.

**🛈 Travelers with Mobility Problems Access Adventures/B. Roberts Travel** ✉ 206 Chestnut Ridge Rd., Scottsville, NY 14624 ☎ 585/889-9096 ⊕ www.brobertstravel.com ✎ dltravel@prodigy.net, run by a former physical-rehabilitation counselor. **Accessible Vans of America** ✉ 9 Spielman Rd., Fairfield, NJ 07004 ☎ 877/282-8267, 888/282-8267, 973/808-9709 reservations ᴁ 973/808-9713 ⊕ www.accessiblevans.com. **CareVacations** ✉ No. 5, 5110-50 Ave., Leduc, Alberta, Canada T9E 6V4 ☎ 780/986-6404 or 877/478-7827 ᴁ 780/986-8332 ⊕ www.carevacations.com, for group tours and cruise vacations. **Flying Wheels Travel** ✉ 143 W. Bridge St., Box 382, Owatonna, MN 55060 ☎ 507/451-5005 ᴁ 507/451-1685 ⊕ www.flyingwheelstravel.com.

**🛈 Travelers with Developmental Disabilities New Directions** ✉ 5276 Hollister Ave., Suite 207, Santa Barbara, CA 93111 ☎ 805/967-2841 or 888/967-2841 ᴁ 805/964-7344 ⊕ www.newdirectionstravel.com. **Sprout** ✉ 893 Amsterdam Ave., New York, NY 10025 ☎ 212/222-9575 or 888/222-9575 ᴁ 212/222-9768 ⊕ www.gosprout.org.

## DISCOUNTS & DEALS

Be a smart shopper and compare all your options before making decisions. A plane ticket bought with a promotional coupon from travel clubs, coupon books, and direct-mail offers or purchased on the Internet may not be cheaper than the least expensive fare from a discount ticket agency. And always keep in mind that what you get is just as important as what you save.

## DISCOUNT RESERVATIONS

To save money, look into discount reservations services with Web sites and toll-free numbers, which use their buying power to get a better price on hotels, airline tickets ( ⇨ Air Travel), even car rentals. When booking a room, always **call the hotel's local toll-free number** (if one is available) rather than the central reservations number—you'll often get a better price. Always ask about special packages or corporate rates.

**7** Airline Tickets **Air 4 Less** ☎ 800/AIR4LESS; low-fare specialist.

**7** Hotel Rooms **Accommodations Express** ☎ 800/444-7666 or 800/277-1064 ⊕ www. accommodationsexpress.com. **Hotels.com** ☎ 800/ 246-8357 ⊕ www.hotels.com. **Quikbook** ☎ 800/ 789-9887 ⊕ www.quikbook.com. **RMC Travel** ☎ 800/245-5738 ⊕ www.rmcwebtravel.com. **Turbotrip.com** ☎ 800/473-7829 ⊕ www. turbotrip.com.

## PACKAGE DEALS

Don't confuse packages and guided tours. When you buy a package, you travel on your own, just as though you had planned the trip yourself. Fly/drive packages, which combine airfare and car rental, are often a good deal. In cities, ask the local visitor's bureau about hotel packages that include tickets to major museum exhibits or other special events.

## EATING & DRINKING

You'll find almost any type of cuisine in Portland. Pacific Northwest cuisine highlights regional seafood and locally grown produce, often prepared in styles that reflect an Asian influence. In each price category, the restaurants we list are the cream of the crop, and unless otherwise noted, they are open daily for lunch and dinner.

| CATEGORY | COST |
| --- | --- |
| $$$$ | over $30 |
| $$$ | $20-$30 |
| $$ | $15-$20 |
| $ | $10-$15 |
| ¢ | under $10 |

*Restaurant prices are per person for a main course at dinner.*

## RESERVATIONS & DRESS

Reservations are always a good idea; we mention them only when they're essential or not accepted. Book as far ahead as you can, and reconfirm as soon as you arrive. (Large parties should always call ahead to check the reservations policy.) We mention dress only when men are required to wear a jacket or a jacket and tie.

## WINE, BEER & SPIRITS

Oregon is a particular joy for beer and pinot noir fans. Beyond the state's breweries and wineries, beer and some wine, depending on the alcohol percentage, can be found in grocery stores. Even though a recent law gives liquor stores the opportunity to open on Sunday, many are only open Monday–Saturday.

You must be 21 to buy alcohol in Oregon.

## ECOTOURISM

The citizens of Oregon are actively interested in preserving their environment; protesters have been known to take residence in trees that they don't want razed. Oregon's ailing timber economy has received some federal funding, allowing the state to focus on tourism while managing the environment. While visiting, consider all wild plants and vegetation off-limits; to play it safe, don't pick anything. It is also important not to stray off paths in parks to avoid erosion. Protection of marine mammals is also of particular concern, and whale-watching is a big business here.

As anywhere, be careful to discard cigarette butts in designated receptacles to help prevent forest fires.

## EMERGENCIES

**7** For **police, ambulance,** or **other emergencies** in Oregon, dial 911. Oregon State Police ☎ 800/452-7888.

## GAY & LESBIAN TRAVEL

A majority of Oregon's gay bars are in Portland. During the third week of June, the Portland Pride Parade & Festival takes place at Tom McCall Waterfront Park. Also in June is the Eugene/Springfield Lesbian, Gay, Bisexual, and Transgender event and the Eugene Gay Pride Celebration.

*Just Out* is an Oregon-based publication and Web site with expansive information for the gay and lesbian community.

As a community resource, Portland has a hot line for gay and lesbian residents and travelers.

For more details about the gay and lesbian scene, consult *Fodor's Gay Guide to the USA* (available in bookstores everywhere).
📱 Resources **Hotline (Portland)** ☎ 800/777-2437. **Just Out** ☎ 503/236-1252 ⊕ www.justout.com.
📱 Gay- & Lesbian-Friendly Travel Agencies **Different Roads Travel** ⊠ 8383 Wilshire Blvd., Suite 520, Beverly Hills, CA 90211 ☎ 323/651-5557 or 800/429-8747 [Ext. 14 for both] 📠 323/651-3678
✍ lgernert@tzell.com. **Kennedy Travel** ⊠ 130 W. 42nd St., Suite 401, New York, NY 10036 ☎ 212/840-8659, 800/237-7433 📠 212/730-2269 ⊕ www.kennedytravel.com. **Now, Voyager** ⊠ 4406 18th St., San Francisco, CA 94114 ☎ 415/626-1169 or 800/255-6951 📠 415/626-8626 ⊕ www.nowvoyager.com. **Skylink Travel and Tour** ⊠ 1455 N. Dutton Ave., Suite A, Santa Rosa, CA 95401 ☎ 707/546-9888 or 800/225-5759 📠 707/636-0951; serving lesbian travelers.

## HOLIDAYS

Major national holidays are New Year's Day (Jan. 1); Martin Luther King Day (3rd Mon. in Jan.); Presidents' Day (3rd Mon. in Feb.); Memorial Day (last Mon. in May); Independence Day (July 4); Labor Day (1st Mon. in Sept.); Columbus Day (2nd Mon. in Oct.); Thanksgiving Day (4th Thurs. in Nov.); Christmas Eve and Christmas Day (Dec. 24 and 25); and New Year's Eve (Dec. 31).

## INSURANCE

The most useful travel-insurance plan is a comprehensive policy that includes coverage for trip cancellation and interruption, default, trip delay, and medical expenses (with a waiver for preexisting conditions).

Without insurance you'll lose all or most of your money if you cancel your trip, regardless of the reason. Default insurance covers you if your tour operator, airline, or cruise line goes out of business. Trip-delay covers expenses that arise because of bad weather or mechanical delays. Study the fine print when comparing policies.

Always **buy travel policies directly from the insurance company**; if you buy them from a cruise line, airline, or tour operator

that goes out of business you probably won't be covered for the agency or operator's default, a major risk. Before making any purchase, review your existing health and home-owner's policies to find what they cover away from home.
📱 Travel Insurers In the U.S.: **Access America** ⊠ 6600 W. Broad St., Richmond, VA 23230 ☎ 800/284-8300 📠 804/673-1491 or 800/346-9265 ⊕ www.accessamerica.com. **Travel Guard International** ⊠ 1145 Clark St., Stevens Point, WI 54481 ☎ 715/345-0505 or 800/826-1300 📠 800/955-8785 ⊕ www.travelguard.com.

## FOR INTERNATIONAL TRAVELERS

For information on customs restrictions, *see* Customs & Duties, *above*.

### CAR RENTAL

When picking up a rental car, non-U.S. residents need a reservation voucher for any prepaid reservations that were made in the traveler's home country, a passport, a driver's license, and a travel policy that covers each driver.

### CAR TRAVEL

In Oregon, gasoline costs $1.39–$1.77 a gallon. Stations are plentiful. Most stay open late (24 hours along large highways and in big cities), except in rural areas, where Sunday hours are limited and where you may drive long stretches without a refueling opportunity. Highways are well paved. Interstate highways—limited-access, multilane highways whose numbers are prefixed by "I-"—are the fastest routes. Interstates with three-digit numbers encircle urban areas, which may have other limited-access expressways, freeways, and parkways as well. So-called U.S. highways and state highways are not necessarily limited-access but may have several lanes.

Along larger highways, roadside stops with rest rooms, fast-food restaurants, and sundries stores are well spaced. State police and tow trucks patrol major highways and lend assistance. If your car breaks down on an interstate, pull onto the shoulder and wait for help, or have your passengers wait while you walk to an emergency phone. If you carry a cell phone, dial *55, referring to the small green roadside mileage markers to note your location.

Driving in the United States is on the right. Do **obey speed limits** posted along roads and highways. Watch for lower limits in small towns and on back roads. All passengers are required to wear seat belts. In Portland on weekdays between 6 and 10 AM and again between 4 and 7 PM **expect heavy traffic.**

Bookstores, gas stations, convenience stores, and rest stops sell maps (about $3) and multiregion road atlases (about $10).

## CURRENCY

The dollar is the basic unit of U.S. currency. It has 100 cents. Coins are the copper penny (1¢); the silvery nickel (5¢), dime (10¢), quarter (25¢), and half-dollar (50¢); and the golden $1 coin, replacing a now-rare silver dollar. Bills are denominated $1, $5, $10, $20, $50, and $100, all green and identical in size; designs vary. In addition, you may come across a $2 bill, but the chances are slim. The exchange rate at this writing was US$1.65 per British pound, 74¢ per Canadian dollar, 68¢ per Australian dollar, and 60¢ per New Zealand dollar.

## ELECTRICITY

The U.S. standard is AC, 110 volts/60 cycles. Plugs have two flat pins set parallel to each other.

## EMERGENCIES

For police, fire, or ambulance, **dial 911** (0 in rural areas).

## INSURANCE

Britons and Australians need extra medical coverage when traveling overseas.
**F** Insurance Information In the U.K.: **Association of British Insurers** ✉ 51 Gresham St., London EC2V 7HQ ☎ 020/7600-3333 🖷 020/7696-8999 🌐 www.abi.org.uk. In Australia: **Insurance Council of Australia** ✉ Insurance Enquiries and Complaints, Level 3, 56 Pitt St., Sydney, NSW 2000 ☎ 1300/363683 or 02/9251-4456 🖷 02/9251-4453 🌐 www.iecltd.com.au. In Canada: **RBC Insurance** ✉ 6880 Financial St., Mississauga, Ontario L5N 7Y5 ☎ 800/565-3129 🖷 905/813-4704 🌐 www. rbcinsurance.com. In New Zealand: **Insurance Council of New Zealand** ✉ Level 7, 111-115 Customhouse Quay, Box 474, Wellington ☎ 04/472-5230 🖷 04/473-3011 🌐 www.icnz.org.nz.

## MAIL & SHIPPING

You can buy stamps and aerograms and send letters and parcels in post offices.

Stamp-dispensing machines can occasionally be found in airports, bus and train stations, office buildings, drugstores, and the like. You can also deposit mail in the stout, dark-blue steel bins at strategic locations everywhere and in the mail chutes of large buildings; pickup schedules are posted. You can deposit packages at public collection boxes as long as the parcels are affixed with proper postage and weigh less than one pound. Packages weighing one or more pounds must be taken to a post office or handed to a postal carrier.

For mail sent within the United States, you need a 37¢ stamp for first-class letters weighing up to 1 ounce (23¢ for each additional ounce) and 23¢ for postcards. You pay 80¢ for 1-ounce airmail letters and 70¢ for airmail postcards to most other countries; to Canada and Mexico, you need a 60¢ stamp for a 1-ounce letter and 50¢ for a postcard. An aerogram—a single sheet of lightweight blue paper that folds into its own envelope, stamped for overseas airmail—costs 70¢.

To receive mail on the road, have it sent c/o General Delivery at your destination's main post office (use the correct five-digit ZIP code). You must pick up mail in person within 30 days and show a driver's license or passport.

## PASSPORTS & VISAS

When traveling internationally, carry your passport even if you don't need one (it's always the best form of ID) and **make two photocopies of the data page** (one for someone at home and another for you, carried separately from your passport). If you lose your passport, promptly call the nearest embassy or consulate and the local police.

Visitor visas aren't necessary for Canadian or European Union citizens, or for citizens of Australia who are staying fewer than 90 days.
**F** Australian Citizens **Passports Australia** ☎ 131-232 🌐 www.passports.gov.au. **United States Consulate General** ✉ MLC Centre, Level 59, 19-29 Martin Pl., Sydney, NSW 2000 ☎ 02/9373-9200, 1902/941-641 fee-based visa-inquiry line 🌐 usembassy-australia.state.gov/sydney.
**F** Canadian Citizens **Passport Office** ✉ to mail in applications: 200 Promenade du Portage, Hull, Québec J8X 4B7 ☎ 819/994-3500, 800/567-6868, 866/255-7655 TTY 🌐 www.ppt.gc.ca.

🇳🇿 New Zealand Citizens **New Zealand Passports Office** ✉ for applications and information, Level 3, Boulcott House, 47 Boulcott St., Wellington ☎ 0800/22-5050 or 04/474-8100 ⊕ www.passports.govt.nz. **Embassy of the United States** ✉ 29 Fitzherbert Terr., Thorndon, Wellington ☎ 04/462-6000 ⊕ usembassy.org.nz. **U.S. Consulate General** ✉ Citibank Bldg., 3rd floor, 23 Customs St. E, Auckland ☎ 09/303-2724 ⊕ usembassy.org.nz.

🇬🇧 U.K. Citizens **U.K. Passport Service** ☎ 0870/521-0410 ⊕ www.passport.gov.uk. **American Consulate General** ✉ Queen's House, 14 Queen St., Belfast, Northern Ireland BT1 6EQ ☎ 028/9032-8239 📠 028/9024-8482 ⊕ www.usembassy.org.uk. **American Embassy** ✉ for visa and immigration information [enclose an SASE], Consular Information Unit, 24 Grosvenor Sq., London W1 1AE ✉ to submit an application via mail, Visa Branch, 5 Upper Grosvenor St., London W1A 2JB ☎ 09068/200-290 recorded visa information or 09055/444-546 operator service, both with per-minute charges, 0207/499-9000 main switchboard ⊕ www.usembassy.org.uk.

## TELEPHONES

All U.S. telephone numbers consist of a three-digit area code and a seven-digit local number. Within many local calling areas, you dial only the seven-digit number. Within some area codes, you must dial "1" first for calls outside the local area. To call between area-code regions, dial "1" then all 10 digits; the same goes for calls to numbers prefixed by "800," "888," "866," and "877"—all toll free. For calls to numbers preceded by "900" you must pay—usually dearly.

For international calls, dial "011" followed by the country code and the local number. For help, dial "0" and ask for an overseas operator. The country code is 61 for Australia, 64 for New Zealand, 44 for the United Kingdom. Calling Canada is the same as calling within the United States. Most local phone books list country codes and U.S. area codes. The country code for the United States is 1.

For operator assistance, dial "0." To obtain someone's phone number, call directory assistance at 555–1212 or occasionally 411 (free at public phones). To have the person you're calling foot the bill, phone collect; dial "0" instead of "1" before the 10-digit number.

At pay phones, instructions often are posted. Usually you insert coins in a slot (usually 25¢–50¢ for local calls) and wait for a steady tone before dialing. When you call long-distance, the operator tells you how much to insert; prepaid phone cards, widely available in various denominations, are easier. Call the number on the back, punch in the card's personal identification number when prompted, then dial your number.

## LODGING

Hotels in the major tourist destinations are often filled in July and August, so it's important to **book reservations in advance.** The lodgings we list are the cream of the crop in each price category. We always list the facilities that are available, but we don't specify whether they cost extra; when pricing accommodations, always ask what's included and what costs extra. Properties are assigned price categories based on the range between their least and most expensive standard double room at high season (excluding holidays). Properties marked ✕🏨 are lodging establishments whose restaurants warrant a special trip.

Assume that hotels operate on the European Plan (EP, with no meals) unless we specify that they use either the Continental Plan (CP, with a Continental breakfast), Breakfast Plan (BP, with a full breakfast), or the Modified American Plan (MAP, with breakfast and dinner) or are all-inclusive (including all meals and most activities).

| CATEGORY | COST |
| --- | --- |
| $$$$ | over $180 |
| $$$ | $140–$180 |
| $$ | $100–$140 |
| $ | $60–$100 |
| ¢ | under $60 |

*Hotel prices are for a standard double room, excluding room tax, which varies 6%–91/2% depending on location.*

### APARTMENT & VILLA RENTALS

If you want a home base that's roomy enough for a family and comes with cooking facilities, consider a furnished rental. These can save you money, especially if you're traveling with a group. Home-exchange directories sometimes list rentals as well as exchanges.

🏠 International Agents **Hideaways International** ✉ 767 Islington St., Portsmouth, NH 03801 ☎ 603/430-4433 or 800/843-4433 📠 603/430-4444 ⊕ www.hideaways.com; membership $145.

**F** Local Agents Portland: **French Home Rentals** ☎ 503/219-9190. Seattle: **Vacation Getaways** ☎ 206/283-5829.

**F** Rental Listings **Discover Sunriver Vacation Rentals** ✉ Sunriver Village Mall No. 9, Box 3247, Sunriver, OR 97707 ☎ 541/593-2482 or 800/544-0300 ⊕ www.discoversunriver.com. **Falcon Cove Ocean Front Getaway** ☎ 503/698-8217, 800/617-8564. **Pacifica House** ✉ 1902 N.W. Cunard St., Waldport ☎ 541/563-7742 ⊕ oregoncoastpacifica.com.

## BED-AND-BREAKFASTS

The Pacific Northwest is known for its many bed-and-breakfast properties, in urban areas, in country settings, and along the coast. Most B&Bs provide Continental breakfasts, some offer full breakfasts, and some have kitchens that guests can use.

The organizations listed below can provide information on reputable establishments. One of them, American Bed & Breakfast, Inter-Bed Network, allows you to book a B&B before leaving the United Kingdom.

**F** Reservation Services **Oregon** ☎ 800/944-6196. **Northwest Bed & Breakfast Reservation Service** ✉ 610 S.W. Broadway, Portland, OR 97205 ☎ 503/243-7616 or 877/243-7782. **American Bed & Breakfast, Inter-Bed Network** ✉ 31 Ernest Rd., Colchester, Essex CO7 9LQ ☎ 0206/223162.

## CAMPING

Oregon has excellent government-run campgrounds. A few accept advance camping reservations, but most do not. Privately operated campgrounds sometimes have extra amenities such as laundry rooms and swimming pools. For more information, contact the state or provincial tourism department.

## HOME EXCHANGES

If you would like to exchange your home for someone else's, join a home-exchange organization, which will send you its updated listings of available exchanges for a year and will include your own listing in at least one of them. It's up to you to make specific arrangements.

**F** Exchange Clubs **Digsville Home Exchange** ✉ 1100 Valley Brook Ave., Lyndhurst, NJ 07071 ☎ 800/856-9059 or 201/964-9044 ⊕ www.digsville.com; $49.95 yearly dues. **HomeLink International** ✉ Box 47747, Tampa, FL 33647 ☎ 813/975-9825 or 800/638-3841 ☎ 813/910-8144 ⊕ www.homelink.org; $110 yearly for a listing, online access, and catalog; $70 without catalog. **Inter-**

**vac U.S.** ✉ 30 Corte San Fernando, Tiburon, CA 94920 ☎ 800/756-4663 ☎ 415/435-7440 ⊕ www.intervacus.com; $125 yearly for a listing, on-line access, and a catalog; $50 without catalog.

## HOSTELS

No matter what your age, you can save on lodging costs by staying at hostels. In some 4,500 locations in more than 70 countries around the world, Hostelling International (HI), the umbrella group for a number of national youth-hostel associations, offers single-sex, dorm-style beds and, at many hostels, rooms for couples and family accommodations. Membership in any HI national hostel association, open to travelers of all ages, allows you to stay in HI-affiliated hostels at member rates; one-year membership is about $28 for adults (C$35 for a two-year minimum membership in Canada, £13.50 in the U.K., A$52 in Australia, and NZ$40 in New Zealand); hostels charge about $10–$30 per night. Members have priority if the hostel is full; they're also eligible for discounts around the world, even on rail and bus travel in some countries.

**F** Organizations **Hostelling International–USA** ✉ 8401 Colesville Rd., Suite 600, Silver Spring, MD 20910 ☎ 301/495-1240 ☎ 301/495-6697 ⊕ www.hiayh.org. **Hostelling International–Canada** ✉ 205 Catherine St., Suite 400, Ottawa, Ontario K2P 1C3 ☎ 613/237-7884 or 800/663-5777 ☎ 613/237-7868 ⊕ www.hihostels.ca. **YHA England and Wales** ✉ Trevelyan House, Dimple Rd., Matlock, Derbyshire DE4 3YH, U.K. ☎ 0870/870-8808, 0870/770-8868, 0162/959-2700 ☎ 0870/770-6127 ⊕ www.yha.org.uk. **YHA Australia** ✉ 422 Kent St., Sydney, NSW 2001 ☎ 02/9261-1111 ☎ 02/9261-1969 ⊕ www.yha.com.au. **YHA New Zealand** ✉ Level 4, Torrens House, 195 Hereford St., Box 436, Christchurch ☎ 03/379-9970 or 0800/278-299 ☎ 03/365-4476 ⊕ www.yha.org.nz.

## HOTELS

Always ask about special packages or corporate rates when booking your room. Many properties offer special weekend rates, sometimes up to 50% off regular prices. However, these deals are usually not extended during peak summer months, when hotels are normally full. All hotels listed have private bath unless otherwise noted.

**F** Toll-Free Numbers **Best Western** ☎ 800/528-1234 ⊕ www.bestwestern.com. **Choice** ☎ 800/424-6423 ⊕ www.choicehotels.com. **Comfort Inn** ☎ 800/424-6423 ⊕ www.choicehotels.com. **Days**

Inn ☎ 800/325-2525 ⊕ www.daysinn.com. **Dou-bletree Hotels** ☎ 800/222-8733 ⊕ www.doubletree.com. **Embassy Suites** ☎ 800/362-2779 ⊕ www.embassysuites.com. **Fairfield Inn** ☎ 800/228-2800 ⊕ www.marriott.com. **Hilton** ☎ 800/445-8667 ⊕ www.hilton.com. **Holiday Inn** ☎ 800/465-4329 ⊕ www.sixcontinentshotels.com. **Howard Johnson** ☎ 800/446-4656 ⊕ www.hojo.com. **Hyatt Hotels & Resorts** ☎ 800/233-1234 ⊕ www.hyatt.com. **La Quinta** ☎ 800/531-5900 ⊕ www.laquinta.com. **Marriott** ☎ 800/228-9290 ⊕ www.marriott.com. **Quality Inn** ☎ 800/424-6423 ⊕ www.choicehotels.com. **Radisson** ☎ 800/333-3333 ⊕ www.radisson.com. **Ramada** ☎ 800/228-2828, 800/854-7854 international reservations ⊕ www.ramada.com or www.ramadahotels.com. **Red Lion and WestCoast Hotels and Inns** ☎ 800/733-5466 ⊕ www.redlion.com. **Sheraton** ☎ 800/325-3535 ⊕ www.starwood.com/sheraton. **Sleep Inn** ☎ 800/424-6423 ⊕ www.choicehotels.com. **Westin Hotels & Resorts** ☎ 800/228-3000 ⊕ www.starwood.com/westin.

## MEDIA

### NEWSPAPERS & MAGAZINES

There are about 15 daily newspapers and about 31 non-daily newspapers in Oregon. The *Oregonian,* Portland's daily paper, has an extensive entertainment and travel section. The *Register-Guard,* a family-owned paper in Eugene, also has a good entertainment section. The *Statesman Journal* in Salem has good overall news and entertainment coverage. The *Portland Alliance,* a free monthly newspaper, is heavy on liberal politics and covers progressive entertainment.

### RADIO & TELEVISION

KBOO 90.7 FM in Portland, 91.9 FM in the Columbia River Gorge, and 100.7 FM in the Willamette Valley are community non-profit stations aimed at a diverse audience. KLCC 89.7 FM in Eugene is an independent public radio station. KWAX 91.1 FM, owned and operated by the University of Oregon, Eugene, programs classical music 24 hours a day. For all-classical music in Portland, tune in KBPS 89.9 FM. Oregon Public Broadcasting can be found at KOPB 91.5 FM in Portland and KOAC 550 AM from Oregon State University in Corvallis.

The ABC network affiliate is KEZI in Eugene, KDKE in Klamath Falls, KDRV in Medford, and KATU in Portland. CBS affiliates are KCBY in Coos Bay, KVAL in Eugene, KTVL in Medford, and KOIN in Portland. NBC affiliates are KTVZ in Bend, KMTR/KMTX in Eugene, KOBI/KOTI in Medford, and KGW in Portland. Public Broadcasting stations can be found statewide on KEPB, KOAB, KOPB, KTVR, and KOAC. In Medford, PBS is on SOPT.

## MONEY MATTERS

Prices for meals and accommodations in Oregon are generally lower than in other major North American regions. Prices for first-class hotel rooms in Portland range from $100 to $200 a night, although you can still find some "value" hotel rooms for $65–$90 a night.

As a rule, costs outside the major cities are lower, but prices for rooms and meals at some of the major deluxe resorts can rival or exceed those at the best big-city hotels.

Prices throughout this guide are given for adults. Substantially reduced fees are almost always available for children, students, and senior citizens.

### ATMS

You'll find numerous ATMs in Portland, Eugene, Salem, and Corvallis. You may have to do some hunting in the smaller communities, though many grocery stores have ATMs available.
🄵 **ATM Locations Cirrus** ☎ 800/424-7787. **Plus** ☎ 800/843-7587.

### CREDIT CARDS

Throughout this guide, the following abbreviations are used: **AE**, American Express; **D**, Discover; **DC**, Diners Club; **MC**, MasterCard; and **V**, Visa.
🄵 **Reporting Lost Cards American Express** ☎ 800/441-0519. **Diners Club** ☎ 800/234-6377. **Discover** ☎ 800/347-2683. **MasterCard** ☎ 800/622-7747. **Visa** ☎ 800/847-2911.

## NATIONAL PARKS

Look into discount passes to save money on park entrance fees. For $50, the National Parks Pass admits you (and any passengers in your private vehicle) to all national parks, monuments, and recreation areas, as well as other sites run by the National Park Service, for a year. (In parks that charge per person, the pass admits you, your spouse and children, and your parents, when you arrive together.)

Camping and parking are extra. The $15 Golden Eagle Pass, a hologram you affix to your National Parks Pass, functions as an upgrade, granting entry to all sites run by the NPS, the U.S. Fish and Wildlife Service, the U.S. Forest Service, and the Bureau of Land Management. The upgrade, which expires with the parks pass, is sold by most national-park, Fish and Wildlife, and BLM fee stations. A percentage of the proceeds from pass sales funds National Parks projects.

Both the Golden Age Passport ($10), for U.S. citizens or permanent residents who are 62 and older, and the Golden Access Passport (free), for those with disabilities, entitle holders (and any passengers in their private vehicles) to lifetime free entry to all national parks, plus 50% off fees for the use of many park facilities and services. (The discount doesn't always apply to companions.) To obtain them, you must show proof of age and of U.S. citizenship or permanent residency—such as a U.S. passport, driver's license, or birth certificate—and, if requesting Golden Access, proof of disability. The Golden Age and Golden Access passes are available only at NPS-run sites that charge an entrance fee. The National Parks Pass is also available by mail and via the Internet.
🏛 **National Park Foundation** ✉ 11 Dupont Circle NW, 6th floor, Washington, DC 20036 ☎ 202/238-4200 ⊕ www.nationalparks.org. **National Park Service** ✉ National Park Service/Department of Interior, 1849 C St. NW, Washington, DC 20240 ☎ 202/208-6843 ⊕ www.nps.gov. **National Parks Conservation Association** ✉ 1300 19th St. NW, Suite 300, Washington, DC 20036 ☎ 202/223-6722 ⊕ www.npca.org.
🏛 Passes by Mail & Online **National Park Foundation** ⊕ www.nationalparks.org. **National Parks Pass** ✍ Box 34108, Washington, DC 20043 ☎ 888/467-2757 ⊕ www.nationalparks.org; include a check or money order payable to the National Park Service, plus $3.95 for shipping and handling, or call for passes by phone.

## PACKING

Residents of Oregon are generally informal by nature and wear clothing that reflects their disposition. Summer days are warm, but evenings can cool off substantially. Your best bet is to **dress in layers**—sweatshirts, sweaters, and jackets are removed or put on as the day progresses. If you plan to explore the region's cities

on foot, or if you choose to hike along mountain trails or beaches, take comfortable walking shoes. Locals tend to dress conservatively when going to the theater or symphony, but it's not uncommon to see some patrons wearing jeans. In other words, almost anything is acceptable for most occasions.

It's a good idea to **take a collapsible umbrella or a rain slicker,** especially if you're traveling to western Oregon in winter. If you plan on hiking or camping during the summer, insect repellent is a must.

In your carry-on luggage, pack an extra pair of eyeglasses or contact lenses and enough of any medication you take to last a few days longer than the entire trip. You may also ask your doctor to write a spare prescription using the drug's generic name, as brand names may vary from country to country. In luggage to be checked, **never pack prescription drugs, valuables, or undeveloped film.** And don't forget to carry with you the addresses of offices that handle refunds of lost traveler's checks. Check *Fodor's How to Pack* (available at online retailers and bookstores everywhere) for more tips.

To avoid customs and security delays, carry medications in their original packaging. Don't pack any sharp objects in your carry-on luggage, including knives of any size or material, scissors, and corkscrews, or anything else that might arouse suspicion.

To avoid having your checked luggage chosen for hand inspection, don't cram bags full. The U.S. Transportation Security Administration suggests packing shoes on top and placing personal items you don't want touched in clear plastic bags.

### CHECKING LUGGAGE

You're allowed to carry aboard one bag and one personal article, such as a purse or a laptop computer. Make sure what you carry on fits under your seat or in the overhead bin. Get to the gate early, so you can board as soon as possible, before the overhead bins fill up.

Baggage allowances vary by carrier, destination, and ticket class. On international flights, you're usually allowed to check two bags weighing up to 70 pounds (32 kilograms) each, although a few airlines allow checked bags of up to 88 pounds

(40 kilograms) in first class. Some international carriers don't allow more than 66 pounds (30 kilograms) per bag in business class and 44 pounds (20 kilograms) in economy. On domestic flights, the limit is usually 50 to 70 pounds (23 to 32 kilograms) per bag. In general, carry-on bags shouldn't exceed 40 pounds (18 kilograms). Most airlines won't accept bags that weigh more than 100 pounds (45 kilograms) on domestic or international flights. Check baggage restrictions with your carrier before you pack.

Airline liability for baggage is limited to $2,500 per person on flights within the United States. On international flights it amounts to $9.07 per pound or $20 per kilogram for checked baggage (roughly $640 per 70-pound bag), with a maximum of $634.90 per piece and $400 per passenger for unchecked baggage. You can buy additional coverage at check-in for about $10 per $1,000 of coverage, but it often excludes a rather extensive list of items, shown on your airline ticket.

Before departure, itemize your bags' contents and their worth, and label the bags with your name, address, and phone number. (If you use your home address, cover it so potential thieves can't see it readily.) Include a label inside each bag, and **pack a copy of your itinerary.** At check-in, make sure each bag is correctly tagged with the destination airport's three-letter code. Because some checked bags will be opened for hand inspection, the U.S. Transportation Security Administration recommends that you leave luggage unlocked or use the plastic locks offered at check-in. TSA screeners place an inspection notice inside searched bags, which are re-sealed with a special lock.

If your bag has been searched and contents are missing or damaged, file a claim with the TSA Consumer Response Center as soon as possible. If your bags arrive damaged or fail to arrive at all, file a written report with the airline before leaving the airport.
🛈 Complaints **U.S. Transportation Security Administration Consumer Response Center** ☎ 866/289-9673 ⊕ www.tsa.gov.

## SENIOR-CITIZEN TRAVEL
To qualify for age-related discounts, mention your senior-citizen status up front when booking hotel reservations (not when checking out) and before you're seated in restaurants (not when paying the bill). Be sure to have identification on hand. When renting a car, ask about promotional car-rental discounts, which can be cheaper than senior-citizen rates.
🛈 Educational Programs **Elderhostel** ⊠ 11 Ave. de Lafayette, Boston, MA 02111-1746 ☎ 877/426-8056, 978/323-4141 international callers, 877/426-2167 TTY 🖷 877/426-2166 ⊕ www.elderhostel.org. **Interhostel** ⊠ University of New Hampshire, 6 Garrison Ave., Durham, NH 03824 ☎ 603/862-1147 or 800/733-9753 🖷 603/862-1113 ⊕ www.learn.unh.edu.

## SHOPPING
Oregon is not well known for its preponderance of malls, outlets, or markets, but there are enough to mollify shoppers, especially in a state devoid of sales tax. The Made in Oregon stores are prevalent; one is in Portland's Lloyd Center, the largest mall in the state; head to customer service on the first floor to learn about benefits and incentives for out-of-town shoppers. The Columbia Gorge Premium Outlets, 15 minutes from Portland International Airport, and Harry and David Country Village in Medford are also popular stops, especially for last-minute or one-stop-shopping souvenir buying. For last-minute shopping, also consider the stores at Portland International Airport: Made in Oregon, Nike, Pendleton, and Powell's World of Books are among the merchants with outposts there.

If you are coast bound and it's raining, Pony Village Mall is the only covered shopping mall from Astoria to the California border along U.S. 101. The Eugene Saturday Market is the oldest weekly open-air venue for crafts in the United States, with about 300 vendors, 24 food booths, and local entertainment. It's open early April through mid-November, Saturday 10–5.

The Portland Saturday Market has 350 artisan vendors and 26 food booths. It's between Front Avenue and Southwest 1st Avenue under the Burnside Bridge and is open Saturday 10–5 and Sunday 11–4:30.
🛈 Malls, Markets & Outlets **Columbia Gorge Premium Outlets** ⊠ 450 N.W. 257th Ave., Troutdale 97060 ☎ 503/669-8060. **Eugene Saturday Market** ⊠ at 8th and Oak Sts. ☎ 541/686-8885 ⊕ www.eugenesaturdaymarket.org. **Harry and David Country Village** ⊠ 1314 Center Dr., Suite A, Medford 97501 ☎ 541/864-2278 ⊕ www.harryanddavid.com. **Made**

in Oregon ☎ 503/273-8719, 800/828-9673 ⌨ 503/222-6855 ⊕ www.madeinoregon.com. **Pony Village Mall** ✉ 1611 Virginia Ave., North Bend 97459. **The Portland Saturday Market** ✉ 108 W. Burnside ☎ 503/222-6072 ⊕ www.saturdaymarket.org.

## SPORTS & THE OUTDOORS

### BICYCLING

The Oregon Bikeway Program has information about biking throughout the state. Call for a free bicycle map of the Coast/U.S. 101 route. Bicycle Paper is a great source on biking in the Pacific Northwest.

Prominent bike-touring outfits include Mid-Valley Bicycle Club, the Portland Wheelmen Touring Club, and Rolling Pub Crawl Pacific Northwest Cycle Tours.

🎟 Bike Resources **Bicycle Paper** ✉ 68 S. Washington St., Seattle, WA 98104 ☎ 206/903-1333 ⊕ www.bicyclepaper.com. **Oregon Bikeway Program** ✉ Room 210, Transportation Bldg., 355 Capitol St. NE, Salem 97310 ☎ 503/986-3556 ⊕ www.odot.state.or.us.

🎟 Bike Tours **Mid-Valley Bicycle Club** ✉ Box 1373, Corvallis 97339. **Portland Wheelmen Touring Club** ☎ 503/257-7982 ⊕ www.pwtc.com. **Rolling Pub Crawl Pacific Northwest Cycle Tours** ✉ 818 S. W. 3rd Ave., No. 99, Portland, 97204 ☎ 503/720-6984 ⊕ www.rollingpubcrawl.com.

### CLIMBING & MOUNTAINEERING

🎟 Eugene: **Obsidians** ✉ Box 322, Eugene 97440 ⊕ www.obsidians.org. Portland: **Mazama Club** ☎ 503/227-2345 ⊕ www.mazamas.org. **Portland Mountain Rescue** ✉ Box 5391, Portland 97228-5391 ☎ 503/972-7743 ⊕ www.pmru.org. Salem: **Chemeketans Outdoor Club** ✉ Box 864, Salem 97308 ⊕ www.chemeketans.org.

### FISHING

To fish in most areas of Oregon, out-of-state visitors need a yearly (about $48.50), seven-day ($34.75), or daily ($8) nonresident angler's license. Additional tags are required for those fishing for salmon or steelhead ($11), sturgeon ($6), or halibut ($6); these tags are available from any local sporting-goods store. For more information, contact the Sport Fishing Information Line.

🎟 Information/Licenses **Oregon Department of Fish and Wildlife** ✉ Box 59, Portland, OR 97207 ☎ 503/872-5268 general information, 503/872-5275 license information ⊕ www.dfw.state.or.us. **Sport Fishing Information Line** ☎ 800/275-3474.

### HIKING

Many of Oregon's hiking trails are shared by horses, dogs, bikes, and pedestrians. Some hiking areas call for a trailhead parking permit, $5 a day or $30 for the season, available at a Forest Service office or at outdoor stores.

🎟 Passes & Information **Nature of Oregon Information Center** ✉ 800 N.E. Oregon St., Suite 177, Portland 97232 ☎ 503/872-2750, TDD 503/872-2752 ⊕ www.naturenw.org.

### SKIING

Sno-Park permits, distributed by the Oregon Department of Transportation, are required for parking at winter recreation areas from mid-November to April. The permits may be purchased for one day ($2), three days ($5), or a full season ($12) at DMV offices and retail agents—sporting-goods stores, markets and gas stations, usually near the areas—which sometimes charge slightly more than the listed price. Permits can often be purchased upon arrival at a ski area, but it's best to call ahead.

🎟 Passes & Information **Oregon Department of Transportation** ☎ 800/977-6368 or 503/986-3006.

## STUDENTS IN OREGON

Student identification can often get you a break on admissions prices at tourist sites. Many of the Rose Festival events in Portland give half off to students.

🎟 IDs & Services **STA Travel** ✉ 10 Downing St., New York, NY 10014 ☎ 212/627-3111, 800/777-0112 24-hr service center ⌨ 212/627-3387 ⊕ www.sta.com. **Travel Cuts** ✉ 187 College St., Toronto, Ontario M5T 1P7, Canada ☎ 800/592-2887 in the U.S., 416/979-2406 or 866/246-9762 in Canada ⌨ 416/979-8167 ⊕ www.travelcuts.com.

## TAX

Sales tax varies among areas. Oregon has no sales tax, although many cities or counties levy a tax on hotel rooms and car rentals.

## TIME

Oregon is in the Pacific time zone and observes daylight saving time from early April to late October. Oregon is in the same time zone as Los Angeles. Chicago is 2 hours ahead, New York is 3 hours ahead, London is 8 hours ahead, and Sydney is 17 hours ahead.

## TIPPING

Tips and service charges are usually not automatically added to a bill in the United States or Canada. If service is satisfactory, customers generally give waiters, waitresses, taxi drivers, barbers, hairdressers, and so forth a tip of 15%–20% of the total bill. Bellhops, doormen, and porters at airports and railway stations are generally tipped $1 for each item of luggage.

## TOURS & PACKAGES

Because everything is prearranged on a prepackaged tour or independent vacation, you spend less time planning—and often get it all at a good price.

### BOOKING WITH AN AGENT

Travel agents are excellent resources. But it's a good idea to collect brochures from several agencies, as some agents' suggestions may be influenced by relationships with tour and package firms that reward them for volume sales. If you have a special interest, find an agent with expertise in that area; the American Society of Travel Agents (ASTA; ⇨ Travel Agencies) has a database of specialists worldwide. You can log on to the group's Web site to find an ASTA travel agent in your neighborhood.

Make sure your travel agent knows the accommodations and other services of the place being recommended. Ask about the hotel's location, room size, beds, and whether it has a pool, room service, or programs for children, if you care about these. Has your agent been there in person or sent others whom you can contact?

Do some homework on your own, too: local tourism boards can provide information about lesser-known and small-niche operators, some of which may sell only direct.

### BUYER BEWARE

Each year consumers are stranded or lose their money when tour operators—even large ones with excellent reputations—go out of business. So check out the operator. Ask several travel agents about its reputation, and try to **book with a company that has a consumer-protection program.** (Look for information in the company's brochure.) In the United States, members of the National Tour Association and the United States Tour Operators Association are required to set aside funds to cover

payments and travel arrangements in the event that the company defaults. It's also a good idea to choose a company that participates in the American Society of Travel Agents' Tour Operator Program; ASTA will act as mediator in any disputes between you and your tour operator.

Remember that the more your package or tour includes, the better you can predict the ultimate cost of your vacation. Make sure you know exactly what is covered, and beware of hidden costs. Are taxes, tips, and transfers included? Entertainment and excursions? These can add up.

🖪 Tour-Operator Recommendations **American Society of Travel Agents** (⇨ Travel Agencies). **National Tour Association (NTA)** ✉ 546 E. Main St., Lexington, KY 40508 ☎ 859/226–4444 or 800/682–8886 🖷 859/226–4404 ⊕ www.ntaonline.com. **United States Tour Operators Association (USTOA)** ✉ 275 Madison Ave., Suite 2014, New York, NY 10016 ☎ 212/599–6599 🖷 212/599–6744 ⊕ www.ustoa.com.

## TRAIN TRAVEL

**Amtrak,** the U.S. passenger rail system, has daily service to the Pacific Northwest from the Midwest and California. The *Empire Builder* takes a northern route through Minnesota and Montana from Chicago to Spokane, whence separate legs continue to Seattle and Portland. Part of the route to Portland runs through the Columbia River Gorge. The *Cascades* train travels once daily between Seattle and Vancouver and several times a day between Seattle, Portland, and Eugene. The *Coast Starlight,* which runs between Seattle and Los Angeles, passes through the Willamette Valley, serving Portland, Salem, Albany (near Corvallis), Eugene, and Klamath Falls.

🖪 Railway Company **Amtrak** ☎ 800/872–7245 ⊕ www.amtrak.com.

## TRAVEL AGENCIES

A good travel agent puts your needs first. Look for an agency that has been in business at least five years, emphasizes customer service, and has someone on staff who specializes in your destination. In addition, **make sure the agency belongs to a professional trade organization.** The American Society of Travel Agents (ASTA)—the largest and most influential in the field with more than 20,000 members in some 140 countries—maintains and enforces a strict code of ethics and will step in to help mediate any agent-client disputes involving ASTA members if necessary. ASTA (whose motto is "Without a travel agent, you're on your own") also maintains a Web site that includes a directory of agents. (If a travel agency is also acting as your tour operator, *see* Buyer Beware *in* Tours and Packages.)

🔢 Local Agent Referrals **American Society of Travel Agents (ASTA)** ✉ 1101 King St., Suite 200, Alexandria, VA 22314 ☎ 703/739-2782 or 800/965-2782 24-hr hot line 🖷 703/739-3268 ⊕ www. astanet.com. **Association of British Travel Agents** ✉ 68-71 Newman St., London W1T 3AH ☎ 020/7637-2444 🖷 020/7637-0713 ⊕ www.abta.com. **Association of Canadian Travel Agencies** ✉ 130 Albert St., Suite 1705, Ottawa, Ontario K1P 5G4 ☎ 613/237-3657 🖷 613/237-7052 ⊕ www.acta.ca. **Australian Federation of Travel Agents** ✉ Level 3, 309 Pitt St., Sydney, NSW 2000 ☎ 02/9264-3299 🖷 02/9264-1085 ⊕ www.afta.com.au. **Travel Agents' Association of New Zealand** ✉ Level 5, Tourism and Travel House, 79 Boulcott St., Box 1888, Wellington 6001 ☎ 04/499-0104 🖷 04/499-0786 ⊕ www. taanz.org.nz.

## VISITOR INFORMATION

Oregon tourist-information centers are marked with blue "i" signs on main roads. Opening and closing times vary, depending on the season and the individual office; call ahead for hours.

🔢 Tourist Information **Bend Chamber of Commerce** ✉ 777 N.W. Wall St., Bend 97701 ☎ 541/382-3221 ⊕ www.bendchamber.org. **Bend Visitor & Convention Bureau** ✉ 63085 N. Hwy. 97, Bend 97701 ☎ 541/382-8048 ⊕ www.visitbend.com. **Central Oregon Visitors Association** ✉ 572 S.W. Bluff Dr., Suite C, Bend 97702 ☎ 541/389-8799 or 800/800-8334 ⊕ www.visitcentraloregon.org. **Convention & Visitors Association of Lane County Oregon** ✉ 115 W. 8th, Suite 190, Eugene 97401 ☎ 541/484-5307 or 800/547-5445 🖷 541343-6335 ⊕ www.cvalco.org.

**Hood River County Chamber of Commerce** ✉ 405 Portway Ave., Hood River 97031 ☎ 541/386-2000 or 800/366-3530 ⊕ www.hoodriver.org. **National Park Service Pacific Northwest Regional Office** ☎ 206/220-4000. **Oregon Coast Visitors Association** ✉ 137 N.E. 1st St., Newport 97365. **Oregon State Park Information Center** ☎ 800/551-6949. **Oregon Tourism Commission** ✉ 775 Summer St. NE, Salem 97310 ☎ 503/986-0000 or 800/547-7842 ⊕ www. traveloregon.com. **Portland Oregon Visitors Association** ✉ 1000 S.W. Broadway, Suite 2300, 97205 ☎ 800/962-3700 ⊕ www.pova.com. **U.S. Forest Service Recreation Information Center** ☎ 503/872-2750, 877/444-6777 campground reservations. **Yamhill Valley Visitors Association** ✉ 417 N.W. Adams St., McMinnville 97128 ☎ 503/883-7770 ⊕ www.oregonwinecountry.org.

🔢 Government Advisories **Consular Affairs Bureau of Canada** ☎ 800/267-6788 or 613/944-6788 ⊕ www.voyage.gc.ca. **U.K. Foreign and Commonwealth Office** ✉ Travel Advice Unit, Consular Division, Old Admiralty Building, London SW1A 2PA ☎ 020/7008-0232 or 020/7008-0233 ⊕ www.fco. gov.uk/travel. **Australian Department of Foreign Affairs and Trade** ☎ 02/6261-1299 Consular Travel Advice Faxback Service ⊕ www.dfat.gov.au. **New Zealand Ministry of Foreign Affairs and Trade** ☎ 04/439-8000 ⊕ www.mft.govt.nz.

## WEB SITES

Do check out the World Wide Web when planning your trip. You'll find everything from weather forecasts to virtual tours of famous cities. Be sure to visit Fodors.com (⊕ www.fodors.com), a complete travel-planning site. You can research prices and book plane tickets, hotel rooms, rental cars, vacation packages, and more. In addition, you can post your pressing questions in the Travel Talk section. Other planning tools include a currency converter and weather reports, and there are loads of links to travel resources.

# THE OREGON COAST

**FODOR'S CHOICE**

Cape Perpetua, *south of Yachats*

Columbia River Maritime Museum, *Astoria*

Fort Clatsop National Memorial, *Astoria*

La Serre, *seafood in Yachats*

Newport Belle Bed & Breakfast, *Newport*

Panini Bakery, *Newport*

Siltcoos River Canoe Trail, *Florence*

Tu Tu' Tun Lodge, *Gold Beach*

Yaquina Head Outstanding Natural Area, *Newport*

**HIGHLY RECOMMENDED**

RESTAURANTS    Blue Heron Bistro, *Coos Bay*

Dining Room at Salishan, *Gleneden Beach*

The Bistro, *Cannon Beach*

HOTELS    Chetco River Inn, *Brookings*

Stephanie Inn, *Cannon Beach*

SIGHTS    Oregon Coast Aquarium, *Newport*

Oregon Dunes National Recreation Area, *Florence*

Sea Lion Caves, *Heceta Head*

Three Capes Loop, *south of downtown Tillamook*

Yaquina Head Lighthouse, *Newport*

By Donald S.
Olson

Updated by
Lori Tobias

**NOT ONE GRAIN** of Oregon's 300 mi of white-sand beaches is privately owned. Public access to the beach has been a concern for Oregonians since the late 19th century, when travel north or south was often possible only on the flat corridor the beaches provided. By 1913, former Governor Oswald West had led the legislature to declare the shore a state highway, preventing the privatization of the beaches. And in 1967, a Beach Bill was enacted to make public parts of the beach from the water all the way up to the line of vegetation. Coastal forests and more land were purchased by the State Highway Commission and turned into state parks. U.S. 101, known as Highway 101 by most Oregonians (it sometimes appears this way in addresses as well) or, simply, as the coastal highway, parallels the coast along the length of the state. It winds past sea-tortured rocks, brooding headlands, hidden beaches, historic lighthouses, and tiny ports, with the gleaming gun-metal-gray Pacific Ocean always in view. With its seaside hamlets and small hotels and resorts, the coast seems to have been created with pleasure in mind. South of Newport, the pace slows. The scenery and fishing and outdoor activities are just as rich as those in the towns to the north, but the area is less crowded and the commercialism less obvious.

## Exploring the Oregon Coast

U.S. 101 is anchored at its northernmost terminus by the historic fishing town of Astoria, the oldest community west of the Mississippi; at the southernmost point is the sleepy town of Brookings, sometimes referred to as the banana belt for its temperate climate. In between, the highway winds through forests of grand fir, pine, and spruce, along rugged coastal cliffs—where views open to the Pacific in all its mighty power—and through lush farming communities and tiny oceanfront communities. Towns are covered from north to south, but you can reverse the journey or use any of the stops along the way as your starting point. Whether you're doing the coast as a day trip or a multiday excursion, you will almost certainly want to do it by car. U.S. 101, accessible from I–5 via a number of secondary highways throughout the state, is generally in good condition, with passing lanes and abundant pullovers for taking in the view; however, in places it also winds through tight curves and hilly stretches, which can make the trip slower than typical highway driving. Small airports throughout the area also provide access, and car rental agencies are available in many towns. If you're forsaking wheels, Greyhound also offers service to a number of the communities along the coast.

### About the Restaurants
Whether you're dining at a tiny café or a posh inn, odds are you'll find ample ways to enjoy Dungeness crab, salmon, oysters, albacore tuna, and halibut. Chefs along the coast are particularly proud of their clam chowder and seafood stews. Dress is almost always casual, and even at finer dining establishments, the norm is khakis and a collared shirt for men, casual slacks or a dress for women. Many of the hotel restaurants host Friday, Sunday, and holiday seafood brunch buffets.

### About the Hotels
Accommodations along the coast vary from simple beachside cabins to resort hotels to luxurious boutique inns. While the upscale lodgings may include complimentary wine, deluxe breakfast, in-room spas, and turndown service, even moderately priced rooms often come with ocean views and beachfront access. Lodging can be pricey in several coastal towns, including Cannon Beach, Seaside, and Gleneden, though you'll find bargains up and down the coast, particularly mid-week and off season.

These itineraries follow the north to south orientation of the chapter, carving up the 300 mi of the coast. Consider just one, or combine them all, depending on your schedule.

*Numbers in the text correspond to numbers in the margin and on the Oregon Coast map.*

**1**

**If you have**
**3 days**

On your first day begin in 🏛 **Astoria ❶** ☞ at the top of the 125-foot-tall Astoria Column, where the view takes in miles of scenery, including the Coast Range and Columbia River. Downtown, stop by the Flavel House for a look at the 19th-century lifestyle of one of the city's richest families; then navigate the exhibit halls of Columbia Maritime Museum. Although the town of **Seaside ❷**, 12 mi south of Astoria, is often criticized for its touristy feel, you can spend a fun afternoon walking through the many shops, arcades, and amusement centers. The "promenade," a 2-mi boardwalk referred to locally as "the prom," is ideal for strolling along the beach without getting sand in your shoes; be warned that during spring break, this place is a favorite with fun-seeking teens. Spend the night in Astoria or Seaside. Spend day two in 🏛 **Cannon Beach ❸**, 8 mi south of Seaside, and the most upscale of the coastal communities, with art galleries; antiques, gift, and specialty shops; and the oft-photographed Haystack Rock. Nearby, Ecola State Park, **Oswald West State Park ❹**, and Saddle Mountain State Park have lush coastal rain forests, hiking trails, and excellent vantage points for bird and marine-life viewing. Overnight in Cannon Beach. On day three, head south on U.S. 101. Here the road hugs the Coast Range, dropping in and out of tiny coastal towns and farming communities; you'll find plenty of mom-and-pop shops, particularly in **Tillamook ❼**. Sample the cheese that put the town on the map at the Tillamook County Creamery; then head west on 3rd Street and follow the signs to **Three Capes Loop ❽**, a 35-mi drive that winds past magnificent headlands, Cape Meares, Cape Lookout, and Cape Kiwanda before reconnecting with U.S. 101 south of **Pacific City ❾**.

**If you have**
**5 days**

Follow the three-day itinerary, spending the night in 🏛 **Pacific City ❾**, and on day four, travel the 16 mi from Pacific City to **Lincoln City ❿**. What this touristy town lacks in charm it more than makes up for in amenities; you'll find Oregon's only beachfront casino, Chinook Winds, along with an outlet mall and blocks of small shops. Eleven miles south, tiny **Depoe Bay ⓬** is the self-proclaimed whale-watching capital of the world, but don't overlook the spouting holes or rock formations in the water that channel the ocean waves into soaking fountains. If you're determined to get an up-close look from the sidewalk above, carry an umbrella. In 🏛 **Newport ⓭**, visit the still operational Yaquina Head Lighthouse and the Yaquina Bay Lighthouse, now a museum and said to come with a ghost all its own. In the newly renovated neighborhood of Nye Beach, while away a few hours in the specialty shops. Over on the bayfront, with one of the largest fishing fleets in the state, wander the docks where fresh seafood is always for sale, or browse through the art and souvenir shops. Overnight in Newport; as you leave on day five, signs on the south side of the picturesque Yaquina Bay Bridge will direct you to the worthy Oregon Coast Aquarium. Twenty-three miles south, the town of **Yachats** ⑮ is an artsy little community favored by those seeking an escape from the crowds. Just outside of town, **Cape Perpetua** ⑯ towers 800 feet over the Pacific Ocean, offering the highest vantage point on the Oregon coast. For more information on this 2,700-acre scenic area, popular with hikers, beachcombers, campers, and naturalists, stop by the Cape Perpetua Visitor's Center.

If you have<br>**8 days**

Follow the five-day itinerary, overnighting on evening five in ⬚ **Heceta Head** ⑰, 10 mi south of Cape Perpetua. On day six, head 11 mi south of Cape Perpetua, where an elevator drops you 208 feet down to the **Sea Lion Caves** ⑱. Wild sea lions gather here to breed and calve. From here, the restored waterfront Old Town in ⬚ **Florence** ⑲ is 13 mi south; shop, enjoy the seafood, and spend the night. The town serves as the jumping-off point on day seven for the Oregon Dunes National Recreation Area, a 41-mi-long stretch with forests, lakes, and camping facilities. In **Reedsport** ⑳, a short drive south, you may want to stop at the Umpqua Discovery Center, where the main attraction is the *Hero*, the laboratory ship used by Admiral Byrd on his expeditions to the Antarctic. Some of the highest sand dunes on the coast are at the **Umpqua Lighthouse Park** ㉑ (turnoff 6 mi south of Reedsport on U.S. 101). The Umpqua River Lighthouse, built in 1861, flashes its warning beacon from a bluff overlooking the south side of Winchester Bay. The former logging community of **Coos Bay** ㉓, the largest natural harbor between San Francisco and Seattle's Puget Sound, is not particularly attractive, but 7 mi west on Newmark Avenue (which becomes Cape Arago Highway), in the tiny fishing village of Charleston, lie three of the area's prettiest state parks: Sunset Bay State Park, Shore Acres State Park, and Cape Arago State Park; the last overlooks the Oregon Islands National Wildlife Refuge, where offshore rocks, beaches, islands, and reefs provide breeding grounds for seabirds and marine mammals. Backtrack to U.S. 101, which will lead to ⬚ **Bandon** ㉔, a town of 3,000 on the mouth of the Coquille River. Follow the signs to Old Town Bandon, with galleries, boutiques, and plenty of seafood. Overnight in Bandon. On day eight, head for **Gold Beach** ㉗. The town's seasonal tourist industry is based largely on fishing and jet-boat trips up the Rogue River. Twenty-seven miles south, you'll reach the last town on U.S. 101 in Oregon, **Brookings** ㉘, where some 90% of the nation's Easter lilies are cultivated.

| WHAT IT COSTS | | | | |
|---|---|---|---|---|
| **$$$$** | **$$$** | **$$** | **$** | **¢** |
| RESTAURANTS over $30 | $20–$30 | $15–$20 | $10–$15 | under $10 |
| HOTELS over $180 | $140–$180 | $100–$140 | $60–$100 | under $60 |

Restaurant prices are per person for a main course at dinner. Hotel prices are for a standard double room, excluding room tax, which varies 6%–9 1/2% depending on location.

## Timing

May through September, when the temperatures are mild and skies sunny, is high season on the Oregon coast. It's an ideal time for strolling the beach, moseying through the local shops, flying a kite, or building an evening bonfire on the beach. Do make hotel reservations several months in advance, particularly on weekends, when visitors from cities from all over the Northwest come to get away from it all. October through February, when shops and beaches are uncrowded, can be delightful in their own right; it's the season of winter storms, when the high seas roil and churn, the wind howls along the headlands, and the rain falls not in drops but sheets blown horizontal. When it all blows over and the high seas have calmed, you'll want to head to the beach to find those odd treasures the waves have carried in. This time of year, expect lower prices and an even slower-than-usual pace.

## Astoria

**①** *96 mi northwest of Portland on U.S. 30.*

The mighty Columbia River meets the Pacific at Astoria, which was founded in 1811. The city was named for John Jacob Astor, then America's wealthiest man, who financed the original fur-trading colony here. Modern Astoria is a placid amalgamation of small town and hard-working port city. Settlers built sprawling Victorian houses on the flanks of Coxcomb Hill. Many of the homes have since been restored and are no less splendid as bed-and-breakfast inns. With so many museums, inns, and recreational offerings, Astoria should be one of the Northwest's prime tourist destinations. Yet the town remains relatively undiscovered, even by Portlanders.

The **Columbia River Maritime Museum**, on the downtown waterfront, explores the maritime history of the Pacific Northwest and is one of the two most interesting man-made tourist attractions on the Oregon coast (Newport's aquarium is the other). Beguiling exhibits include the personal belongings of some of the ill-fated passengers of the 2,000 ships that have foundered here since 1811. Also here are an observation tower of the World War II submarine USS *Rasher* (complete with working periscopes), the fully operational U.S. Coast Guard Lightship *Columbia*, and a 44-foot Coast Guard motor lifeboat. ✉ *1792 Marine Dr., at 17th St.* ☎ *503/325–2323* ⊕ *www.crmm.org* ✆ *$5* ☼ *Daily 9:30–5.*

The **Astoria Column**, a 125-foot monolith atop Coxcomb Hill that was patterned after Trajan's Column in Rome, rewards your 164-step, spiral-stair climb with views over Astoria, the Columbia River, the Coast Range, and the Pacific. ✚ *From U.S. 30 downtown take 16th St. south 1 mi to the top of Coxcomb Hill* ✆ *Free* ☼ *Daily 9–dusk.*

The prim **Flavel House** was built between 1884 and 1886. Its Victorian-era furnishings, including six handcrafted fireplace mantels carved from different hardwoods and accented with tiles imported from Asia and Europe, yield insight into the lifestyle of a wealthy 19th-century shipping tycoon. Visits start in the Carriage House interpretive center. ✉ *441 8th St., at Duane St.* ☎ *503/325–2203* ⊕ *www.clatsophistoricalsociety.org* ✆ *$5* ☼ *May–Sept., daily 10–5; Oct.–Apr., daily 11–4.*

"Ocean in view! O! The joy!" recorded William Clark, standing on a spit of land south of present-day Astoria in the fall of 1805. **Fort Clatsop National Memorial** is a faithful replica of the log stockade depicted in Clark's journal. Park rangers, who dress in period garb during the summer and perform such early-19th-century tasks as making fire with flint and steel, lend an air of authenticity, as does the damp and lonely feel of the fort itself. ✉ *Fort Clatsop Loop Rd., (5 mi south of Astoria; from U.S. 101 cross Youngs Bay Bridge, turn east on Alt. U.S. 101, and follow signs)* ☎ *503/861–2471* ⊕ *www.nps.gov.focl* ✆ *$5 per vehicle* ☼ *Mid-June–Labor Day, daily 8–6; Labor Day–mid-June, daily 8–5.*

Fodor'sChoice

The earthworks of 37-acre **Fort Stevens**, at Oregon's northwestern tip, were mounded up during the Civil War to guard the Columbia against a Confederate attack. No such event occurred, but during World War II, Fort Stevens became the only mainland U.S. military installation to come under enemy (Japanese submarine) fire since the War of 1812. The fort's abandoned gun mounts and eerie subterranean bunkers are a memorable destination. The corroded skeleton of the *Peter Iredale*, a century-old English four-master ship, protrudes from the sand west of the campground, a stark testament to the temperamental nature of the Pacific. ⊠ *Fort Stevens Hwy., (from Fort Clatsop, take Alt. U.S. 101 west past U.S. 101, turn north onto Main St.–Fort Stevens Hwy., and follow signs)* ☎ *503/861–2000* ⊕ *www.visitfortstevens.com* ✉ *$3 per vehicle, park tours in summer $2.50* ☉ *Mid-May–Sept., daily 10–6; Oct.–mid-May, daily 10–4.*

One of the Oregon coast's oldest commercial smokehouses, **Josephson's** uses alderwood for all processing and specializes in Pacific Northwest chinook and coho salmon. You can also buy smoked sturgeon, tuna, oysters, mussels, scallops, and prawns by the pound or in sealed gift packs. An exhibit of photos and magazine articles provides a history of the smokehouse. ⊠ *106 Marine Dr., 97103* ☎ *503/325–2190* 🖷 *503/325–4075* ⊕ *www.josephsons.com* ✉ *Free* ☉ *Weekdays 9–5:30, Sat. 10–5:30, Sun. 10–5.*

In a 100-year-old Colonial Revival building originally used as the city hall, the **Heritage Museum** has two floors of exhibits detailing the history of the early pioneers, Native Americans, and logging and marine industries of Clatsop County, the oldest American settlement west of the Mississippi. The research library, where you may research local family and building history, is also open to the public. ⊠ *1618 Exchange St.* ☎ *503/338–4849* ✉ *$3* ☉ *May–Labor Day, daily 10–5; Labor Day–Apr., daily 11–4.*

Old equipment, including hand-pulled and horse-drawn fire engines, and a collection of photos of some of Astoria's most notable fires make up the exhibits at **Uppertown Firefighters Museum.** Built in the late 1880s as a brewpub, the building was converted to a firehouse during prohibition in 1928. Plans are under way to add a children's museum, which will have educational safety and history programs. ⊠ *2968 Marine Dr.* ☎ *503/325–0920* ✉ *$3* ☉ *Wed.–Sat. 11–2.*

The **Astoria Riverfront Trolly**, also known as "Old 300," is a beautifully restored 1913 streetcar travels for 4 miles along Astoria's historic riverfront. Get a close-up look at the waterfront, from the Port of Astoria to the East Morring Basin; the Columbia River; and points of interest in between; while reliving the past through guided and narrated historical tours. ⊠ *1095 Dwayne St.* ☎ *503/325–6311* ⊕ *www.oldoregon.com* ✉ *$1 per boarding; $2 all-day pass* ☉ *Memorial Day–Labor Day, weekdays 3–9, weekends noon–9; Labor Day–Memorial Day, weekends noon–dusk.*

## Where to Stay & Eat

**$$–$$$$**  ✕ **Pier 11 Feed Store Restaurant.** Open beams and old wood floors give this restaurant overlooking the Columbia River an old-fashioned rustic feel. Seafood entrées are made from seafood fresh off the boat, and there is an assortment of steak and chicken dishes as well. ⊠ *77 11th St.* ☎ *503/325–0279* ▤ *AE, D, MC, V.*

**$$$**  ✕ **Home Spirit Bakery Café.** In an 1891 Queen Anne–style house with a river view, this spot is filled with antiques from the 1902–1912 Arts and Crafts period, including Stickley furniture, textiles, and lighting fixtures.

**1**

## Beachcombing
Beachcombing in Oregon can turn up unexpected finds, including—despite the rough and rugged surf—some perfectly preserved shells. The careful comber might find white limpet shells, delicate sand dollars, the smooth and curving purple olive shell, or the twisted chocolate whelk. Nonetheless, the real prize for which beachcombers here vie are the agates, translucent stones of many sizes that might be frosty white, yellow, orange, dark gray, or even a rare powder blue. A common misperception is that the translucent rocks are swept in from the ocean; rather, they are washed from the headlands and cliffs inland from the sea onto the sand. The changing tide constantly rearranges the sand, often exposing agate beds where yesterday there were none and hiding those that once yielded great treasure. Agate hunters should seek out stretches of sand where there is gravel dotting the water line. The best time to look is about two hours before low tide, when the water continues to move away from the shore but much of the beach is already exposed.

## Whale-watching
Twice a year during official Whale Watch Weeks—usually the last weeks of December and March—volunteers man 29 sites along the coast to help passersby spot gray whales migrating south in December to calve and in March north again. Outside of these designated weeks, you still might spot a gray whale if you are patient; also not uncommon in the waters along the coast are orcas, a.k.a. killer whales, which can be seen year-round. From land, the best chance of catching a glimpse is to find a high vantage point, where you might able to see an outline of the whale's body. Generally the first sign of a gray whale will be the spray of water in the air as it breathes, often just before it breaches the water. Killer whales can be spotted by their large dorsal fin, which breaks the water before their body. One marine expert says your best chance of catching sight of a whale is to be patient and to spend an hour or more watching from the same point.

## Crabbing
In virtually every town, from public docks or rental boats, crabbing for Dungeness crab is a favorite activity. And no wonder: there's no permit necessary, you can rent equipment easily, and with a little luck you'll have dinner by the end of the day. A few rules do apply. It's illegal to keep female or male crabs smaller than 5¾ inches, and catch is limited to 12 per person per day. Most of what you need to know about crabbing you'll likely find at the local marine store, where there may also be crab rings for rent and no doubt some insider's advice on the best place to try your luck. At the end of the day, boil the catch—some marine shops will do it for you—and cook it over the campfire with a pot of garlic butter on the side.

---

It's known locally and beyond for its homemade organic fare. Everything is made to order and showcases seasonal produce and seafood. The owners serve lunch four days a week. Thursday through Saturday there's a prix-fixe dinner with a choice of four entrées: seafood, chicken, red meat, and vegetarian. ⊠ *1585 Exchange St., 97103* ☎ *503/325–6846* ▱ *No credit cards* ⊘ *Closed Sun.–Tues. No dinner Wed.*

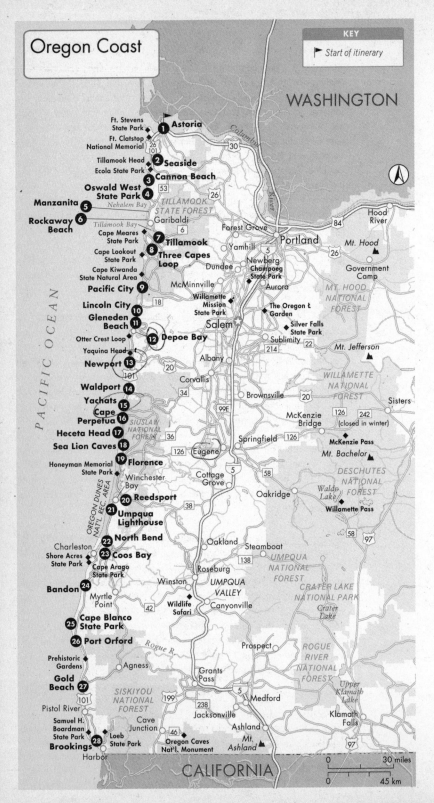

Oregon Coast

WASHINGTON

Ft. Stevens State Park
① Astoria
Ft. Clatstop National Memorial
Tillamook Head
② Seaside
Ecola State Park
③ Cannon Beach
Oswald West State Park ④
Manzanita ⑤
Nehalem Bay
Rockaway Beach ⑥
Tillamook Bay
Garibaldi
Cape Meares State Park ⑦ Tillamook
Cape Lookout State Park ⑧ Three Capes Loop
Cape Kiwanda State Natural Area
Pacific City ⑨
Lincoln City ⑩
Gleneden Beach ⑪
Otter Crest Loop
⑫ Depoe Bay
Yaquina Head
Newport ⑬
Waldport ⑭
Yachats ⑮
Cape Perpetua ⑯
Heceta Head ⑰
Sea Lion Caves ⑱
Florence ⑲
Honeyman Memorial State Park
Winchester Bay
⑳ Reedsport
㉑ Umpqua Lighthouse
Charleston
Shore Acres State Park ㉒ North Bend
㉓ Coos Bay
Cape Arago State Park
Bandon ㉔
Myrtle Point
㉕ Cape Blanco State Park
㉖ Port Orford
Prehistoric Gardens
Gold Beach ㉗
Pistol River
Samuel H. Boardman State Park
Brookings ㉘ Loeb State Park
Harbor

TILLAMOOK STATE FOREST
Forest Grove
Portland
Yamhill
Newberg
Champoeg State Park
Dundee
Aurora
McMinnville
Willamette Mission State Park
Salem
The Oregon Garden
Silver Falls State Park
Sublimity
Albany
Corvallis
Brownsville
McKenzie Bridge
Springfield
Eugene
Cottage Grove
Oakridge
Oakland
Steamboat
Roseburg
Winston
UMPQUA VALLEY
Wildlife Safari
Canyonville
Prospect
Agness
Grants Pass
Medford
Jacksonville
Cave Junction
Oregon Caves Nat'l. Monument
Mt. Ashland
Ashland
Klamath Falls

Hood River
Mt. Hood
Government Camp
MT. HOOD NATIONAL FOREST
Mt. Jefferson
WILLAMETTE NATIONAL FOREST
Sisters
McKenzie Pass
Mt. Bachelor
DESCHUTES NATIONAL FOREST
Waldo Lake
Willamette Pass
UMPQUA NATIONAL FOREST
CRATER LAKE NATIONAL PARK
Crater Lake
ROGUE RIVER NATIONAL FOREST
Upper Klamath Lake

SISKIYOU NATIONAL FOREST

PACIFIC OCEAN

OREGON DUNES NATL. REC. AREA

SIUSLAW NATIONAL FOREST

CALIFORNIA

0        30 miles
0        45 km

$–$$$  ✕ **Columbian Cafe.** Locals love this unpretentious diner with such tongue-in-cheek south-of-the-border decor as chili-pepper-shape Christmas lights. Simple food—crepes with broccoli, cheese, and homemade salsa for lunch; grilled salmon and pasta with a lemon-cream sauce for dinner—is served by a staff that usually includes the owner. Come early; this place always draws a crowd. ⊠ *1114 Marine Dr.* ☎ *503/325–2233* ⊟ *No credit cards* ⊘ *No dinner Sun.–Tues.*

¢–$$$  ✕ **Ship Inn.** The Ship Inn is well known among locals and savvy tourists for its casual style and famous fish-and-chips (with halibut), as well as English specialties, such as bangers and mash and chicken pasty. Inside, oversize windows overlook the river; outside, there's a new patio for dining on fair-weather days. ⊠ *1 2nd St., 97103* ☎ *503/325–0033* ⊟ *AE, D, MC, V.*

$–$$  ✕ **Cannery Cafe.** Original fir floors, windows, and hardware combine with expansive views of the Columbia River to give this restaurant in a renovated 1879 cannery an authentic nautical feel. Homemade breakfast fare, often with crab or salmon, comes with potato pancakes and buttermilk biscuits. Fresh salads, large sandwiches, clam chowder, and crab cakes are lunch staples. The dinner menu emphasizes seafood, including cioppino, an Italian fish stew, and homemade southern Italian pasta dishes. ⊠ *1 6th St.* ☎ *503/325–8642* ⊟ *AE, D, DC, MC, V.*

$–$$$  ▦ **Benjamin Young Inn.** On the National Register of Historic Places, this handsome 5,500-square-foot Queen Anne–style inn is surrounded by century-old gardens. Among the ornate original details are faux graining on frames and molding, shutter-blinds in windows, and Povey stained glass. The spacious guest rooms mix antiques with contemporary pieces and have views of the Columbia River from their tall windows. City tennis courts are right next door. There's a two-night minimum on holiday and July–August weekends. ⊠ *3652 Duane St., 97103* ☎ *503/325–6172 or 800/201–1286* ⊕ *www.benjaminyounginn.com* ⇆ *4 rooms, 1 two-bedroom suite* ⌂ *Some in-room hot tubs; no a/c, no smoking, no TV in some rooms* ⊟ *AE, D, MC, V* ⦿ *BP.*

$–$$$  ▦ **Rosebriar Hotel.** Built in 1902, this building was once used as a convent, and it still retains its stained-glass windows, hardwood floors, and wainscoting. In the carriage house, which predates the house by 17 years, French doors open to a private courtyard, and in the new Captain's Suite, a soaking tub takes in views of the Columbia River. All of the rooms have antiques and quality linens; some have fireplaces and views of the Columbia River and downtown. ⊠ *636 14th St., 97103* ☎ *503/325–7427 or 800/487–0224* 🖶 *503/325–6937* ⇆ *12 rooms* ⌂ *Some in-room hot tubs, business services; no a/c* ⊟ *MC, V* ⦿ *BP.*

$–$$  ▦ **Franklin Street Station Bed & Breakfast.** Ticking grandfather clocks and mellow light filtering through leaded-glass windows set the tone at this velvet-upholstered Victorian built in 1900 on the slopes above downtown Astoria. Breakfasts are huge, hot, and satisfying, and there's always a plate of goodies and a pot of coffee in the kitchen. ⊠ *1140 Franklin St., 97103* ☎ *503/325–4314 or 800/448–1098* ⊕ *www.franklin-st-station-bb.com* ⇆ *6 rooms* ⊟ *MC, V* ⦿ *BP.*

¢–$$  ▦ **Crest Motel.** High on a hill on 1½ acres, this older, no-frills motel has views of the Columbia River, the city of Astoria, and the Washington State shoreline. There is a large backyard where you can watch the river traffic. Rooms are clean and well maintained. ⊠ *5366 Leif Erickson Dr., 97103* ☎ *503/325–3141 or 800/421–3141* ⇆ *40 rooms* ⌂ *Some refrigerators, cable TV, hot tub, laundry facilities, business services, some pets allowed; no a/c* ⊟ *AE, D, DC, MC, V* ⦿ *CP.*

¢–$$   ⊞ **Grandview Bed & Breakfast.** This turreted mansion lives up to its name—decks look out over Astoria, with the Columbia River and Washington State beyond. The interior is bright, with scrubbed hardwood floors and lace-filled rooms. The breakfast specialty is bagels with cream cheese and smoked salmon from Josephson's ( ⇨ Shopping). ⊠ *1574 Grand Ave., 97103* ☎ *503/325–5555 or 800/488–3250* ⊕ *www. go-to.com/grandviewbedandbreakfast* ⇝ *9 rooms, 7 with bath* ⊟ *D, MC, V* ⏐◯⏐ *BP.*

$   ⊞ **Astoria Dunes.** Across from the Maritime Memorial Park and on the banks of the Columbia, the motel is within easy access of the Astoria Riverfront Trolley, and many of the clean, plain rooms have a view of the river. There is also an indoor heated pool and hot tub. ⊠ *288 W. Marine Dr., 97103* ☎ *503/325–7111 or 800/441–3319* 🖷 *503/325–0804* ⇝ *58 rooms* ♿ *Cable TV, indoor pool, hot tub, laundry facilities, business services; no a/c in some rooms* ⊟ *AE, D, DC, MC, V.*

$   ⊞ **Astoria Inn.** This Queen Anne–style farmhouse with gingerbread trim sits atop a hill in a quiet residential area high above the Columbia River. The views are inspiring, especially from the appropriately named Cape Lookout guest room. The rooms and a library are filled with antiques and wing back chairs. The innkeeper loves to show off her passion for cooking with breakfasts of crab quiche or Mariner French toast, and fresh-baked cookies are a house specialty. ⊠ *3391 Irving Ave., 97103* ☎ *503/325–8153 or 800/718–8153* ⊕ *www.astoriainnbb.com* ⇝ *4 rooms* ♿ *No smoking, no room TVs* ⊟ *D, MC, V* ⏐◯⏐ *BP.*

⚠ **Fort Stevens State Park.** A historic military site with diverse amenities, the park includes 9 mi of biking trails and 6 mi of hiking trails; two swimming areas; and paddle boats, canoes and kayaks for rent. ♿ *Flush toilets, full hookups, partial hookups, dump station, drinking water, showers, fire pits, picnic tables, electricity, swimming.* ⇝ *174 full hookups, 303 partial hookups, 42 tent sites, 15 yurts, 4 group sites, hiker/biker camping by request.* ⊠ *Off U.S. 101, 10 mi south of Astoria (follow signs)* ☎ *800/452–5687 reservations, 800/551–6949 information only* ⊕ *www.oregonstateparks.org* 🖷 *Full hookups $22, electrical hookups $22, tent sites $17, primitive/overflow $9, yurts $29, hiker/biker $4, group $65* ⚠ *Reservations essential* ⊙ *Campsites and yurts closed Sept. 10–May 21.*

## Sports & the Outdoors

KAYAKING  **Pacific Wave** ( ⊠ 21 U.S. 101, Warrenton ☎ 888/223–9794) has a full line of skate, snow, and kite boards as well as kayaks and apparel. Kayak rentals, instruction, and custom tours are available.

## Shopping

More than 100 vendors bring their handmade, hand-grown, and hand-gathered goods to the **Astoria Sunday Market** ( ⊠ 12th St. between Marine and Exchange Sts.), set up downtown on the main thoroughfare, which is closed to traffic. Admission to the market is free; entertainment is provided by local bands with streetside seating available, and local restaurants offer above-average street-fair fare at the international food court. The market is open from Mother's Day through the first Sunday in October. **Josephson's** ( ⊠ 106 Marine Dr. ☎ 503/325–2190) is one of the Oregon coast's oldest commercial smokehouses, preparing Columbia River chinook salmon in the traditional alder-smoked and lox styles. Smoked shark, tuna, oysters, mussels, sturgeon, scallops, and prawns are also available by the pound or in sealed gift packs. The owners of **Let It Rain** ( ⊠ 1124 Commercial St. ☎ 503/325–7728) claim they carry

# ASTORIA'S COLORFUL PAST

Winter at Fort Clatsop near present-day Astoria was not the most enjoyable experience for Lewis and Clark. Meat rotted, even as it was being smoked over the fire. The explorers' buckskin clothing fell apart in the wet weather. The men suffered from colds, dysentery, rheumatism, and unbearable infestations of fleas. The winter was one of the wettest on record—only six days without rain from December to March.

Even Christmas, the day the Corps moved into the unfinished fort, was miserable. "We should have Spent this day the nativity of Christ in feasting, had we any thing either to raise our Sperits or even gratify our appetites," wrote Clark. "Our Diner concisted of pore Elk, So much Spoiled that we eate it thro' mear necessity . . ."

Miserable as they were, President Jefferson's men knew a valuable piece of real estate when they saw one. When they returned to the East and told Jefferson that the area now known as Astoria had potential as an important fur trade post, a wealthy New York businessman took notice. Just five years after Lewis and Clark packed up and eagerly returned home, Lewis and Clark's dot on the map became Fort Astoria. In 1811, John Jacob Astor, a wealthy German-born fur and real estate magnate from New York who once owned the land that today is Times Square, sent members of his Pacific Fur Company to build Fort Astoria and stake America's claim to the western shore.

The establishment of Fort Astoria was the first permanent American settlement west of the Rockies. But it would not remain in American hands for long. At war with America, the British sent troops and warships to Astoria to demand the surrender of the fort in 1813, only to find the British Hudson's Bay Company had already bought it. In 1818, five years after the British took over, Astoria became American again.

However, it wasn't until 1846 that the official boundaries of the United States were finally drawn at the 49th parallel. Until then, British and American citizens alike were allowed to settle in Oregon Country. As it turned out, mostly people of Scandinavian descent settled the town.

In 1840, the first U.S. Customs Office opened in Astoria. And by 1860, almost 500 pioneers called the city home. Twenty years later, it was a bawdy port town of 7,000. Stories of shanghaied sailors, brothels, and gambling dens color the city's now celebrated past. For nearly two decades, a local theater group has produced "Shanghaied in Astoria," a musical melodrama based on the city's history.

Today, Astoria is a rural community of 10,000—so rural, in fact, that a small LearJet hit an elk while taking off from the local airport not long ago.

---

the largest line of umbrellas in the Pacific Northwest. The store also has raincoats, hats, and rubber boots. Exhibits at **Riversea Gallery** (✉ 1160 Commercial St. ☎ 503/325–1270) change monthly and typically showcase regional artists working in glass, pottery, wood, bronze, paint, fiber, and jewelry. The shop also has unique and edgy art as well as jewelry for sale.

## Seaside

❷ *12 mi south of Astoria on U.S. 101.*

The now busy resort town of Seaside has grown up around the spot where the Lewis and Clark expedition finally reached the Pacific Ocean. A bronze statue of the two explorers commemorates the end of their trail and faces the ocean at the center of Seaside's historic Promenade. The Prom was originally built in 1908 as a wooden walkway, and in 1920 it was extended to its current length, 1½ mi, with concrete sidewalks.

For years Seaside had a reputation as a garish arcade-filled town. But it cleaned up its act and now supports a bustling tourist trade with hotels, condominiums, and restaurants surrounding a long beach. Only 90 mi from Portland, Seaside is often crowded, so it's not the place to come if you crave solitude. Peak times include February, during the Trail's End Marathon; mid-March, when hordes of teenagers descend on the town during spring break; and July, when the annual Miss Oregon Pageant is in full swing.

Just south of town, waves draw surfers to the Cove, a spot jealously guarded by locals.

It's a 2½-mi hike from the parking lot of **Saddle Mountain State Park** to the summit of Saddle Mountain. It's much cooler at that elevation. The campground, which is 14 mi north of Seaside, has 10 primitive sites. ✉ *Off U.S. 26* ☎ *503/861–1671 or 503/436–2844* 🎫 *$3 per vehicle day-use fee* ☉ *Mar.–Nov., daily.*

Jellyfish, giant king crab, octopus, moray eels, wolf eels, and other sea life are swimming in 35 tanks at **Seaside Aquarium**, on the 1½ mi beachfront Promenade. You can feed the harbor seals. ✉ *200 N. Promenade* ☎ *503/738–6211* 🎫 *$6.50* ☉ *Daily 9–5.*

## Where to Stay & Eat

$–$$$  ✕ **Ambrosia.** In a former bank building, this stylish restaurant serves organic fare with flair. Specialties include ahi tuna with soba buckwheat noodles and Caesar salad. The former bank safe, now known as the Vault Room, is open to diners or for private groups. ✉ *210 S. Holladay* ☎ *503/738–7199* ▣ *AE, D, DC, MC, V* ☉ *Closed Mon. No lunch.*

$–$$$  ✕ **Shilo Restaurant and Lounge.** Sixteen windows give you a view of the ocean outside, while inside, candlelight glints off brass rails in this two-level dining room. A familiar entrée list is enhanced by beautiful plate presentation and such specialties as razor clams, grilled herb-crusted salmon, and a wide selection of steaks. The lounge has nightly entertainment. ✉ *30 N. Promenade, 97138* ☎ *503/738–8481* ▣ *AE, D, DC, MC, V.*

¢–$$  ✕ **Doogers.** The original branch of this Northwest chain is much loved by local families. The seafood is expertly prepared, and the creamy clam chowder may be the best on the coast. A collection of oil paintings by Oregon women artists colors the dining-room walls. ✉ *505 Broadway* ☎ *503/738–3773* ☝ *Reservations not accepted* ▣ *AE, D, MC, V.*

¢–$  ✕ **Sam's Seaside Café.** A half a block from the boardwalk and beach, this casual, quiet place is the spot for inexpensive burgers, salads, seafood dishes, and homemade cakes and pies at lunch and dinner. Fresh flowers and a wall-size sea mural give the café a cheery feel, and Sam's stays open late, too. ✉ *104 Broadway* ☎ *503/717–1725* ▣ *AE, MC, V.*

¢–$  ✕ **Salvatore's Cafe.** This family restaurant in a Best Western serves steaks, chicken, seafood, and pastas. Try the Oregon crab cakes or be a rebel and have Alaskan salmon and halibut. Plan on having the Oregon blueberry-and-white chocolate cheesecake for dessert. ✉ *414 N. Promenade* ☎ *503/738–3334 or 800/234–8439* ▣ *AE, D, MC, V.*

$$–$$$$  ▦ **Convention Center Inn.** Two-bedroom and group-size hospitality suites are available at this motel on the Necanicum River a few blocks from the Promenade. The inn is an easy walk to restaurants and shopping, and you'll find the *Oregonian* at your door each morning. ✉ *441 2nd*

*Ave.* ☎ *503/738–9581 or 800/699–5070* 🖶 *503/738–3212* 🛏 *48 rooms* 🔥 *Some kitchenettes, some refrigerators, cable TV, indoor pool, hot tub, laundry facilities, business services, some pets allowed (fee)* 🖃 *AE, D, DC, MC, V* ⎮⊙⎮ *CP.*

**$$–$$$$** 🏨 **Gearhart by the Sea.** Four separate buildings make up this beachfront resort 3 mi from Seaside. Units have ocean views and fireplaces, with one- or two-bedroom floor plans available. ✉ *1157 N. Marion Ave., Gearhart 97138* ☎ *503/738–8331 or 800/547–0115* 🖶 *503/738–0881* 🛏 *90 apartments* 🔥 *Restaurant, kitchenettes, cable TV, 18-hole golf course, indoor pool, bar, laundry facilities; no a/c* 🖃 *D, MC, V.*

**$–$$$$** 🏨 **Seashore Resort Motel.** If you want a convenient motel directly on the beach, this is the place. Some rooms have a view of the ocean, and a new elevator provides easy access to the upper floors. The motel is a short walk from the heart of Seaside. ✉ *60 N. Promenade, 97138* ☎ *503/738–6368 or 888/738–6368* 🖶 *503/738–8314* 🌐 *www.seashoreinnor.com* 🛏 *54 rooms* 🔥 *Some kitchenettes, some microwaves, some refrigerators, cable TV, pool, hot tub; no a/c* 🖃 *AE, D, DC, MC, V* ⎮⊙⎮ *CP.*

**$–$$$** 🏨 **Ebb Tide.** Right on the beach, this motel has some rooms with ocean views. All rooms are nicely finished with newer furnishings and bright colors. ✉ *300 N. Promenade, 97138* ☎ *503/738–8371 or 800/468–6232* 🖶 *503/738–0938* 🛏 *99 rooms* 🔥 *In-room data ports, some kitchenettes, refrigerators, cable TV, indoor pool, hot tub, gym, business services* 🖃 *AE, D, DC, MC, V.*

**$–$$$** 🏨 **Hi-Tide.** Some rooms at this small beachfront motel have fireplaces, and most rooms have ocean views. It's close to shopping and restaurants and only three blocks from the city center's "famous turn around." ✉ *30 Ave. G, 97138* ☎ *503/738–8414 or 800/621–9876* 🖶 *503/738–0875* 🛏 *64 rooms* 🔥 *Kitchenettes, cable TV, indoor pool, hot tub, business services; no a/c* 🖃 *AE, D, DC, MC, V.*

**$$** 🏨 **Gilbert Inn Bed and Breakfast.** This Queen Anne–style Victorian, built in 1892, is one of Seaside's prettiest lodging properties. In the common area you'll find the original brick fireplace, fir floors, and tongue-and-groove wood ceilings. Rooms are furnished in French-country prints and antiques, including cherry four-poster and brass beds and, in one room, a claw-foot tub. The Turret Room is popular for its turret windows, while the fourth-floor Garret has a view of the ocean. ✉ *341 Beach Dr., 97138* ☎ *503/738–9770 or 800/410–9770* 🖶 *503/717–1070* 🛏 *9 rooms, 1 suite* 🔥 *Cable TV, airport shuttle; no a/c, no smoking* 🌐 *www. gilbertinn.com* 🖃 *AE, D, MC, V* ⊙ *Closed Jan.* ⎮⊙⎮ *BP.*

**$** 🏨 **Hillcrest Inn.** The Hillcrest is only one block from both the beach and the convention center and three blocks from the downtown area and several restaurants and shops. The inn has been owned by the same family for more than two decades, and friendliness, cleanliness, and convenience are bywords here. You're welcome to use the picnic tables, lawn chairs, and even the barbecue on the grounds. ✉ *118 N. Columbia St., 97138* ☎ *503/738–6273 or 800/270–7659* 🖶 *503/717–0266* 🛏 *19 rooms, 4 suites, 3 two-bedroom cottages, 1 five-bedroom house* 🔥 *Picnic area, some in-room hot tubs, some kitchenettes, microwaves, refrigerators, cable TV, sauna, laundry facilities; no a/c in some rooms* 🖃 *AE, DC, MC, V.*

**$** 🏨 **Royale.** This small motel right in the center of downtown is on the Necanicum River, 3½ blocks from the beach and in very close walking distance to shopping and restaurants. Some rooms have river views. There's ample off-street parking. ✉ *531 Ave. A, 97138* ☎ *503/738–9541* 🛏 *26 rooms* 🔥 *No a/c* 🖃 *D, DC, MC, V.*

A brisk 2-mi hike from U.S. 101 south of Seaside leads to the 1,100-foot-high viewing point atop **Tillamook Head.** The view from here takes in the **Tillamook Rock Light Station,** which stands a mile or so out to sea. The lonely beacon, built in 1881 on a straight-sided rock, towers 41 feet above the surrounding ocean. In 1957 the lighthouse was abandoned; it is now a columbarium. Eight miles south of Seaside, U.S. 101 passes the entrance to **Ecola State Park,** a playground of sea-sculpted rocks, sandy shoreline, green headlands, and panoramic views. The park's main beach can be crowded in summer, but the **Indian Beach** area contains an often-deserted cove and explorable tidal pools. ☎ *800/551–6949* ✉ *$3 per vehicle* ☼ *Daily dawn–dusk.*

## Sports & the Outdoors

SURFING **Cleanline Surf** (✉ 719 1st Ave. ☎ 503/738–7888) rents body, surf, and skim boards. Prices for body and surfboards and all the accessories are $35 per day; skim boards, $15.

## Shopping

Fans of saltwater taffy should have no trouble finding a favored flavor at the **Candy Man** (✉ 21 N. Columbia ☎ 503/738–5280). Not only does this sweets shop have 185 flavors of the sticky stuff, there's also ice cream by the scoop, chocolates, fudge, jelly beans, and licorice whips.

# Cannon Beach

❸ *10 mi south of Seaside on U.S. 101, 80 mi west of Portland on U.S. 26.*

Cannon Beach is Seaside's refined, artistic alter ego, a more mellow yet trendy place (population 1,400) for Portlanders to take the sea air. One of the most charming hamlets on the coast, the town has beachfront homes and hotels and a weathered-cedar downtown shopping district. On the downside, the Carmel of the Oregon coast is expensive, crowded, and afflicted with a subtle, moneyed hauteur (such as the town's ban on vacation-home rentals) that may grate on more plebeian nerves.

The town got its name when a cannon from the wrecked schooner USS *Shark* washed ashore in 1846 (the piece is on display a mile east of town on U.S. 101). Towering over the broad, sandy beach is **Haystack Rock,** a 235-foot-high monolith that is supposedly the most-photographed feature of the Oregon coast. The rock is temptingly accessible during some low tides, but the coast guard regularly airlifts stranded climbers from its precipitous sides, and falls have claimed numerous lives over the years. Every May the town hosts the Cannon Beach Sandcastle Contest, for which thousands throng the beach to view imaginative and often startling works in this most transient of art forms.

Shops and galleries selling kites, upscale clothing, local art, wine, coffee, and food line **Hemlock Street,** Cannon Beach's main thoroughfare.

The road takes hair-raising curves as it climbs to 700 feet above the Pacific around the flank of 1,661-foot **Neahkahnie Mountain,** south of Cannon Beach. The views are dramatic. Carvings on nearby beach rocks and old Native American legends gave rise to a tale that a fortune in gold doubloons from a sunken Spanish galleon is buried somewhere on the mountainside. ✉ *U.S. 101.*

## Where to Stay & Eat

**$–$$$$** ✕**Doogers.** Like the original Doogers in Seaside, the Cannon Beach branch serves superb seafood. The restaurant is in a shingle-sided building typical of regional architecture. Clam-chowder fans can take home the Doogers clam-chowder kit to re-create the famous soup at home. ⊠ *1371 S. Hemlock St.* ☎ *503/436–2225* ▭ *AE, D, MC, V.*

★ **$–$$$** ✕ **The Bistro.** Flowers, candlelight, and classical music convey romance at this 11-table restaurant. The menu includes imaginative Continental-influenced renditions of local seafood and pasta dishes as well as specialty salads. The signature dish is the fresh seafood stew. ⊠ *263 N. Hemlock St.* ☎ *503/436–2661* ▭ *MC, V* ☉ *Closed Tues. and Wed. Nov.–Jan. No lunch.*

**¢–$** ✕ **Lazy Susan Cafe.** Entrées at this laid-back spot—*the* place to come for breakfast in Cannon Beach—include quiche, omelets, hot cereal, and a substantial order of waffles topped with fruit and orange syrup. Don't leave without tasting the fresh-baked scones and the home fries. ⊠ *Coaster Sq., 126 N. Hemlock St.* ☎ *503/436–2816* ⌂ *Reservations not accepted* ▭ *No credit cards* ☉ *Closed Tues. No dinner Mon.–Thurs.*

★ **$$$–$$$$** ✕▥ **Stephanie Inn.** Superior service, luxurious rooms, and tastefully decorated public areas make this three-story inn the premier oceanfront hotel in Cannon Beach. Impeccably maintained, with country-style furnishings, fireplaces, large bathrooms with whirlpool tubs, and balconies commanding outstanding views of Haystack Rock, the rooms are so comfortable you may never want to leave—except perhaps to enjoy the four-course prix-fixe dinners of innovative Pacific Northwest cuisine. Generous country breakfasts are included in the room price, as are evening wine and hors d'oeuvres. ⊠ *2740 S. Pacific St., 97110* ☎ *503/436–2221 or 800/633–3466* ᐁ *503/436–9711* ⊕ *www.stephanie-inn.com* ⇥ *50 rooms* ⌂ *Dining room, in-room VCRs, minibars, refrigerators, massage, library* ▭ *AE, D, DC, MC, V.*

**$$$$** ▥ **Ocean Lodge.** Designed to capture the feel of a 1940s beach resort, this lodge is right on the beach. Most of the rooms have full oceanfront views, and all have open wood beams, simple but sophisticated furnishings, gas fireplaces, and balconies or decks. The lobby floor is reclaimed spruce wood, while stairs were fashioned from old stadium bleachers. A massive rock fireplace anchors the lobby, and there is a second fireplace in the second-floor library. Bungalows across the street do not have ocean views but are large and private. An expanded Continental breakfast is served in the second-floor breakfast room. ⊠ *2864 S. Pacific St., 97110* ☎ *888/777–4047* ᐁ *503/436–2159* ⊕ *www.theoceanlodge.com* ⇥ *45 rooms* ⌂ *Some in-room hot tubs, kitchenettes, cable TV, some pets allowed (fee); no a/c in some rooms, no smoking* ▭ *AE, D, MC, V.*

**$$$$** ▥ **Surfsand Resort.** Many of the bright, modern rooms at this resort, within walking distance of downtown, have views of Haystack Rock and the Pacific Ocean; some are oceanfront. Many rooms have fireplaces. There are in-room DVD players and movies. ⊠ *Ocean and Gower St., 97110* ☎ *503/436–2274 or 800/547–6100* ᐁ *503/436–9116* ⊕ *www.surfsand.com* ⇥ *86 rooms; houses* ⌂ *Restaurant, some in-room hot tubs, some kitchenettes, refrigerators, cable TV, indoor pool, hot tub, beach, bar, laundry facilities, airport shuttle, some pets allowed (fee); no a/c* ▭ *AE, D, DC, MC, V.*

**$$$–$$$$** ▥ **Inn at Cannon Beach.** Opened in 2000, the inn is one of the area's newer hotels. Rooms in rustic two-story bungalows have fireplaces and decks. There's a koi pond, gardens, and generous secluded lawns with Adirondack chairs for guests' use. The property is one block from the beach. A deluxe Continental breakfast is served in an on-site art gallery. ⊠ *3215 N. Hemlock, 97110* ☎ *503/436–9085 or 800/321–6304* ᐁ *503/436–8510* ⊕ *www.atcannonbeach.com* ⇥ *40* ⌂ *Some in-room hot tubs, kitch-*

*enettes, cable TV, in-room VCRs, some pets allowed (fee); no a/c, no smoking* ⊟ *AE, D, MC, V.*

**$$–$$$$** ⊡ **Webb's Scenic Surf.** Small and family-operated, this beachfront hotel is a throwback to simpler times in Cannon Beach, before trendiness translated into big resorts and $500 weekends. Many of the tidy rooms have kitchenettes and fireplaces. ⊠ *255 N. Larch St., 97110* ☎ *503/436–2706 or 800/374–9322* 🖷 *503/436–1229* ⊕ *www.at-e.com/webbsurf* 🛏 *14 rooms* ⟐ *Some kitchenettes* ⊟ *AE, DC, MC, V.*

**¢–$$$$** ⊡ **Hallmark Resort at Cannon Beach.** Large suites with fireplaces, whirlpool tubs, kitchenettes, and great views make this triple-decker oceanfront resort a good choice for families or for couples looking for a romantic splurge. The rooms, all with spacious balconies and oak-tile baths, have soothing color schemes. The least-expensive units do not have views. Pets are welcome for a $10 charge. ⊠ *1400 S. Hemlock St., 97110* ☎ *503/436–1566 or 888/448–4449* 🖷 *503/436–0324* 🛏 *132 rooms, 4 rental homes, 24 units in town* ⟐ *Restaurant, in-room data ports, refrigerators, indoor pool, wading pool, gym, sauna, bar, laundry service, business services, meeting room, some pets allowed (fee)* ⊟ *AE, D, DC, MC, V.*

**¢–$$$** ⊡ **Cannon Beach Hotel.** Walk to the beach and downtown shopping from this restored, turn-of-the-20th-century, European-style inn close to Haystack Rock. There's a cozy fireplace in the lobby, and some rooms have fireplaces, too. ⟐ *Restaurant, some in-room hot tubs, cable TV, hot tub, business services.* ⊠ *1116 S. Hemlock* ☎ *503/436–1392* 🖷 *503/436–2101* ⊕ *www.cannonbeachhotel.com* 🛏 *9 rooms* ⊟ *AE, D, DC, MC, V.*

**$** ⊡ **Grey Whale Inn.** This small, charming inn dates from 1948. It is in a very quiet residential neighborhood, a 5-minute walk to the beach or a 20-minute walk to Haystack Rock. All the rooms are individually decorated with original artwork, done either by the family or local artists. The rooms have shower facilities only. ⊠ *164 Kenai St., 97110* ☎ *503/ 436–2848* 🛏 *5 rooms* ⟐ *Some kitchenettes, cable TV, in-room VCRs; no a/c, no smoking* ⊟ *MC, V.*

**en route** | South of Cannon Beach, U.S. 101 climbs 700 feet above the Pacific, providing dramatic views and often hair-raising curves as it winds along the flank of **Neahkahnie Mountain.** Cryptic carvings on beach rocks near here and centuries-old Native American legends of shipwrecked Europeans gave rise to a tale that the survivors of a sunken Spanish galleon buried a fortune in doubloons somewhere on the side of the 1,661-foot-high mountain.

## Sports & the Outdoors

HORSEBACK RIDING | In Cannon Beach, **Sea Ranch Stables** (⊠ 415 Alt. U.S. 101 N ☎ 503/ 436–2815) leads summer guided rides by Haystack Rock and to geological sites along the coast as well as night rides.

SURFING | You'll find beach accessories for rent at **Cannon Beach Surf & Mercantile** (⊠ 1088 S. Hemlock ☎ 503/436–0475). Among the items on hand are wet suits ($20 per day), surf and body boards ($25 per day or wet suit and board $40), bikes ($8 an hour), jogging strollers ($20 per day), sand wheelchairs ($35 per day), metal detectors ($15 per day), beach carts ($15 per day), and kayaks ($40 per day, including life vest). The store also carries a line of beach wear. Rent skim, body, and surf boards and all the other necessary accessories at **Cleanline Surf** (⊠ 171 Sunset Blvd. ☎ 503/436–9726). Skim boards rent for about $15; adult surf- and bodyboard packages start at $35.

# BELOVED LOUSY WEATHER

O N A FALL DAY IN A NEWPORT store, a young clerk remarks to a coastal newcomer, "Oh, you will hate it here in the winter. All it does is rain." And later, in a conversation about coastal weather, one woman asks another, "But don't you mind the gray?"

The Oregon coast rarely fails to inspire awe for its breathtaking scenery, but when it comes to the weather, well, some folks find it less than laudable. There are others, however, who will tell you that the moody weather—the sunny days that suddenly evaporate in a trailing wrap of foggy gray, the rain that comes down in sheets blown horizontal, the wind that blasts through in a steady howl—is a prized part of the coast's singular charm.

Sunny days are undeniably glorious—noble Grand firs towering dark and green against endless blue sky; foam-tipped waves tumbling against water sometimes blue, sometimes green, sometimes a color solely the ocean's own. You will find those days any time of year, most predictably during the summer but often in the spring and fall, and, unexpectedly, though not at all that uncommon, in the midst of January. And even on that winter day when other places lie dormant beneath freezing snow, the temperatures on the coast might be a balmy 55°F.

There's much to be said for the sunny day, but in terms of high drama and displays of nature's sheer force, the winter storm reigns supreme. From November to February, give or take a week or two on either side, storms can be a common and sudden event. Dark clouds will roll in, the skies will open, the wind will unleash itself, and for hours on end, beach communities north and south will undergo relentless batterings. On those days, ocean swells are said to curl up to four stories high—no time to be on the beach. But then, just as quickly as it rolled in, the rain will stop, the wind will slow, the ocean will quiet—there may even be a peek of that glorious sunny blue sky. And storm watchers everywhere will descend on the beach in search of some small find stirred up by the storm and left waiting in the sand.

Many people think you come to the coast only for those glorious sunny days. A few intrepid souls know better.

— By Lori Tobias

## Shopping

Find an eclectic mix of antiques, gifts, linens, jewelry, and local art at **Castaways** (✉ 1088 S. Hemlock ☎ 503/436–0903). Glass and crystal are the specialties at **Rare Discoveries** (✉ 480 N. Hemlock ☎ 503/436–0119), which also carries jewelry and pottery.

## Oswald West State Park

❹ *10 mi south of Cannon Beach on U.S. 101.*

Adventurous travelers will enjoy a sojourn at one of the best-kept secrets on the Pacific coast, **Oswald West State Park,** at the base of Neahkahnie Mountain. Park in one of the two lots on U.S. 101 and use a park-provided wheelbarrow to trundle your camping gear down a ½-mi trail. An old-growth forest surrounds the 36 primitive campsites (reservations not accepted), and the spectacular beach contains caves and tidal pools.

The trail to the summit, on the left about 2 mi south of the parking lots for Oswald West State Park (marked only by a HIKERS sign), rewards the intrepid with unobstructed views over surf, sand, forest, and mountain. Come in December or March and you might spot pods of gray whales. ⊠ *Ecola Park Rd.* ☎ *503/368–5943 or 800/551–6949* ⊕ *www. oregonstateparks.org* ⊒ *Day use free, campsites $16* ⊙ *Day use daily dawn–dusk; camping Mar.–Oct., daily dawn–dusk.*

---

**en route** | After passing through several small fishing, logging, and resort towns, U.S. 101 skirts around **Tillamook Bay,** where the Miami, Kilchis, Wilson, Trask, and Tillamook rivers enter the Pacific. The bay rewards sportfishing enthusiasts with quarry that includes sea-run cutthroat trout, bottom fish, and silver, chinook, and steelhead salmon, along with mussels, oysters, clams, and the delectable Dungeness crab. Charter-fishing services operate out of the **Garibaldi** fishing harbor 10 mi north of Tillamook. For some of the best rock fishing in the state, try Tillamook Bay's North Jetty.

---

# Manzanita

**❺** *20 mi south of Cannon Beach on U.S. 101.*

Manzanita is a secluded seaside community with only 500 full-time residents. It's on a sandy peninsula peppered with tufts of grass on the northwestern side of Nehalem Bay. It is a tranquil small town, but its restaurants, galleries, and 18-hole golf course have increased its appeal to tourists. Manzanita and Nehalem Bay both have become popular windsurfing destinations.

Established in 1974, **Nehalem Bay Winery,** the sixth-oldest winery in Oregon, is known for its pinot chardonnay and blackberry and plum fruit wines. You can taste them here, in a building that was once the Mohler Cheese Factory, and enjoy the picnic area. The winery also has a busy schedule of events with concerts, barbecues, an occasional pig roast, children's activities, performances at the Theatre Au Vin, and a bluegrass festival the third week of August. ⊠ *34965 Hwy. 53, Nehalem 97131* ☎ *503/368–9463 or 888/368–9463* ⊟ *503/368–5300* ⊕ *www. nehalembaywinery.com* ⊙ *Daily 9–6.*

### Where to Stay & Eat

¢–$$$  ✕ **Blue Sky Cafe.** Stained glass, a jungle of plants, and funky furnishings lend a quirky air to this casual hole-in-the-wall café. Try the chive crepes with asparagus, leeks, and morel mushrooms; Thai peanut chicken with mint cilantro and fresh-picked cucumbers; or the prawn posole. Save room for one of the rich desserts. ⊠ *154 Laneda St., off U.S. 101* ☎ *503/368–5712* ⊟ *No credit cards* ⊙ *Closed Mon. and Tues. Oct.–June. No lunch.*

$$–$$$  ⊡ **Inn at Manzanita.** This 1987 Scandinavian structure, filled with light-color woods, beams, and glass, is half a block from the beach. Shore pines on the property give upper-floor patios a tree-house feel, all rooms have decks, and two have skylights. A nearby café serves breakfast, and area restaurants are nearby. In winter the inn is a great place for storm watching. There's a two-day minimum stay on weekends. ⊠ *67 Laneda Ave.* ⊙ *Box 243, 97130* ☎ *503/368–6754* ⊟ *503/368–5941* ⊕ *www. innatmanzanita.com* ⊅ *13 rooms in 4 buildings* ⚲ *In-room hot tubs,*

*some kitchenettes, some microwaves, refrigerators, cable TV; no a/c in some rooms, no phones in some rooms, no smoking ═ MC, V.*

⚠ **Nehalem Bay State Park.** Close enough to the ocean that you'll potentially be lulled to sleep by the waves, the park is on the edge of Nehalem Bay, which is popular for kayaking, crabbing, and fishing. ♿ *Flush toilets, partial hookups, dump station, drinking water, showers, fire pits, picnic tables, electricity, swimming (ocean)* ⚐ *267 electrical sites, 18 yurts, 17 sites with corrals.* ═ *MC, V* ✉ *Off U.S. 101, 3 mi south of Manzanita Junction* ☎ *800/452–5687 reservations, 800/551–5687 information* ⊕ *www.oregonstateparks.org.* ⚑ *Reservations essential* 💳 *Electrical hookups $20, tent sites $17, horse camp $16, yurts $27.*

### Sports & the Outdoors

KAYAKING   Midway between Manzanita and Rockaway Beach, the tiny **Nehalem Bay Kayak Company** (✉ 395 U.S. 101, Wheeler ☎ 503/368–6055) sells kayaks, surfboards, and outdoor wear and has equipment rentals, lessons, and kayak tours.

## Rockaway Beach

❻  *28 mi south of Cannon Beach on U.S. 101*

Rockaway Beach, a small community of over 1,000 residents, sits between Nehalem Bay and the Manzanita area to the north and Tillamook Bay and Tillamook dairy-farming country to the south. Rockaway originated in the early 1900s as a summer-vacation destination for Portlanders, a role it now fills for visitors from elsewhere in the state and country.

### Where to Stay & Eat

¢–$  ✕ **Beach Pancake and Dinner House.** This cozy restaurant's specialty is homemade chicken and dumplings; it has a children's menu, offers senior-citizen discounts, is wheelchair accessible, and serves breakfast—voted by locals the best in Tillamook County—all day. Authentic Mexican dishes add south-of-the-border zest to the down-home menu. ✉ *202 N. U.S. 101, 97136* ☎ *503/355–2411* ═ MC, V.

$$–$$$  🏨 **Silver Sands.** Each room in this beachfront motel has a balcony and view of the ocean. It's central to local shopping and restaurants and is right in the middle of town; it's also an easy and scenic drive from here to the northern coast. ✉ *215 S. Pacific St., 97136* ☎ *503/355–2206 or 800/457–8972* 🖷 *503/355–9690* ⚐ *64 rooms* ♿ *Some kitchenettes, refrigerators, cable TV, indoor pool, hot tub; no a/c* ═ AE, D, DC, MC, V.

## Tillamook

❼  *30 mi south of Oswald West State Park and Neahkahnie Mountain on U.S. 101.*

Tillamook County is something of a wet Wisconsin-on-the-Pacific. More than 100 inches of annual rainfall and the confluence of three rivers contribute to the lush green pastures around Tillamook, probably best known for its thriving dairy industry and cheese factory. The Tillamook County Cheese Factory ships about 40 million pounds of cheese around the world every year. Both Tillamook and the Blue Heron French Cheese Factory offer you a look at their cheese-making processes.

Just south of town is the largest wooden structure in the world, one of two gigantic buildings constructed in 1942 by the U.S. Navy to shelter blimps that patrolled the Pacific Coast during World War II. Hangar A was destroyed by fire in 1992, and Hangar B was subsequently converted to the Tillamook Naval Air Station Museum.

The Three Capes Loop over Cape Meares, Cape Lookout, and Cape Kiwanda offers spectacular views of the ocean and coastline. A lighthouse and an old Indian burial Sitka spruce, Octopus Tree, are worth the trip to Cape Meares, while Cape Lookout is one of the Northwest's best whale-watching viewpoints. Along the route from Tillamook's small resort area of Oceanside, take a look at Three Arch Rocks, a National Wildlife Refuge, with hundreds of sea lions and seals and nesting habitat for as many as 200,000 birds.

☺ The **Pioneer Museum** in Tillamook's 1905 county courthouse has an intriguing if old-fashioned hodgepodge of Native American, pioneer, logging, and natural-history exhibits, along with antique vehicles and military artifacts. ✉ *2106 2nd St.* ☎ *503/842–4553* ✍ *$3* ☼ *May–Sept., Mon.–Sat. 8:30–5, Sun. 12:30–5.*

The **Latimer Quilt and Textile Center** is dedicated to the preservation, promotion, creation, and display of the fiber arts. Spinners, weavers, beaders, and quilters can be found working on projects in the Quilting Room and may engage you in hands-on demonstrations. Rotating exhibits range from costumes, cloth dolls, crocheted items from the 1940s and 1950s, exquisite historical quilts dating from the early to mid 1800s, basketry, and weavings. ✉ *2105 Wilson River Loop Rd.* ☎ *503/842–8622* ✍ *$2.50* ☼ *Tue.–Sat. 10–4, Sun. noon–4.*

More than 750,000 visitors annually press their noses against the spotlessly clean windows at the **Tillamook County Creamery,** the largest cheese-making plant on the West Coast. Here the rich milk from the area's thousands of Holstein and brown Swiss cows becomes ice cream, butter, and cheddar and Monterey Jack cheeses. Exhibits at the visitor center, where free samples are dispensed, explain the cheese-making process. ✉ *4175 U.S. 101 N, 2 mi north of Tillamook* ☎ *503/815–1300* ⊕ *www.tillamookcheese.com* ✍ *Free* ☼ *Mid-Sept.–May, daily 8–6; June–mid-Sept., daily 8–8.*

The **Blue Heron French Cheese Company** specializes in French-style cheeses—Camembert, Brie, and others. There's a petting zoo for kids, a sit-down deli, wine and cheese tastings, and a gift shop that carries wines and jams, mustards, and other products from Oregon. ✉ *2001 Blue Heron Dr. (watch for signs from U.S. 101)* ☎ *503/842–8281* ✍ *Free* ☼ *Memorial Day–Labor Day, daily 8–8; Labor Day–Memorial Day, daily 8:30–5.*

In the world's largest wooden structure, a former blimp hangar south of town, the **Tillamook Naval Air Station Museum** displays one of the finest private collections of vintage aircraft from World War II, including a B-25 Mitchell and an ME-109 Messerschmidt. The 20-story building is big enough to hold half a dozen football fields. ✉ *6030 Hangar Rd. (½ mi south of Tillamook; head east from U.S. 101 on Long Prairie Rd. and follow signs)* ☎ *503/842–1130* ✍ *$9.50* ☼ *Daily 10–5.*

## Where to Stay & Eat

$–$$$ ✕ **Roseanna's.** Nine miles west of Tillamook in Oceanside, Roseanna's is in a rustic 1915 building on the beach opposite Three Arch Rock, so you might be able to watch sea lions and puffins while you eat. The calm of the beach is complemented in the evening by candlelight and fresh flowers. Have halibut or salmon half a dozen ways, or try the poached baked oysters or Gorgonzola seafood pasta. ✉ *1490 Pacific Ave., Oceanside 97134* ☎ *503/842–7351* ⌘ *Reservations not accepted* ▭ *MC, V.*

$–$$ ✕ **Artspace.** You'll be surrounded by artwork as you enjoy homemade creations at Artspace in Bay City, 6 mi north of Tillamook. The menu may include garlic-grilled oysters, vegetarian dishes, and other specials, all beautifully presented, often with edible flowers. And if you reserve in advance, you'll get a complimentary appetizer for your thoughtfulness. ⊠ *9120 5th St., Bay City 97107* ☎ *503/377–2782* 🖷 *503/377–2010* ▤ *No credit cards* ⊘ *Closed Mon.*

**$–$$** ✕ **Cedar Bay.** Locally owned for 15 years, this casual restaurant downtown is popular with locals for its steaks, prime rib, and seafood. There's a kids' menu. ⊠ *2015 1st St., 97141* ☎ *503/842–8288* ▤ *MC, V.*

**$$–$$$** 🏨 **Sandlake Country Inn.** Tucked into a bower of old roses on 2 acres, this intimate bed-and-breakfast is in a farmhouse built of timbers that washed ashore from a shipwreck in 1890. It is listed on the Oregon Historic Registry and filled with antiques. The Timbers Suite has a massive, king-size wood canopy bed and two-person jetted tub; the Starlight Suite occupies four rooms on the second floor and includes a canopy queen bed and double-sided fireplace. ⊠ *8505 Galloway Rd., Sandlake 97112* ☎ *503/965–6745 or 877/726–3525* 🖷 *503/965–7425* ⊕ *www.sandlakecountryinn.com* 🛏 *4 rooms, 1 suite* 🍴 *Some kitchenettes, cable TV, in-room VCRs, hot tub; no a/c, no phones in some rooms, no smoking* ▤ *D, MC, V* ⦿l *BP.*

**$$** 🏨 **Hudson House.** The son of the original owner of this 1906 farmhouse was a photographer who captured the area's rough beauty on postcards. The larger suite is downstairs, with a parlor and private porch overlooking the Nestucca Valley. The more popular, upstairs suite has a bedroom in the house's turret. The two guest rooms are under the high-gabled roof. The house has a wraparound porch from which you can enjoy a view of the surrounding woods. ⊠ *37700 U.S. 101 S, Cloverdale 97112* ☎ *503/392–3533 or 888/835–3533* ⊕ *www.hudsonhouse.com* 🛏 *2 rooms, 2 suites* 🍴 *Picnic area, some in-room data ports, hot tub, library; no kids under 12, no room phones, no room TVs, no smoking* ▤ *MC, V* ⦿l *BP.*

**$–$$** 🏨 **Marclair Inn.** This family-owned hotel is on a landscaped garden abloom with flowers. It's 2½ mi from the Tillamook Naval Air Station Museum and within walking distance of restaurants. Rooms are generous in size and well maintained with credenzas, small tables, and good lighting. ⊠ *11 Main Ave., 97141* ☎ *503/842–7571 or 800/331–6857* 🛏 *47 rooms* 🍴 *Restaurant, some kitchenettes, pool, hot tub, some pets allowed (fee)* ▤ *AE, D, MC, V.*

**$** 🏨 **Whiskey Creek Bed and Breakfast.** The builder of this 1900 cedar-shingle house owned a sawmill where he made spruce oars, using the leftovers to panel the interior. Surrounded by forest, the house is unfussy and comfortable and filled with the artist owner's oil and watercolor landscapes. The two small rooms upstairs have terraces overlooking Netarts Bay. The apartment downstairs has one bedroom, plus bathroom and kitchen. In winter the inn is a retreat, with yoga and shiatsu massage on site. ⊠ *7500 Whiskey Creek Rd., 97141* ☎ *503/842–2408* 📧 *whiskeycreek@oregoncoast.com* 🛏 *2 rooms, 1 apartment* 🍴 *Picnic area, some kitchenettes, some microwaves, some refrigerators, cable TV, library, baby-sitting; no a/c in some rooms, no smoking, no TV in some rooms* ▤ *No credit cards* ⊘ *Closed Dec.* ⦿l *BP.*

### Sports & the Outdoors

GOLF **Alderbrook Golf Club** (⊠ 7300 Alderbrook Rd. ☎ 503/842–6413) is an 18-hole, par-69 golf course. The greens fees are $27 for 18 holes and $15 for 9. Optional cart costs are $25 and $15, respectively.

## Three Capes Loop

★ ⑧ *Starts south of downtown Tillamook off 3rd St.*

The Three Capes Loop, a 35-mi byway off U.S. 101, is one of the coast's most thrilling driving experiences. The loop winds along the coast between Tillamook and Pacific City, passing three distinctive headlands—Cape Meares, Cape Lookout, and Cape Kiwanda. Bayocean Road heading west from Tillamook passes what was the thriving resort town of Bay Ocean. More than 30 years ago, Bay Ocean washed into the sea—houses, a bowling alley, everything—during a raging Pacific storm.

Nine miles west of Tillamook, trails from the parking lot at the end of Bay Ocean Spit lead through the dunes to a usually uncrowded and highly walkable white-sand beach.

**Cape Meares State Park** is on the northern tip of the Three Capes Loop. Cape Meares was named for English navigator John Meares, who voyaged along this coast in 1788. The restored **Cape Meares Lighthouse**, built in 1890 and open to the public May–September, provides a sweeping view over the cliff to the caves and sea-lion rookery on the rocks below. A many-trunked Sitka spruce known as the Octopus Tree grows near the lighthouse parking lot. ✥ *Three Capes Loop 10 mi west of Tillamook* ☎ *800/551-6949* 🖃 *Free* ⊗ *Park daily dawn–dusk. Lighthouse May–Sept., daily 11–4; Mar., Apr., and Oct., weekends 11–4.*

**Cape Lookout State Park** lies south of the beach towns of Oceanside and Netarts. A fairly easy 2-mi trail—marked on the highway as WILDLIFE VIEWING AREA—leads through giant spruces, western red cedars, and hemlocks to views of Cascade Head to the south and Cape Meares to the north. Wildflowers, more than 150 species of birds, and migrating whales passing by in early April make this trail a favorite with nature lovers. The park has a picnic area overlooking the sea and a year-round campground. ✥ *Three Capes Loop 8 mi south of Cape Meares* ☎ *800/ 551-6949* 🖃 *Day use $3, campsites $18–$22* ⊗ *Daily dawn–9 PM.*

Huge waves pound the jagged sandstone cliffs and caves at **Cape Kiwanda State Natural Area.** The much-photographed, 327-foot-high **Haystack Rock** juts out of Nestucca Bay south of here. Surfers ride some of the longest waves on the coast, hang gliders soar above the shore, and beachcombers explore tidal pools and take in unparalleled ocean views. ✥ *Three Capes Loop 15 mi south of Cape Lookout* ☎ *800/551-6949* 🖃 *Free* ⊗ *Daily dawn–dusk.*

## Pacific City

**⑨** *1½ mi south of Cape Kiwanda on Three Capes Loop.*

The beach at Pacific City, the town visible from Cape Kiwanda, is one of the few places in the state where fishing dories (flat-bottom boats with high, flaring sides) are launched directly into the surf instead of from harbors or docks. During the commercial salmon season in late summer, it's possible to buy salmon directly from the fishermen.

A walk along the flat white-sand beach at **Robert Straub State Park** leads down to the mouth of the Nestucca River, considered by many to be the best fishing river on the north coast. ✉ *West from main intersection in downtown Pacific City across Nestucca River (follow signs)* ☎ *800/ 551-6949* 🖃 *Free* ⊗ *Daily dawn–dusk.*

off the beaten path

**NATURE CONSERVANCY CASCADE HEAD TRAIL –** The trail at one of the most unusual headlands on the Oregon coast winds through a rain forest where 250-year-old Sitka spruces and a dense green undergrowth of mosses and ferns is nourished by 100-inch annual rainfalls. After the forest comes grassy and treeless Cascade Head, a rare example of a maritime prairie. Magnificent views down to the Salmon River and west to the Coast Range open up as you continue along the headland, where black-tailed deer often graze and turkey vultures soar in the strong winds. You need to be in fairly good shape for the first and steepest part of the hike, which can be done in about an hour. The 270-acre area has been named a United Nations Biosphere Reserve. Coastal bluffs make this a popular hang-gliding and kite-flying area. A campground has 54 full hookups, 1 electrical and 191 tent sites, and 4 yurts. ⊠ *Savage Rd., 6 mi south of Neskowin off U.S. 101 (turn west on Three Rocks Rd. and north on Savage)* ☎ *503/230–1221* ☎ *Free* ⊙ *July–Dec., daily dawn–dusk.*

The small 350-foot stretch of **Mugg Estuarine Park**, on the Nestucca River, is an ideal bird-watching vantage point. All facilities are accessible by people with disabilities. ⊹ *2 blocks from center of town, across bridge* ☎ 503/965–6161.

## Where to Stay & Eat

¢–$$$  ✕ **Riverhouse.** Fresh seafood, sandwiches, and home-baked desserts are the specialties at this casual dining spot overlooking the Nestucca River. Original, all-natural salad dressings are a big hit with guests and available for sale in gift packs. ⊠ *34450 Brooten Rd.* ☎ *503/965–6722* ☐ *MC, V.*

¢–$$  ✕ **Pelican Pub and Brewery.** Breakfast, lunch, and dinner are served daily at this oceanfront restaurant. The large windows provide a majestic view of Cape Kiwanda to Cascade Head. Dine outdoors on a patio right on the beach. The menu includes steaks, fresh fish, pizza, burgers, and beer brewed in-house. ⊠ *33180 Cape Kiwanda Dr., 97135* ☎ *503/965–7007* ☐ *AE, D, MC, V.*

$$–$$$  ▥ **Inn at Cape Kiwanda.** All the rooms at this three-story inn built in 1998 on the Three Capes Scenic Loop have gas fireplaces, minibars, and a view of the ocean. The inn is a short stroll to shops, galleries, restaurants, and the beach. ⊠ *33105 Cape Kiwanda Dr., 97135* ☎ *503/965– 7001* ☐ *503/965–7002* ⊕ *www.innatcapekiwanda.com* ⤳ *35 rooms* ☖ *In-room data ports, gym, laundry facilities, some pets allowed; no smoking* ☐ *AE, D, DC, MC, V.*

$$  ▥ **Eagles View Bed and Breakfast.** This small inn was built in 1995 and is set amid tall trees overlooking the Nestucca Bay and River about 1 mi from town. Furnishings are themed around original and limited-edition art. All rooms have a view of either the forest or the bay. Children under 12 and pets are not permitted. ⊠ *37975 Brooten Rd., 97135* ☎ *503/965–7600 or 888/846–3292* ⊕ *eaglesviewbb.com* ⤳ *5 rooms* ☖ *Some in-room hot tubs, outdoor hot tub; no kids under 12, no smoking* ☐ *AE, D, MC, V* ⊙ *BP.*

*Pacific City* [handwritten margin note]

$  ▥ **Inn at Pacific City.** Family owned and operated, this ground-level inn is five blocks from the beach and near the Nestucca River. Area restaurants are also nearby. ⊠ *35215 Brooten Rd.* ⏍ *Box 1000, 97135* ☎ *503/965–6366 or 888/722–2489* ☐ *503/965–6812* ⤳ *16 rooms* ☖ *Kitchenettes, microwaves, refrigerators, some pets allowed (fee), no-smoking rooms* ☐ *AE, D, DC, MC, V.*

# Lincoln City

🔟 *16 mi south of Pacific City on U.S. 101, 78 mi west of Portland on Hwy. 99 W and Hwy. 18.*

Once a series of small villages, Lincoln City is a sprawling, suburban-ish town without a center. But the endless tourist amenities make up for whatever it lacks in charm. Clustered like barnacles on the offshore reefs are fast-food restaurants, gift shops, supermarkets, candy stores, antiques markets, dozens of motels and hotels, a factory-outlet mall, and a busy casino. Lincoln City is the most popular destination city on the Oregon coast, but its only real geographic claim to fame is the 445-foot-long **D River**, stretching from its source in Devil's Lake to the Pacific; *Guinness World Records* lists the D as the world's shortest river.

The only casino built directly on the beach in Oregon, **Chinook Winds** has slot machines, blackjack, poker, keno, and off-track betting. The entry atrium is accented with a two-story waterfall and natural rocks, trees, and plants to replicate the fishing ground of the Confederated Tribes of the Siletz, who own the casino. The Siletz Room has good food, and there is an all-you-can-eat buffet, a snack bar, and a lounge. An arcade will keep the kids busy while you are on the gambling floor. Big-name entertainers perform in the showroom. ✉ *1777 N.W. 44th St., 97367* ☎ *541/996–5825 or 888/244–6665.*

The imaginative craftspeople at the **Alder House II** studio turn molten glass into vases and bowls, which are available for sale. It is the oldest glass-blowing studio in the state. ✉ *611 Immonen Rd.* ☎ *541/996–2483* ⊕ *www.alderhouse.com* ✆ *Free* ☺ *Mid-Mar.–Nov., daily 10–5.*

Canoeing and kayaking are popular on the small lake at **Devil's Lake State Park,** which is in turn popular with coots, loons, ducks, cormorants, bald eagles, and grebes. It's the only Oregon-coast campground within the environs of a city. There are 32 full hookups, 55 tent sites, and 10 yurts. ✉ *1452 N.E. 6th St.* ☎ *541/994–2002 or 800/551–6949* ✆ *Free* ☺ *Daily.*

The community performing arts center **Theatre West** showcases local talent in a year-round schedule of popular plays. ✉ *3536 S.E. U.S. 101* ☎ *541/994–5663* ☺ *Thurs.–Sat.; call for hrs.*

### Where to Stay & Eat

$–$$$ ✕ **Bay House.** Inside a charming bungalow, this restaurant serves meals to linger over while you enjoy views across sunset-gilded Siletz Bay. The seasonal Pacific Northwest cuisine includes Dungeness crab cakes with roasted-chili chutney, fresh halibut Parmesan, and roast duckling with cranberry compote. The wine list is extensive, the service impeccable. ✉ *5911 S.W. U.S. 101, about 5 mi south of Lincoln City* ☎ *541/996–3222* ☰ *AE, D, MC, V* ☺ *Closed Mon. and Tues. Nov.–Apr. No lunch.*

$–$$ ✕ **Kyllo's.** Light-filled Kyllo's rests on stilts beside the D River. It's one of the best places in Lincoln City to enjoy casual but well-prepared seafood, pasta, and meat dishes. ✉ *1110 N.W. 1st Ct.* ☎ *541/994–3179* ☰ *AE, D, MC, V.*

$–$$ ✕ **Lighthouse Brew Pub.** This westernmost outpost of the Portland-based McMenamin brothers' microbrewery empire has the same virtues as their other establishments: fresh local ales; good, unpretentious sandwiches, burgers, and salads; and cheerfully eccentric furnishings that include psychedelic art by Pacific Northwest painters. Try the stout-ale milk shake. ✉ *4157 N. U.S. 101* ☎ *541/994–7238* ⚓ *Reservations not accepted* ☰ *AE, D, MC, V.*

$–$$ ✕ **Rogue River Room.** On the upper floor of the Chinook Winds Casino, this restaurant overlooks the Pacific, and every candlelit table has an ocean view. Locals come regularly for the salmon and prime rib, but there are plenty more surf or turf selections, which might include Dungeness crab, escargots, coconut-rum-butter prawns, or rack of lamb. ✉ *1777 N.W. 44th St., 97367* ☎ *541/996–5825 or 888/244–6665* 🖷 *541/996–5852* ☰ *AE, D, MC, V.*

¢–$$ ✕ **Dory Cove.** For more than 25 years, this spot has been serving up an extensive menu of seafood and steak. The clam chowder is remarkable. There's also a large selection of low-cholesterol dishes. Some booths have ocean views; nautical and aeronautical knickknacks accent wood-panel walls. ⊠ *5819 Logan Rd., 97367* ☎ *541/994–5180* ⊟ *AE, D, MC, V.*

¢–$$ ✕ **Fathoms Restaurant and Bar.** From this bright and airy space on the 10th floor of the Inn at Spanish Head, you'll have a fine view of the ocean, along with worthy seafood dishes, such as lobster wontons, salmon in parchment paper, and Nawlin's barbecued shrimp, as well as steaks, pasta, and vegetarian choices. Fish-and-chips is a specialty, and the Sunday seafood brunch is one of the best in the region. ⊠ *4009 S. W. U.S. 101, 97367* ☎ *541/996–2161 or 800/452–8127* ☎ *541/996– 4089* ⊟ *AE, D, DC, MC, V.*

$$$–$$$$ ⌂ **Inn at Spanish Head.** You'll find tidal pools right outside your door at this condominium resort set on a bluff. All of the bright, contemporary units have ocean views. Choose from one-bedroom suites, deluxe studios, or deluxe rooms. ⊠ *4009 S. U.S. 101, 93767* ☎ *541/996–2161 or 800/452–8127* ☎ *541/996–4089* ⊕ *www.spanishhead.com* ⇒ *120 rooms, 25 suites ⌂ Restaurant, bar, room service, cable TV, pool, exercise equipment, hot tub, Ping-Pong, billiards, business services* ⊟ *AE, D, DC, MC, V.*

$–$$$$ ⌂ **All Seasons Vacation Rentals.** The property rents condominiums and houses on the beach, with ocean views; on lakes; and on the bay front. Accommodations run from the very simple to luxurious; some in secluded areas; some in the heart of town. ⊠ *4515 N. U.S. 101, 97367* ☎ *800/ 362–5229* ⊕ *www.allseasonsvacation.com* ⊟ *D, MC, V.*

$$–$$$ ⌂ **Coho Inn.** Close to the center of the city, in a residential neighborhood, the inn has rooms overlooking the ocean. After a day on the beach, soak in the indoor spa, where views take in the waves crashing only yards away. ⊠ *1635 N.W. Harbor Ave., 97367* ☎ *541/994–3684 or 800/848– 7006* ☎ *541/994–6244* ⊕ *www.thecohoinn.com* ⇒ *50 rooms ⌂ Some kitchenettes, cable TV, hot tub, business services, some pets allowed (fee); no a/c* ⊟ *AE, D, MC, V.*

$$–$$$ ⌂ **Dock of the Bay.** The spacious one- and two-bedroom condominium units at this small property have fireplaces. A shuttle bus leaves for the Chinook Winds Casino every hour. All the rooms have furnished patios overlooking Siletz Bay. ⊠ *1116 S.W. 51st St., 97367* ☎ *541/996– 3549 or 800/362–5229* ☎ *541/996–4759* ⇒ *20 suites ⌂ Hot tub* ⊟ *MC, V.*

$–$$$ ⌂ **Cozy Cove Beach Front Resort.** Some rooms at this comfortable inn on the beach have fireplaces, while half the rooms have ocean views and balconies. The casino is less than 2 mi away. ⊠ *515 N.W. Inlet Ave., 97367* ☎ *541/994–2950 or 800/553–2683* ☎ *541/996–4332* ⇒ *70 rooms ⌂ Picnic area, some in-room hot tubs, some kitchenettes, cable TV, pool, hot tub, business services* ⊟ *D, DC, MC, V.*

$–$$$ ⌂ **Liberty Inn.** The big Liberty Inn still manages to look like a large private home in this quiet and prosperous residential area on the north side of town. Ivory with green trim, and surrounded by trees, flowers, and shrubbery, the inn blends smoothly into the scenery. The modern rooms are spacious, done in dark green and burgundy with cherry-wood furnishings. You can walk to both the Chinook Winds Casino and Lighthouse Brew Pub. ⊠ *4990 N. Logan Rd., 97367* ☎ *541/994–1777 or 877/ 994–1777* ☎ *541/994–1888* ⊕ *www.libertyinn.com* ⇒ *76 rooms ⌂ Inroom data ports, some in-room hot tubs, microwaves, refrigerators, cable TV, pool, hot tub, laundry facilities* ⊟ *AE, D, DC, MC, V* ⊙ *CP.*

¢–$$$ ⌂ **The Orca Inn.** This inn is at the south end of town. The bay beach is across the road, and the Pacific beach is only 1 mi away. You can eat at the local branch of Mo's, which is opposite the entrance. This is a cozy, older inn, and some rooms have heart-shape hot tubs along with gas fireplaces, balconies, and bay views. ⊠ *861 S.W. 51st St., 97367* ☎ *541/996–3996 or 800/843–4940* ☎ *541/994–7554* ⇒ *29 rooms, 11* suites ⑁ *Some in-room hot tubs, some kitchenettes, some refrigerators, cable TV; no a/c* ▭ *MC, V.*

**$–$$**  ▣ **Pelican Shores Inn.** All of the oceanfront rooms here have views of the surf. Rooms are furnished in standard motel style with nautical accents, and some rooms have oceanfront patios with small lawns and barbecues. ✉ *2645 N.W. Inlet Ave., 97367* ☎ *541/994–2134 or 800/705–5505* 🖷 *541/994–4963* ⊕ *www.pelicanshores.com* ➦ *36 rooms, 19 suites* ⑁ *Some kitchenettes, cable TV, indoor pool, laundry facilities, business services* ▭ *AE, D, DC, MC, V.*

### Sports & the Outdoors

GOLF  The greens fee at the 18-hole, par-66 course at the **Lakeside Golf & Racquet Club** (✉ 3245 Clubhouse Dr. ☎ 541/994–8442) is $35–$40; an optional cart costs $25.

WATER SPORTS  Rent kayaks, surfboards, body boards, skim boards, and all necessary accessories at the **Oregon Surf Shop** (✉ 4933 S.W. U.S. 101 ☎ 541/996–3957), which also sells new and used kayaks, boards, wet suits, clothing, and sunglasses. **Lincoln City Surf Shop** (✉ 4792 S.E. U.S. 101 ☎ 541/996–7433) sells surf, skate, and boogie boards. The shop also rents equipment and gives surf lessons.

### Shopping

The **Factory Stores at Lincoln City** (✉ 1500 S.E. Devil's Lake Rd., 97367 ☎ 541/996–5000) has 65 outlet stores, including Eddie Bauer, Coldwater Canyon, Reebok, Mikasa, and Samsonite. Items are 20%–70% off regular retail prices.

# Gleneden Beach

⓫  *7 mi south of Lincoln City on U.S. 101.*

**Salishan,** the most famous resort on the Oregon coast, perches high above placid Siletz Bay. This expensive collection of guest rooms, vacation homes, condominiums, restaurants, golf fairways, tennis courts, and covered walkways blends into a forest preserve; if not for the signs, you'd scarcely be able to find it.

The long-established **Gallery at Salishan** has a well-informed staff that will guide you through the collections of work by Northwest artists, including paintings (pastels, oils, and watercolors), glassworks, bronze and metal, furniture, and ceramics and porcelain. ✉ *7755 N. U.S. 101, 97388* ☎ *541/764–2318 or 800/764–2318* ⊙ *Memorial Day–Labor Day, Mon.–Sat. 10–6, Sun. 10–5; Labor Day–Memorial Day, daily 10–5.*

### Where to Stay & Eat

**$$–$$$**  ✕ **Sidedoor Cafe.** This dining room with a high ceiling, exposed beams, a fireplace, and many windows under the eaves shares a former tile factory with the Eden Hall performance space. The menu changes constantly—fresh preparations have included mushroom-crusted rack of lamb and broiled swordfish with citrus-raspberry vinaigrette over coconut-ginger basmati rice. ✉ *6675 Gleneden Beach Loop Rd., 97388* ☎ *541/764–3825* ▭ *MC, V* ⊙ *Closed Tues. Sept.–Apr.*

★ **$–$$$**  ✕ **Dining Room at Salishan.** The Salishan resort's main dining room, a multilevel expanse of hushed waiters, hillside ocean views, and snow-white linen, serves Pacific Northwest cuisine. House specialties include fresh local fish, game, beef, and lamb. By all means make a selection from the wine cellar, which has more than 10,000 bottles. ✉ *7760 N. U.S. 101* ☎ *541/764–2371* ⑁ *Reservations essential* ▭ *AE, D, DC, MC, V* ⊙ *No lunch.*

**$$$$** ⊡ **Cavalier Beachfront Condominiums.** Every condo in this three-story build-ing has two bedrooms, a private deck, and an ocean view. There is lit-tle traffic noise at this place at the end of the road: you hear only the waves. When you do venture out, the shops and golf at the Salishan are minutes away and Lincoln City and Depoe Bay attractions are a 10-minute drive. The property charges $15 per additional person. ⊠ *325 N.W. Lancer St., 97388* ☎ *888/454–0880* ⤶ *30 condos* ᐃ *Cable TV, indoor pool, beach, library* ⊟ *MC, V.*

**$$$$** ⊡ **Salishan Lodge and Golf Resort.** From the soothing, silvered cedar of its rooms, divided among eight units in a hillside forest preserve, to its wood-burning fireplaces, Salishan embodies a uniquely Oregonian ele-gance. Each of the quiet rooms has a balcony, and original works by North-west artists. Given all this, plus fine food, you'll understand why the timeless lodge also carries one of the steepest price tags on the coast. ⊠ *7760 N. U.S. 101, 97388* ☎ *541/764–3600 or 800/452–2300* ᕸ *541/764–3681* ⊕ *www.salishan.com* ⤶ *205 rooms* ᐃ *2 restaurants, in-room data ports, minibars, room service, indoor pool, hair salon, massage, sauna, driving range, 18-hole golf course, putting green, 4 tennis courts, gym, hiking, beach, billiards, piano, library, bar, baby-sitting, playground, laundry service, dry cleaning, concierge* ⊟ *AE, D, DC, MC, V.*

**$$–$$$$** ⊡ **Beachcombers Haven Vacation Rentals.** Most of the homes and con-dos for rent are on the beach, and all have ocean views and easy beach access. Furnishings are contemporary, and all rentals are convenient to area attractions. Choose from one-, two-, or three-bedroom units. ⊠ *7045 N.W. Glen Ave., 97388* ☎ *541/764–2252 or 800/428–5533* ᕸ *541/764–4094* ⊕ *www.beachcombershaven.com* ⤶ *15 properties* ᐃ *Some in-room hot tubs, kitchenettes, in-room VCRs, laundry facil-ities* ⊟ *D, MC, V.*

## Sports & the Outdoors

GOLF **Salishan Golf Links** (⊠ 7760 N. U.S. 101 ☎ 541/764–3632) is an 18-hole, par-72, often windy seaside course. The greens fee is $95 (public) or $80 (lodge guest) and includes cart and token (for driving range). Without a cart the rate is $75 (public) and $60 (lodge guests). The twilight rate after 4 PM is $35.

## Shopping

**Allegory Books & Music** (⊠ The Marketplace at Salishan, 7755 U.S. 101 N ☎ 541/764–2020) has literary and mainstream books, as well as mag-azines and CDs.

Shop **Toujours** (⊠ The Marketplace at Salishan, 7755 U.S. 101 N ☎ 541/ 764–5254) for men's and women's natural-fiber clothing, shoes, and jew-elry from all over the world. Offering what may be the most varied and extensive selection of toys on the coast, the **Wooden Duck** (⊠ The Mar-ketplace at Salishan, 7755 U.S. 101 N ☎ 541/764–2489) is packed with everything from the old classics to beach fun, collectibles, and educa-tional toys.

# Depoe Bay

⓬ *12 mi south of Lincoln City on U.S. 101.*

The small town of Depoe Bay was founded in the 1920s and named in honor of Charles DePoe, of the Siletz tribe, who in turn was named for his employment at a U.S. Army depot in the late 1800s. Depoe Bay calls itself the whale-watching capital of the world.

**Depoe Bay Park.** The park runs along the beach in front of the town's retail district. With a narrow channel and deep water, the tiny harbor is also one of the most protected on the coast. It supports a thriving fleet of commercial- and charter-fishing boats. The Spouting Horn, a natural cleft in the basalt cliffs on the waterfront, blasts seawater skyward during heavy weather. ⊠ *South on U.S. 101* ☎ *541/765–2889* ⊕ *www. stateoforegon.com/depoe_bay/chamber* ☞ *Free* ☉ *Daily.*

**Fogarty Creek State Park.** Bird-watching and viewing the tidal pools are the key draws here, but hiking and picnicking are also popular at this park 4 mi north of Depoe Bay on U.S. 101. Wooden footbridges arch through the forest. The beach is rimmed with cliffs. ⊠ *U.S. 101* ☎ *541/ 265–9278 or 800/551–6949* ⊕ *www.prd.state.or.us* ☞ *$3 per vehicle day-use fee* ☉ *Daily.*

**Tradewinds.** Every year a few of the gigantic gray whales migrating along the coast decide to linger in Depoe Bay, and for more than six decades, Tradewinds has operated whale-watching cruises. The skippers are all marine naturalists who give a running commentary, and the boats can accommodate from 6 to 40 passengers (daylight hours only). The ticket office is on U.S. 101 at the north end of Depoe Bay Bridge. ⊠ *U.S. 101 97341* ☎ *541/765–2345 or 800/445–8730* ☎ *541/765–2282* ⊕ *www.tradewindscharters.com* ☞ *One hour $15, two hours $20.*

## Where to Stay & Eat

$$–$$$    ✕ **Whale Cove Inn.** Known for its homemade jumbo cinnamon rolls, this little restaurant overlooking the cove from which it takes its name has pasta, seafood, steaks, ribs, and chowders. Every table and booth has an ocean view. The property came under new ownership in 2001 and has been completely remodeled. ⊠ *2345 S.W. U.S. 101* ☎ *541/765–2255* ⊟ *AE, D, MC, V.*

$–$$    ✕ **Sea Hag.** This friendly restaurant has been specializing in fresh seafood for more than 30 years. There's a seafood buffet on Friday night, while Saturday the focus is on prime rib with Yorkshire pudding. Several booths at the front of the restaurant have views of the "spouting horns" across the highway. The restaurant is kid friendly, and there's an adjoining grown-up–friendly bar. ⊠ *53 U.S. 101* ☎ *541/765–2734* ⊟ *AE, D, DC, MC, V.*

$–$$    ✕ **Tidal Rave.** Every table at this locally popular seafood grill has an ocean view. There are fresh fish specials every day: try crab casserole, Thai barbecue prawns, or breaded halibut. ⊠ *279 N.W. U.S. 101, 97341* ☎ *541/ 765–2995* ⚓ *Reservations essential* ⊟ *MC, V.*

$–$$$$    ⊡ **Channel House.** Some of the rooms in this cliffside inn have whirlpool tubs with views of the Pacific; most have fireplaces and balconies, and all have private baths. Each of the rooms, such as the Admiral's Suite and the Crow's Nest, incorporates different nautical themes and furnishings. A buffet breakfast is included in the room rate. ⊠ *35 Ellington St., Depoe Bay 97341* ☎ *541/765–2140 or 800/447–2140* ☎ *541/ 765–2191* ⊕ *www.chanelhouse.com* ☜ *14 rooms* ⚲ *Some in-room hot tubs; no smoking* ⊟ *AE, D, MC, V* ○ *BP.*

$–$$$$    ⊡ **Inn at Arch Rock.** White with black trim, this 1930s inn is between two coves on the cliffs above the ocean, but it's still within walking distance of town. Some of the warmly decorated rooms have fireplaces. The penthouse suite has two bedrooms, a fireplace, a massive hot tub, and two private decks. All but one of the rooms have views of the ocean, the town, and some dramatic spouting horns. The property also rents neighboring condominiums. ⊠ *70 N.W. Sunset St., 97341* ☎ *541/765–2560 or 800/767–1835* ☎ *541/765–3036* ⊕ *www. innatarchrock.com* ☜ *10 rooms, 3 suites* ⚲ *Picnic area, some in-room hot tubs, some kitchenettes, refrigerators, cable TV; no a/c* ⊟ *AE, D, MC, V* ○ *CP.*

**$$**  □ **Inn at Otter Crest.** Surrounded by thousands of rhododendrons and 35 acres of forest, this inn 5 mi south of Depoe Bay is a great spot for a getaway. The beach and tidal pools are right out the door, and the contemporary-furnished rooms are spacious and bright. ⊠ *301 Otter Crest Loop, Otter Rock 97369* ☎ *541/765–2111 or 800/452–2101* 📠 *541/765–2047* ⊕ *www.ottercrest.com* ⇥ *120 rooms, 40 suites* ♢ *Restaurant, some microwaves, refrigerators, cable TV, pool, hot tub, tennis courts, bar, laundry facilities, business services* ▭ *AE, D, DC, MC, V.*

**$–$$**  □ **Crown Pacific Inn.** This 1999 cedar-shingle inn is on a hillside across the highway from the ocean. Every room has a balcony with an ocean view, and some rooms have fireplaces. You're welcome to use the barbecue and picnic tables on the grounds. ⊠ *U.S. 101 and Bechill St., 97341* ☎ *541/765–7773 or 888/845–5131* 📠 *541/765–7740* ⊕ *www.crownpacificinn.com* ⇥ *31 rooms* ♢ *Some in-room hot tubs, microwaves, refrigerators, cable TV, hot tub; no a/c* ▭ *AE, MC, V* ⦿⦿ *CP.*

**$–$$**  □ **Surfrider Oceanfront Resort.** There are six buildings on 5 landscaped acres, 2 mi from the center of Depoe Bay. Every room has an oceanfront deck and direct access to the beach. The resort is close to whalewatching, and you can enjoy bald eagles nesting within view of the property. ⊠ *3115 N.W. U.S. 101, 97341* ☎ *541/764–2311 or 800/662–2378* 📠 *541/764–2634* ⊕ *www.surfriderresort.com* ⇥ *50 rooms* ♢ *Restaurant, some in-room hot tubs, some kitchenettes, cable TV, indoor pool, hot tub, bar, airport shuttle, some pets allowed; no a/c* ▭ *AE, D, DC, MC, V.*

**en route**  Five miles south of Depoe Bay off U.S. 101 (watch for signs), the **Otter Crest Loop,** another scenic byway, winds along the cliff tops. Only parts of the loop are now open to vehicles, but you can drive to points midway from either end and turn around. The full loop is open to bikes and hiking. British explorer Captain James Cook named the 500-foot-high **Cape Foulweather,** at the south end of the loop, on a blustery March day in 1778. Backward-leaning shore pines lend mute witness to the 100-mph winds that still strafe this exposed spot. At the viewing point at the **Devil's Punchbowl,** 1 mi south of Cape Foulweather, you can peer down into a collapsed sandstone sea cave carved out by the powerful waters of the Pacific. About 100 feet to the north in the rocky tidal pools of the beach known as **Marine Gardens,** purple sea urchins and orange starfish can be seen at low tide. The Otter Crest Loop rejoins U.S. 101 about 4 mi south of Cape Foulweather near **Yaquina Head,** which has been designated an Outstanding Natural Area. Harbor seals, sea lions, cormorants, murres, puffins, and guillemots frolic in the water and on the rocks below **Yaquina Bay Lighthouse**—a gleaming white tower activated in 1873.

## Sports & the Outdoors

WHALE-WATCHING  **Tradewinds** (⊠ U.S. 101 near Coast Guard Boat Basin Rd. ☎ 541/765–2345 or 800/445–8730) operates $12 whale-watching cruises on the hour (10 AM–5 or 6 PM) when conditions permit. The ticket office is at the north end of the Depoe Bay Bridge. There is a resident group of gray whales that stays in the Depoe Bay area year-round.

## Shopping

Amid blocks of souvenir shops, **Dancing Coyote Gallery** stands alone as a noted fine arts gallery. Browsers will find fine jewelry, hand-blown glass, bronze work, and paintings all by Pacific Northwest artists. If you're looking for a gift or enjoy singular artwork, this is the place to stop. ⊠ 34 N.E. U.S. 101 ☎ 541/765–3366.

# Newport

**⑬** *12 mi south of Depoe Bay on U.S. 101; 114 mi from Portland, south on I–5 and west on Hwy. 34 and U.S. 20.*

Newport was transformed after Keiko, the orca star of the movie *Free Willy,* arrived at the Oregon Coast Aquarium in 1996. The small harbor and fishing town with about 8,000 residents became one of the most-visited places on the coast. The surge of tourists brought new prosperity to a town feeling the pinch of federally imposed fishing restrictions that had cut into its traditional economy. Keiko moved to Iceland in 1998, so the crowds have diminished, but thanks to its easily accessible beach, a lively Performing Arts Center, and the local laid-back attitude, Newport remains a favorite both with regional travelers looking for a weekend escape and those who come for longer stays.

Newport exists on two levels: the highway above, threading its way through the community's main business district, and the old **Bayfront** along Yaquina Bay below (watch for signs on U.S. 101). With its high-masted fishing fleet, well-worn buildings, seafood markets, and art galleries and shops, Newport's Bayfront is an ideal place for an afternoon stroll. So many male sea lions in Yaquina Bay loiter near crab pots and bark from the waterfront piers that locals call the area the Bachelor Club. Visit the docks to buy fresh seafood or rent a small boat or kayak to explore Yaquina Bay.

**Nye Beach,** a neighborhood west of the highway, preserves a few remnants of Newport's crusty past—you can still get an idea of the simple beach architecture that once characterized most of the Oregon coast—but in the aftermath of a $2.5 million face-lift, many old cottages and other sites have been gentrified. One of the first beachside communities on the Oregon coast, Nye Beach once had a sanitarium with hot sea-water baths and the popular Natatorium, a looming bluffside structure with an indoor saltwater-fed pool, dance floors, and miniature golf. Those old buildings are long gone, replaced today by the Yaquina Art Center, parking, and access to the beach. The graceful 3,280-foot **Yaquina Bay Bridge,** a Work Projects Administration structure completed in 1936, leads to Newport's southern section.

★ ⓒ  The **Oregon Coast Aquarium,** a 4½-acre complex, has re-creations of off-shore and near-shore Pacific marine habitats, all teeming with life: playful sea otters, comical puffins, fragile jellyfish, and even a 60-pound octopus. There's a hands-on interactive area for children and North America's largest seabird aviary. For a few years the biggest attraction was Keiko, the 4-ton killer whale brought to the aquarium to be rehabilitated. Since 1998, when Keiko was moved, the aquarium has developed new attractions. Permanent exhibits include Passages of the Deep, a trio of tanks linked by a 200-foot underwater tunnel with 360-degree views of sharks, wolf eels, halibut and other sea life. Large coho salmon and sturgeon can be viewed in a naturalistic setting through a window wall 9 feet high and 20 feet wide. Keiko's former home has been transformed into a deep-sea exhibit complete with a wrecked ship. ✉ *2820 S.E. Ferry Slip Rd., (heading south from Newport, turn right at southern end of Yaquina Bay Bridge and follow signs)* ☎ *541/867–3474* ⊕ *www.aquarium.org* ✇ *$10.75* ☉ *Daily 10–5.*

ⓒ  Interactive and interpretive exhibits at Oregon State University's **Hatfield Marine Science Center,** which is connected by a trail to the Oregon Coast Aquarium, explain current marine research from global, bird's-eye, eye-level, and microscopic perspectives. The star of the show is a large octopus in a touch tank near the entrance. She seems as interested in human visitors as they are in her; guided by a staff volunteer, you can sometimes reach in to stroke her suction-tipped tentacles. ⊠ *2030 S. Marine Science Dr., (heading south from Newport, cross Yaquina Bay Bridge on U.S. 101 S and follow signs)* ☎ *541/867–0100* ✍ *Suggested donation $4* ☉ *Memorial Day–Labor Day, daily 10–6; Labor Day–Memorial Day, Thurs.–Mon. 10–5.*

**Mariner Square** has several touristy attractions. **Ripley's Believe It or Not** (✍ call for prices ☉ mid-June–mid-Sept., daily 9–9; mid-Sept.–Oct. and mid-Feb.–mid-June, daily 10–5; Nov.–mid-Feb. daily 11–4) has strange but true exhibits. **Undersea Gardens** (✍ call for prices ☉ mid-June–mid-Sept., daily 9–9; mid-Sept.–Oct. and mid-Feb.–mid-June, daily 10–5; Nov.–mid-Feb. daily 11–4) has scuba-diving shows, marine plants, and animal exhibits. **Wax Works** (✍ call for prices ☉ mid-June–mid-Sept., daily 9–9; mid-Sept.–Oct. and mid-Feb.–mid-June, daily 10–5; Nov.–mid-Feb., daily 11–4) has wax-figure exhibits of famous people. ⊠ *250 S.W. Bay Blvd.* ☎ *541/265–2206.*

**Marine Discovery Tours** conducts narrated whale-watching cruises in the bay. The 65-foot excursion boat *Discovery*, with inside seating for 49 and two viewing levels, departs from the Newport bayfront in the morning and afternoon. You can also watch from outside. The best viewing is March–October, though tours run year-round except during storms. While they can't guarantee you'll see a whale, 95% of outings are successful. There is a resident population of gray whales that stays near Newport year-round, including young mothers with calves who feed less than 1 mi from shore. During summer they often come right up to the boat. *Discovery* is wheelchair accessible. ⊠ *345 S.W. Bay Blvd., Newport 97365* ☎ *800/903–2628* ✍ *$25* ⊟ *D, MC, V.*

Seven mi north of Newport, beachfront **Beverly Beach State Park** extends from Yaquina Head to the headlands of Otter Rock. It has a campground with 53 full hookups, 76 electrical and 136 tent sites, and 14 yurts. ⊠ *U.S. 101* ☎ *541/265–9278 or 800/551–6949* ⊕ *www.prd.state.or.us* ✍ *Free* ☉ *Daily.*

A rocky shoreline separates the day-use **Devil's Punch Bowl State Natural Area** from the surf. It's a popular whale-watching site 9 mi north of Newport and has excellent tidal pools. ⊠ *U.S. 101* ☎ *541/265–9278* ✍ *Free* ☉ *Daily.*

The **Lincoln County Historical Society Museums** include a log cabin and an 1895 Victorian house. Exhibits focus on Native American, maritime, and coastal settlement history. ⊠ *579 S.W. 9th St.* ☎ *541/265–7509* ✍ *Donations accepted* ☉ *June–Sept., Tues.–Sun. 10–5; Oct.–May, Tues.–Sun. 11–4.*

The day-use **Ona Beach State Park** is a popular beachcombing and picnic spot, 5 mi south of Newport. ⊠ *U.S. 101 S* ☎ *541/867–7451* ✍ *Free* ☉ *Daily.*

Ray Kowalski invented the art of chain-saw sculpture. For years he displayed 300 of his sculptures of cowboys, Indians, trolls, gnomes, and other figures at a park here called **Sea Gulch**, 10 mi south of Newport. The park is gone now, fallen victim to flashier tourist attractions, but Ray still presides over the busy workshop where his sons turn out new figures, mostly of bears. You're welcome to come by, take a look at the workshop, and buy small wooden sculptures in a small shop. You'd do best to call ahead. ⊠ *U.S. 101 97376* ☎ *541/563–2727* ✍ *Free.*

Fishing, crabbing, boating, windsurfing, hiking, and beachcombing are popular at **South Beach State Park.** A campground has 238 electrical and 6 primitive sites as well as 16 yurts. ⊠ *U.S. 101 S* ☎ *541/867–4715 or 541/867–7451* ⬚ *Free* ☉ *Daily.*

At the north end of Yaquina Bay near its outlet to the Pacific, **Yaquina Bay State Park** has a historic lighthouse that in more recent years was used as a Coast Guard Lifeboat Station. It's been restored and is now open to the public. ⊠ *U.S. 101 S* ☎ *541/867–7451* ⬚ *Free* ☉ *Daily.*

★ ☻ The tallest lighthouse on the Oregon Coast is the 93-foot **Yaquina Head Lighthouse,** which is on a rocky peninsula. Guided morning tours are limited to 15 people. ⊠ *4 mi north of bridge in Newport* ☎ *541/574–3100* ⬚ *Call for prices* ☉ *Mid-June–mid-Sept., daily noon–4; in winter, call ahead.*

FodorsChoice  In addition to the Yaquina Head Lighthouse, the **Yaquina Head Outstanding**
★  **Natural Area** is the site of man-made tidal pools universally accessible, as well as natural tidal pools, and Cobble Beach, a stretch of round basalt rocks believed to have originated from volcano eruptions 14 million years ago in the Columbia Gorge 300 mi away. Thousands of birds—cormorants, gulls, common murres, pigeon guillemots—make their home beyond shore on Pinnacle and Colony Rocks, and nature trails wind through fields of sea-grass and wildflowers, leading to spectacular views. There is also an interpretive center, where you can view a short video about the area, read old lighthouse log books and listen to the songs of seabirds and whales. It's a great place to pass a rainy day. ⊠ *750 N.W. Lighthouse Dr.* ☎ *541/574–3100* ⬚ *$5 per vehicle (9 passengers or fewer)* ☉ *Daily dawn–dusk.*

## Where to Stay & Eat

$$  ✕ **Tables of Content.** The well-plotted prix-fixe menu at the restaurant of the outstanding Sylvia Beach Hotel changes nightly. Chances are the main dish will be fresh local seafood, perhaps a moist grilled salmon fillet in a sauce Dijonnaise, served with sautéed vegetables, fresh-baked breads, rice pilaf; a decadent dessert is also included. The interior is functional and unadorned, with family-size tables. Come for the food, not the furnishings. ⊠ *267 N.W. Cliff St. (from U.S. 101 head west on 3rd St.)* ☎ *541/265–5428* ⚱ *Reservations essential* ▭ *AE, MC, V* ☉ *No lunch.*

¢–$$  ✕ **Canyon Way Restaurant and Bookstore.** Cod, Dungeness crab cakes, bouillabaisse, and Yaquina Bay oysters are among the specialties of this Newport dining spot up the hill from the center of the Bayfront. There's also a deli counter for takeout. The restaurant, which has an outdoor patio, is to one side of a well-stocked bookstore. The new Fast Eddie's Bar serves lighter fare and lunch sandwiches as well as light dinners. ⊠ *S. W. Canyon Way off Bay Front Blvd.* ☎ *541/265–8319* ▭ *AE, MC, V* ☉ *Closed Sun.*

¢–$$  ✕ **Quimby's.** A recent addition to the Nye Beach scene, this is a casual restaurant with limited views of the ocean and friendly service. The menu is heavy on seafood and also has the unexpected. The vanilla custard French toast is popular at breakfast, while a lunch favorite is the Monte Cristo, a sandwich of ham and turkey deep-fried in tempura batter. Servings are generous and doggie bags the norm. For dinner try the seafood stew, crab omelet, or swordfish tacos. ⊠ *740 W. Olive* ☎ *541/265–9919* ▭ *AE, MC, V* ☉ *No dinner Sun.*

¢–$  ✕ **Nye Beach Cafe.** This roomy café in the Nye Beach hotel has a limited bar—wine, beer, some simple mixed drinks—a grand piano, a fireplace, and a deck that stretches out over the beach. It specializes in spicy seafood dishes. The clam chowder is popular, and so is the cioppino; desserts include homemade flan and chocolate carrot cake. Consider stopping by for breakfast, too, to try the Scotch eggs (hard-boiled and covered with sausage) or the Mexican quiche. ⊠ *219 N.W. Cliff St., 97365* ☎ *541/265–3334* 🖷 *541/265–3622* 🖃 *AE, D, MC, V.*

¢–$  ✕ **Whale's Tale.** Casual and family oriented, this Bayfront restaurant serves local seafood, thick clam chowder, fish-and-chips, burgers, and sandwiches. Tucked in a storefront opposite the bay, the restaurant has a nautical theme. ⊠ *452 S.W. Bay Blvd.* ☎ *541/265–8660* 🖃 *AE, D, DC, MC, V* ⊗ *Closed Wed. Nov.–Apr.*

¢  ✕ **Champagne Patio.** Serving lunch for 23 years, this spot is one of those local secrets that you'll feel lucky to discover. Chef Christina Swafford cooks up daily specials that might one day be Mexican in origin, the next Swedish; she bakes breads and prepares desserts daily. The restaurant serves wine that comes from the adjoining wine shop, operated by Joe Swafford, who pens the local weekly newspaper column on wines. ⊠ *1630 N. Coast Hwy.* ☎ *541/265–3044* 🖃 *AE, D, MC, V* ⊗ *No lunch Mon.–Sat.*

¢  ✕ **Panini Bakery.** The young couple who operate this bakery and espresso
**Fodor's**Choice  bar—a local favorite after a few years in existence—pride themselves
★  on hearty and home-roasted meats, hand-cut breads, and friendly service. The coffee's organic, the eggs free range, the orange juice fresh squeezed, and just about everything is made from scratch. Take a seat inside, or, in good weather, streetside tables are a great place to view the Nye Beach scene. ⊠ *232 N.W. Coast Hwy.* ☎ *541/265–5033* 🖃 *No credit cards* ⊗ *Closed Tues. and Wed.*

$$–$$$  🏨 **Little Creek Cove.** The units at this condominium property have access to the beach as well as ocean and beach views from private decks. All the units are individually furnished and have fireplaces. Agate Beach Golf Course is across the street. ⊠ *3641 N.W. Ocean View Dr., 97365* ☎ *541/265–8587 or 800/294–8025* 🖷 *541/265–4576* ⊕ *www. newportnet.com/lcc* 🛏 *29 rooms* ☆ *Kitchenettes, microwaves, cable TV, in-room VCRs, business services* 🖃 *AE, D, DC, MC, V.*

$$–$$$  🏨 **Newport Belle Bed & Breakfast.** This fully operational stern-wheeler
**Fodor's**Choice  stays permanently moored at the Newport Marina, where you have front-
★  row seats to all the boating activity in the bay. Five rooms have themes that run from the Australian Outback to Montana's West. The main salon is cozy, with hardwood floors, a woodstove, and comfortable furniture. Facilities, such as Internet access, TV and phones, not found in guest rooms, are all available in the salon. ⊠ *H Dock, Newport Marina, 97365* ☎ *541/867–6290 or 800/348–1922* 🖷 *541/867–6291* ⊕ *www. newportbelle.com* 🛏 *5 rooms* ☆ *No a/c, no kids under 7, no room phones, no room TVs, no smoking* 🖃 *AE, D, MC, V* ⊗ *BP.*

$$–$$$  🏨 **Ocean House.** Marie and Bob Garrard are the gracious hosts of this Cape Cod B&B on a bluff overlooking Agate Beach. The Inn is noted for its extensive coastal gardens and has a walkway leading directly to the beach. Each of the 7 rooms has been updated or completely remodeled in the past three years and a new cottage with rock fireplace and bedroom loft was added in 2002. All of the rooms have designer furnishings, fine linens, antiques, art, and views of the beach, ocean, and lighthouse. ⊠ *4920 N.W. Woody Way, 97365* ☎ *541/265–6158* ⊕ *www. oceanhouse.com* 🛏 *7 guest rooms, 1 cottage* ☆ *In-room hot tubs; no kids, no room phones, no room TVs* 🖃 *AE, D, DC, MC, V* ⊗ *BP.*

$$–$$$  🏨 **Tyee Lodge Oceanfront Bed & Breakfast.** *Tyee* means "chinook salmon" in the Indian trading language. This 1940s house in Agate Beach is on a bluff, and a nearby trail leads down to the beach. The guest rooms all have pine furniture, gas fireplaces, and views of the ocean through towering Sitka spruce trees. Breakfast is served family-style in a bay-window room facing the ocean. Composer Ernest Bloch lived nearby. ⊠ *4925 N.W. Woody Way, 97365* ☎ *541/265–8953 or 888/553–8933*

⊕ *www.tyeelodge.com* ⚲ *5 rooms* ⚿ *No a/c, no kids under 16, no room phones, no room TVs, no smoking* ▭ *AE, D, MC, V* ⦙◯⦙ *BP.*

$–$$$ ▦ **The Hallmark Resort Newport.** All rooms have balconies from which you can enjoy ocean views. Some rooms have fireplaces. Room configurations vary: choose from one queen-size bed with a small sitting area, two queen-size beds and a full living room and kitchenette, three queen-size beds (with one tucked up in a loft space), or a king-size bed with a hot tub. There's also an oceanfront restaurant on the premises, Georgie's Beachside Grill, which has an extensive menu of northwest cuisine. Favorite items are encrusted halibut, stuffed Pacific sole, or crab and artichoke fondue. ⚿ *Restaurant, in-room data ports, some kitchenettes, indoor pool, laundry facilities, some pets allowed (fee).* ⊠ *744 SW Elizabeth St., 97365* ☎ *888/448–4449 or 541/265–2600* ⊕ *www. hallmarkinns.com* ⚲ *158 rooms* ▭ *AE, D, MC, V.*

$–$$$ ▦ **Nye Beach Hotel.** Despite its century-old appearance, suitable to the historic Nye Beach district, the Nye Beach Hotel was built in 1992. It's on a cliff above the beach, and all rooms have balconies with ocean views, private baths, and fireplaces. The pastel colors and potted tropical plants in the lobby remind some guests of Key West. Keep an eye out for the macaw and the African love birds. ⊠ *219 N.W. Cliff St., 97365* ☎ *541/ 265–3334* ⊟ *541/265–3622* ⊕ *www.nyebeach.com* ⚲ *18 rooms* ⚿ *Restaurant, some in-room hot tubs, cable TV* ▭ *AE, D, MC, V.*

$–$$$ ▦ **Sylvia Beach Hotel.** Make reservations far in advance for this 1913-vintage beachfront hotel, whose antiques-filled rooms are named for famous writers. A pendulum swings over the bed in the Poe room. The Christie, Twain, and Colette rooms are the most luxurious; all have fireplaces, decks, and great ocean views. A well-stocked split-level upstairs library has decks, a fireplace, slumbering cats, and too-comfortable chairs. Complimentary mulled wine is served here nightly at 10. ⊠ *267 N.W. Cliff St., 97365* ☎ *541/265–5428 or 888/795–8422* ⊕ *www. sylviabeachhotel.com* ⚲ *20 rooms* ⚿ *Restaurant, library; no room phones, no room TVs* ▭ *AE, MC, V* ⦙◯⦙ *BP.*

$$ ▦ **The Embarcadero.** At the east end of Bay Boulevard, this resort of vacation rental condominiums has great views of Yaquina Bay and its graceful bridge. Spacious suites have one or two bedrooms, with a bayside deck, a fireplace, and a kitchen. ⊠ *1000 S.E. Bay Blvd., 97365* ☎ *541/ 265–8521 or 800/547–4779* ⊟ *541/265–7844* ⊕ *www.embarcadero-resort.com* ⚲ *85 units* ⚿ *Restaurant, bar, indoor pool, outdoor hot tub, sauna, gym, dock, boating, fishing* ▭ *AE, D, DC, MC, V.*

$–$$ ▦ **Whaler.** All rooms at this motel have ocean views; some have fireplaces. In a residential area across from the city park and the beach, it's a short walk to the Yaquina Bay Lighthouse. ⊠ *155 S.W. Elizabeth St., 97465* ☎ *541/265–9261 or 800/433–9444* ⊟ *541/265–9515* ⚲ *73 rooms* ⚿ *Some microwaves, some refrigerators, cable TV, laundry facilities, airport shuttle, some pets allowed* ▭ *AE, D, DC, MC, V* ⦙◯⦙ *CP.*

⚞ **South Beach State Park.** The park is close to fishing, crabbing, boating, windsurfing, and beachcombing, as well as the Yaquina Bay Lighthouse, Hatfield Marine Science Center, and Oregon Coast Aquarium. ⚿ *Flush toilets, full hookups, dump station, drinking water, showers, fire pits, picnic tables, electricity.* ⚲ *228 electrical, 6 primitive, 27 yurts, 3 group sites.* ⊠ *Off U.S. 101, 2 mi south of Newport (follow signs)* ☎ *800/452–5687 reservations, 800/551–6949 information* ⊕ *www.oregonstateparks.org* ⚲ *Full hookups $21, partial hookups $21, tent sites $9, yurts $29, group $64* ⚞ *Reservations essential* ▭ *MC, V.*

## Nightlife & the Arts

The only facility of its kind on the Oregon coast, the **Newport Performing Arts Center** hosts performers from all over the world and also serves as a showcase for local theater companies. On any given evening, a performance may include tango dancers, a reading by nationally known actors and actresses, or a symphony performance. It also hosts an international film series. ⊠ *777 W. Olive St.* ☎ *541/265–2787* ⊕ *www. coastarts.org.*

## Sports & the Outdoors

Fossils, clams, mussels, and other aeons-old marine creatures, easily dug from soft sandstone cliffs, make **Beverly Beach State Park,** 5 mi north of Newport, a favorite with young beachcombers. Explore the Yaquina Bay by motorized boat or kayak, try your hand at crabbing, or venture out into the ocean on body or surf board. Be sure to wear the proper safety equipment and know the tide. Tide books indicating low and high tides are available free in shops all over the area.

BOATING   **Embarcadero Resort Marine** (⊠ 1000 S.E. Bay Blvd. ☎ 541/265–8521) rents two-man kayaks for $15 an hour or $65 for six hours and small boats for $60 for four hours. Crab rings can be rented for an additional charge, but life jackets are included. **Sawyer's Landing** (⊠ 4098 Yaquina Bay Rd. ☎ 541/265–3907) rents small boats with crab rings and all safety equipment for $60 a day.

SURFING   **Ocean Pulse Surfboards** (⊠ 429 S.W. Coast Hwy. ☎ 541/265–7745) carries surfboards, body boards, and accessories. **Ossie's Surf Shop** (⊠ 4860 N. Coast Hwy. ☎ 541/574–4634) rents boards, wet suits, and other items and is directly across the highway from a very popular surfing spot at the north end of Agate Beach. They also give lessons.

## Shopping

On Newport's **Bay Boulevard** you'll find the finest group of fresh seafood markets on the coast. **Englund Marine Supply** (⊠ S.W. Bay Blvd. ☎ 541/265–9275) carries nautical supplies. **Mainsale** (⊠ 338 S. W. Bay Blvd. ☎ 541/265–3940) stocks marine- and nature-related gift items. **Wood Gallery** (⊠ 818 S.W. Bay Blvd. ☎ 541/265–6843) sells wood crafts and paintings.

**Oregon Oyster Farms** (⊠ 6878 Yaquina Bay Rd. ☎ 541/265–5078) raises and sells many kinds of oysters, as well as shucking knives, sauces, and T-shirts. Search for that out-of-print classic or the slightly used edition of the latest best-seller at **Nye Beach Books** (⊠ 727 N.W. 3rd St. ☎ 541/ 265–6840), where three rooms are lined floor-to-ceiling with old and new tomes. Wendy Engler, owner of the **Nye Beach Gallery** (⊠ 715 N. W. 3rd ☎ 541/265–3291 ⊕ www.nyebeach.org) scours the world over for the fine wines and artisan cheeses that fill the shelves of this streetfront shop. On Saturdays, stop by to sample wine and cheese and admire (or buy) Lon Brusselback's bronze sculptures. Shop for fresh-baked goods, local produce, plants, crafts, and homemade dog goodies at Newport's **Saturday Market** (⊠ U.S. 101 in Armory parking lot), open late May–late October, Saturday 9 AM–2 PM. Joseph Swafford, owner of **Swafford's Oregon** (⊠ 1630 N. U.S. 101 ☎ 541/265–3044), pens a weekly wine column for the local newspaper and visitors to this little wine shop can benefit from his expertise. The inventory of domestic and imported wines numbers in the thousands. Gift baskets and special wine dinners are also available. Shop at **Toujours** (⊠ 704 Nye Beach Dr. ☎ 541/574–6404) for clothing and accessories. The boutique carries natural-fiber women's wear, shoes, jewelry, unique hair combs and barrettes, purses, and a line of Brighton watches and sunglasses. Paint a piece of ready-made pottery or throw your own at **Tsunami Ceramics** (⊠ 310 N. W. Coast St. ☎ 541/574–7958). If it's not ready to go when you are, they'll ship it to your home.

# CloseUp

## LIGHTHOUSE LORE

TEN LIGHTHOUSES STAND on the 360 mi of Oregon's rocky, rugged coastline. But it's a wonder that they're standing at all. It's in the nature of lighthouses to take the brunt of storms, but Oregon's sentinels have occasionally crumbled before the winter onslaughts of rain and wind.

The Cape Arago Lighthouse at Coos Bay was first built in 1866. It had to be replaced with a new structure in 1908 and then again in 1934. (There's a good view of the current lighthouse from Shore Acres Botanical Gardens.) But Reedsport's Umpqua River Lighthouse fared even less well than that. Built in 1857, it quickly succumbed to the slings and arrows of outrageous winter storms and came crashing down only four years later. It was replaced in 1894.

The Cape Blanco Lighthouse qualifies for several titles. Not only is it Oregon's most southerly lighthouse, it's also the most westerly, the longest in continuous service (since 1870) and, at 245 feet, it's the highest above sea level. The light's first keeper, James Langlois, served here for 42 years; his name is preserved in the village of Langlois, north of Cape Blanco on U.S. 101. Another title goes to Cleft of the Rock Lighthouse in Yachats. It's the only Oregon light that is privately owned and operated. Maritime writer and former lighthouse keeper Jim Gibbs now has one of his very own.

Most interesting is Tillamook Rock at Cannon Beach. "Terrible Tilly," as local people know it, stands on a small rock island 1½ mi offshore, and Tilly's dark history began early. During construction in 1880, the land surveyor on the job drowned at the base of the rock. A century later, after the light was decommissioned, a private party bought the lighthouse and turned it into the Eternity at Sea Columbarium, its interior lined with shelves of urns containing the ashes of departed souls who wanted to be buried at sea, but not quite. The management's literature invites you to "be part of a preservation." Literally!

From south to north, Oregon's 10 lighthouses are Cape Blanco (Port Orford), Coquille River (Bandon), Cape Arago (Coos Bay), Umpqua River (Reedsport), Heceta Head (Florence), Cleft of the Rock (Yachats), Yaquina Bay and Yaquina Head (Newport), Cape Meares (Tillamook), and Tillamook Rock (Cannon Beach).

— Alan Ryan

## Waldport

⑭ 15 mi south of Newport on U.S. 101, 67 mi west of Corvallis on Hwy. 34 and U.S. 20.

Long ago the base of the Alsi Indians, Waldport later became a gold-rush town and a logging center. In the 1980s it garnered national attention when local residents fought the timber industry and stopped the spraying of dioxin-based defoliants in the Coast Range forests. Waldport attracts many retirees and those seeking an alternative to the expensive beach resorts nearby.

At **Alsea Bay Bridge Interpretive Center,** displays recount the construction of the Oregon Coast highway and its many graceful bridges through dioramas, bridge models, photography, and time lines. ⊠ *620 N.W. Spring St. (off U.S. 101 at south end of bridge)* ☎ *541/563–2002* 🖾 *Free* ⊙ *Daily 10–5.*

The **Drift Creek Wilderness** east of Waldport holds some of the rare old-growth forest that has triggered battles between the timber industry and environmentalists. Hemlocks hundreds of years old grow in parts of this 9-square-mi area. The 2-mi **Harris Ranch Trail** winds through these an-cient giants—you may even spot a spotted owl. The Siuslaw National Forest–Waldport Ranger Station provides directions and maps. ⊠ *Risely Creek Rd., (from Waldport, take Hwy. 34 east for 7 mi to Alsea River crossing)* ☎ *541/563–3211* ⊙ *Daily 8–4.*

### Where to Stay

$$ 🏠 **Cliff House Bed-and-Breakfast.** The view from Yaquina John Point, on which this B&B sits, is magnificent. The house, which in livelier days was a bordello, is done in a mix of classic American antiques and com-fortable overstuffed furniture. Plush rooms all have ocean views; three have balconies and wood-burning stoves. A glass-front terrace looking out over 8 mi of white-sand beach leads down to the garden. ⊠ *1450 Adahi Rd., 1 block west of U.S. 101, 97394* ☎ *541/563–2506* 🖨 *541/563–3903* ⊕ *www.cliffhouseoregon.com* 🛏 *4 rooms* 🛁 *In-room VCRs, hot tub* ⊟ *MC, V* 🍴 *BP.*

### Sports & the Outdoors

BOATING **McKinley's Marina** (⊠ Hwy. 34 ☎ 541/563–4656) rents boats and crab pots to those who want to take advantage of the excellent crabbing in Alsea Bay.

# Yachats

🔟 *8 mi south of Waldport on U.S. 101.*

A tiny burg of 685 inhabitants, Yachats (pronounced "yah-*hots*") has acquired a reputation among Oregon beach lovers that is disproportionate to its size. The small town is at the mouth of the Yachats River, and from its rocky shoreline, which includes the highest point on the Oregon coast, trails lead to beaches and dozens of tidal pools. A relaxed alternative to the more touristy communities to the north, Yachats has all the coastal pleasures: B&Bs, good restaurants, deserted beaches, tidal pools, surf-pounded crags, fishing, and crabbing. The town's name is a Na-tive American word meaning "foot of the mountain."

At **Neptune State Park** you can look for animals, watch the surf, or re-flect on the view over Cumming Creek from the benches set on the cliff above the beach. It's also a great spot for whale watching. Low tide pro-vides access to a natural cave and tidal pools. ⊠ *U.S. 101 S* ☎ *800/551–6949* ⊕ *www.prd.state.or.us* 🖾 *Free* ⊙ *Daily.*

Six miles south of Yachats, **Sea Rose** sells seashells from Oregon and around the world, plus gift items and souvenirs, and serves both casual collectors and serious shell aficionados. A free museum displays shells and sea life. There's an exhibit of glass fishing floats, but a favorite item is the giant clam. ⊠ *95478 U.S. 101, 97498* ☎ *541/547–3005* 🖨 *541/547–5197* ⊙ *Memorial Day–Labor Day, daily 9:30–6; Labor Day–Memorial Day, daily 10–5.*

The oceanside **Tillicum Beach Campground** 3½ mi north of Yachats is so popular there is a 10-day-stay limit. Stairs provide access to the beach. Open year-round, there are 61 sites. ⊠ *U.S. 101* ☎ *541/563–3211* 🖾 *Day use free* ⊙ *Daily.*

The Yachats River meets the Pacific Ocean at **Yachats Ocean Road State Recreation Area,** 1 mi from Yachats. Whale-watching is a popular activity. ⊠ *U.S. 101 to Yachats Ocean Rd.* ☎ *541/997–3851 or 800/551–6949* ⊕ *www.prd.state.or.us* ☒ *Free* ☺ *Daily.*

## Where to Stay & Eat

$–$$$  ✕ **Adobe Restaurant.** The food at the dining room of the Adobe Hotel doesn't always measure up to the extraordinary ocean views, but if you stick to the seafood, you'll come away satisfied. The Baked Crab Pot is a rich, bubbling casserole filled with Dungeness crab and cheese in a shallot cream sauce; best of all is the Captain's Seafood Platter, heaped with prawns, scallops, grilled oysters, and razor clams. ⊠ *1555 U.S. 101* ☎ *541/547–3141* ☰ *AE, D, DC, MC, V.*

$–$$$  ✕ **La Serre.** Don't be dismayed by the vaguely steak-and-salad-bar feel
Fodor'sChoice  at this skylit, plant-filled restaurant—the chef's deft touch with fresh
★  seafood attracts knowledgeable diners from as far away as Florence and Newport. Try the tender geoduck clam, breaded with Parmesan cheese and flash-fried in lemon-garlic butter. A reasonably priced wine list and mouthwatering desserts complete the package. ⊠ *2nd and Beach Sts.* ☎ *541/547–3420* ☰ *AE, MC, V* ☺ *Closed Jan. and Tues. No lunch.*

$–$$$  ✕ **Yachats Crab & Chowder House.** Overlooking the Yachats River, this spot has many fresh seafood dishes. The seafood chowder is outstanding, and you can't go wrong with a bucket of steamers or fresh crab cakes. Vintage prints recall the Yachats of yesterday. ⊠ *131 U.S. 101* ☎ *541/547–4132* ☰ *AE, D, DC, MC, V* ☺ *Closed Mon.*

$$$–$$$$  ▦ **Seaquest.** Eight miles south of Yachats and right on the ocean, this bed-and-breakfast has a massive fireplace and a TV in the main sitting area, where breakfast is served. All rooms have queen-size beds and views of the ocean, where you might see a migrating whale pass by. ⊠ *95354 U.S. 101, 97498* ☎ *541/547–3782, 800/341–4878 reservations* 🖷 *541/547–3719* ⊕ *www.seaq.com* 🖅 *5 rooms* ⚬ *In-room hot tubs, beach; no kids under 14, no room phones, no room TVs, no smoking* ☰ *MC, V* ⦿ *BP.*

$$$  ▦ **Kittiwake.** This modern oceanfront home 7 mi south of Yachats was designed to include comfortable guest rooms with large bathrooms and scenic views. Two rooms have window seats, and the decks overlook the pounding surf. The 2½-acre grounds attract deer, birds, and butterflies, and there are tidal pools to explore below the bluff. Both beach and rain gear are provided, along with a big German breakfast. ⊠ *95368 U.S. 101, 97498* ☎ *541/547–4470* 🖷 *541/547–4415* ⊕ *www.kittiwakebandb. com* 🖅 *3 rooms* ⚬ *Some in-room hot tubs; no a/c, no kids, no room phones, no smoking, no TV in some rooms* ☰ *AE, D, MC, V* ⦿ *BP.*

$$$  ▦ **Ziggurat.** You have to see this four-story cedar-and-glass pyramid 6½ mi south of Yachats to believe it. And you need to spend a night or two, serenaded by the wind and sea, to fully appreciate it. Odd angles, contemporary furnishings, and works of art gathered on the owners' world travels lend a discerning, sophisticated air. Two first-floor suites open out to grassy cliffs; the smaller, fourth-floor bedroom has two balconies and dramatic views. ⊠ *95320 U.S. 101, 97498* ☎ *541/547–3925* ⊕ *www.newportnet.com/ziggurat* 🖅 *1 room, 2 suites* ⚬ *No kids under 14, no smoking* ☰ *No credit cards* ⦿ *BP.*

$$–$$$  ▦ **Serenity.** With many genuine Bavarian touches because of the owners' origins, this inn sits on 10 peaceful acres in a wooded area above the Yachats River, 6 mi inland from the town of Yachats. One of the accommodations is a detached second-floor suite with a canopy bed and windows overlooking rolling lawns where deer often congregate. All the rooms have stereos. ⊠ *5985 Yachats River Rd., 97498* ☎ *541/547–3813*

↵ *3 suites* ⚤ *Picnic area, in-room hot tubs, refrigerators, some in-room VCRs; no room phones, no smoking* 🖃 *MC, V* ⧄❗ *BP.*

**$-$$** ⊞ **The Adobe.** The knotty-pine rooms in this unassuming resort motel are on the smallish side but are warm and inviting. High beam ceilings and picture windows frame majestic views. Most rooms have fireplaces; all have coffeemakers. ✉ *1555 U.S. 101, 97498* ☎ *541/547–3141 or 800/522–3623* 🖷 *541/547–4234* ⊕ *www.adoberesort.com* ↵ *108 units, 8 suites* ⚤ *Restaurant, refrigerators, cable TV, in-room VCRs, health club, indoor pool, wading pool, hot tub, sauna* 🖃 *AE, D, DC, MC, V.*

**$-$$** ⊞ **Fireside Motel.** The Fireside Motel, the sister property to the Overleaf Lodge, offers a more casual atmosphere. The setting is no less spectacular and most rooms have oceanfront views and balconies on which to enjoy them. Some units have gas fireplaces. ✉ *1881 U.S. 101 N, 97498* ☎ *541/547–3636 or 800/336–3573* 🖷 *541/547–3152* ↵ *43 rooms, 1 house* ⚤ *Refrigerators, cable TV, some pets allowed (fee)* 🖃 *D, MC, V.*

**$-$$** ⊞ **Overleaf Lodge.** Revel in the rugged beauty of crashing waves against the rocky shoreline from an oceanfront room—or from the shoreline trail that meanders in front of the lodge. Framed art with poetry and driftwood sculptures hang in the hallways and rooms. Accommodations are spacious and many offer patios, balconies or picture windows to admire dramatic coastal sunsets. Excellent, warm service includes guided nature walks and marshmallow bonfire sing-alongs on summer weekends. ⚤ *Some kitchenettes, microwaves, in-room VCR's, exercise equipment, massage, laundry facilities.* ✉ *280 Overleaf Lodge Lane, 97498-0036* ☎ *541/547–4880 or 800/338–0507* ⊕ *www.overleaflodge. com* ↵ *39 rooms* 🖃 *AE, D, MC, V* ⧄❗ *CP.*

**$-$$** ⊞ **Shamrock Lodgettes.** On the beach, these "lodgettes" include individual log cabins as well as rooms. The grounds are beautifully and elaborately landscaped; some people come just to walk through the gardens. All rooms have ocean or Yachats River views. ✉ *105 U.S. 101, 97498* ☎ *541/547–3312 or 800/845–5028* 🖷 *541/547–3843* ⊕ *www.shamrocklodgettes. com* ↵ *19 rooms, 7 cabins* ⚤ *Some in-room hot tubs, some kitchenettes, refrigerators, cable TV, some pets allowed (fee)* 🖃 *AE, DC, MC, V.*

**¢-$** ⊞ **Ocean Cove Inn.** These comfortable, spacious ocean-view quarters have wicker furnishings, handmade quilts, and hardwood floors. Decks to watch the beautiful sunsets, affordable rates, and excellent service make this a great choice. Prospect Avenue is off of Highway 101, at the south end of downtown. ⚤ *Microwaves, minibars, cable TV.* ✉ *180 Prospect Ave., 97498* ☎ *541/547–3900* ⊕ *www.oceancoveinn.com* ↵ *4 rooms* 🖃 *MC, V.*

## Shopping

Visitors stop by **Raindogs** as much to see Sam the dog as to shop. But shoppers looking for unique and classy gifts will find much to browse. Shelves are stocked with items for babies and pets as well as bath and body care; there are also jewelry and home accessories. ✉ *162 Beach Ave.* ☎ *541/547–3000* ⊕ *www.raindogsonline.com.*

en route    About 1 mi south of the bevy of upscale B&Bs at the southern boundary of Yachats (6 mi from the town itself), an easy trail leads down from the parking lot at **Devil's Churn State Park** to the deep, tide-cut fissure for which the park was named. Surging waves funneled into this narrow cleft in the basaltic embankment explode into "spouting horns" and sea spray. At nearby **Strawberry Hill State Park** (U.S. 101, west side, no phone), a ½-mi path leads to a small area of tidal pools, a great spot to observe shore life at low tide.

# Cape Perpetua

**16**  *9 mi south of Yachats town on U.S. 101.*

Fodor'sChoice
★

With the highest lookout point on the Oregon coast, Cape Perpetua towers 800 feet above the rocky shoreline. Named by Captain Cook on St. Perpetua's Day in 1778, the cape is part of a 2,700-acre scenic area popular with hikers, campers, beachcombers, and naturalists. General information and a map of 10 trails are available at the **Cape Perpetua Visitors Center,** on the east side of the highway, 2 mi south of Devil's Churn. The easy 1-mi **Giant Spruce Trail** passes through a fern-filled rain forest to an enormous 500-year-old Sitka spruce. Easier still is the marked Auto Tour; it begins about 2 mi north of the visitor center and winds through Siuslaw National Forest to the ¼-mi **Whispering Spruce Trail.** Views from the rustic rock shelter here extend 150 mi north and south and 37 mi out to sea. The **Cape Perpetua Interpretive Center,** in the visitor center, has educational movies and exhibits about the natural forces that shaped Cape Perpetua. ⊠ *U.S. 101* ☎ *541/547-3289* ☜ *Visitor center free, interpretive center $3* ☉ *Memorial Day–Labor Day, daily 9–5; Labor Day–Memorial Day, weekends 10–4.*

# Heceta Head

**17**  *10 mi south of Cape Perpetua on U.S. 101; 65 mi from Eugene, west on Hwy. 126 and north on U.S. 101.*

A ½-mi trail from the beachside parking lot at **Devil's Elbow State Park** leads to **Heceta Head Lighthouse,** whose beacon, visible for more than 21 mi, is the most powerful on the Oregon coast. The trail passes **Heceta House,** a pristine white structure said to be haunted by the wife of a lighthouse keeper whose child fell to her death from the cliffs shortly after the beacon was lit in 1894. The house is one of Oregon's most remarkable bed-and-breakfasts. ⊠ *U.S. 101* ☎ *541/997-3851* ☜ *Day use $3, lighthouse tours free* ☉ *Lighthouse Mar.–Oct., daily noon–5; park daily dawn–dusk.*

In 1880 a sea captain named Cox rowed a small skiff into a fissure in a 300-foot-high sea cliff. Inside, he was startled to discover a vaulted chamber in the rock, 125 feet high and 2 acres in area. Hundreds of massive sea lions—the largest bulls weighing 2,000 pounds or more—covered every available horizontal surface. Cox had no way of knowing it, but his discovery would eventually become one of the Oregon coast's premier tourist attractions, **Sea Lion Caves.** An elevator near the cliff-top ticket office descends to the floor of the cavern, near sea level, where Steller's and California sea lions and their fuzzy pups can be viewed from behind a wire fence. This is the only known hauling-out area and rookery for wild sea lions on the mainland in the Lower 48, and it's an awesome—if aromatic—sight and sound. In the spring and summer the mammals usually stay on the rocky ledges outside the cave; in fall and winter they move inside. You'll also see several species of sea birds here, including migratory pigeon guillemots, cormorants, and three varieties of gulls. Gray whales are visible during their northern and southern migrations, October–December and March–May. ⊠ *91560 U.S. 101, 1 mi south of Heceta Head* ☎ *541/547-3111* ☜ *$7* ☉ *Opens at 9 AM daily; closing times vary.*

★ ☮ **18**

## Where to Stay

$$–$$$$  ▥ **Heceta House.** On a windswept promontory, this unusual B&B is surrounded by a white-picket fence. The late-Victorian house, owned by the U.S. Forest Service, is managed by Mike and Carol Korgan, certified ex-

ecutive chefs who prepare a seven-course breakfast (included in the room rate) each morning. The nicest of the simply furnished rooms is the Mariner's, with a private bath and an awe-inspiring view. Filled with period detailing and antiques, the common areas are warm and inviting. If you're lucky, you may hear Rue, the resident ghost, in the middle of the night. ✉ *92072 U.S. 101 S, Yachats 97498* ☎ *541/547–3696* ⊕ *www. hecetalighthouse.com* ⤳ *3 rooms, 1 with bath* ☰ *MC, V* ⍣ *BP.*

**en route**  South of Heceta Head, U.S. 101 jogs inland, and the frowning headlands and cliffs of the north coast give way to the beaches, lakes, rivers, tidal estuaries, and rolling dunes of the south. Historic bridges span many of the famous fishing rivers that draw anglers from around the world. **Darlingtona Botanical Wayside** (✉ Mercer Lake Rd. ☎ no phone), 6 mi south of Sea Lion Caves on the east side of U.S. 101, is an example of the rich plant life found in the marshy terrain near the coast. It's also a surefire child pleaser. A short paved nature trail leads through clumps of insect-catching cobra lilies, so named because they look like spotted cobras ready to strike. This wayside area is the most interesting in May, when the lilies are in bloom. Admission is free.

## Florence

**⑲**  *12 mi south of Heceta Head on U.S. 101, 63 mi west of Eugene on Hwy. 126.*

Tourists and retirees have been flocking to Florence in ever greater numbers in recent years. Its restored waterfront Old Town has restaurants, antiques stores, fish markets, and other diversions. But what really makes the town so appealing is its proximity to remarkable stretches of coastline. Seventy-five creeks and rivers empty into the Pacific Ocean in and around Florence, and the Siuslaw River flows right through town. When the numerous nearby lakes are added to the mix, it makes for one of the richest fishing areas in Oregon. Salmon, rainbow trout, bass, perch, crabs, and clams are among the water's treasures. Fishing boats and pleasure craft moor in Florence's harbor, forming a pleasant backdrop for the town's restored buildings. South of town, miles of white-sand dunes lend themselves to everything from solitary hikes to rides aboard all-terrain vehicles.

★ ⌘  Florence is the gateway to the **Oregon Dunes National Recreation Area,** a 41-mi swath of undulating camel-color sand. The dunes, formed by eroded sandstone pushed up from the sea floor millions of years ago, have forests growing on them, water running through them, and rivers that have been dammed by them to form lakes. **Honeyman Memorial State Park,** 522 acres within the recreation area, is a base camp for dune-buggy enthusiasts, mountain bikers, hikers, boaters, horseback riders, and dogsledders (the sandy hills are an excellent training ground). The dunes are a vast and exuberant playground for children, particularly the slopes surrounding cool **Cleawox Lake.** ✉ *Oregon Dunes National Recreation Area office, 855 U.S. 101, Reedsport 97467* ☎ *541/271–3611* 🚗 *Day use $5* ⊙ *Daily dawn–dusk.*

Ride year-round along the Oregon Dunes National Recreation Area at **C and M Stables,** spotting not only marine life—sea lions, whales, and all manner of coast bird—but also bald eagles, red-tailed fox, and deer. Choose a 10-minute corral ride or take a horse out for the day to explore the beach or dunes. Children must be at least eight years old for the beach ride or six years old for the dune trail rides. There are also six overnight RV spaces. ✉ *90241 U.S. 101 N* ☎ *541/997–7540* ⊕ *www.touroregon.com/horses/index.html* 🖃 *$25–$40 per hr* ☉ *Daily 10–dusk.*

A small, homey business, **Siuslaw River Coffee Roasters** (✉ 1240 Bay St. ☎ 541/997–3443) serves cups of drip-on-demand coffee— you select the roast and they grind and brew it on the spot. Beans are roasted on site, muffins and breads are freshly baked, and a view of the namesake river can be savored from the deck out back.

The focus at **Siuslaw Pioneer Museum,** formerly a Lutheran church, is on pioneer and Native American history. ✉ *85294 U.S. 101 S* ☎ *541/997– 7884* 🖃 *$1 suggested donation* ☉ *Jan.–Nov., Tues.–Sun. 10–4.*

A trail from **Carl G. Washburne Memorial** park connects you to the Heceta Head trail, which you can use to reach the Heceta Head lighthouse. The campground has 58 full hookups, 2 tent sites, and 2 yurts. ✉ *93111 U.S. 101 N* ☎ *541/547–3416* ⊕ *www.prd.state.or.us* 🖃 *$3 per vehicle* ☉ *Daily.*

The Victorian *Westward Ho!* **Sternwheeler** leaves from the Old Town Docks and cruises the Siuslaw River past forests and the Oregon Dunes National Recreation Area. ✉ *Bay and Maple Sts.* ☎ *541/997–9691* ⊕ *www. westward-ho.com* 🖃 *$14, sunset dinner cruise $33* ☉ *Apr.–Oct., daily; call for schedules.*

Beginning at the Siltcoos Lake, where cottages float on calm waters, the **Siltcoos River Canoe Trail** winds through thick rain forest, past towering sand dunes, emerging some 4 mi later at white-sand beaches and the blue waters of the Pacific, where seals and snowy plovers rest. The river is a Class I with no rapids, but there are a few trees to navigate and one very short portage around a small dam.

*Fodor's*Choice
★

## Where to Stay & Eat

**$–$$$** ✕ **Bridgewater Seafood Restaurant.** Freshly caught seafood—25 to 30 choices nightly—is the mainstay of this creaky-floored Victorian-era restaurant in Florence's Old Town. The cooking is plain and not exactly inspired, but that may be part of its appeal. ✉ *1297 Bay St.* ☎ *541/ 997–9405* ▤ *MC, V.*

**$–$$$** ✕ **Clawson's Windward Inn.** One of the south coast's most elegant eateries, this tightly run ship prides itself on its vast seafood-heavy menu, master wine list, and fresh and fine desserts. The chinook salmon fillets poached in Riesling and the shrimp and scallops sautéed in white wine are delectable. ✉ *3757 U.S. 101 N* ☎ *541/997–8243* ▤ *D, MC, V.*

**¢–$$** ✕ **Mo's.** Going hand in hand at Mo's are clear bayfront views and a creamy bowl of clam chowder. This coastal institution has been around for more than 40 years, consistently providing fresh seafood and down-home service. ✉ *1436 Bay St.* ☎ *541/997–2185* ▤ *D, MC, V.*

**$–$$$** ▥ **Driftwood Shores Surfside Resort Inn.** The chief amenity of this resort is its location directly above Heceta Beach, one of the longest sand beaches on the south coast. The simple rooms have ocean views and kitchens; the three-bedroom suites have fireplaces and balconies. ✉ *88416 1st Ave. (from U.S. 101 take Heceta Beach Rd. west about 3 mi north of Florence), 97439* ☎ *541/997–8263 or 800/422–5091* 🖷 *541/997–5857* ⊕ *www.driftwoodshores.com* ⇆ *108 rooms, 28 suites* ♨ *Restaurant, indoor pool, hot tub, beach, bar* ▤ *AE, D, DC, MC, V.*

**$$** ▥ **Johnson House.** The single accommodation here is the one-room Rose cottage, overlooking the gardens. Hardwood floors, a claw-foot tub, and period furniture lend this little place an old country charm. You can drive to the beach in 10 minutes, and it's a short walk to the antiques shops, crafts boutiques, and eateries on the bay dock. While it is sometimes possible to get a room even with only a night's notice, travelers set on staying here will want to make reservations at least two months in advance during the summer season and one month in advance the rest of the year. ⊠ *216 Maple St., 97439* ☎ *541/997–8000 or 800/768–9488* 🖷 *541/997–2364* ⊕ *www.touroregon.com/thejohnsonhouse* ⤴ *1 cottage* ⚴ *No a/c, no kids under 12, no smoking* ⊟ *D, MC, V* ⦿ *BP.*

⚠ **Jessie M. Honeyman Memorial State Park.** Two miles of sand dunes separate this park from the ocean. The second-largest overnight camp in the state, the park has two natural freshwater lakes, and from October through April, direct access from the campsite to the Oregon Dunes National Recreation Area. ⚴ *Flush toilets, full hookups, dump station, drinking water, showers, fire pits, picnic tables, electricity, swimming.* ⤴ *47 full hookups, 119 electrical, 191 tent sites, 6 group tent sites 10 yurts* ⊠ *Off U.S. 101, 3 mi south of Florence* ☎ *800/452–5687 reservations, 800/551–6949 information* ⊕ *www.oregonstateparks.org* ⊠ *Full hookups $21, electrical hookups $21, tent sites $17, primitive/overflow $9, hiker/biker $4, yurts $29* ⚴ *Reservations essential* ⊟ *MC, V.*

## Sports & the Outdoors

BOATING · **Central Coast Watersports** (⊠ 1901 U.S. 101 ☎ 541/997–1812) rents kayaks and sand boards and sells boats, diving equipment, and accessories.

DUNE BUGGIES · **Sandland Adventures** (⊠ 85366 U.S. 101, ☎ 541/997–8087), 1 mi south of town, rents ATVs and single-person dune buggies. Beginning at the property there's an 8-mi stretch of sand dunes to explore. There's also miniature golf and a go-cart track.

GOLF · **Ocean Dunes Golf Links** (⊠ 3345 Munsel Lake Rd. ☎ 541/997–3232) is an 18-hole, par-71 course. The greens fee is $38, and an optional cart costs $26. **Sandpines Golf Course** (⊠ 1201 35th St. ☎ 541/997–1940) is an 18-hole, par-72 course. Greens fees are $55 during the week, $59 on weekends; an optional cart costs $26.

## Shopping

**Bay Street** in Old Town Florence is filled with gift shops, souvenirs, and collectibles. **Incredible & Edible Oregon** (⊠ 1350 Bay St. ☎ 541/997–7018) in Old Town is devoted to Oregon products: wine, fruit preserves, books, and gift items. Especially popular are Pendleton blankets and items made from Oregon's unique myrtlewood. **Reigning Cats and Dogs** (⊠ 1384 Bay St. ☎ 541/997–8982) caters to pet lovers with gifts, art, and souvenirs in animal themes. Look for sun catchers and handmade glass ornaments at the **Raindrop Factory** (⊠ 1287 Bay St. ☎ 541/997–5228). **Bonjour! Boutique** (⊠ 1336 Bay St. ☎ 541/997–8194) is all about feminine style and exotic fashion. Get your T-shirts at the **Old Town T-Shirt Co.** (⊠ 1431 Bay St. ☎ 541/902–9408). Buy kites and wind socks at **Catch the Wind** (⊠ 1250 Bay St. ☎ 541/997–9500).

# Reedsport

**㉒** *20 mi south of Florence on U.S. 101, 90 mi west of Eugene on I–5 and Hwy. 38.*

The small town of Reedsport owes its existence to the Umpqua River, one of the state's great steelhead fishing streams. Exhibits at the **Umpqua Discovery Center** in the waterfront area give a good introduction to the Lower Umpqua estuary and surrounding region. The center's chief attraction is the *Hero,* the laboratory ship Admiral Byrd used on his expeditions to the Antarctic. ⊠ *409 Riverfront Way* ☎ *541/271–4816* ⊠ *Museum $5, tour of ship $3* ⊙ *May–Sept., daily 10–6; Oct.–Apr., daily 10–4.*

The natural forces that created the towering sand dunes along this section of the Oregon coast are explained in interpretive exhibits at the Reedsport **Oregon Dunes National Recreation Area Visitors Center.** The center, which also sells maps, books, and gifts, is a good place to pick up free literature on the area. ⊠ *855 Highway Ave., south side of Umpqua River Bridge* ☎ *541/271–3611* ✆ *Free* ☉ *Memorial Day–Labor Day, daily 8:30–5; hrs vary rest of year.*

A herd of wild Roosevelt elk, Oregon's largest land mammal, roams within sight of the **Dean Creek Elk Viewing Area.** Abundant forage and a mild winter climate enable the elk to remain at Dean Creek year-round. The best viewing times are early morning and before dusk. ⊠ *Hwy. 38, 3 mi east of Reedsport (watch for signs)* ✆ *Free* ☉ *Daily dawn–dusk.*

Two miles south of Reedsport at the mouth of the Umpqua River, **Salmon Harbor** is one of the largest marinas on the Oregon coast. An RV park is near the county-operated facility. ⊠ *U.S. 101* ☎ *541/271–3407* ✆ *Free* ☉ *May–Sept., daily; Oct.–Apr., weekdays.*

On Eel Lake near the town of Lakeside, the little-known **William M. Tugman State Park** is surrounded by a dense forest of spruce, cedar, fir, and alder. Recreational activities include fishing, swimming, canoeing, and sailing. A campground has 115 electrical sites and 3 yurts. ⊠ *U.S. 101 S* ☎ *541/888–4902 or 800/551–6949* ⊕ *www.prd.state.or.us* ✆ *$3 per vehicle day-use fee* ☉ *Daily.*

en route

A public pier at **Winchester Bay's Salmon Harbor,** 3¼ mi south of Reedsport, juts out over the bay and yields excellent results for crabbers and fishermen (especially those after rockfish). There's also a full-service marina with a fish market.

## Where to Stay

$ ⌂ **Salbasgeon Inn of the Umpqua.** In the heart of fishing country, this inn takes its name from salmon, striped bass, and sturgeon. It overlooks the Umpqua River, and all rooms have river views. ⊠ *45209 Rte. 38, 97467* ☎ *541/271–2025* ⊕ *www.salbasgeon.com or www.umpquariver.com* ✆ *12 rooms* ♨ *Picnic area, some kitchenettes, cable TV, putting green, some pets allowed (fee)* ▭ *AE, D, DC, MC, V.*

¢–$ ⌂ **Anchor Bay Inn.** Right in the center of Reedsport, this motel has easy access to the dunes. Elk viewing is only 4 mi away. ⊠ *1821 Winchester Ave., 97467* ☎ *541/271–2149 or 800/767–1821* 🖨 *541/271–1802* ✉ *anchorbay@presys.com* ✆ *21 rooms* ♨ *Some kitchenettes, some microwaves, some refrigerators, cable TV, pool, laundry facilities, business services, some pets allowed (fee)* ▭ *AE, D, MC, V* ⧈⧉ *CP.*

# Umpqua Lighthouse Park

㉑ *6 mi south of Reedsport on U.S. 101.*

Some of the highest sand dunes in the country are found in the 50-acre Umpqua Lighthouse Park. The first **Umpqua River Lighthouse,** built on the dunes at the mouth of the Umpqua River in 1857, lasted only four years before it toppled over in a storm. It took local residents 33 years to build another one. The "new" lighthouse, built on a bluff overlooking the south side of Winchester Bay and operated by the U.S. Coast Guard, is still going strong, flashing a warning beacon out to sea every five seconds. The **Douglas County Coastal Visitors Center** adjacent to the lighthouse has a museum and can arrange lighthouse tours. ⊠ *Umpqua Hwy., west side of U.S. 101* ☎ *541/271–4118* ✆ *Donations appreciated* ☉ *Lighthouse May–Sept., Wed.–Sat. 10–4, Sun. 1–4.*

# North Bend

**㉒** *20 mi south of Reedsport on U.S. 101.*

Named by the town's founder, sea captain and shipbuilder Asa Simpson, for its location on the north bend of Coos Bay, this town continues a decades-long tradition by making its livelihood from forest products, fishing, agriculture, and tourism. North Bend and its neighbors Coos Bay and Charleston make up the Bay Area, the largest urban area on the Oregon coast; North Bend sits at the south end of the 41-mi-long Oregon Dunes National Recreation Area.

The highlight here at **Coos County Historical Society Museum** is a 1922 steam locomotive used in Coos County logging. On display are a formal 1900 parlor, a pioneer kitchen, and exhibits on Native American history, agriculture, and industry such as logging, shipping, and mining. ✉ *1220 Sherman St.* ☎ *541/756–6320 or 541/756–4847* ☞ *$2* ☉ *Tues.–Sat. 10–4.*

The complex at **Mill Casino-Hotel** has a casino with 350 slots, blackjack, poker, and bingo. There's a waterfront restaurant and a showroom. ✉ *3201 Tremont Ave., 97459* ☎ *541/756–8800 or 800/953–4800* 🖷 *541/756–0431* ⊕ *www.themillcasino.com* ☞ *Free* ☉ *Daily.*

## Where to Stay & Eat

**$–$$$** ✕ **Hilltop House.** A dining tradition on the coast for 40 years, Hilltop House offers specialties that include Bouillabaisse Marseillaise, Salmon Neptune, rack of lamb, and lobster Newberg. Enjoy views of the bay, harbor, and sand while dining in the many-window dining room. ✉ *166 N. Bay Dr., 97459* ☎ *541/756–4160* ⊟ *AE, MC, V.*

**¢–$$** ✕ **Plank House.** The Plank House menu is designed to satisfy many tastes, whether with a simple home-style meat loaf, the local seafood catch of the day, or a tender cut of steak. All the baking, including chocolate decadence tortes and cheesecakes, is done right here. The restaurant, part of the Mill Casino-Hotel, serves breakfast, lunch, and dinner, and the outside deck, though not for eating, has a fantastic view of Coos Bay. ✉ *3201 Tremont Ave., 97459* ☎ *541/756–8800 or 800/953–4800* 🖷 *541/756–0431* ⊟ *AE, D, MC, V.*

**$$–$$$** ▥ **Mill Casino-Hotel.** The grounds here are landscaped with native greenery, and signs explain how each plant is used by the Coquille Indians, who own the resort. The hotel and room designs follow through with a Northwest flavor; the lobby has open beams and a stone fireplace, and guest rooms have rustic hickory beds. About half the rooms have a view of Coos Bay. ✉ *3201 Tremont Ave., 97459* ☎ *541/756–8800 or 800/953–4800* 🖷 *541/756–0431* ⊕ *www.themillcasino.com* ↬ *112 rooms, 3 suites* ⌂ *2 restaurants, in-room data ports, some in-room hot tubs, some refrigerators, room service, cable TV, shops, 2 bars, laundry service, business services* ⊟ *AE, D, MC, V* ⦿ *CP.*

**¢–$** ▥ **Bay Bridge.** This small motel is on Pacific Bay with views of the bay. The rooms are simple and basic. ✉ *33 U.S. 101, 97459* ☎ *541/756–3151 or 800/557–3156* ↬ *16 rooms* ⌂ *Some kitchenettes, some refrigerators, cable TV, some pets allowed (fee)* ⊟ *AE, D, DC, MC, V.*

# Coos Bay

**㉓** *27 mi south of Reedsport on U.S. 101; 116 mi southwest of Eugene, I–5 to Hwy. 38 to U.S. 101.*

The Coos Bay–Charleston–North Bend metropolitan area, collectively known as the Bay Area (population 25,000), is the gateway to rewarding recreational experiences. The town of Coos Bay lies next to the largest natural harbor between San Francisco Bay and Seattle's Puget Sound.

A century ago vast quantities of lumber cut from the Coast Range were milled in Coos Bay and shipped around the world. Coos Bay still has a reputation as a rough-and-ready port city, but with mill closures and dwindling lumber reserves it has begun to look in other directions, such as tourism, for economic prosperity. One former mill has even been converted into a casino.

To see the best of the Bay Area head west from Coos Bay on Newmark Avenue for about 7 mi to **Charleston**. Though it's a Bay Area community, this quiet fishing village at the mouth of Coos Bay is a world unto itself. As it loops into town the road becomes the Cape Arago Highway and leads to several oceanfront parks.

At **Charleston Marina Complex** there's a launch ramp, a store with tackle and marine supplies, a 110-space RV park, a motel, restaurants, and gift shops. Fishing charters also set out from here. ⊠ *4535 Kingfisher Dr., Charleston 97420* ☎ *541/888–2548* ⊕ *www.charlestonmarina.com* ⊠ *Free* ☼ *Daily.*

A placid semicircular lagoon protected from the sea by overlapping fingers of rock and surrounded by reefs, **Sunset Bay State Park** is one of the few places along the Oregon coast where you can swim without worrying about the currents and undertows. Only the hardiest souls will want to brave the chilly water, however. ⊹ *2 mi south of Charleston off Cape Arago Hwy.* ☎ *800/551–6949* ⊠ *Free* ☼ *Daily dawn–dusk.*

At **Shore Acres State Park,** an observation building on a grassy bluff overlooking the Pacific marks the site that held the mansion of lumber baron Louis J. Simpson. The view over the rugged wave-smashed cliffs is splendid, but the real glory of Shore Acres lies a few hundred yards to the south, where an entrance gate leads into what was Simpson's private garden. Beautifully landscaped and meticulously maintained, the gardens incorporate formal English and Japanese designs. From March to mid-October the grounds are ablaze with blossoming daffodils, rhododendrons, azaleas, roses, and dahlias. In December the entire garden is decked out with a dazzling display of holiday lights. ⊠ *10965 Cape Arago Hwy., 1 mi south of Sunset Bay State Park* ☎ *800/551– 6949* ⊠ *$3 per vehicle day-use fee* ☼ *Daily 8–dusk.*

The distant barking of sea lions echoes in the air at **Cape Arago State Park.** A trio of coves connected by short but steep trails, the park overlooks the **Oregon Islands National Wildlife Refuge**, where offshore rocks, beaches, islands, and reefs provide breeding grounds for seabirds and marine mammals. ⊠ *End of Cape Arago Hwy., 1 mi south of Shore Acres State Park* ☎ *800/551–6949* ⊠ *Free* ☼ *Daily dawn–dusk.*

On a rock island 12 mi offshore south of Coos Bay, **Cape Arago Lighthouse** has had several iterations; the first lighthouse was built here in 1866, but it was destroyed by storms and erosion. A second, built in 1908, suffered the same fate. The current white tower, built in 1934, is 44 feet tall and towers 100 feet above the ocean. If you're here on a foggy day, listen for its unique foghorn. The lighthouse is connected to the mainland by a bridge. Neither is open to the public, but there's an excellent spot to view this lonely guardian and much of the coastline. From U.S. 101, take Cape Arago Highway to Gregory Point, where it ends at a turnaround, and follow the short trail.

The wreck of the *New Carissa* freighter in winter 1999 was considered a serious threat to the fragile ecosystem at **South Slough National Estuarine Research Reserve,** but not much leaking oil reached the slough. The mudflats and tidal estuaries of Coos Bay support everything from algae to bald eagles and black bears. More than 300 species of birds have been sighted at the reserve; an interpretive center, guided walks (summer only), and nature trails give you a chance to see things up close. ⊠ *Seven Devils Rd., 4 mi south of Charleston* ☎ *800/551–6949* ⚑ *Free* ☉ *Trails daily dawn–dusk, interpretive center daily 8:30–4:30.*

Both a gift shop and a factory, the **Oregon Connection** produces more than 200 myrtlewood items and sells Oregon food and wine, homemade fudge, Pendleton woolen clothes, and jewelry. You can take a free tour of the factory. ⊠ *1125 S. 1st St.* ☎ *541/267–7804 or 800/255–5318* ⚑ *Free* ☉ *Daily 9–5.*

## Where to Stay & Eat

$–$$   ✕ **Portside Restaurant.** The fish at this gem of a restaurant overlooking the Charleston boat basin comes straight to the kitchen from the dock outside. Try the steamed Dungeness crab with drawn butter. On Friday night come for the all-you-can-eat seafood buffet. The nautical furnishings—vintage bayside photos, boat lamps, navigational aids, coiled rope—reinforce the view of the harbor through the restaurant's picture windows. ⊠ *8001 Kingfisher Rd., (follow Cape Arago Hwy. from Coos Bay)* ☎ *541/888–5544* ▤ *AE, DC, MC, V.*

★ ¢–$$   ✕ **Blue Heron Bistro.** You'll find subtle preparations of local seafood, chicken, and homemade pasta at this busy bistro. There are no flat spots on the far-ranging menu; even the innovative soups and desserts are excellent. The skylit tile-floor dining room seats about 70 amid natural wood and blue linen. The seating area outside has blue awnings and colorful Bavarian window boxes that add a festive touch. Espresso and 18 microbrewery beers are available. ⊠ *100 W. Commercial St.* ☎ *541/267–3933* ▤ *AE, D, MC, V* ☉ *Closed Sun. Oct.–May.*

¢–$   ✕ **Kum-Yon's.** The preparations at this small pan-Asian restaurant on Coos Bay's main drag are average, and the interior resembles nothing so much as a Seoul Burger King, but the portions of sushi, kung-pao shrimp, and other dishes are satisfying, and the prices are ridiculously low. ⊠ *835 S. Broadway* ☎ *541/269–2662* ▤ *AE, D, MC, V.*

$   ▥ **Coos Bay Manor.** Built in 1912 on a quiet residential street in Coos Bay, this 15-room Colonial Revival manor is listed on the National Register of Historic Places. Hardwood floors, detailed woodwork, high ceilings, and antiques and period reproductions offset the red-and-gold-flecked wallpaper. An unusual open balcony on the second floor leads to the large rooms. Innkeeper Pam Bate serves a full breakfast (included in the rates) in the wainscoted dining room. ⊠ *955 S. 5th St., 97420* ☎ *541/269–1224 or 800/269–1224* 🖷 *541/269–1224* ⚏ *5 rooms, 3 with bath* ⚐ *Airport shuttle* ▤ *D, MC, V* ⊠ *BP.*

▵ **Sunset Bay State Park.** A short walk from the beach, the park has a network of hiking trails linking the nearby Shore Acres and Cape Arago state parks. ⚐ *Flush toilets, full hookups, drinking water, showers, fire pits, picnic tables, electricity* ⚏ *29 full hookups, 36 electrical, 66 tent sites, 8 yurts, 11 group tent sites* ⊠ *Off U.S. 101, 12 mi south of Coos Bay* ☎ *800/452–5687 reservations, 800/551–6949 information* ⊕ *www.oregonstateparks.org* ⚑ *Full hookups $20, electrical hookups $20, tent sites $16, hiker/biker $4, yurts $27, group $60* ⚐ *Reservations essential* ▤ *MC, V.*

## Sports & the Outdoors

GOLF   **Kentuck Golf Course** (⊠ 675 Golf Course La., North Bend ☎ 541/756–4464) is an 18-hole, par-70 course. The greens fee is $18 on weekdays, $22 on weekends; a cart costs $24. **Sunset Bay Golf Course** (⊠ 11001 Cape Arago Hwy. ☎ 541/888–9301) is a 9-hole, par-36 course. The greens fee is $22, plus $25 for a cart.

off the
beaten
path

**GOLDEN AND SILVER FALLS STATE PARK** – Deep in old-growth forest sprinkled with delicate maidenhair ferns, this park has two of the region's natural wonders. Silver Falls is an arresting sight as it pours over a 200-foot-high semicircular rock ledge. One-quarter mile to the northwest, Golden Falls, another giant cataract formed by the thundering waters of Glenn Creek, is even more impressive, especially in the spring. ⊠ *U.S. 101, 24 mi northeast of Coos Bay (follow signs)* ☎ *800/551–6949* ⊠ *Free* ⊙ *Daily dawn–dusk.*

## Bandon

**24** *25 mi south of Coos Bay on U.S. 101.*

Referred to by some who cherish its romantic lure as Bandon-by-the-Sea, Bandon is both a harbor town and a popular vacation spot. Bandon is famous for its cranberry products and its cheese factory, as well as its artists' colony, complete with galleries and shops. Two National Wildlife Refuges, Oregon Islands and Bandon Marsh, are within the city limits. Newly developed on natural rolling dune land along the Pacific Ocean, the Bandon Dunes links-style course is attracting interest from golfers worldwide.

It may seem odd that tiny Bandon, built above a beach notable for its gallery of photogenic sea stacks, bills itself as the cranberry capital of Oregon. But 10 mi north of town lie acres of bogs and irrigated fields where tons of the tart berries are harvested every year. Each October a Cranberry Festival, complete with a parade and a fair, takes place.

The town, almost entirely rebuilt after a devastating fire in 1936, has fine restaurants, resort hotels, and a busy boat basin on the Coquille River estuary. A few of the buildings in the Old Town area a block north of the boat basin hark back to the early 20th century, when Bandon was a booming port of call for passengers traveling from San Francisco to Seattle by steamship.

The **Bandon Historical Society Museum,** in the old City Hall building, documents the town's past through dioramas, historic photos, and artifacts, such as marine and logging equipment. ⊠ *270 Fillmore St.* ☎ *541/347–2164* ⊠ *$1* ⊙ *May–Sept., Mon.–Sat. 10–4, Sun. noon–3.*

The tiny **Bandon Beach State Park,** along the Beach Loop Road 5 mi south of Bandon, has access to beaches, fishing, and hiking trails. ⊠ *Bradley Lake Rd.* ☎ *541/347–3501 or 800/551–6949* ⊕ *www.prd.state.or.us* ⊠ *Free* ⊙ *Daily.*

The octagonal **Coquille Lighthouse** at **Bullards Beach State Park,** built in 1896 and no longer in use, stands lonely sentinel at the mouth of the Coquille River. From the highway the 2-mi drive to reach it passes through the Bandon Marsh, a prime bird-watching and picnicking area. The beach beside the lighthouse is a good place to search for jasper, agate, and driftwood. ⊠ *U.S. 101, 2 mi north of Bandon* ☎ *800/551–6949* ⊠ *Free* ⊙ *Daily dawn–dusk.*

In the old City Hall building, the **Coquille River Museum** documents Bandon's past with displays of pioneer furniture, glassware, and clothing, plus exhibits on the Bandon fire of 1936 and the local lumber, cranberry, creamery, and maritime industries. ⊠ *270 Fillmore St., 97411* ☎ *541/347–2164* ⊠ *$2* ⊙ *Oct.–Memorial Day, Mon.–Sat. 10–4; Memorial Day–Sept., Mon.–Sat. 10–4, Sun. noon–3.*

Throughout the year, the 250-seat **Sprague Community Theater** presents live productions of musicals, comedies, and concerts from the Bandon

Playhouse, Bandon Youth Theater, and other community groups. Quality musicals such as *Chicago, Man of La Mancha,* and *The Nutcracker* draw regular patrons as well as visitors. Call for show and ticket information. ⊠ *Bandon City Park, 1202 11th St. SW* ☎ *541/347–7426.*

The stone sculptures of **Face Rock Wayside,** formed only by wind and rain, have names such as Elephant Rock, Table Rock, and Face Rock. To reach them follow signs from Bandon south along Beach Loop Road; then walk down a stairway to the sand. ☒ *Free* ☾ *Daily.*

The "walk-through safari" on 21 acres of **West Coast Game Park** has free-roaming wildlife: 450 animals and 75 species including lions, tigers, snow leopards, bears, chimps, cougars, and camels, make it one of the largest wild-animal petting parks in the United States. The big attractions here are the young animals: bear cubs, tiger cubs, whatever is suitable for actual handling. It is 7 mi south of Bandon on U.S. 101. ⊠ *U.S. 101* ☎ *541/347–3106* ⊕ *www.gameparksafari.com* ☒ *$11* ☾ *Mid-June–Labor Day, daily 9–7; spring and early fall, daily 9–5.*

## Where to Stay & Eat

**$–$$$** ✕ **Lord Bennett's.** His lordship has a lot going for him: a cliff-top setting, a comfortable and spacious dining area, sunsets visible through picture windows overlooking Face Rock Beach, and musical performers on weekends. The rich dishes include prawns sautéed with sherry and garlic and steaks topped with shiitake mushrooms. A Sunday brunch is served. ⊠ *1695 Beach Loop Rd.* ☎ *541/347–3663* ☐ *AE, D, MC, V.*

**¢–$$$** ✕ **Wheelhouse Restaurant & Crowsnest Lounge.** As any restaurant with an ocean view should, the Wheelhouse has great seafood—fresh oysters, clams, prawns, and salmon are some of the choices. Additionally impressive is the extensive selection of aged steaks, rich pastas, and chicken dishes such as cilantro pesto chicken, charbroiled with feta cheese and jalapeño. The wine list favors Pacific Northwest vintages. ⊠ *125 Chicago St.* ☎ *541/347–9331* ☐ *MC, V.*

**¢–$$** ✕ **Bandon Boatworks.** A local favorite, this romantic jettyside eatery serves its seafood, steaks, and prime rib with a view of the Coquille River harbor and lighthouse. Try the panfried oysters flamed with brandy and anisette or the quick-sautéed seafood combination, which is heavy on scampi and scallops. ⊠ *S. Jetty Rd. off 1st St.* ☎ *541/347–2111* ☐ *AE, D, MC, V.*

**¢** ✕ **Bandon Baking Company & Deli.** The only scent stronger than the salty sea air is the aroma of fresh-baked bread emanating from this establishment. You'll have a tough time deciding between the huge selection of loaves, especially the cinnamon swirl, cranberry nut, or jalapeño and cheese. There are also muffins, scones, bagels, pastries, and cookies—including snickerdoodles and a molasses ginger concoction. For something hearty, you can build your own sandwich. Note that the bakery closes at 5 PM. ⊠ *160 Second St.* ☎ *541/347–9440* ⊕ *www.bandonbakingco.com* ☐ *No dinner* ☐ *No credit cards.*

**$$–$$$$** ▦ **The Lighthouse.** Wide windows and a porch off the dining room of this 1980 cedar home on Bandon's waterfront, within walking distance of Old Town and restaurants, provide great views of the Coquille River Lighthouse across the estuary. The simple furnishings include antiques and plants. Three guest rooms have dramatic ocean and sunset views, and guests say the Gray Whale Room has the best view on the Oregon coast, right from the room's hot tub. ⊠ *650 Jetty Rd., 97411* ☎ *541/347–9316* ⊕ *www.lighthouselodging.com* ⇆ *5 rooms* ♨ *Some in-room hot tubs; no kids under 12, no smoking, no TV in some rooms* ☐ *MC, V* ⦿ *BP.*

**$$$** ▦ **Bandon Beach Vacation Rentals.** These vacation homes across the street from the beaches and Bandon State Park are a nice option for large families—and they're brimming with little comforts of home, such as books, games, and videos. Basics, such as pots, pans, and linens, are also provided. ⊠ *54515 Beach Loop Rd., 97411* ☎ *541/347–4801 or 888/441– 8030* ⊕ *www.bandonbeachrentals.com* ♺ *4 cottages* ⚲ *Kitchens, in-room VCRs.* ⊟ *AE, D, MC, V.*

¢–$$  🏨 **Sunset Motel.** Many rooms at this rustic property have decks with ocean views, and some have fireplaces. Beach houses are also available. ⊠ *1755 Beach Loop Rd., 97411* ☎ *541/347–2453 or 800/842–2407* 🖷 *541/347–3636* ⊕ *www.sunsetmotel.com* ♺ *58 rooms, 5 beach houses* ⚲ *Restaurant, some kitchenettes, cable TV, hot tub, laundry facilities, business services, airport shuttle, some pets allowed (fee)* ⊟ *AE, D, DC, MC, V.*

$  🏨 **Harbor View Motel.** Rooms at this motel on the Coquille River have ocean views. It's close to Old Town shopping and restaurants. ⊠ *355 U.S. 101, 97411* ☎ *541/347–4417 or 800/526–0209* 🖷 *541/347–3616* ♺ *59 rooms* ⚲ *Refrigerators, cable TV* ⊟ *AE, D, DC, MC, V* ⏨ *CP.*

### Sports & the Outdoors

GOLF  **Bandon Dunes Golf Resort** (⊠ Round Lake Dr. ☎ 541/347–4380 or 888/ 345–6008) has two 18-hole courses with a lodge, shop, and full practice facilities. The greens fee is $160 for guests, $200 for nonguests, June–October; call for seasonal rates. This is a walking-only course.

KAYAKING  The waterfront shop **Adventure Kayak** (⊠ 315 First Street ☎ 541/347– 3480) sells and rents kayaks and hosts tours and classes. There's also a selection of kites and windsocks for sale.

### Shopping

**Bandon Mercantile & Timeless Accents** (⊠ U.S. 101 and Elmira ☎ 541/ 347–4341) has bed-and-bath essentials, kitchen gadgets, clothing, and coffees. **Cranberry Sweets** (⊠ 1005 Newmark Ave. ☎ 541/347–9475) specializes in delectable handmade candies—cranberry jellies, "lemon pies" (white chocolate around a lemon jelly center), and other delicacies. **Northwest Country Gift Shop** (⊠ 325 2nd St. ☎ 541/347–5348) has furnishings and accessories you might expect to find in a mountain lodge. The selection includes Pendleton blankets and clothing, Big Sky furniture, carved decoys, Boyd's Bears, and Lang cards and calendars, as well as T-shirts and stuffed animals. **Spirit of Oregon** (⊠ 112 2nd Ave. ☎ 541/ 347–4311) has pottery, sea-kelp and sea-grass baskets, and unique jewelry all handcrafted by regional artists. In addition, there is custom clothing imported annually from Bali and African art. If you're looking for a book on outdoor adventure or travel in the northwest, odds are **Winter River Books** (⊠ 170 2nd St. SE ☎ 541/347–4111) will have it. The selection also includes spiritual, music, and reference books as well as one of the largest children's selections on the coast.

## Cape Blanco State Park

🅝 *27 mi south of Bandon on U.S. 101.*

Cape Blanco is the westernmost point in Oregon and perhaps the windiest—gusts clocked at speeds as high as 184 mph have twisted and battered the Sitka spruces along the 6-mi road from U.S. 101 to the **Cape Blanco Lighthouse.** The lighthouse, atop a 245-foot headland, has been in continuous use since 1870, longer than any other in Oregon. No one knows why the Spaniards sailing past these reddish bluffs in 1603 called them *blanco* (white). One theory is that the name refers to the fossilized shells that glint in the cliff face. Campsites at the 1,880-acre **Cape Blanco State Park** are available on a first-come, first-served basis. Saturday-evening tours are available in summer, with a donation suggested.

✉ *Cape Blanco Rd. (follow signs from U.S. 101)* ☎ *541/332–6774 state park, 541/332–2750 lighthouse* 🖼 *Day use free, campsites $13–$18* ⊙ *Park daily dawn–dusk; lighthouse Apr.–Oct., Thurs.–Mon. 10–3:30.*

**en route** | U.S. 101 between Port Orford and Brookings, often referred to as the "fabulous fifty miles," soars up green headlands, some of them hundreds of feet high, and past a seascape of cliffs and sea stacks. The ocean is bluer and clearer—though not appreciably warmer—than it is farther north, and the coastal countryside is dotted with farms, grazing cattle, and small rural communities. As you round a bend between Port Orford and Gold Beach you'll see one of those sights that make grown-ups groan and kids squeal with delight: a huge, open-jawed Tyrannosaurus rex, with a green brontosaurus peering out from the forest beside it. The **Prehistoric Gardens** (✉ 36848 U.S. 101 ☎ 541/332–4463) are filled with life-size replicas of these primeval giants. The complex is open daily 9 AM–dusk. Admission is $7.

# Port Orford

㉖ *27 mi south of Bandon on U.S. 101.*

The most westerly incorporated city in the contiguous United States, Port Orford is surrounded by forests, rivers, lakes, and beaches of the Pacific Ocean. The jetty at Port Orford offers little protection from storms, so every night the fishing boats are lifted out and stored on the docks. Commercial fishing boats search for crab, tuna, snapper, and salmon in the waters out of Port Orford, and diving boats gather sea urchins for Japanese markets. The area is a favorite spot for sport divers because of the near-shore, protected reef and for whale watchers in fall and early spring.

Six miles south of Port Orford, **Humbug Mountain State Park** is especially popular with campers. The park usually has warm weather, thanks to the nearby mountains, which block the ocean breezes. Windsurfing and scuba diving are popular here. Hiking trails lead to the top of Humbug Mountain. The campground has 30 electrical and 78 tent sites. ✉ *U.S. 101* ☎ *541/332–6774 or 800/551–6949* ⊕ *www.prd.state.or.us* 🖼 *$3 per vehicle day-use fee* ⊙ *Daily.*

## Where to Stay

**$$** 🏠 **Floras Lake House by the Sea.** This cedar home rests beside freshwater Floras Lake, spring-fed and separated from the ocean by only a sand spit. The owners run a windsurfing school on the lake. The interior of the house is light, airy, and comfortable, with picture windows, exposed beams, contemporary couches, and a woodstove. Two rooms have fireplaces, and all have private deck entrances. Outside, there's a garden, with a sauna beside the lake. ✉ *92870 Boice Cope Rd., Langlois 97450* ☎ *541/348–2573* 🖨 *541/348–9912* ⊕ *www.floraslake.com* ⇄ *4 rooms* ⚬ *Lake, sauna; no room phones, no room TVs, no smoking* ▭ *D, MC, V* ⊙ *Closed mid-Nov.–mid-Feb.* ⑩ *BP.*

**$–$$** 🏠 **Home by the Sea.** On a headland jutting into the Pacific is this 1985 three-story shingle house. A nearby path leads down to the beach. Both guest rooms have views of the ocean, as does the lower-level solarium and breakfast room, a great spot for watching whales (October–May is the best time) and winter storms. Both rooms have myrtlewood beds. ✉ *444 Jackson St., 97465* ☎ *541/332–2855* ⊕ *www.homebythesea.com* ⇄ *2 rooms* ⚬ *Refrigerators, in-room data ports, cable TV, laundry facilities, Internet; no a/c, no smoking* ▭ *MC, V* ⑩ *BP.*

# Gold Beach

**㉗** *35 mi south of Cape Blanco on U.S. 101.*

The fabled **Rogue River,** which empties into the Pacific at Gold Beach, has been luring anglers and outdoors enthusiasts for more than a century. Zane Grey, in such books as *Rogue River Feud,* was among the writers who helped establish the Rogue's reputation as a renowned chinook salmon and steelhead stream. Celebrities as diverse as Winston Churchill, Clark Gable, and Ginger Rogers, who had a home on the Rogue, have all fished here. It's one of the few U.S. rivers to merit Wild and Scenic status from the federal government.

From spring to late fall an estimated 50,000 visitors descend on the town to take one of the daily jet-boat excursions that roar upstream from Wedderburn, Gold Beach's sister city across the bay, into the Rogue River Wilderness Area. Some of the boats go to Agness, 32 mi upstream, where the riverside road ends and the Wild and Scenic portions of the Rogue begin. Other boats penetrate farther, to the white-knuckle rapids at Blossom Bar, 52 mi upstream. Black bears, otters, beavers, ospreys, egrets, and bald eagles are regularly seen on these trips. From Grave Creek to Watson Creek, along the 40-mi stretch classified as Wild, a National Recreation Trail grants access to this "vestige of primitive America."

Gold Beach is very much a seasonal town, thriving in the summer and nearly deserted the rest of the year. It marks the entrance to Oregon's banana belt, where mild, California-like temperatures take the sting out of winter and encourage a blossoming trade in lilies and daffodils.

The parking lots at **Cape Sebastian State Park** are more than 200 feet above sea level. At the south parking vista you can see up to 43 mi north to Humbug Mountain. Looking south, you can see nearly 50 mi toward Crescent City, California, and the Point Saint George Lighthouse. A deep forest of Sitka spruce covers most of the park. There's a 1½-mi walking trail. ⊠ *U.S. 101* ☎ *541/469–2021 or 800/551–6949* ⊕ *www.prd.state.or.us* ⊠ *Free* ☉ *Daily.*

Area Native American baskets, historic photos, and documents fill the diminutive **Curry County Historical Museum** on the Curry County Fairgrounds. ⊠ *920 S. Ellensburg* ☎ *541/247–6113* ⊠ *Free* ☉ *June–Sept., Tues.–Sat. noon–4; Oct.–May, Sat. 10–4.*

## Where to Stay & Eat

**$$–$$$$** ✕ **Nor'Wester Seafood Restaurant.** At the mouth of the Rogue River, this 24-year-old casual eatery has a cedar interior, fireplace, and waterfront views. Refined fare includes fresh-caught salmon, clam chowder, and fettuccine tapenade. Specialty salads, razor clams, and choice cut steaks are also menu favorites, and the wine list is varied and full. ⊠ *Port of Gold Beach* ☎ *541/247–2333* ⊟ *AE, MC, V* ☉ *No lunch.*

**$$–$$$** ✕ **Chives.** With some of the finest dining on the southern coast, this spot has an ever-changing menu of eclectic regional seafood and meat dishes. Specials might include local Pistol River shiitake mushrooms in Madeira cream, swordfish, fresh Hawaiian ono, scallops, or King salmon purchased that day from the dock. The restaurant faces the ocean and has a 1,200-foot patio with fire pit. ⊠ *29212 U.S. 101* ☎ *541/247–4121* ⊟ *AE, D, MC, V* ☉ *Closed Mon.–Tues.*

**¢** ✕ **Grant's Pancake and Omelette House.** What better way to start your morning than with a heaping stack of buttermilk pancakes topped with melted butter and raspberry syrup or a fluffy omelet stuffed with goodies? Light lunch items such as sandwiches and salads are also available. ⊠ *29790 Ellensburg* ☎ *541/247–7208* ☉ *No dinner* ⊟ *D, MC, V.*

$$$–$$$$     ▣ **Tu Tu' Tun Lodge.** Pronounced "too-*too*-tin," this well-known fishing
**Fodor'sChoice**   resort is on the Rogue River, 7 mi upriver from Gold Beach. Salmon and
★       steelhead fishing made the Tu Tu' Tun's name, but jet-boat excursions,
golf, and other outdoor activities are also draws. All the units in this
small establishment are rustically elegant. Some have hot tubs, others
have fireplaces, and a few have both; private decks overlook the river.
Two deluxe rooms have tall picture windows, tile baths, and outdoor
soaking tubs with river views. The dining room (closed November–April)
serves breakfast, lunch, and dinner; the last, open to nonguests (though
reservations are hard to come by), consists of a five-course prix-fixe meal
that changes nightly. ⊠ *96550 N. Bank Rogue, 97444* ☎ *541/247–6664*
🖷 *541/247–0672* ⊕ *www.tututun.com* 🛏 *18 rooms, 3-bedroom house*
⚷ *Restaurant, 4-hole golf course, pool, dock, boating, fishing, hiking,*
*horseshoes, bar* ⊟ *D, MC, V.*

$$–$$$     ▣ **Inn at Nesika Beach.** The beautifully decorated rooms at this intimate
Victorian-style B&B, 6 mi north of Gold Beach, have hardwood floors
and ocean views. ⊠ *33026 Nesika Rd., 97444* ☎ *541/247–6434*
⊕ *www.moriah.com/nesika* 🛏 *4 rooms* ⚷ *In-room hot tubs; no room*
*phones, no smoking* ⊟ *No credit cards* ⏐⚪⏐ *BP.*

$–$$     ▣ **Inn of the Beachcomber.** As the name suggests, this is a great place for
beachcombing and hunting for beach agates, sand dollars, and other trea-
sures. The hotel is no more than 300 feet from the water, and most rooms
have a view of the ocean. You can walk to restaurants and the county
fairgrounds. ⊠ *29266 Ellensburg Rd. (U.S. 101), 97444* ☎ *541/247–*
*6691 or 888/690–2378* 🖷 *541/247–7981* ⊕ *www.beachcomber-inn.com*
🛏 *43 rooms, 5 suites* ⊟ *AE, D, MC, V.*

$     ▣ **Ireland's Rustic Lodges.** Seven original one- and two-bedroom cabins
filled with rough-hewn charm and 33 motel rooms are available on a
landscaped beachside. Some units have wood-burning fireplaces and decks
overlooking the sea. For the price, you can't beat this accommodation.
⊠ *29330 Ellensburg Ave. (U.S. 101), 97444* ☎ *541/247–7718* 🖷 *541/*
*247–0225* 🛏 *33 rooms, 7 cabins* ⚷ *No-smoking rooms* ⊟ *MC, V.*

## Sports & the Outdoors

GOLF     **Cedar Bend Golf Course** (⊠ 34391 Squaw Valley Rd. ☎ 541/247–6911)
is a 9-hole, par-36 course. The greens fee for 18 holes (play twice) is
$18; a cart costs $20. As you play you may encounter deer, elk, hawks,
eagles, and other wildlife that inhabit the valley around Cedar Fork Creek.

JET-BOAT   **Jerry's Rogue River Jet Boat Trips** (⊠ 29985 Harbor Way ☎ 541/247–4571
EXCURSIONS   or 800/451–364) includes 64-, 80-, or 104-mi round-trip treks up the
Wild and Scenic–designated section of the Rogue River. The trips last
from six to eight hours and leave from the Rogue River Bridge at the
port of Gold Beach Boat Basin. **Official Rogue River Mail Boat Hydro-Jet**
**Trips** (⊠ Mail Boat Dock ☎ 541/247–7033 or 800/458–3511 ⊕ www.
mailboat.com ☺ May–Oct., daily; call for hrs), slightly upstream from
the north end of Rogue River Bridge in Wedderburn, has provided more
than 100 years of continuous postal service, and you can ride along on
its 64-, 80-, or 104-mi trips along the Rogue River. Bring along a picnic lunch, although reasonably priced meals are available at one of
three lodges in Agness. Keep an eye out for bears.

⬚ **en route**   Between Gold Beach and Brookings, you'll cross Thomas Creek
Bridge, the highest span in Oregon. Take advantage of the off-road
coastal viewing points along the 10-mi-long **Samuel H. Boardman**
**State Park**—especially in summer, when highway traffic becomes
heavy and rubbernecking can be dangerous.

# Brookings

**28** *27 mi south of Gold Beach on U.S. 101.*

The little town of Brookings, on the southern Oregon Coast north of the California border, calls itself Oregon's banana belt and, in fact, is often noted for having the highest temperatures in the state. As a result, Brookings also bills itself as the home of winter flowers. The area supplies the majority of lilies in the United States. A botanical garden and an azalea park are among the town's prized assets.

A startling 90% of the pot lilies grown in the United States come from a 500-acre area inland from Brookings. Strangely enough, these white symbols of peace probably wouldn't be grown here in such abundance if not for the fact that in 1942 Brookings experienced the only wartime aerial bombing attack on the U.S. mainland. A Japanese air raid set trees ablaze and understandably panicked the local residents; the imminent ban on Japanese flowers set them to work cultivating the Easter lilies that appear in stores across the country every spring. Mild temperatures along this coastal plain provide ideal conditions for flowering plants of all kinds—even a few palm trees, a rare sight in Oregon.

The town is equally famous as a commercial and sportfishing port at the mouth of the turquoise-blue **Chetco River.** If anything, the Chetco is more highly esteemed among fishermen and wilderness lovers than is the Rogue. A short jetty, used by many local crabbers and fishermen, provides easy and productive access to the river's mouth; salmon and steelhead weighing 20 pounds or more swim here.

Brookings celebrates its horticultural munificence on Memorial Day weekend with an Azalea Festival in **Azalea Park** (⊠ N. Bank Rd. off U.S. 101 downtown) amid blossoming wild azaleas, some of them hundreds of years old. Take the kids to Kidtown to play on its wooden playground equipment.

The **Chetco Valley Historical Museum,** inside a mid-19th-century stagecoach stop and trading post, has some unusual items and is worth a brief visit. An iron casting that bears a likeness to Queen Elizabeth I has led to speculation that it was left during an undocumented landing on the Oregon coast by Sir Francis Drake. On a hill near the museum stands the **World Champion Cypress Tree,** 99 feet tall and with a 27-foot circumference. ⊠ *5461 Museum Rd.* ☎ *541/469–6651* ☞ *$1* ⊙ *Memorial Day–Labor Day, Wed.–Sun. noon–5; Labor Day–Memorial Day, Fri.–Sun. noon–5.*

**Loeb State Park** contains 53 riverside campsites and some fine hiking trails, including one that leads to a hidden redwood grove. There's also a grove of myrtlewood trees, which you'll find only in southwest Oregon and northern California. ⊹ *North bank of Chetco River, 10 mi east of Brookings (follow signs from U.S. 101)* ☎ *541/469–2021* ☞ *Reservations not accepted* ☞ *Day use free, campsites $13–$16* ⊙ *Daily dawn–dusk.*

There is plenty to see and do at **Harris Beach State Park,** where you can watch the gray whales migrate in spring and winter. Bird Island, also called Goat Island, is a National Wildlife Sanctuary and a breeding site for rare birds. There is a campground with 34 full hookups, 52 electrical and 66 tent sites, and 4 yurts. ⊠ *U.S. 101* ☎ *541/469–2021 or 800/ 551–6949* ⊕ *www.prd.state.or.us* ☞ *Free* ⊙ *Daily.*

Witness the art of brandy-making the old-fashioned way at the family-owned **Brandy Peak Distillery.** Fruits are ripened to peak flavor, fermented, and slowly distilled in wood-fired pot stills for natural flavoring and aromas—no additional coloring or flavoring is added. Samples of grappa, pear and grape brandies are provided. The distillery is north of Brookings on Highway 101; take Carpenterville Road and drive 4 mi to Tetley Road, and turn right. ⊠ *18526 Tetley Rd.* ☎ *541/469–0194* ⊕ *www.brandypeak.com* ⊗ *Mar.–Jan., Tues.–Sat. 1–5; Jan.–Mar. by appointment only.*

### Where to Stay & Eat

**$–$$$** ✕ **Smuggler's Cove.** Fishing vessels docked in the adjacent boat basin and picture windows looking out to the sea lend a salty feel to this low-key restaurant. The daily seafood specials—usually halibut and salmon—are the best bets. For lunch try the fish-and-chips or the crab melt, and for a real dinner treat, dive into the steak and lobster for $55.95. ⊠ *16011 Boat Basin Rd.* ☎ *541/469–6006* ⊟ *MC, V.*

**¢–$** ✕ **Chetco Seafood Co.** Homemade chowder is the house specialty here; fish favorites are the grilled cod or halibut. All dishes comes with generous, hearty sides such as baked potatoes and coleslaw. ⊠ *16182 Lower Harbor Rd.* ☎ *541/469–9251* ⊟ *MC, V.*

★ **$$–$$$** ☷ **Chetco River Inn.** Forty acres of private forest surround this remote inn 17 mi from Brookings up the North Bank Road along the Chetco River. The house stands only 100 feet from one of the cleanest rivers in the country, so you can swim in summer and fish in fall and winter. Guests also come here to hike, hunt wild mushrooms, and relax in the library or in front of the fireplace. There's a lavender and herb garden, as well. The host cooks delicious dinners that sometimes star a nickel-bright salmon fresh from the stream. Rooms have thick comforters and panoramic river and forest views. A full breakfast is included. ⊠ *21202 High Prairie Rd., 97415* ☎ *541/670–1645 or 800/327–2688* ⊟ *541/469–4341* ⊕ *www.chetcoriverinn.com* ⊲ *5 rooms, 1 cottage* ⟡ *Picnic area, some in-room hot tubs, boating, fishing, library, laundry facilities; no a/c, no room phones, no smoking* ⊟ *MC, V* ⏍ *BP.*

**¢–$** ☷ **Spindrift Motor Inn.** For simple but clean accommodations at a bargain price, consider this motel, on a cliff overlooking the ocean. All the rooms have balconies and good views. ⊠ *1215 Chetco Ave. (U.S. 101), 97415* ☎ *541/469–5345 or 800/292–1171* ⊟ *541/469–5213* ⊲ *35 rooms* ⟡ *Refrigerators, cable TV, business services* ⊟ *AE, D, DC, MC, V.*

△ **Harris Beach State Park.** Winter brings dramatic storms; summer, warm days and mild nights; and fall, some of the best sunsets of the year at this park with plentiful wildlife viewing. ⟡ *Full hookups, dump station, drinking water, showers, fire pits, picnic tables, electricity, swimming.* ⊠ *Off U.S. 101, north side of Brookings* ⊲ *36 full hookups, 50 electrical, 63 tent sites, 6 yurts.* ☎ *800/452–5687 reservations, 800/551–6949 information* ⊕ *www.oregonstateparks.org* ⊠ *Full hookups $21, electrical hookups $21, tent sites $17, yurts $29* ⊲ *Reservations essential* ⊟ *MC, V.*

# THE OREGON COAST A TO Z

*To research prices, get advice from other travelers, and book travel arrangements, visit www.fodors.com.*

### AIRPORTS

The North Bend Municipal Airport (OTH) is the only airport on the coast serviced by a major carrier; Horizon Air flies into North Bend from Portland four times daily. Regional service is provided at the Newport Municipal Airport (ONP) by two shuttle services, Sky Taxi and Central Oregon Coast Air Service.

🛈 Airport Information **Central Oregon Coast Air Service** ☎ 800/424–3655. **Horizon Air** ☎ 800/547–9308. **Newport Municipal Airport** ☎ 541/867–7422. **North Bend Municipal Airport** ☎ 541/756–8531. **Sky Taxi** ☎ 866/759–8294.

## BIKE TRAVEL

The Coastal Bike Trail follows U.S. 101 but dips in and out of community back roads. Maps, though dated, can be found at local bike shops, and a designated bike lane is marked in white where it parallels the highway. Most larger communities have at least one bike rental shop with mountain and touring bikes available.

🚲 Rentals **The Bike Shop** ⊠ 223 N.W. Nye St., Newport ☎ 541/265-7824. **High Tide Rentals** ⊠ 8073 Cape Arago Hwy., Coos Bay ☎ 541/888-3664. **Wheel Fun Rentals** ⊠ 151 Ave. A, Seaside ☎ 503/738-7412.

## BUS TRAVEL

Greyhound serves Astoria (inside Mini Mart's Video City store), Brookings (inside Fiji Tanning), Coos Bay, Florence, Newport, and other coastal cities. Sunset Empire Transportation provides service on the north coast from Astoria to Cannon Beach, and Porter Stage lines connects the Coos Bay area with Eugene.

🚌 Depots **Greyhound Astoria** ⊠ 95 W. Marine Dr. ☎ 503/325-4162. **Greyhound Brookings** ⊠ 66 Railroad ☎ 541/469-3326. **Greyhound Coos Bay** ⊠ 275 N. Broadway ☎ 541/267-4436. **Greyhound Gold Beach** ⊠ 29770 Colvin St. ☎ 541/247-7710. **Greyhound Newport** ⊠ 956 S.W. 10th St. ☎ 800/231-2222 or 541/265-2253.

🚌 Lines **Greyhound** ☎ 800/231-2222. **Porter Stage Lines** ☎ 541/269-7183. **Sunset Empire Transportation** ☎ 503/325-6500.

## CAR RENTALS

🚗 Agencies **Enterprise** ⊠ 644 W. Marine Dr., Astoria ☎ 503/325-6500 ⊠ 1 Main Ave., Tillamook ☎ 503/842-1076 ⊠ 533 E. Olive St., Newport ☎ 541/574-1999 ⊠ 455 N. Broadway, Coos Bay ☎ 541/266-7100. **Hertz** ⊠ 1492 Duane, Astoria ☎ 503/325-7700 ⊠ 2348 Colorado St., North Bend ☎ 541/746-4416.

## CAR TRAVEL

U.S. 101 runs the length of the coast, sometimes turning inland for a few miles. The highway enters coastal Oregon from Washington State at Astoria and from California near Brookings. U.S. 30 heads west from Portland to Astoria. U.S. 20 travels west from Corvallis to Newport. Highway 126 winds west to the coast from Eugene. Highway 42 leads west from Roseburg toward Coos Bay.

## CHILDREN ON THE OREGON COAST

Rainy days are not unusual on the coast. But depending on the area, a number of options exist for getting out of the rain. On the north end of the coast, visit the Columbia River Maritime Museum and the Children's Museum in Astoria, or spend the day at play at Seasides's arcade. In Tillamook, visit the Tillamook County Creamery. In Newport, tour the Yaquina Head Lighthouse and Yaquina Bay Lighthouse, spend an afternoon at the Oregon Coast Aquarium, or get creative at Tsunami Ceramics, where shelves of pottery await painting. Farther south there are the Sea Lion Caves in Florence and the *Westward Ho!* stern-wheeler on the Siuslaw River.

🎡 **Funland Entertainment Center** ⊠ 201 Broadway, Seaside ☎ 503/738-7361. **Tsunami Ceramics** ⊠ 310 N.W. Coast St. ☎ 541/574-7958. *Westward Ho!* **Sternwheeler** ⊠ by docks near Mo's Restaurant in Florence ☎ 541/997-9691.

## DISABILITIES & ACCESSIBILITY

Travelers with disabilities will find many coastal parks, shops, and attractions easy to maneuver. Yaquina Head Outstanding Natural Area includes Quarry Cove, reportedly the first man-made, universally accessible, barrier-free intertidal zone in the world.

🚹 Local Resources **Yaquina Head Outstanding Natural Area** ⊠ 7580 N.W. Lighthouse Dr., Newport ☎ 541/574-3100

## EMERGENCIES
For any emergency, dial 911 and the appropriate service will be dispatched.

## HEALTH
Keep an eye out for warnings of "red tides," which indicate it is unsafe to eat sea life taken from that area.

## MAIL & SHIPPING
While Internet cafés are few and far between, many community libraries offer Internet access.

🏷 Post Offices **Astoria Post Office** ✉ 750 Commercial St. ☎ 503/338-0316. **Bandon Post Office** ✉ 105 12th St. SE ☎ 541/347-1160. **Brookings Post Office** ✉ 711 Spruce St. ☎ 541/412-0117. **Cannon Beach Post Office** ✉ 163 N. Hemlock St. ☎ 503/436-2822. **Coos Bay Post Office** ✉ 470 Golden Ave. ☎ 541/267-0379. **Florence Post Office** ✉ 770 Maple St. ☎ 541/997-9406. **Lincoln City Post Office** ✉ 1501 S.E. East Devil's Rd. ☎ 541/994-7910. **Newport Post Office** ✉ 310 S.W. 2nd St. ☎ 541/574-6746. **Seaside Post Office** ✉ 300 Ave. A ☎ 503/738-5190. **Tillamook Post Office** ✉ 2200 1st St. ☎ 503/842-2517.

🏷 Internet Cafés & Sites **Coos Bay Public Library** ✉ 525 Anderson Ave. ☎ 541/269-1101. **Mail Boxes Etc.** ✉ 3639 Broadway, North Bend ☎ 541/267-4444. **Newport Public Library** ✉ 35 N.W. Nye ☎ 541/265-2153. **North Bend Public Library** ✉ 1800 Sherman Ave. ☎ 541/756-0400. **Photo Run Plus** ✉ 1241 N. Coast Hwy., Newport ☎ 541/265-5300. **Scanners** ✉ 715 S.W. Hurbert St., Newport ☎ 541/574-3333.

## MEDIA
Nearly every community has a small local newspaper, generally a weekly or semi-weekly publication. Newspapers from nearby cities, Portland, Salem, and Eugene are generally also available depending on the area. In smaller communities, there may not be a local radio station; however, you can usually pick up a station from the next-larger town. The *Oregon Coast Magazine,* a bimonthly publication, has stories and information exclusively about the Oregon coast and can be found at most newsstands and grocery stores.

RADIO & TELEVISION In Astoria, try KAST, 92.9 FM, for soft rock and 1370 AM for news/talk. In Brookings, KURY, 95.3 FM is the contemporary station. In Cannon Beach/Seaside, try KCBZ, 96.5 FM, for adult contemporary. In Coos Bay: KDCQ, 93.5 FM, plays oldies. In Newport, try KNCU, 92.7 FM, for country; KNTT, 1310 AM, for news/talk; and KSND, 95.1 FM, for pop.

The following stations are NPR affiliates. On the north coast: KMUN, 91.9 (Astoria); 89.5 (Cannon Beach); 90.1 (Tillamook). On the central coast: KLCC, 90.5 FM. On the southern coast: KLFR, 89.1 FM (Reedsport); KLFO, 88.1 FM (Florence).

## SPORTS & THE OUTDOORS
Surfing, body boarding, and kayaking are popular along the coast. Stop by the local surf shop for pointers on the places to observe participants and for information on equipment rentals.

🏷 Water Sports **Adventure Kayak** ✉ 315 1st St., Bandon ☎ 541/347-3480. **Big Air Wind Surfing** ✉ 48435 U.S. 101, Langlois ☎ 541/348-2213. **Central Coast Watersports** ✉ 1901 U.S. 101, Florence ☎ 541/997-1812. **Cleanline Surf** ✉ 719 1st Ave., Seaside ☎ 503/738-7888. **Lincoln City Surf Shop** ✉ 4792 S.E. U.S. 101, Lincoln City ☎ 541/996-7433. **Nehalem Bay Kayak Company** ✉ 395 U.S. 101, Nehalem ☎ 503/368-6055. **Ocean Pulse Surfboards** ✉ 429 S.W. Coast Hwy., Newport ☎ 541/265-7745. **Ossie's Surf Shop** ✉ 4860 N. Coast Hwy., Newport ☎ 541/574-4634. **Pacific Wave** ✉ 21 U.S. 101, Warrenton ☎ 888/223-9794.

## TAXIS

While you might spot a taxi passing by, in most communities companies are small and you'll want to call ahead.

🚖 Companies **Royal Cab of Astoria** ☎ 503/325-5818. **Old Gray Cab, Astoria** ☎ 503/338-6030. **Arrow Taxi, Seaside** ☎ 503/738-4005. **Newport Express/Yaquina Cab Company, Newport** ☎ 541/265-9552. **Jerry's Taxi, Coos Bay** ☎ 541/751-0085. **Yellow Cab, Brookings** ☎ 541/469-4838.

## TOURS

Tours on the coast are generally from boats for the purpose of whale- or marine-life-watching.

🚤 Charter & Tour Companies **Depoe Bay Ocean Charters** ⊠ 110 S.E. U.S. 101, Depoe Bay ☎ 541/765-3474. **Jerry's Rogue River Jet Boats** ⊠ U.S. 101 at the Rogue River, Gold Beach ☎ 541/247-4571. **Marine Discovery Tours** ⊠ junction of U.S. 101 and Rte. 20, Newport ☎ 800/903-2628. **Tiki Charters** ⊠ 350 Industry St., Astoria ☎ 503/325-7818.

## TRAIN TRAVEL

With the exception of Astoria, which is serviced by Amtrak from Portland, train travel is not an option on the coast.

## VISITOR INFORMATION

🛈 Tourist Information **Astoria-Warrenton Area Chamber of Commerce** ⊠ 143 S. U.S. 101, Astoria 97103 ☎ 503/861-1031 or 800/875-6807 ⊕ www.oldoregon.com. **Bay Area Chamber of Commerce** ⊠ 50 E. Central St., Coos Bay 97420 ☎ 541/269-0215 or 800/824-8486 ⊕ www.oregonsbayareachamber.com. **Brookings Harbor Chamber of Commerce** ⊠ 16330 Lower Harbor Rd., 97415 ☎ 541/469-3181 or 800/535-9469 ⊕ www.brookingsoregon.com. **Cannon Beach Chamber of Commerce** ⊠ 2nd and Spruce Sts., 97110 ☎ 503/436-0910 ⊕ www.cannonbeach.org. **Florence Area Chamber of Commerce** ⊠ 270 U.S. 101, 97439 ☎ 541/997-3128 or 800/524-4864 ⊕ www.florencechamber.com. **Greater Newport Chamber of Commerce** ⊠ 555 S.W. Coast Hwy., 97365 ☎ 503/265-8801 or 800/262-7844 ⊕ www.newportchamber.org. **Lincoln City Visitors Center** ⊠ 801 S.W. U.S. 101, Suite 1, 97367 ☎ 541/994-8378 or 800/452-2151 ⊕ www.oregoncoast.org. **Seaside Visitors Bureau** ⊠ 7 N. Roosevelt Ave., 97138 ☎ 503/738-6391 or 800/444-6740 ⊕ www.clatsop.com/seaside. **Tillamook Chamber of Commerce** ⊠ 3705 U.S. 101 N, 97141 ☎ 503/842-7525. **Yachats Area Chamber of Commerce** ⊠ U.S. 101 near 2nd St., 97498 ☎ 541/547-3530 ⊕ www.yachats.org.

# PORTLAND

## FODOR'S CHOICE

Heathman Hotel, *downtown*
Higgins, *downtown contemporary fare*
Japanese Garden, *landscaping in Washington Park*
Lion and the Rose, *B&B east of the Willamette*
Montage, *spicy Cajun east of the Willamette*
Paley's Place, *Nob Hill bistro*
Portland Classical Chinese Garden, *harmony in Old Town/ Chinatown*
Portland Saturday Market, *Old Town*
Powell's City of Books, *Pearl District*

## HIGHLY RECOMMENDED

**RESTAURANTS**   Couvron, *downtown*
Genoa, *near Hawthorne District*
Three Doors Down, *Hawthorne District*
Nicholas' Restaurant, *near the Morrison Bridge*
Pambiche, *near Laurelhurst*
The Heathman, *downtown*

**HOTELS**   Benson Hotel, *downtown*
5th Avenue Suites Hotel, *downtown*
Governor Hotel, *downtown*
Inn @ Northrup Station, *Nob Hill*
MacMaster House, *Washington Park area*
McMenamins Kennedy School, *near Alberta District*
Portland's White House, *Irvington*

**SIGHTS**   International Rose Test Garden, *Washington Park*
Oregon History Center, *downtown*
Oregon Museum of Science and Industry, *under the Hawthorne Bridge*
Oregon Zoo, *Washington Park*
Pittock Mansion, *north of Washington Park*
Portland Art Museum, *downtown*

By Donald S.
Olson

Updated by
Sarah Kennedy

**PORTLAND IS LOADED WITH ENERGY.** For decades this inland port on the Willamette River was the undiscovered gem of the West Coast, often overlooked by visitors seeking more sophisticated milieus. But in the past decade, people have begun flocking here in unprecedented numbers—to visit and to live.

The city's proximity to mountains, ocean, and desert adds an element of natural grandeur to its urban character. Majestic Mt. Hood, about 70 mi to the east, acts as a kind of mascot, and on a clear day several peaks of the Cascade Range are visible, including Mt. St. Helens, which dusted the city with ash when it erupted in 1980. The west side of town is built on a series of forested hills that descend to the downtown area, the Willamette River, and the flatter east side. Filled with stately late-19th-century and modern architecture, linked by an effective transit system, and home to a vital arts scene, Portland is a place where there's much to do day or night, rain or shine.

The quality of life remains a high and constant priority here. As far back as 1852, Portland began setting aside city land as parks. This legacy has added immeasurably to the city's attractiveness and environmental mystique. Included among Portland's 250 parks, public gardens, and greenways are the nation's largest urban wilderness, the world's smallest park, and the only extinct volcano in the lower 48 states within a city's limits.

A temperate climate and plenty of precipitation keep Portland green year-round, ideal for the state's gardeners. The City of Roses, as it's known, celebrates its favorite flower with a monthlong Rose Festival—a June extravaganza with auto and boat races, visiting navy ships, and a grand parade second in size only to Pasadena's Rose Parade. But the floral spectacle really starts three months earlier, when streets and gardens bloom with the colors of flowering trees, camellias, rhododendrons, and azaleas.

Portland, which began as an Indian clearing of about 1 square mi, has become a metropolis of more than 2 million people; within its 132-square-mi borders are 90 diverse and distinct neighborhoods. A center for sports and sportswear makers, the four-county metropolitan area, which includes the burgeoning city of Vancouver across the state line in Washington, contains the headquarters and factories of Jantzen, Nike, Columbia Sportswear, and Pendleton. The city's western suburbs of Beaverton and Hillsboro have been called the Silicon Forest because of their high concentration of high-tech manufacturing plants, including those of Intel, Tektronix, and Fujitsu. High-tech shipbuilding, furniture, fabricated metals, and other manufacturers have broadened the region's economic base even further. And its prime location at the confluence of the Columbia and Willamette rivers has helped Portland become the third-largest port on the West Coast. Five main terminals export automobiles, steel, livestock, grain, and timber products. Shipyards repair tankers, tugboats, cruise ships, and navy vessels.

The arts here flourish in unexpected places: there's artwork in police stations, office towers, banks, playgrounds, and on the sides of buildings. The brick-paved transit mall downtown is virtually an outdoor gallery of fountains and sculptures. As for the performing arts, Portland has several professional theater companies, the Oregon Symphony, the Portland Opera, and Chamber Music Northwest, to name a few. Those into nightlife will also find some of the best live-band and club action in the country. Families have plenty of kid-friendly attractions to enjoy, including the Oregon Zoo, Oaks Amusement Park, and Oregon Museum of Science and Industry.

2

*Numbers in the text correspond to numbers in the margin and on the Down-town, the Pearl District & Old Town/Chinatown; Washington Park & Forest Park; and East of the Willamette River maps.*

**If you have**
**1 day**

Spend the morning exploring downtown. Visit the **Portland Art Museum 6** ► or the **Oregon History Center 5**, stop by the historic **First Congregational Church 4** and **Pioneer Courthouse Square 1**, and take a stroll along the Park Blocks or Waterfront Park. Eat lunch and do a little shopping along Northwest 23rd Avenue in the early afternoon, and be sure to walk down a few side streets to get a look at the beautiful historic homes in Nob Hill. From there, drive up into the northwest hills by the **Pittock Mansion 50**, and finish off the afternoon at the **Japanese Garden 46** and the **International Rose Test Garden 45** in Washington Park. If you still have energy, head across the river for dinner on Hawthorne Boulevard; then drive up to **Mt. Tabor Park 54** for Portland's best view of sunset.

**If you have**
**3 days**

On your first day, follow the one-day itinerary above, exploring downtown, Nob Hill, and Washington Park, but stay on the west side for dinner, and take your evening stroll in Waterfront Park. On your second morning, visit the **Portland Classical Chinese Garden 29** in Old Town, and then head across the river to the **Sellwood District 57** for lunch and antiquing. Stop by the **Crystal Springs Rhododendron Garden 56**; then head up to **Hawthorne District 53** in the afternoon. Wander through the Hawthorne and Belmont neighborhoods for a couple hours, stop by **Laurelhurst Park 55**, and take a picnic dinner up to **Mt. Tabor Park 54**. In the evening, catch a movie at the Bagdad Theatre, or get a beer at one of the east side brewpubs. On day three, take a morning hike in **Hoyt Arboretum 44** or **Forest Park 51**; then spend your afternoon exploring the galleries in the Pearl District and on northeast Alberta Street. Drive out to the Grotto, and then eat dinner at the Kennedy School or one of the other McMenamins brewpubs.

**If you have**
**7 days**

With a whole week to enjoy the city, you can take a little more time to absorb it all. Spend your first day in downtown alone, devoting a few hours each to the **Portland Art Museum 6** ► and the **Oregon History Center 5**. Wander along the park blocks and through Riverfront Park, and stop into some of the historic buildings described in the walking tours, such as the **Old Church 7** and **City Hall 19**. On day two, spend the morning at the **Portland Classical Chinese Garden 29**, and take the early part of the afternoon to explore the galleries and shops in the trendy Pearl District. For a mid-afternoon break, stop by the Ecotrust building, get a cup of coffee at World Cup Coffee, and drink it while sitting on the "eco-roof," where you can get a good overview of the neighborhood; then stop by **Powell's City of Books 33** to browse for a little while. In the late afternoon drive out to **Forest Park 51** and take a hike in the country's largest urban wilderness.

On your third day, stop by Whole Foods Supermarket on West Burnside, pack a picnic lunch, and spend the day at Washington Park. Start out with a hike through the **Hoyt Arboretum 44**; then visit the **Forest Discovery Center Museum 48** and the **Oregon Zoo 47**. Spend the afternoon at the **Japa-**

nese Garden ④ and the **International Rose Test Garden** ④, and if you have
time, take a tour of **Pittock Mansion** ⑤. Spend the first part of your fourth
day exploring Northwest 23rd Avenue and Nob Hill. Visit some of the unique
shops, take the walking tour of the neighborhood's historic homes, and drink
a cup of coffee at one the area's myriad coffeehouses. In the afternoon drive
to **Mt. Tabor Park** ⑤ for a short walk.

Devote yourself to the east side of the river for the next two days. On day
five, spend at least a few hours exploring the Hawthorne shopping district,
stop by **Laurelhurst Park** ⑤ for a scenic break in the action, and eat lunch
on Hawthorne or Belmont Street. Head up to the northeast in the afternoon,
winding your way through the streets of historic Irvington, just north of
Broadway, to see some of the most beautiful Victorian homes in the city. Spend
some time in the galleries and shops on Alberta Street, and, if you have
time, head out to 82nd Avenue to see the Grotto. If you enjoyed your visit
to Edgefield, stop by the Kennedy School to see another fascinating McMenamins
renovation project; you can get dinner here, watch a movie in the evening,
or get a drink at one of their bars. On day six, go to the **Oregon Museum
of Science and Industry (OMSI)** ⑤ in the morning; then keep heading south
to **Sellwood District** ⑤ for lunch and some antiques shopping. Take a walk
at the **Crystal Springs Rhodendron Garden** ⑤ and through Reed College campus. On your last day, you might want to see a little of the surrounding area
of Portland. If so, you can take a drive along the Columbia River Gorge via
I–84, or take a day trip to the coast on U.S. 26. If you're happy to stay
closer to Portland, you might want to visit Sauvie Island to see some wildlife,
pick berries, or walk along the beach. Or, you might want to revisit some
of your favorite neighborhoods and explore them a little more fully.

---

Northeast Alberta Street has emerged as an art center, with more than
two dozen art galleries and studios and a growing number of coffeehouses, restaurants, barbecues, and specialty shops. Galleries and businesses host the "Art on Alberta" sidewalk event on the last Thursday
evening of each month. A street fair in September enlivens the neighborhood with arts-and-crafts booths, music, and food vendors.

Although Portland is now the 22nd largest metropolitan area in the nation, it has only one major-league sports team—the National Basketball Association's Portland Trail Blazers. In spring 2001, an extensive
renovation of Portland's old Civic Stadium—renamed PGE Park—was
completed, with hopes of attracting a major-league baseball team.

For all its focus on the future, though, Portland has not forgotten its
past. Architectural preservation is a major preoccupation, particularly
when it comes to the 1860s brick buildings with cast-iron columns and
the 1890s ornate terra-cotta designs that grace areas like the Skidmore
Old Town, Yamhill, and Glazed Terra-Cotta national historic districts.
In the Pearl District, older industrial buildings are being given new life
as residential lofts, restaurants, office space, galleries, and boutiques. It
has also become the center of the metro area's plan to more efficiently
use available urban space by revitalizing existing neighborhoods. Not
all Portlanders are happy with the results, which have brought increased
traffic congestion and constant construction. But the new century also
brought a renewed emphasis on mass transit. An extension of the MAX
light-rail line to Portland International Airport opened in fall 2001, and
the Portland Central City Streetcar began operation in summer 2001,

connecting Portland State University, downtown, and the Pearl District and Nob Hill neighborhood. The city's farsighted approach to growth and its pitfalls means it reaps all of the benefits and few of the problems of its boom. As a result, Portland is better than ever, cultivating a new level of sophistication, building on enhanced prosperity, and bursting with fresh energy.

# EXPLORING PORTLAND

The Willamette River is Portland's east–west dividing line. Burnside Street separates north from south. The city's 200-foot-long blocks make them easy to walk, but you can also explore the downtown core and Nob Hill by MAX light rail, the Central City Streetcar, or Tri-Met buses ( ⇨ Portland A to Z). Closer to the downtown core are the Pearl District and Old Town/Chinatown. Both the Old Town and Pearl District have a plethora of restaurants, specialty shops, and nightspots.

## Downtown

Portland has one of the most attractive and inviting downtown urban cores in the United States. Clean, compact, and filled with parks, plazas, and fountains, it holds a mix of new and historic buildings. Hotels, shops, museums, restaurants, and entertainment can all be found here, and the entire downtown area is part of the Tri-Met transit system's Fareless Square, within which you can ride MAX, the Central City Streetcar, or any bus for free.

*Numbers in the text correspond to numbers in the margin and on the Downtown, the Pearl District & Old Town/Chinatown map.*

**a good walk**

Begin at Southwest Morrison Street and Southwest 6th Avenue at **Pioneer Courthouse Square** ❶ ▶. From the square, walk west on Yamhill for three blocks. Between Yamhill and Taylor streets on 10th Avenue is the **Central Library** ❷. Continue on 10th Avenue for two blocks and turn left on Main Street. Cross over the **South Park Blocks** and find the **Portland Center for the Performing Arts** ❸ between Park Avenue and Broadway. Back along the Park Blocks, the **First Congregational Church** ❹ will be on your left on the corner of Madison, followed by the **Oregon History Center** ❺, directly across the street, impossible to miss under the mural of Lewis and Clark and the Oregon Trail along the side of the building. West on Jefferson across the Park Blocks is the **Portland Art Museum** ❻. Walk west on Jefferson and south on 11th Avenue to reach the **Old Church** ❼. Loop back east to the South Park Blocks along Columbia Street and head south on Park Avenue to Market Street, where the campus of **Portland State University** ❽ begins.

Continue east on Market to 3rd Avenue to reach the **Keller Auditorium** ❾, which has a waterfall fountain. **KOIN Center** ❿, the most distinctive highrise in downtown Portland, occupies the next block to the north. From here, head east on Clay Street to the waterfront and, crossing Naito Parkway, take a leisurely stroll through **Governor Tom McCall Waterfront Park** ⓫ past the **Salmon Street Fountain.** Heading back west along Taylor, you are now in the **Yamhill National Historic District** ⓬ of cast-iron and other buildings. Turn left on 2nd Avenue and proceed one block south toward the **World Trade Center** ⓭.

After wandering around the complex, continue west on Salmon Street. At the corner of Salmon and 3rd Avenue sits the **Mark O. Hatfield U.S. Courthouse** ⓮. The **State of Oregon Sports Hall of Fame** ⓯ sits nearby, between 3rd and 4th avenues on Salmon. Cross the street and find yourself in **Chapman and Lownsdale squares** ⑯, which abut the **Justice Center** ⑰, across 3rd Avenue. **Terry Schrunk Plaza** ⑱ sits one block south, and you can pass directly through the plaza into **City Hall** ⑲ across 4th Avenue. Walk through City Hall and exit onto 5th Avenue. Turn right and head north on 5th Avenue, stopping at the **Portland Building** ⑳ on the next block. Head one more block up 5th Avenue and turn left on Salmon Street, to find **Niketown** ㉑ at the corner of 6th and Salmon. If you are interested in art and architecture, continue on 6th back past Pioneer Courthouse Square, and explore the area between Oak and Yamhill on 5th and 6th avenues. This is the heart of the **Glazed Terra-Cotta National Historic District** ㉒.

TIMING  The entire downtown walk can be accomplished in about two hours. If you're planning to stop at the Oregon History Center or Portland Art Museum (both closed on Monday), add at least one to two hours for each. Allot 15 or 30 minutes for the Sports Hall of Fame, which is closed on Sunday.

## What to See

❷ **Central Library.** The elegant central staircase and elaborate ceiling ornamentation make this no ordinary library. With a gallery space on the second floor, frequent musical performances in the spacious upper-floor lobbies, and a Starbucks in the first-floor reading room, this renovated building is well worth a walk around. ⊠ *801 S.W. 10th Ave., Downtown* ☎ *503/988–5123* 🎟 *Free* ⊗ *Tues.–Thurs. 9–9, Fri. and Sat. 9–6, Sun. 1–5.*

⑯ **Chapman and Lownsdale squares.** During the 1920s, these parks were segregated by sex: Chapman, between Madison and Main streets, was reserved for women, and Lownsdale, between Main and Salmon streets, was for men. The elk statue on Main Street, which separates the parks, was given to the city by former mayor David Thompson. It purportedly honors an elk that grazed here in the 1850s.

⑲ **City Hall.** Portland's four-story, granite-faced City Hall, which was completed in 1895, is an example of the Renaissance Revival style popular in the late 19th century. Italian influences can be seen in the porch, the pink scagliola columns, the cornice embellishments, and other details. The building was renovated in the late 1990s. ⊠ *1220 S.W. 5th Ave., Downtown* ☎ *503/823–4000* ⊗ *Weekdays 8–5.*

❹ **First Congregational Church.** This Venetian Gothic church, modeled after Boston's Old South Church, was completed in 1895, and you still can hear its original bell, purchased in 1871, ringing from its 175-foot tower. The church provided much of the land on which the Portland Center for the Performing Arts was built. ⊠ *1126 S.W. Park Ave., Downtown* ☎ *503/228–7219* 🎟 *Free.*

㉒ **Glazed Terra-Cotta National Historic District.** A century ago terra-cotta was often used in construction because of its availability and low cost; it could also be easily molded into the decorative details that were popular at the time. Elaborate lions' heads, griffins, floral displays, and other classical motifs adorn the rooflines of the district's many buildings that date from the late 1890s to the mid-1910s. Public art lines 5th and 6th avenues. On 5th is a sculpture that reflects light and changing colors, a nude woman made of bronze, a copper and redwood creation inspired by the Norse god Thor, and a large limestone cat in repose. Sixth Avenue has a steel-and-concrete matrix, a granite-and-brick fountain, and an abstract modern depiction of an ancient Greek defending Crete. ⊠ *S.W. 5th and S.W. 6th Aves. between S.W. Oak and S.W. Yamhill Sts., Downtown.*

2

## Biking

Portland has been called the best city in the country for biking, and with bike lanes galore, mild weather year-round, and a beautiful waterfront to ride along, it's no wonder. With all this encouragement, cyclists in Portland have gotten creative: not only does cycling provide an excellent form of transportation around here, it also has evolved into a medium of progressive politics and public service. Riders gather at least once every month to ride en masse through the streets of the city in an event called Critical Mass to show solidarity as a powerful alternative to an auto-society, and they have been known to gather force for the purpose of political protest. In addition, several bike co-ops have sprung up throughout the city in the past several years, devoted to providing used bikes at decent prices to members of the community, as well as to teaching bike maintenance and the economic and environmental benefits of becoming a commuter on two wheels.

## Brews and Views

Everyone knows that Oregon loves its microbrews and that good beer drinking makes for some of Oregon's favorite pastimes, but Portlanders have taken this a step further, creating a recreational venue fondly called the Brew and View; that is, a movie theater showing second-run, classic, or cult films for $2 or $3, where you can buy a pitcher of good locally brewed beer and a slice of pizza to enjoy while watching. The McMenamins brothers are largely to thank for this phenomenon, being the masterminds behind such popular spots as the Bagdad Theatre, the Mission Theatre, and the St. John's Pub, but unaffiliated establishments like the Laurelhurst Theatre manage to edge in on the action as well.

## Bridges

With a river running through the center of the city, Portland has one of the most interesting urban landscapes in the country, due in no small part to the several unique bridges that span the width of the Willamette River. Five of the city's ten bridges are drawbridges, frequently raised to let barges go through, and there is something awe-inspiring and anachronistic in watching a portion of a city's traffic and hubbub stand still for several minutes as a slow-moving vessel floats through still water. Each bridge is beautiful and different: the St. John's Bridge has elegant 400-foot towers, the Broadway Bridge is a rich red hue, the arches of the huge two-level Fremont Bridge span the river gracefully, and the Steel Bridge has a pedestrian walkway just 30 feet above the water, allowing walkers and bikers to get a fabulous view of the river.

---

**⑪ Governor Tom McCall Waterfront Park.** The park named for a former governor of Oregon revered for his statewide land-use planning initiatives stretches north along the Willamette River for about a mile to Burnside Street. Broad and grassy, it yields what may be the finest ground-level view of downtown Portland's bridges and skyline. The park, on the site of a former expressway, hosts many events, among them the Rose Festival, classical and blues concerts, and the Oregon Brewers Festival. The five-day **Cinco de Mayo Festival** (☎ 503/222–9807) in early May celebrates Portland's sister-city relationship with Guadalajara, Mexico. Next to the Rose Festival, this is one of Portland's biggest get-togethers. Food

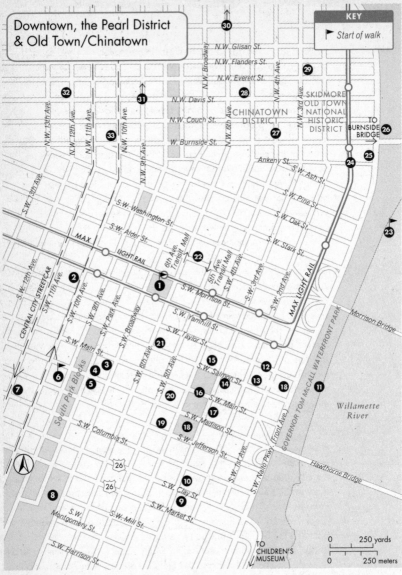

Downtown, the Pearl District & Old Town/Chinatown

KEY

▶ Start of walk

N.W. Glisan St.
N.W. Flanders St.
N.W. Everett St.
N.W. Davis St.
N.W. Couch St.
W. Burnside St.
Ankeny St.
S.W. Ash St.
S.W. Pine St.
S.W. Oak St.
S.W. Stark St.
S.W. Washington St.
S.W. Alder St.
S.W. Morrison St.
S.W. Yamhill St.
S.W. Taylor St.
S.W. Salmon St.
S.W. Main St.
S.W. Madison St.
S.W. Jefferson St.
S.W. Columbia St.
S.W. Clay St.
S.W. Market St.
S.W. Mill St.
S.W. Montgomery St.
S.W. Harrison St.

N.W. 13th Ave.
N.W. 12th Ave.
N.W. 11th Ave.
N.W. 10th Ave.
N.W. 9th Ave.
N.W. 6th Ave.
N.W. 4th Ave.
N.W. 3rd Ave.
S.W. 13th Ave.
S.W. 12th Ave.
S.W. 11th Ave.
S.W. 10th Ave.
S.W. 9th Ave.
S.W. Park Ave.
S.W. Broadway
S.W. 6th Ave.
S.W. 5th Ave.
S.W. 4th Ave.
S.W. 3rd Ave.
S.W. 2nd Ave.
S.W. Nalto Pkwy. (Front Ave.)

CHINATOWN DISTRICT
SKIDMORE OLD TOWN NATIONAL HISTORIC DISTRICT
TO BURNSIDE BRIDGE

MAX LIGHT RAIL
CENTRAL CITY STREETCAR
6th Ave. Transit Mall
5th Ave. Transit Mall

GOVERNOR TOM McCALL WATERFRONT PARK
South Park Blocks

Willamette River

Morrison Bridge
Hawthorne Bridge

26

TO CHILDREN'S MUSEUM

0    250 yards
0    250 meters

American Advertising Museum .......... 28

Central Library ........ 2

Chapman and Lownsdale Squares .... 16

Chinatown Gate ...... 27

City Hall .............. 19

First Congregational Church ............ 4

Glazed Terra-Cotta National Historic Distict ............ 22

Governor Tom McCall Waterfront Park ..... 11

Japanese-American Historical Plaza ...... 26

Jean Vollum Natural Capital Center ....... 31

Justice Center ........ 17

Keller Auditorium ..... 9

KOIN Center ......... 10

Mark O. Hatfield U.S. Courthouse ..... 14

Niketown ........... 21

Old Church ........... 7

Oregon History Center .............. 5

Oregon Maritime Center and Museum ........ 23

Pioneer Courthouse Square .............. 1

Portland Art Museum .......... 6

Portland Building .... 20

Portland Center for the Performing Arts .. 3

Portland Classical Chinese Garden ...... 29

Portland Institute for Contemporary Art ... 32

Portland Saturday Market ............. 25

Portland State University ........... 8

Powell's City of Books .......... 33

Skidmore Fountain ... 24

State of Oregon Sports Hall of Fame ... 15

Terry Schrunk Plaza ............... 18

Union Station ........ 30

World Trade Center .............. 13

Yamhill National Historic District ...... 12

and arts-and-crafts booths, stages with mariachi bands, and a carnival complete with a Ferris wheel line the riverfront for the event. Bikers, joggers, and roller and in-line skaters enjoy the area year-round. The arching jets of water at the **Salmon Street Fountain** change configuration every few hours and are a favorite cooling-off spot during the dog days of summer. ⊠ *S.W. Naito Pkwy. (Front Ave.) from south of Hawthorne Bridge to Burnside Bridge, Downtown.*

**⑰ Justice Center.** This modern building houses the county courts and support offices and, on the 16th floor, the **Police Museum** (☎ 503/823–0019 🖃 free ☉ Mon.–Thurs. 10–3), which has uniforms, guns, and badges worn by the Portland Police Bureau. Thanks to a city ordinance requiring that 1% of the development costs of new buildings be allotted to the arts, the center's hallways are lined with travertine sculptures, ceiling mosaics, stained-glass windows, and photographic murals. You're welcome to peruse the works of art. ⊠ *1111 S.W. 2nd Ave., Downtown.*

**❾ Keller Auditorium.** Home base for the Portland Opera, the former Civic Auditorium also hosts traveling musicals and other theatrical extravaganzas. The building itself, part of the Portland Center for the Performing Arts, is not particularly distinctive, but the **Ira Keller Fountain,** a series of 18-foot-high stone waterfalls across from the front entrance, is worth a look. ⊠ *S.W. 3rd Ave. and Clay St., Downtown* ☎ *503/274–6560* ⊕ *www.pcpa.com.*

**❿ KOIN Center.** An instant landmark after its completion in 1984, this handsome tower with a tapering form and a pyramidal top takes its design cues from early art deco skyscrapers. Made of brick with limestone trim and a blue metal roof, the tower has offices (including those of the CBS-TV affiliate and a radio station), a multiplex cinema, and, on its top floors, some of the most expensive condominiums in Portland. ⊠ *S.W. Columbia St. and S.W. 3rd Ave., Downtown.*

**⑭ Mark O. Hatfield U.S. Courthouse.** The New York architectural firm Kohn Pedersen Fox designed this skyscraper, which was completed in 1997. The sophisticated exterior is clad in Indiana limestone, and the courtroom lobbies have expansive glass walls. Rooftop terraces yield grand city views but, due to heightened security, are not always open to the public; ask the security guards whether the roof is open. ⊠ *S.W. 3rd Ave. between Main and Salmon Sts., Downtown.*

> **need a break?** Stop at **Martinotti's** (⊠ 404 S.W. 10th Ave., Downtown ☎ 503/224–9028), on the Central City streetcar line, for a glass of wine and a deli sandwich. You can also shop for kitchen gadgets, bottled wines, and packaged snacks.

**㉑ Niketown.** This futuristic F. A. O. Schwarz for the athletically inclined is a showplace for Nike, the international sportswear giant headquartered in suburban Beaverton. A life-size plaster cast of Michael Jordan captured in mid-jump dangles from the ceiling near the basketball shoes. Autographed sports memorabilia, video monitors, and statuary compete for your attention with the many products for sale. But don't expect any bargains: prices are full retail, and the word "sale" is almost as taboo around here as the name Reebok. If you don't get your fill at this branch, there's an outpost at Portland International Airport. ⊠ *930 S.W. 6th Ave., Downtown* ☎ *503/221–6453* ⊕ *www.niketown.com* ☉ *Mon.–Thurs. and Sat. 10–7, Fri. 10–8, Sun. 11:30–6:30.*

# CloseUp

## COMING UP ROSES

EVERY JUNE SINCE 1905, PORTLAND, the City of Roses, has rolled out its rosy red carpet and welcomed thousands of visitors from around the world to its annual **Rose Festival**. The monthlong extravaganza now draws a total of some 2 million people, making it the event of Portland's year. During the festival, the roses in the 4½-acre International Rose Test Garden—and all over the city—are at their finest.

The festivities begin on the first Friday in June, with the naming and crowning of a rose queen, chosen each year from among candidates representing 14 Portland high schools. The ceremony is held at the Arlene Schnitzer Concert Hall. In honor of each rose queen, a bronze star is embedded in a sidewalk in the International Rose Test Garden, and a fireworks spectacular downtown lights up the sky over the Willamette River after the coronation. On the day after the coronation, about 350,000 people turn out to see the dozens of illuminated floats in the **Starlight Parade** downtown.

The highlight of the 25 days of events and festivities is the **Grand Floral Parade** on the second Saturday in June, when around half a million people jam downtown streets to watch dozens of all-floral floats, marching bands, and equestrian performers. The parade is the second-largest all-floral parade in North America, second only to the Tournament of Roses Parade in Pasadena, California. Many people camp out overnight on downtown streets to hold a good spot along the parade route, but you can reserve a paid seat ($10–$20) in special viewing areas.

The Rose Festival coincides with **Fleet Week**, which usually gets under way around June 10. Thousands of sailors and marines cruise into town on dozens of military ships that dock downtown, along the seawall on the west side of the Willamette River. Tens of thousands of people board the many cutters, destroyers, and frigates of the U.S. Navy, U.S. Coast Guard, and Royal Canadian Navy for free tours. On the Up River/Down River Cruises you can pay about $20 to ride a U.S. Navy or U.S. Coast Guard ship along the Columbia River from Longview, Washington, to Portland (cruises restricted to those age eight and over).

In late June the **Rose Festival Airshow,** one of the nation's best, draws huge crowds to the Hillsboro Airport in suburban Portland. Dozens of aircraft, from biplanes to fighter jets, buzz the west side of town during the three-day event. The U.S. Air Force's Thunderbirds have appeared in past shows. The show costs about $10 for general admission, but reserved seating is also available.

Contending with the glory of the roses, the works of 125 juried artists from Oregon and around the United States appear at the **Portland Arts Festival** during three days in late June. Sculpture, jewelry, paintings, and photography fill the South Park Blocks near Portland State University, amid live music and food booths. The Portland Rose Society's **Annual Spring Rose Show** at Lloyd Center's Ice Chalet is the largest and longest-running rose show in the country. Local growers show off their best buds and compete for trophies on the Thursday and Friday before the Grand Floral Parade.

**Portland Rose Festival** (✉ 202 N.W. 2nd Ave., Portland 97209 ☎ 503/227–2681 ⊕ www.rosefestival.org).

**7 Old Church.** This building erected in 1882 is a prime example of Carpenter Gothic architecture. Tall spires and original stained-glass windows enhance its exterior of rough-cut lumber. The acoustically resonant church hosts free classical concerts at noon each Wednesday. If you're lucky you'll get to hear one of the few operating Hook and Hastings tracker pipe organs. ✉ *1422 S.W. 11th Ave., Downtown* ☎ *503/222–2031* ⊕ *www.oldchurch.org* ✉ *Free* ☉ *Weekdays 11–3, Sat. by appointment.*

★ **5 Oregon History Center.** Impressive eight-story-high trompe l'oeil murals of Lewis and Clark and the Oregon Trail (the route the two pioneers took from the Midwest to the Oregon Territory) cover two sides of this downtown museum, which follows the state's story from prehistoric times to the present. Recent renovations include the construction of a new entrance and lobby space as well as several new spaces for large exhibits and public gatherings. Anticipated exhibits include "Oregon History A to Z," a comprehensive overview of the state's past; "Oregon Country"; and the "Lewis and Clark National Bicentennial Exhibition," showcasing the largest collection of artifacts from the expedition ever assembled. The center's research library is open to the public; its bookstore is a good source for maps and publications on Pacific Northwest history. ✉ *1200 S.W. Park Ave., Downtown* ☎ *503/222–1741* ⊕ *www.lewisandclarktrail.com* ✉ *$6* ☉ *Tues.–Sat. 10–5, Sun. noon–5.*

▶ **1 Pioneer Courthouse Square.** Downtown Portland's public heart and commercial soul are centered in this amphitheatrical brick piazza, whose design echoes the classic central plazas of European cities. Special events often take place in this premier people-watching venue, where the neatly dressed office crowd mingles with some of the city's stranger elements. If you're here at noon on a day when all systems are operational, you might be lucky enough to see the goofy weather machine blast a fanfare and a shining sun, stormy dragon, or blue heron rise out of a misty cloud to confirm the day's weather. On Sunday, **vintage trolley** cars run from the MAX station here to Lloyd Center, with free service every half hour between noon and 6 PM. Call to check on the current schedule (☎ 503/323–7363). You can pick up maps and literature about the city and the state here at the **Portland/Oregon Visitors Association** (☎ 503/275–8355 ⊕ www.pova.com ☉ weekdays 8:30–5:30, Sat. 10–4, Sun. 10–2). Directly across the street is one of downtown Portland's most familiar landmarks, the classically sedate **Pioneer Courthouse.** Built in 1869, it's the oldest public building in the Pacific Northwest. ✉ *701 S. W. 6th Ave., Downtown.*

★ ▶ **6 Portland Art Museum.** The treasures at the Pacific Northwest's oldest visual- and media-arts facility span 35 centuries of Asian, European, and American art. A high point is the Center for Native American Art, with regional and contemporary art from more than 200 tribes. Keep an eye out for the large winter festival dish, the *potlatch,* and the transformation masks that really do transform. The film center presents the annual Portland International Film Festival in February and March and the Northwest Film Festival in early November. Also take a moment to linger in the peaceful outdoor sculpture garden. ✉ *1219 S.W. Park Ave., Downtown* ☎ *503/226–2811, 503/221–1156 film schedule* ⊕ *www.pam.org* ✉ *$10* ☉ *Tues., Wed., and weekends 10–5, Thurs. and Fri. 10–8.*

**20 Portland Building.** *Portlandia,* the second-largest hammered-copper statue in the world, surpassed only by the Statue of Liberty, kneels on the second-story balcony of one of the first postmodern buildings in the United States. The building itself generates strong feelings; chances are you'll either love it or hate it. The controversial structure, architect Michael Graves's first major design commission, is buff-colored, with brown and blue trim and exterior decorative touches. The interior spaces are dark and clumsily executed. A permanent exhibit of public art includes a huge fiberglass mold of Portlandia's face and original works by local artists. ⊠ *1120 S.W. 5th Ave., Downtown* ⊡ *Free* ⊙ *Weekdays 8–6.*

❸ **Portland Center for the Performing Arts.** The "old building" and the hub of activity here is the **Arlene Schnitzer Concert Hall,** host to the Oregon Symphony, musical events of many genres, and lectures. Across Main Street, but still part of the center, is the 292-seat **Delores Winningstad Theater,** used for plays and special performances. Its stage design and dimensions are based on those of an Elizabethan-era stage. The 916-seat **Newmark Theater,** which houses Portland Center Stage, a highly regarded resident theater company, is also part of the complex. The section of the street connecting the old and new buildings is sometimes blocked off for food fairs, art shows, and other events. ⊠ *S.W. Broadway and S.W. Main St., Downtown* ☎ *503/796–9293* ⊕ *www.pcpa.com* ⊙ *Free tours Wed. at 11* AM, *Sat. every ½ hr 11–1, and 1st Thurs. of month at 6* PM.

❽ **Portland State University.** The state's only university in a major metropolitan area takes advantage of downtown's South Park Blocks to provide trees and greenery for its 15,000 students. The compact campus, between Market Street and I–405, spreads west from the Park Blocks to 12th Avenue and east to 5th Avenue. Seven schools offer undergraduate, master's, and doctoral degrees. ⊠ *Park Ave. and Market St., Downtown* ☎ *503/725–3000* ⊕ *www.pdx.edu.*

⓯ **State of Oregon Sports Hall of Fame.** This museum has two multimedia theaters and sports memorabilia associated with prominent Oregonian athletes and organizations such as Heisman Trophy winner Terry Baker, the Portland Trail Blazers professional basketball team, and baseball player Mickey Lolich, who pitched for the Detroit Tigers in three World Series. ⊠ *321 S.W. Salmon St., Downtown* ☎ *503/227–7466* ⊕ *www.pova. com* ⊡ *$4* ⊙ *Mon.–Sat. 10–5.*

⓲ **Terry Schrunk Plaza.** A terraced amphitheater of green lawn and brick, shaded by flowering cherry trees, the plaza is a popular lunch spot for the office crowd. ⊠ *Between S.W. 3rd and 4th Aves. and S.W. Madison and Jefferson Sts., Downtown.*

⓭ **World Trade Center.** The three sleek, handsome World Trade Center buildings, designed by the Portland architectural firm Zimmer Gunsel Frasca, are connected by sky bridges. Retail stores, a restaurant, coffee shops, banks, and travel agencies occupy the ground floors. ⊠ *Salmon St. between S.W. 2nd Ave. and S.W. Naito Pkwy., Downtown.*

⓬ **Yamhill National Historic District.** Many examples of 19th-century cast-iron architecture have been preserved within this district's six square blocks. Because the cast-iron facade helped support the main structure, these buildings traditionally did not need big, heavy walls to bear the weight; the interior spaces could therefore be larger and more open. North and west of this area, along 2nd Avenue, galleries exhibit fine art, ceramics, photography, and posters. On Southwest Naito Parkway at Taylor Street is **Mill Ends Park,** which sits in the middle of a traffic island. This patch of urban tranquillity, at 24 inches in diameter, has been recognized by *Guinness World Records* as the world's smallest official city park. ⊠ *Between S.W. Naito Pkwy. and S.W. 3rd Ave. and S.W. Morrison and S.W. Taylor Sts., Downtown.*

| off the beaten path | **LEWIS & CLARK COLLEGE** – The college was founded by Presbyterian pioneers as Albany Collegiate Institute in 1867. The school moved to the former Lloyd Frank estate in Portland's southwest hills in 1942 and took the name Lewis & Clark College. The campus is in a wooded residential area 6 mi from downtown Portland. ⊠ *S.W. Palatine Hill Rd.* ☎ *503/768–7000* ⊕ *www.lclark.edu* ✉ *Free* ⊗ *Weekdays.* |
|---|---|

## Pearl District & Old Town/Chinatown

The Skidmore Old Town National Historic District, commonly called Old Town/Chinatown, is where Portland was born. The 20-square-block section, bounded by Oak Street to the south and Everett Street to the north, includes buildings of varying ages and architectural designs. Before it was renovated, this was skid row, and vestiges of that condition remain. One of Portland's newest attractions is here: the Portland Classical Chinese Garden, which opened in summer 2000. In addition to yielding many Chinese restaurants and gift shops, the area is home to several gay bars and restaurants. MAX serves the area with a stop at the Old Town/Chinatown station.

Bordering Old Town to the northwest is the Pearl District. Formerly a warehouse area along the railroad yards, the Pearl District is the fastest-growing part of Portland. Mid-rise residential lofts have sprouted on almost every block, and boutiques, galleries, and trendy restaurants line the streets. The new Central City streetcar line passes through here on its way from Nob Hill to downtown and Portland State University.

*Numbers in the text correspond to numbers in the margin and on the Downtown, the Pearl District & Old Town/Chinatown map.*

a good walk

Begin in Waterfront Park at the **Oregon Maritime Center and Museum** ㉓ ▶. Cross Southwest Ash Street and walk north on Southwest 1st Avenue to **Skidmore Fountain** ㉔, which is the centerpiece of Ankeny Square. On Saturday and Sunday the area west of the fountain near 2nd Avenue is the site of the **Portland Saturday Market** ㉕. Go north one block on Naito Parkway past the Burnside Bridge to the **Japanese-American Historical Plaza** ㉖. Walk west on Burnside Street to Northwest 4th Avenue and the **Chinatown Gate** ㉗, the official entrance to the Chinatown District. Continue through the gate, down 4th Avenue to Davis Street, and turn left. Head west one block to the **American Advertising Museum** ㉘. Head down 5th Avenue to Everett Street and turn right; the **Portland Classical Chinese Garden** ㉙ is two blocks east.

Head back west along Everett and turn right on 6th Avenue. Walk about five blocks to its terminus at **Union Station** ㉚. Head back along 6th Avenue for two blocks, and turn right on Hoyt Street. Follow Hoyt Street to 9th Avenue, and look for the **Jean Vollum Natural Capital Center** ㉛ one block to your right, at the corner of 9th Avenue and Irving Street. Back on Hoyt Street, turn right and walk three blocks north. Turn left on 12th Avenue, and proceed three blocks to the **Portland Institute for Contemporary Art** ㉜. Walk two blocks farther on 12th Avenue and turn left on Burnside. Two blocks south on Burnside, at the corner of 10th Avenue, is **Powell's City of Books** ㉝.

TIMING    You can easily walk through Old Town/Chinatown and the Pearl District in an hour or two. However, a visit to the Portland Classical Chinese Garden is a must, so allow some extra time. If you also visit the American Advertising Museum or PICA, or plan on delving into the shelves at Powell's, allow a half day in the area.

## What to See

**㉘ American Advertising Museum.** This museum is devoted exclusively to advertising. Exhibits celebrate memorable campaigns, print advertisements, radio and TV commercials, and novelty and specialty products. The museum also has the industry's most comprehensive collection of advertising and business artifacts. ⊠ *211 N.W. 5th Ave., Old Town/ Chinatown* ☎ *503/226-0000* ⊕ *www.admuseum.com* ✉ *$5* ⊘ *Thurs.–Sat. 11–5.*

**㉗ Chinatown Gate.** Recognizable by its five roofs, 64 dragons, and two huge lions, the Chinatown Gate is the official entrance to the **Chinatown District.** During the 1890s, Portland had the second-largest Chinese community in the United States. Today's Chinatown is compressed into several blocks with restaurants (though many locals prefer Chinese eateries outside the district), shops, and grocery stores. ⊠ *N.W. 4th Ave. and Burnside St., Old Town/Chinatown.*

**㉖ Japanese-American Historical Plaza.** Take a moment to study the evocative figures cast into the bronze columns at the plaza's entrance; they show Japanese-Americans before, during, and after World War II— living daily life, fighting in battle for the United States, and marching off to internment camps. More than 110,000 Japanese-Americans were interned by the American government during the war. This park was created to commemorate their experience and contributions. Simple blocks of granite carved with haiku poems describing the war experience powerfully evoke this dark episode in American history. ⊠ *East of Naito Pkwy. between W. Burnside and N.W. Davis Sts., Old Town/Chinatown.*

> **need a break?**
>
> For a break from sightseeing and shopping, head back south under the Burnside Bridge into cool, dark **Kell's Irish Restaurant & Pub** (⊠ 112 S.W. 2nd Ave., between S.W. Ash and S.W. Pine Sts., Skidmore District ☎ 503/227–4057) for a pint of Guinness and authentic Irish pub fare—and be sure to ask the bartender how all those folded-up dollar bills got stuck to the ceiling.

**㉛ Jean Vollum Natural Capital Center.** Known to most locals simply as the Ecotrust Building, this building has a handful of environment-friendly businesses and organic-friendly retail spaces including Hot Lips Pizza, World Cup Coffee, and Patagonia (outdoor clothes). Originally built in 1895 and purchased by Ecotrust in 1998, the building has been significantly adapted to serve as a landmark in sustainable, "green" building practices. Take the self-guided tour of the building, which begins with the original "remnant wall" on the west side of the parking lot; proceeds throughout the building; and ends on the "eco-roof," a grassy rooftop used to provide temperature insulation, where you can get a great view of the Pearl District. ⊠ *721 N.W. 9th Ave., Pearl District* ☎ *503/ 227–6225* ⊕ *www.ecotrust.org* ✉ *Free* ⊘ *Weekdays 9–5; ground-floor businesses also evenings and weekends.*

**㉓ Oregon Maritime Center and Museum.** Local model makers created most of this museum's models of ships that plied the Columbia River. Contained entirely within the stern-wheeler steamship *Portland,* docked at the foot of Southwest Pine Street on the seawall in Tom McCall Waterfront Park, this small museum provides an excellent overview of Oregon's maritime history. ⊠ *On steamship at the end of S.W. Pine St., in Waterfront Park, Skidmore District* ☎ *503/224–7724* ⊕ *www. oregonmaritimemuseum.org* ✉ *$4* ⊘ *Fri.–Sun. 11–4.*

**㉙ Portland Classical Chinese Garden.** In a twist on the Joni Mitchell song, the
Fodor'sChoice   city of Portland and private donors took down a parking lot and unpaved
★   paradise, as it were, when they created this wonderland abutting the Pearl
District and Old Town/Chinatown. It's the largest Suzhou-style garden outside China, with a large lake, bridged and covered walkways, koi- and water
lily-filled ponds, rocks, bamboo, statues, waterfalls, and courtyards. A team
of 60 artisans and designers from China literally left no stone unturned—
500 tons of stone were brought here from Suzhou—in their efforts to give
the windows, roof tiles, gateways, including a "moongate," and other architectural aspects of the Garden some specific meaning or purpose, and
you could easily spend hours during multiple visits pondering the construction, design, or situation of the different elements. You will, for instance, never encounter a straight path here—the walkways wind through
the landscape to encourage you to slow down; there are even spots where
you're encouraged to walk barefoot. Everchanging vantage points make
you feel like you're the only one in the garden even if it's crowded, but try
to arrive right at opening time for a maximum dose of serenity. Also on
the premises are a gift shop and a two-story teahouse overlooking the lake
and garden. ⊠ *N.W. 3rd Ave. and Everett St., Old Town/Chinatown*
☎ *503/228–8131* ⊕ *www.chinesegarden.org* ✉ *$7* ⊗ *Nov.–Mar., daily
10–5; Apr.–Oct., daily 9–6. Tours daily at noon and 1.*

**㉜ Portland Institute for Contemporary Art (PICA).** Founded in 1995, PICA seeks
to advance new ideas in art by bringing innovative artists working in
all mediums (visual arts, dance, music, theatre) to Portland to showcase
their work. Exhibits and performances vary greatly throughout the
year; call ahead or visit the Web site to find out what to expect. ⊠ *219
N.W. 12th Ave., Pearl District* ☎ *503/242–1419* ⊕ *www.pica.org* ✉ *$3*
⊗ *Wed.–Sat. noon–6.*

**㉕ Portland Saturday Market.** On weekends from March to Christmas, the
Fodor'sChoice   west side of the Burnside Bridge and the Skidmore Fountain environs
★   has North America's largest open-air handicraft market. This is not upscale shopping by any means, but if you're looking for crystals, yard
goods, beaded hats, stained glass, birdhouses, jewelry, flags, wood and
rubber stamps, or custom footwear and decorative boots, you stand a
good chance of finding them. Entertainers and food and produce booths
add to the festive feel. ⊠ *Under west end of Burnside Bridge, from S.
W. Naito Pkwy. to Ankeny Sq., Skidmore/Old Town* ☎ *503/222–6072*
⊕ *www.saturdaymarket.org* ⊗ *Mar.–Dec., Sat. 10–5, Sun. 11–4:30.*

**㉝ Powell's City of Books.** The largest independent bookstore in the world,
Fodor'sChoice   with more than 1.5 million new and used books, Powell's is a Portland
★   landmark that can easily consume you for several hours if you're not
careful. Rooms and ample signs are helpfully color-coded according to
the types of books, so you'll have a blueprint for wandering. Be sure to
espy the pillar bearing signatures of prominent sci-fi authors who have
passed through the store—the scrawls are protected by a jagged length
of Plexiglas. At the very least, stop into Powell's for a peek just to say
you've seen it, or grab a cup of coffee at the adjoining branch of World
Cup Coffee. Should you miss the store or require another dose, there's
a branch at Portland International Airport that's useful for whiling
away an hour or two. ⊠ *1005 W. Burnside St., Pearl District* ☎ *503/
228–4651* ⊕ *www.powells.com* ⊗ *Daily 9 AM–11 PM.*

**㉔ Skidmore Fountain.** This unusually graceful fountain built in 1888 is
the centerpiece of **Ankeny Square,** a plaza around which many community activities take place. Two nymphs uphold the brimming basin
on top; citizens once quenched their thirst from the spouting lions' heads
below, and horses drank from the granite troughs at the base of the

fountain. ⊠ *S.W. Ankeny St. between S.W. Naito Pkwy. and 1st Ave., Skidmore District.*

**㉚ Union Station.** You can always find your way to Union Station by heading toward the huge neon GO BY TRAIN sign that looms high above the station. The vast lobby area, with high ceilings and marble floors, is particularly worth a brief visit if you hold any nostalgia for the heyday of train travel in the United States. It's a far cry from the Greyhound station next door. ⊠ *800 N.W. 6th Ave., Old Town/Chinatown* ☎ *503/ 273–4866.*

# Nob Hill & Vicinity

The showiest example of Portland's urban chic is Northwest 23rd Avenue—sometimes referred to with varying degrees of affection as "trendy-third"—a 20-block thoroughfare that cuts north–south through the neighborhood known as Nob Hill. Fashionable since the 1880s and still filled with Victorian residential architecture, the neighborhood is a mixed-use cornucopia of old Portland charm and new Portland hip. With its cafés, restaurants, galleries, and boutiques, it's a delightful place to stroll, shop, and people-watch. More restaurants, shops, and nightspots can be found on Northwest 21st Avenue, a few blocks away. Finding parking in this neighborhood has become such a challenge that the city put in a streetcar line. The Central City streetcar line runs from Legacy Good Samaritan Hospital in Nob Hill, through the Pearl District on 10th and 11th avenues, connects with MAX light rail near Pioneer Courthouse Square downtown, and then continues on to Portland State University. The line will eventually extend to RiverPlace on the Willamette River.

*Numbers in the text correspond to numbers in the margin and on the Nob Hill & Vicinity map.*

### Two Good Walks

Northwest 23rd Avenue between West Burnside Street and Northwest Lovejoy Street—the east–west-running streets are in alphabetical order—is the heart of Nob Hill. There's such a profusion of coffee bars and cafés along the avenue that some locals call it Latte-land Central. You don't need a map of the avenue, just cash or credit cards. Some of the shops and restaurants are in newly designed quarters, and others are tucked into restored Victorian and other century-old homes and buildings. As it continues north past Lovejoy Street, the avenue begins to quiet down. Between Overton and Pettygrove streets, a block of open-porch frame houses converted into shops typifies the alternative, new-age side of Portland. The **Pettygrove House** ㉞ ▶, a Victorian gingerbread on the corner of 23rd Avenue and Pettygrove Street, was built by the man who gave Portland its name. Continue on 23rd Avenue past Pettygrove to Quimby Street to reach the **Clear Creek Distillery** ㉟.

There's much more to Nob Hill than Northwest 21st and 23rd avenues, something you'll discover if you walk among the neighborhood's Victorian residences. Most of the noteworthy structures are private residences and do not have identifying plaques, nor do they admit visitors. Begin at 23rd Avenue and Flanders Street, with the 1891 **Trevett-Nunn House** ㊱ ▶, an excellent example of the Colonial Revival style. Continue east to the 1907 **Day Building** ㊲, an apartment building fronted by Corinthian columns. Farther east is the Byzantine **Temple Beth Israel** ㊳, completed in 1928. At Flanders and 17th Avenue head north (to the left) to Irving Street. The **Campbell Townhouses** ㊴ are the only known example of brick row-house construction in Oregon. Continue west on Irving and north (to the right) on 18th Avenue to the **Ayer-Shea House** ㊵, an elegant Colonial Revival house.

Heading west on Johnson Street, you'll pass the Italianate-style Sprague-Marshall-Bowie House, built in 1882, and the 1893 Albert Tanner House, a rare Stick-style residence with a wraparound porch and richly decorated front gables. The 2½-story **Mary Smith House** ㊷ offers an unusual variation on the Colonial Revival style. At 22nd Avenue, turn south (left) to reach the **Nathan Loeb House** ㊷, a fine late-19th-century Queen Anne–style structure. Continue south on 22nd Avenue and turn east (left) on Hoyt Street to reach the Joseph Bergman House, a High Victorian Italianate-style home built in 1885. Head two blocks east to 20th Avenue and two blocks south (to the right) to reach the rare, Shingle-style **George Huesner House** ㊸.

TIMING    Strolling along 23rd Avenue from Burnside Street to Pettygrove Street can take a half hour or half a day, depending on how many eateries or shops lure you in along the way. The tour of neighborhood Victorian residences can be done in about an hour.

## What to See

㊵   **Ayer-Shea House.** This Colonial Revival house was built in 1892 by Whidden and Lewis, who also designed Portland's City Hall. ⊠ *1809 N.W. Johnson St., Nob Hill.*

㊴   **Campbell Townhouses.** These six attached buildings with Queen Anne–style detailing, reminiscent of row houses in San Francisco and along the East Coast, have undergone virtually no structural modification since they were built in 1893. ⊠ *1705–1719 N.W. Irving St., Nob Hill.*

㉟   **Clear Creek Distillery.** The distillery keeps such a low profile that it's practically invisible. But ring the bell and someone will unlock the wrought-iron gate and let you into a dim, quiet tasting room where you can sample Clear Creek's world-famous Oregon apple and pear brandies and grappas. ⊠ *1430 N.W. 23rd Ave., near Quimby St., Nob Hill* ☎ *503/248–9470* ⊕ *www.clearcreekdistillery.com* ☉ *Weekdays 8:30–4:30 or by appointment.*

**need a break?**   You won't have any trouble finding a place to sit and caffeinate in this Northwest Portland neighborhood. **Coffee Time** (⊠ *710 N.W. 21st Ave., Nob Hill* ☎ *503/497–1090*) serves all the requisite brews and pastries. Inside, discover a surprising labyrinth of dark, cozy rooms with couches, small tables, and floor lamps. Retreat into its depths or sit outdoors at a sidewalk table.

㊲   **Day Building.** This 1907 example of the Colonial Revival style offers a front facade of large, fluted columns rising more than 30 feet to ornate Corinthian capitals. ⊠ *2068 N.W. Flanders St., Nob Hill.*

㊸   **George Huesner House.** Typical of the Shingle style that came into vogue in the 1890s, this home was designed by Edgar Lazarus, architect of landmarks such as Vista House in the Columbia River Gorge. ⊠ *333 N.W. 20th Ave., Nob Hill.*

㊷   **Mary Smith House.** Dating from 1906, this home has a central second-story bow window and a full-length veranda with a central bowed portico supported by Ionic columns. ⊠ *2256 N.W. Johnson St., Nob Hill.*

㊷   **Nathan Loeb House.** One of the most ornate Victorians in Portland, the Loeb House has turned-wood posts, wood arches with central pendants and sunburst spandrel patterns, and a projecting ground-floor section with an ornamental three-bay round-arch window. ⊠ *726 N.W. 22nd Ave., Nob Hill.*

Ayer-Shea
House ...... 40

Campbell
Town-
houses ..... 39

Clear Creek
Distillery .... 35

Day
Building .... 37

George
Huesner
House ...... 43

Mary Smith
House ...... 41

Nathan Loeb
House ...... 42

Pettygrove
House ...... 34

Temple Beth
Israel ....... 38

Trevett-Nunn
House ...... 36

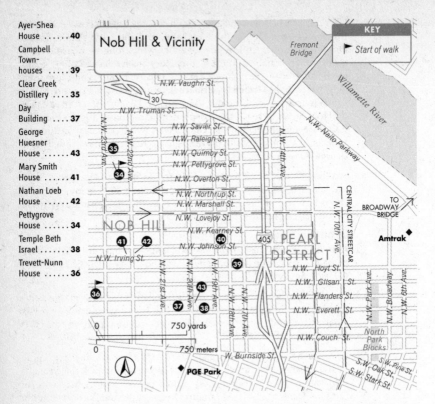

**34 Pettygrove House.** Back in 1845, after he'd bought much of what is now downtown Portland for $50, Francis Pettygrove and his partner, Asa Lovejoy, flipped a coin to decide who would name the still unbuilt city. Pettygrove won and chose Portland, after a town in his native Maine. His beautifully restored Victorian gingerbread house was built in 1892. Inside, **Vivace** creperie and coffee house has several laid-back and decorative sitting areas with colorful walls and comfortable chairs spread among rooms on both levels of the house. ✉ *2287 N.W. Pettygrove St., Nob Hill.*

**38 Temple Beth Israel.** The imposing sandstone, brick, and stone structure with a massive domed roof and Byzantine styling was completed in 1928 and still serves a congregation first organized in 1858. ✉ *1972 N.W. Flanders St., Nob Hill.*

**36 Trevett-Nunn House.** Built in 1891, this Colonial Revival home is the oldest extant residence designed by Whidden and Lewis, Portland's most distinguished late-19th-century architectural firm. ✉ *2347 N.W. Flanders St., Nob Hill.*

# Washington Park & Forest Park

*Numbers in the text correspond to numbers in the margin and on the Washington Park & Forest Park map.*

**a good tour**

The best way to get to Washington Park is via MAX light rail, which travels through a tunnel deep beneath the city's West Hills. Be sure to check out the Washington Park station, the deepest (260 feet) transit station in North America. Graphics on the walls depict life in the Portland area during the past 17 million years. There's also a core sample of the bedrock taken from the mountain displayed along the walls. If you're driving, head west of downtown on West Burnside Street and south (turn left) on Southwest Tichner Drive to reach 322-acre Washington Park, home to the **Hoyt Arboretum** ㊹, the **International Rose Test Garden** ㊺, and the **Japanese Garden** ㊻. By car, the **Oregon Zoo** ㊼, **Forest Discovery Center Museum** ㊽, and **Children's Museum** ㊾ can best be reached by heading west on U.S. 26. North of the park is the opulent **Pittock Mansion** ㊿. Also north of Washington Park is **Forest Park** (51).

TIMING You could easily spend a day at either Washington Park or Forest Park. Plan on at least two hours at the zoo; an hour or more at the arboretum, rose garden, and Japanese Garden; and an hour to tour the Pittock Mansion and its grounds.

## What to See

㊾ **Children's Museum.** In summer 2001 this museum for kids 12 and under moved from downtown to Washington Park across from the Oregon Zoo. Hands-on play is the order of the day, with rotating exhibits, a clay shop, and a child-size grocery store. The zoo parking lot provides free parking. Take MAX light rail to Washington Park station. ✉ *4015 S.W. Canyon Rd., Washington Park (U.S. 26, Zoo exit)* ☎ *503/223–6500* *$5.50* ⏲ *Tues.–Sun. 9–5.*

㊽ **Forest Discovery Center Museum.** The two-level center, across from the Oregon Zoo, takes its arboreal interests seriously—its spokesperson is a 70-foot-tall talking tree. Outside, a 1909 locomotive and antique logging equipment are displayed, and inside is the multi-image "Forests of the World," a collection of 100-year-old wood, and a gift shop. Take MAX to the Washington Park station. ✉ *4033 S.W. Canyon Rd., Washington Park* ☎ *503/228–1367* 🌐 *www.worldforest.org* *$5* ⏲ *Daily 9–5.*

(51) **Forest Park.** The nation's largest (5,000 acres) urban wilderness, this city-owned park, with more than 100 species of birds and 50 species of mammals, has more than 50 mi of trails. The **Portland Audubon Society** (✉ 5151 N.W. Cornell Rd. ☎ 503/292–9453) supplies free maps and sponsors a bevy of bird-related activities in the heart of the only old-growth forest in a major U.S. city. Programs include guided bird-watching events, and there's a hospital for injured and orphaned birds as well as a gift shop stocked with books, feeders, and bird lovers' paraphernalia. ✥ *Take N.W. Lovejoy St. west to where it becomes Cornell Rd. and follow to the park, past Nob Hill in the Northwest* ☎ *503/823–7529* *Free* ⏲ *Daily dawn–dusk.*

㊹ **Hoyt Arboretum.** Ten miles of trails wind through the arboretum, which has more than 800 species of plants and one of the nation's largest collections of coniferous trees; pick up trail maps at the visitor center. Also here are the Winter Garden and a memorial to veterans of the Vietnam War. ✉ *4000 S.W. Fairview Blvd., Washington Park* ☎ *503/228–8733* 🌐 *www.portlandparks.org* *Free* ⏲ *Arboretum daily dawn–dusk, visitor center daily 9–4.*

★ ㊺ **International Rose Test Garden.** Despite the name, these grounds are not an experimental greenhouse laboratory but three terraced gardens, set on 4 acres, where 10,000 bushes and 400 varieties of roses grow. The flowers, many of them new varieties, are at their peak in June and July and September and October. From the gardens, you can see highly photogenic views of the downtown skyline and, on fine days, the Fuji-shape slopes of Mt. Hood, 50 mi to the east. Summer concerts take place in the garden's amphitheater. Take MAX light rail to Washington Park station and transfer to Bus No. 63. ✉ *400 S.W. Kingston Ave., Wash-*

Children's
Museum .... **49**

Forest
Discovery
Center
Museum .... **48**

Forest Park .. **51**

Hoyt
Arboretum ... **44**

International
Rose
Test Garden .. **45**

Japanese
Garden ..... **46**

Oregon Zoo .. **47**

Pittock
Mansion .... **50**

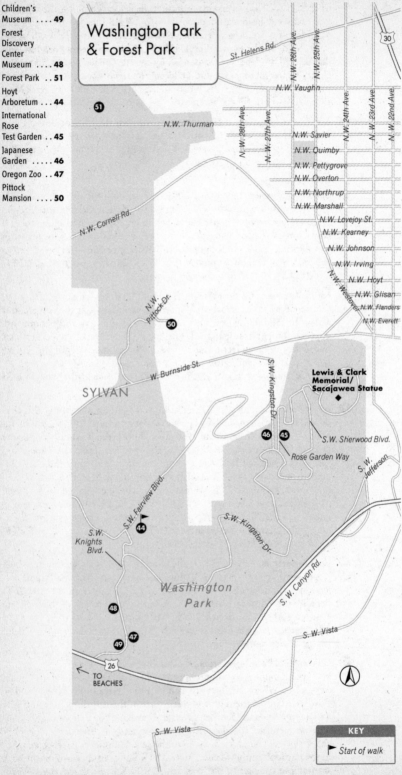

# Washington Park & Forest Park

St. Helens Rd.

30

N.W. Vaughn

N.W. 26th Ave.

N.W. 25th Ave.

N.W. 24th Ave.

N.W. 23rd Ave.

N.W. 22nd Ave.

**51**

N.W. Thurman

N.W. 28th Ave.

N.W. 27th Ave.

N.W. Savier

N.W. Quimby

N.W. Pettygrove

N.W. Overton

N.W. Northrup

N.W. Marshall

N.W. Lovejoy St.

N.W. Kearney

N.W. Johnson

N.W. Irving

N.W. Hoyt

N.W. Glisan

N.W. Flanders

N.W. Everett

N.W. Cornell Rd.

N.W. Westover

N.W. Pittock Dr.

**50**

W. Burnside St.

SYLVAN

**Lewis & Clark
Memorial/
Sacajawea Statue**

◆

S.W. Kingston Dr.

**46** **45**

S.W. Sherwood Blvd.

Rose Garden Way

S.W. Jefferson

S.W. Fairview Blvd.

**44**

S.W. Kingston Dr.

S.W.
Knights
Blvd.

*Washington
Park*

S.W. Canyon Rd.

**48**

**47**

**49**

S.W. Vista

26

← TO
BEACHES

S.W. Vista

*ington Park* ☎ *503/823–3636* ⊕ *www.parks.ci.portland.or.us* ✉ *Free* ⊙ *Daily dawn–dusk.*

**㊻ Japanese Garden.** The most authentic Japanese garden outside Japan is
**Fodor'sChoice** nestled among 5½ acres of Washington Park above the International Rose
★ Test Garden. This serene spot, designed by a Japanese landscape master and opened to the public in 1967, represents five separate garden styles: Strolling Pond Garden, Tea Garden, Natural Garden, Sand and Stone Garden, and Flat Garden. The Tea House was built in Japan and reconstructed here. The west side of the Pavilion has a majestic view of Portland and Mt. Hood. Take MAX light rail to Washington Park station and transfer to Bus No. 63. ✉ *611 S.W. Kingston Ave., Washington Park* ☎ *503/223–1321* ⊕ *www.japanesegarden.com* ✉ *$6.50* ⊙ *Oct.–Mar., Mon. noon–4, Tues.–Sun. 10–4; Apr.–Sept., Mon. noon–7, Tues.–Sun. 10–7.*

★ ☺ **㊼ Oregon Zoo.** This beautiful animal park in the West Hills is famous for its Asian elephants. Major exhibits include an African section with rhinos, hippos, zebras, and giraffes. Steller Cove, a state-of-the-art aquatic exhibit, has two Steller sea lions and a family of sea otters. Other exhibits include polar bears, Siberian tigers, chimpanzees, an Alaska Tundra exhibit with wolves and grizzly bears, a penguinarium, and habitats for beavers, otters, and reptiles native to the west side of the Cascade Range. During the summer a 4-mi round-trip narrow-gauge train operates from the zoo, chugging through the woods to a station near the International Rose Test Garden and the Japanese Garden. Take the MAX light rail to the Washington Park station. ✉ *4001 S.W. Canyon Rd., Washington Park* ☎ *503/226–7627* ⊕ *www.oregonzoo.org* ✉ *$8; free 2nd Tues. of month after 1PM* ⊙ *Oct.–Mar., daily 9–4, Apr.–Sept., daily 9–6.*

★ **㊿ Pittock Mansion.** Henry Pittock, the founder and publisher of the *Oregonian* newspaper, built this 22-room mansion, which combines French Renaissance and Victorian styles. The opulent manor, built in 1914, is filled with art and antiques of the 1880s. The 46-acre grounds, north of Washington Park and 1,000 feet above the city, have superb views of the skyline, rivers, and the Cascade Range. There's a tea house and a small hiking trail. ✉ *3229 N.W. Pittock Dr. (from W. Burnside St. heading west, turn right on N.W. Barnes Rd. and follow signs), north of Washington Park* ☎ *503/823–3624* ⊕ *www.portlandparks.org* ✉ *$5.25* ⊙ *June–Aug., daily 11-4, Sept.–Dec. and Feb.–May, daily noon–4.*

## East of the Willamette River

Portland is known as the City of Roses, but the 10 distinctive bridges spanning the Willamette River have also earned it the name Bridgetown. The older drawbridges, near downtown, open several times a day to allow passage of large cargo ships and freighters. You can easily spend a couple of days exploring the attractions and areas on the east side of the river.

*Numbers in the text correspond to numbers in the margin and on the East of the Willamette River map.*

**a good tour**

Most people visit Portland's east-side destinations separately, and by car rather than public transportation. At the western end of Hawthorne Boulevard, along the banks of the Willamette River, is the **Oregon Museum of Science and Industry** ㊲ ▶. After visiting OMSI head east on busy Hawthorne Boulevard through the **Hawthorne District** ㊳, where there are interesting shops and restaurants. Hawthorne runs into **Mt. Tabor Park** ㊴ at its eastern end. Park your car and hike up the mountain for a spectacular view of the city and surrounding mountains. Head back toward town and stop at **Laurelhurst Park** 55, a stately enclave. Head south to **Crystal Springs Rhododendron Garden** 56, and then make your way back toward the river and the shops of the **Sellwood District** 57. At river's edge stands **Oaks Amusement Park** 58, a good spot for kids; another option is to drive to **North Clackamas Aquatic Park** 59, where you can all unwind in the wave pool.

TIMING    You could spend a pleasant hour or so strolling through each of the parks, gardens, and neighborhoods here. Plan to spend two to three hours each at either the Oregon Museum of Science and Industry or the amusement park.

## What to See

56 **Crystal Springs Rhododendron Garden.** For much of the year this 7-acre retreat near Reed College is used by bird-watchers and those who want a restful stroll. But starting in April, thousands of rhododendron bushes and azaleas burst into flower. The peak blooming season for these woody shrubs is May; by late June the show is over. ⊠ *S.E. 28th Ave. (west side, 1 block north of Woodstock Blvd.), Sellwood/Woodstock area* ☎ *503/771–8386* ⊕ *www.portlandparks.org* ⊠ *$3 Mar.–Labor Day, Thurs.–Mon. 10–6; otherwise free* ⊙ *Daily dawn–dusk.*

At the **Bagdad Theatre and Pub** (⊠ 3702 S.E. Hawthorne Blvd., Hawthorne District ☎ 503/236–9234) you can buy a pint of beer and a slice of pizza and watch a movie.

53 **Hawthorne District.** Though it has become more upscale in recent years, this neighborhood stretching from the foot of Mt. Tabor to 30th Avenue tends to attract a slightly younger, more "alternative" crowd than downtown or Nob Hill, and it is one of the most crowded and popular areas east of the Willamette. With many bookstores, coffeehouses, taverns, restaurants, antiques stores, used-CD shops, and boutiques filling the streetfront, it is easy to spend a few hours wandering the street. Finding a parking space can be a real challenge on Hawthorne; be prepared to look on a few side streets. ⊠ *S.E. Hawthorne Blvd. between 30th and 42nd Aves., Hawthorne District.*

55 **Laurelhurst Park.** Manicured lawns, stately trees, and a wildfowl pond make this 25-acre southeast Portland park a favorite urban hangout. Laurelhurst, one of the city's most beautiful neighborhoods, surrounds the park. ⊠ *S.E. 39th Ave. between S.E. Ankeny and Oak Sts., Laurelhurst* ⊕ *www.portlandparks.org* ⊙ *Daily dawn–dusk.*

54 **Mt. Tabor Park.** Dirt trails and an asphalt road wind through forested hillsides and past good picnic areas to the top of Mt. Tabor, which provides a panoramic view of Portland's West Hills and Cascade mountain peak. Mt. Tabor is an extinct volcano; the buttes and conical hills east of the park are evidence of the gigantic eruptions that formed the Cascade Range millions of years ago. Said to be the best place in the city to watch the sunset, the park is also a popular place to bike, hike, picnic, or just throw a Frisbee. ⊠ *S.E. 60th Ave. and Salmon St., east of Hawthorne District* ☎ *503/823–7529* ⊕ *www.portlandparks.org.*

off the
beaten
path

**THE GROTTO** – Owned by the Catholic Church, the National Sanctuary of Our Sorrowful Mother, as it's officially known, displays more than 100 statues and shrines in 62 acre of woods. The grotto was carved into the base of a 110-foot cliff and has a replica of Michelangelo's *Pietà*. The real treat is found after ascending the cliff face via elevator, as you enter a wonderland of gardens, sculptures and shrines, and a glass-walled cathedral with an awe-inspiring view

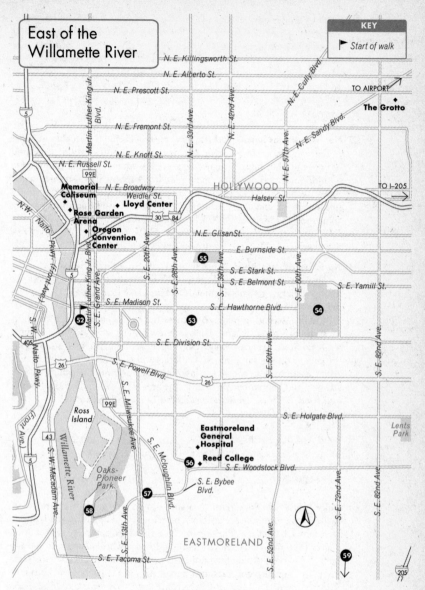

# East of the Willamette River

**KEY**

▶ Start of walk

N.E. Killingsworth St.

N.E. Alberto St.

N.E. Prescott St.

TO AIRPORT

N.E. 42nd Ave.

N.E. Cully Blvd.

**The Grotto**

N.E. Fremont St.

N.E. 33rd Ave.

Martin Luther King Jr. Blvd.

N.E. Knott St.

N.E. Sandy Blvd.

N.E. 57th Ave.

N.E. Russell St.

99E

**Memorial Coliseum**

N.E. Broadway

HOLLYWOOD

TO I-205

Weidler St.

**Lloyd Center**

Halsey St.

30  84

**Rose Garden Arena**

**Oregon Convention Center**

N.E. Glisan St.

E. Burnside St.

5

S.E. 20th Ave.

S.E. 28th Ave.

S.E. 39th Ave.

55

S.E. Stark St.

S.E. Belmont St.

N.W. Naito Pkwy. (Front Ave.)

S.E. Yamill St.

S.E. 50th Ave.

S.E. Madison St.

S.E. Hawthorne Blvd.

54

52

S.E. Grand Ave.

Martin Luther King Jr. Blvd.

53

S.E. Division St.

S.W. Naito Pkwy.

405

S.E. 50th Ave.

S.E. 82nd Ave.

26

S.E. Powell Blvd.

26

Ross Island

99E

S.E. Milwaukee Ave.

S.E. Holgate Blvd.

Lents Park

**Eastmoreland General Hospital**

43

Willamette River

Oaks-Pioneer Park

5

S.W. Macadam Ave.

S.E. McLoughlin Blvd.

56  **Reed College**

S.E. Woodstock Blvd.

57

S.E. Bybee Blvd.

58

S.E. 13th Ave.

S.E. 72nd Ave.

S.E. 82nd Ave.

EASTMORELAND

S.E. 52nd Ave.

59

205

S.E. Tacoma St.

Crystal Springs Rhododendron Garden ............. 56

Hawthorne District .... 53

Laurelhurst Park ...... 55

Mt. Tabor Park ....... 54

North Clackamas Aquatic Park ........ 59

Oaks Amusement Park ..... 58

Oregon Museum of Science and Industry ........ 52

Sellwood District ..... 57

of the Columbia River and the Cascades. There's a dazzling Festival of Lights at Christmastime (late November–December), with 250,000 lights, and holiday concerts in the 600-seat chapel. Sunday masses are held here, too. ⊠ *Sandy Blvd. at N.E. 85th Ave., near airport* ☎ *503/254–7371* ⊕ *www.thegrotto.org* 🖃 *Plaza level free; elevator to upper level $3* ⊙ *Mid-May–Labor Day, daily 9–7:30; Labor Day–late Nov., daily 9–5:30; late Nov.–Jan., daily 9–4:30; Feb.–mid-May, daily 9–5:30.*

**⑲ 59 North Clackamas Aquatic Park.** If you're visiting Portland with kids any time of the year and are looking for a great way to cool off—especially on one of Portland's hot July or August days—check out this 45,000-square-foot, all-indoor attraction, whose main pool has 4-foot waves and three super slides. There's also a 25-yard-long lap pool, a wading pool, an adults-only hot whirlpool, and a café. Children under age 8 must be accompanied by someone 13 or older. ⊠ *7300 S.E. Harmony Rd., Milwaukie* ☎ *503/557–7873* ⊕ *www.co.clackamas.or.us/ncap* 🖃 *$9.50* ⊙ *Mon., Wed., and Fri. 4–8, weekends 11–8 (no open swim weekends 3–4).*

**Northeast Alberta Street.** More than two dozen art galleries and studios, alongside coffeehouses, restaurants, and specialty shops, line this street in this quickly gentrifying neighborhood in northeast Portland. The neighborhood, which has undergone rapid transition since the mid-'90s, is a fascinating place to witness the intersection of cultures and lifestyles in a growing city. There are few other places in Portland with a Mexican grocery, a vintage-clothing store, a barbecue joint, and an art gallery on the same block. Galleries and businesses host the Art on Alberta sidewalk event on the last Thursday evening of each month. A street fair in September showcases the area with arts-and-crafts booths and food vendors. ⊠ *Between Martin Luther King Jr. Blvd. and 30th Ave., Alberta District.*

**NORTHWEST ALPACAS RANCH –** The kids can pet the llamalike animals at this ranch southwest of Portland. A gift shop sells sweaters made from alpaca wool. ⊠ *11785 S.W. River Rd., Scholls* ☎ *503/628–3110* ⊕ *www.alpacas.com* 🖃 *Free* ⊙ *Fri.–Sun. 10–5.*

**⑲ 58 Oaks Amusement Park.** There's a small-town charm to this park, with thrill rides and miniature golf in summer and roller-skating year-round. In summer 1999 Oaks Park opened Acorn Acres, complete with a 360-degree loop roller coaster, carousel, and Ferris wheel. The skating rink, built in 1905, is the oldest continuously operating one in the United States. There are outdoor concerts in summer. Also in the park is the **Ladybug Theater** (☎ 503/232–2346), which presents shows for children. ⊠ *S. E. Spokane St. east of Willamette River (from east side of Sellwood Bridge, take Grand Ave. north and Spokane west), Sellwood* ☎ *503/233–5777* ⊕ *www.oakspark.com* 🖃 *Park free, 5-hr ride passes $8.50–$11, individual-ride tickets $1.25* ⊙ *Mid-June–Labor Day, weekends noon–7; late Mar.–mid-June and Labor Day–Oct., weekends noon–5.*

**★ ⑲ ⏩ 52 Oregon Museum of Science and Industry** (OMSI). An Omnimax theater and planetarium are among the main attractions at the Northwest's largest astronomy educational facility, which also has a hands-on computer center, a space wing with a mission-control center, and many permanent and touring scientific exhibits. Moored in the Willamette as part of the museum is a 240-foot submarine, the USS *Blueback*. ⊠ *1945 S.E. Water Ave., south of Morrison Bridge, under Hawthorne Bridge* ☎ *503/797–6674 or 800/955–6674* ⊕ *www.omsi.edu* 🖃 *Full package $16, museum*

*$8, planetarium $3.50, Omnimax $7, submarine $3.50* ⊙ *Memorial Day–Labor Day, Fri.–Wed. 9:30–7, Thurs. 9:30–8; Labor Day–Memorial Day, Tues.–Sun. 9:30–5:30.*

**57** **Sellwood District.** The browsable neighborhood that begins east of the Sellwood Bridge was once a separate town. Annexed by Portland in the 1890s, it retains a modest charm. On weekends the antiques stores along 13th Avenue do a brisk business. Each store is identified by a plaque that tells the date of construction and the original purpose of the building. More antiques stores, specialty shops, and restaurants are near the intersection of Milwaukie and Bybee. ⊠ *S.E. 13th Ave. between Malden and Clatsop Sts., Sellwood.*

# WHERE TO EAT

First-time visitors to Portland are often surprised by how diverse and inexpensive many restaurants are. Lovers of ethnic foods can choose from restaurants serving Chinese, French, Indian, Italian, Japanese, Middle Eastern, Tex-Mex, Thai, and Vietnamese specialties. Pacific Northwest cuisine also dominates; Portlanders view salmon with passion, and likewise other regional seafood including halibut, crab, oysters, and mussels. Many restaurants are devoted to organic, locally grown produce such as wild mushrooms, hazelnuts, and berries, as well as free-range local beef and poultry.

Portland claims to have more restaurants per capita than any other city in the country, so while it is easy to stumble upon some great food, it is also worth doing a little research to find some of the out-of-the-way places that have much to offer. Many of the city's trendier restaurants are in Nob Hill and the Pearl District, and downtown is filled with many diverse, quality menus at some of the city's long-running old reliables. But an incredible smattering of cuisines can be found on the east side of town as well, near Hawthorne Boulevard and Alberta Street and tucked away in myriad neighborhoods in between.

Restaurants are arranged first by neighborhood and then by type of cuisine served.

| WHAT IT COSTS | | | | |
|---|---|---|---|---|
| $$$$ | $$$ | $$ | $ | ¢ |
| RESTAURANTS over $30 | $20–$30 | $15–$20 | $10–$15 | under $10 |

Restaurant prices are per person for a main course at dinner.

## Downtown

### American

**$–$$$** ✕ **Jake's Grill.** Not to be confused with the Jake's of seafood fame, this eatery in the Governor Hotel has more turf than surf. Steaks and the Sunday brunch are popular draws. Private booths with green velvet curtains make for a cozy, intimate dinner. The bar is famous for its Bloody Marys. ⊠ *611 S.W. 10th Ave., Downtown* ☎ *503/220–1850* ▤ *AE, D, DC, MC, V.*

**$–$$$** ✕ **Red Star Tavern & Roast House.** Cooked in a wood-burning oven, smoker, rotisserie, or grill, the cuisine at Red Star can best be described as American comfort food inspired by the bounty of the Pacific Northwest. Spit-roasted chicken, maple-fired baby-back ribs with a brown-ale glaze, charred salmon, and crayfish étouffée are some of the better

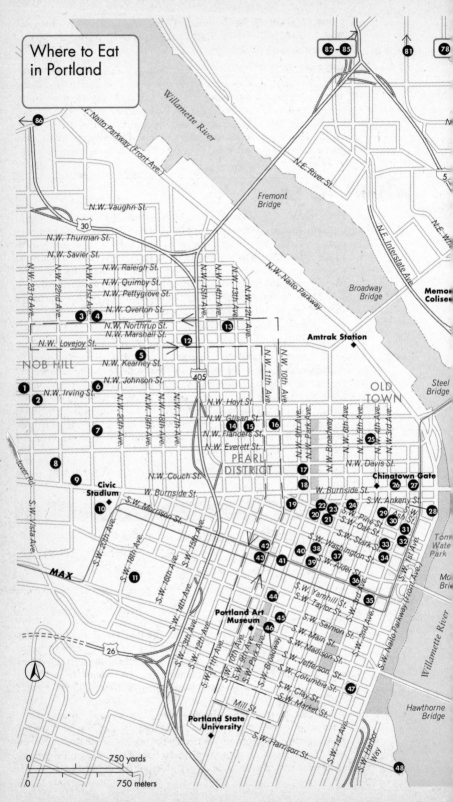

Where to Eat in Portland

Abou Karim . . . . . . . . . **31**
Alameda Brewhouse . . **80**
Al-Amir . . . . . . . . . . . . **33**
Alessandro's . . . . . . . . **36**
Alexis . . . . . . . . . . . . . **26**
Assaggio . . . . . . . . . . . **52**
Bastas . . . . . . . . . . . . **7**
Bernie's Sourthern
Bistro . . . . . . . . . . . . **84**
Bijou Cafe . . . . . . . . . **30**
Bread & Ink . . . . . . . . **61**
Brewhouse Taproom . . **86**
BridgePort BrewPub
& Restaurant . . . . . . . **13**
Bush Garden . . . . . . . **41**
Cafe Azul . . . . . . . . . **17**
Cafe des Amis . . . . . . **5**
Caprial's . . . . . . . . . . **53**
Castagna . . . . . . . . . . **57**
Chart House . . . . . . . . **51**
Chez Grill . . . . . . . . . **60**
Colosso . . . . . . . . . . . **76**
Couvron . . . . . . . . . . **11**
Cup and Saucer . . . . . **63**
Dan & Louis's
Oyster Bar . . . . . . . . **28**
El Gaucho . . . . . . . . . **22**
Esparza's
Tex-Mex Cafe . . . . . . **69**
Fong Chong . . . . . . . **25**
Fujin . . . . . . . . . . . . . **58**
Genoa . . . . . . . . . . . . **66**
The Heathman . . . . . . **45**
Higgins . . . . . . . . . . . **46**
Hokkaido . . . . . . . . . **73**
Il Fornaio . . . . . . . . . . **8**
Il Piatto . . . . . . . . . . . **68**
Ivy House . . . . . . . . . **55**
Jake's Famous
Crawfish . . . . . . . . . . **19**
Jake's Grill . . . . . . . . **42**
Jazz de Opus . . . . . . **27**
Koji Osakaya . . . . . . . **39**
Kornblatt's . . . . . . . . . **2**
Le Happy . . . . . . . . . **12**
Little Wing Cafe . . . . . **14**
London Grill . . . . . . . . **20**
Lucy's Table . . . . . . . . **6**
Mandarin Cove . . . . . **47**
Mayas Taqueria . . . . . **43**
McCormick
& Schmick's . . . . . . . **32**
McMenamins Kennedy
School Courtyard
Restaurant . . . . . . . . **79**
Montage . . . . . . . . . . **64**
Mother's Bistro . . . . **34**
Newport Bay at
RiverPlace . . . . . . . . . **48**

Nicholas's
Restaurant . . . . . . . . . **67**
Oba! . . . . . . . . . . . . . **15**
Old Spaghetti
Factory . . . . . . . . . . . **49**
Original
Pancake House . . . **50**
Paley's Place . . . . . . . **4**
Pambiche . . . . . . . . . **70**
Papa Haydn/Jo bar . . **1**
Pazzo . . . . . . . . . . . **38**
Pearl Bakery . . . . . . . **18**
Perry's on Fremont . . . **78**
Pho Van . . . . . . . . . . **16**
Pizzicato . . . . . . . . . **40**
Plainfield's Mayur . . . . **10**
Poor Richard's . . . . . . **77**
Portland City Grill . . . . **24**
Portland Steak &
Chophouse . . . . . . . **29**
Red Star Tavern . . . . . **37**
Rheinlander . . . . . . . . **74**
The Ringside . . . . . . . **9**
Rock Bottom
Brewing . . . . . . . . . . **35**
Saigon Kitchen . . . . . **71**
Salty's on the
Columbia . . . . . . . . . **81**
Saucebox . . . . . . . . . **23**
Saylor's Old Country
Kitchen . . . . . . . . . . . **54**
Southpark . . . . . . . . **44**
Sylvia's Class Act . . . . **75**
Tennessee Red's . . . **56**
Thai Noon . . . . . . . . **83**
Thanh Thao . . . . . . . . **59**
Three Doors Down . . . . **62**
Tin Shed
Garden Cafe . . . . . . . **82**
Typhoon! . . . . . . . . . **21**
Vita Cafe . . . . . . . . . . **85**
Wild Abandon . . . . . . **65**
Wildwood . . . . . . . . . **3**
Winterborne . . . . . . . **72**

entrées. The wine list includes regional and international vintages, and 12 microbrews are on tap. The spacious restaurant, in the 5th Avenue Suites Hotel, has tufted leather booths, murals, and copper accents. ⊠ *503 S.W. Alder St., Downtown* ☎ *503/222–0005* ▭ *AE, D, DC, MC, V.*

¢–$$ ✕ **Mother's Bistro.** The menu is loaded with home-style favorites—macaroni and cheese with extra ingredients of the day, soups, pierogi, chicken and dumplings, pot roast, and meat loaf. For vegetarians there's a couscous stew. The high ceilings in the well-lit dining room lend an air of spaciousness, but the tables are a bit close together. The bar is open late Friday and Saturday. ⊠ *409 S.W. 2nd Ave., Downtown* ☎ *503/464–1122* ▭ *AE, D, DC, MC, V* ☯ *Closed Mon.*

¢–$$ ✕ **Rock Bottom Brewing Co.** Some locals might balk at the idea of a corporate brewpub in a city that prides itself on its outstanding local microbrews, but this slightly upscale establishment manages to do just fine and serves some tasty dinner options, including burgers, pasta, and salads. With a full bar, pool upstairs, and rustic decor, there is plenty to please the after-work crowd. Brewery tours are available. ⊠ *210 S.W. Morrison St.* ☎ *503/796–2739* ▭ *AE, D, MC, V.*

## Chinese

$–$$$ ✕ **Mandarin Cove.** One of Portland's best Chinese restaurants has Hunan- and Szechuan-style beef, chicken, pork, seafood, and vegetarian dishes. There are almost two dozen seafood choices. Try the sautéed scallops simmered in spicy tomato sauce. ⊠ *111 S.W. Columbia St., 97201* ☎ *503/222–0006* ▭ *AE, DC, MC, V* ☯ *No lunch Sun.*

## Contemporary

$$–$$$$ ✕ **Portland City Grill.** On the 30th floor of the US Bank Tower, Portland City Grill has one of the best views in town. You can sit at a windowside table and enjoy the Portland skyline while eating fine steak and seafood with an Asian flair; it's no wonder that this restaurant, opened in 2002, has quickly become a favorite hot spot for the city's jet-set. The adjoining bar and lounge has comfortable arm chairs all along its windowed walls, which are the first to get snatched up during the extremely popular happy hour each day. ⊠ *111 S.W. 5th Ave., Downtown* ☎ *503/ 450–0030* ▭ *AE, D, DC, MC, V* ☯ *No lunch weekends.*

$$–$$$ ✕ **Higgins.** Chef Greg Higgins, former executive chef at the Heathman
FodorśChoice Hotel, focuses on ingredients from the Pacific Northwest and on or-
★ ganically grown herbs and produce while incorporating traditional French cooking styles and other international influences into his menu. Start with a salad of warm beets, asparagus, and artichokes or the country-style terrine of venison, chicken, and pork with dried sour cherries and a roasted-garlic mustard. Main courses change seasonally and might include dishes made with Alaskan spot prawns, halibut, duck, or pork loin. Vegetarian items are available. A bistro menu is available in the adjoining bar, where comfortable leather booths and tables provide an alternative to the main dining room. ⊠ *1239 S.W. Broadway, Downtown* ☎ *503/222–9070* ▭ *AE, MC, V* ☯ *No lunch weekends.*

★ $–$$$ ✕ **The Heathman.** Chef Philippe Boulot revels in fresh ingredients of the Pacific Northwest. His menu changes with the season and includes entrées made with grilled and braised fish, fowl, veal, lamb, and beef. Among the chef's Northwest specialties are a delightful Dungeness crab, mango, and avocado salad and a seafood paella made with mussels, clams, shrimp, scallops, and chorizo. Equally creative choices are available for breakfast and lunch. The dining room, scented with wood smoke and adorned with Andy Warhol prints, is a favorite for special occasions. ⊠ *Heathman Hotel, 1001 S.W. Broadway, Downtown* ☎ *503/790–7752* ▭ *AE, D, DC, MC, V.*

¢–$   ✕ **Bijou Cafe.** This spacious, sunny, high-ceiling restaurant has some of the best breakfasts in town: French-style crepes and oyster hash are a few popular favorites, along with fabulous pancakes and French toast. Breakfast is served all day, and at lunch there are burgers, sandwiches, and soups, as well as delectable daily specials. ✉ *132 S.W. 3rd Ave., Downtown* ☎ *503/222–3187* ▭ *MC, V* ☺ *No dinner.*

## Continental

$$$–$$$$   ✕ **London Grill.** The plush, dimly lit dining room in the historic Benson Hotel serves classic dishes made with fresh, seasonal local ingredients with an Asian influence. Try the salmon glazed with sake and ginger. With one of the longest wine lists around and a good chance of live harp or piano music, this a place to truly indulge. Breakfast is also available. ✉ *309 S.W. Broadway* ☎ *503/295–4110* 🏛 *Jacket required* ▭ *AE, D, DC, MC, V.*

## French

★ $$$$   ✕ **Couvron.** Understated elegance defines this crown jewel for contemporary French cuisine. Chef Anthony Demes prepares prix-fixe menus—vegetarian, seasonal, and grand—each of which includes an appetizer, lobster or vegetable soup, and signature dishes such as honey-glazed Oregon duck breast with curry and anise, and scallops with braised short ribs ravioli. The full-service wine pairings to match each course are a special treat. ✉ *1126 S.W. 18th Ave., Downtown* ☎ *503/225–1844* ⚓ *Reservations essential* ▭ *AE, MC, V* ☺ *Closed Sun. and Mon. No lunch.*

## Italian

$$–$$$   ✕ **Alessandro's.** This cozy eatery turns out Roman-style Italian pastas and entrées made with seafood, poultry, and veal. Try the cioppino, or filetti Rossini, two fillet medallions with Portobello mushrooms and pancetta bacon, laced with a red wine sauce. ✉ *301 S.W. Morrison St., 97204* ☎ *503/222–3900* ▭ *AE, DC, MC, V* ☺ *Closed Sun.*

¢–$$$   ✕ **Pazzo.** The aromas of roasted garlic and wood smoke greet patrons of the bustling, street-level dining room of the Hotel Vintage Plaza. Pazzo's frequently changing menu relies on deceptively simple new Italian cuisine—creative pastas, risottos, and grilled meats, fish, and poultry as well as antipasti and appetizers. All the baked goods are made fresh in the Pazzoria Bakery & Cafe next door. The decor is a mix of dark wood, terra-cotta, and dangling garlands of garlic. Breakfast is served daily. ✉ *627 S.W. Washington St., Downtown* ☎ *503/228–1515* ▭ *AE, D, DC, MC, V.*

## Japanese

$–$$$   ✕ **Bush Garden.** This authentic Japanese restaurant, which opened in 1960, is known for its sashimi and sukiyaki but also offers traditional favorites such as udon noodles, bento, tempura, and teriyaki. There is karaoke singing Monday–Saturday. ✉ *900 S.W. Morrison St., 97205* ☎ *503/226–7181* ▭ *AE, D, DC, MC, V* ☺ *No lunch Sun.*

¢–$   ✕ **Koji Osakaya.** Inside this little storefront, sushi and sashimi reign supreme. The *uni* (sea urchin), *hamachi* (yellowtail tuna), *saba* (mackerel), and *kasu* (cod) are all outstanding. The menu also includes teriyaki, tempura, and udon. Small tables and a sushi bar at the back fill the cozy, L-shape space. ✉ *606 S.W. Broadway, Downtown* ☎ *503/294–1169* ▭ *AE, MC, V.*

## Lebanese

$–$$   ✕ **Al-Amir.** Upon entering the restaurant and moving beyond the small bar in the front, through the elaborately large and ornate Middle Eastern gateway into a dark, stylish dining room, choose between excellent broiled kebabs, falafel, hummus, tabbouleh, and baba ghanouj. There's live music and belly dancing on the weekends. ✉ *223 S.W.*

*Stark St., 97204* ☎ *503/274–0010* ▭ *AE, D, DC, MC, V* ☉ *No lunch weekends.*

¢–$ ✕ **Abou Karim.** More than half the menu is vegetarian, but the leg of lamb served on a bed of rice with lentil soup or a full salad is a favorite. A special menu of meals low in saturated fats targets health-conscious diners. The laid-back restaurant's two dining areas are decorated simply, with white linen and dark wood. You can dine outside on sidewalk tables in summer. ✉ *221 S.W. Pine St., Downtown* ☎ *503/223–5058* ▭ *AE, MC, V* ☉ *Closed Sun. No lunch Sat.*

## Mexican

¢ ✕ **Mayas Taqueria.** Part of a local chain, this downtown outpost is within walking distance of many downtown shopping areas. Give your order cafeteria style, and then sit along the window inside or at one of the sidewalk tables in warmer months and watch the MAX light-rail trains and streetcars pass by. The delicious taco, with a generous heap of your choice of grilled meat and beans and served with fresh salsa and tortilla chips, is one of the best deals in town. ✉ *1000 S.W. Morrison St., Downtown* ☎ *503/226–1946* ▭ *AE, D, DC, MC, V.*

## Pan-Asian

$–$$ ✕ **Saucebox.** Creative pan-Asian cuisine and many creative cocktails draw the crowds to this popular restaurant and nightspot near the big downtown hotels. Inside the long and narrow space with closely spaced tables draped with white cloths, Alexis Rockman's impressive and colorful 24-foot painting *Evolution* spans the wall over your head, and mirrored walls meet your gaze at eye level. The menu includes Korean baby-back ribs, Vietnamese pork tenderloin, and Indonesian roasted Javanese salmon. An excellent late-night menu is served after 10 PM. ✉ *214 S. W. Broadway, Downtown* ☎ *503/241–3393* ▭ *AE, DC, MC, V* ☉ *Closed Sun. and Mon. No lunch.*

## Pizza

¢ ✕ **Pizzicato.** This local chain serves pies and slices topped by inventive combinations such as chanterelles, shiitakes, and Portobellos, or andouille sausage, shrimp, and smoked mozzarella. The menu includes large salads to share, antipasti, and panini. The restaurant interiors are clean, bright, and modern. Beer and wine are available. ✉ *705 S.W. Alder St., Downtown* ☎ *503/226–1007* ✉ *505 N.W. 23rd Ave., Nob Hill* ☎ *503/242–0023* ▭ *AE, D, DC, MC, V.*

## Seafood

$–$$$ ✕ **Jake's Famous Crawfish.** Diners have been enjoying fresh Pacific Northwest seafood in Jake's warren of wood-panel dining rooms for more than a century. The back bar came around Cape Horn during the 1880s, and the chandeliers hanging from the high ceilings date from 1881. The restaurant gained a national reputation in 1920 when crawfish was added to the menu. White-coated waiters take your order from an almost endless sheet of daily seafood specials year-round, but try to come during crawfish season (May–September), when you can sample the tasty crustacean in pie, cooked Creole style, or in a Cajun-style stew over rice. ✉ *401 S.W. 12th Ave., Downtown* ☎ *503/226–1419* ▭ *AE, D, DC, MC, V* ☉ *No lunch weekends.*

$–$$$ ✕ **McCormick & Schmick's.** The seafood is flawless at this lively restaurant, where you can dine in a cozy, private wooden booth downstairs or upstairs overlooking the bar. Fresh Pacific Northwest oysters and Alaskan halibut are favorites; specialties include Dungeness crab cakes with roasted red-pepper sauce. A new menu is printed daily with a list of more than two dozen fresh seasonal choices. Oregon and California vineyards take center stage on the wine list. The popular bar has bargain happy-hour appetizers and a wide selection of top-shelf, single-malt scotches. ⊠ *235 S.W. 1st Ave., Downtown* ☎ *503/224–7522* ⊟ *AE, D, DC, MC, V* ⊙ *No lunch Sun.*

**$–$$$**    ✗ **Newport Bay at RiverPlace.** When it comes to river, bridge, and city-skyline views, there's not a bad seat in this circular glass dining room, which floats on the Willamette River. The regional chain's menu includes seafood and chicken salads, seasonal specials, and creative seafood fare. The oven-roasted jumbo prawns are stuffed with crab, Brie, and roasted garlic and topped with béarnaise sauce. Upstairs, a comfortable lounge has a popular happy hour every day in the late afternoon and before closing. ⊠ *RiverPlace, 0425 S.W. Montgomery St., Downtown* ☎ *503/ 227–3474* ⊟ *AE, D, DC, MC, V.*

**$–$$**    ✗ **Southpark Seafood Grill & Wine Bar.** Wood-fired seafood is served in this comfortable, art deco-tinged room with two bars. Chef Ronnie Mac-Quarrie's Mediterranean-influenced menu includes grilled grape-leaf-wrapped salmon with pomegranate and sherry glaze as well as tuna au poivre with mashed potatoes and red wine demi-glace. There's a wide selection of fresh Pacific Northwest oysters and fine regional wines available by the glass. Some of the desserts are baked to order. There is no smoking. ⊠ *901 S.W. Salmon St., Downtown* ☎ *503/326–1300* ⊟ *AE, D, DC, MC, V.*

**¢–$$**    ✗ **Dan & Louis's Oyster Bar.** Oysters at this Portland landmark near the river come fried, stewed, or on the half shell. The clam chowder is tasty, but the crab stew is a rare treat. Combination dinners let you mix your fried favorites. The collection of steins, plates, and marine art has grown since the restaurant opened in 1907 to fill beams, nooks, crannies, and nearly every inch of wall. ⊠ *208 S.W. Ankeny St., Downtown* ☎ *503/ 227–5906* ⊟ *AE, D, DC, MC, V.*

## Steak

**$$$–$$$$**    ✗ **El Gaucho.** Three dimly lit dining rooms with blue walls and striped upholstery invite those with healthy pocketbooks. The specialty here is 28-day, dry-aged, certified Angus beef, but chops, ribs, and chicken entrées are also cooked in the open kitchen. The chateaubriand for two is carved tableside. Seafood lovers might want to try the tomato fennel bouillabaisse. Service is impeccable at this Seattle transplant in the elegant Benson Hotel. Each night live Latin guitar music serenades the dinner guests. Visit the full-service cigar lounge for a brandy and a smoke. ⊠ *319 S.W. Broadway, Downtown* ☎ *503/227–8794* ⊟ *AE, DC, MC, V* ⊙ *No lunch.*

**¢–$$$$**    ✗ **Portland Steak & Chophouse.** Expensive cuts of steak and prime rib are the draw at this steak house in the Embassy Suites hotel. The menu includes wood-fired pizzas, pasta, and café meals. Surf lovers can choose the ahi chop, cioppino, or seafood linguine. Lunch is served until 4:30 weekdays, and brunch is served on weekends. The bar menu draws a loyal happy-hour crowd. ⊠ *121 S.W. 3rd Ave., Downtown* ☎ *503/223– 6200* ⊟ *AE, D, MC, V.*

## Thai

**$–$$$**    ✗ **Typhoon!** A Buddha statue with burning incense watches over diners at this popular restaurant in the Lucia Hotel. Come enjoy the excellent food in a large, modern dining room filled with colorful art and sleek red booths. The spicy chicken or shrimp with crispy basil, the curry and noodle dishes, and the vegetarian spring and salad rolls are standouts. If tea is your thing, 145 varieties are available, from $2 a pot to $55 for some of the world's rarest. ⊠ *400 S.W. Broadway, Downtown* ☎ *503/ 224–8285* ⊟ *AE, D, DC, MC, V.*

# Pearl District & Old Town/Chinatown

## American

$–$$$ ✕ **Jazz de Opus.** The draw here is live jazz, but this dark Old Town establishment, which centers on the bar and a small stage, also turns out decent seafood and prime rib. Panfried oysters and crab cakes are popular, and specialties include the jambalaya and the mesquite-grilled salmon Oscar, topped with fresh Dungeness crab and drizzled with béarnaise. ✉ *33 N.W. 2nd Ave., Old Town* ☎ *503/222–6077* ▭ *AE, MC, V* ⊗ *No lunch.*

¢ ✕ **BridgePort BrewPub & Restaurant.** The hops- and ivy-covered, century-old industrial building seems out of place among its neighbors, but once inside you'll be clear about the business here: serving thick, hand-thrown pizza on sourdough crust to boisterous crowds, who wash it down with frothy pints of BridgePort's ale, brewed on the premises. The India Pale Ale is a specialty, but a treat for the indecisive is the seven glass sampler that might also include "Old Knucklehead," the brewery's barley wine–style ale. Handmade focaccia, sandwiches, including a tasty chicken almond salad sandwich, upscale pub snacks like figs marsala—baked figs with blue cheese—and salads are also available, and pizza is served by the pie, half pie, and the slice. During the summer the flower-festooned loading dock is transformed into a beer garden. ✉ *1313 N. W. Marshall St., Pearl District* ☎ *503/241–3612* ▭ *MC, V.*

## Cafés

¢–$$ ✕ **Little Wing Cafe.** In the heart of the Pearl District, the small and friendly Little Wing Cafe manages to be a refreshingly unpretentious place for simple lunches and elegant, quality dinners; evening entrées might include pork tenderloin with cherry sauce and apple-fennel relish or braised lamb shoulder with butternut-squash curry. Vegan and vegetarian dishes are available. ✉ *529 N.W. 13th Ave., Pearl District* ☎ *503/228–3101* ⚒ *Reservations not accepted* ▭ *AE, MC, V* ⊗ *Closed Sun. No dinner Mon.*

¢ ✕ **Pearl Bakery.** A light breakfast or lunch can be had at this popular spot known for its excellent fresh breads, pastries, cakes, and sandwiches. The cakes, cookies, croissants, and Danish are some of the best in the city. ✉ *102 N.W. 9th Ave., Pearl District* ☎ *503/827–0910* ▭ *No credit cards* ⊗ *Closed Sun. No dinner.*

## Chinese

¢–$ ✕ **Fong Chong.** Considered by some to be Chinatown's best Chinese restaurant, Fong Chong serves dim sum every day. The family-style eatery has dumplings filled with shrimp, pork, or vegetables, accompanied by plenty of different sauces. If you haven't eaten dim sum before, just take a seat: the food is brought to you on carts. Pick what you want as the food carts come by. The menu also lists traditional entrées. ✉ *301 N. W. 4th Ave., Chinatown* ☎ *503/220–0235* ▭ *MC, V.*

## French

¢–$$ ✕ **Le Happy.** This tiny creperie just outside of the hubbub of the Pearl District can serve as a romantic dinner-date spot or just a cozy place to enjoy a drink and a snack. You can get sweet crepes with fruit, cheese, and cream or savory ones with meats and cheeses; in addition, the dinner menu is rounded out with steaks and salads. It's a classy joint, but not without a sense of humor: Le Trash Blanc is a bacon and cheddar crepe, served with a can of Pabst. ✉ *1011 N.W. 16th Ave., Pearl District* ☎ *503/226–1258* ⊗ *Closed Sun.*

## Greek

$ ✕ **Alexis.** The Mediterranean furnishings here consist only of white walls and basic furnishings, but the authentic Greek flavor keeps the

# MICROBREWS
# OF THE PACIFIC NORTHWEST

THE CUSTOMER TIPS BACK HIS GLASS and takes a long, thirsty swallow. The ale cascades along his tongue, tweaking taste buds that for years have known only pale, flavorless industrial lagers. A blast of sweet malt explodes at the back of his mouth, counterpointing the citrusy sting of the hops. This is flavor, something missing from American beer for far too long.

There's something inherently noble about a well-crafted pint, something ancient and universal. Anthropologists theorize that agriculture and brewing may have provided the stimulus for the very foundation of human civilization. Certainly there is nothing new in the idea of a city or region being served by a number of small, distinctive breweries. More than 5,000 years ago, in Egypt, the many breweries of ancient Pelusium were as famous as the city's university. (Even then, books, beer, and scholarly contemplation went hand in hand.) The ancient Greeks and Romans, though more partial to wine than grain beverages, drank beer; evidence shows that there were more than 900 public houses in Herculaneum before Mt. Vesuvius sounded its fateful "last call" in AD 79.

It may be a coincidence that during the 1970s Britain's Campaign for Real Ale movement—credited with single-handedly restoring fine ale to United Kingdom pubs—paralleled the resurgence in the British economy and national pride. It may also be a coincidence that the return of the microbrewery ale to the Northwest signaled the end of a bitter recession here, and the beginning of a rapid climb into prosperity.

The best place to sample the Northwest's handcrafted ale is in a well-run brewpub, which stimulates the human spirit with conviviality, pleasant warmth, intelligent conversation, the scent of malt, and hearty food. Combatting the region's chilly, damp climate, brewpubs become places of refuge where you can shake the tears of a hostile world from your umbrella, order a pint of cask-conditioned bitter, and savor a complex substance that caresses the senses.

Microbreweries (companies producing fewer than 20,000 kegs per year) can be found from Minneapolis to Maui, but it all started in the Pacific Northwest. On any given evening, several dozen locally brewed beers and ales are available for tasting in pubs in Portland and Seattle. Most East Coast entries in the microbrewing sweepstakes produce German-style lagers—the most familiar brewing style to American palates—but the microbrewers of the Pacific Northwest go for wildly adventuresome bitters, stouts, and porters.

With all these beers to choose from, where do you begin? What should you look for in a microbrewery ale? First and foremost, variety. At any given time in Portland and Seattle, there are several dozen fresh, locally made brews on tap. They range in strength from a standard 3½% alcohol to an ominous 8½%.

And the flavor? Well, you'll just have to taste for yourself. There is the rich sweetness of malt, counterbalanced by good bitter hops. There are the mocha java overtones of roasted barley, used in stouts and porters, and the spiciness of malted wheat. There are sweet ales and tart ales, mild inconsequential ales, and ales so charged with flavor they linger on the palate like a fine Bordeaux.

Above all else, you should look for an ale you can savor, an ale you can taste without wanting to swallow too quickly. The dearest emotion to a brewer's heart is the beer drinker's feeling of regret that the last swig is gone.

— By Jeff Kuechle

crowds coming for *kalamarakia* (deep-fried squid served with *tzatziki*, a yogurt dip), *horiatiki* (a Greek salad combination with feta cheese and kalamata olives), and other traditional dishes. If you have trouble making up your mind, the gigantic Alexis platter includes a little of everything. ⊠ *215 W. Burnside St., Old Town* ☎ *503/224–8577* ⊟ *AE, D, DC, MC, V* ⊗ *No lunch weekends.*

### Latin

$–$$$ ✕ **Oba!** Many come to Oba! for the upscale bar scene, but this Pearl District salsa hangout also serves excellent Latin American cuisine, including coconut prawns, ahi tuna, roasted vegetable enchiladas and tamales, and other seafood, chicken, pork, and duck dishes. The bar is open late Friday and Saturday. ⊠ *555 N.W. 12th Ave., Pearl District* ☎ *503/228–6161* ⊟ *A, D, MC, V* ⊗ *No lunch.*

### Mexican

$$–$$$ ✕ **Cafe Azul.** This busy restaurant retains the building's Pearl District industrial feel with a simple yet elegant brick-wall interior. The plates may seem pricey if you're accustomed to the other Mexican food offerings in the city, but these authentic and beautifully prepared dishes are nothing like most other Mexican food found nearby, and your palate won't be disappointed. Owner and chef Claire Archibald's menu includes innovative creations made with fish, chicken, lamb, beef, and pork. The complex sauces, such as the 28-ingredient Oaxacan mole, are spectacular. ⊠ *112 N.W. 9th Ave., Pearl District* ☎ *503/525–4422* ⊟ *D, MC, V* ⊗ *Closed Sun. and Mon. No lunch.*

### Vietnamese

¢–$$ ✕ **Pho Van.** This spacious, minimalist restaurant is the newer and trendier of the two Pho Van locations in Portland—the other is on the far east side, on 82nd Avenue. A big bowl of pho noodle soup is delicious, enough to fill you up, and costs only $7 or $8. The knowledgeable and friendly waitstaff will gladly help you work your way through the lengthy menu and will make suggestions to give you the best sampling of Vietnamese cuisine. ⊠ *1012 N.W. Glisan St., Pearl District* ☎ *503/248–2172* ⊟ *MC, D, V* ⊗ *Closed Sun.* ⊠ *1919 S.E. 82nd Ave.* ☎ *503/788–5244.*

## Nob Hill & Vicinity

### American

$$–$$$$ ✕ **The Ringside.** This Portland institution has been famous for its beef for more than 50 years. Dine in cozy booths on rib eye, prime rib, and New York strip, which come in regular- or king-size cuts. Seafood lovers will find plenty of choices: a Chilean platter with an 8-ounce lobster tail, Dungeness crab, oysters, jumbo prawns, and Oregon bay shrimp. The onion rings, made with Walla Walla sweets, are equally renowned. ⊠ *2165 N.W. Burnside St., close to Nob Hill* ☎ *503/223–1513* ⊟ *AE, D, DC, MC, V* ⊗ *No lunch.*

¢–$$$ ✕ **Papa Haydn/Jo Bar.** Many patrons come to this bistro just for the luscious desserts. Favorite dinner entrées include oven-roasted sea bass, fresh four-cheese ravioli, and pan-seared rib eye. Wood-fired, rotisserie-cooked meat, fish, and poultry dishes plus pasta and pizza are available next door at the jazzy **Jo Bar**, which also serves bar munchies and Sunday brunch (reservations essential). ⊠ *701 N.W. 23rd Ave., Nob Hill* ☎ *503/228–7317 Papa Haydn, 503/222–0048 Jo Bar* ⊟ *AE, MC, V* ⊗ *No dinner Sun.*

### Contemporary

$$–$$$$ ✕ **Wildwood.** The busy center bar, stainless-steel open kitchen, and blond-wood chairs set the tone at this restaurant serving fresh Pacific

Northwest cuisine. Chef Cory Schreiber's entrées include dishes made with lamb, pork loin, chicken, steak, and seafood. There's also a vegetarian selection. Wildwood also has a Sunday brunch and a family-style Sunday supper menu with selections for two or more people. ✉ *1221 N.W. 21st Ave., Nob Hill* ☎ *503/248–9663* 🗏 *AE, MC, V.*

**$–$$$** ✕ **Lucy's Table.** Amid this corner bistro's regal purple and gold interior, chef Alex Pitts creates Northwest cuisine with a mix of Italian and French accents. The seasonal menu includes lamb, steak, pork, and seafood dishes. For dessert try the *boca negra*, chocolate cake with Frangelico whipped cream and cherries poached with port and walnut Florentine. Valet parking is available Wednesday–Saturday. ✉ *706 N.W. 21st Ave., Nob Hill* ☎ *503/226–6126* 🗏 *AE, MC, DC, V* ☾ *Closed Sun. No lunch.*

**¢–$** ✕ **Brewhouse Taproom.** The copper beer-making equipment at the door tips you off to the specialty of the house—beer. The restaurant is part of a 27,000-square-foot MacTarnahan's brewery complex. Try the MacTarnahan's fish-and-chips: the batter is made with the Brewhouse's signature ale. The haystack back ribs with garlic rosemary fries are popular. Asparagus-artichoke lasagne served with salad is a good vegetarian option. Eat it all on the patio overlooking the landscaped garden. ✉ *2730 N.W. 31st Ave., 97210* ☎ *503/228–5269* 🗏 *AE, MC, V.*

## Delicatessen

**¢** ✕ **Kornblatt's.** This kosher deli and bagel bakery evokes a 1950s diner. Thick sandwiches are made with fresh bread and lean fresh-cooked meats, and the tender home-smoked salmon and sablefish are simply mouthwatering. For breakfast try the poached eggs with spicy corned-beef hash. ✉ *628 N.W. 23rd Ave., Nob Hill* ☎ *503/242–0055* 🗏 *MC, V.*

## French

**$$–$$$** ✕ **Paley's Place.** This charming bistro serves French cuisine Pacific Northwest–style. Among the entrées are dishes with duck, New York steak, chicken, pork tenderloin, and halibut. A vegetarian selection is also available. Paley's has a fine selection of Willamette Valley and French wines. There are two dining rooms and a classy bar. In warmer months outdoor seating is available on the front porch and back patio. ✉ *1204 N.W. 21st Ave., Nob Hill* ☎ *503/243–2403* 🗏 *AE, MC, V* ☾ *No lunch.*

FodorsChoice ★

**$–$$$** ✕ **Cafe des Amis.** This established, romantic bistro in a small vine-covered brick building serves fine French provincial cuisine. The menu focuses on entrées with lamb, pork, beef, and duck. Seafood is limited primarily to the appetizer selections. French varieties dominate the wine list, which includes a dozen by the glass. ✉ *1987 N.W. Kearney St., Nob Hill* ☎ *503/295–6487* 🗏 *AE, MC, V* ☾ *Closed Sun. No lunch.*

## Indian

**$$–$$$** ✕ **Plainfield's Mayur.** Portland's finest Indian cuisine is served in an elegant Victorian house. The tomato-coconut soup with fried curry leaves and the vegetarian and vegan dishes are highlights. Appetizers include the authentic Bombay *bhel* salad with tamarind dressing and the *dahi wadi* (crispy fried lentil croquettes in a spicy yogurt sauce). Meat and seafood specialties include lobster in brown onion sauce and tandoori chicken or lamb. This family-owned restaurant consistently wins accolades from *Wine Spectator*. ✉ *852 S.W. 21st Ave., one block south of Burnside, close to Nob Hill* ☎ *503/223–2995* 🗏 *AE, D, DC, MC, V* ☾ *No lunch.*

## Italian

**$–$$$** ✕ **Il Fornaio.** This outpost of the San Francisco–based trattoria and bakery serves handmade pastas, pizzas, and sandwiches. For the first two weeks of every month, cuisine from a different region of Italy is highlighted in addition to the basic menu. Many dishes are cooked in a wood-burning pizza oven and rotisserie. An open kitchen, warm redbrick walls, and vines with baskets of grapes and garlic hanging from the ceiling contribute to the restaurant's festive and welcoming character. ⊠ *115 N.W. 22nd Ave., 97210* ☎ *503/248–9400* ▤ *AE, D, MC, V.*

$–$$ ✕ **Bastas.** In a funky converted Tastee-Freeze, this bistro serves dishes from all over Italy. The walls are painted with Italian earth tones, and a small side garden provides alfresco dining in good weather. The menu includes veal scaloppine, grilled chicken, lamb chops, and creative pasta dishes. ⊠ *410 N.W. 21st Ave., Nob Hill* ☎ *503/274–1572* ▤ *AE, MC, V* ⊙ *No lunch Sat.–Wed.*

# East of the Willamette

### American

¢–$$ ✕ **Poor Richard's.** With an old-fashioned menu of burgers, steak, fish-and-chips, and potpies, this home-style restaurant has stuck to the reliable, no-frills environment that has kept it in business since 1959. With comfortable booths, a large and casual dining room, and a smoking lounge, this is the place to go to if you've had enough of the hip, innovative menus that abound in the city and just want to find some comfort food. ⊠ *3907 N.E. Broadway, Hollywood District, 97232* ☎ *503/288–5285* ▤ *AE, D, MC, V* ⊙ *No lunch Sat.*

### American/Casual

¢–$$ ✕ **Alameda Brewhouse.** A spacious dining room and bar in a high-ceiling room with light wood and stainless steel gives this brewhouse a feeling of urban chic while still managing to remain friendly and casual. Many people come for the excellent microbrews made on premises, but the food must not be overlooked; this is no pub grub. With creative pasta dishes such as mushroom-artichoke linguine, salmon gyros, ahi tacos, and delicious burgers, it is clear that this restaurant has as much thought going into its menu and ingredients as it does into its brewing. ⊠ *4675 N.E. Fremont St., Alameda* ☎ *503/460–9025* ▤ *AE, MC, V.*

¢–$ ✕ **McMenamins Kennedy School Courtyard Restaurant.** Whether you are coming to the Kennedy School to stay overnight at the hotel, to watch a movie, or just to enjoy dinner and drinks, the Courtyard Restaurant can add to your evening. The huge restaurant, with additional outdoor seating in the courtyard, is a hopping place every night of the week, and you may have to wait for a table, but there is so much to do on the premises that it doesn't really matter. The food, ranging from burgers, salads, and pizzas to fish-and-chips, pasta, prime rib, and beef stew, can satisfy most any appetite. Several standard McMenamins microbrews are always available, in addition to seasonal specialty brews. ⊠ *5736 N.E. 33rd Ave., near Alberta District* ☎ *503/249–3983* ▤ *AE, D, DC, MC, V.*

### Barbecue

¢–$ ✕ **Tennessee Red's.** The best barbecue is arguably found in raw, out-of-the-way places, and this spot fits the bill—a corner rib joint in a laid-back neighborhood. The portions, served with a choice of five sauces and corn bread, are more than generous. In addition to the requisite ribs and brisket, you can get chicken, sausage, and blackened catfish. All entrées come with a choice of two southern-style side dishes. ⊠ *2133 S.E. 11th Ave., near Ladd's Addition* ☎ *503/231–1710* ▤ *MC, V.*

### Cafés

¢ ✕ **Cup and Saucer.** This casual diner-style restaurant is extremely popular with hip young locals and is always packed on the weekends, especially for breakfast and lunch. The long menu includes all-day-breakfast, quiches, burgers, sandwiches, soups, and salads, with plenty of vegetarian and vegan options. ⊠ *3566 S.E. Hawthorne Blvd., Hawthorne District* ☎ *503/236–6001* ⌲ *Reservations not accepted* ▤ *No credit cards.*

¢  ✕ **Tin Shed Garden Cafe.** This small restaurant has been a popular break-fast spot since opening in 2002, growing widely known for its shredded potato cakes, biscuits and gravy, sweet-potato cinnamon French toast, creative egg and tofu scrambles, and breakfast burritos. The lunch and dinner menu has creative items like a creamy artichoke sandwich, and a chicken sandwich with bacon, Gorgonzola and apple, in addition to burg-ers, salads, and soups. A comfortable outdoor patio doubles as a beer garden on warm spring and summer evenings, and the adjacent community garden rounds off the property with a peaceful sitting area in which to wait for a table, sip coffee, or listen to music on a summer night. ⊠ *1438 N.E. Alberta St., Alberta District* ☏ *503/288–6966* ⟡ *Reservations not accepted* ⊟ *MC, V* ⊙ *Closed Tues. No dinner Sun. or Mon.*

## Cajun/Creole

¢–$  ✕ **Montage.** Spicy Cajun is the jumping-off point for the chef at this sassy bistro under the Morrison Bridge on Portland's east side. Jambalayas, blackened pork, chicken, and catfish, linguine, and old-fashioned mac-aroni dishes are served up from around noon until the wee hours in a spot that's loud, crowded, and casually hip. The wine list includes more than 100 varieties. ⊠ *301 S.E. Morrison St., between Martin Luther King Jr. Blvd. and Morrison Bridge* ☏ *503/234–1324* ⟡ *Reservations not accepted* ⊟ *No credit cards* ⊙ *No lunch weekends.*

FodorsChoice  
★

## Chinese

¢  ✕ **Fujin.** Although the place looks a bit tattered, this family-run neigh-borhood restaurant consistently serves good wok-cooked favorites at rea-sonable prices. The fried tofu dishes and sesame-crusted shrimp are tasty. Check the specials, which change daily. ⊠ *3549 S.E. Hawthorne Blvd., Hawthorne District* ☏ *503/231–3753* ⊟ *D, MC, V* ⊙ *No lunch Sun.*

## Contemporary

$$–$$$$  ✕ **Salty's on the Columbia.** Pacific Northwest salmon (choose blackened or grilled, a half or full pound) is what this comfortable restaurant over-looking the Columbia River is known for. Try the seafood pesto fettuccine with prawns, scallops, halibut, salmon, grape tomatoes, and pine nuts. The menu includes chicken and steak offerings. There is a heated, cov-ered deck and an uncovered deck for open-air dining. ⊠ *3839 N.E. Ma-rine Dr., 97211* ☏ *503/288–4444* ⊟ *AE, D, DC, MC, V.*

$$$  ✕ **Castagna.** Enjoy the bouillabaisse or one of the inventive Mediterranean seafood entrées at this tranquil Hawthorne restaurant. The pan-seared scallops with mushrooms are the signature dish. Next door is the more casual **Cafe Castagna** (☏ *503/231–9959*), a bistro and bar open nightly serving pizzas and other slightly less expensive, lighter fare. ⊠ *1752 S. E. Hawthorne Blvd., Hawthorne District* ☏ *503/231–7373* ⊟ *AE, MC, V* ⊙ *Closed Sun. and Mon. No lunch.*

$$–$$$  ✕ **Caprial's.** PBS cooking-show star Caprial Pence serves Mediterranean-inspired creations at her bustling, brightly lit bistro with an open kitchen, full bar, and velvet armchairs. The dinner menu changes monthly and is limited to four or five choices, which have included pan-roasted salmon as well as smoked and grilled pork loin chop. The wine "wall" (you pick the bottle) has more than 200 varieties. ⊠ *7015 S.E. Milwaukie Ave., Sellwood* ☏ *503/236–6457* ⊟ *MC, V* ⊙ *Closed Sun. and Mon.*

$–$$$  ✕ **Perry's on Fremont.** This diner, still famous for burgers, chicken pot-pies, and fish-and-chips, has gone a bit more upscale with the addition of pricier menu items such as steak and salmon. Eat outside on the large patio among the flowers, and don't pass up one of the desserts. ⊠ *2401 N.E. Fremont St.* ☏ *503/287–3655* ⊟ *AE, D, MC, V* ⊙ *Closed Sun. No dinner Sat.*

$-$$ ✕ **Ivy House.** This restaurant combines the unlikely duo of an extremely kid-centric dining environment and carefully prepared, elegant entrées for the adults who accompany them. Grown-ups might gravitate toward the shiitake mushroom risotto with Portuguese goat cheese, or seared duck breast with oyster mushroom ragout, while the little ones will likely be itching to retire to one of two play areas. There is seating outside on the patio in the center of a blooming rose garden. ⊠ *1605 S.E. Bybee Blvd.* ☎ *503/231–9528* ☒ *MC, V.*

¢–$$ ✕ **Bread and Ink.** The old-fashioned elegance will strike you as soon as you walk in, but the high-ceiling dining room, done in cream and forest green, is not trendy in any way, and it is partly this earnest no-frills dedication to quality food that has helped it gain its name as a neighborhood landmark. Breakfast is a specialty and might include brioche French toast and smoked fish. Lunch and dinner yield good choices, including burgers, poached salmon, and crab cakes. You can get the legendary blintzes at every meal. ⊠ *3610 S.E. Hawthorne Blvd., Hawthorne District* ☎ *503/239–4756* ☒ *AE, D, MC, V.*

¢–$$ ✕ **Wild Abandon and the Red Velvet Lounge.** Inside this small, bohemian-looking building, chef Michael Cox creates an inventive Mediterranean-influenced menu that includes fresh seafood, pork, beef, and pasta entrées. Vegetarian selections might be ziti, panfried tofu, or polenta lasagna made with roasted eggplant, squash, and spinach. The popular Sunday brunch includes omelets, Benedict dishes, breakfast burritos, and sandwiches. ⊠ *2411 S.E. Belmont St., near Hawthorne District* ☎ *503/232–4458* ☒ *AE, D, DC, MC, V* ☻ *Closed Tues. No lunch weekdays.*

## Cuban

★ ¢–$ ✕ **Pambiche.** Locals know that you can drive by Pambiche any night of the week and find it packed. With traditional Cuban fare including plantains, roast port, mojitos, and Cuban espresso, it is no surprise why. If you have some time to wait for a table, you should stop by and make an evening of it at this hopping neighborhood hot spot. Don't miss out on the incredible dessert here; it is the sole reason why some people make the trip. ⊠ *2811 N.E. Glisan St., near Laurelhurst* ☎ *503/233–0511* ⌕ *Reservations not accepted* ☒ *MC, V.*

## German

$-$$ ✕ **Rheinlander.** A strolling accordionist and singing servers entertain as patrons dine on authentic traditional German food, including sauerbraten, hasenpfeffer, schnitzel, sausage, and rotisserie chicken. **Gustav's,** the adjoining pub and grill, serves slightly less expensive entrées, including sausages, cabbage rolls, and German meatballs, in an equally festive, if slightly more raucous, environment. ⊠ *5035 N.E. Sandy Blvd., 97213* ☎ *503/288–5503* ☒ *AE, MC, V.*

## Italian

★ $$$$ ✕ **Genoa.** Widely regarded as the finest restaurant in Portland, Genoa serves a prix-fixe menu (seven courses on Friday and Saturday evenings, four courses on weekdays), focusing on authentic Italian cuisine, that changes every two weeks. In a space that evokes Tuscany, seating is limited to a few dozen diners, so service is excellent. Smoking is permitted in a separate sitting room. ⊠ *2822 S.E. Belmont St., near Hawthorne District* ☎ *503/238–1464* ⌕ *Reservations essential* ☒ *AE, D, DC, MC, V* ☻ *No lunch.*

★ $$–$$$ ✕ **Three Doors Down.** Just half a block away from the busy shopping district around Hawthorne, this small Italian restaurant is known for quality Italian food, with exquisite seafood dishes, skillful pasta concoctions, and decadent desserts. Reservations aren't accepted, but the intimate restaurant's reputation brings people coming back again and again, even though they might have to wait on the sidewalk for close to an hour. ⊠ *1429 S.E. 37th Ave., Hawthorne District* ☎ *503/236–6886* ⚑ *Reservations not accepted* ▭ *A, D, DC, MC, V* ☉ *Closed Sun. and Mon. No lunch.*

**$–$$** ✕ **Il Piatto.** On a quiet residential street, this laid-back trattoria and espresso house turns out inventive dishes and classic Italian favorites. A tasty sun-dried-tomato–pesto spread instead of butter accompanies the bread. Entrées include ahi tuna ravioli with roasted red peppers, capers, and dill in a lemon cream sauce with leeks. The vegetarian lasagna with grilled eggplant, zucchini, and yams is rich and satisfying. The extensive wine selection focuses on varieties from Tuscany. ⊠ *2348 Ankeny St., near Laurelhurst* ☎ *503/236–4997* ▭ *AE, MC, V* ☉ *No lunch Sat.–Mon.*

**$–$$** ✕ **Sylvia's Class Act.** This combo restaurant–dinner theater offers multiple dining options: Dine in a private candlelit booth, family style, in a banquet-room setting, in the lounge away from the kids, or in the theater. The food is classic southern Italian. Try the spinach lasagne or fettuccine Ricardo, with strips of boneless chicken breast, zucchini, and onions tossed in an Alfredo sauce. ⊠ *5115 N.E. Sandy Blvd., 97213* ☎ *503/288–6828* ▭ *AE, D, DC, MC, V* ☉ *No lunch.*

**$** ✕ **Assaggio.** In an age of canned music, it's pleasant to enter a restaurant and hear opera arias. But then, everything about this Sellwood trattoria is extraordinarily pleasant. Many dishes are available as family-style samplers, perfect for sharing. The pasta menu favors vegetarian entrées, but dishes made with chicken or pork sausages are served as well. An excellent wine cellar highlights Italian vintages. The interior, painted in a burnt-sienna shade and accented with classical architectural motifs, lovingly evokes Italy. ⊠ *7742 S.E. 13th Ave., Sellwood* ☎ *503/232–6151* ▭ *AE, D, MC, V* ☉ *Closed Sun. and Mon. No lunch.*

## Japanese

**¢–$** ✕ **Hokkaido.** The soothing sound of water flowing over a rock fountain into a pool with koi greets diners at this Zen-inspired restaurant with a sushi bar. It's better than many Asian restaurants between 42nd and 70th avenues. The large selection of sushi and sashimi is impeccably fresh. The menu includes teriyaki and tempura favorites as well as udon. ⊠ *6744 N.E. Sandy Blvd., near airport* ☎ *503/288–3731* ▭ *MC, V* ☉ *Closed Mon. No lunch Sun.*

## Lebanese

**★ ¢** ✕ **Nicholas' Restaurant.** In a small streetfront along an unimpressive stretch of Grand Avenue, this hidden gem serves some of the best Lebanese food in Portland, for prices that can't be beat. Everything from the fresh homemade pita to the hummus, falafel, baba ghanouj, and kebabs is delicious and comes in enormous portions. No alcohol is served here. ⊠ *318 S.E. Grand Ave., near Morrison Bridge* ☎ *503/235–5123* ▭ *No credit cards.*

## Mexican

**¢–$** ✕ **Chez Grill.** Creative Mexican cuisine, including grilled mushroom fajitas, Baja grilled pork, prawn quesadillas, and lamb tacos, is prepared lovingly at this large, festive restaurant. The fun and unusual feel is created by the combination of disparate elements including exposed forest-green ceiling pipes, crystal chandeliers, sculpted metal handrails and doorways, and Mexican figurines. ⊠ *2229 S.E. Hawthorne Blvd., Hawthorne District* ☎ *503/239–4002* ▭ *D, MC, V* ☉ *No lunch.*

## Seafood

**$$–$$$** ✕ **Winterborne.** French flourishes enliven seafood served at this intimate retreat. The baked or sautéed selections on the seasonal menu come with soup, fresh vegetables, and salad, which is served after the main course.

Add reasonable prices and quality service, and a satisfying dining experience unfolds. ✉ *3520 N.E. 42nd Ave., Beaumont* ☎ *503/249–8486* 🍴 *Reservations essential* 🟰 *AE, D, MC, V* 🕐 *Closed Sun.–Tues. No lunch.*

## Southern

**$–$$$** ✕ **Bernie's Southern Bistro.** You definitely won't find finer soul food in Portland. At first glance, Bernie's may seem fairly expensive for the cuisine, but then, this food is in a different realm from that of your garden variety fried chicken. Restaurant specialties include crisp fried green tomatoes, crawfish, and catfish, in addition to delectable fried chicken, collard greens, and black-eyed peas. The inside of the restaurant is painted in warm oranges, and the outdoor patio is one of Portland's best. ✉ *2904 N.E. Alberta St.* ☎ *503/282–9864* 🟰 *AE, D, MC, V* 🕐 *Closed Sun. and Mon. No lunch.*

## Southwestern

**¢–$** ✕ **Esparza's Tex-Mex Cafe.** Be prepared for south-of-the-border craziness at this beloved local eatery. Wild West kitsch festoons the walls, but it isn't any wilder than some of the entrées that emerge from chef-owner Joe Esparza's kitchen. Look for such creations as lean smoked-sirloin tacos—Esparza's is renowned for its smoked meats—and, for the truly adventurous diner, ostrich enchiladas. ✉ *2725 S.E. Ankeny St., at S.E. 28th Ave., near Laurelhurst* ☎ *503/234–7909* 🟰 *AE, D, MC, V* 🕐 *Closed Sun. and Mon.*

## Spanish

**¢–$** ✕ **Colosso.** A dimly lit tapas bar and restaurant, Colosso is one of the most hip and romantic places to dine in northeast Portland. The best way to get the full experience of the place is to order a pitcher of sangria and split a few of the small tapas plates between you and your companions. In the evening the restaurant is usually crowded with folks drinking cocktails late into the night. ✉ *1932 N.E. Broadway, Broadway District* ☎ *503/288–3333* 🟰 *MC, V* 🕐 *No lunch.*

## Steak

**$–$$$** ✕ **Sayler's Old Country Kitchen.** Home of the massive 72-ounce steak (free if you can eat it in an hour), Sayler's complements its steak-focused menu with a few seafood and chicken dinners. With no pretense of being trendy or hip, this large family-style restaurant and lounge near Gresham has been around since 1946 and relies today on the same old-fashioned menu and quality it did back then. There's brunch on Sunday. ✉ *10519 S.E. Stark St., 97216* ☎ *503/252–4171* 🟰 *AE, D, MC, V* 🕐 *No lunch.*

## Thai

**¢–$** ✕ **Thai Noon.** Opened in 2003 along the bustling stretch of Alberta's art and shopping district, Thai Noon is a popular spot that serves excellent traditional dishes including red, green, and yellow curry; stir fries; and noodle dishes in a simple, attractive dining room with only about 12 tables. You can choose the spiciness of your meal, but beware that although "medium" may be milder than "extra hot," it is still quite spicy. Try the fried banana split or the mango ice cream for dessert. ✉ *2635 N.E. Alberta St., Alberta District* ☎ *503/282–2021* 🟰 *MC, V.*

## Vegetarian

**¢** ✕ **Vita Cafe.** Vegan mac and cheese and vegetarian biscuits and gravy are but a few of the old favorites with a new spin. This trendy restaurant along Alberta Street has a large menu with American, Mexican, Asian, and Middle-Eastern-inspired entrées, and both herbivores and carnivores are sure to find something. There is plenty of free-range, organic meat to go around, in addition to the vegan and vegetarian options. Finish off your meal with a piece of decadent German chocolate cake or a peanut-butter fudge bar. ✉ *3024 N.E. Alberta St., Alberta District* ☎ *503/335–8233* 🖃 *No credit cards.*

### Vietnamese

¢–$$ ✕ **Saigon Kitchen.** Consistently good Vietnamese-Thai food and friendly service have made this restaurant a citywide favorite. The interior is no-nonsense diner, but don't let that deter you. Huge portions of wok-cooked seafood, meat, and vegetable entrées join Thai coconut-milk soups and pad thai on the extensive menu. The healthy spring rolls (meat or tofu) served with peanut sauce are a must. ✉ *835 N.E. Broadway, Lloyd District* ☎ *503/281–3669* 🖃 *AE, D, MC, V.*

¢–$ ✕ **Thanh Thao.** This busy Asian diner in the heart of Portland's bohemian Hawthorne neighborhood has an extensive menu of Vietnamese stir-fries, noodles, soups, and Thai favorites. Be prepared to wait for *and* at your table: the place is almost always packed, and service is famously slow. But the food and generous portions are worth the wait. ✉ *4005 S.E. Hawthorne Blvd., Hawthorne District* ☎ *503/238–6232* 🖃 *D, MC, V.*

## West of Downtown

### American/Casual

¢–$ ✕ **Original Pancake House.** Not to be confused with any chain imitations, this pancake house is the real deal. Faithful customers have been coming for close to 50 years to wait for a table at this bustling, cabin-like local landmark, and you can expect to find a contented crowd of locals and tourists alike from the time the place opens at 7 AM until afternoon. With pancakes starting at $7, it's not the cheapest place to get a stack, but with 20 varieties and some of the best waffles and crepes around, it's worth the trip. ✉ *8600 S.W. Barbur Blvd. Burlingame 97219* ☎ *503/246–9007* 🖃 *No credit cards* ⊘ *Closed Mon. and Tues. No dinner.*

### Contemporary

$$–$$$ ✕ **Chart House.** On a hill high above the Willamette River, the Chart House has a stunning view of the city and the surrounding mountains from almost all of its tables. Prime rib is a specialty, but the seafood dishes, including coconut-crunchy shrimp deep-fried in tempura batter and the Cajun spiced yellowfin ahi are just as tempting. ✉ *5700 S.W. Terwilliger Blvd., 97206* ☎ *503/246–6963* 🖃 *AE, D, DC, MC, V* ⊘ *No lunch weekends.*

### Italian

¢–$ ✕ **Old Spaghetti Factory.** An old trolley car, oversize velvet chairs, dark wood, and fun antiques fill this huge restaurant overlooking the Willamette River. With a lounge upstairs, room for 500 diners, and a great view of the river, the flagship location of this nationwide restaurant chain is a great place for families, with a crowd-pleasing menu of basic pasta dishes and a kids' menu. ✉ *0715 S.W. Bancroft St., 97201* ☎ *503/222–5375* ⌖ *Reservations not accepted* 🖃 *AE, D, DC, MC, V.*

# WHERE TO STAY

Many of the elegant hotels near the city center or on the riverfront appeal because of their proximity to the city's attractions. MAX light rail is within easy walking distance of most properties. Many downtown hotels cater to business travelers and offer special discounts on weekends. Additional accommodations clustered near the Convention Center and the airport are almost exclusively chain hotels and tend to be slightly less expensive than those found downtown. An alternative to the standard hotels in the city are the several beautiful B&Bs spread throughout residential neighborhoods in the northwest and northeast,

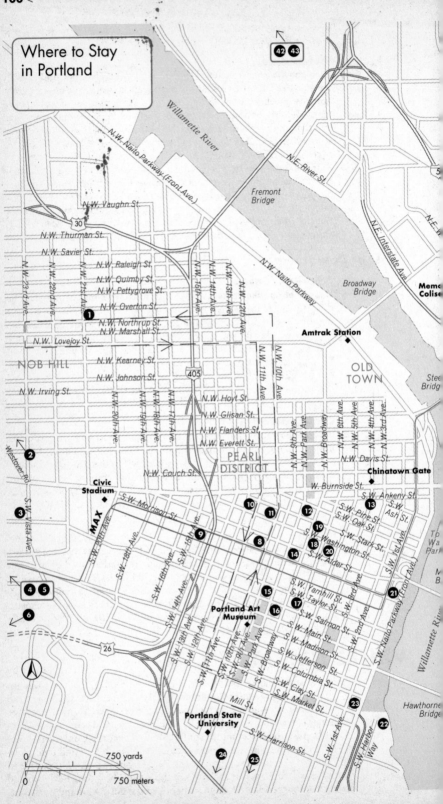

## Where to Stay in Portland

Benson Hotel . . . . . . . . . . . . . **12**
Clyde Hotel . . . . . . . . . . . . . . **11**
Courtyard Airport . . . . . . . . **40**
Doubletree Columbia River . . . **43**
Doubletree Downtown . . . . . . .**25**
Doubletree Hotel
Jantzen Beach . . . . . . . . . . . **42**
Doubletree Hotel
Portland–Lloyd Center . . . . . . **30**
Embassy Suites . . . . . . . . . . . **13**
Embassy Suites Airport . . . . . . **38**
5th Avenue Suites Hotel . . . . **20**
Four Points Sheraton . . . . . . . **21**
Georgian House . . . . . . . . . . .**35**
Governor Hotel . . . . . . . . . . . . **8**
Hawthorne Inn and Suites . . . **27**
Heathman Hotel . . . . . . . . . . **16**
Heron Haus . . . . . . . . . . . . . . **2**
Hillsboro Courtyard
by Marriott . . . . . . . . . . . . . . .**4**
Hilton Garden Inn
Beaverton . . . . . . . . . . . . . . . . **6**
Hilton Portland . . . . . . . . . . . **17**
Hotel Vintage Plaza . . . . . . . **19**
Inn at the
Convention Center . . . . . . . . . **28**
Inn at Northrup Station . . . . . . .**1**
Lion and the Rose . . . . . . . . .**36**
MacMaster House . . . . . . . . . . **3**
Mallory Hotel . . . . . . . . . . . . . **9**
Mark Spencer . . . . . . . . . . . .**10**
Marriott City Center . . . . . . . **18**
Marriott Residence Inn–
Hillsboro . . . . . . . . . . . . . . . . .**5**
Marriott Residence Inn–
Lloyd Center . . . . . . . . . . . . .**33**
McMenamin's
Kennedy School . . . . . . . . . . .**41**
Paramount . . . . . . . . . . . . . . **15**
Portland Guest House . . . . . . **34**
Portland Marriott
Downtown . . . . . . . . . . . . . . **23**
Portland's White House . . . . . **37**
Radisson Hotel . . . . . . . . . . .**31**
Ramada Inn Rose Quarter . . . **32**
Red Lion Hotel
Convention Center . . . . . . . . .**29**
RiverPlace Hotel . . . . . . . . . . **22**
Shilo Suites Airport . . . . . . . . **39**
Sweetbriar Inn . . . . . . . . . . . .**24**
Tudor House . . . . . . . . . . . . . .**26**
Westin . . . . . . . . . . . . . . . . . . **14**

where there are lovely homes, unique and luxurious guest rooms, deluxe home-cooked breakfasts, and friendly and knowledgeable innkeepers.

| WHAT IT COSTS | | | | |
|---|---|---|---|---|
| $$$$ | $$$ | $$ | $ | ¢ |
| HOTELS | over $180 | $140–$180 | $100–$140 | $60–$100 | under $60 |

Hotel prices are for a standard double room, excluding room tax, which varies 6%–9 1/2% depending on location.

## Downtown

★ **$$$–$$$$** 🏨 **Governor Hotel.** With its mahogany walls and mural of Pacific Northwest Indians fishing in Celilo Falls, the clubby lobby of the distinctive Governor sets the overall tone for the hotel's 1920s Arts and Crafts style. Painted in soothing earth tones, the tastefully appointed guest rooms have large windows, honor bars, and bathrobes. Some have whirlpool tubs, fireplaces, and balconies. Jake's Grill is off the lobby, the street-car runs right out front, and the hotel is one block from MAX. Guests may purchase a one-day pass to the adjoining independent health club for $8. ⊠ *611 S.W. 10th Ave., Downtown, 97205* ☎ *503/224–3400 or 800/554–3456* ☏ *503/241–2122* ⊕ *www.govhotel.com* ⟿ *68 rooms, 32 suites* ⟐ *Restaurant, room service, in-room data ports, minibars, video games, health club, bar, dry cleaning, laundry service, concierge, business services, meeting rooms, parking (fee), no-smoking rooms* ⊟ *AE, D, DC, MC, V.*

**$$$–$$$$** 🏨 **Portland Marriott Downtown.** The large rooms at Marriott's 16-floor corporate-focused waterfront property are decorated in off-whites; the best ones face east with a view of the Willamette and the Cascades. All rooms have work desks, high-speed Internet access, and voice mail. Champions Lounge, filled with sports memorabilia, is a singles' hot spot on weekends. It's six blocks from MAX light rail. ⊠ *1401 S.W. Naito Pkwy., Downtown, 97201* ☎ *503/226–7600 or 800/228–9290* ☏ *503/221–1789* ⊕ *www.marriott.com* ⟿ *503 rooms, 6 suites* ⟐ *Restaurant, coffee shop, room service, in-room data ports, indoor pool, hot tub, health club, bar, shop, laundry facilities, dry cleaning, laundry service, concierge, business services, convention center, airport shuttle, meeting rooms, parking (fee), no-smoking rooms* ⊟ *AE, D, DC, MC, V.*

★ **$$–$$$$** 🏨 **Benson Hotel.** Portland's grandest hotel was built in 1912. The hand-carved Russian Circassian walnut paneling and the Italian white-marble staircase are among the noteworthy design touches in the public areas. In the guest rooms expect to find small crystal chandeliers, inlaid mahogany doors, and the original ceilings. Extra touches include fully stocked private bars, bathrobes, and nightly turn-down service. ⊠ *309 S.W. Broadway, Downtown, 97205* ☎ *503/228–2000 or 800/549–9099* ☏ *503/471–3920* ⊕ *www.bensonhotel.com* ⟿ *286 rooms* ⟐ *2 restaurants, coffee shop, room service, in-room data ports, minibars, cable TV with movies and video games, gym, bar, lobby lounge, laundry service, concierge, Internet, business services, meeting rooms, parking (fee)* ⊟ *AE, D, DC, MC, V.*

**$$–$$$$** 🏨 **Paramount.** Inside this 15-story boutique-style property—two blocks from Pioneer Square, MAX, and the Portland Art Museum—earth tones, plush dark-wood furnishings, dried flowers, honor bars, and granite baths adorn the cozy rooms. Some have outdoor balconies and whirlpool tubs. The grand suites, which also have wet bars and gas fireplaces, have magnificent views of the city. ⊠ *808 S.W. Taylor St., Downtown, 97205* ☎ *503/223–9900* ☏ *503/223–7900* ⊕ *www.paramounthotel.net* ⟿ *154 rooms* ⟐ *Restaurant, room service, in-*

*room data ports, minibars, refrigerators, room TVs with video games, gym, dry cleaning, laundry service, business services, meeting rooms, concierge, parking (fee), no-smoking floors* ⊟ *AE, D, DC, MC, V.*

**$$–$$$$** 🖳 **Westin.** Opened in 1999, this European-style boutique property combines luxury with convenience. Its tastefully appointed rooms include entertainment-center armoires, work desks, plush beds covered with layers of down, and granite bathrooms with separate showers and tubs. Pioneer Square and MAX are two blocks away. The Oritalia restaurant combines the best of Mediterranean and Asian cuisines. ⊠ *750 S.W. Alder St., Downtown, 97205* ☎ *503/294–9000 or 888/625–5144* 🖷 *503/241– 9565* 🖫 *205 rooms* ♿ *Restaurant, room service, in-room data ports, in-room safes, refrigerators, gym, bar, dry cleaning, laundry service, concierge, business services, meeting rooms, parking (fee)* ⊟ *AE, D, DC, MC, V.*

★ **$$$** 🖳 **5th Avenue Suites Hotel.** The 1912 Lipman Wolfe Department Store reopened as this boutique hotel in 1997. A tall vestibule with a marble mosaic floor leads to the art-filled lobby, where guests gather by the fireplace for an early-evening glass of wine or a cup of coffee. Warm fall colors, stripes, and floral prints adorn the 10-story property's 550-square-foot suites, divided by curtained sliding doors. Upholstered chairs, fringed ottomans, and other appointments in the sitting areas will make you feel right at home (or wish you had one like this). The large bathrooms are stocked with every amenity, including samplers of Aveda products—a nod to the Aveda Lifestyle Spa at the hotel. ⊠ *506 S.W. Washington St., Downtown, 97205* ☎ *503/222–0001 or 888/207– 2201* 🖷 *503/222–0004* ⊕ *www.5thavenuesuites.com* 🖫 *82 rooms, 137 suites* ♿ *Restaurant, room service, in-room data ports, minibars, room TVs with movies and video games, massage, health club, dry cleaning, laundry service, business services, meeting rooms, parking (fee), some pets allowed, no-smoking rooms* ⊟ *AE, D, DC, MC, V.*

**$$$** 🖳 **Heathman Hotel.** Superior service, a renowned restaurant, a central down-

Fodor'sChoice ★ town location (adjoining the Performing Arts Center), and swank public areas have earned the Heathman its reputation for quality. From the teak-panel lobby hung with Warhol prints to the rosewood elevators and marble fireplaces, this hotel exudes refinement. The earth-tone guest rooms are luxuriously comfortable, and the bathrooms have plenty of marble and mirrors. The second-floor mezzanine, with a small art gallery with works changing every several weeks and a small library (primarily filled with the works of notable Heathman guests), overlooks the high-ceiling Tea Court, which becomes a popular gathering spot in the evening. ⊠ *1009 S.W. Broadway, Downtown, 97205* ☎ *503/241–4100 or 800/ 551–0011* 🖷 *503/790–7110* ⊕ *www.heathmanhotel.com* 🖫 *117 rooms, 33 suites* ♿ *Restaurant, room service, in-room data ports, minibars, gym, bar, library, dry cleaning, laundry service, concierge, Internet, meeting rooms, parking (fee), no-smoking floors* ⊟ *AE, D, DC, MC, V.*

**$$$** 🖳 **Hilton Portland.** Built in 1963, the Hilton became Oregon's largest hotel in 2002 when it opened its Executive Tower across the street, at the corner of 6th and Taylor. Together, the two buildings comprise a gargantuan complex of luxuriously contemporary bedrooms, meeting rooms, restaurants, and athletic facilities, including two indoor swimming pools. The property is within walking distance of the Performing Arts Center, Pioneer Courthouse Square, the Portland Art Museum, and MAX light rail. Alexander's restaurant offers a fantastic view of the Portland area from the 23rd floor. More than 60 restaurants are within a few blocks. ⊠ *921 S.W. 6th Ave., Downtown, 97204* ☎ *503/226– 1611 or 800/HILTONS* 🖷 *503/220–2565* ⊕ *www.hilton.com* 🖫 *773 rooms, 9 suites* ♿ *3 restaurants, in-room data ports, room TVs with movies and video games, 2 indoor pools, gym, hot tub, massage, sauna,* *steam room, 2 bars, shop, Internet, business services, convention center, parking (fee), no-smoking rooms = AE, D, DC, MC, V.*

**$$$** RiverPlace Hotel. With its bright rooms, wing chairs, teak tables, and feather pillows, this hotel evokes a European setting, complete with landscaped courtyard. It has one of the best views in Portland, overlooking the river, the marina, and skyline. ⌗ *1510 S.W. Harbor Way, Downtown, 97201* ☎ *503/228–3233 or 800/227–1333* ⎙ *503/295–6161* ⊕ *www.riverplacehotel.com* ⤺ *39 rooms, 45 suites* & *Restaurant, room service, in-room data ports, minibars, hot tub, sauna, concierge, business services, meeting rooms, parking (fee), no-smoking rooms* = *AE, D, DC, MC, V* ⎟⊙⎟ *CP.*

**$$–$$$** Embassy Suites. The grand lobby welcomes you at this Old Town property in the historic Multnomah Hotel building. The spacious accommodations in the all-suites property have large windows, sofa beds, and wet bars and come with terry bathrobes. The basement-level pool and exercise area is a special treat. A complimentary van will take you anywhere within a 2-mi radius. A full breakfast, cooked to order, and happy-hour cocktails are included in the room rate. The riverfront and MAX light rail are within walking distance. ⌗ *319 S.W. Pine St., Downtown, 97204* ☎ *503/279–9000 or 800/362–2779* ⎙ *503/497–9051* ⊕ *www.embassysuites.com* ⤺ *276 suites* & *Restaurant, in-room data ports, microwaves, refrigerators, indoor pool, gym, hot tub, spa, steam room, bar, laundry service, concierge, business services, meeting room, parking (fee)* = *AE, D, DC, MC, V* ⎟⊙⎟ *BP.*

**$$–$$$** Four Points Sheraton. If you're concerned about location, consider this five-story hotel on the MAX light-rail line. Starwood Hotels converted the former Riverside into this boutique hotel in 1999. Some of the rooms have balconies; east-facing rooms offer views of the Willamette River and the Governor Tom McCall Waterfront Park. Guests have privileges at Bally's Total Fitness nearby. ⌗ *50 S.W. Morrison St., Downtown, 97204* ☎ *503/221–0711 or 800/899–0247* ⎙ *503/484–1417* ⊕ *www.fourpointsportlaned.com* ⤺ *140 rooms* & *Restaurant, room service, room TVs with movies and video games, bar, dry cleaning, laundry service, business services, meeting rooms, parking (fee), some pets allowed, no-smoking floors* = *AE, D, DC, MC, V.*

**$$–$$$** Hotel Vintage Plaza. This historic landmark takes its theme from the area's vineyards. Guests can fall asleep counting stars in top-floor rooms, where skylights and wall-to-wall conservatory-style windows rate highly among the special details. Hospitality suites have extra-large rooms with a full living area, and the deluxe rooms have a bar. All are appointed in warm colors and have cherry-wood furnishings; some rooms have hot tubs. Complimentary wine is served in the evening, and an extensive collection of Oregon vintages is displayed in the tasting room. Two-story town house suites are named after local wineries. ⌗ *422 S.W. Broadway, Downtown, 97205* ☎ *503/228–1212 or 800/243–0555* ⎙ *503/228–3598* ⊕ *www.vintageplaza.com* ⤺ *107 rooms, 21 suites* & *Restaurant, room service, in-room data ports, minibars, gym, bar, concierge, business services, meeting room, parking (fee)* = *AE, D, DC, MC, V.*

**$$–$$$** Mallory Hotel. The years have been kind to this 1920s-vintage hotel eight blocks from the downtown core. Its gilt-ceiling lobby has fresh white paint and floral carpeting; crystal chandeliers and a leaded-glass skylight hark back to a more genteel era. The rooms are old-fashioned but clean and cheerful and have been refurbished; corner suites and rooms on the east side of the building have impressive skyline views. The hotel is a favorite with visiting singers, writers, and artists of every stripe. The staff is friendly and knowledgeable. ⌗ *729 S.W. 15th Ave., Downtown, 97205* ☎ *503/223–6311 or 800/228–8657* ⎙ *503/223–0522*

⊕ *www.malloryhotel.com* ⮌ *130 rooms* ⏃ *Restaurant, in-room data ports, refrigerators, bar, free parking, some pets allowed (fee), no-smoking rooms* ⊟ *AE, D, DC, MC, V* ⫴❂⫴ *CP.*

$$-$$$ ⊞ **Marriott City Center.** The lobby of this 20-story boutique property, in the heart of the downtown arts and dining area, is accented with a grand staircase, maple paneling, and marble floors. The plush rooms, designed for business travelers, have voice mail, large work desks, and coffeemakers. The MAX light rail is two blocks away. ⊠ *520 S.W. Broadway, Downtown, 97205* ☎ *503/226–6300 or 800/228–9290* ⎙ *503/227–7515* ⊕ *www.marriott.com* ⮌ *249 rooms, 10 suites* ⏃ *Restaurant, room service, in-room data ports, hot tub, gym, bar, laundry service, concierge, business services, meeting rooms, parking (fee)* ⊟ *AE, D, DC, MC, V.*

$-$$$ ⊞ **Clyde Hotel.** Built in 1902, this historic building has been restored to its original design. Today it operates as a limited-service historic hotel. Rooms have claw-foot tubs, and there are a few romantic suites. Don't expect all the amenities of the other downtown hotels here; the focus is on the historic charm, not luxury. Several shared-bath rooms are also available for slightly lower rates. ⊠ *1022 S.W. Stark St., 97205* ☎ *503/224–8000* ⎙ *503/224–9999* ⮌ *36 rooms* ⏃ *Cable TV; no room phones* ⊟ *AE, D, MC, V* ⫴❂⫴ *CP.*

$$ ⊞ **Doubletree Downtown.** Close to Portland State University and Oregon Health Sciences University, this hotel provides extremely comfortable and spacious accommodations for less money than many other downtown hotels. Close to the waterfront, it is in a convenient spot for walking to most downtown destinations. ⊠ *310 S.W. Lincoln, 97201* ☎ *503/221–0450* ⎙ *503/225–4303* ⊕ *www.doubletree.com* ⮌ *235 rooms* ⏃ *Restaurant, in-room data ports, cable TV, pool, gym, laundry facilities, meeting rooms, parking (fee)* ⊟ *AE, D, DC, MC, V.*

$-$$ ⊞ **Mark Spencer.** Near Portland's gay bar district and Powell's City of Books, the Mark Spencer has one of the best values in town. The rooms are clean and comfortable, and all have full kitchens. Other amenities include free high-speed wireless Internet and a rooftop garden deck open to all guests. The hotels bills itself as a major supporter of the arts in the area and has acted as housing sponsor for the America Repertory Theatre, Portland Opera, and Center Stage. Special room-rate packages are available that include theater tickets to local performances. ⊠ *409 S.W. 11th Ave., 97205* ☎ *503/224–3293 or 800/548–3934* ⎙ *503/223–7848* ⊕ *www.markspencer.com* ⮌ *101 rooms* ⏃ *In-room data ports, kitchens, cable TV, laundry facilities, dry cleaning, meeting rooms, some pets allowed (fee)* ⊟ *AE, D, DC, MC, V* ⫴❂⫴ *CP.*

## East of the Willamette

$$-$$$ ⊞ **Doubletree Hotel Portland—Lloyd Center.** This busy and business-oriented hotel maintains a huge traffic in meetings and special events. The public areas are a tasteful mix of marble, rose-and-green carpet, and antique-style furnishings. The large rooms, many with balconies, have views of the mountains or the city center. Lloyd Center and the MAX light-rail line are across the street; the Oregon Convention Center is a five-minute walk away. ⊠ *1000 N.E. Multnomah St., Lloyd District, 97232* ☎ *503/281–6111 or 800/222–8733* ⎙ *503/284–8553* ⊕ *www.doubletree. com* ⮌ *476 rooms* ⏃ *2 restaurants, coffee shop, room service, in-room data ports, pool, gym, bar, dry cleaning, laundry service, concierge, business services, meeting rooms, parking (fee)* ⊟ *AE, D, DC, MC, V.*

★ $$-$$$ ⊞ **Portland's White House.** Hardwood floors with Oriental rugs, chandeliers, antiques, and fountains create a warm and romantic mood at this elegant bed-and-breakfast inn in a Greek Revival mansion in the historic Irvington District. The mansion, built in 1911 and on the National Register of Historic Landmarks, was remodeled in 1997. Rooms have private baths and mahogany canopy or four-poster queen- and king-size beds. The Garden Room overlooks a courtyard from its own portico. A full breakfast is included in the room rate, and the owners offer vegetarian or low-fat options. Smoking and pets are not permitted. ⊠ *1914 N.E. 22nd Ave., Irvington, 97212* ☎ *503/287–7131 or 800/ 272–7131* 🖷 *503/249–1641* ⊕ *www.portlandswhitehouse.com* ➴ *9 suites* ♿ *Dining room, in-room data ports, library, free parking; no smoking* ▭ *AE, D, MC, V* ⦿| *BP.*

**$$**   **Lion and the Rose.** This 1906 Queen Anne-style mansion is one of Portland's premier B&Bs and the city's only Victorian one. Oak and mahogany floors, original light fixtures, antique silver, and the coffered dining-room ceiling set a tone of formal elegance, while the wonderfully friendly, accommodating, and knowledgeable innkeepers make sure that you feel perfectly at home. A two-course breakfast and evening snacks are served daily, and afternoon tea is available upon request. In a beautiful residential neighborhood, you are just a block from the shops and restaurants that fill northeast Broadway and within an easy walk of a free MAX ride downtown. ⊠ *1810 N.E. 15th Ave., 97212* ☎ *503/287– 9245 or 800/955–1644* 🖷 *503/287–9247* ⊕ *www.lionrose.com* ➴ *6 rooms* ♿ *In-room data ports, in-room VCRs, business services, free parking; no kids under 7, no smoking* ▭ *AE, D, MC, V.*

Fodor'sChoice
★

**$$**   **Marriott Residence Inn–Lloyd Center.** With large, fully equipped suites and a short walk both to the Lloyd Center and a MAX stop within Fareless Square, this three-level apartment-style complex is perfect for extended-stay visitors or for tourists. Rooms come equipped with full kitchens and ample seating space, and many have wood-burning fireplaces. In addition to a large complementary breakfast buffet each morning, on weekday evenings an hors d'oeuvres reception presents a small meal such as minestrone soup or chicken wings. ⊠ *1710 N.E. Multnomah St., Lloyd District, 97232* ☎ *503/288–1400 or 800/331–3131* 🖷 *503/288–0241* ⊕ *www.residenceinnportland.com* ➴ *168 rooms* ♿ *In-room data ports, kitchens, microwaves, pool, outdoor hot tub, basketball, volleyball, lobby lounge, laundry facilities, meeting rooms, business services, free parking, some pets allowed (fee), no-smoking rooms* ⦿| *BP.*

**$$**   **Radisson Hotel.** This sleek, modern hotel is very close to the Rose Quarter, the Coliseum, and the Convention Center and is within easy walking distance of Lloyd Center, the MAX line, and the Broadway Bridge leading to downtown. Between its attractive rooms and its ample facilities, it provides a reliable and convenient option for both business travelers and tourists. ⊠ *1441 N.E. 2nd Ave., 97232* ☎ *503/233–2401* 🖷 *503/238–7016* ⊕ *www.radisson.com* ➴ *238 rooms* ♿ *Restaurant, in-room data ports, cable TV, pool, gym, bar, business services, meeting rooms* ▭ *AE, D, DC, MC, V.*

**$–$$**   **Georgian House.** This redbrick Georgian Colonial–style house with neoclassical columns is on a quiet, tree-lined street in the Irvington neighborhood. The gardens in back can be enjoyed from a solarium and from a vine-canopied deck and gazebo. The largest and sunniest of the guest rooms is the Lovejoy Suite, with a tile fireplace and brass canopy bed. ⊠ *1828 N.E. Siskiyou St., 97212* ☎ *503/281–2250 or 888/282– 2250* 🖷 *503/281–3301* ⊕ *www.thegeorgianhouse.com* ➴ *3 rooms, 2 with shared bath; 1 suite* ♿ *No room phones, no smoking, no TV in some rooms* ▭ *MC, V* ⦿| *BP.*

**$–$$**   **Inn at the Convention Center.** In 2002 this old Best Western changed hands and is now an independently run hotel with many of the same features. Directly across the street from the Convention Center, four blocks from Lloyd Center, and right along the MAX line, this no-frills hotel offers convenience as its main asset. Many of the simple and comfort-

able rooms at the six-story facility have refrigerators and/or minibars.
✉ *420 N.E. Holladay St., Lloyd District/Convention Center, 97232*
☎ *503/233–6331* 🖷 *503/233–2677* ⟿ *97 rooms* ♻ *Some minibars, some
refrigerators, laundry facilities, dry cleaning, laundry service, free parking, no-smoking rooms* ▤ *AE, D, DC, MC, V.*

★ **$-$$** 🏨 **McMenamins Kennedy School.** In a renovated elementary school in north-
east Portland, the Kennedy School may well be one of the most unusual
hotels you'll ever encounter. With all of the guest rooms occupying former classrooms, complete with the original chalkboards and cloak-
rooms, and with small bars known as Detention Bar (with cigars and
the only television on site) and Honors Bar (with classical music and
cocktails), the McMenamins brothers have created a multi-use facility
that is both luxurious and fantastical. Room rates include breakfast for
two, movie admission, and use of the outdoor soaking pool. ✉ *5736
N.E. 33rd Ave., near Alberta District, 97211* ☎ *503/249–3983* ⊕ *www.
kennedyschool.com* ⟿ *35 rooms* ♻ *Restaurant, in-room data ports, outdoor hot tub, 4 bars, cinema, shop, meeting rooms, free parking; no room
TVs, no smoking* ▤ *AE, D, DC, MC, V* ⦿| *BP.*

**$-$$** 🏨 **Portland Guest House.** Inside a northeast Portland working-class Vic-
torian home with a dusty-heather exterior paint job, this cozy B&B near
the Lloyd Center contains rooms with antique walnut furniture, original Pacific Northwest artwork, and phones. The rates include a full breakfast. No smoking is permitted. ✉ *1720 N.E. 15th St., Irvington, 97212*
☎ *503/282–1402* ⊕ *www.teleport.com/~pgh* ⟿ *7 rooms, 5 with bath*
♻ *Free parking; no smoking* ▤ *AE, DC, MC, V* ⦿| *BP.*

**$-$$** 🏨 **Red Lion Hotel Convention Center.** Across the street from the Conven-
tion Center and adjacent to the MAX, this hotel is as convenient as can
be for both business travelers and tourists. Though a hotel has occu-
pied this spot for quite some time, it became a Red Lion only in 2003,
and the rooms and facilities were renovated during the transition. It provides a few more on-site amenities than some of the other hotels right
by the Convention Center (Shilo Inn and Inn at the Convention Center
are right across the street), which is reflected in its slightly higher rates.
✉ *1021 N.E. Grand Ave., 97232* ☎ *503/235–2100 or 800/RED–LION*
🖷 *503/238–0132* ⊕ *www.redlion.com* ⟿ *174 rooms* ♻ *Restaurant, room
service, in-room data ports, refrigerators, cable TV with movies and video
games, gym, lounge, meeting rooms, business services, parking (fee).*

**$-$$** 🏨 **Tudor House.** This 5,400-square-foot bed-and-breakfast, set on extensive
grounds edged with laurel bushes, hawthorne trees, and azaleas, resembles a Tudor manor. Antiques crowd the house, the guest rooms, and the
dining room, where breakfast is served. ✉ *2321 N.E. 28th Ave., 97212*
☎ *503/287–9476* 🖷 *503/288–8363* ⊕ *www.tudor-house.com* ⟿ *3 dou-
ble rooms, 1 suite* ♻ *Cable TV; no smoking* ▤ *AE, D, MC, V* ⦿| *BP.*

**$** 🏨 **Ramada Inn Rose Quarter.** Remodeled in 1999, rooms at this Ramada
have pastel walls, floral-print bedspreads, and mauve drapes. You're also
only two blocks from the Rose Garden arena, Memorial Coliseum, the
Oregon Convention Center, and MAX light rail. The Mucho Grande
Restaurant and Lounge, adjoining the hotel, claims to be "Home of the
World's Largest Margarita." ✉ *10 N.E. Weidler St., Rose Quarter,
97227* ☎ *503/287–9900* 🖷 *503/287–3500* ⊕ *www.ramada.com* ⟿ *180
rooms* ♻ *Restaurant, room service, in-room data ports, indoor pool,
bar, dry cleaning, laundry service, business services, free parking, no-
smoking floors* ▤ *AE, D, DC, MC, V.*

## West of Downtown

**$$-$$$$** 🏨 **Heron Haus.** This lovely, bright B&B is inside a stately, 100-year-old
three-floor Tudor-style mansion near Forest Park. Special features in-

clude a tulip-shape bathtub in one room and a tile, seven-head antique shower in another. You can enjoy a relaxing afternoon in the secluded sitting garden. All rooms have phones, work desks, and fireplaces. Breakfast, included in the room rate, is a fancy Continental affair. ⊠ *2545 N.W. Westover Rd., Nob Hill, 97210* ☎ *503/274–1846* 🖷 *503/ 248–4055* ⊕ *www.heronhaus.com* 📠 *6 rooms* 🕭 *In-room data ports, library, business services, free parking; no smoking* ▭ *MC, V* ᵀᴼᴵ *CP.*

★ **$–$$$** 🖼 **Inn @ Northrup Station.** Bright colors, original artwork, retro designs, and extremely luxurious suites fill this hotel in Nob Hill. Just moments from the shopping and dining on Northwest 21st Avenue, the inn looks like a stylish apartment building from the outside, with patios or balconies adjoining most of the suites, and a garden terrace for all guests to use. The striking colors and bold patterns found on bedspreads, armchairs, pillows, and throughout the halls and lobby manage to be charming, elegant, and fun, never falling into the kitschiness that plagues many places that strive for "retro" decor. All rooms have full kitchens, two TVs, three phones, and large sitting areas. ⊠ *2025 N.W. Northrup St., Nob Hill, 97209* ☎ *503/224–0543 or 800/224–1180* 🖷 *503/273–2102* ⊕ *www.northrupstation.com* 📠 *70 suites* 🕭 *In-room data ports, kitchens, room TVs with movies and video games, free parking; no smoking* ▭ *AE, D, DC, MC, V* ᵀᴼᴵ *CP.*

**$$** 🖼 **Hilton Garden Inn Beaverton.** This four-level Hilton in suburban Beaverton brings a much-needed lodging option to Portland's west side. The property offers bright rooms with plush carpeting, work desks, and microwaves. It's right off U.S. 26. ⊠ *15520 N.W. Gateway Ct., Beaverton* ☎ *503/439–1717 or 800/445–8667* 🖷 *503/439–1818* ⊕ *www. hilton.com* 📠 *150 rooms* 🕭 *Restaurant, room service, in-room data ports, microwaves, refrigerators, cable TV with movies, indoor pool, hot tub, exercise equipment, bar, business services, meeting rooms, free parking, no-smoking rooms* ▭ *AE, D, DC, MC, V.*

★ **$$** 🖼 **MacMaster House.** On King's Hill, next to Washington Park's Japanese and rose gardens, this 17-room Colonial Revival mansion built in the 1890s is comfortable, funky, and fascinating. A hybrid assortment of Victorian furniture and antiques fills the parlors, and the guest rooms on the second and third floors are charming without being too cute. The two suites with large, private, old-fashioned baths are the ones to choose, especially the spacious Artist's Studio, tucked garretlike under the dormers, with a high brass bed and fireplace. A two-night minimum stay is required on the weekends. ⊠ *1041 S.W. Vista Ave., Washington Park area, 97205* ☎ *503/223–7362 or 800/774–9523* 🖷 *503/224– 8808* ⊕ *www.macmaster.com* 📠 *5 rooms with shared bath, 2 suites* 🕭 *Cable TV, free parking* ▭ *AE, D, DC, MC, V* ᵀᴼᴵ *BP.*

**$$** 🖼 **Marriott Residence Inn Hillsboro.** Near the west side's many high-tech offices and fabrication plants, this all-suites motel is popular with people relocating to Portland and perfect for extended stays. It's within walking distance of several restaurants, a shopping center, and a multiplex theater. The homey suites, some with fireplaces, have full kitchens. ⊠ *18855 N.W. Tanasbourne Dr., Hillsboro 97124* ☎ *503/531–3200 or 800/331–3131* 🖷 *503/645–1581* ⊕ *www.marriott.com* 📠 *122 suites* 🕭 *In-room data ports, kitchens, cable TV, in-room VCRs, tennis court, pool, hot tub, gym, laundry facilities, laundry service, business services, meeting room, free parking, some pets allowed (fee), no-smoking rooms* ▭ *AE, D, DC, MC, V* ᵀᴼᴵ *BP.*

**$–$$** 🖼 **Hillsboro Courtyard by Marriott.** Next door to the Residence Inn, this hotel offers easy access to shopping and restaurants in Hillsboro, as well as quick access onto U.S. 26 toward Portland. With large, comfortable rooms, it is perfect for business travelers, or for tourists who don't mind being several miles from downtown Portland. ⊠ *3050 N.W. Stucki Pl.,*

*Hillsboro 97124* ☎ *503/690–1800 or 800/321–2211* 🖷 *503/690–0236* ⊕ *www.marriott.com* 🛏 *149 rooms, 6 suites* ⬩ *Restaurant, room service, in-room data ports, cable TV with movies, indoor pool, hot tub, gym, lounge, dry cleaning, laundry facilities, business services, meeting rooms, no-smoking rooms* ☰ *AE, D, DC, MC, V.*

$  🖸 **Sweetbrier Inn.** Set on landscaped grounds among fir and pine trees just off I–5 several miles south of Portland, this two-story manor-style property in Tualatin provides a peaceful lodging option for those who don't mind being a bit farther away from the action of the city. The majority of the bright, hardwood-furnished rooms in the L-shape complex are accessible via an outside walkway that winds around the complex, and many of them look out onto an inner courtyard. It's near golf courses, tennis courts, and a jogging track. ⊠ *7125 S.W. Nyberg Rd., Tualatin 97062* ☎ *503/692–5800 or 800/551–9167* 🖷 *503/692–3079* 🛏 *98 rooms, 32 suites* ⬩ *Restaurant, room service, in-room data ports, pool, gym, bar, playground, laundry service, meeting rooms, free parking* ☰ *AE, D, DC, MC, V.*

## Portland International Airport Area

$$$–$$$$  🖸 **Embassy Suites Airport.** Suites in this eight-story atrium hotel have beige walls and blond-wood furnishings. The lobby has a waterfall and pond with koi. All suites come with separate bedrooms and living areas with sleeper sofas. A full breakfast is included, and cocktails are free at happy hour. It's on the new MAX airport line. ⊠ *7900 N.E. 82nd Ave., Airport, 97220* ☎ *503/460–3000* 🖷 *503/460–3030* 🛏 *251 suites* ⬩ *Restaurant, room service, in-room data ports, microwaves, refrigerators, minibars, cable TV, indoor pool, hot tub, gym, laundry service, concierge, meeting rooms, airport shuttle, business services, free parking* ☰ *AE, D, DC, MC, V* 🍽 *BP.*

$–$$$  🖸 **Doubletree Hotel Jantzen Beach.** The four-story Doubletree, on the Columbia River, has larger-than-average rooms, many with balconies and good views of the river and Vancouver, Washington. Public areas glitter with brass and bright lights that accentuate the greenery and the burgundy, green, and rose color scheme. The menu at Maxi's Seafood Restaurant highlights ingredients fresh from Pacific Northwest fields, farms, and waters. ⊠ *909 N. Hayden Island Dr. (east of I–5's Jantzen Beach exit), Jantzen Beach, 97217* ☎ *503/283–4466 or 800/222–8733* 🖷 *503/283–4743* ⊕ *www.doubletree.com* 🛏 *320 rooms* ⬩ *2 restaurants, room service, in-room data ports, cable TV with movies, pool, hot tub, tennis court, gym, bar, laundry facilities, dry cleaning, business services, meeting room, no-smoking rooms* ☰ *AE, D, DC, MC, V.*

$$  🖸 **Courtyard Airport.** This six-story Marriott inn is designed for business travelers. Rooms are brightly decorated in earth tones and have sitting areas, work desks, and high-speed Internet access. It's ¾ mi east of I–205. ⊠ *11550 N.E. Airport Way, Airport, 97220* ☎ *503/252–3200 or 800/321–2211* 🖷 *503/252–8921* ⊕ *www.courtyard.com* 🛏 *150 rooms, 10 suites* ⬩ *Restaurant, room service, coffee shop, in-room data ports, cable TV with movies, pool, hot tub, gym, bar, dry cleaning, laundry facilities, laundry service, business services, meeting rooms, free parking, no-smoking rooms* ☰ *AE, D, DC, MC, V.*

$$  🖸 **Shilo Suites Airport.** Each room in this large, four-level all-suites inn is bright, with floral-print bedspreads and drapes, and has a microwave, wet bar, and two oversize beds. The indoor pool and hot tub are open 24 hours. Local calls are free. ⊠ *11707 N.E. Airport Way, Airport, 97220* ☎ *503/252–7500 or 800/222–2244* 🖷 *503/254–0794* ⊕ *www.shiloinns.com* 🛏 *200 rooms* ⬩ *Restaurant, room service, in-room data ports, refrigerators, microwaves, minibars, cable TV with movies, indoor pool,*

# CloseUp

## THE SHANGHAI TUNNELS

TODAY PORTLAND IS RENOWNED as one of America's most livable cities, but just a short century and a half ago, it was infamously regarded as one of the most dangerous port cities on the West Coast, if not the world. Why? The answers, and many more questions, lie in a part of Portland that few people know about and even fewer have laid eyes on: the Portland Underground, a.k.a. the Shanghai Tunnels.

In Portland's Victorian heyday in the second half of the 19th century, the neighborhoods near the waterfront saw the seedier side of the city's activities, with saloons, bordellos, and boardinghouses catering to the sailors and other working folk who passed through Portland looking for a night of relaxation after a day or month of hard labor. But a night of drinking turned into an ongoing nightmare for thousands of unsuspecting young men, when they woke up the next morning on a ship bound for Asia. They had been Shanghaied.

That is, their drink had been drugged, and their unconscious bodies carried through a series of underground tunnels leading to the waterfront, where they were sold to a ship's captain as slave labor, not to awaken until they were at sea, with no way to escape, and no options but to work or die. It might sound like a far-fetched legend told to wide-eyed children to keep them away from the unsavory parts of town, but this cautionary tale is no myth. If it helps to prove it, you can take a tour of the very tunnels into which unwitting victims vanished.

Historian Michael Jones has worked for many years to discover, explore, restore, and preserve the labyrinth of underground passageways that still exists under the stores, restaurants, and apartment buildings of Old Town, Chinatown, and Downtown Portland. Working with the Cascade Geographic Society, he provides guided tours of the "Shanghai Tunnels," where visitors can see the tunnels, holding cells, and trap doors through which victims were literally dropped from a saloon or boardinghouse into the underground. The underground used to extend all the way to Northwest 23rd, but a large portion is inaccessible today; what is clearly evident, however, is that all tunnels eventually led to the waterfront, where the inconspicuously transported bodies were passed between the hands of the "crimp" and the sea captain, who paid upwards of $50 per head—not a bad price for a sailor who, to ever return to Portland, would have to work for at least six years (the duration of two full passages).

Not surprisingly, this subterranean haven of abduction, abuse, and corruption has piqued the interest not only of history buffs but enthusiasts of the tales of the supernatural as well. Where better than in the musty, abandoned, underground sites of century-old kidnappings to discover apparitions of the undead? Indeed, Northwest Paranormal Investigations has declared the Shanghai Tunnels to be the most haunted place in Oregon. For those interested in the creepier side of an already creepy place, the Cascade Geographic Society offers the "Shanghai Tunnels Ghost Tours" in addition to the standard "Heritage Tour."

All tours must be booked in advance by calling the Cascade Geographic Society (☎ 503/622–4798). Tours depart from Hobo's Restaurant, cost $11, and last about an hour and a half.

— By Sarah Kennedy

*hot tub, steam room, gym, bar, laundry facilities, dry cleaning, laundry service, business services, meeting rooms, airport shuttle, free parking, no-smoking floor* ⊟ *AE, D, DC, MC, V* ⊠ *CP.*

**$–$$** ⊡ **Doubletree—Columbia River.** On Hayden Island between Portland and Vancouver, Washington, close to the Jantzen Beach shopping area, this Doubletree overlooks the Columbia River and is directly next to the Doubletree Jantzen Beach, its sister hotel. It is an easy drive to downtown and the airport, although nothing terribly interesting is within walking distance. Rooms are decorated in earth tones and many have riverfront views and balconies. ⊠ *1401 N. Hayden Island Dr., 97217* ☎ *503/283–2111* 🖨 *503/283–4718* ⇩ *351 rooms* ⟡ *2 restaurants, room service, in-room data ports, cable TV with movies, pool, hair salon, putting green, business services, airport shuttle, some pets allowed (fee)* ⊟ *AE, D, DC, MC, V.*

**$** ⊡ **Hawthorne Inn and Suites.** Although it is in Gresham, this hotel's proximity to I–205 makes for easy access to downtown, and it's just a short ride to the airport. Rooms are spacious and comfortable, and much of the hotel's interior has a woodsy flair that distinguishes it from many other chain hotels. Suites include kitchenettes, and a hot breakfast buffet is offered every morning. ⊠ *2323 N.E. 181st Ave., Gresham, 97230* ☎ *503/492–4000* 🖨 *503/492–3271* ⇩ *71 rooms, 23 suites* ⟡ *In-room data ports, some kitchenettes, cable TV with movies, indoor pool, gym, hot tub, laundry facilities, meeting rooms, business services, free parking, some pets allowed, no-smoking rooms* ⊟ *AE, D, DC, MC, V* ⊠ *BP.*

# NIGHTLIFE & THE ARTS

"A&E, The Arts and Entertainment Guide," published each Friday in the *Oregonian*, contains listings of performers, productions, events, and club entertainment. *Willamette Week*, published free each Wednesday and widely available throughout the metropolitan area, contains similar, but hipper, listings. *Just Out*, the city's gay and lesbian newspaper, is published bimonthly.

## Nightlife

Portland's flourishing music scene encompasses everything from classical concerts to the latest permutations of rock and roll and hip-hop. The city has become something of a base for young rock bands, which perform in dance clubs scattered throughout the metropolitan area. Good jazz groups perform nightly in clubs and bars. Top-name musicians and performers in every genre regularly appear at the city's larger venues.

### Bars & Lounges

DOWNTOWN Many of the best bars and lounges in Portland are found in its restaurants.

**Brasserie Montmartre** (⊠ 626 S.W. Park Ave., Downtown ☎ 503/224–5552) is a popular late-night spot with live jazz. At the elegant **Heathman Hotel** (⊠ 1001 S.W. Broadway, Downtown ☎ 503/241–4100) you can sit in the marble bar or the wood-panel Tea Court. **Huber's Cafe** (⊠411 S.W. 3rd Ave., Downtown ☎ 503/228–5686), the city's oldest restaurant, is noted for its Spanish coffee and old-fashioned feel. The young and eclectic crowd at the **Lotus Cardroom and Cafe** (⊠ 932 S.W. 3rd Ave., Downtown ☎ 503/227–6185) comes to drink, dance to modern sounds, and play pool. At **Oba!** (⊠ 555 N.W. 12th Ave., Pearl District ☎ 503/228–6161), plush tans and reds with lime-green backlit walls set a backdrop for South American salsa. The **Rialto** (⊠ 529 S.W. 4th Ave. ☎ 503/228–7605) is a large, dark bar with several pool tables and enthusiastic pool players as well as some of the best Bloody Marys in town.

**Saucebox** (✉ 214 S.W. Broadway, Downtown ☎ 503/241–3393) attracts a sophisticated crowd who enjoy colorful cocktails and trendy DJ music. At **Veritable Quandary** (✉ 1220 S.W. 1st Ave., Downtown ☎ 503/228–5672), along the river, you can sit in the cozy tree-filled outdoor patio or in the glass atrium.

NOB HILL   Boisterous **Gypsy** (✉ 625 N.W. 21st Ave., Nob Hill ☎ 503/796–1859) has 1950s-like furnishings. Young hipsters pack **Muu-Muus** (✉ 612 N.W. 21st Ave., Nob Hill ☎ 503/223–8169) on weekend nights. **21st Avenue Bar & Grill** (✉ 721 N.W. 21st Ave., Nob Hill ☎ 503/222–4121) is open till 2:30 AM and has a patio and outdoor bar. The upscale martini set chills at **Wildwood** (✉ 1221 N.W. 21st Ave., Nob Hill ☎ 503/248–9663).

EAST PORTLAND   An artsy, hip east-side crowd, not to be mistaken for the downtown jet-setters, hangs and drinks martinis and wine at the minimalist **Aalto Lounge** (✉ 3356 S.E. Belmont St. ☎ 503/239–4698). One of few bars on northeast Alberta Street, **Bink's** (✉ 2715 N.E. Alberta St. ☎ 503/293–4430) is a small, friendly neighborhood spot with cozy seats around a fireplace, a pool table, and a good jukebox. It serves only beer and wine. **Colosso** (✉ 1932 N.E. Broadway ☎ 503/288–3333), a popular tapas bar, draws a cocktail-sipping crowd of hipsters at night. A laid-back beer-drinking crowd fills the **Horse Brass Pub** (✉ 4534 S.E. Belmont St. ☎ 503/232–2202), as good an English-style pub as you will find this side of the Atlantic, with nearly 50 beers on tap and air thick with smoke. **Noble Rot** (✉ 2724 S.E. Ankeny St. ☎ 503/233–1999) is a chic east-side wine bar with excellent food and red leather booths.

## Brewpubs, Brew Theaters & Microbreweries

Dozens of small breweries operating in the metropolitan area produce pale ales, bitters, bocks, barley wines, and stouts. Some have attached pub operations, where you can sample a foaming pint of house ale. "Brew theaters," former neighborhood movie houses, whose patrons enjoy food, suds, and recent theatrical releases, are part of the microbrewery phenomenon.

The **Bagdad Theatre and Pub** (✉ 3702 S.E. Hawthorne Blvd., Hawthorne District ☎ 503/225–5555 Ext. 8830) screens recent Hollywood films and serves microbrews. The first McMenamins brewpub, the **Barley Mill Pub** (✉ 1629 S.E. Hawthorne Blvd. Hawthorne District ☎ 503/231–1492), is filled with Grateful Dead memorabilia and concert posters and is a fun place for families. **BridgePort BrewPub & Restaurant** (✉ 1313 N. W. Marshall St., Pearl District ☎ 503/224–4400), Portland's oldest microbrewery, prepares hand-tossed pizza (⇨ Where to Eat) to accompany its ales. The **Mission Theater** (✉ 1624 N.W. Glisan St., Nob Hill ☎ 503/225–5555 Ext. 8830) was the first brew theater to show recent Hollywood offerings and serve locally brewed McMenamins ales. In an old church, the **St. John's Pub** (✉ 8203 N. Ivanhoe, St. John's ☎ 503/224–4400) is another McMenamins brewpub and includes a beer garden and a movie theater. **Tugboat Brewery** (✉ 711 S.W. Ankeny St., Downtown ☎ 503/226–2508) is a small, cozy brewpub with books and games, picnic tables, and experimental jazz several nights a week.

The McMenamins chain of microbreweries includes some pubs in restored historic buildings. **Ringlers** (✉ 1332 W. Burnside St., Downtown ☎ 503/225–0543) occupies the first floor of the building that houses the famous Crystal Ballroom (⇨ Dancing). **Ringlers Annex** (✉ 1223 S. W. Stark St., Downtown ☎ 503/525–0520), one block away from Ringlers, is a pie-shape corner pub where you can puff a cigar while drinking beer, port, or a single-malt scotch. **Widmer Brewing and Gasthaus** (✉ 955 N. Russell St., North Portland, near Fremont Bridge ☎ 503/

281–3333) brews German-style beers and has a full menu; you can tour the adjacent brewery Monday–Saturday.

## Coffeehouses & Teahouses

DOWNTOWN With independent coffee shops nearly everywhere you go in Portland, you can get your fix without setting foot in a Starbucks, but if you are craving the old familiar blends, rest assured that you will find a branch on nearly every corner.

Traditional English teas, complete with scones and Devonshire cream, are served with authentic English accents at the **British Tea Garden** (⊠ 725 S.W. 10th Ave., Downtown ☎ 503/221–7817). **Three Lions Bakery** (⊠ 1138 S.W. Morrison St., Downtown ☎ 503/224–3429) turns out excellent pastries as well as strong java; sandwiches, fresh-made quiches, and salads are also served.

NOB HILL & **Anna Bannanas** (⊠ 1214 N.W. 21st Ave., Nob Hill ☎ 503/274–2559)
VICINITY serves great espresso and coffee, veggie sandwiches, soup, and smoothies; there's outdoor seating out front. **Coffee People** (⊠ 533 N.W. 23rd Ave., Nob Hill ☎ 503/221–0235) is a local chain that draws crowds from early in the morning until late in the evening. **Torrefazione Italia** (⊠ 838 N.W. 23rd Ave., Nob Hill ☎ 503/228–1255) has several locations in Portland and beyond but manages to feel like a real Italian espresso house, with the best cappuccino in town. One of the newer additions to the Portland coffee scene, **World Cup Coffee and Tea** (⊠ 1740 N.W. Glisan St. ☎ 503/228–5503) sells excellent organic coffee and espresso in Nob Hill, as well as at its store in the Pearl District at the Ecotrust building and at Powell's City of Books on Burnside. **Village Coffee** (⊠ 1037 N.W. 23rd St., Nob Hill ☎ 503/225–0746) is a sleek coffee shop right in the center of the shopping district on Northwest 23rd and offers free Internet to customers.

EAST PORTLAND **Common Grounds** (⊠ 4321 S.E. Hawthorne Blvd., East Portland ☎ 503/236–4835) has plush couches and serves desserts plus sandwiches and soup. **Palio Coffee and Dessert House** (⊠ 1996 S.E. Ladd St., Ladd's Addition, near Hawthorne District ☎ 503/232–9412), in the middle of peaceful residential Ladd's Addition, has delicious desserts and espresso, and is open later than many coffee shops in the area. Twentysomething sippers lounge on sofas and overstuffed chairs at **Pied Cow** (⊠ 3244 S.E. Belmont St., East Portland ☎ 503/230–4866), a laid-back alternative to more yuppified establishments. **Rimsky Korsakoffee House** (⊠ 707 S. E. 12th Ave., East Portland ☎ 503/232–2640), one of the city's first coffeehouses, is still one of the best, especially when it comes to desserts. **Torrefazione Italia** (⊠ 1403 N.E. Weidler St., East Portland ☎ 503/288–1608) is just off the Broadway strip in a busy area near Lloyd Center.

## Comedy

**Harvey's Comedy Club** (⊠ 436 N.W. 6th Ave., Old Town ☎ 503/241–0338) presents stand-up comics nightly except Monday; its menu includes bar appetizers, burgers, chicken, and fish.

## Dancing

**McMenamins Crystal Ballroom** (⊠ 1332 W. Burnside St., Downtown ☎ 503/225–0047) is a famous Portland dance hall that dates from 1914. Rudolph Valentino danced the tango here in 1923, and you may feel like doing the same once you step out onto the 7,500-square-foot "elastic" floor (it's built on ball bearings) and feel it bouncing beneath your feet. Bands perform everything from swing to hillbilly rock nightly except Monday. **Polly Esther's Culture Club** (⊠ 424 S.W. 4th Ave., Downtown ☎ 503/221–1970) is a dance bar with several levels and a DJ playing a '70s–'80s nostalgia mix.

## Gay & Lesbian Clubs

**Boxxes/Panorama** (⊠ Stark St. between 10th and 11th Aves., Downtown ☎ 503/221–7262) is a bar-disco-restaurant complex with a video bar, poker machines, a pool table, late-night dancing Friday and Saturday in the cavernous Panorama, and outdoor seating at the Red Cap Café. **C. C. Slaughters** (⊠ 219 N.W. Davis Ave., Old Town ☎ 503/248–9135) is a male-oriented bar with a restaurant and a dance floor that's crowded on weekend nights; weeknights yield karaoke and country dancing. **Egyptian Room** (⊠ 3701 S.E. Division St., south of Hawthorne District ☎ 503/236–8689), Portland's lesbian bar-disco, has pool tables, video poker, and a medium-size dance floor. **Fox and Hounds** (⊠ 217 N.W. 2nd Ave., Old Town ☎ 503/243–5530) is popular with gay men and lesbians. A full menu is served in the evenings, and the place is packed for Sunday brunch. **Scandals** (⊠ 1038 S.W. Stark St., Downtown ☎ 503/227–5887) is low-key and has plate-glass windows with a view of Stark Street and the city's streetcars. The lower level has video poker and a pool table, and the adjoining Other Side bar serves light food.

## Live Music

BLUES, FOLK & ROCK

The **Aladdin Theater** (⊠ 3017 S.E. Milwaukie St., ☎ 503/224–4400), in an old movie theater, is one of the best music venues in town and serves microbrews and pizza. The **B Complex** (⊠ 320 S.E. 2nd Ave., under Burnside Bridge ☎ 503/235–4424), in an industrial loft building with brick walls and exposed duct work, is a great venue for all kinds of live music, including jazz, hip-hop, and electronica. No alcohol is served.

**Berbati's Pan** (⊠ 10 S.W. 3rd Ave., Old Town ☎ 503/248–4579), on the edge of Old Town, has dancing and presents live music, everything from big band and swing to acid jazz, rock, and R&B. **Candlelight Room** (⊠ 2032 S.W. 5th Ave., Downtown ☎ 503/222–3378) presents blues nightly. **Dublin Pub** (⊠ 6821 S.W. Beaverton–Hillsdale Hwy., Beaverton ☎ 503/297–2889), on the west side, pours more than 100 beers on tap and hosts Irish bands and rock groups. **Kell's Irish Restaurant & Pub** (⊠ 112 S.W. 2nd Ave., Old Town ☎ 503/227–4057) serves terrific Irish food and presents Celtic music nightly. Locals crowd the **Laurelthirst Public House** (⊠ 2958 N.E. Glisan St., Laurelhurst ☎ 503/232–1504) to eat tasty food, sit in cozy red booths, and listen to folk, jazz, country, or bluegrass music on its tiny stage. There are pool tables in an adjoining room. **Meow Meow** (⊠ 527 S.E. Pine St., east side, near Burnside Bridge ☎ 503/230–2111) hosts punk-rock acts in a nonalcohol environment for all ages. **Produce Row Cafe** (⊠ 204 S.E. Oak St., east side, near Burnside Bridge and I–5 ☎ 503/232–8355) has a huge beer list, a great beer garden, a down-to-earth flavor, and live bluegrass, folk, and acoustic music most nights of the week. **Satyricon** (⊠ 125 N.W. 6th Ave., Old Town ☎ 503/243–2380) is Portland's leading outlet for grunge, punk, and other alternative rock music.

During the Rose Festival–dominated month of June, **Beaverton SummerFest** (⊠ Griffith Park, at intersection of Hwys. 10 and 217, Beaverton ☎ 503/644–0123) attracts big-name entertainers to a three-day bash in suburban Beaverton. A food pavilion presents Pacific Northwest specialties while the bands play on. The **North by Northwest Music Festival** (☎ 512/467–7979), an annual new music conference, spotlights hundreds of up-and-coming musicians from around the West in late September. The focus is on alternative rock, but other musical genres are represented as well. One admission price gets you into about two dozen downtown clubs during the three-day event. There are also panels, workshops, and a music trade show.

COUNTRY & WESTERN  The **Drum** (✉ 14601 S.E. Division St., close to Gresham ☎ 503/760–1400) books traditional country and contemporary country-rock performers. The Ponderosa Lounge at **Jubitz Truck Stop** (✉ 10210 N. Vancouver Way, ☎ 503/283–1111) presents live country music and dancing nightly—not your ordinary truck stop.

JAZZ  **Brasserie Montmartre** (✉ 626 S.W. Park Ave., Downtown ☎ 503/224–5552) presents duos on weeknights and quartets and larger groups on weekends; its European-style bistro serves Pacific Northwest cuisine. **Jazz de Opus** (✉ 33 N.W. 2nd Ave., Old Town ☎ 503/222–6077) books local musicians with national reputations seven nights a week; its menu focuses on seafood and prime rib.

Since 1982 the **Mt. Hood Jazz Festival** (✉ 26000 S.E. Stark St., Gresham ☎ 503/224–4400 ⊕ www.mthoodjazz.com) has drawn big names as well as new talent to this three-day event in August. Past years have seen appearances by Ella Fitzgerald, Sarah Vaughan, and George Benson. The festival is held on the campus of Mount Hood Community College in suburban Gresham. Take MAX light rail to Gresham Transit Center and transfer to Bus 26.

# The Arts

When it comes to public arts funding, Oregon ranks low compared with other states, yet Portland has a symphony orchestra, opera and dance companies, and a number of theater companies. Most Portland-based performing arts groups have their own box-office numbers; *see* individual listings. For tickets to most events, call **Ticketmaster** (☎ 503/224–4400) or **Fastixx** (☎ 503/224–8499).

During the summer half-price tickets for almost any event are available the day of the show at Ticket Central in the **Visitor Information and Services Center** (✉ Pioneer Courthouse Sq., Downtown ☎ 503/275–8358 after 10 AM), open Monday–Saturday 9–4:30. This is an outlet for tickets from Ticketmaster and Fastixx. Credit cards are accepted, but you must buy tickets in person.

## Classical Music

CHAMBER MUSIC  **Chamber Music Northwest** (✉ 522 S.W. 5th Ave. Suite 725, Downtown ☎ 503/294–6400 ⊕ www.cnmw.org) presents some of the most sought-after soloists, chamber musicians, and recording artists from the Portland area and abroad for a five-week summer concert series; performances take place at Reed College and Catlin Gabel School.

ORCHESTRAS  The **Oregon Symphony** (✉ 923 S.W. Washington ☎ 503/228–1353 or 800/228–7343 ⊕ www.orsymphony.org) presents more than 40 classical, pop, children's, and family concerts each year at the Arlene Schnitzer Concert Hall.

The **Portland Baroque Orchestra** (☎ 503/222–6000 ⊕ www.pbo.org) performs works on period instruments in a season that runs October–April. Performances are held at **Reed College's Kaul Auditorium** (✉ 3203 S.E. Woodstock Blvd., Reed/Woodstock) and downtown at **First Baptist Church** (✉ 1425 S.W. 20th Ave., Downtown).

OPERA  **Portland Opera** (✉ 222 S.W. Clay St. ☎ 503/241–1802 ⊕ www.portlandopera.org) and its orchestra and chorus stage five productions annually at the Keller Auditorium.

## Dance

**Body Vox** (☎ 503/229–0627 ⊕ www.bodyvox.com) performs energetic contemporary dance–theater works at several locations in Portland.

**Do Jump! Extremely Physical Theatre** (✉ 1515 S.E. 37th Ave. ☎ 503/ 231–1232 ⊕ www.dojump.org) showcases its creative acrobatic work at the Echo Theatre near Hawthorne.

Founded in 1982, the **Northwest Afrikan American Ballet** (⌂ P.O. Box 11143 Portland 97211 ☎ 503/287–8852) was the first traditional African dance company in the Northwest United States, and it continues to offer excellent authentic and electrifying performances in and outside Portland.

**Oregon Ballet Theatre** (✉ 818 S.E. Sixth Ave. ☎ 503/222–5538 or 888/ 922–5538 ⊕ www.obt.org) produces five classical and contemporary works a year, including a much-loved holiday *Nutcracker*. Most performances are at Keller Auditorium.

**White Bird** (⌂ P.O. Box 99 Portland 97207 ☎ 503/245–1600 ⊕ www. whitebird.org) is a non-profit organization committed to enhancing the performance offerings in the city through presenting traveling companies, commissioning new work, and otherwise helping to make myriad dance events possible. Many of the stellar performers and troupes that make their way through Portland are there in connection with White Bird.

## Film

**Cinema 21** (✉ 616 N.W. 21st Ave., Nob Hill ☎ 503/223–4515) is an art-movie house in Nob Hill; it also hosts the annual gay and lesbian film festival in June.

**Cinemagic** (✉ 2021 S.E. Hawthorne Blvd., Hawthorne District ☎ 503/ 231–7919), in the Hawthorne District, shows progressive and cult films.

A seventy-year-old landmark, the **Hollywood Theatre** (✉ 4122 N.E. Sandy Blvd., Hollywood District ☎ 503/281–4215) shows everything from obscure foreign art films to old American classics and second-run Hollywood hits.

For Hollywood blockbusters, new foreign films, and interesting low-budget sleepers, check out **KOIN Center Cinemas** (✉ 222 S.W. Columbia Blvd., Downtown ☎ 503/225–5555 Ext. 4608).

The **Laurelhurst Theatre** (✉ 2735 E. Burnside ☎ 503/232–5511) is a beautiful theater and pub showing excellent second-run features and cult classics for only $2–$3.

Not-to-be-missed Portland landmarks when it comes to movie-viewing, the **McMenamins theatres and brewpubs** offer beer, pizza, and inexpensive tickets to second-run blockbusters in uniquely renovated buildings that avoid any hint of corporate streamlining. Local favorites include the Bagdad Theatre (✉ 3702 S.E. Hawthorne Blvd. ☎ 503/225–5555 Ext. 8831), the Mission Theatre (✉ 1624 N.W. Glisan ☎ 503/225–5555 Ext. 8832), and the Kennedy School (✉ 5736 N.E. 33rd St. ☎ 503/225– 5555 Ext. 8833), found in a renovated elementary school along with a bed-and-breakfast and a restaurant.

The **Northwest Film and Video Center** (✉ 1219 S.W. Park Ave., Downtown ☎ 503/221–1156), a branch of the Portland Art Museum, screens all manner of art films, documentaries, and independent features and presents the three-week Portland International Film Festival in February and March. Films are shown at the Whitsell Auditorium, next to the museum, and at the Guild Theatre (✉ 879 S.W. Park Ave.).

## Performance Venues

The 2,776-seat **Arlene Schnitzer Concert Hall** (✉ Portland Center for the Performing Arts, S.W. Broadway and Main St., Downtown ☎ 503/

796–9293), built in 1928 in Italian rococo revival style, hosts rock stars, choral groups, lectures, and concerts by the Oregon Symphony and others.

With 3,000 seats and outstanding acoustics, **Keller Auditorium** (✉ 222 S.W. Clay St., Downtown ☎ 503/796–9293) hosts performances by the Portland Opera and Portland Ballet as well as country and rock concerts and touring shows.

**Memorial Coliseum** (✉ 1 Center Ct., Rose Quarter, Lloyd Center District ☎ 503/235–8771), a 12,000-seat venue on the MAX light-rail line, books rock groups, touring shows, the Ringling Brothers circus, ice-skating extravaganzas, and sporting events.

Remodeled in 2001, **PGE Park** (✉ 1844 S.W. Morrison St., Downtown/ Nob Hill ☎ 503/553–5400 ⊕ www.pgepark.com) is home to the Portland Beavers Triple-A baseball team and the Portland Timbers soccer team. The 20,000-seat stadium also hosts concerts and other sporting events. No parking is available at the park; MAX light rail is the most convenient option. Your game ticket entitles you to a free round-trip.

**Portland Center for the Performing Arts** (✉ 1111 S.W. Broadway, Downtown ☎ 503/796–9293 ⊕ www.pcpa.com) hosts opera, ballet, rock shows, symphony performances, lectures, and Broadway musicals in its three venues (⇨ Downtown *in* Exploring Portland).

The 21,000-seat **Rose Garden** (✉ 1 Center Ct., Broadway and N. Interstate Ave., Lloyd Center District ☎ 503/235–8771) is home to the Portland Trail Blazers basketball team and the site of other sporting events and rock concerts. The arena is on the MAX light-rail line.

The **Roseland Theater** (✉ 8 N.W. 6th Ave., Old Town/Chinatown ☎ 503/224–2038), which holds 1,400 people, primarily stages rock and blues shows.

### Theater

**Artists Repertory Theatre** (✉ 1516 S.W. Alder St., Downtown ☎ 503/241– 1278 ⊕ www.artistrep.org) stages seven productions a year—regional premieres, occasional commissioned works, and selected classics.

**Imago Theatre** (✉ 17 S.E. 8th Ave. ☎ 503/231–9581 ⊕ www.imagotheatre. com) is considered by some to be Portland's most outstanding innovative theater company, specializing in movement-based work for both young and old.

**Oregon Children's Theatre** (☎ 503/228–9571 ⊕ www.octc.org) puts on three or four shows a year at major venues throughout the city for school groups and families.

**Oregon Puppet Theater** (☎ 503/236–4034) stages five children's productions a year at different locations in town.

**Portland Center Stage** (✉ 1111 S.W. Broadway, Downtown ☎ 503/274– 6588) produces six contemporary and classical works between October and April in the 800-seat Newmark Theater.

**Stark Raving Theatre** (✉ 2257 N.W. Raleigh St. ☎ 503/232–7072 ⊕ www. starkravingtheatre.org) provides a forum for cutting-edge dramatic work, producing four shows a year at the CoHo Theatre in the Northwest.

# SPORTS & THE OUTDOORS

Portlanders are definitely oriented to the outdoors. Hikers, joggers, and mountain bikers take to the city's hundreds of miles of parks, paths, and trails. The Willamette and Columbia rivers are used for boating and water sports; however, it's not easy to rent any kind of boat for casual use. Big-sports fervor is reserved for Trail Blazer games, held at the Rose Quarter arena on the east side. The Portland/Oregon Visitors Association (⇨ Visitor Information *in* Portland A to Z) provides information on sports events and outdoor activities in the city.

## Participant Sports

### Bicycling

*Bicycling* magazine has named Portland the number one cycling city in the United States, and you will soon find out why; aside from the sheer numbers of cyclists you are bound to see on every road and pathway, notable bike-friendly aspects of this city include well-marked bike lanes on many major streets, bike paths meandering through parks and along the shoreline of the Willamette River, street signs reminding motorists to yield to cyclists at many intersections, and bike racks on the front of all Tri-Met buses.

Despite the occasionally daunting hills and frequent wintertime rain, cycling remains one of the best ways to see some of what Portland has to offer. Bike paths on both the east and west sides of the Willamette River continue south of downtown, and you can easily make a several-mile loop by crossing bridges to get from one side to the other. (Most bridges, including the Broadway Bridge, the Steel Bridge, the Hawthorne Bridge, and the Sellwood Bridge, are accessible to cyclists.)

Forest Park's Leif Erikson Drive is an 11-mi ride through Northwest Portland's Forest Park, accessible from the west end of Northwest Thurman Street. Parts of this ride and other Forest Park trails are recommended only for mountain bikes. Bicycling on Sauvie Island is a rare treat, with a 12-mi loop around the island with plenty of spots for exploring. To get to Sauvie Island from Portland, you can brave the 10-mi ride in the bike lane of U.S. 30, or you can shuttle your bike there via Tri-Met bus 17. The Springwater Corridor, when combined with the Esplanade ride on the east side of the Willamette, can take you all the way from downtown to the far reaches of southeast Portland along a former railroad line. The trail heads east beginning near Sellwood, close to Johnson Creek Boulevard.

For more information on bike routes and resources in and around Portland, visit the **Department of Transportation** Web page (⊕ www.trans.ci. portlande.or.us/bicycles). Here, you can download maps, or order "Bike There," a glossy detailed bicycle map of the metropolitan area.

Bikes can be rented at several places in the city. Rentals can run anywhere from $20 to $50 per day and commonly are available for cheaper weekly rates, running from $75 to $150 per week. Bike helmets are generally included in the cost of rental. Good hybrid bikes for city riding are available at **City Bikes Workers Cooperative** (✉ 714 S.E. Ankeny St., near Burnside and Martin Luther King Jr.Blvd. ☎ 503/222–2376) on the east side. For treks in Forest Park, mountain bikes can be rented at **Fat Tire Farm** (✉ 2714 N.W. Thurman St., near Forest Park ☎ 503/222–3276). In the Northwest, rentals are offered at **Northwest Bicycles** (✉ 916 N.W. 21st Ave., Nob Hill ☎ 503/248–9142). For jaunts along the Willamette, try **Waterfront Bicycle Rentals** (✉ 36015 S.W. Montgomery St., Suite 3, Downtown ☎ 503/227–1719).

### Fishing

The Columbia and Willamette rivers are major sportfishing streams with opportunities for angling virtually year-round. Though salmon can still be caught here, runs have been greatly reduced in both rivers in recent years, and the Willamette River is still plagued by pollution. Nevertheless, the Willamette still offers prime fishing for bass, channel catfish, sturgeon, crappies, perch, panfish, and crayfish. It is also a good winter steelhead stream. June is the top shad month, with some of the best fishing occurring below Willamette Falls at Oregon City. The Columbia River is known for its salmon, sturgeon, walleye, and smelt. The Sandy and Clackamas rivers, near Mt. Hood, are smaller waterways popular with local fishermen.

OUTFITTERS　Outfitters throughout Portland operate guide services. Few outfitters rent equipment, so bring your own or be prepared to buy. **Countrysport Limited** (⊠ 126 S.W. 1st Ave., Old Town ☎ 503/221–3964) specializes in all things fly fishing, including tackle, rentals, and guided outings.

**G.I. Joe's** (⊠ 3900 S.E. 82nd Ave., near Powell Blvd. ☎ 503/283–0312) sells rods, reels, tackle, accessories, and fishing licenses. You can find a broad selection of fishing gear, including rods, reels, and fishing licenses, at **Stewart Fly Shop** (⊠ 23830 N.E. Halsey St., near Troutdale ☎ 503/666–2471).

REGULATIONS　Local sport shops are the best sources of information on current fishing hot spots, which change from year to year. Detailed fishing regulations are available from the **Oregon Department of Fish and Wildlife** (⊠ 2501 S.W. 1st Ave., 97207 ☎ 503/872–5263).

## Golf

**Broadmoor Golf Course** (⊠ 3509 N.E. Columbia Blvd., near airport, 97211 ☎ 503/281–1337) is an 18-hole, par-72 course where the greens fee runs $22–$26 and an optional cart costs $22.

At the 18-hole, par-70 **Colwood National Golf Club** (⊠ 7313 N.E. Columbia Blvd., near airport, 97218 ☎ 503/254–5515), the greens fee is $26–$28, plus $22 for an optional cart. On mornings and weekends, the $31 greens fee includes a cart.

**Eastmoreland Golf Course** (⊠ 2425 S.E. Bybee Blvd., Sellwood, 97202 ☎ 503/775–2900) has a highly regarded 18-hole, 72-par course close to the Rhododendron Gardens, Crystal Springs Lake, and Reed College. The greens fee is $21–$23.

**Glendoveer Golf Course** (⊠ 14015 N.E. Glisan St., near Gresham, 97230 ☎ 503/253–7507) has two 18-hole courses, one par-71 and one par-73, and a covered driving range. The greens fee is $17–$19; carts are $13 for 9 holes, $25 for 18 holes.

**Heron Lakes Golf Course** (⊠ 3500 N. Victory Blvd., west of airport, off N. Marine Dr., 97217 ☎ 503/289–1818) consists of two 18-hole, par-72 courses: the less-challenging Greenback and the Great Blue, generally acknowledged to be the most difficult links in the greater Portland area. The greens fee at the Green, as it is locally known, is $19–$21, while the fee at the Blue is $31 at all times. An optional cart at either course costs $24.

**Pumpkin Ridge Golf Club** (⊠ 12930 N.W. Old Pumpkin Ridge Rd., Cornelius 97133 ☎ 503/647–4747 or 888/594–4653 ⊕ www.pumpkinridge. com) has 36 holes, with the 18-hole Ghost Creek par-71 course open to the public. According to *Golf Digest,* Ghost Creek is one of the best public courses in the nation. Pumpkin Ridge hosted the U.S. Women's Open in 1997 and will again in 2004. The greens fee is $40–$120; the cart fee is $15.

**Rose City Golf Course** (✉ 2200 N.E. 71st Ave., east of Hollywood District, 97213 ☎ 503/253–4744) has one 18-hole, par-72 course. Greens fees are $19–$21; carts are $13 for 9 holes, $25 for 18 holes.

### Ice-Skating
**Ice Chalet at Lloyd Center** (✉ Multnomah St. and N.E. 9th Ave., Lloyd District ☎ 503/288–6073) has open skating and skate rentals ($9 admission includes skate rental). The indoor rinks are open year-round. You can skate year-round on the indoor rink at **Ice Chalet at Clackamas Town Center** (✉ 12000 S.E. 82nd Ave., Clackamas ☎ 503/786–6000). The $9 admission includes skate rental. The indoor rink is open year-round.

### Skiing
**Mountain Shop** (✉ 628 N.E. Broadway, Lloyd District/Irvington, 97232 ☎ 503/288–6768) rents skis and equipment. **REI** (✉ 1798 Jantzen Beach Center, Jantzen Beach ☎ 503/283–1300) can fill all your ski-equipment rental needs.

### Swimming & Sunbathing
**Blue Lake Regional Park** (✉ 20500 N.E. Marine Dr., Troutdale ☎ 503/797–1850) has a swimming beach that's packed on hot summer days. You can also fish and rent small boats here. This is a great place for a hike on the surrounding trails or for a picnic.

If you feel like tanning au naturel, drive about a half hour northwest of downtown to **Sauvie Island,** a wildlife refuge with a secluded beachfront that's popular (and legal) with nude sunbathers. If the sky is clear, you'll get a spectacular view from the riverbank of three Cascade mountains—Hood, St. Helens, and Adams. Huge oceangoing vessels cruise by on their way to and from the Port of Portland. To get here, take U.S. 30 north to Sauvie Island bridge, turn right, and follow Reeder Road until you hit gravel. Look for the Collins Beach signs. There's plenty of parking, but a permit is required. You can buy it ($3.50 for a one-day permit, $11 for an annual permit) at the Cracker Barrel country store just over the bridge on the left side of the road.

### Tennis
**Lake Oswego Indoor Tennis Center** (✉ 2900 S.W. Diane Dr., Lake Oswego ☎ 503/635–5550) has four indoor tennis courts. **Portland Parks and Recreation** (☎ 503/823–7529) operates more than 100 outdoor tennis courts (many with night lighting) at Washington Park, Grant Park, and many other locations. The courts are open on a first-come, first-served basis year-round, but you can reserve one, starting in March, for play May–September. The **Portland Tennis Center** (✉ 324 N.E. 12th Ave., just south of I-84 ☎ 503/823–3189) operates four indoor courts and eight lighted outdoor courts. The **St. John's Racquet Center** (✉ 7519 N. Burlington Ave., St. John's ☎ 503/823–3629) has three indoor courts.

# Spectator Sports

### Auto Racing
**Portland International Raceway** (✉ West Delta Park, 1940 N. Victory Blvd., west of I–5, along the Columbia Slough ☎ 503/823–7223) presents bicycle and drag racing and motocross on weeknights and sports-car, motorcycle, and go-cart racing on weekends April–September.

**Portland Speedway** (✉ 9727 N. Martin Luther King Jr. Blvd., at I–5 along Columbia Slough ☎ 503/285–9511) hosts demolition derbies and NASCAR and stock-car races April–September. In June it hosts the Budweiser Indy Car World Series, a 200-mi race that lures the top names on the Indy Car circuit.

### Baseball

The **Portland Beavers** (☎ 503/553–5555), Portland's Triple-A team, play at the downtown **PGE Park** (✉ 1844 S.W. Morrison St., Downtown ☎ 503/553–5400) April–September.

### Basketball

The **Portland Trail Blazers** (✉ 1 Center Ct., Rose Quarter ☎ 503/797–9617) of the National Basketball Association play in the Rose Garden.

### Dog Racing

Greyhounds race at the **Multnomah Greyhound Park** (✉ 944 N.E. 223rd Ave., Wood Village, Gresham, 97060 ☎ 503/667–7700) from early May to mid-October.

### Horse Racing

Thoroughbred and quarter horses race, rain or shine October–April, at **Portland Meadows** (✉ 1001 N. Schmeer Rd., between I–5 and Martin Luther King Jr. Blvd., along Columbia Slough ☎ 503/285–9144 or 800/944–3127).

### Ice Hockey

The **Portland Winter Hawks** (☎ 503/236–4295) of the Western Hockey League play home games September–March at **Memorial Coliseum** (✉ 300 N. Winning Way, Rose Quarter) and at the **Rose Garden** (✉ 1 Center Ct., Rose Quarter).

# SHOPPING

Portland's main shopping area is **downtown,** between Southwest 2nd and 10th avenues and between Southwest Stark and Morrison streets. The major department stores are scattered over several blocks near Pioneer Courthouse Square. Northeast **Broadway** between 10th and 21st avenues is lined with boutiques and specialty shops. **Nob Hill,** north of downtown along Northwest 21st and 23rd avenues, is home to eclectic clothing, gift, book, and food shops. Most of the city's fine-art galleries are concentrated in the booming **Pearl District,** north from Burnside Street to Marshall Street between Northwest 8th and 15th avenues, along with furniture and design stores. **Sellwood,** 5 mi from the city center, south on Naito Parkway and east across the Sellwood Bridge, has more than 50 antiques and collectibles shops along southeast 13th Avenue, plus specialty shops and outlet stores for sporting goods. You'll find the largest concentration near the intersection of Milwaukie Boulevard and Bybee. **Hawthorne Boulevard** between 30th and 42nd avenues has an often countercultural grouping of bookstores, coffeehouses, antiques stores, and boutiques.

The open-air **Portland Saturday Market** (✉ Burnside Bridge, underneath west end, Old Town ☎ 503/222–6072), open on weekends, is a good place to find handcrafted items. *See* Old Town/Chinatown *in* Exploring Portland.

Portland merchants are generally open Monday–Saturday 9 or 10 AM–6 PM and on Sunday noon–6. Most shops in downtown's Pioneer Place, the east side's Lloyd Center, and the outlying malls are open until 9 Monday–Saturday and until 6 on Sunday.

## Malls & Department Stores

### Downtown/City Center

**Meier & Frank** (✉ 621 S.W. 5th Ave., Downtown ☎ 503/223–0512), a Portland department store that dates from 1857, has 10 floors of general merchandise at its main location downtown.

Seattle-based **Nordstrom** (✉ 701 S.W. Broadway, Downtown ☎ 503/224–6666) sells fine-quality apparel and accessories and has a large footwear department. Bargain lovers should head for the **Nordstrom Rack** (✉ 401 S.W. Morrison St., Downtown ☎ 503/299–1815) outlet across from Pioneer Place mall.

**Pioneer Place** (✉ 700 S.W. 5th Ave., Downtown ☎ 503/228–5800) has 70 upscale specialty shops (including Williams-Sonoma, Coach, J. Crew, Godiva, and Caswell-Massey) in a three-story, glass-roof atrium setting. You'll find good, inexpensive ethnic foods from more than a dozen vendors in the Cascades Food Court in the basement.

**Saks Fifth Avenue** (✉ 850 S.W. 5th Ave., Downtown ☎ 503/226–3200) has two floors of men's and women's clothing, jewelry, and other merchandise.

## Beyond Downtown

NORTHEAST PORTLAND **Lloyd Center** (✉ N.E. Multnomah St. at N.E. 9th Ave., Northeast Portland ☎ 503/282–2511), which is on the MAX light-rail line, has more than 170 shops (including Nordstrom, Sears, and Meier & Frank), an international food court, a multiscreen cinema, and an ice-skating pavilion. The mall is within walking distance of northeast Broadway, which has many specialty shops, boutiques, and restaurants.

SOUTHEAST PORTLAND **Clackamas Town Center** (✉ Sunnyside Rd. at I–205's Exit 14, Southeast Portland ☎ 503/653–6913) has four major department stores, including Nordstrom and Meier & Frank; more than 180 shops; and an ice-skating rink. Discount stores are nearby.

SOUTHWEST PORTLAND **Washington Square** (✉ 9585 S.W. Washington Square Rd., at S.W. Hall Blvd. and Hwy. 217, Tigard ☎ 503/639–8860) contains five major department stores, including Meier & Frank and Sears; a food court; and 140 specialty shops. Discount and electronics stores are nearby.

The **Water Tower** (✉ 5331 S.W. MacAdam Ave., Southwest Portland ☎ 503/242–0022), in the John's Landing neighborhood on the Willamette River, is a pleasant mall with more than 20 specialty shops and nine restaurants.

# Specialty Stores

## Antiques

**Portland Antique Company** (✉ 2929 S.E. Powell, Pearl District ☎ 503/232–4001) spreads over 35,000 square feet. It has the Pacific Northwest's largest selection of European and English antiques.

**Moreland House** (✉ 826 N.W. 23rd, Nob Hill ☎ 503/222–0197) has eclectic antiques and gifts, with a notable selection of dog collectibles, old printing-press type, and fresco tiles.

**Shogun's Gallery** (✉ 206 N.W. 23rd Ave., Nob Hill ☎ 503/224–0328) specializes in Japanese and Chinese furniture, especially the lightweight wooden Japanese cabinets known as *tansu*. Also here are chairs, tea tables, altar tables, armoires, ikebana baskets, and Chinese wooden picnic boxes, all of them at least 100 years old and at extremely reasonable prices.

**Stars Antique Mall** (✉ 7027 S.E. Milwaukie, Sellwood ☎ 503/239–0346), Portland's largest antiques mall, with three stores in the Sellwood neighborhood, rents its space to 300 antiques dealers; you might find anything from low-end 1950s kitsch to high-end treasures. The stores are within walking distance of each other.

## Art Dealers & Galleries

**Butters Gallery, Ltd.** (✉ 520 N.W. Davis, Pearl District ☎ 503/248–9378) has monthly exhibits of the works of nationally known and local artists in its Pearl District space.

**Graystone Gallery** (✉ 3279 S.E. Hawthorne Blvd., Hawthorne District ☎ 503/238–0651) takes up two floors of a large house on Hawthorne and is filled with pottery and paintings, as well as some kitschy gift items and jewelry.

**In Her Image Gallery** (✉ 3208 S.E. Hawthorne Blvd., Hawthorne ☎ 503/231–3726) specializes in statues, totems, and works of art dedicated to the great earth goddesses.

**Margo Jacobsen Gallery** (✉ 1039 N.W. Glisan St., Pearl District ☎ 503/224–7287) exhibits works by local and nationally known artists and has a large selection of glass, ceramics, sculpture, paintings, and photography.

**Our Dream Gallery** (✉ 2315 N.E. Alberta St., Alberta District ☎ 503/288–3024) displays contemporary works by local African-American artists.

**Photographic Image Gallery** (✉ 240 S.W. 1st Ave., Old Town ☎ 503/224–3543) carries prints by nationally known nature photographers Christopher Burkett and Joseph Holmes, among others, and has a large supply of photography posters.

**Pulliam/Deffenbaugh Gallery** (✉ 522 N.W. 12th Ave., Pearl District ☎ 503/228–6665) generally shows contemporary figurative and expressionistic works by Pacific Northwest artists.

**Quintana's Galleries of Native American Art** (✉ 501 S.W. Broadway, Downtown ☎ 503/223–1729 or 800/321–1729) focuses on Pacific Northwest coast, Navajo, and Hopi art and jewelry, along with photogravures by Edward Curtis.

**Talisman Gallery** (✉ 1476 N.E. Alberta St., Alberta District ☎ 503/284–8800) is a cooperative gallery formed in 1999 that showcases two artists each month, including local painters and sculptors.

**Twist** (✉ 30 N.W. 23rd Pl., Nob Hill ☎ 503/224–0334 ✉ Pioneer Place ☎ 503/222–3137) has a huge space in Nob Hill and a smaller shop downtown. In Nob Hill are contemporary American ceramics, glass, furniture, sculpture, and handcrafted jewelry; downtown carries an assortment of objects, often with a pop, whimsical touch.

## Books

**Broadway Books** (✉ 1714 N.E. Broadway, Broadway District ☎ 503/284–1726) is a fabulous independent bookstore with books on all subjects including Judaica literature and information on the Pacific Northwest.

**In Other Words** (✉ 3734 S.E. Hawthorne Blvd., Hawthorne District ☎ 503/232–6003) is a non-profit feminist bookstore that carries feminist literature, as well as acting as a community resource for feminist events and readings.

**New Renaissance Bookshop** (✉ 1338 N.W. 23rd Ave., Nob Hill ☎ 503/224–4929), between Overton and Pettygrove, is dedicated to new-age and metaphysical books and tapes.

**Powell's City of Books** (✉ 1005 W. Burnside St., Downtown ☎ 503/228–4651), the largest used- and new retail bookstore in the world (with more than 1.5 million volumes), covers an entire city block on the edge of the Pearl District. It also carries rare hard-to-find editions.

**Powell's for Cooks and Gardeners** (✉ 3747 Hawthorne Blvd., Hawthorne District ☎ 503/235–3802), on the east side, has a small adjoining grocery. There's also a small store in the Portland International Airport.

**Twentythird Ave. Books** (✉ 1015 N.W. 23rd Ave., Nob Hill ☎ 503/224–5097) is a cozy independent bookstore that makes for great browsing if you want to escape the bustle of 23rd Avenue.

## Clothing

**Clogs 'n' More** (✉ 717 S.W. Alder, Downtown ☎ 503/279–9358 ✉ 3439 S.E. Hawthorne, Hawthorne District ☎ 503/232–7007), with locations both on the west and east sides of the city, carries quality clogs and other shoes.

**Eight Women** (✉ 3614 S.E. Hawthorne, Hawthorne District ☎ 503/236–8878) is a tiny boutique "for mother and child," with baby clothes, women's nightgowns, jewelry, and handbags.

**Elizabeth Street and Zelda's Shoe Bar** (✉ 635 N.W. 23rd Ave., Nob Hill ☎ 503/243–2456), two connected boutiques in Nob Hill, carry a sophisticated, highly eclectic line of women's clothes, accessories, and shoes.

**Imelda's Designer Shoes** (✉ 1431 S.E. 37th Ave., Hawthorne District ☎ 503/233–7476) is an upscale boutique with funky, fun shoes for women with flair.

**Jane's Obsession** (✉ 521 S.W. Broadway, Downtown ☎ 503/221–1490), a porch-level shop in one of Northwest 23rd Avenue's "house boutiques," sells luxurious French and Italian lingerie.

**Mario's** (✉ 921 S.W. Morrison St., Downtown ☎ 503/227–3477), Portland's best store for fine men's clothing, carries designer lines by Canali, Armani, Vestimenta, Donna Karan, and Calvin Klein, among others.

**Mario's for Women** (✉ 811 S.W. Morrison St., Downtown ☎ 503/241–8111) stocks Armani, Calvin Klein, and Vesti.

**Mimi and Lena** (✉ 823 N.W. 23rd Ave., Nob Hill ☎ 503/224–7736) is a small boutique with expensive but beautifully feminine and unique designer clothing.

**Nob Hill Shoes and Repair** (✉ 921 N.W. 23rd Ave., Nob Hill ☎ 503/224–8682), a tiny spot, sells men's and women's Naot sandals from Israel and Swedish Bastad clogs.

**Norm Thompson Outfitters** (✉ 1805 N.W. Thurman St., Nob Hill ☎ 503/221–0764) carries classic fashions for men and women, innovative footwear, and one-of-a-kind gifts.

**Portland Outdoor Store** (✉ 304 S.W. 3rd Ave., Downtown ☎ 503/222–1051) stubbornly resists all that is trendy, both in clothes and decor, but if you want authentic western gear—saddles, Stetsons, boots, or cowboy shirts—head here.

**Portland Pendleton Shop** (✉ S.W. 4th Ave. and Salmon St., Downtown ☎ 503/242–0037) stocks clothing by the famous local apparel maker.

**M. Sellin, Ltd.** (✉ 3556 S.E. Hawthorne Blvd., Hawthorne District ☎ 503/239–4605) has quality clothing for women as well as shoes and jewelry.

**Tumbleweed** (✉ 1804 N.E. Alberta St., Alberta District ☎ 503/335–3100) carries fun and stylish designer clothing you might describe as "country chic," for the woman who likes to wear flirty feminine dresses with cowboy boots. There is also unique baby and toddler clothing.

## Gifts

**Babik's** (✉ 730 N.W. 23rd, Nob Hill ☎ 503/248–1771) carries an enormous selection of hand-woven rugs from Turkey, all made from hand-spun wool and all-natural dyes.

The **Backyard Bird Shop** (✉ 3574 S.E. Hawthorne Blvd., Hawthorne District ☎ 503/230–9557) has everything for the bird lover: bird feeders, birdhouses, a huge supply of bird seed, and quality bird-theme gifts ranging from wind chimes to stuffed animals.

**Christmas at the Zoo** (✉ 118 N.W. 23rd Ave., Nob Hill ☎ 503/223–4048 or 800/223–5886) is crammed year-round with decorated trees and has Portland's best selection of European hand-blown glass ornaments and plush animals.

**Gai-Pied** (✉ 2544 N.E. Broadway, near Lloyd District ☎ 503/331–1125) carries periodicals, books, gifts, and videos of interest to the gay community.

**Greg's** (✉ 3707 S.E. Hawthorne Blvd., Hawthorne District ☎ 503/235–1257) has the feel of an upscale vintage shop, with a fun poster art, postcards, '20s-style gifts, and artsy home furnishings.

**Hawthorne Coffee Merchant** (✉ 3562 Hawthorne Blvd., Hawthorne District ☎ 503/230–1222) will lure you in with its aroma of coffee and candy, and once you're inside, you will find coffeepots and teapots, coffee and tea blends, espresso makers, and candy.

**Heaven and Earth Home and Garden** (✉ 3206 S.E. Hawthorne Blvd., Hawthorne District ☎ 503/230–7033) is a lovely small store with gifts for home and garden as well as plants and flowers.

**Kathmandu to You** (✉ 511 N.W. 21st Ave., Nob Hill ☎ 503/221–9986) sells clothing, incense, and Eastern religious artifacts and gifts.

**La Bottega de Mamma Ro** (✉ 940 N.W. 23rd, Nob Hill ☎ 503/241–4960) carries Italian tabletop and home accessories, including a colorful line of dishes and cloth for tablecloths and napkins.

**Made in Oregon** (☎ 800/828–9673), which sells books, smoked salmon, local wines, Pendleton woolen goods, carvings made of myrtle wood, and other products made in the state, has shops at Portland International Airport, the Lloyd Center, the Galleria, Old Town, Washington Square, and Clackamas Town Center.

**Moonstruck** (✉ 526 NW 23rd, Nob Hill ☎ 503/542–3400), even without its nod from Oprah, is doing well for itself as a chocolatier extraordinaire. Just a couple of the rich confections might sustain you if you're nibbling—water is available for palate cleansing in between treats—but whether you're just grazing or boxing some up for the road, try The Ocumarian Truffle, chocolate laced with chili pepper; the unusual kick of sweetness and warmth is worth experiencing.

**Pastaworks** (✉ 3735 S.E. Hawthorne Blvd., Southeast Portland ☎ 503/232–1010) sells cookware, fancy deli food, organic produce, beer, wine, and pasta.

At **Stella's on 21st** (✉ 1108 N.W. 21st Ave., Nob Hill ☎ 503/295–5930), there are eccentric, colorful, and artsy items for the home, including lamps, candles, and decorations, as well as jewelry.

## Jewelry

**Carl Greve** (✉ 731 S.W. Morrison St., Downtown ☎ 503/223–7121), in business since 1922, carries exclusive designer lines of fine jewelry, such as Mikimoto pearls, and has the state's only Tiffany boutique. The second floor is reserved for china, stemware, and housewares.

## Music

**Artichoke Music** (✉ 3130 S.E. Hawthorne Blvd., Hawthorne District ☎ 503/232–8845) is a friendly family-owned business that sells guitars, banjos, mandolins, and other instruments that might come in handy for a bluegrass bands. Music lessons are led in two sound-proof practice rooms, and music performances and song-circles are held in the café in the back.

**Classical Millennium** (✉ 3144 E. Burnside St., Laurelhurst ☎ 503/231–8909) has the best selection of classical CDs and tapes in Oregon.

**Django Records** (✉ 404 N.W. 10th, Pearl District ☎ 503/227–4381) is a must for collectors of music and video. There is an extensive used-CD selection.

**Music Millennium Northwest** (✉ 801 N.W. 23rd Ave., Nob Hill ☎ 503/248–0163) stocks a huge selection of CDs and tapes in every possible musical category, from local punk to classical.

## Outdoor Supplies

**Andy and Bax** (✉ 324 S.E. Grand Ave., near Morrison Bridge ☎ 503/234–7538) is an army-navy/outdoors store, with good prices on everything from camo-gear to rafting supplies.

**Countrysport Limited** (✉ 126 S.W. 1st Ave., Old Town ☎ 503/221–4545) is a fly-fishing specialty shop and a fascinating place to wander whether or not you're an angler.

**Next Adventure Sports** (✉ 426 S.E. Grand Ave., near Morrison Bridge ☎ 503/233–0706) carries new and used sporting goods, including camping gear, snowboards, kayaks, and mountaineering supplies.

### Perfume

**Aveda Lifestyle Store and Spa** (✉ 500 S.W. 5th Ave., Downtown ☎ 503/248–0615) sells the flower-based Aveda line of scents and skin-care products.

**Perfume House** (✉ 3328 S.E. Hawthorne Blvd., Hawthorne District ☎ 503/234–5375) carries hundreds of brand-name fragrances for women and men.

### Toys

**Finnegan's Toys and Gifts** (✉ 922 S.W. Yamhill St., Downtown ☎ 503/221–0306), downtown Portland's largest toy store, stocks artistic, creative, educational, and other types of toys.

**Kids at Heart** (✉ 3445 S.E. Hawthorne Blvd. Hawthorne District ☎ 503/231–2954) is a small, colorful toy store on Hawthorne with toys, models, and stuffed animals for kids of all ages.

# PORTLAND A TO Z

*To research prices, get advice from other travelers, and book travel arrangements, visit www.fodors.com.*

### ADDRESSES

The Willamette River and Burnside Street divide the metro area into four quarters. Addresses containing a northwest designation are north of Burnside and west of the river, southwest designations are south of Burnside and west of the river, and so forth. Downtown is in the southwest, and Hawthorne Boulevard is in the southeast. Numbered roads in Portland are avenues and run north–south, and named roads are streets, generally running east–west, with several exceptions, including Martin Luther King Jr. Blvd., Grand Avenue, S.W. Broadway, and S.W. Park. House numbers on east–west streets correspond to the numbered avenue on the closest cross street (for example, 601 Burnside would be on the corner of 6th Avenue and Burnside Street), and house numbers on north–south streets correspond to the number of blocks north or south of Burnside (for example, 500 S.W. 6th Ave. is five blocks south of Burnside). On the west side, the streets north of Ankeny are alphabetized: Ankeny, Burnside, Couch, Davis, etc., all the way to Thurman, Vaughn, and Wilson in the far northwest.

### AIR TRAVEL

Portland International Airport (PDX) is a sleek, modern airport with service to many international destinations, as well as all over the United States. It is easily accessible from downtown Portland and is easy to navigate once inside. Even if your final destination is in another city in Oregon, you may choose to fly into Portland and rent a car to get there, because all other airports in the state are small regional airports with limited service. It is possible, however, to get a connecting flight from Portland airport to smaller cities in Oregon. Portland Airport is served by all major airlines as well as by several smaller regional carriers.

🛪 Carriers **Air B.C.** ☎ 888/247-2262 🌐 www.aircanada.ca **Alaska Airlines** ☎ 800/252-7522 🌐 www.alaskaairlines.com **America West** ☎ 800/235-9292 🌐 www.americawest.com **American** ☎ 800/433-7300 🌐 www.im.aa.com **Continental** ☎ 800/523-3273 🌐 www.continental.com **Delta** ☎ 800/221-1212 🌐 www.delta.com **Frontier Air** ☎ 800/

432-1359 ⊕ www.frontierairlines.com **Hawaiian** ☎ 800/367-5320 ⊕ www.hawaiianair. com **Horizon** ☎ 800/547-9308 ⊕ www.alaskaairlines.com **Lufthansa** ☎ 800/645-3880 ⊕ www.lufthansa-usa.com **Mexicana** ☎ 800/531-7921 **Northwest** ☎ 800/225-2525 ⊕ www.nwa.com **Southwest** ☎ 800/435-9792 ⊕ www.southwest.com **Sky West** ☎ 800/ 453-9417 ⊕ www.skywest.com **United/United Express** ☎ 800/241-6522 ⊕ www.ual.com

## AIRPORTS

For flights departing from Portland International Airport (PDX), you should arrive at least an hour early for domestic flights and two hours early for international flights. Security lines can be long, and you will not necessarily get bumped to the front of the line just because you are running late.

🚩 Airport Information **Portland International Airport** ✉ N.E. Airport Way at I-205 ☎ 877/739-4636 ⊕ www.portlandairportpdx.com.

**AIRPORT TRANSFERS** Gray Line buses leave from the airport every 45 minutes and serve most major downtown hotels. The fare is $15 one-way. Tri-Met trains and buses also serve the airport ( ⇨ Bus Travel Within Portland).
🚩 **Gray Line** ☎ 503/285-9845 or 800/422-7042.

## BUSINESS HOURS

**BANKS & OFFICES** Most banks are open Monday–Friday 10 AM–4 PM. Many are open Saturday morning.

**GAS STATIONS** Stations are open seven days a week, and many are open 24 hours a day. Several are on northeast Broadway near the Rose Garden arena.

**MUSEUMS & SIGHTS** Most museums and attractions are open Tuesday–Sunday.

**SHOPS** Most retail businesses are open Monday–Saturday 10 AM–6 PM and Sunday noon–6 PM. Shopping centers are open Monday–Saturday until 9 PM and Sunday noon–6 PM.

## BUS TRAVEL TO & FROM PORTLAND

Greyhound is a good way to get between destinations in Oregon for a reasonable price if you don't have a car at your disposal. It is cheaper than the train but often takes longer and makes frequent stops. Portland is the main hub for nearly all routes in the state, making it the most practical starting and ending point for most bus excursions. One route heads north on I–5 to Seattle and beyond, and south through Salem, Eugene, and Ashland. An east–west route follows I–84 through Pendleton, La Grande, and Ontario, and another route dips down to Bend and follows Route 97 to Klamath Falls. Finally, a coast route runs down to California on U.S. 101. Keep in mind that many small towns in Oregon may not be regularly accessible by bus and that there may be no public transportation or car rental locations in many towns you visit. Buses arrive at and depart from the Greyhound terminal next to the Amtrak station in Old Town. You can book tickets ahead of time by phone or on-line, but it is generally unnecessary. The only way to guarantee a seat on a given bus is to get there early enough and be on line before the bus fills up. Often, during peak travel times, Greyhound will send an additional bus if there are too many passengers for one vehicle.
🚩 Depots **Greyhound Terminal** ✉ 550 N.W. 6th Ave., Old Town ☎ 503/243-2310 or 800/231-2222, 503/243-2337 baggage, 503/243-2361 customer service ⏱ daily 5 AM–11:30 PM and midnight–1 AM.

## BUS TRAVEL WITHIN PORTLAND

Tri-Met operates an extensive system of buses, streetcars, and light-rail trains. The Central City streetcar line runs between Legacy Good Samaritan hospital in Nob Hill, the Pearl District, downtown, and Portland

State University. To Nob Hill it travels along 10th Avenue and then on Northwest Northrup; from Nob Hill it runs along Northwest Lovejoy and then on 11th Avenue. Trains stop every few blocks. MAX light-rail trains run between downtown, the airport, and the western and eastern suburbs and stop at the zoo, the Rose Garden arena, PGE Park, and Lloyd Center.

A 5½-mi extension of the MAX light-rail system, running from the Gateway Transit Center (at the intersection of I–84 and I–205) directly to and from the airport, opened in fall 2001. Trains arrive at and depart from inside the passenger terminal near the south baggage-claim area. The trip takes about 35 minutes from downtown. Tri-Met Bus 12, which runs about every 15 minutes, also serves the airport. The fare to or from the airport on MAX or the bus is $1.25.

**FARES & SCHEDULES**  Bus, MAX, and streetcar fare is $1.25 for one or two zones, which cover most places you will have cause to go, and $1.55 for three zones, which includes all of the outlying areas of the city. Ask the driver if you are uncertain whether you are traveling within Zones 1 and 2. A "fareless square" extends from downtown all the way to the Lloyd Center on the east side. If you are riding only within this area, your ride is free; just say "fareless" as you board the bus, and be sure to get off before you pass into a fare zone; drivers really do take note of who is riding for free, and may ask you to get off the bus. Day passes for unlimited system-wide travel cost $4. Three-day and monthly passes are available. As you board the bus, the driver will hand you a transfer ticket that is good for one to two hours, depending on the time of day, on all buses and MAX trains. Be sure to hold on to it whether you are transferring or not; it also serves as proof that you have paid for your ride. MAX trains run every 10 minutes Monday–Saturday before 8 PM and every 15 minutes after 8 PM and all day Sunday and holidays. Buses can operate as frequently as every five minutes or once an hour. Bikes are allowed on designated areas of MAX trains, and there are bike racks on the front of all buses that everyone is free to use.

🚻 **Bus Information Tri-Met/MAX** ✉ 6th Ave. and Morrison St., Downtown ☎ 503/238-7433 🌐 www.tri-met.org, www.portlandstreetcar.org.

## CAR RENTALS
Most major rental companies have rental offices in the Portland airport and downtown. (For rental-company 800 numbers, *see* Car Rentals *in* Smart Travel Tips).

🚻 **Local Agencies, Portland Airport Alamo** ☎ 503/249-4907 🌐 www.alamo.com. **Avis** ☎ 503/249-4953 🌐 www.avis.com. **Budget** ☎ 503/249-4556 🌐 www.budget.com. **Dollar** ☎ 503/249-4792 🌐 www.dollar.com. **Hertz** ☎ 503/249-8216 🌐 www.hertz.com. **National** ☎ 503/249-4907 🌐 www.nationalcar.com.

🚻 **Local Agencies, Downtown Enterprise** ☎ 503/252-1500 🌐 www.enterprise.com **Thrifty** ☎ 503/254-6563

## CAR TRAVEL
I–5 enters Portland from the north and south. I–84, the city's major eastern corridor, terminates in Portland. U.S. 26 and U.S. 30 are primary east–west thoroughfares. Bypass routes are I–205, which links I–5 and I–84 before crossing the Columbia River into Washington, and I–405, which arcs around western downtown. Most city-center streets are one-way only, and Southwest 5th and 6th avenues between Burnside and Southwest Madison streets are limited to bus traffic.

From the airport to downtown, take I–205 south to westbound I–84. Drive west over the Willamette River and take the City Center exit. If going to the airport, take I–84 east to I–205 north; follow I–205 to the airport exit.

EMERGENCY SERVICES ⬛ **American Automobile Association** ☎ 503/222–6777 or 800/AAA–HELP. **Oregon State Police** ☎ 503/731–3030.

PARKING Most parking meters are patrolled Monday–Saturday 8 AM–6 PM. Meters, which accept credit cards, cost $1 an hour, emitting a transferrable parking sticker that you can affix to your car window. Many streets have parking time limits or prohibited parking during rush hour. To avoid the hassle of moving your car every two hours, consider one of the reasonably priced "Smart Park" parking garages downtown. Meter parking is free on Sunday and major holidays. The meters, representing one of Portland's many efforts to maintain sustainability, are solar powered.

TRAFFIC Traffic on I–5 north and south of downtown and on I–84 and I–205 east of downtown is heavy between 6 AM and 9 AM and between 4 and 8 PM. Four-lane U.S. 26 west of downtown can be bumper-to-bumper any time of the day going to or from downtown.

## CHILDREN IN PORTLAND

Portland has green parks scattered throughout the city, making it a great place to travel with kids. Washington Park can provide a day's worth of outdoor fun, but the smaller parks found all over the east side of the city also provide endless opportunity for picnics, ball games, or just a short jaunt on a playground. Attractions specifically geared toward children include the Children's Museum, the Oregon Museum of Science and Industry, Oaks Amusement Park, and the Oregon Zoo. If you've been to all the museums, and encounter another rainy day, the children's room of the public library downtown has computers with kids' programs that can provide a couple hours of entertainment, and you can always spend some time ice skating at the Lloyd Center.

## CONSULATES

Belgium, Cyprus, Denmark, Germany, Italy, Japan, Mexico, the Netherlands, Sweden, Thailand, and the United Kingdom all have consulates in the Portland area.

⬛ **Belgium** ✉ 2812 N.W. Imperial Terr. ☎ 503/228–0465. **Cyprus** ✉ 1130 S.W. Morrison St., Suite 510 ☎ 503/248–0500. **Denmark** ✉ 888 S.W. 5th Ave., ☎ 503/802–2131. **Germany** ✉ 200 S.W. Market St. ☎ 503/222–0490. **Italy** ✉ 4507 S.E. Milwaukie Ave., Suite A ☎ 503/287–2578. **Japan** ✉ 1300 S.W. 5th Ave., Suite 2700 ☎ 503/221–1811. **Mexico** ✉ 1234 S.W. Morrison St. ☎ 503/274–1442. **Netherlands** ✉ 520 S.W. Yamhill St., Suite 600 ☎ 503/222–7957. **Sweden** ✉ 111 S.W. 5th Ave., Suite 2900 ☎ 503/227–0634. **Thailand** ✉ 121 S.W. Salmon St., Suite 1430 ☎ 503/221–0440. **United Kingdom** ✉ 520 S.W. Yamhill St., Suite 800 ☎ 503/227–5665.

## DISABILITIES & ACCESSIBILITY

In many areas, Portland is exemplary for the measures it has taken to assist travelers and residents with disabilities. All Tri-Met buses and MAX trains are wheelchair accessible, and the Portland airport has received praise for the excellent access it provides for deaf and hearing-impaired travelers. Most restaurants and hotels are accessible for travelers who use wheelchairs, although several historical inns and B&Bs may not be. Independent Living Resources is an excellent source for people with disabilities living and traveling in the Portland area and has information on facilities, assistance, and basic rights for people with disabilities.

⬛ **Local Resources Independent Living Resources** ✉ 2410 S.E. 11th Ave. ☎ 503/232–7411.

## DISCOUNTS & DEALS

The Portland Oregon Visitors Association is an excellent resource for information on discounts and promotional deals that may save you money on lodging, dining, and area attractions. The Big Deal is sponsored by POVA and is geared toward providing discounts for hotels, restaurants, and attractions between October and May, to promote tourism during the "off-season." Discounts vary in size from $1 off museum admission to as much as 50% off the advertised room rates for several lovely area hotels. Visit the POVA Web site or call to find out what establishments are participating. Ticket Central has half-price tickets every day for theater and musical performances to be held that night, depending on availability. Call after 10 AM to hear the day's offerings. You must go in person to purchase tickets. It's open Monday–Friday 10–5, Saturday 10–2, and is closed Sunday.

🛈 **The Big Deal** ☎ 877/678-5263 ⊕ www.pova.com. **Ticket Central** ✉ in visitor center in Pioneer Sq. ☎ 503/275-8358.

## EMERGENCIES

🛈 Doctors & Dentists **Tanasbourne Urgent Care** ✉ 1881 N.W. 185th Ave., Hillsboro ☎ 503/690-6818. **Willamette Dental Group PC** ✉ 1933 S.W. Jefferson St., Goose Hollow, near Downtown ☎ 503/644-3200.

🛈 Emergency Services **Ambulance, fire, police** ☎ 911.

🛈 Hospitals **Eastmoreland Hospital** ✉ 2900 S.E. Steele St., Eastmoreland ☎ 503/234-0411. **Legacy Emanuel Hospital and Health Center** ✉ 2801 N. Gantenbein Ave., North Portland, near Fremont Bridge ☎ 503/413-2200. **Legacy Good Samaritan Hospital & Medical Center** ✉ 1015 N.W. 22nd Ave., Nob Hill ☎ 503/413-7711. **Providence Portland Medical Center** ✉ 4805 N.E. Glisan St., near Laurelhurst ☎ 503/215-1111. **Providence St. Vincent Hospital** ✉ 9205 S.W. Barnes Rd., west of Downtown ☎ 503/216-1234.

🛈 Hotlines **Poison Center** ☎ 503/494-8968.

🛈 24-Hour Pharmacy **Walgreens** ✉ 940 S.E. 39th Ave., Hawthorne District ☎ 503/238-6053.

## LODGING

While vacation rental homes and cabins abound in areas outside of Portland, around Mt. Hood, and on the coast, in the city you are mostly limited to fairly standard hotels, motels, and B&Bs. If you are planning a long-term stay, however, many hotels, such as the Marriott Residence Inn, offer weekly or monthly rates. If you intend to spend more than a month in the city, you might look into short-term rental options, such as sublets. You can peruse the options for independently arranged short-term rentals in the newspaper classifieds. The *Oregonian* and *Willamette Week* both make their classified ads available on-line. If you are looking for a standard hotel or motel, POVA runs a room reservation service that may be of assistance if you find yourself at a loss for where to stay; it's open Monday–Friday 8:30–5.

🛈 Resources **The *Oregonian*** ⊕ www.oregonlive.com. **The *Willamette Week*** ⊕ www.wweek.com. **POVA** ✉ in Pioneer Courthouse Sq. ☎ 877/678-5263.

BED-AND-BREAKFASTS Bed-and-breakfasts abound in Portland, and most offer lovely, carefully tended rooms; full breakfast; and knowledgeable and helpful owners. It might be difficult to choose between them. The Oregon Bed & Breakfast Guild can provide detailed information to help you make up your mind, but it is not a reservation service; Northwest Bed & Breakfast Reservation Service can take you the whole way to booking a room.

🛈 Resources **Oregon Bed & Breakfast Guild** ☎ 541/201-0511 or 800/944-6196 ⊕ www.obbg.org. **Northwest Bed & Breakfast Reservation Service** ✉ 610 S.W. Broadway, Portland ☎ 503/243-7616.

## MAIL & SHIPPING

🅵 Post Offices **Central Station Post Office** ✉ 204 S.W. 5th Ave. ☎ 503/294-2564.
**Pioneer Station** ✉ 520 S.W. 5th Ave., across from Pioneer Courthouse Sq. ☎ 503/294-
2564. **Main Post Office** ✉ 715 N.W. Hoyt, Pearl District ☎ 800/275-8777. **University
Station** ✉ 1505 S.W. 6th Ave.

## MEDIA

NEWSPAPERS &
MAGAZINES
The *Oregonian* is Portland's daily newspaper. The *Portland Tribune* is
distributed free Tuesday and Friday. *Willamette Week* is a free weekly
published every Friday. *Just Out,* published twice monthly, is the city's
gay newspaper. The *Skanner* is the city's African-American weekly.

RADIO &
TELEVISION
NBC: KGW Channel 8; ABC: KATU Channel 4; CBS: KOIN Channel
6; UPN: KPTV Channel 12; PBS: KOPB Channel 10; Fox: KPDX Chan-
nel 49; WB: KWBP Channel 32. NPR: KOPB-FM 91.5; News/talk:
KXL-AM 750.

## TAXIS

Taxi fare is $2.50 at flag drop plus $1.50 per mile. The first person pays
by the meter, and each additional passenger pays $1. Cabs cruise the
city streets, but it's better to phone for one. The major companies are
Broadway Cab, New Rose City Cab, Portland Taxi Company, and
Radio Cab. The trip between downtown Portland and the airport takes
about 30 minutes by taxi. The fare is about $20.

🅵 Companies **Broadway Cab** ☎ 503/227-1234. **New Rose City Cab** ☎ 503/282-
7707. **Portland Taxi Company** ☎ 503/256-5400. **Radio Cab** ☎ 503/227-1212.

## TELEPHONES

AREA CODES
The area codes for the Portland metro area are 503 and 971.

PHONE CARDS
**AT&T** (☎ 800/321-0288). **MCI/Worldcom** (☎ 800/444-3333). **Sprint**
(☎ 800/877-8000).

PUBLIC PHONES
Local calls at most pay phones cost 50¢. Before making a long-distance
call from a pay phone, check to see which long-distance provider is being
used. Use a calling card if you have one.

## TOURS

BIKE TOURS
Rose City Bike Tours has regularly scheduled tours of the Portland
area.

🅵 Tour Operator **Rose City Bike Tours** ✉ 2080 S.E. Caruthers St., south of Hawthorne
District ☎ 503/241-0340.

BOAT TOURS
Sternwheeler Riverboat Tours' *Columbia Gorge* departs year-round
from Tom McCall Waterfront Park on two-hour excursions of the
Willamette River; there are also Friday-night dinner cruises. During the
summer the stern-wheeler travels up the Columbia River. Yachts-O-Fun
Cruises operates dinner and Sunday-brunch cruises, Portland harbor excursions, and historical tours.

🅵 Tour Operator **Sternwheeler Riverboat Tours** ✉ S.W. Naito Pkwy. and Stark St.,
Riverfront Park ☎ 503/223-3928. **Yachts-O-Fun Cruises** ✉ S.E. Marion Street ☎ 503/
234-6665.

BUS TOURS
Gray Line operates city tours year-round and scheduled service to Chinook Winds Casino in Lincoln City; call for departure times.

🅵 Fees & Schedules **Gray Line** ☎ 503/285-9845.

TROLLEY TOURS
The Willamette Shore Trolley company operates vintage double-decker
electric trolleys that provide scenic round-trips between suburban Lake
Oswego and downtown, along the west shore of the Willamette River.
The 7-mi route, which the trolley traverses in 45 minutes, passes over
trestles and through Elk Rock tunnel along one of the most scenic

stretches of the river. The line, which opened in 1885, was electrified in 1914, and Southern Pacific Railway operated dozens of trips daily along this route in the 1920s. Passenger service ended in 1929, and the line was taken over by the Oregon Electric Railway Historical Society. Reservations are recommended. The trolley ($8 round-trip) departs Lake Oswego at noon and 2:30 PM and Portland at 1 and 3:15 on Saturday and Sunday from April through September. Charters are available.

🚋 **Willamette Shore Trolley** ✉ 311 N. State St., Lake Oswego ✉ south of RiverPlace Marina, at Sheridan and Moody Sts., Portland ☎ 503/222-2226.

WALKING TOURS   The Portland Oregon Visitors Association (⇨ Visitor Information, which is open on weekdays 9–5 and Saturday 9–4, has brochures, maps, and guides to art galleries and select neighborhoods.

### TRAIN TRAVEL

Amtrak serves Union Station. The *Coast Starlight* operates daily between Seattle, Portland, and Los Angeles. The *Empire Builder* travels between Portland and Chicago via Spokane and Minneapolis. The *Cascades,* modern European trains, operate daily between Eugene, Portland, Seattle, and Vancouver, B.C.

Metropolitan Area Express, or MAX, links the eastern and western Portland suburbs with downtown, Washington Park and the Oregon Zoo, the Lloyd Center district, the Convention Center, and the Rose Quarter. From downtown, trains operate daily 5:30 AM–1 AM, with a fare of $1.25 for travel through one or two zones, $1.55 for three zones, and $4 for an unlimited all-day ticket. A three-day visitor pass is also available for $10. Trains run about every 10 minutes Monday–Saturday and every 15 minutes on Sunday and holidays.

🚋 Information & Reservations **Amtrak** ✉ 800 N.W. 6th Ave., Old Town ☎ 800/872-7245. **MAX** ☎ 503/228-7246.

### TRANSPORTATION AROUND PORTLAND

Tri-Met operates bus service throughout the greater Portland area. The fares are the same for buses and the MAX light-rail system, and tickets can be used on either system. Travel is free throughout the entire downtown "Fareless Square," whose borders are Northwest Irving Street to the north, I–405 to the west and south, and the Willamette River to the east. The Portland Central City Streetcar, which began operation in summer 2001, travels between Portland State University, the Pearl District, and the popular Nob Hill neighborhood northwest of downtown. The Tri-Met information office at Pioneer Courthouse Square is open weekdays 9–5.

🚋 **Tri-Met** ✉ 6th Ave. and Morrison St., Pioneer Courthouse Sq. ☎ 503/238-7433 🌐 www.tri-met.org or www.portlandstreetcar.org.

### VISITOR INFORMATION

🚋 Tourist Information **Portland Oregon Visitors Association** ✉ 1000 S.W. Broadway, Suite 2300, 97205 ☎ 800/962-3700 🌐 www.pova.com. **Portland Oregon Visitors Association Information Center** ✉ Pioneer Courthouse Sq. ☎ 503/275-8355 or 877/678-5263, is open weekdays 8:30-5:30, Saturday 10-4, Sunday 10-2.

# THE COLUMBIA RIVER GORGE & THE OREGON CASCADES

3

## FODOR'S CHOICE

Beacon Rock, *Stevenson landmark*

The Cascade Room at Dolce Skamania Lodge, *Stevenson*

Dolce Skamania Lodge, *Stevenson*

McMenamins Edgefield, *Troutdale B&B*

Metolius Recreation Area, *northwest of Sisters*

Metolius River Resort, *Camp Sherman*

Multnomah Falls Lodge, *Multnomah Falls*

Timberline Lodge, *Mt. Hood*

## HIGHLY RECOMMENDED

RESTAURANTS  Cascade Dining Room, *Mt. Hood*

KC's Espresso & Deli, *Detroit*

HOTELS  The Cabins Creekside at Welches, *Welches*

Lakecliff Bed & Breakfast, *Hood River*

SIGHTS  Goldendale Observatory State Park and Interpretive Center, *Goldendale*

Mt. Hood National Forest, *60 mi east of Portland*

Suttle Lake Resort and Marina, *Metolius Recreation Area*

Updated by
Janna Mock-
Lopez

**THOUSANDS OF YEARS INTERACTING WITH NATURE'S VOLCANOES,**
lava flows, Ice Age floodwaters, and glaciers left behind the Columbia
River Gorge's dramatic landscape. Native Americans hunted and fished
for many millenniums along the Columbia River, equally rich in history
as it is in beauty, and a natural divide between Oregon and Washington. Only in the last few hundred years have pioneers, including Lewis
and Clark, forged towards the west over the Cascades to discover the
Columbia Gorge. Local Native American tribes still have exclusive fishing rights on many areas of the river.

A tour of the Columbia River Gorge and the Oregon Cascades rewards
you with a combination of recreation and spectacular scenery. Sightseers,
hikers, and skiers find contentment in this robust region and won't regret packing extra rolls of film for the never-ending views, particularly
in spring, when dozens of accessible waterfalls are full. Out of the
Columbia Gorge's 70-plus waterfalls, 11 cascade over 100 feet. During
fall and spring, the drama of fast-moving mixtures of clouds and sun
will likely be pierced by a rainbow arching across the sky.

Highlights of the Columbia River Gorge, where the mighty waterway
is dwarfed by steep, basalt cliffs, include Multnomah Falls, Bonneville
Dam, and the windsurfing hub and rich orchard land of Hood River.
To the south of Hood River lie the skiing and other alpine attractions
of the 11,239-foot-high Mt. Hood. From Portland, the Columbia
Gorge–Mt. Hood Loop is the easiest way to see the gorge and the
mountain. Take I–84 east to Troutdale and follow U.S. 26 to Bennett
Pass (near Timberline), where Highway 35 heads north to Hood River;
then follow I–84 back to Portland. Or make the loop in reverse.

Winter weather in the Columbia Gorge and the Mt. Hood area is much
more severe than that in Portland and western Oregon. Even I–84 may
be closed because of snow and ice. If you're planning a winter visit, be
sure your car has chains and carry plenty of warm clothes. Travelers canvassing farther south over the 4,800-foot Santiam Pass of the Cascade
Range, via the North Santiam Highway, will see a stark transition between the western Cascade's dominance of cedar and the eastern slopes
of pine. Exploration leads to pristine lakes and a panorama of all-season snow-capped vistas. In early fall brilliant red and gold leaves burst
from vine maple, tamarack and aspen. During winter, chains are a requirement for traveling over mountain passes.

## Exploring the Columbia River Gorge & Oregon Cascades

Bring comfortable, sturdy shoes and an adventurous attitude for heavy-
duty hiking or walking through what seem to be endless wilderness trails.
Pick from the Columbia Gorge's 21 state parks that border the mam-
moth Columbia River to picnic, watch wildlife, gaze at waterfalls, or
test hiking fitness. Mt. Hood is a star attraction, with more than 70 campgrounds and an extensive trail system that blankets 187,000 acres of
wilderness. Cast a fishing line or swim at serene locations such as Trillium Lake or Salmon River. With so many miles of sights, a car will most
likely be the primary mode of transportation. The 35-mi Hood River
valley Fruit Loop leads bicyclists and motorists through a scenic valley,
lovely orchards producing spectacular fruit, farmlands, and forest.
Towns like Troutdale, Hood River, Stevenson, and The Dalles have fascinating museums covering regional geology, culture, and history, as well
as shops brimming with local handcrafted and specialty wares.

Farther south, unique highlights of both Western and Eastern Cascades
can be easily accessed from Portland in less than a three-hour drive. From

Depending on what season you visit, activities in this region will vary in their desirability; consult visitor information resources or call individual properties before touring.

*Numbers in the margin correspond to points of interest on the Columbia River Gorge and Cascades map.*

**3**

**If you have
3 days**

Oregon's varied topography is highlighted in this driving tour. Begin your first day in **Troutdale ❷ ►**, 13 mi east of Portland on I–84. This marks the beginning of the Columbia River Gorge National Scenic Area. Continue along the Historic Columbia River Highway until **Crown Point State Park ❸**, where Vista House has displays about the Columbia Gorge and U.S. 101. Overlooking the Columbia River, you'll get a stunning view of five mountains and the gorge. Continue on to **Multnomah Falls ❹**, the nation's fifth-highest waterfall, and have lunch in the area. Continue east on 1–84 until Cascade Locks and cross the Bridge of the Gods. To the west is Bonneville Dam, and to the east is the Columbia Gorge Interpretive Center and Dolce Skamania Lodge. Go back over the bridge up 1–84 to ⬛ **Hood River ❽** and spend the afternoon shopping, exploring museums, or taking a ride on the Mt. Hood Railroad. Overnight in Hood River. On day two, drive up to **Mt. Hood ❿** via Highway 36 and stop at fruit farms along the way for picnic items. Hike, walk, or picnic in one of the many Mt. Hood parks and lakes on your way through ⬛ **Government Camp ⑪**, and up to Timberline Lodge. Overnight in Government Camp or farther west on Highway 26. On your third day, as you head toward **Gresham ❶**, take your pick between a hike along the Salmon River, year-round activities at Mt. Hood Ski Bowl, or fishing at Rainbow Trout Fishing Farm.

**If you have
5 days**

Spend your first two days exploring the many historical and scenic wonders of the Columbia River Gorge, beginning at the mouth of the gorge in **Troutdale ❷ ►** and heading east toward the Bridge of the Gods. Cross over to the Washington State side and visit the Bonneville Dam. Take a hike up to Beacon Rock and then head east to see the Columbia Gorge Interpretive Center. In the afternoon take a two-hour side excursion either on the sternwheeler *Colombia Gorge* or by saddle through Greyhorse Trails. Either drive east on the Washington side of the Columbia River via Highway 14 or cross back over the Bridge of the Gods to take I–84, until you reach ⬛ **Hood River ❽**. Overnight in Hood River. On day two, tour the shops, museums, and other sights in Hood River and **The Dalles ❾**. If time permits, include Maryhill Museum of Art on the Washington side of the river. On day three head south up to ⬛ **Mt. Hood ❿** via Highway 35 through the gorgeous scenery of fruit orchards of Hood River valley. Spend the day exploring the route's parks, lakes, and forest as you near the summit; area highlights are Trillium Lake and Barlow Pass. Overnight in Mt. Hood. Spend the morning of day four on the approximately 2½-hour drive to ⬛ **Camp Sherman ⑮** on the eastern slope of the Cascades. Head southeast on Highway 26 until you reach Madras and pick up 97 south. When you reach Redmond, go west on 126 until you reach the Camp Sherman turnoff. Grab some picnic goodies at the Camp Sherman Store. For a beautiful view of Mt. Jefferson and a short, peaceful walk through ponderosa forest, have lunch at the head of the Metolius River.

From there, visit Wizard Falls Fish Hatchery. Spend the rest of the day fly fishing, hiking, or relaxing riverside. Overnight in Camp Sherman. On day five take in wondrous snowcapped views by driving west on Highway 126, scenic McKenzie-Santiam Pass. Places to visit depending on the time of year are Suttle Lake, where you can rent canoes or paddleboats, or Hoodoo Ski Area, where you can hit the slopes. Continue west on Highway 22 toward **Detroit** ⑬ and the Detroit Lake Recreation Area, to hike, fish, rent a boat, or take in the sights of the Detroit Dam. From there you're less than 50 mi east of Salem and I–5.

**If you have**
**8 days**

Follow the five-day itinerary above, adding a day to each of the primary areas: the Columbia Gorge, Mt. Hood, and the Cascades south of Mt. Hood. Begin by visiting the small galleries and shops in **Troutdale** ② ➤. Drive east on the Historic Columbia River Highway and stop to hike one of the accessible trails near one of the many waterfalls along the way; being sure to include **Oneonta Gorge** ⑤ among your stops. Continue with other sites mentioned above; after visiting the Columbia Gorge Interpretive Center, stay on Highway 14 and check out endless surprises at the Wind River Trading Post antiques store. Go west to return to I–84, where you'll continue east; or, if you're feeling adventurous, stay east on Highway 14 until Hood River and cross the bridge south over the Columbia River at Highway 35. Spend time as described above in **Hood River** ⑧ and **the Dalles** ⑨, staying overnight in either place. Add a full day for a side trip to Goldendale, Washington, seeing Maryhill Museum of Art, Horsethief Lake State Park and Goldendale Observatory. Stay in Goldendale or drive back to the Dalles for the night.

Spend day three canvassing the beautiful Hood River valley. Take a Mt. Hood Railroad excursion, visit local farms, or shop in the town of Parkdale. Stay overnight at or near **Mt. Hood** ⑩. Day four through six explore the natural wonder and beauty of the mountain's highlights. In warmer months, sights choose myriad hiking, swimming, canoeing, fishing, and picnic locations, including a cluster of tranquil waters such as Trillium Lake, Timothy Lake, Summit Lake, Clear Lake, and Little Create Lake. Winter activities might encompass spending time at one of the several large ski resorts or gliding across a quiet mountain meadow either by snow shoe or cross-country skis. Timberline Lodge, 6 mi north of **Government Camp** ⑪, is an attraction year-round. Spend the last few days exploring the Cascades south of Mt. Hood where the western side of the Willamette Forest merges into eastern slopes of the Deschutes. Early on day six you'll travel over the Western Cascades Scenic Byway and the McKenzie Pass Scenic Byway. Go to the **Metolius Recreation Area** ⑭ for the remainder of the day to fish, hike or relax, and consider visiting the head of the Metolius River and Wizard Falls Fish Hatchery. Spend the night in 🏠 **Camp Sherman** ⑮. On day seven visit Suttle Lake or Blue Lake, Oregon's third-deepest lake; explore Sawyers Ice Cave, a lava tube several hundred feet long, off Highway 126/20 just west of Highway 22. Make your way west until you arrive at 🏠 **Detroit** ⑬ and the Detroit Lake Recreation Area, where you'll spend your final night and day. Aside from all the great fishing, boating, hiking, and picnicking activities, other area highlights include Breitenbush Hot Springs, for a soak in healing waters or walk in ancient forest; the Canyon Life Museum in Mill City; and numerous lake and riverside parks off Highway 22. I–5 in Salem is 47 mi west of Detroit.

Salem to Sisters over Highway 22 you'll be traveling through segments of two scenic byways: the West Cascades and the McKenzie Pass-Santiam Pass Scenic Byways. The terrain delivers you to a diversity of waterfalls, snow-capped volcanoes, raging rivers, wilderness, and high desert. Several months out of the year you can ski in the morning at higher elevations, then play a round of golf or fly fish in the afternoon at the lower elevations. Detroit Lake Recreation Area, 47 mi east of Salem, has 33 mi of shoreline parks and campgrounds perfect for picnicking, fishing, or boating. Continuing southeast over the Cascades, expect volcanic remnants, including lava flows, old-growth forests, and dramatic snow-clad peaks. Before reaching the town of Sisters, the official boundary of Central Oregon, you'll pass through the Metolius Recreation Area, a dry, high-desert environment that incorporates an 86,000-acre conservation zone to protect a unique ecological blend of wildlife, such as spotted owls and bald eagles, plant life like the old-growth yellow-bellied ponderosa, and scenery, such as the spring-fed Metolius River.

## About the Restaurants

Restaurants within this region love to flaunt creativity in their use of fresh, local ingredients such as fish—mostly salmon and trout—and fruit, like huckleberries, pears, and apples. Since berries are seasonal and prevalent in this region, restaurants will throw them into everything, making scrumptious treats from pancakes, cobblers, taffies, and pies. Most dishes are enhanced by using a multitude of fresh seasonings and methods of cooking such as planks and wood ovens. Dining establishments, whether they serve up burgers or rib eyes, typically ensure that you'll be able to try one of the many beer or ale microbrews found in this region.

## About the Hotels

If you prefer an outdoor camping adventure, you'll have a hard time choosing among the amazing variety of campsites found in the Columbia Gorge, Mt. Hood, and the Cascades. For everyone else there's an equal amount of choice: regal historic lodges that transport you back in time, first class resorts where every amenity is offered, or charming, cozy B&Bs. From June through September, entire properties in the Mt. Hood area, including Government Camp, are booked months in advance by summer camps; area lodging may be difficult to find, but you may find rooms in Sandy to the west and Parkdale or Hood River to the north. Late June into early September is considered "peak" travel season; therefore room rates may be higher. When possible, peak rates have been indicated; however, call ahead to check availability and current pricing.

| WHAT IT COSTS | | | | |
| --- | --- | --- | --- | --- |
| **$$$$** | **$$$** | **$$** | **$** | **¢** |
| RESTAURANTS over $30 | $20–$30 | $15–$20 | $10–$15 | under $10 |
| HOTELS over $180 | $140–$180 | $100–$140 | $60–$100 | under $60 |

Restaurant prices are per person for a main course at dinner. Hotel prices are for a standard double room, excluding room tax, which varies 6%–9 1/2% depending on location.

## Timing

There are two factors to consider when visiting this region: temperamental weather and summer crowds, with travelers and natives alike capitalizing on the sunnier, warmer weather. Throughout summer hiking trails and attractions are busy, and many establishments require reservations months in advance. Premium touring alternatives are spring, with seas of pastel wildflowers spilling over hillsides, and fall, which ignites brilliant gold and scarlet foliage. During winter, the risk of icy, volatile road conditions increases the higher you go in elevation.

# Gresham

❶ *10 mi east of Portland off I–84.*

Gresham was founded in the mid-1800s by westward-bound pioneers who cut a trail in the wilderness as they descended Mt. Hood. Today, it remains a well-traveled passageway between the Columbia River Gorge and the Mt. Hood recreation areas.

With a population of about 91,000, Gresham is Oregon's fourth-largest city and is recognized as Portland's largest suburb to the east, with light manufacturing, technology, and agriculture forming its employment infrastructure. Gresham calls itself the "city of music" for the festivals that have flourished in its midst. The first and most notable is the annual Mt. Hood Jazz Festival, hosted by Gresham and Mt. Hood Community College in early August.

Learn about this city's logging and agricultural roots at **Gresham History Museum,** in the beautiful former Carnegie Library building built in 1913. The English Tudor exterior is complemented by an artfully crafted interior with original clear lead-glass windows, finely-finished wood and trim. Authentic artifacts and an extensive gallery of more than 3,000 photos are on display. Even the bathroom has its own gallery. ✉ *410 N. Main Ave.* ☎ *503/661–0347* ✎ *Free, donations accepted.* ☉ *Tues. and Thurs. 10–4, Sat. noon–4.*

> **need a break?**

Pull into the Gresham Station Mall for the fresh handmade ice cream, at **Cold Stone Creamery** (✉ *1044 N.W. Civic Dr. 97080* ☎ *503/ 491–5920*). Base flavors are rolled on a frozen granite stone and combined with such swell mix-ins as peanut butter, fudge, or fruit. The waffle cones are baked fresh daily. Expect the crew to serenade you for a tip.

In downtown Gresham, **Main City Park** has more than 17 acres of tree-filled outdoor space for picnics, basketball, and other recreational activities. A 4½-mi stretch of the **Springwater Trail Corridor,** which runs through the park and connects to a regional 40-mi loop, is a beautiful spot for walking, biking, and horseback riding. The park is open from dawn to dusk. ✉ *219 S. Main Ave.* ⊕ *www.parks.ci.portland.or.us.*

## Where to Stay & Eat

$–$$$ ✕ **Persimmon Grille.** The Grille is at the Persimmon Country Club, tucked away in the hills 5 mi from Gresham. On the lower level of the hillside clubhouse, this light and airy room overlooks the golf course with a view of Mt. Hood in the background. Northwest touches accent the menu of Black Angus prime rib, charbroiled salmon, baked halibut, Dungeness crab, and shrimp salad, as well as a very special local dessert, marionberry cobbler. ✉ *500 S.E. Butler Rd., 97080* ☎ *503/666–4797* 🖷 *503/ 667–3885* ▭ *AE, D, MC, V* ☉ *No dinner Mon. and Tues. Oct.–Mar.*

$ ✕ **Rose's Tea Room.** Take tea in this converted 1928 home while being serenaded in three-part harmony by Rose and her two daughters. Rose's specialty is a four-tier royal high tea with some contemporary twists. The first tier is seasonal soup served with scones and Devonshire cream; the second is fresh fruit, traditional tea sandwiches, and savories; the third has desserts that might include English sticky toffee pudding or tarts. Leave room for the final tier, a chocolate course, with truffles and

**3**

## Windsurfing & Kiteboarding

The Columbia River Gorge is known for its beauty but is world-famous for its windsurfing and kiteboarding. Exceptional and consistent strong winds are siphoned through the only sea-level route in the Cascades, creating unique and extremely desirable conditions that attract top-notch international talent. Kiteboarding is exploding on the outdoor recreation scene. Unlike windsurf boards, the kites aren't attached to the boards themselves. Thrill rides are created by having the kite work in tandem with the wind. Boards are 5 to 5 ½ feet long. In windsurfing, the sail is attached directly to the board, and motion manifests by tacking against the wind. Windsurfing boards are 8–9 feet long on average. In either form, the wind opposing the river current lifts waves high above the surface, taking men, women, and teens on rides of their lives. There are more than 50 approved sites where you can launch into the river's air torrent, and it's a thrill for spectators to watch hundreds of colorful sails become one with the mighty river, slicing through infinite whitecaps as they rip in the wind.

## Hood River Valley Fruit

A remarkable combination of natural occurrences makes this 15,000-acre region of the world a delicious hub for growing fruit, including pears, cherries, apples, and peaches. Fertile volcanic soil yielded from numerous Mt. Hood eruptions over thousands of years is complemented by centuries of decomposed organic materials, thus creating a mineral-laden concoction. Add pure glacier water and warm sunny days into the mix, and results are crops harvesting 220,000 tons of apples, cherries, and pears every year. Half of the nation's winter pears are picked off these trees, and the highest grade of Pippens found anywhere is here. The Dalles is the largest cherry-growing district in Oregon, with 7,500 acres producing two-thirds of the state's sweet-cherry output. There are ample, seasonal opportunities to pick fruit, and depending upon where you live, fruit may be shipped to meet specific government regulations and personal travel requirements. For details, visit ⊕ www.hoodriverfruitloop.com.

## Waterfalls

Thousands of years of geological occurrences have created steep canyon cliffs drenched in accessible waterfalls. More than 75 waterfalls cascade down rocky inclines, fan over large rocks, or spray over boulder terraces. Short hikes, picnic areas, and canopies of dense forest alive with mist provide travelers with memories to last a lifetime. The Historic Columbia Highway is a golden gateway to Loutrell Falls, Shepperds Dell, Bridal Veil Falls, Multnomah Falls, Oneonta Falls, and Horsetail Falls, to name a few. What makes waterfall watching even more tantalizing is seeing how many variations there are in width, flow, height, and setting.

---

cakes. The lunch menu also has a selection of other sandwiches, soups, and salads. ⊠ *155 S.E. Vista Ave. 97080* ☎ *503/665–7215* ▭ *MC, V* ☼ *Closed Sun. and Mon. No dinner.*

$ ▣ **Hampton Inn.** Heavy on extras, this Hilton family property is a convenient base for either the beginning or end of your Columbia Gorge tour. Service is excellent, rooms are spacious, and a complimentary newspaper is delivered to your door each morning. ⊠ *3039 N.E. 181st Ave., 97230* ☎ *503/669–7000* 🖷 *503/669–7755* ⊕ *www.hamptoninn. com* 🖙 *60 rooms* ⟡ *In-room data ports, cable TV with movies, indoor pool, exercise equipment, laundry service, business services* ⊟ *AE, D, MC, V* 🍴 *CP.*

$ 🖳 **Sleep Inn.** This Sleep Inn, within sight of Exit 13 from I–84, blends economy and convenience. It's 13 mi from downtown Portland and only a few miles from the Columbia River Gorge. It's also within walking distance of restaurants, and half a block away you can visit the Candy Basket Factory Outlet, with its chocolate waterfall. The indoor pool is heated. ⊠ *2261 N.E. 181st Ave., 97230* ☎ *503/618–8400 or 866/ 753–3796* 🖷 *503/618–9711* ⊕ *www.sleepinn-portland.com* 🖙 *75 rooms* ⟡ *In-room data ports, some microwaves, cable TV, some in-room hot tubs, indoor pool, exercise equipment, laundry facilities, laundry service, business services, free parking* ⊟ *AE, D, DC, MC, V* 🍴 *CP.*

### Nightlife & the Arts

**Mt. Hood Repertory Theater Company** (⊠ Box 1644, 97030 ☎ 503/491–5950) produces quality family-oriented plays. Year-round shows run from small staged readings to full productions, including the signature American Classics Theater Festival, which showcases plays by American playwrights as originally written and performed from the 1930s to 1950s. The company performs in two venues, **Mt. Hood Community College** (⊠ 26000 S.E. Stark St. ☎ 503/491–6422) and **Reynolds Middle School** (⊠ 1200 N.E. 201st, Fairview ☎ 503/665–8166).

### Shopping

Gresham has two shopping hubs. The **historic downtown district,** situated largely on Main Street, has cute shops with antiques, children's clothing, toys, jewelry, books, and home accessories. Right off Main Street at Division and Eastman Parkway is **Gresham Station,** one of the largest mixed-use development projects in Oregon. Retail stores include independent merchants and such larger chains as Gap, Old Navy, Cost Plus World Market, and Eddie Bauer.

Every Saturday from Mother's Day to the end of October, rain or shine, you can buy fresh produce and flowers from local growers at the outdoor **Gresham Farmers' Market** (⊠ 3rd St. between N. Main and N.W. Miller). Other vendors sell honey, coffees, and baked goods, and there's musical entertainment, too. Admission to the market is free.

# Troutdale

▶ **2** *13 mi east of Portland on I–84.*

An eastern suburb of Portland on the Columbia River, Troutdale was named by its founder for the fish ponds he built and stocked and is the gateway to the Columbia River Gorge. Upscale galleries, antiques stores, and specialty gift shops stretching ½ mi adorn this charming community. Extending into the gorge from Troutdale is the 22-mi-long **Historic Columbia River Highway,** U.S. 30 (also known as the Columbia River Scenic Highway and the Scenic Gorge Highway), which leaves I–84 and begins its climb to the forested riverside bluffs high above the interstate. Completed in 1915, the serpentine highway was the first paved road in the gorge built expressly for automotive sightseers.

**3** East of Troutdale, a few miles on U.S. 30 is **Crown Point State Park,** a 730-foot-high bluff with an unparalleled 30-mi view down the Columbia River Gorge. **Vista House,** the two-tier octagonal structure on the side of the cliff, opened its doors to visitors in 1918; the rotunda has displays about the gorge and the highway. ⊠ *U.S. 30* ☎ *503/695–2230* ⊕ *www.vistahouse.com* ✉ *Free* ◷ *Mid-Apr.–mid-Oct., daily 9–6.*

About 4 mi east of the Troutdale bridge, **Dabney State Park** has boating, hiking, and fishing. It's also a popular summer swimming hole. There's also an 18-hole disc golf course. A boat ramp is open from October through May—when no one is swimming. ⊠ *Rte. 30* ☎ *800/551–6949* ⊕ *www.oregonstateparks.org* ✉ *Day use $3 per vehicle* ◷ *Daily dawn–dusk.*

The most famous beach lining the Columbia River, **Rooster Rock State Park** is below Crown Point; access is from the interstate only. Three miles of sandy beaches, panoramic cascades, and a large swimming area make this a popular spot. True naturists appreciate that one of Oregon's only two designated nude beaches is at Rooster Rock at the east end, not visible to conventional sunbathers. ⊠ *I–84, 7 mi east of Troutdale* ☎ *503/ 695–2261* ✉ *Day use $3 per vehicle* ◷ *Daily 7 AM–dusk.*

## Where to Stay & Eat

**$$$**   ✕ **Black Rabbit.** At McMenamins Edgefield, this restaurant in the main lodge serves all day and offers northwestern cuisine, such as fresh green curry mussels steamed with green curry coconut milk, lime juice, and basil, and traditional favorites, such as New York steak. A kids' menu is also available. Dine indoors or in the outdoor courtyard. ⊠ *2126 S. W. Halsey St., 97060* ☎ *503/492–3086* ☐ *AE, D, MC, V.*

**$**   ✕ **Stromboli's.** Hearty flavors come across in sizzling Philly-cheese steak sandwiches and hoagies. Stromboli's really makes the cheese steaks by hand, from preparing its own meat to grinding its own cheese. A favorite is the Bombsteak, a combination of green chilies, onions, mushrooms, strip steak, and cheeses. There are also pizza, salads, and soups. ⊠ *177 E. Historic Columbia River Hwy. 97060* ☎ *503/674–2654* ⊕ *www. strombolis.com* ☐ *MC, V* ◷ *No dinner Mon.*

**$–$$**   **McMenamins Edgefield.** This European-style bed-and-breakfast hotel in
FodorsChoice   a historic Georgian Revival–style manor is a tranquil getaway. Its 38
★   acres of gardens and vineyards include a winery, brewery, distillery, several small bars and gathering areas, an 18-hole pitch-and-putt golf course, gardens, and a movie theater. Relaxing and enjoying simple pleasures are the focus here. Rooms have no telephones, and most share separate men's and women's bathrooms. The only television on the grounds is found in the Ice House, a tiny cigar bar decorated with old sports memorabilia. There's also a wine-tasting room here. Massage service is available on site, and a full country breakfast is included. ⊠ *2126 S.W. Halsey St., Troutdale 97060* ☎ *503/669–8610 or 800/669–8610* ✑ *103 rooms* △ *2 restaurants, 18-hole golf course, massage, 4 bars, beer garden, pub, cinema, shop, meeting rooms, free parking; no smoking* ☐ *AE, DC, MC, V* ⦿ *BP.*

**$**   ◫ **Phoenix Inn Suites—Troutdale.** This all-suites hotel near the mouth of the Columbia River Gorge has spacious suites with microwaves and refrigerators. Other handy extras are an iron with ironing board, free local calls, and pool, spa, and fitness center. Factory outlet stores are nearby. ⊠ *477 N.W. Phoenix Dr., 97060* ☎ *503/669–6500 or 800/824–6824* 🖷 *503/669–3500* ✑ *73 rooms* △ *Cable TV, indoor pool, hot tub, business services, airport shuttle, some pets allowed (fee)* ☐ *AE, D, DC, MC, V* ⦿ *CP.*

## Shopping

Save a bundle on your favorite brand-name products at **Columbia Gorge Factory Stores** (⊠ 450 N.W. 257th Ave., ☎ 503/669–8060), near the entrance to the gorge. This outlet mall has more than 45 shops, including

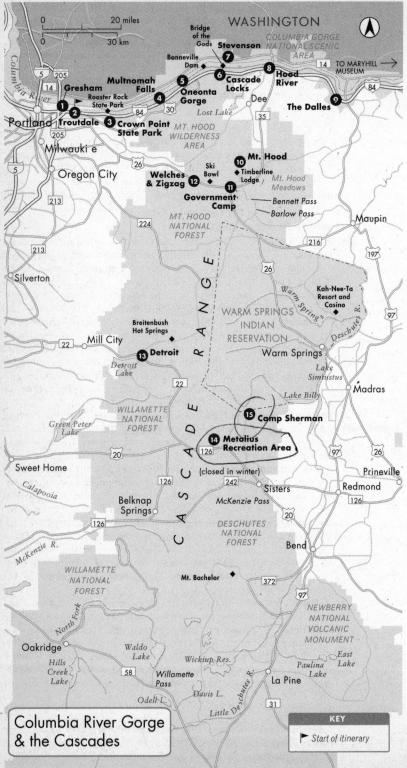

20 miles

30 km

WASHINGTON

COLUMBIA GORGE
NATIONAL SCENIC
AREA

Bridge
of the
Gods

Stevenson **7**

Bonneville
Dam

Columbia River

5    205

14

Gresham

**1** **2**

Rooster Rock
State Park

Multnomah
Falls

**4**

**5**

Oneonta
Gorge

84

30

**6** Cascade
Locks

TO MARYHILL
MUSEUM

14

Hood
River

**8**

84

Dee

Portland

Troutdale **3** Crown Point
State Park

35

The Dalles **9**

205

Lost Lake

MT. HOOD
WILDERNESS
AREA

Milwauki e

5

Oregon City

26

213

213

Silverton

**10** Mt. Hood

Ski
Bowl

Welches
& Zigzag **12**

Timberline
Lodge

Mt. Hood
Meadows

**11**

Government
Camp

Bennett Pass

Barlow Pass

Maupin

224

MT. HOOD
NATIONAL
FOREST

216

197

26

Warm Springs

Kah-Nee-Ta
Resort and
Casino

Green Peter
Lake

22

Mill City

Breitenbush
Hot Springs

**13** Detroit

Detroit
Lake

WARM SPRINGS
INDIAN
RESERVATION

Warm Springs

Deschutes R.

97

Lake
Simtustus

Madras

C
A
S
C
A
D
E

R
A
N
G
E

WILLAMETTE
NATIONAL
FOREST

22

Lake Billy

**15** Camp Sherman

**14** Metolius
Recreation Area

126

97

26

Sweet Home

20

126

Calapooia

(closed in winter)

242

Sisters

McKenzie Pass

20

Redmond

126

Prineville

Belknap
Springs

126

DESCHUTES
NATIONAL
FOREST

Bend

McKenzie R.

WILLAMETTE
NATIONAL
FOREST

North Fork

Mt. Bachelor

372

97

NEWBERRY
NATIONAL
VOLCANIC
MONUMENT

Oakridge

Hills
Creek
Lake

Waldo
Lake

58

Willamette
Pass

Wickiup Res.

Paulina
Lake

East
Lake

Davis L.

La Pine

31

Odell L.

Little Deschutes R.

# Columbia River Gorge
# & the Cascades

Mikasa, Adidas, Harry and David, Bass, Levi's, Carter's, Big Dog Sportswear, Great Outdoor Clothing Co., and Norm Thompson. Take I–84 east to Exit 17.

**Gallery G** (✉ 219 E. Historic Columbia River Hwy. ☎ 503/661–5847) showcases noteworthy glass, metal, and painted works of Northwest artists.

If you're looking to appease your wine palate, **Sandy River Cellars** (✉ 119 E. Historic Columbia River Hwy. ☎ 503/492–2387) has an international selection of wines, with an emphasis on Northwest harvests.

Shop for locally crafted gifts before or after a delicious cup of salmon chowder or a sweet-potato black-eyed pea salad at the **Troutdale General Store** (✉ 289 E. Historic Columbia River Hwy. ☎ 503/492–7912). Sip a brew on tap or glass of wine on the outdoor deck.

en route | From Crown Point, the Columbia River Highway heads downhill over graceful stone bridges built by Italian immigrant masons and winds through quiet forest glades. More than a dozen waterfalls pour over fern- and lichen-covered cliffs in a 10-mi stretch. Latourell, Bridal Veil, Wahkeena, and Horsetail falls are the most impressive. All have parking areas and hiking trails.

## Multnomah Falls

**④** *20 mi east of Troutdale on I–84 or Historic Columbia River Hwy. (U.S. 30).*

Multnomah Falls, a 620-foot-high double-decker torrent, the fifth-highest waterfall in the nation, is by far the most spectacular of the cataracts east of Troutdale. The scenic highway leads down to a parking lot; from there, a paved path winds to a bridge over the lower falls. A much steeper trail climbs to a viewing point overlooking the upper falls.

### Where to Eat

$-$$ ✕ **Multnomah Falls Lodge.** The lodge, built in 1925 and listed on the
FodorsChoice National Register of Historic Places, has vaulted ceilings and classic
★ stone fireplaces. Wonderful service complements a wide selection of delicious food prepared in generous helpings such as a zesty apple-wood-grilled salmon, slow-roasted prime rib, and grilled flat-iron steak. Other favorites are blueberry pancakes and traditional French onion soup. ✉ *50000 Historic Columbia River Hwy. (Exit 31 off I–84), Bridal Veil,* ☎ *503/695–2376* ⊕ *www.multnomahfallslodge.com* ⊟ *AE, D, MC, V.*

## Oneonta Gorge

**⑤** *2 mi east of Multnomah Falls on Historic Columbia River Hwy.*

Following the old highway east from Multnomah Falls, you come to a narrow, mossy cleft with walls hundreds of feet high. Oneonta Gorge is most enjoyable during the summer, when you can walk up the streambed through the cool green canyon, where hundreds of plant species—some found nowhere else—flourish under the perennially moist conditions. At other times of the year, take the trail along the west side of the canyon. The clearly marked trailhead is 100 yards west of the gorge, on the south side of the road. The trail ends at Oneonta Falls, about ½ mi up the stream. Bring boots or submersible sneakers—plus a strong pair of ankles—because the rocks are slippery. East of Oneonta Gorge, the scenic highway returns to I–84.

# GREAT RIVER OF THE WEST

**E**TCHED IN NEAT SCRIPT on one of the hand-drawn government maps Lewis and Clark carried with them on their journey are the words, "Oragon or R. of the West." This was the river of the explorers' dreams—the Great River of the West, as the Columbia was called. This massive waterway would become a river highway, connecting East and West and ensuring the extension of American agrarian society across the continent. American sea captain Robert Gray found the Columbia's mouth in 1792. His descriptions, along with those of British and Spanish explorers, led President Thomas Jefferson to believe that the huge river must stretch east to the Rockies.

To Lewis's and Clark's disappointment, it did not. And just as the Rockies were not gentle and forgiving like the mountains of Virginia, as Jefferson had imagined them, the Columbia was not placid and smooth. Unlike the river we know today, subdued by dams, it was wild and mighty, twisting and turning north from its headwaters in Canada, then south, then sharply west through the Cascades, and finally swinging north again to the Pacific. Huge rapids dogged the expedition beginning at its confluence with Snake River. This white water was an aftereffect of the Missoula floods—the violent breakup of a glacier ice sheet over an ice dam 12,000–14,000 years before. Some rapids took entire days to portage.

But despite the explorers' initial disappointment, the Columbia did eventually become the Great River of the West. It was at once a trade route, a great natural resource, and a regional icon. The story of this river, which quenches desert thirst and sustains miles of estuaries after it rushes headlong past the basalt and granite of the Columbia River Gorge cliffs, and through rain forests before tumbling into the surf of the Pacific, is a story of cataclysmic geologic events, complex ecosystems, and persistent human engineering.

Many rivers cross mountain ranges, but few cut their way through at near sea level as the Columbia does on its route through the Cascades. Despite the dams, the Columbia River Gorge remains one of the most scenic places on earth; some have called it the Rhine River of the Pacific Northwest. The river itself is a place where desert, forest, and sea compete and converge, shadowed by 8,000-foot basalt and granite cliffs and ancient forests. The snow-charged Columbia reaches across 1,200 mi, and its watershed drains 259,000 square mi and includes portions of seven states. Of the North American rivers to reach the Pacific Ocean, the Columbia is the third longest.

When Lewis and Clark made their way down the river, it was pristine, naturally diverse, and naturally balanced—undammed, unpolluted, and not overfished. Today, the river's rapids and falls are silent. Where the river was once narrow and fast, it is now wide and slow. According to the Portland State University Center for Columbia River History, the Columbia is, with the dams along its entire length, "the most hydroelectrically developed hydroelectric river system in the world." During the past 200 years, it has been altered by dikes, channels, locks, and dams to become a series of lakes that sustain huge agricultural economies in arid regions of the West and send electricity buzzing in all directions. At the Celilo Converter Station on a hilltop near The Dalles, the Bonneville Dam hydroelectric station transmits enough power for all of Los Angeles and Hollywood.

The Columbia may not sound or look the same as it did 200 years ago. But it is still the Great River of the West.

# Cascade Locks

**6** *7 mi east of Oneonta Gorge on Historic Columbia River Hwy. and I–84, 30 mi east of Troutdale on I–84.*

In pioneer days, boats needing to pass the bedeviling rapids near the town of Cascade Locks had to portage around them. The locks that gave the town its name were completed in 1896, allowing waterborne passage for the first time. Native Americans still use the locks for their traditional dip-net fishing.

The first federal dam to span the Columbia, **Bonneville Dam** was dedicated by President Franklin D. Roosevelt in 1937 and may be the state's most impressive man-made attraction. Its generators (visible from a balcony during self-guided powerhouse tours) have a capacity of nearly a million kilowatts, enough to supply power to more than 200,000 single-family homes. There is a modern visitor center on Bradford Island, complete with underwater windows for viewing migrating salmon as they struggle up fish ladders. The best viewing times are between April and October. In recent years the dwindling runs of wild Columbia salmon have made the dam a subject of much environmental controversy. ⊠ *From I–84 take Exit 40, head northeast, and follow signs 1 mi to visitor center* ☎ *541/374–8820* ☜ *Free* ☉ *Visitor center daily 9–5.*

Below Bonneville Dam, the ponds at the **Bonneville Fish Hatchery** teem with fingerling salmon, fat rainbow trout, and 6-foot-long sturgeon. The hatchery raises Chinook and coho salmon; from mid-October to late November, you can watch as staff members spawn the fish, beginning a new hatching cycle, or feed the trout with food pellets from a coin-operated machine. ✢ *From I–84 take Exit 40 and follow signs northeast 1 mi to hatchery* ☎ *541/374–8393* ☜ *Free* ☉ *Hatchery grounds daily dawn–dusk, spawning room daily 7:30–4:30.*

Cascade Locks is the home port of the 600-passenger stern-wheeler ***Columbia Gorge.*** Between mid-June and early October the relic ship churns upriver, then back again, on two-hour excursions through some of the Columbia River Gorge's most impressive scenery. The ship's captain will talk about the gorge's fascinating 40-million-year geology and about pioneering spirits and legends, such as Lewis and Clark, who once triumphed over this very same river. ⊠ *Cruises leave from Marine Park in Cascade Locks* ☎ *541/374–8427* ⊕ *www.sternwheeler.com* ☝ *Reservations essential* ☜ *2-hr cruises (no meal) $12.95, longer cruises with meals $26–$36* ☉ *2-hr cruises June–Sept., daily at 10, 12:30, and 3; dinner cruise Fri. at 7 PM, Sat. at 6 PM; brunch cruise weekends at 12:30 PM* ☱ *AE, MC, V.*

## Where to Stay & Eat

**$–$$** ✕**Char Burger Restaurant.** Arrowheads, rifles, and wagon-wheel chandeliers carry out the western motif of this dining room overlooking the Columbia River. Hamburgers, sandwiches, and breakfast favorites are served cafeteria-style. ⊠ *745 S.W. Wanapa St.* ☎ *541/374–8477* ☱ *AE, MC, V.*

**¢–$$** ✕**Salmon Row Pub.** A woodsy tavern with cedar-shake walls, historical photos, and a stone fireplace provides hearty servings of starters, salads, and main courses, including smoked salmon chowder and oven-roasted chicken accompanied by house-specialty horseradish. Sit outside in the adjacent courtyard and take in mountain and river views while sipping one of 11 featured microbrews. ⊠ *500 Wanapa St.* ☎ *541/374–9310* ☱ *D, MC, V* ☉ *No lunch Mon. or Tues.*

**¢** ▦ **Bridge of the Gods Motel and RV Park.** One block from the historic Bridge of the Gods and within walking distance of Cascade Locks activities, this locally owned business offers clean, spacious rooms with modest furnishings, including microwaves. Some have kitchenettes, patios, and balconies. ⊠ *630 Wanapa, Box 278, 97014* ☎ *541/374–8628* 🖶 *541/374–9056* ⤴ *15 rooms* ⚭ *Some kitchenettes, microwaves, laundry facilities, some pets allowed (fee)* ⊟ *AE, D, MC, V.*

## Stevenson, Washington

**❼** *Across the river from Cascade Locks via the Bridge of the Gods and 4 mi east on Washington State Hwy. 14.*

For a magnificent vista from high above the Columbia, pay the 75¢ toll and take the truss bridge, called the **Bridge of the Gods**, above Cascade Locks over to the Washington side. Slightly west of the bridge, hikers gain access to the Oregon-Washington link of the Mexico-to-Canada **Pacific Crest Trail.** Travel east on Highway 14 for about 10 minutes to reach the small town of Stevenson, with several antiques shops and good places to grab a bite.

Fodor's Choice
★

For several hundreds years, 800-foot **Beacon Rock** was a landmark for river travelers, including Native Americans, who recognized this point as the last rapid of the Columbia River. Lewis and Clark were reportedly the first white men to see the volcanic remnant in 1805. Picnic atop old lava flows after hiking a 1-mi trail, steep but safe, which leads to tremendous views of the Columbia Gorge and river. A round-trip hike takes 45 minutes to one hour. The site is a few miles west of the Bridge of the Gods.

The **Columbia Gorge Interpretive Center,** below the dramatic basaltic cliffs on the north bank of the Columbia River Gorge, has exhibits that explain the volcanic forces that shaped the gorge landscape and the cultural history of the area. On display are a huge fish wheel and native dip nets used for salmon fishing, a Native American pit house, and artifacts pertaining to the explorers, missionaries, fur trappers, and soldiers who came through the gorge. ⊠ *990 S.W. Rock Creek Dr., Stevenson, WA, (1 mi east of Bridge of the Gods on Hwy. 14)* ☎ *509/427–8211* ⊕ *www.columbiagorge.org* ⊠ *$6* ☉ *Daily 10–5.*

### Where to Stay & Eat

$-$$$
Fodor's Choice
★

✕ **The Cascade Room at Dolce Skamania Lodge.** Gaze at the perfect fusion of sky, river, and cliffscapes through the Cascade Room's expansive windows during an exquisite dining experience. Alder-plank potlatch salmon and oat-crusted trout stuffed with Northwest potatoes and herbs are signature dishes; also try the garlic sizzling shrimp and sautéed forest mushrooms. Melt-in-your-mouth chocolate soufflé and fresh mixed-berry cobbler are grand finales. Breakfast specialties include hazelnut pancakes and fresh berry crepes. The Gorge Harvest Buffet brunch is offered on Sunday, and the seafood, salads, sushi, and pasta draw patrons from miles around. ⚓ *Skamania Lodge Way north of Hwy. 14, 2 mi east of the Bridge of the Gods* ☎ *509/427–2508* ⚑ *Reservations essential* ⊟ *AE, D, DC, MC, V.*

¢-$ ✕ **Big River Grill.** The fare at this appealing storefront grill on Stevenson's main street is simple—chili, soup, sandwiches, and burgers. High-back wooden booths line one side; photos and memorabilia provide insight into the local past. ⊠ *192 S.W. 2nd St.* ☎ *509/427–4888* ⊟ *MC, V.*

¢ ✕ **It's a Wrap.** Dozens of healthy burrito-like wraps are served at this café-style eatery. Patrons favor the Garden Wrap, a tomato tortilla stuffed with lettuce, cucumbers, and jasmine rice smothered in sesame dressing, and the Gorge Wrap, eggs, cheese, onions, tomato, green pepper, and hash browns packed in a garlic tortilla. Also choose from homemade soups and salads. Take-out is available. ✉ *220 2nd St.* ☎ *509/427–7725* ▭ *MC, V.*

**$$$–$$$$** 🏨 **Bonneville Hot Springs Resort.** The pampering at this 6,000-square-foot property has a history; local lore says that the same 97°F hot-springs ground waters being fed into present-day resort spa treatments, pools, and hot tubs were once used by Native American tribes seeking health and healing. The expansive three-story lobby has floor-to-ceiling windows overlooking lush forest and an equally tall two-sided river-rock fireplace. Impressive use of stone, fiber, and wood finishes throughout includes a 25-meter redwood-panel indoor lap pool and an outdoor patio garden with an 8-foot stone waterfall wall, soaking pool, and attractive garden sculptures. Massage, mineral and herbal baths, and wraps are administered by candlelight. Rooms are spacious with upscale furnishings. ⊕ *3 mi west of Bridge of the Gods on Hwy. 14, right on Hot Springs Way, right on E. Cascade Dr. follow for ½ mi.* ✉ *1252 E. Cascade Dr., North Bonneville, WA 98639* ☎ *509/427–9720 or 866/459–1678* 🖷 *509/427–7733* ⊕ *www.bonnevilleresort.com* 🛏 *78 rooms* ⚒ *Restaurant, bar, indoor pool, indoor and outdoor hot tubs, massage* ▭ *AE, D, MC, V.*

**$$$–$$$$** 🏨 **Dolce Skamania Lodge.** Because this grand lodge is situated high on a forested knoll overlooking the Columbia River, the natural touches of endless windows, pine floors, and an immense river-rock fireplace leave an organic imprint. The rooms, many with fireplaces and gorgeous views, have lodge-style furniture covered with handwoven fabrics. Breathe in the surrounding beauty by walking one of the lodge's mile-plus wooded nature trails or replenish your spirit in the beautiful spa. Outstanding recreational facilities make this a premier resort on the Columbia. ⊕ *Skamania Lodge Way north of Hwy. 14, 1½ mi east of the Bridge of the Gods* ☎ *509/427–7700 or 800/221–7117* 🖷 *509/427–2547* ⊕ *www.dolce.com/skamania* 🛏 *254 rooms* ⚒ *Restaurant, bar, indoor pool, indoor and outdoor hot tubs, massage, sauna, 18-hole golf course, 2 tennis courts, gym, hiking, volleyball, bicycles, cross-country skiing, library, business services, some pets allowed (fee)* ▭ *AE, D, DC, MC, V.*

FodorsChoice ★

**¢–$** 🏨 **Carson Mineral Hot Springs Resort.** People have been coming to this funky place for decades to soak in the hot mineral-laden water pumped up to the two bathhouses (virtually unchanged since they opened in 1923) from the Wind River. After a soak in an old claw-foot tub, you're wrapped in sheets and blankets for a blissful snooze. The bathhouses are open daily 8:45 AM–7 PM. Call ahead if you want a massage; baths ($10) are available to nonguests on a first-come, first-served basis. The hotel, dating from 1897, is clean, if charmless, with spartan rooms and cabins. The restaurant's open all day. ✉ *372 St. Martin's Springs Rd., Carson, WA 98610, (4 mi east of Stevenson on Hwy. 14)* ☎ *509/427–8292 or 800/607–3678* 🖷 *509/427–7242* 🛏 *9 rooms share 4 baths; 1 suite; 14 cabins with ½ bath; 2 cabins with bath* ⚒ *Restaurant, some kitchens, 18-hole golf course* ▭ *AE, MC, V.*

## Sports & the Outdoors

HORSEBACK RIDING An adventurous and relaxing way to absorb the magnificent views of the Columbia River Gorge is by saddle. The owners of **Greyhorse Trails** (✉ Beacon Rock State Park, North Bonneville, WA 98639 ☎ 866/604–6773), the only horse concession operating in the gorge, have more than 80 years' combined horse experience. Rates are based on trail rides, not hours. There are five rides, lasting from 90 minutes to all day. Rides are available for those seven and older seven days a week, including holidays. Advance reservations are required. To reach the trails, head west from the Bridge of the Gods on Highway 14 to Beacon Rock State Park, turn right, and go about a mile up Kueffler Road.

**Shopping**

For a one-of-a-kind shopping experience and leisurely afternoon, consider **Wind River Trading Post** (✉ 981 Wind River Hwy. ☎ 509/427–4766). Wall-to-wall aisles are overstuffed with historical artifacts that conjure up imagery about who previously owned these treasures. Comb through dishes, books, postcards, photographs, vintage jewelry, farming tools, magazines, handmade quilts, and many odds and ends in between. Only cash and checks are accepted. The shop is 3 mi east of Stevenson; go left at the Carson turnoff at the flashing yellow light and take the Wind River Highway for about 1½ mi. It's closed on Monday.

# Hood River

**8** *17 mi east of Cascade Locks on I–84.*

For years the incessant easterly winds at the town of Hood River, where the Columbia Gorge widens and the scenery changes to tawny, wheat-covered hills, were nothing but a nuisance. Then somebody bolted a sail to a surfboard, and a new recreational craze was born. A fortuitous combination of factors—mainly the reliable gale-force winds blowing against the current—has made Hood River the self-proclaimed boardsailing capital of the world. Especially in the summer, this once-somnolent town swarms with colorful "boardheads," many of whom have journeyed from as far away as Europe and Australia. In winter, many of these same athletes stay in town but turn south to ski on mountain slopes that are only a short drive away. Other outdoor enthusiasts find the area's fishing, boating, swimming, and hiking venues the best in the region.

Hood River's rich pioneer past is reflected in its downtown historic district. The City of Hood River publishes a free, informative self-guided walking tour (available through the City of Hood River government office or the Hood River chamber of commerce) that takes you roughly 10 blocks to more than 40 civic and commercial buildings dating from 1893 to the 1930s, a handful of which are listed in the National Register of Historic Places.

Either by car or bicycle, tour Hood River valley's **Fruit Loop,** whose vast orchards surround the Hood River. You'll see apples, pears, cherries, and peaches fertilized by volcanic soil, pure glacier water, and a conducive harvesting climate. Along the 35 mi of farms are a host of delicious baked goods, wines, flowers, and nuts. Festive farm activities from April to November also give a taste of the agricultural life. While on the loop, consider stopping at the town of **Parkdale** to lunch, shop, and snap a photo of Mt. Hood's north face. There are well-marked signs on the entire 35-mi loop. ✉ *Route begins on Hwy. 35* ⊕ *www. hoodriverfruitloop.com.*

The **Hutson Museum** exhibits Native American dolls, taxidermy, and a rare rock collection, which includes thousands of rough specimens, polished slabs, spheres and eggs. More than 2,500 arrow and spear points, stone bowls, mortars, grinding tools, and specialized tools are prized for their regional geological and historical value. The Mt. Hood excursion train terminates at the museum. ✉ *4967 Baseline Dr., Parkdale* ☎ *541/ 352–6808* 🖅 *$1* ⊙ *Oct.–Apr., Wed.–Fri. 11–4; Sat. 11–6.*

On the river downtown, **Columbia Gorge Sailpark** has a boat basin, swimming beach, jogging trails, picnic tables, and rest rooms. ✉ *Port Marina, Exit 64 off I–84* ☎ *541/386–1645.*

An efficient and relaxing way to survey Mt. Hood and the Hood River, the **Mt. Hood Scenic Railroad and Dinner Train** was established in 1906 as a passenger and freight line. Chug alongside the Hood River through vast fruit orchards before climbing up steep forested canyons, glimpsing Mt. Hood along the way. There are four trip options: a four-hour excursion (serves light concessions with two daily departures, morning and afternoon), dinner, brunch, and themed murder-mystery dinner. Choose from brunch fare such as quiche stuffed with mushrooms, caramelized onions, bacon, cottage and cheddar cheeses, or fresh berry crepes. Favorite dinner selections are the herbed fillet of salmon served with chardonnay-lime butter or roasted chicken breast filled with shallots, mushrooms, and spinach. Exceptional service is as impressive as the scenery. ⊠ *110 Railroad Ave.* ☎ *541/386–3556 or 800/872–4661* ⊕ *www.mthoodrr.com* ⊠ *Excursion $23, brunch $57, dinner $70, murder mystery dinner $80* ⊙ *Apr.–Dec., call for schedule.*

**need a break?**   A glass-walled microbrewery with a windswept deck overlooking the Columbia, the **Full Sail Tasting Room and Pub** (⊠ 506 Columbia St. ☎ 541/386–2247) has won major awards at the Great American Beer Festival. Savory snack foods complement fresh ales.

An amalgam of education, history, and fun, ☺ **Oregon's International Museum of Carousel Art** has the world's largest and most comprehensive collection of antique carousel art. Admire, without touching, the master craftsmanship and beauty of 150 restored animals, including horses, tigers, and dragons. ⊠ *304 Oak St.* ☎ *541/387–4622* ⊠ *$5* ⊙ *Wed.–Sun. 11–3.*

In the scenic Hood River valley, **Flerchinger Vineyards** has a 6-acre vineyard nearby where Riesling and chardonnay grapes are grown. ⊠ *4200 Post Canyon Dr.* ☎ *541/386–2882 or 800/516–8710* ⊕ *www.flerchinger. com* ⊠ *Free* ⊙ *Daily 11–5.*

Sauvignon blanc, cabernet sauvignon, and merlot are among the varieties produced at the 12-acre, family-owned **Hood River Vineyards,** which overlook the Columbia River Gorge and Hood River valley. Bottles are sold individually; best-sellers are the pinot noir and chardonnay. ⊠ *4693 Westwood Dr.* ☎ *541/386–3772* ⊠ *Free* ⊙ *Mar.–Dec., daily 11–5.*

**off the beaten path**   **LOST LAKE –** The waters of one of the most-photographed sights in the Pacific Northwest reflect towering Mt. Hood and the thick forests that line the lakeshore. Cabins are available for overnight stays, and because no motorboats are allowed on Lost Lake, the area is blissfully quiet. ⊠ *Lost Lake Rd., (take Hood River Hwy. south from Hood River to town of Dee and follow signs)* ☎ *541/386–6366* ⊠ *Day use $5.*

## Where to Stay & Eat

$–$$$   ✕ **Stonehedge Gardens.** Unique to this dinner-only spot is a five-level Italian stone terrace for outdoor summer dining. The 1898 house rests on 6½ acres of gardens and a wooded area. The interior is embellished by fine woodwork detail and stained-glass windows. The menu has a mix of Northwest and Continental dishes that includes locally raised organic beef filet mignon and seared ahi tuna. Complement your meal with a glass of wine from the extensive cellar. Listen to folk music or jazz on Wednesday nights during July and August. ⊠ *3405 Cascade St. 97031* ☎ *541/386–3940* ⊟ *AE, MC, V.*

$–$$   ✕ **6th Street Bistro and Loft.** The menu here changes weekly but concentrates on Pacific Northwest flavors, right down to the coffee and salads. Try the grilled fresh fish and chicken or, in season, local fresh steamer clams and wild coral mushrooms. This restaurant uses only local and organic food products. The deck and patio have great outdoor seating and views of the Columbia River. ⊠ *509 Cascade Ave.* ☎ *541/386–5737* ☰ *MC, V.*

**$$$** ✕⊡ **Columbia Gorge Hotel.** One selling point of this grande dame of gorge hotels is the view of a 208-foot-high waterfall. Rooms with plenty of wood, brass, and antiques overlook the formal gardens. Rates include a seven-course breakfast, dubbed the World Famous Farm Breakfast (nonguests pay $24.95). While watching the sun set on the Columbia River, you can dine in the hotel's restaurant, also open to non-guests, where selections might include breast of pheasant with pear wine, hazelnuts, and cream, as well as grilled venison, breast of duck, Columbia River salmon, or sturgeon. ⊠ *4000 Westcliff Dr., 97031, off I–84's Exit 62* ☎ *541/386–5566 or 800/345–1921* ☎ *541/387–5414* ⊕ *www.columbiagorgehotel.com* ☞ *46 rooms* ☾ *Restaurant, bar* ☰ *AE, D, DC, MC, V* ⋈ *BP.*

○ **$$$** ⊡ **Old Parkdale Inn.** This fanciful B&B is decorated in the spirit and with reproductions of famed artists: for example, the Gauguin Room, inspired by Paul Gauguin's love of the tropics, or the O'Keeffe Suite, which has a colorful yet subtle decor meant to evoke creativity and serenity. The inn encourages stays of children and families and provides lots of toys and kids' books. ⊠ *4932 Baseline Rd.* ✆ *Box 474, 97041* ☎ *541/352–5551* ⊕ *www.hoodriverlodging.com* ☞ *3 rooms* ☰ *MC, V* ⋈ *BP.*

**$$–$$$** ⊡ **Inn of the White Salmon.** Quiet and cozy, this European-style two-story brick inn on the Washington side of the Columbia River was built in 1937. The common areas and sleeping rooms are filled with antiques and artifacts that deliver you back in time. Sit outside and admire the pristine garden with colorful flowers and plants. All rooms have private bathrooms. Breakfast is a treat and available to the public; choose from more than 20 pastries, tarts, cakes, breads, and rolls. Entrées include artichoke or Italian frittatas, broccoli quiche, and chiles rellenos. ⊠ *172 W. Jewett, White Salmon, WA 98672* ☎ *509/493–2335 or 800/972–5226* ⊕ *www.innofthewhitesalmon.com* ☞ *11 rooms, 5 suites* ☾ *Hot tub, some pets allowed (fee)* ☰ *AE, D, DC, MC, V* ⋈ *CP.*

★ **$$–$$$** ⊡ **Lakecliff Bed & Breakfast.** Architect A. E. Doyle, who designed the Multnomah Falls Lodge, the Classical Revival public library, and Benson Hotel in Portland, also designed the summer home that's now a bed-and-breakfast inn. The 1908 house, built on a cliff overlooking the river, is a popular site for weddings and is beautifully maintained and exceptionally comfortable. A deck at the back of the house, fireplaces in three of the rooms, and top-notch service ensure a relaxing stay. For summer months, reservations are required at least three months in advance. ⊠ *3820 Westcliff Dr. (head east from I–84's Exit 62), 97031* ☎ *541/386–7000* ☎ *541/386–1803* ⊕ *www.lakecliffbnb.com* ☞ *4 rooms* ☰ *MC, V.*

¢–**$$$** ⊡ **Hood River Hotel.** Public areas at this 1913 landmark are rich in beveled glass, warm wood, and tasteful jade-and-cream-color fabrics. Rooms have fir floors, Oriental carpets, four-poster beds, and skylights. The suites, all with kitchens, can sleep five. There's a lively lobby bar and a Mediterranean-inspired restaurant. ⊠ *102 Oak St., 97031* ☎ *541/386–1900* ☎ *541/386–6090* ⊕ *www.hoodriverhotel.com* ☞ *33 rooms, 9 suites* ☾ *Restaurant, café, gym, hot tub, sauna, bar* ☰ *AE, D, DC, MC, V.*

**$** ⊡ **Beryl House.** A 1910 Craftsman-style farmhouse stands amid apple and pear trees 4 mi from Hood River and 3 mi from the Columbia River Gorge. Upstairs, braided rugs, Mission-style furnishings, and the original fir floors, plus robes and slippers for guests, add up to a comfortable stay. There's a wraparound porch, and breakfast may be served on a sundeck overlooking the pear trees. There's a TV in the common area. ⊠ *4079 Barrett Dr., 97031* ☎ *541/386–5567* ⊕ *www.berylhouse.com* ☞ *4 rooms* ☾ *No room phones, no room TVs, no smoking* ☰ *MC, V* ⋈ *BP.*

¢–$ 🏠 **Vagabond Lodge.** On 5 acres of quiet, wooded grounds, this property is at the edge of the Columbia River Gorge cliffs. Most rooms have views of the river, and some have fireplaces. Ponderosa pines tower 110 feet over the courtyard. ✉ *4070 Westcliff Dr.,* ☎ *541/386–2992* 📠 *541/386–3317* 🛏 *42 rooms, 7 suites in 5 buildings* 🍴 *Picnic area, some kitchenettes, some in-room hot tubs, cable TV, playground, some pets allowed* 🟰 *AE, DC, MC, V.*

## Sports & the Outdoors

BICYCLING  Every Saturday morning year-round, **Discover Bicycles** (✉ 205 Oak St. ☎ 541/386–4820), with the largest rental and demo fleet in the Northwest, hosts two separate two-hour rides. The 8 AM ride is for hard-core riders who seek to travel at least at a 20- to 23-mph pace. The 10 AM ride is more scenic and guides motivated beginner and intermediate riders 20–30 mi round-trip to places like Hood River valley or Rowena overlook. Rides are free and the staff is knowledgeable. Bikes rent for $5–$10 an hour.

GOLF  In the hills and fruit orchards of Hood River valley, the public, 18-hole **Indian Creek Golf Course** (✉ 3605 Brookside Dr. ☎ 866/386–7770) gives spectators golfing pleasure among 360-degree views of mountainous scenery, including the snowcaps of Mt. Hood and Mt. Adams. Divots Clubhouse Restaurant has an extensive menu and lots of windows to view the enchantment.

WATER SPORTS  Expect an exhilarating experience on one of four nearby rivers with **All Adventures Rafting** (✉ 20 Forest La., BZ Corner, White Salmon, WA 98672 ☎ 877/641–7238). An outdoor rafting team will guide you on half-day floats covering miles of winding and splashing white water. Trips are designed for first timers and families with children six and older. Guides have 20-plus years' experience in rafting, white-water rescue, first aid, and CPR. All gear is provided, and reservations are required. A year-round windsurfing school, **Brian's Windsurfing** (✉ Hood River Marina Park ☎ 541/386–1423) provides lessons and top-grade equipment rental. A former U.S. National and Masters Racing champion, Brian himself has 20 years' teaching experience, and he and his staff are dedicated to instructing anyone willing to learn.

## Shopping

A must for any adult traveling with children, **G. Willikers** (✉ 202 Oak St. ☎ 541/387–2229) carries toys that promote interaction, learning, and creativity. Kites and beach toys are among the useful items, and there are plenty of other goodies on hand to keep the kids busy during drives or hotel stays. To bring home an authentic piece of the Northwest, stop by **Twiggs** (✉ 305 Oak St. ☎ 541/386–6188) for products handcrafted by local artists. Peruse classic and contemporary silver jewelry, hand-stitched bags made from colorful textures and fibers, watercolor and acrylic paintings of Columbia River Gorge scenery, vibrant ceramics, and handmade furniture.

# The Dalles

❾ *20 mi east of Hood River on I–84.*

The Dalles lies on a crescent bend of the Columbia River where the river narrows and once spilled over a series of rapids, creating a flagstone effect. French voyagers christened it *dalle,* or "flagstone." The Dalles is the seat of Wasco County and the trading hub of north-central Oregon. It gained fame early in the region's history as the town where the Oregon Trail branched, with some pioneers departing to travel over Mt. Hood on Barlow Road and the others continuing down the Columbia River.

This may account for the small-town Old West feeling that still permeates the area. Several historical Oregon moments as they relate to The Dalles's past are magnificently illustrated on eight murals painted by renowned Northwest artists. They're downtown within short walking distance of one another.

Outstanding exhibits at the 130-year-old **Wasco County Courthouse** illustrate the trials and tribulations of those who traveled the Oregon Trail. ⊠ *410 W. 2nd Pl.* ☎ *541/296–4798* ⬚ *Free (donation suggested)* ☺ *Mon., Tues., Fri., and Sat. 10–4.*

The 1856-vintage Fort Dalles Surgeon's Quarters is the site of the **Fort Dalles Museum,** the oldest history museum in Oregon. On display in these authentic hand-hewn log buildings are the personal effects of some of the region's settlers and a collection of early automobiles. The entrance fee gains you admission to the **Anderson House** museum across the street, which also has pioneer artifacts. ⊠ *15th and Garrison Sts.* ☎ *541/296–4547* ⬚ *$3* ☺ *Daily 10–5.*

A favorite of windsurfers, **Celilo Park** also has swimming, sailboarding, and fishing. It's 7 mi east of The Dalles. ⊠ *Exit 99 off I–84* ☎ *541/296–1181* ⬚ *Free* ☺ *Daily.*

Exhibits at **Columbia Gorge Discovery Center—Wasco County Historical Museum** highlight the geological history of the Columbia Gorge, back 40 million years when volcanoes, landslides, and floods carved out the area. The museum focuses on 10,000 years of Native American life and exploration of the region by white settlers. ⊠ *5000 Discovery Dr.* ☎ *541/296–8600* ⊕ *www.gorgediscovery.org* ⬚ *$6.50* ☺ *Daily 10–6.*

At **The Dalles Dam and Reservoir,** a hydroelectric dam just east of the Bonneville Dam, you can ride the free Dalles Dam Tour Train to the fish ladder and powerhouse. There's also a sturgeon pond at the visitor center. ⊠ *Exit 87 (in summer) or Exit 88 other times off I–84* ☎ *541/296–1181* ⬚ *Free* ☺ *Daily; tour train departs mid-Apr.–Labor Day, Wed.–Sun. 8–4; Labor Day–Memorial Day, daily 8–5.*

Built in 1897, **Old St. Peter's Landmark** is a Gothic brick church with brilliant stained glass, hand-carved pews, marble altars, and an immense pipe organ. Steamboat captains once used the steeple, which rises 176 feet, as a navigational benchmark. The landmark now functions as a nondenominational, nonprofit organization that makes the space available for tours, weddings, and other private functions. ⊠ *3rd and Lincoln Sts.* ☎ *541/296–5686* ⬚ *Free (donations accepted)* ☺ *Feb.–Dec., Tues.–Fri. 11–3, weekends 1–3.*

View the lower part of **Mayer State Park** from the top of Rowena Crest. Recreational activities include swimming, boating, fishing, and picnicking. ⊠ *Exit 77 off I–84* ☎ *800/551–6949* ⊕ *www.prd.state.or.us* ⬚ *Day use $3 per vehicle* ☺ *Daily.*

## Where to Stay & Eat

**$–$$$** ✕ **Bailey's.** The fine western-style food at this restaurant with friendly, competent service has a Continental twist. It's hard to go wrong when choosing an entrée—try a thick slab of prime rib or the veal Oscar—especially when it's accompanied by a selection from the well-conceived wine list. ⊠ *515 Liberty St.* ☎ *541/296–6708* ⊟ *AE, MC, V* ☺ *Closed Sun. and Mon. No lunch.*

**¢–$** ✕ **Cousin's Restaurant and Saloon.** Home cooking rules at this family restaurant with a frontier motif. Try the pot roast or turkey supper with all the trimmings. A kids' menu is available, as is a breakfast menu. ⊠ *2114 W. 6th St., 97058* ☎ *541/298–2771* ⊟ *AE, D, DC, MC, V.*

$ ▦ **Columbia House.** A period feel lingers at this enormous late-1930s house on a cliff overlooking the Columbia. The rooms have king-size beds; two have river views. On a quiet wooded acre three blocks from downtown, the B&B has three decks out back, perfect for relaxing or, in good weather, enjoying the breakfast served up by the owner. ⊠ *525 E. 7th St., 97058* ☎ *541/298–4686 or 800/807–2668* ⇆ *4 rooms, 1 with shared bath* ⬦ *Airport shuttle* ⊟ *MC, V* ⦿⦿ *BP.*

$ ▦ **Cousin's Country Inn.** Locally owned, close to shopping, and 2 mi from downtown, this inn has standard but comfortable rooms spread throughout three buildings. Cousin's Restaurant is part of the property. ⊠ *2114 W. 6th St., 97058* ☎ *541/298–5161* 🖷 *541/298–6411* ⇆ *93 rooms* ⬦ *Restaurant, in-room data ports, some kitchenettes, cable TV, pool, hot tub, laundry facilities, business services, some pets allowed (fee)* ⊟ *AE, D, DC, MC, V.*

¢ ▦ **Inn at the Dalles.** This property sits up on a hill and offers views of the Columbia River, Mt. Hood, and the Dalles Dam. As an affordable alternative, rooms are functional with decent furnishings and book up in the summer. ⊠ *3550 S.E. Frontage Rd., 97058* ☎ *541/296–1167 or 800/982–3496* 🖷 *541/296–3920* ⇆ *45 rooms* ⬦ *Some kitchenettes, cable TV, indoor pool, business services, airport shuttle* ⊟ *AE, D, DC, MC, V.*

### Shopping

Inside the Discovery Center and Museum, the **Columbia River Trading Company** (⊠ 5000 Discovery Dr. 97058 ☎ 541/296–8600) has an appealing blend of souvenirs that aim to inspire appreciation and stewardship of the history, artistry, and beauty of the Columbia River Gorge region. Local artists' crafts include toys, jewelry, books, and specialty foods. Museum admission is not required to shop here. Describing itself as Oregon's largest antiques mall and gallery east of Portland, **Honald's 2nd Street Place** (⊠ Lincoln and 2nd Sts. ☎ 541/296–8500) has two floors of aisles filled with fun, collectible toys, jewelry, prints, dolls, tools, books, furniture, and original works of art. A short drive across the Columbia River will lead you to **TiPi Indian Craft** (⊹ ¼ mi west of junction of U.S. 197 and Hwy. 14, Dallesport, WA ☎ 509/767–2202), a world of Native American blankets, leather products, and music. The beaded moccasins, medicine bags, medallions, earrings, and dream catchers are handcrafted by members of neighboring tribes including the Warm Springs and Yakima. Other handmade goods are from Northwest reservations including the Umatilla, Nez Perce, Blackfeet, and Flathead. The shop is closed Sunday and Monday, and hours vary during the year.

# Mt. Hood

⑩ *About 60 mi east of Portland on I–84 and U.S. 26; 65 mi from The Dalles, west on I–84 and south on Hwy. 35 and U.S. 26.*

Majestically towering 11,235 ft above the Columbia River Gorge, Mt. Hood is what remains of the original north wall and rim of a volatile crater. Although the peak no longer spews ash or fire, active steam vents can be spotted high on the mountain. Native Americans in the area named it Wy'east, after a great chief who mystically became the mountain. In anger, Wy'east spouted flames and threw rocks toward the sky. The name was changed when in 1792 the British Royal Navy, the first recorded Caucasians sailing down the Columbia River, spotted the mountain and named it after the ship's admiral, Hood.

Mt. Hood offers the only year-round skiing in the lower 48 states, with three major ski areas and 26 lifts, as well as extensive areas for cross-country skiing and snowboarding. Many of the ski runs turn into mountain bike trails during the summer. The mountain is also popular with climbers and hikers. In fact, some hikes follow parts of the Oregon Trail, and signs of the pioneers' passing are still evident.

★ The fourth-highest peak in the Cascades, towering at 11,000 feet and crowned by year-round snow, is a focal point of the 1.1-million-acre **Mt. Hood National Forest,** an all-season playground attracting more than 7 million visitors annually. Twenty miles southeast of Portland, it extends south from the Columbia River Gorge for more than 60 mi and includes 189,200 acres of designated wilderness. These woods are perfect for hikers, horseback riders, mountain climbers, and cyclists. Within the forest are more than 80 campgrounds and 50 lakes stocked with brown, rainbow, cutthroat, brook, and steelhead trout. The Sandy, Salmon, and other rivers are known for their fishing, rafting, canoeing, and swimming. Both forest and mountain are crossed by an extensive trail system for hikers, cyclists, and horseback riders. The **Pacific Crest Trail,** which begins in British Columbia and ends in Mexico, crosses at the 4,157-foot-high Barlow Pass. As with most other mountain destinations within Oregon, weather can be temperamental, and snow and ice may affect driving conditions as early as October and as late as May. Bring tire chains and warm clothes as a precaution.

For a glimpse into the area's vivid history stop at the **Mt. Hood Information Center** (⊠ 65000 E. Hwy. 26, Welches 97067 ☎ 503/622–7674 or 503/622–3360) in the Mt. Hood Village RV park and pick up a copy of the *Barlow Road.* This is a great navigational map of the first emigrant road over the Cascades where pioneers traveled west via ancient Indian trails to avoid the dangers of the mighty Columbia River. Since this forest is close to the Portland metro area, campgrounds and trails are potentially crowded over the summer months, especially on weekends. If camping, contact the forest service desk while you're at the Mt. Hood Information Center. Prepare yourself by gathering information about the more than 80 campgrounds, including a string of neighboring campgrounds that rest on the south side of Mt. Hood: Trillium Lake, Still Creek, Timothy Lake, Little Crater Lake, Clackamas Lake, Summit Lake, Clear Lake and Frog Lake. Each varies in what it offers and in price. The mountain is overflowing with day-use areas, and passes can be obtained for $5. There are also Mt. Hood National Forest maps with details about well-marked trails. ⊠ *Information center 3 mi west of town of Zigzag on north side of U.S. 26* ☎ *503/622–7674* ⊕ *www.mthood.org* ⊠ *Day use free–$5, campsites $12–$14* ☉ *Information center daily 8–6, most campgrounds open year-round.*

## Where to Stay & Eat

★ **$$–$$$$** ✕ **Cascade Dining Room.** If the large windows in this room at Timberline Lodge aren't coated with snow, a clear day or night will yield a spectacular view of five mountain peaks, including the Three Sisters, Mt. Jefferson, and Broken Top. Inside, wooden beams and a wood-plank floor, handcrafted furniture, and a huge stone fireplace with a rendering of a forest scene create a warmth complemented by an attentive staff and a highly-regarded wine list. Entrées lean toward game: you might choose free range bison, Kobe or Angus beef, or rack of lamb, and elk occasionally makes an appearance on the specials list. The grilled salmon is also worthy; finish up with the house crème brûlée. The lunch menu includes sandwiches, salads, and inventive starters. ⊠ *Timberline Rd., Timberline, 97028* ☎ *503/622–0700 or 800/547–1406* 🖷 *503/727–3710* 🖃 *AE, D, MC, V.*

**$–$$$$** 🏨 **Timberline Lodge.** Depression-era workers built it, FDR dedicated it, and howling winter storms and intermittent disrepair dogged it, but the one question staffers answer several times a day is, "Was *The Shining*

filmed here?" (Yes, but only some exteriors.) And once you make the intimidating 6-mi drive midway up the slope of Mt. Hood and get a glimpse of the place, a Work Projects Administration structure and a National Historic Landmark, you'll understand why. At once awesome and formidable, the lodge is gargantuan: the buildings, especially the head house, were constructed to complement the size and majesty of the mountain it's on—the lodge itself is built from huge timbers and stone, and bannisters were crafted from old telephone poles. Once inside, notions of whether Jack Nicholson will make an appearance give way to cozier thoughts. Much of what you see looks handcrafted, and is, from the massive beams and wooden chairs to the curtains, quilts, and rugs. Rooms incorporate different handmade pieces and artwork that hark back to the lodge's beginnings in 1937. Don't miss a peek at the low-ceiling Blue Ox Bar, with stained-glass murals of Paul Bunyan and fronted by a wrought-iron gate, and treat yourself to some exceptional cooking in the Cascade Dining Room. ⊠ *Timberline Rd., Timberline 97028, (north from U.S. 26; follow signs)* ☎ *503/231–5400 or 800/547– 1406* 🖷 *503/727–3710* ⊕ *www.timberlinelodge.com* ⏋ 60 rooms 👌 *Restaurant, pool, outdoor hot tub, sauna, cross-country skiing, downhill skiing, bar* ⊟ *AE, D, MC, V.*

### Sports & the Outdoors

SKIING One of the longest ski seasons in North America unfolds at **Timberline Lodge Ski Area** (⊠ off U.S. 26, Timberline ☎ 503/272–3311). The U.S. ski team conducts summer training at this full-service ski area—the only ski area in the lower 48 states that's open year-round—which welcomes snowboarders. Timberline is famous for its Palmer chairlift, which takes skiers to a high glacier for summer skiing. There are five double chairs and two high-speed quad chairs. The top elevation is 8,500 feet, with a 3,600-foot vertical drop, and the longest run is 3 mi. Facilities include a day lodge with fast food and a ski shop; lessons and equipment rental and repair are available. Parking requires a Sno-Park permit. Lift tickets weekdays are $31, $34 on weekends. The area is open Sunday–Tuesday 9–5 and Wednesday–Saturday 9 AM–10 PM; the lift is open June–August, daily 7 AM–1:30 PM.

## Government Camp

⑪ *45 mi from The Dalles, south on Hwy. 35 and west on U.S. 26; 54 mi east of Portland on I–84 and U.S. 26.*

Government Camp, an alpine resort village, has a fair amount of hotels and restaurants. It's a convenient drive from here to Mt. Hood's five ski resorts or to Welches, which has restaurants and a resort.

### Where to Stay & Eat

¢–$ ✕ **Charlie's Mountainview.** Old and new skis plaster the walls, lift chairs now function as furniture, and photos of famous skiers and other memorabilia are as abundant as the menu selections. Steaks and hamburgers are worthy here, but house specialties include creamy mushroom soup and chicken Caesar salad with dressing made from scratch. Top it off with apple dumplings when they're in season. There's also a full bar, with live music on weekends year-round. ⊠ *88462 Government Camp Loop* ☎ *503/272–3333* ⊟ *AE, D, MC, V.*

¢–$ ✕ **Mt. Hood Brew Pub.** Pizza, pasta, steak, and seafood are among the popular and hearty choices at this family-style pub. Espresso drinks, Oregon wines, and freshly brewed ales—including root beer—are available. Arrive early if you want outdoor seating in the summertime. ⊠ *87304 E. Government Camp Loop* ☎ *503/622–0724* ⊕ *www.mthoodbrewing. com* ⊟ *AE, D, MC, V.*

¢ ✕ **Huckleberry Inn.** Whether it's 2 AM or 2 PM, Huckleberry Inn welcomes you 24 hours a day with soups, milk shakes, burgers, sandwiches, and omelets. Well-known treats are made with huckleberries and include pie, pancakes, tea, jelly, and huckleberry-vinaigrette salad dressing. ⊠ *E. Government Camp Loop, 97028* ☎ *503/272–3325* ⊕ *www.huckleberry-inn.com* ▭ *MC, V.*

$–$$$ ✕▥ **Falcon's Crest Inn.** Rooms at this sophisticated cedar-and-glass chalet are theme-oriented. Safari, Mexi-Cali, and French provincial are among the guest-room styles. You'll be greeted by a complimentary glass of wine, soft drink, and appetizers upon arrival. A nightly six-course dinner (open to nonguests; reservations essential) includes such entrées as chicken stuffed with shrimp in a sauce of champagne and Pernod. The room rates include a full breakfast. ⊠ *87287 Government Camp Loop Hwy., 97028* ☎ *503/272–3403 or 800/624–7384* ▤ *503/272–3454* ⊕ *www.falconscrest.com* ⇌ *5 rooms* ⚹ *Restaurant* ▭ *AE, D, DC, MC, V* ❙◯❙ *BP.*

$$–$$$ ▥ **Mt. Hood Inn.** The Mt. Hood National Forest is right outside the east windows of this comfortable, contemporary inn. Rooms facing the southwest have a remarkable view of the Mt. Hood Ski Bowl, which is just across the street. Accommodations come in many sizes, from spacious standards to king-size suites. Among the amenities are complimentary ski lockers and a ski-tuning room. ⊠ *Government Camp Loop* ⌂ *Box 400, Government Camp, 97028* ☎ *503/272–3205 or 800/443–7777* ▤ *503/272–3307* ⇌ *56 rooms, 4 suites* ⚹ *Picnic area, some refrigerators, some in-room hot tubs, cable TV, hot tub, cross-country skiing, downhill skiing, laundry facilities, business services, some pets allowed (fee)* ▭ *AE, D, DC, MC, V* ❙◯❙ *CP.*

$–$$$ ▥ **Thunderhead Lodge.** Jaw-dropping mountain views and the night lights of the Mt. Hood Ski Bowl are among the sights at this fun and friendly condominium lodge. Room sizes and capacities vary according to your needs, and there's a rec room with foosball, a pool table, wet bar, and fireplace. The outdoor pool is heated. ⊠ *W. Government Camp Loop, 97028* ☎ *866/622–1142, 503/272–3368* ⊕ *www.thunderheadlodge.com* ⇌ *10 units* ⚹ *Pool, laundry facilities* ▭ *MC, V.*

$ ▥ **Huckleberry Inn.** In the heart of Government Camp, this inn is near ski areas, hiking trails, and mountain lakes. Room sizes vary and can accommodate from 2-14 people. Pine wood furnishings and old photos of historical Government Camp decorate the rooms. Some units have lofts. A 24-hour family-style restaurant draws patrons around the clock. Huckleberry pancakes are a specialty. ⊠ *East Government Camp Loop, 97028* ☎ *503/272–3325* ⊕ *www.huckleberry-inn.com* ⇌ *17 rooms* ⚹ *Restaurant* ▭ *MC, V.*

## Sports & the Outdoors

CROSS-COUNTRY SKIING   Nearly 120 mi of cross-country ski trails lace the **Mt. Hood National Forest**; try the trailheads at Government Camp, Trillium Lake, or the Cooper Spur Ski Area, on the mountain's northeast flank.

DOWNHILL SKIING   On the eastern slope of Mt. Hood, **Cooper Spur Ski and Recreation Area** (✛ follow signs from Hwy. 35 for 3½ mi to ski area ☎ 541/352–7803) caters to families and has two rope tows and a T-bar. The longest run is ⅔ mi, with a 500-foot vertical drop. Facilities and services include rentals, instruction, repairs, and a ski shop, day lodge, snack bar, and restaurant. Call for hours. Mt. Hood's largest resort, **Mt. Hood Meadows Ski Resort** (✛ 10 mi east of Government Camp on Hwy. 35 ☎ 503/337–2222 or 800/754–4663) has more than 2,000 skiable acres, dozens of runs, seven double chairs, one triple chair, one quad chair, a top elevation of 7,300 feet, a vertical drop of 2,777 feet, and a longest run of 3 mi. Facilities include a day lodge, seven restaurants, two lounges, a ski school, and a ski shop; equipment rental and repair are also available. The ski area closest to Portland, **Mt. Hood Ski Bowl** (⊕ 53 mi east of Portland, across U.S. 26 from Government Camp ☏ 503/272–3206) has 63 trails serviced by four double chairs and five surface tows, a top elevation of 5,050 feet, a vertical drop of 1,500 feet, and a longest run of 3½ mi. Night skiing is a major activity here. You can take advantage of two day lodges, a mid-mountain warming hut, three restaurants, and two lounges. Sleigh rides are conducted, weather permitting. The longest run at the **Summit Ski Area** (⊕ Government Camp Loop Hwy., east end, Government Camp ☏ 503/272–0256) is ½ mi, with a 400-foot vertical drop; there's one chairlift and one rope tow. Facilities include instruction, a ski shop, a cafeteria, and a day lodge. Bike rentals are available in summer.

SUMMER SPORTS During the summer months, **Ski Bowl** (✉ 87000 E. Hwy. 26, at Mile Post ☾ 53 ☏ 503/222–2695) has go-carts, mountain- and alpine-bike rentals, and pony rides. The **Alpine Slide** gives the intrepid a chance to whiz down the slopes on a European-style toboggan run. This is heady stuff, with a marvelous view. **Eastside Action Park,** ½ mi to the east, has more than 20 kid-oriented attractions, including something called the Rapid Riser, a sort of reverse bungee-jumping device that catapults riders 80 feet in the air.

# Welches & Zigzag

⑫ *14 mi west of Government Camp on U.S. 26; 40 mi east of Portland, I–84 to U.S. 26.*

Find restaurants and other services in these two small towns at the base of Mt. Hood. Drop by the **Mt. Hood Visitors Center** (✉ 65000 E. Hwy. 26 ☏ 503/622–3017) in Welches for detailed information on all the Mt. Hood area attractions.

## Where to Stay & Eat

$$$–$$$$ ✕ **Tartans Pub and Steakhouse.** Enjoy a view of the resort at the mountain's lush, green golf course and Mt. Hood foothills from your indoor or outdoor table. This classy-casual dining spot offers dishes such as the house-smoked barbecue baby-back ribs and smoked chicken with mushrooms, spinach, and Asiago cream sauce poured over penne pasta. There's an inexpensive kids' menu, and breakfast is also available. ✉ *68010 E. Fairway Ave., Welches 97067* ☏ *503/622–3101 or 800/669–7666* ▤ *AE, D, DC, MC, V.*

$–$$ ✕ **Don Guidos Italian Cuisine.** Cap off a day of skiing, hiking, or touring with chicken piccata or seafood fettuccine, cooked from fresh, local ingredients. Lengthy booths, red carpet, and a two-sided hearth fireplace give warmth and charm to this restored log lodge. Tiramisu made from scratch is a favorite, as is the espresso-bar coffee service. ✉ *73330 E. Hwy. 26, Rhododendron 97049* ☏ *503/622–5141* ⊕ *www.donguidos. com* ▤ *AE, D, MC, V* ⊘ *Closed Mon.–Wed. Sept.–June.*

$–$$ ✕▥ **Resort at the Mountain.** In the burly Cascade foothills, this sprawling golf and ski resort is the most complete in the Mt. Hood area. Outdoor activities are plentiful, including fly-fishing on the Salmon River, horseback riding, white-water rafting, and croquet. Accommodations run from double rooms to two-bedroom condos. Each of the tastefully decorated rooms has a deck or patio overlooking the forest, courtyard, or a fairway. The resort is about a one-hour drive east of Portland. ✉ *68010 E. Fairway Ave. (follow signs south from U.S. 26 in Welches), 97067* ☏ *503/622–3101 or 800/669–7666* ☐ *503/622–2222* ⊕ *www. theresort.com* ⤳ *160 rooms* ⚂ *2 restaurants, picnic area, in-room data ports, some kitchenettes, 27-hole golf course, putting green, 4 tennis courts, pool, indoor hot tub, outdoor hot tub, health club, bicycles, horseback* *riding, 2 bars, laundry facilities, business services, meeting room* ⊟ *AE, D, DC, MC, V.*

$–$$$    ⊞ **Old Welches Inn.** A simple white clapboard house and an 8-foot-high stone fireplace on a covered patio are all that remain of the bustling 1890 Welches Hotel, the first structure and oldest hotel on Mt. Hood. Floral-pattern drapes and comforters complement antique and pine interiors. The largest of the guest rooms overlooks Resort at the Mountain's 27-hole golf course and has views of Hunchback Mountain and the Salem River. The cabin, which dates from 1901, overlooks the first hole of the golf course and has a fireplace and kitchen. There's a two-night minimum on holiday weekends. ⊠ *26401 E. Welches Rd., Welches 97067* ☎ *503/622–3754* 🖷 *503/622–5370* ⊕ *www.lodging-mthood.com* 🖃 *4 rooms, 1 two-bedroom cabin* ⚲ *Picnic area, some microwaves, some refrigerators; no kids under 10, no room phones, no smoking, no TV in some rooms* ⊟ *AE, D, DC, MC, V* ⦿ *BP.*

$$    ⊞ **Brightwood Guest House Bed & Breakfast.** Set on the shoulder of beautiful Mt. Hood, this small working ranch has a breathtaking view of Mt. Hood and Mt. Adams. The guest house is surrounded by tall firs and nestled in a Japanese garden with a footbridge and miniature koi pond. There's a cozy sitting area and a kitchenette stocked with exotic teas and microwave popcorn. The featherbed in the sleeping loft has a view of the water garden. Kimonos and slippers are provided, too. Weekends in summer months book up quickly. ⊠ *64725 E. Barlow Trail Rd., Brightwood 97011* ☎ *503/622–5783 or 888/503–5783* 🖷 *503/622–5783* ⊕ *www.mounthoodbnb.com* 🖃 *1 guest house* ⚲ *Picnic area, microwaves, refrigerators, pond, laundry facilities; no kids under 13, no smoking* ⊟ *AE, MC, V* ⦿ *BP.*

★ $    ⊞ **The Cabins Creekside at Welches.** Affordability, accessibility to recreational activities, and wonderful hosts make this a great lodging choice in the Mt. Hood area. Comfortable, large studio units have knotty-pine vaulted ceilings and log furnishings. As a bonus, full-size kitchens make cooking "at home" a breeze. Surrounding woods offer privacy. Patios on each unit face the seasonal creek, and each cabin has lock-storage units large enough to hold bikes, skis, or snowboards. ⊠ *25086 E. Welches Rd., 97067* ☎ *503/622–4275* ⊕ *mthoodcabins.com* 🖃 *10 cabins* ⚲ *Kitchens, microwaves, refrigerators, ski storage, laundry facilities* ⊟ *AE, D, MC, V.*

### Shopping

A three-building complex, **Arrah Wanna Rendezvous Center** (⊠ Hwy. 26, ½ mi west of main light, Welches) has several gift shops, including Enchanted Beadin Path, with beads, stones, custom jewelry, candles, and clothing; Uff Da Antiques, with vintage trinkets and glassware; and the Wy'east Book Shoppe and Gallery, with more than 5,000 new books, handcrafted works from more than 100 artists, classes, workshops, and poetry readings.

### Sports & the Outdoors

MINIATURE GOLF    An optimal spot for family enjoyment, **Mountain Air Miniature Golf** (⊠ east of Sandy at mile post 36 ☎ 503/622–4759) has a highly landscaped 18-hole putt-putt minigolf course blended into the forest pine trees. The course is accented by authentic farming, mining, and logging artifacts from Oregon Trail pioneers. The facility also has horseshoes, a picnic area, snack bar, and gift shop.

# THE OREGON CASCADES

Oregon's segment of the Cascade Range begins with Mt. Hood and pushes on south, covering millions of wilderness acres until Mt. McLoughlin in southern Oregon. Slightly below Mt. Hood in the Cascade Range are hundreds of tranquil campgrounds as well as trails friendly to all levels of hikers. In a relatively short west-to-east route over the range (which encompasses large pieces of two scenic byways, McKenzie-Santiam Pass and West Cascades Scenic Byways), you'll get a geographical sampling of the state. Just 47 mi east of Salem along the North Santiam River is the Detroit Lake Recreation Area, controlled by the Detroit Dam. Only 10 mi north of Detroit Lake, but a secluded world apart, is Breitenbush Hot Springs Retreat and Conference Center, a spiritual healing and renewal community surrounded by old-growth forest.

Other popular spots within this region are Hoodoo Ski Bowl near the crest of the Cascades at Santiam Pass, and over on the eastern slope within the Deschutes National Forest is the serenity of Suttle Lake. If you're looking to fly fish or relax by listening to stands of ponderosa pine whisper on a warm, lazy afternoon, consider the Metolius Recreation Area. The Metolius River, flowing through the small town of Camp Sherman, has biking and walking trails along its banks in addition to cabins and several other lodgings.

# Detroit

**⑬** *40 mi. east of Salem on Hwy. 22.*

A small town with fewer than 300 residents, Detroit was founded in the late 1800s during construction of the Oregon Pacific Railroad. Its name was chosen because many of the earlier settlers were from Detroit, Michigan. Because Detroit Lake is surrounded by tree-laden mountains and national and state forests, it will not grow much beyond its current size. It's also near a wealth of trails and creeks, many of which are more secluded and tranquil than those in the Mt. Hood area. Detroit's elevation is 1,573 feet, so getting here through winter snow likely won't be a problem. One waterway influencing the water level of Detroit Lake is **Detroit Dam** (☎ 503/897–2385 tours), which rises 463 feet above its foundation in the steep, narrow slopes of North Santiam Canyon. The dam creates 33 mi of shoreline along Detroit Lake conducive to boating, fishing, camping, and picnicking. Guided tours of the lake are available, though in winter the lake is lowered, so depending on snow pack, lake activities may be suspended. Three miles downstream from Detroit Dam, **Big Cliff Dam** rises 191 feet above its foundation into the canyon and also feeds Detroit Lake.

off the beaten path

**CANYON LIFE MUSEUM –** As you travel to or from Detroit Lake via Salem, stop at the yellow Southern Pacific train depot, site of this small but insightful repository in Mill City, about 10 mi west of Detroit. Lore, photos, and artifacts related to the bygone era of logging, mills, railroads, and farm life are on display. Visitors are welcome during scheduled hours or outside posted hours by appointment; call to schedule. ⊠ *143 Wall St. NE, Mill City* ☎ *503/ 897–4088, 503/897–2877* ⊠ *Free (donations accepted)* ☉ *Apr., May, and Sept. Thurs. and Fri. 1:30–4:30; June–Aug., Wed.–Fri. 1:30–4:30; Oct.–Mar., call for appointment.*

## Where to Stay & Eat

¢–$  ✕ **The Cedars Restaurant and Lounge.** The open dining room in this wood-panel, lodge-style spot complements the counter seating, lengthy booths, and lumberjack motif of painted rusty saw blades. Have healthy portions of buttery biscuits and gravy made from scratch, juicy burgers, or the owner-recommended seasoned pork chops. Toward the back is a dim lounge with a full bar, separated from the main dining area; country music hums from a jukebox while patrons shoot pool, throw darts, or watch a sporting event glowing from a big-screen TV. The heaping Nachos Supreme is the appetizer of choice for lounge patrons. ⊠ *200 Detroit Ave. 97342* ☎ *503/854–3636* ▤ *MC, V.*

¢–$ ✕ **Korner Post Restaurant & Cathy's Korner Gift Shop.** Authentic antique household artifacts on the walls depict simpler times. Enjoy a simmering bowl of homemade chili or gravy-smothered chicken-fried steak; salads and veggie burgers are also available. Visit the adjoining gift shop to find unique creations like hand-carved wooden eagles or flower vases made from stone. ⊠ *100 S. Detroit Ave., 97342* ☎ *503/854–3735* ⊕ *www.kornerpost.com* ▤ *AE, D, MC, V.*

★ ¢ ✕ **KC's Espresso & Deli.** In this friendly deli and gift shop with locally handmade goodies, order such house specialties as homemade soup and potato salad, the meat-loaf sandwich, or the fresh mocha or strawberry shakes. Sit outside with your lunch and a large scoop of ice cream on hot summer days. The shop carries its own line of products, some seasonal, including huckleberry lotions, taffy, tea, and muffins. ⊠ *155 N. Detroit Ave. 97342* ☎ *503/854–3145* ⊕ *www.kcsespresso.com* ▤ *MC, V.*

$–$$$$ ▥ **KC's Detroit Lake Cabins.** Completely furnished cabins including fully equipped kitchens are either lakeside or hillside. Each rental varies in size, price, and availability to suit your travel fancy, from the studio cabin perfect for a family of four, to the three-bedroom lakefront cabin, which sleeps nine. There's a three-night minimum stay, and a $50 nonrefundable cleaning fee is required. ⊠ *155 N. Detroit Ave., 97342* ☎ *503/854–3145* ⊕ *www.kcsespresso.com* ⊅ *4 cabins* ⌂ *Kitchens* ▤ *MC, V.*

$ ▥ **Repose and Repast Bed & Breakfast.** In a custom home built as a labor of love, two modestly decorated and spacious rooms upstairs have a shared bath; downstairs, in an expansive, cozy living room, you can quietly read by the flames from the stove. The smells of breakfast cooking will likely get your tummy rumbling in the morning. ⊠ *165 S. Detroit Ave., 97342* ☎ *503/854–3204 or 503/859–8085* 🖷 *503/854–5702* ⊕ *www.reposeandrepast.com* ⊅ *2 rooms* ▤ *No credit cards* ⦿ *BP.*

¢–$ ▥ **Breitenbush Hot Springs Retreat and Conference Center.** A cooperative community, tucked away on 150 acres that went uninhabited for 11,000 years, bonds to protect the forest, heal the soul, and provide solitude. Power sources throughout the facility are geo- and hydrothermal. Retreat prices include modest cabins, three vegetarian meals per day, well-being programs—including yoga, ancient forest walks, and meditation—and the use of 45 naturally occurring hot-springs pools. Bathing in the hot springs is clothing optional. ✛ *Just east of Detroit, turn north on Hwy. 46 off Hwy. 22; 10 mi past Cleator Bend Campground turn right onto single-lane bridge crossing Breitenbush River. Road is gravel after bridge and has three forks in its 1½-mi course. Go left at every fork until parking lot* ⊠ *Detroit 97342* ☎ *503/854–3314* 🖷 *503/854–3819* ⊕ *www.breitenbush.com* ⊅ *42 cabins* ⌂ *Massage, sauna, hiking* ▤ *MC, V* ⦿ *FAP.*

¢–$ ▥ **Lakeside Motel.** Friendly on-site owners and decent rates compensate for the lack of frills at this motel, the only one on the lake. Clean grounds surrounded by towering pine and fir trees are within feet of the lake's marina and dock area. ⊠ *110 Santiam Ave., 97342* ☎ *503/854–3376* 🖷 *503/854–3752* ⊕ *www.lakesidemotel.com* ⊅ *10 rooms* ⌂ *Some kitchens, microwaves, refrigerators, cable TV, some pets allowed (fee)* ▤ *AE, D, MC, V.*

⛺ **Detroit Lake Campground and Mongold Day Use.** It hardly feels like "roughing it" on the 1½ mi of waterfront at this campground, where water glistens in the sun, towering fir hovers over well-spaced campsites, and plentiful amenities deliver a comfortable outdoor experience.

# BREITENBUSH: A SPA WITH A CONSCIENCE

CLOTHING-OPTIONAL BATHING, meditation classes, and vegetarian meals make it easy for outsiders to classify Breitenbush Hot Springs Retreat and Conference Center as "new age." It's true—even though there's not a prescribed religion defining the essence of Breitenbush, the living practices and ideologies manifested there may not mirror what some are accustomed to in everyday life. But it's also true that these social mores are precisely what make Breitenbush so unique. The deeper story of how this "community" has intentionally been created around a primary set of principles—"to dedicate themselves to living mindfully in the spirit of love, unity, honesty and service"—and to protect the environment in spite of a complicated world, is admirable.

The community of Breitenbush—the people, the land, and the philosophy that binds the two—represents an evolving social and environmental paradigm implicit to Oregon. Breitenbush, and its 45 naturally occurring hot springs, at last peacefully rests on 150 dense forest acres, many of them old growth, within land uninhabited for 11,000 years. Native Americans were the first humans to visit the springs, with tribes traveling hundreds of miles to partake in healing and purification rituals. Their luxury of remaining undisturbed to practice traditions was temporary; Europeans began to penetrate the Pacific Northwest. The bounty and beauty of the hot-springs region were no longer obscure, and everyone who came to the region identified with its richness. Some internalized the environmental contributions—the ecological habitat and tranquillity—while others prized the bounty, deeming the land a gold mine for logging and timber sales. The stage was perfectly set for social and environmental battles.

From the mid-1800s all the way until the mid-1990s, the land was caught in the cross fire of preservation battles, turnstile political administrations, and contested environmental policies. Decades of legal battles ensued after the original settlements, and with the support of the Oregon Natural Resource Council, Breitenbush eventually prevailed to protect and grow its social and environmental community after scars of more than 60-acres of clear cut were left behind. Thousands of surrounding acres are now protected, and miles of reclaimed trails radiate out from the springs.

Today the land is owned by the 40-plus full-time workers who can, for $500, invest into the cooperative after one year of employment. Breitenbush's business (including the events, workshops, lodging, and hot springs) and community guidelines are collectively established and governed by an elected board and eight functional "teams." Everyone works together to manage the delicate balance between preservation, sustainability, and community growth. The presence of the Breitenbush River, which rushes through the land, in tandem with the hot springs, allows the community to practice ecological stewardship by remaining "off the grid" and use hydroelectric power and geothermal heat to meet energy needs.

Breitenbush openly welcomes people from all philosophical walks of life to immerse themselves in all that is absent in a hurried, disconnected world. Well-being classes and activities focus on the soul, body, and mind connection, but because personal preferences to identify with these forms of engagement vary, guests can choose for offerings to be a focal point or just an experiential backdrop. In other words, if bathing naked is not your thing, don't. Instead, walk among the ranks of majestic ancient forest. Whatever cultural beliefs prevail, guests set aside differences as individuals flock from around the globe for the same purposes: absolute peace, solitude, and sacrament intrinsic to Oregon's preserved nature.

— By Janna Mock-Lopez

A visitor center sells soft drinks, first-aid gear, and souvenirs. There are two boat docks, ramps, and one fishing dock, as well as horseshoe, basketball, and volleyball areas. The day-use area has 83 single-car spaces and 120 RV parking spaces. ♿ *Flush toilets, full hookups, partial hookups (electric and water), sewer, drinking water, showers, fire pits, grills, picnic tables, electricity, public telephone, playground, swimming.* ⬅ *106 full hookups, 72 partial hookups, 133 tent sites, 2 campsites accessible to campers with disabilities.* ✉ *2 mi west of Detroit* ☎ *800/452–5687 or 503/854–3346* ⊕ *www.oregonstateparks.org* ✉ *Full hookups $20, electric hookups $20, tent sites $16; day use $3* ♿ *Reservations essential* ▤ *MC, V.*

### Sports & the Outdoors

WATER SPORTS A full-service facility, **Kanes Marina** (✉ 530 Clester Rd., 97342 ☎ 503/854–3362) rents boats, sells fishing licenses and tackle, and has a fuel dock, slips, moorage, and an RV park. Boats you self-operate and navigate for 4–12 people can be rented by the hour or by the day from $50 to $170, plus fuel. A convenience store carries groceries, sundries, fishing and camping necessities, beer, gifts, and souvenir clothing. Kanes Tavern serves cold draft beer and Northwest wine, and pizza, and has live music on Saturdays for a $5 cover.

Licensed guide Arden Corey uses his knowledge of forestry, wildlife, and fisheries from his 30 years with the U.S. Forest Service to create the **Oregon Experience** (✉ Box 526, Mill City 97360 ☎ 503/897–3291). Whitewater rafting and fishing are among the guided adventures on the crystal clear North Santiam River which flows down from the Cascades into the Willamette Valley. Try drift-boat fishing for spring Chinook salmon or summer and winter steelhead. Equipment, bait, tackle, cleaning, and packaging services are included.

off the beaten path

**PIETY KNOB –** A 177-acre tree-blanketed island, Piety rises out of Detroit Lake, giving the adventurous a chance to gaze at the stars unencumbered by conveniences of modern life. A boat-in campground ½ mi from the marina docks yields 12 lakeside campsites spread over the island, and pit toilets, providing a sense of wilderness and isolation. There are hiking trails and great fishing access. Self-navigated boat rentals are available at Kanes Marina. Pack first-aid gear, plenty of water, and layers of warm clothing—the wind off the water creates extra chill.

# Metolius Recreation Area

**⑭** *9 mi northwest of Sisters, off Hwy. 22.*

Fodor'sChoice ★

On the eastern slope of the Cascades and within the 1.6-million-acre Deschutes National Forest, this bounty of recreational wilderness is drier and sunnier than the western side of the mountains, giving way to bountiful natural history, outdoor activities, and wildlife. Spectacular views of jagged, 10,000-foot snow-capped Cascade peaks—including Broken Top, Three Sisters, and Mt. Jefferson, the second-highest peak in Oregon—sprawl high above the basin of an expansive evergreen valley carpeted by pine.

At the base of **Black Butte**, a dark cinder cone about 5 mi south of Camp Sherman that rises at 6,400 feet, the **Metolius River** springs forth. Witness the birth of this "instant" river by walking a paved ¼-mi path embedded in ponderosa forest, eventually reaching a viewpoint with the dramatic snow-covered peak of **Mt. Jefferson** on the horizon. At this point, water gurgles to the ground's surface and pours into a wide-trickling creek cascading over a cloister of moss-covered rocks. Within feet it funnels outward, expanding its northerly flow; becomes a full size river; and meanders east alongside grassy banks and a dense pine forest to join the Deschutes River 35 mi downstream. Because the river is spring fed, the 48-degree flow of the water remains constant. In 1988, the 4,600-acre corridor of the Metolius was designated a National Wild and Scenic River. Within the area and along the river, there are ample resources for camping, hiking, biking, swimming, and boating. You'll also discover some of the best fly-fishing—for rainbow, brown, and bull trout—in the Cascades.

## Where to Stay & Eat

★ $–$$$  ✕⊠ **Suttle Lake Resort and Marina.** On the eastern side of the 1½ mi shore of Suttle Lake is this superb dining, lodging, and outdoor experience. The 10,000-square-foot Cascadian log-style lodge has 11 elegant guest rooms, each with a fireplace and whirlpool. Lakefront cabins have picnic tables and fire pits outside the front door. Inhale the fresh pine mountain air as you stroll or bike around the lake on a 3.2-mi trail, or troll the waters at dawn and wait for trout to nibble. Paddleboats and canoes are also available. You'll have a lake view wherever you sit in the Boathouse restaurant. Aside from daily Northwest specials of wild game or fresh fish, the chef prepares a signature grilled pistachio chicken and wood-oven-roasted rack of lamb. Creative salads and vegetarian and lighter fare are also available. During summer months sit outside and sip a cold tropical drink; there's live entertainment on some weekends. ⊠ *13300 Hwy. 20, 97759* ☎ *541/595–2628* ⊕ *www.suttlelake.com* ⌑ *11 rooms 14 cabins* ⌂ *Some kitchens, some microwaves, boating, marina, fishing, bicycles, bar* ▤ *MC, V* ⊙ *Boathouse restaurant closed Mon. and Tues. Oct.–May.*

△ **Big Lake.** Many of the 49 campsites at this high-elevation spot blend into the scenery and shadow of Mt. Washington. Because the lake is situated at 4,600 feet and experiences snow pack, it often opens later. For the serious athlete, there are numerous trails for hiking, jogging, or exploring, and waterskiing and fishing are also available. Bring lots of repellent in June to ward off mosquitoes. ⌂ *Pit toilets, drinking water, fire pits, grills, picnic tables.* ⌑ *49 campsites* ⊠ *Hwy. 20 at top of Santiam Pass (turn off Hwy. 20 onto Big Lake Rd. and drive 3½ mi)* ☎ *877/444– 6777 or 541/822–3799* ⊕ *www.hoodoo.com* 🖃 *$12–$14* ▤ *MC, V.*

△ **Suttle Lake.** There are three campground areas at Suttle Lake: Link Creek, South Shore, and Blue Bay. Link Creek, open April through October, is the best RV option because of roomier space lengths and relatively flat surfaces. South Shore is the largest and least crowded of the sites and has a picnic area; boats have launch access from the ramp. Blue Bay has a mixture of shaded and sunny spots and tents might fare better because sites are slightly smaller. Both South Shore and Blue Bay are open May through September. ⌂ *Pit toilets, drinking water, fire pits, grills, picnic tables.* ⌑ *97 rooms* ⊠ *Hwy. 20 at Santiam Pass to Suttle Lake Campground turnoff* ☎ *877/444–6777 or 541/822–3799* ⊕ *www. hoodoo.com* 🖃 *$12–$14* ▤ *MC, V.*

## Sports & the Outdoors

BICYCLING  The east side of the Cascades has 300 sunny days a year, so chances are you'll have sunshine on your shoulders when you rent a bike at Suttle Lake Resort and Marina (⊠ 13300 Hwy. 20, 97759 ☎ 541/595–2628) and ride through miles of gorgeous paved and mountainous routes. Rates are $5 per hour, $15 per half-day, and $25 for a full day. Scout Lake, Camp Tamarack, Camp Sherman, and Hoodoo Ski Area all have perfect paths for pedaling.

SKIING On a 5,711-foot summit, **Hoodoo Ski Area** (⌧ Hwy. 20, 20 mi west of Sisters ☎ 541/822–3799) has 806 acres of skiable terrain. With three quad lifts, one triple lift, one double lift, and 30 downhill runs, skiers of all levels will find suitable thrills. For tranquillity, upper and lower Nordic trails are surrounded by silence. At a 60,000-square-foot lodge at the mountain's base you can take in the view, grab bait, shop, or relax your weary feet. The ski area has kids' activities and child-care services available.

# Camp Sherman

⓯ *10 mi northwest of Sisters on Hwy. 20, 5 mi north on Hwy. 14.*

Surrounded by groves of whispering yellow-bellied ponderosa pines, larch, fir and cedars, and miles of streamside forest trails, this small, peaceful resort community of 250 residents is part of a designated 86,000-acre conservation area. The area's beauty and natural resources are the big draw: the spring-fed Metolius River prominently glides through town. In the early 1900s Sherman County wheat farmers escaped the dry summer heat by migrating here to fish and rest in the cool river environment. To help guide fellow farmers to the spot, devotees nailed a shoebox top with the name CAMP SHERMAN to a tree at a fork in the road. Several original buildings still stand from the homesteader days, including some cabins, a schoolhouse, and a tiny chapel.

## Where to Stay & Eat

¢–$$$ ✕ **Kokanee Cafe.** People from miles around come to this upscale yet casual spot. The juniper-smoked salmon is a winner; also try the free-range chicken rubbed with roasted garlic and fresh thyme or the pan-fried rainbow trout with spicy bacon, roasted corn hash, and chili orange butter. Ginger beef and spinach salad are also popular. ⌧ 25545 S.W. Forest Service Rd. 1419, 97730 ☎ 541/595–6420 ☐ MC, V ☾ Closed Nov.–Apr. and Mon. May–Oct.

¢–$ ✕ **Camp Sherman Store and Fly Shop.** For freshly made deli sandwiches, fine cheeses, or espresso, stop by this general grocery store, grab some picnic goodies, and head to the nearby bank of the Metolius River. There's also a fair selection of Northwest wines to accompany your cheese or, if you prefer, microbrews or soda. Try the locally made cookies. ⌧ 24543 N. Forest Service Rd. 1419, 97730 ☎ 541/595–6711 ⊕ www.campshermanstore.com ☐ MC, V ☾ Closed Mon.–Thurs. Nov.–May.

$ ✕▥ **Waltraute's Bed & Breakfast.** This sun-filled log-house-style lodge is in a meadow and has plenty of windows to take in the views of wandering deer and Canada geese. Living and reading areas are sizable, and the sleeping rooms have A-frame ceilings and skylights. The buffet-style breakfast of fresh-baked Austrian bread, tasty cheeses, and muesli with fruit is a change of pace from bacon and eggs. ⌧ 13210 S.W. Forest Service Rd. 1419, 97730 ☎ 541/595–1930 ⊕ www.waltrautesbnb.com ⇆ 3 rooms ☐ No credit cards ⏀ BP.

$$$$ ▥ **Metolius River Resort.** If you want a sense of what a 1930s alpine fishing village might have looked like, consider this upscale resort. Comfort and elegance merge in these bi-level riverside cedar-shake cabins. Hand-painted bathroom tiles, custom lodgepole furniture, quilted bedding, and wrought-iron accessories complement predominantly knotty-pine interiors. Spacious kitchens are completely equipped. Sit by your cabin's oversized river-rock fireplace with a good book, or kick back on the large deck with the sounds of the nearby Metolius River to soothe you. ⌧ 25551 S.W. Forest Service Rd. 1419 (take U.S. 20 northeast 10 mi from Sisters, turn north on Camp Sherman Rd. and east on Forest Service Rd. 1419), 97730 ☎ 800/818–7688 ⊕ www.

FodorśChoice ★

*metoliusriverresort.com* ⏎ *11 cabins* ♿ *Kitchens, microwaves, some in-room VCRs* ⊟ *MC, V.* ◄──

**$–$$$** ▥ **Metolius River Lodges.** Homespun cottages give you cozy river views, fireplaces, and woodsy interiors complemented by top-notch hospitality. Pick from studiolike four-plex lodges or free-standing lodges with kitchen and bedrooms. Big picture windows bring in the pine scenery and blue sky reflecting off the water. Of the cabins, the Salmonfly is the most popular, as its large front deck overhangs the current. Make reservations well in advance, especially for summer. ✉ *12390 S. W. Forest Service Rd. 1419-700, 97730* ☎ *800/595–6290* ⊕ *www.metoliusriverlodges.com* ⏎ *13 cabins* ♿ *Kitchens, microwaves* ⊟ *MC, V.*

**$$** ▥ **Cold Springs Resort & RV Park.** Of five riverfront cabins, four are smaller but newer, with equipped kitchens and covered porches facing the river; the fifth is a log cabin with a kitchenette and older furnishings. These are the only Camp Sherman cabins that take pets. Nestled under pines are 45 large, shaded RV sites with full-hookups. There's a grassy picnic area with barbecues available. ♿ *Flush toilets, full hookups, drinking water, laundry facilities, showers, fire pits.* ⏎ *5 cabins, 45 RV sites* ✉ *25615 Cold Springs Resort La., 97730* ☎ *541/595–6271* ⊕ *www.coldsprings-resort.com* ⊟ *AE, D, MC, V.*

# SIDE TRIP TO WASHINGTON

On the Washington side of the Columbia River Gorge are several sites that are part of the Goldendale area. This trip could take one to two days, depending upon how much exploring you want to do, and as previously suggested, could be incorporated into an eight-day itinerary.

## Goldendale Area

*70 mi south of Yakima, Washington; 35 mi north of The Dalles; 120 mi east of Portland; and 10 mi north of Hwy. 14 on U.S. 97.*

The county seat of Klickitat County and a commercial center for ranchers and farmers, Goldendale is an attractive area with many old clapboard houses. First settled in 1872, the small community still projects a down-to-earth feel and offers tourists a central "home base" from which to explore the surrounding cultural and natural attractions. Goldendale sits on a fertile plateau, north of the Columbia River and south of the Simcoe Mountains and Yakima Indian reservation. The sprawling scenery includes pine forests, farmland, desolate desert-like land, and lava flows along the Washington side of the Columbia River Gorge.

One of the Columbia Gorge's most unusual cultural attractions, the **Maryhill Museum of Art** is in a castlelike mansion, perched high on a cliff. Built by a colorful character named Sam Hill as a private residence, the house was dedicated as a museum by Queen Marie of Romania in 1923. It contains the largest collection of Rodin sculptures and watercolors west of the Mississippi; prehistoric Native American tools and baskets; and the charming "Théâtre de la Mode," a miniature fashion show devised by French couturiers after World War II. Queen Marie's coronation gown and personal artifacts are also on display. Three miles east of the museum, just off Washington State Highway 14, is an even stranger landmark in this unpopulated high-desert country: a replica of Stonehenge, built by Hill as a memorial to soldiers killed in World War I. ✉ *35 Maryhill Museum Dr., Goldendale, WA* ☎ *509/773–3733* 🎟 *$6.50* ⊙ *Mid-Mar.–mid-Nov., daily 9–5.*

An enchanting 340-acre site, **Horsethief Lake State Park** has 7,500 feet of Columbia River frontage. Petroglyphs embedded in stone, which you can see during a walk on one of the park's trails, attest to the prominence and history of Native American life. There are 12 campsites, and the day-use area has picnic tables, a dump station, hiking trails, and boat launches to the river and the lake. ⊠ *2 mi east of U.S. 197 on Hwy. 14, Goldendale 98620* ☎ *509/767–1159* ☉ *Apr.–Oct., 8 AM–dusk; call for winter schedule.*

★ The 24½-inch reflecting Cassegrain telescope at the **Goldendale Observatory State Park and Interpretive Center** is one of the nation's largest amateur telescopes of its kind available for public viewing. With nothing but dark, smog-free sky above you, you might spot the moon, planets, and constellations. There are lectures on celestial phenomena, slide shows, and knowledgeable staff eager to share their passion for astronomy. ⊠ *1602 Observatory Dr., Goldendale 98620* ☎ *509/773–3141* ⊕ *www. perr.com/gosp.html* ☒ *Free (donations accepted)* ☉ *Wed.–Sun. 2–5 and 8–midnight; call for winter schedule.*

# THE COLUMBIA RIVER GORGE & THE OREGON CASCADES A TO Z

*To research prices, get advice from other travelers, and book travel arrangements, visit www.fodors.com.*

### BIKE TRAVEL

A majority of the bike routes in the Columbia River Gorge and Cascades are intermediate, yet beginners and experts will also discover suitable routes. Shops in Hood River, The Dalles, and Suttle Lake rent mountain and touring bikes, as well as safety gear. For touring books, bicycle touring companies, and maps, contact the State of Oregon, Bicycle & Pedestrian Program.

🛈 **State of Oregon, Bicycle & Pedestrian Program** ⊠ 355 Capitol St. NE, 5th floor, Salem 97301 ☎ 503/986–3555 ⊕ www.odot.state.or.us.
🛈 **Rentals Discover Bicycles** ⊠ 205 Oak St., Hood River 97031 ☎ 541/386–4820 ⊕ www.discoverbicycles.com. **Suttle Lake Resort and Marina** ⊠ 13300 Hwy. 20, 97759 ☎ 541/595–2628 ⊕ www.suttlelake.com.

### BOAT & FERRY TRAVEL

The stern-wheeler *Columbia Gorge* offers excursions on the Columbia River. Two-hour tours, as well as dinner and brunch cruises, depart from the Cascade Locks.

🛈 Ferry Information **Sternwheeler Columbia Gorge** ⊠ Cascade Locks Pier, 97014 ☎ 541/ 374–8427 or 800/643–1354 ⊕ www.sternwheeler.com.

### BUS TRAVEL

Greyhound provides service from Portland to Hood River, The Dalles, and Government Camp. CARTS Canyon Connector offers public transportation from Salem to the North Santiam Canyon area, Monday through Friday, three times a day.

🛈 Lines **CARTS Canyon Connector** ☎ 503/585–5197 or 800/422–7723. **Greyhound** ☎ 800/454–2487.
🛈 Depots **The Dalles Depot** ⊠ 201 Federal St., The Dalles 97058 ☎ 541/296–2421. **Government Camp Depot** ⊠ Huckleberry Inn, Hwy. 26 Business Loop, Government Camp 97028 ☎ 503/272–3325. **Hood River Depot** ⊠ 600 E. Marina Way, Hood River 97031 ☎ 541/386–1212.

### CAR RENTALS

The Enterprise branch in Sandy, open Monday through Friday, has customer pick-up service.

🛈 **Enterprise** ⊠ 37000 Hwy. 26, Sandy 97055 ☎ 503/668–7430 ⊕ www.enterprise.com.

## CAR TRAVEL

I–84 is the main east–west route into the Columbia River Gorge. U.S. 26, heading east from Portland and northwest from Prineville, is the main route into the Mt. Hood area. Portions of I–84 and U.S. 26 that pass through the mountains pose winter-travel difficulties, though the state plows these roadways regularly. The gorge is closed frequently during harsh winters due to ice and mud slides. Extreme winds can also make driving hazardous and potentially result in highway closures.

The Historic Columbia River Highway (U.S. 30) from Troutdale, to just east of Oneonta Gorge, passes Crown Point State Park and Multnomah Falls. I–84/U.S. 30 continues on to The Dalles. Highway 35 heads south from The Dalles to the Mt. Hood area, intersecting with U.S. 26 at Government Camp.

## CHILDREN IN THE COLUMBIA RIVER GORGE & OREGON CASCADES

Many state and forest parks have day-use areas with playgrounds and room for kids to run. If you're hiking with children, procure maps that show the length and degree of difficulty of the trails. Wherever you are in this region, have sunscreen and extra warm clothing on hand, as temperatures can change quickly, particularly at higher elevations.

Local libraries have story times and crafts activities. A good Web site for kids' resources within the gorge is Gorgekids.com, which lists ski camps, museums, kid-friendly trails, parks, and recreational events. 🚩 Local Libraries **Cascade Locks Branch Library** ✉ 140 S.E. Wa-Na-Pa St., Cascade Locks ☎ 541/374–9317. **The Dalles Library** ✉ 722 Court St., The Dalles ☎ 541/296–2815. **Hood River County Library** ✉ 601 State St., Hood River ☎ 541/386–2535.

BABY-SITTING Many ski areas offer children's activities and child care. Just Like Home is an agency in White Salmon, Washington, just across the Columbia River from Hood River, and provides licensed child care by the hour, day, or week. Cathy's Kids in Hood River accepts reservations for care and drop-ins. 🚩 Agencies **Cathy's Kids** ✉ 2246 Montello, Hood River ☎ 541/386–7384. **Just Like Home** ✉ 345 Brislawn Rd. White Salmon, WA ☎ 509/493–8646.

## DISABILITIES & ACCESSIBILITY

Travelers with disabilities will find days-use parks, campgrounds, and points of interest that are accommodating. For convenience, these areas are clearly marked. State-park and national-forest Web sites, as well as ranger stations, provide access information to assist in planning. 🚩 Local Resources **Mt. Hood Information Center** ✉ 65000 E. Hwy. 26, Welches 97067 ☎ 503/622–4822 or 888/622–4822 ⊕ www.mthood.info. **Willamette National Forest Ranger Station (Detroit Lake Recreation Area)** ⌂ HC 73, Box 320, Mill City 97360 ☎ 503/854–4205.

## EMERGENCIES

Since most communities within this region are small, local county sheriffs are the best resource to contact in emergencies. Ranger stations also have access to emergency services. 🚩 Area Hospitals **Detroit Lake Recreation Area Santiam Memorial Hospital** ✉ 1401 N. 10th Ave., Stayton ☎ 503/769–2175. **Goldendale Klickitat Valley Hospital** ✉ 310 S. Roosevelt, Goldendale, WA ☎ 509/773–4022. **Mid-Columbia Medical Center** ✉ 1700 E. 19th St., The Dalles ☎ 541/296–1111. **Providence Hood River Memorial Hospital** ✉ 811 13th St., Hood River ☎ 541/386–3911. **St. Charles Medical Center (Metolius Recreation Area)** ✉ 2500 Neff Rd., Bend ☎ 541/382–4321. **White Salmon Skyline Hospital** ✉ 211 Skyline Dr., White Salmon, WA ☎ 509/493–1101.

# 168 <   The Columbia River Gorge & the Oregon Cascades

## LODGING

Gorge Central Vacation Rentals has apartments, cottages, condos, and houses within the Columbia River Gorge. In the Mt. Hood area, An Oregon Experience rents vacation homes, as does Cascade Property Management–Mt. Hood Vacation Rentals. In Detroit Lake, properties are also available through KC's Cabin Rentals. Roomfinder provides free rate and availability information about B&Bs in the gorge.

🖪 **Local Agents & Services An Oregon Experience** ✉ 11330 S.W. Ambiance Pl., Tigard 97223 ☎ 503/620-0717 🌐 www.anoregonexperience.com. **Cascade Property Management–Mt. Hood Vacation Rentals** ✉ 24403 E. Welches Rd., Suite 104, Welches 97067 ☎ 503/622-5688 or 800/635-5417. **Gorge Central Vacation Rentals** ✉ 555 E. Eastside Rd., Hood River 97031 ☎ 541/386-6109 or 877/386-6109 🌐 www.gorgeres.com. **KC's Cabin Rentals** ✉ 155 N. Detroit Ave., Detroit 97342 ☎ 503/854-3145 🌐 www. kcsespresso.com. **Roomfinder** ✉ 4079 Barrett Dr., Hood River 97031 ☎ 541/386-6767 🌐 www.gorgelodging.com.

## MEDIA

The *Current* is the Columbia River Gorge's biweekly news and cultural events newspaper; *Columbia Gorge Weekly* has local news, features, and entertainment; the *Stayton Mail* is a local weekly community newspaper; *Mill City Enterprise* is a community newspaper published weekly; the *Dalles Chronicle* has international, national, and local news; and the *Mountain Times* provides news and community information for Mt. Hood and the surrounding area.

## SPORTS & THE OUTDOORS

The Oregon Tourism Commission and the Columbia River Gorge Visitors Association ( ⇨ Visitor Information, *below*) can provide information about sports and outdoor recreation in the region. An excellent resource to help refine your campground search is Hoodoo Recreation Services, which manages more than 70 campgrounds on both sides of the Cascades; it also connects visitors to other area recreational services.

🖪 **Bicycling Oregon Bicycle and Pedestrian Program** ✉ 355 Capitol St. NE, 5th floor, Salem 97301 ☎ 503/986-3555 🌐 www.odot.state.or.us.

🖪 **Camping Hoodoo Recreation Services** ✉ Hwy. 20 ☎ 541/822-3799 🌐 www. hoodoo.com.

🖪 **Fishing Oregon Dept. of Fish and Wildlife** ✉ 2501 S.W. 1st Ave., Portland 97201 ☎ 503/872-5268 🌐 www.oregonfishing.com.

🖪 **Golfing Oregon Golf Association** ✉ 2840 Hazelnut Dr., Woodburn 97071 ☎ 503/ 981-GOLF 🌐 www.orgolf.org.

🖪 **Hiking U.S. Forest Service** ✉ 65000 E. Hwy. 26, Welches 97067 ☎ 503/622-7674 🌐 mthood.info. **Friends of the Columbia Gorge** ✉ 205 Oak St., Suite 17, Hood River 97031 ☎ 541/386-5268 🌐 www.gorgefriends.org.

🖪 **Windsurfing Columbia Gorge Windsurfers Association** ✉ 202 Oak St., Suite 150, Hood River 97031 ☎ 541/386-9225 🌐 www.cgwa.net.

## TAXIS

Taxi service is available but somewhat limited in the Columbia River Gorge and Mt. Hood areas. You'll need to phone the cab company for service. Fees may incorporate a pickup charge, mileage rate, price per passenger, and hourly rates. Columbia Gorge Taxi (Spanish speaking and available 24 hours), E&R Taxi, and Hood River Taxi provide transport throughout Cascade Locks, The Dalles, Mt. Hood, Portland, and Stevenson and White Salmon in Washington. Blue Star Shuttle and Columbia Gorge Express provide service from the Portland airport.

🖪 **Companies Blue Star Shuttle** ☎ 800/247-2272. **Columbia Gorge Express Shuttle** ☎ 888/386-6822. **Columbia Gorge Taxi** ☎ 541/806-2085. **E&R Taxi** ☎ 509/493-2592. **Hood River Taxi** ☎ 541/386-2255.

## TOURS

Tour operators throughout the region offer scenic trips throughout the Columbia River Gorge, Mt. Hood, and the outlying areas. Northwest Gold Tours offers tours throughout the state.

🏞 Scenic Tours **Julee's Gorge Tours** ⌂ Box 434, Hood River 97031 ☏ 541/806-1075 ⊕ www.gorgetours.com. **Northwest Gold Tours** ✉ 13195 S.W. Oakwood St., Beaverton 97005 ☏ 503/318-1591 ⊕ www.nwgoldtours.com.

## VISITOR INFORMATION

🏞 Organizations **Columbia River Gorge Visitors Association** ✉ 2149 W. Cascade, Suite 106A, Hood River 97031 ☏ 800/98-GORGE ⊕ www.crgva.org. **Detroit Lake Recreation Area Business Association** ⌂ Box 574, Detroit 97342 ⊕ www.detroitlakeoregon.org. **Hood River County Chamber of Commerce** ✉ Port Marina Park, 97031 ☏ 541/386-2000 or 800/366-3530 ⊕ www.hoodriver.org. **Hoodoo Recreation Services** ✉ Hwy. 20, Sisters 97759 ☏ 541/822-3799 ⊕ www.hoodoocom. **Metolius Recreation Area** ⌂ Box 64, Camp Sherman 97730 ☏ 541/595-6117 ⊕ www.Metoliusriver.com. **Mt. Hood Chamber of Commerce** ✉ 65000 E. Hwy. 26, Welches 97067 ☏ 503/622-4822 or 888/622-4822 ⊕ www.mthood.org. **Mt. Hood Information Center** ✉ 65000 E. Hwy. 26, Welches 97067 ☏ 503/622-7674 ✉ 70220 W. Hwy. 26, Zigzag 97049 ☏ 503/622-3191. **Mt. Hood National Forest Ranger Stations** ✉ 6780 Hwy. 35, Mt. Hood 97041 ☏ 541/352-6002 ✉ Superintendent, 16400 Champion Way, off Hwy. 26, Sandy 97055 ☏ 503/668-1771. **Oregon Tourism Commission** ✉ 775 Summer St. NE, Salem 97301-1282 ☏ 503/986-0000 ⊕ www.traveloregon.com.

# CENTRAL OREGON

4

**FODOR'S CHOICE**

Bend Riverside Motel, *Bend*

Cork, *romantic restaurant in Bend*

Cove Palisades State Park, *Madras*

Depot Deli & Cafe, *Sisters*

High Desert Museum; *Bend*

Lara House Bed & Breakfast Inn, *Bend*

Merenda, *contemporary food in Bend*

Museum at Warm Springs, *Warm Springs*

Smith Rock State Park, *Redmond*

Sunriver Resort, *Sunriver*

**HIGHLY RECOMMENDED**

HOTELS    Kah-Nee-Ta Resort and Casino, *Warm Springs*

Pine Ridge Inn, *Bend*

SIGHTS    Downtown Bend

Peter Skene Ogden Wayside, *Redmond*

Updated by
Zach Dundas

**CENTRAL OREGON CAN BE SEEN AS OREGON'S SPINE:** a region stretching from the Columbia Gorge in the north to the Klamath Basin in the south, an arid and wild western landscape dramatically different from the state's rain-washed coastal rim. Everything about central Oregon is writ large: miles of sun-bleached earth; vast expanses of juniper and sage; gushing rivers; imperial snow-capped mountains. In the not-so-distant past, the area saw vicious range wars and hell-for-leather railroad competition. Today it's a laboratory for a West gripped by rapid change, as recreation and tourism slowly replace extractive industries as the region's economic foundation.

Newcomers lured by central Oregon's spectacular vistas and high-desert climate are flooding into this once-isolated landscape, sparking all the cultural, economic, and political tensions one might expect. Meanwhile, two groups of original Oregonians—three confederated tribes on the 640,000-acre Warm Springs reservation in the north, the Klamath tribe in the south—continue to forge new futures after 150 years of displacement and decline.

The city of Bend is central Oregon's urban center of gravity, a skiing base infused with a heady dose of resort-town chic. Even though exceptional downhill and cross-country skiing is nearby, Bend racks up 250 days of sunshine every year. Given such statistics and its truly magnificent landscape, central Oregon's lure is no mystery.

## Exploring Central Oregon

For an overview of central Oregon, trace it from the region's northern edge, where Mt. Hood's rarified wonderland suddenly gives way to parched high desert, to its southern boundaries, where the bustling city of Bend marks the epicenter of one of Oregon's greatest playgrounds. U.S. 97 more or less cuts straight down the middle of this territory; this chapter is arranged according to the north–south path the highway suggests. And indeed, it makes most sense to conduct any extensive exploration of this rangy, far-flung region by automobile; central Oregon's scattered cities are not well served by mass transit. The region's only major airport, at Redmond, is serviced by daily direct flights from Portland, Seattle, and San Francisco. A couple of modest rail circuits offer sightseeing day trips rather than real point-to-point transportation; Amtrak's only nearby stop is in Chemult, 65 mi south of Bend.

### About the Restaurants

Most of central Oregon is rural and decidedly western; this is largely steak-and-eggs country. Almost every town has at least one old-fashioned diner serving up rib-sticking all-American food, and all the dubious treats of the modern fast-food industry are on offer in and around most towns. That said, this area is no less food-obsessed than any other part of the Northwest. Between the low-cost authentic taquerias frequented by the area's burgeoning Hispanic population and upscale, ambitious eateries aiming for resort goers' dollars, you can eat very well in central Oregon.

### About the Hotels

Destination resorts—like Kah-Nee-Ta, on the Warm Springs Indian Reservation; Sunriver, near Bend; and Black Butte Ranch, near Sisters—constitute central Oregon's high-gloss, high-price lodging options; if you have a taste, and the means, for cushy accommodations in jaw-dropping settings, this may be your thing. The region's larger towns—Madras, Bend, Prineville, Redmond, and Sisters—have plenty of lower-cost hotels and motels, both mom-and-pop operations and national chain affiliates. A vigorous B&B network has grown up in Bend, mostly based in the city's charming century-old residential core.

| WHAT IT COSTS | | | | | |
|---|---|---|---|---|---|
| | **$$$$** | **$$$** | **$$** | **$** | **¢** |
| RESTAURANTS | over $30 | $20–$30 | $15–$20 | $10–$15 | under $10 |
| HOTELS | over $180 | $140–$180 | $100–$140 | $60–$100 | under $60 |

Restaurant prices are per person for a main course at dinner. Hotel prices are for a standard double room, excluding room tax, which varies 6%–9 1/2% depending on location.

### Timing

Central Oregon, especially Mt. Bachelor near Bend, enjoys an exceptionally long winter sports season, often stretching from the first days of October deep into May. Lingering snows in the high country have created an economic boom in the region and an object of cultish devotion among winter recreation enthusiasts. And as skiers flock to the mountains, many of the region's other attractions can be blissfully quiet and uncrowded in winter. Weather in winter will invariably make car travel in and around the region difficult, so prepare your vehicle as you normally would for snowy conditions.

Even as winter keeps a grip on the uplands, spring often comes earlier to the high-desert plateau below than to coastal Oregon or the Willamette Valley. If you're stuck in Portland on a dour April Saturday, there's a good chance the sun is shining on the Warm Springs Reservation just over Mt. Hood: Portlanders have used the resort at Kah-Nee-Ta as a mini–Palm Springs for years. Summer brings bustling events like the Sisters Rodeo, Bend's Pole Pedal Paddle race, and the Warm Springs tribes' major cultural festivals. Take these festive occasions into account when booking accommodations; especially in Bend, hotels switch to high-season rates when something big's going on.

## Warm Springs

▶ ❶ *115 mi southeast of Portland on U.S. 26.*

If, like the many visitors who begin their journey in Portland, you enter the Warm Springs Indian Reservation after traversing the frosty alpine skirt of Mt. Hood, you may feel you've been teleported from *The Sound of Music* into *A Fistful of Dollars*. This austere desert landscape is nothing short of stunning—a country of brooding solitary buttes, lonely pines, and untamed ravines, lorded over by the snow-capped spires of Mt. Jefferson and Mt. Hood. For a crash course in Oregon's thrilling contrasts, you could do no better. A singular museum and the popular desert resort of Kah-Nee-Ta provide cultural and economic bases for the three confederated tribes who live here.

The Confederated Tribes of the Warm Springs Reservation created the **Museum at Warm Springs** south of town to preserve their traditions and keep their legacy alive. On display are tribal heirlooms, beaded artifacts, baskets, historic photographs, ceramics, and traditional dwellings. This haul is the product of years of carefully planned collecting and curating and is seen as a model tribal-run cultural resource. The museum's buildings, with such unmistakable nods to tribal history as conical, teepee-like atriums and sleek modernist lines, received an award from the American Institute of Architects. The museum's gift shop sells Native American crafts. ✉ 2189 U.S. 26 ☎ 541/553-3331 ☜ $6 ☉ Daily 9–5.

FodorsChoice ★

**4**

*Numbers in the text correspond to numbers in the margin and on the Central Oregon and Bend maps.*

**If you have 3 days**

Spend an educational morning in the tribal museum at 🏛 **Warm Springs** ❶ ⟩. There's no better immersion into the land's deeper history. An afternoon dip in the huge mineral-spring-fed pools (hotel guests receive a day pass to the pools; nonguests pay $8) at Kah-Nee-Ta Resort and Casino (11 mi north of Warm Springs), along with a hiking excursion into the resort's extensive network of trails, should help you forge a more personal connection to this unique desert country. Kah-Nee-Ta's accommodations run from luxury suites to bring-your-own-bedroll teepees, so a stay here should be within the reach of most travelers. On your second day, after breakfast at the classic Deschutes Crossing diner on the reservation's border, head for **Madras** ❷. Swing 14 mi west of the city toward Lake Billy Chinook, the heart of Cove Palisades State Park. The drive out alone, on a clear day, is well worth it. Make 🏛 **Bend** ❻–⓯ by evening and sample the delights of downtown's up-and-coming dining and nightlife scenes. Luxe B&Bs, low-cost motels, and the high-desert playground of Sunriver are all possibilities for an overnight. Wake up on day three with a walk or a run along the banks of the Deschutes in **Drake Park** ❻. Shop downtown, or strike out for downhill skiing at **Mt. Bachelor** ⑪ or Sunriver, where walking trails abound. North of Bend, Smith Rock swarms with climbers and is a staggering piece of geology even if you have no intention of roping up. Later in the day, strike out east for **Prineville** ❸, the old-time cow-town and jumping-off point for secluded outdoors adventure in the **Ochoco National Forest** ❺. You have your pick of hikes or drives in Ochoco, which has three small wilderness areas.

**If you have 5 days**

Follow the three-day itinerary above, but take an extra day getting acquainted with 🏛 **Bend** ❻–⓯ and its surroundings. Check out the dramatic, plunging river gorge at the Peter Skene bridge north of 🏛 **Redmond** ❹; you can also see the historic railroad bridge across the 300-foot-deep chasm, which played a key role in the no-holds-barred competition for rail dominion in the region a century ago. Overnight in Bend or Redmond. After visiting **Ochoco National Forest** ❺ on what will be day four, camp in Ochoco or stay over in Redmond, and another day swing west to **Sisters** ⓰, where the main street will remind you of every western you've ever seen. Innumerable mountain hikes, mountain-bike routes, and cross-country ski trails surround Sisters, and the U.S. Forest Service Ranger Station in town can provide information and maps.

**If you have 7 days**

Follow the itinerary suggested for a five-day visit, but before you head east to 🏛 **Prineville** ❸, go south from Bend to take in the surreal vulcanian beauty of **Newberry National Volcanic Monument** ⑭. The drive up **Lava Butte** ⑬ takes you to an observation deck commanding spectacular views of the Cascades. Overnight in Prineville and linger in **Ochoco National Forest** ❺ before heading out to **Sisters** ⓰.

For a seventh day in your itinerary, you might also devote extra time at the beginning of your tour to getting to know the Warm Springs Reservation's pristine, austere high-desert landscape or to floating on or fishing the Deschutes River.

## Where to Stay & Eat

¢ ✕ **Deschutes Crossing.** Even if you're just passing through, this classic diner on the banks of the verdant Deschutes makes a worthy stop. Breakfast, served all day, includes basic eggs, hash browns, and toast configurations, along with pork chops, steak and eggs, and the heart-stopping Cowboy Breakfast of ground beef, eggs, hash browns, and toast. Check out the vintage photos as you consume. ⊠ *Hwy. 26 at Deschutes River* ☎ *541/553–1300* ▭ *MC, V.*

★ **$$** ✕▣ **Kah-Nee-Ta Resort and Casino.** Kah-Nee-Ta means "root digger" in one of the reservation's native tongues, but this modern destination resort doesn't really match that humble moniker. Built around hot mineral springs that feed huge open-air swimming pools, Kah-Nee-Ta has an isolated, exclusive feel that makes a tempting escape from bustling Portland or Bend. The casino, straight out of third-tier Vegas, strikes a depressing and tacky note with its windowless, stifling atmosphere and hordes of mostly unhappy would-be winners. But the rooms are comfortable, and the staff is friendly and helpful. Best of all, however, are the sweeping, sparse desert panoramas; restorative mineral pools; and pristine juniper-scented air, a form of aromatherapy in and of itself. (For those who want to address the health-beauty nexus in a more formal way, Spa Wanapine has massage, reflexology, facials and other new-age treatments.) The Juniper Room serves decent upscale food with a distinct regional inflection; a more affordable seafood buffet is also available. The Warm Springs, Wasco, and Paiute suites, which cost a little extra, have tile fireplaces and hot tubs, big-screen TVs, and king-size beds. An RV park and wood-frame, canvas-covered teepees, for those who don't mind packing their own bedrolls, form the "village" around the hot springs below the main lodge. Kah-Nee-Ta also has a water slide, kayak rentals, and maps to nearby hiking trails. ⊠ *6823 Hwy. 8 (11 mi north of Warm Springs), Hwy. 3 north of U.S. 26 (follow signs), 97761* ☎ *541/553–6123 or 800/831–0100* 🖷 *541/553–6119* ⊕ *www.kah-nee-taresort.com* ⇌ *139 rooms, 21 tepees* ♨ *2 restaurants, 2 pools, hot tub, sauna, 18-hole golf course, tennis court, gym, fishing, mountain bikes, hiking, horseback riding, bar, casino, convention center* ▭ *AE, D, DC, MC, V.*

## Nightlife

Nightlife options are in short supply around Warm Springs, so locals flock to Kah-Nee-Ta's dark **Appaloosa Lounge** (⊠ at Kah-Nee-Ta Resort, 6823 Hwy. 8 [11 mi north of Warm Springs], Hwy. 3 north of U.S. 26 [follow signs] ☎ 541/553–6123 or 800/831–0100) to cut loose. This results in some decidedly weird cultural frissons, as literal cowboys and Indians party in the company of resort guests and loud country-rock bands get down. It's definitely the place to come if you want a raucous, western night out.

## Sports & the Outdoors

Kah-Nee-Ta Resort makes a convenient base for different kinds of outdoor recreation in the dazzling surrounding desert. The resort's front desk provides free maps of nearby hiking trails. You can rent a kayak for an expedition on the Warm Springs River or book a guided horseback ride.

If you plan to camp on the Warm Springs reservation or fish stretches of the Deschutes or Warm Springs River within its borders, be sure your **tribal permits** (⊠ 1233 Veterans St., 97761 ☎ 541/553–3333 🖷 541/553–1924) are in order. You can buy permits at some area sporting-goods stores, even off the reservation, or inquire with the tribal government. Reservation officials can also fill you in on what exactly non-members

4

## Climbing Smith Rock

Smith Rock State Park isn't too big—about 650 acres—but its name carries vast weight in the rock-climbing world. To the daring, often fanatical practitioners of this demanding sport, the blood-red and orange 550-foot-tall slab of compressed volcanic ash poses an endless combination of challenges. There are more than 1,400 climbing routes on the Rock, in various areas bearing strange, poetic and irreverent names like Monkey Face, Pleasure Palace, Spiderman Buttress, and Wombat. If you're not up for vertical pursuits, the park also has miles of hiking trails. A day-use pass is $3, while an annual pass costs $25. The campground within the park itself costs $4 per person, per night, but free camping is available at Skull Hollow Campground, 8 mi east. See the outstanding ⊕ www.smithrock.com for more information and digital panoramas of the park's rugged terrain.

## Rafting the Deschutes

Cyclops. The Elevators. Wreck. Sinister? Not to white-water enthusiasts, who flock to these evocatively named rapids on the Deschutes River in search of thrills. Along much of its length, the Deschutes is as smooth as glass—a polite little river just begging for a fly rod's attention. However, when geography puts on the squeeze, the Deschutes transforms into a bucking beast. Some 66 mi of the river's course are designated Wild & Scenic by the federal government. That means you'll have to buy a boater's pass from the Bureau of Land Management (☎ 541/416–6700 ⊕ www.boaterspass.com); prices run from $2 for a weekday, one-day pass to $75 for a full year. Licensed outfitters arrange passes for trips they organize.

## The White Stuff

Among North American downhill skiers, Bend's Mt. Bachelor hardly needs an introduction. The 7,000-foot Cascades peak enjoys a huge geographical advantage over rival ski hills—it sits at the point where warm Pacific air collides with inland cold, producing extravagant snowfalls between October and May. This bit of luck proved to be Bend's destiny—the onetime timber and ranching outpost is now a full-fledged resort destination, with a year-round ski culture. Nordic skiers also have plenty to do on Mt. Bachelor's miles of cross-country trails. Indeed, all of central Oregon is a cross-country bonanza in winter; Sunriver, the Ochoco National Forest, and the Sisters area are all prime cross-country destinations.

---

are allowed to do within the tribes' sovereign territory, and it makes sense to check in with them, whatever your plans may be.

## Madras

**❷** *120 mi southeast of Portland on U.S. 26.*

Madras, a hard-scrabble community of about 5,000 outside the Warm Springs Reservation's border, is the seat of Jefferson County. This crossroads town at the junction of Highways 26 and 97 has a "tri-cultural" population of Hispanics, Native Americans, and Anglos; thriving Mexican groceries, restaurants, and bakeries add splashes of color to its gritty streets. Though there's not much doing in town, in recent years Madras

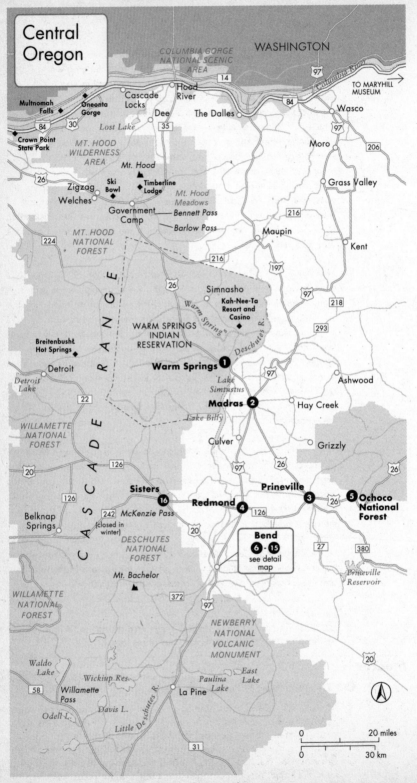

# Central Oregon

WASHINGTON

COLUMBIA GORGE NATIONAL SCENIC AREA

TO MARYHILL MUSEUM

Columbia River

14

97

84

Hood River

Cascade Locks

Multnomah Falls

Oneonta Gorge

Dee

The Dalles

Wasco

84

30

Lost Lake

35

Moro

97

206

Crown Point State Park

MT. HOOD WILDERNESS AREA

Grass Valley

26

Mt. Hood

Zigzag

Ski Bowl

Timberline Lodge

216

Welches

Government Camp

Mt. Hood Meadows

Bennett Pass

Barlow Pass

Maupin

Kent

224

MT. HOOD NATIONAL FOREST

216

197

26

Simnasho

Kah-Nee-Ta Resort and Casino

97

218

Warm Spring

WARM SPRINGS INDIAN RESERVATION

293

Breitenbush Hot Springs

Deschutes R.

Detroit

Warm Springs **1**

Ashwood

Detroit Lake

Lake Simtustus

97

22

Madras **2**

Hay Creek

WILLAMETTE NATIONAL FOREST

Lake Billy

Culver

Grizzly

126

97

26

20

126

Sisters

**16**

Redmond

**4**

Prineville

**3**

**5** Ochoco National Forest

26

26

Belknap Springs

126

242

McKenzie Pass

(closed in winter)

20

126

27

380

DESCHUTES NATIONAL FOREST

Bend

**6** · **15**

see detail map

Prineville Reservoir

Mt. Bachelor

372

WILLAMETTE NATIONAL FOREST

97

NEWBERRY NATIONAL VOLCANIC MONUMENT

20

Waldo Lake

Wickiup Res.

Paulina Lake

East Lake

58

Willamette Pass

Willamette Pass

La Pine

Davis L.

Little Deschutes R.

Odell L.

31

0        20 miles

0        30 km

# THREE NATIONS, ONE LANDSCAPE

A LITTLE MORE THAN A CENTURY and a half ago, the Warm Springs, Wasco, and Paiute tribes were no more a single "nation" than the French, British, and Germans are today. They spoke different languages, claimed different domains, and practiced markedly different ways of life. The Wasco and Warm Springs tribes, traditional trading partners from the Columbia River region, got along fine, but both had a history of enmity with the Paiute, who dwelled in southeastern Oregon. So how did all three of these distinct peoples end up inhabiting the same 640,000 acres of central Oregon's high desert? The short answer: white emigrants.

By the middle of the 19th century, the Oregon Trail brought a gushing stream of white settlers to the region, and it wasn't long before the newly established Oregon Territory sought to clear Indian lands for settlement. In 1855, the Warm Springs and Wasco tribes gave up vast land claims along the Columbia and Deschutes in exchange for exclusive rights to the present-day reservation. (They also retained traditional fishing rights along the Columbia still exercised today.) In 1879, the federal government forced a small group of Paiutes to move from reservations in Washington State after the tribe fought U.S. forces in the Bannock War. More Paiute settlement followed, creating the tri-national mix of today's Warm Springs reservation.

Like reservation-bound tribes elsewhere in the West, the three groups saw their cultures, languages, and economic foundations erode disastrously in the first decades on the reservation. In 1937, however, the first step of what was to be an incremental and perpetual rebirth began when the three tribes voted to confederate under a single tribal government. Under a tribal council including representatives from all three tribes, the peoples of Warm Springs found themselves better able to negotiate with Uncle Sam and make some headway in the modern economy. When a dam project destroyed some sacred fisheries on the Columbia in the late 1950s, the tribes cannily used the $4 million compensation to buy out non-tribal property owners on the reservation. One parcel thus (re)acquired included the mineral-water hot springs now at the center of Kah-Nee-Ta Resort, the reservation's first-class casino, recreation, and lodging money maker, which opened in 1972.

As the tribes established a new economic framework for survival, they also bolstered their now-intertwined cultures. Tribal festivals and long-house meetings keep alive ancient prayer songs and dances. The FM radio station KWSO, launched in the mid-'80s, serves up a heady mix of Top 40 pop and Native culture, broadcasting the latest hip-hop hits alongside indigenous-language programming and traditional music. The Museum at Warm Springs, with a collection of artifacts that took decades to pull together, opened in 1993 to immediate acclaim. Perhaps the most crucial and imperiled aspect of this desert renaissance is the reservation's Tribal Language Program, which races against time to save the tribes' three languages. Although yeoman efforts are under way, only a handful of elders speak the languages fluently, and the tribe reports no fluent speakers under the age of 50.

Make no mistake, the three nations of the Warm Springs Reservation have not fully recovered from displacement and resettlement—unemployment, alcoholism, and other social ills stalk the reservation, which today is home to Oregon's largest concentration of Native Americans. But the efforts of the Wasco, Paiute, and Warm Springs tribes—no less dramatic for being dogged—to reclaim their sovereignty, save their cultures, and forge new futures seem to be paying real dividends at a new century's start.

— By Zach Dundas

has become a popular launchpad for outdoors adventure. Fly-fishing and rafting on the Deschutes River attract river rats, while geology enthusiasts are drawn to the area's abundance of thunder eggs—egg-shape rocks with crystalline agate interiors. Nearby Cove Palisades, a well-maintained state park flanking the dramatic canyon banks of Lake Billy Chinook, lures about 500,000 boaters, anglers, hikers, and sightseers annually.

In the former city hall built in 1917, the tiny **Jefferson County Museum** has pioneer artifacts, with an emphasis on agricultural tools and memorabilia. ⊠ *34 S.E. D St., 97741* ☎ *541/475–3808* 🖾 *Free* ☉ *June–Sept., Tues.–Fri. 1–5.*

Rent boats or fish at **Lake Simtustus RV Park,** 11 miles west of Madras, or swim, picnic, or camp here; it's quieter and less trafficked than Cove Palisades State Park. The park is open year-round, but fishing season runs only from mid-April through October. ⊠ *2750 N.W. Pelton Dam Rd., 97741* ☎ *541/475–1085.*

> **need a break?** Quick caffeine jolts, scoops of homemade hard ice cream, and pastries are plentiful at **Madras Coffee Station** (⊠ 118 S.W. 5th St. ☎ 541/475–6044), a small shop near the edge of downtown Madras.

Fifteen miles north of Madras, **Richardson's Recreational Ranch** has the largest concentration of thunder eggs in North America. You can also hunt for agates here. ⊠ *Off U.S. 97 N* ☎ *541/475–2680* 🖾 *Free* ☉ *Store daily 7–5; must arrive by 3 PM to dig; diggings dependent on weather, call for information.*

Fodor'sChoice ★ The Deschutes, Metolius, and Crooked rivers combine to form Lake Billy Chinook, a glittering stretch of water snaking through the **Cove Palisades State Park,** a mini–Grand Canyon of red-rock cliffs and gorges 14 mi west of Madras. On a clear day, a column of snow-capped Cascades peaks lines the horizon during the drive from town. The Crooked River Day Use Area is the most immediately accessible part of the park, a great place to cast a line into the water, launch a boat, or raid your picnic basket. In addition to 10 mi of hiking trails, a store, restaurant, and full-service marina, Cove Palisades has a driving loop around its craggy rim. A full-service campground has 87 full hookups, 91 electrical and 94 tent sites, houseboats, and cabins. ⊠ *Old Culver Hwy.* ☎ *541/546–3412 or 800/ 551–6949* ⊕ *www.prd.state.or.us* 🖾 *Day use $3 per vehicle* ☉ *Daily.*

## Where to Stay & Eat

¢–$ ✕ **The Black Bear Diner.** Hordes of locals gather to wolf down this attractive family-style café's all-American burgers, sandwiches, and gargantuan Hungry Bear breakfasts. Western-theme knickknacks and whimsical menus printed to look like old newspapers enliven standard family restaurant surroundings. ⊠ *237 S.W. 4th St.* ☎ *541/475–6632* 🖃 *AE, D, MC, V.*

¢–$ ✕ **Pepe's Mexican Bakery & Restaurant.** Mexican eateries line the streets of downtown Madras; this one is particularly lively. Pepe himself may well greet you at the door of his cheery, vine-hung restaurant, ushering you with enviable enthusiasm to one of the deep, wooden booths. Try some of his generous flour tacos, a pair of which—toothsome *lengua* (chopped beef tongue), perhaps, or the spiced-up barbecued pork— make an ample lunch. Burritos, quesadillas, and combo plates flesh out the menu. ⊠ *221 S.E. 5th St., 97741* ☎ *541/475–3286* 🖃 *MC, V* ☉ *Closed Sun.*

¢ ✕ **Great Earth Natural Food Store.** Travelers suffering organic withdrawal in Madras will be happy to find this small but well-stocked whole-foods grocer and deli. Great Earth sells pasta fixings and organic and bulk food, along with deli-style sandwiches and panini, vegetarian soups, and good coffee. ⊠ 60 S.E. 6th St. ☎ 541/475–1813 ☰ MC, V ⊘ Closed Sun.

¢–$$ ⌦ **Sonny's.** This medium-size motel has basic accommodations. It is on the highway, about 12 mi from the lake and water-ski resort areas. One suite includes a "hot tub room." ⊠ 1539 S.W. U.S. 97, 97741 ☎ 541/475–7217 or 800/624–6137 ⌦ 541/475–6547 ⊕ www.sonnysmotel.com ↪ 44 rooms, 2 suites ⌂ Restaurant, some microwaves, some in-room hot tubs, pool, outdoor hot tub, bar, laundry facilities, business services, some pets allowed (fee) ☰ AE, D, DC, MC, V ⏐◉⏐ CP.

¢–$ ⌦ **Madras Hotel/Motel.** A very Old West–looking establishment, the Madras includes both hotel rooms in a 1911 building and more modern, motel-style wings. Every room is different; some have a historical theme appropriate to the main building's vintage look. The hotel's convenient location, off the highway and two blocks from the heart of downtown, puts it within easy walking distance of most shops and restaurants. ⊠ 171 S.W. C St., at 4th St. ☎ 877/475–2345 ↪ 40 rooms ☰ AE, D, MC, V.

¢ ⌦ **Hoffy's Motel.** Hoffy's rooms are in five buildings on landscaped lawns just outside Madras. If you want, you can rent the tepee outside; it sleeps up to six, but you'll need camping gear. A chain Mexican restaurant is opposite the motel, in a building that formerly housed Hoffy's own restaurant. ⊠ 600 N. Hwy. 26, 97741 ☎ 541/475–4633 or 800/227–6865 ⌦ 541/475–7872 ↪ 90 rooms, 8 suites ⌂ In-room data ports, cable TV, some in-room hot tubs, some microwaves, some refrigerators, putting green, indoor pool, basketball, laundry facilities ☰ AE, D, DC, MC, V.

## Sports & the Outdoors

DRAG RACING The great outdoors is all well and good, but many Madras locals prefer to get their recreation in more high-octane form at **Madras Dragstrip** (✛ about 1 mi west of Madras; head west on Depot Rd. from Hwy. 26, south on Glass Rd. ⌀ Box 617, 97741 ☎ 541/815–2107 ⊕ www.madrasdragstrip.com). The green flag drops on several dragster and hot-rod races here throughout the summer; most races charge $7 general admission.

WHITE-WATER RAFTING Madras is near the rafting- and fishing-rich Deschutes River; many of the guide services that lead trips on the river are based in Maupin to the north. **Deschutes River Adventures** (⊠ 602 Deschutes Ave., Maupin 97037 ☎ 541/395–2238) has numerous river excursions, from one-day to multiday outings.

## Shopping

A bargain fanatic's dream come true, **Mountain View Auxiliary Thrift** (⊠ 59 S.W. 5th St. ☎ 541/475–3882) is a hunting ground for local keepsakes and the sort of kitschy, small-town treasures that vanish instantly in big-city thrift stores. If you're looking for a cheap used paperback to while away the hours, **Willow Creek Books & Music** (⊠ 154 S.W. 5th St. ☎ 541/475–3131) is the place to go. In addition to a large stock of mysteries, thrillers, and sci-fi potboilers, there's a solid selection of American literature, drama, and poetry. Regional literature and tomes of local lore make up the bulk of the new-books stock.

# Prineville

❸ 52 mi east of Sisters on Hwy. 126, 35 mi northeast of Bend on Hwy. 126 and U.S. 97.

Prineville is the oldest town in central Oregon and the only incorporated city in Crook County. Surrounded by verdant ranch lands and the purplish hills of the Ochoco National Forest, Prineville will likely interest you chiefly as a jumping-off point for some of the region's more secluded outdoor adventures. The area attracts thousands of anglers, boaters, sightseers, and rock hounds to its nearby streams, reservoirs, and mountains. Rimrocks nearly encircle Prineville, and geology nuts dig for free agates, limb casts, jasper, and thunder eggs on mining claims provided by the local chamber of commerce.

The town itself is dominated by a tire-distribution company owned by local magnate Les Schwab. The dusty streets of the state's unofficial "cowboy capital" have seen woolier days—the city grew up around a disreputable saloon, and range wars between cattlemen and sheep men claimed casualties among all involved species a century ago.

A tough little stone building (it was a bank once, and banks out here needed to be tough) is the site of the museum of the Crook County Historical Society, the **Bowman Museum.** The 1911 edifice is now on the National Register of Historic Places. Prominent are pioneer artifacts—chiefly agricultural implements and deadly weapons—that defined early Prineville. ⊠ *246 N. Main St.* ☎ *541/447–3715* ⊠ *Free* ⊙ *Mar.–Dec., weekdays 10–5, Sat. 11–4.*

Three stolid stories of gray stone anchor the **Crook County Courthouse.** A perpetual memorial flame maintained by the local American Legion burns in front of this stately 1909 building. ⊠ *300 N. 3rd St.* ☎ *541/447–6553.*

Mountain streams flow out of the Ochoco Mountains and join together to create the Crooked River, which is dammed near Prineville. Bowman Dam on the river forms **Prineville Reservoir State Park.** Recreational activities include boating, swimming, fishing, and hiking. A campground has 22 full hookups, 23 electrical and 25 tent sites, and 3 cabins. ⊠ *Juniper Canyon Rd.* ☎ *541/447–4363 or 800/452–5687* ⊕ *www.prd.state. or.us* ⊠ *Day use $3 per vehicle* ⊙ *Daily.*

About ½ mi west of Prineville, **Ochoco Viewpoint** is a scenic overlook that commands a sweeping view of the city and the hills, ridges and buttes beyond. ⊠ *½ mi west of Prineville on U.S. Hwy. 126* ⊠ *Free* ⊙ *Daily.*

## Where to Stay & Eat

**$–$$$** ✕ **Crooked River Railroad Company Dinner Train.** Dine aboard this excursion train as it winds through the rimrock-lined Crooked River valley between Redmond and Prineville. The ride and show are the draw here; the food is nothing special. Murder mysteries are played out on Saturday nights year-round and on Friday nights from June to September, while a simulated Jesse James train robbery keeps the Sunday champagne brunch hopping with live entertainment. Call for reservations and departure times. ⊠ *525 S.W. 6th St., Redmond* ☎ *541/548–8630* ⊟ *AE, D, MC, V.*

**$** ✕ **Dad's Place.** A typical American diner, Dad's dishes out no-nonsense breakfasts and lunches at no-nonsense prices. If you're not afraid of fat and cholesterol, try the sandwich of ham, bacon, cheese, and egg on a toasted biscuit. ⊠ *229 N. Main St.* ☎ *541/447–7059* ⊟ *MC, V* ⊙ *Closed Sun. No dinner.*

**$** ▦ **Elliott House.** With its thick green lawns, wraparound porch, Tuscan columns, and bay windows, this B&B stands out like a well-groomed dowager in an otherwise undistinguished neighborhood. Century-old furnishings and accessories fill the house. One of the two rooms contains a double cast-iron bed and an embroidered quilt, and the large shared bathroom has original brass fixtures and a marble-top sink. Breakfast is served on antique china. ⊠ *305 W. 1st St., 97754* ☎ *541/416–0423* ⊕ *www.empnet.com/elliotthouse/* ⊐ *2 rooms with shared bath* ⚲ *Nosmoking room* ⊟ *No credit cards* ⊙ *BP.*

¢ 🖼 **Rustler's Inn.** From the old-style covered walkways to the large, antiques-furnished rooms, this motel is Old West all the way. Each room is decorated differently—if you call in advance, the managers will attempt to match your room furnishings to your personality. Some rooms have kitchenettes. The Rustler's allows pets to stay for a onetime $10 fee. ⊠ *960 W. 3rd St. (U.S. 26), 97754* ☎ *541/447–4185* ⊕ *www.majestyhotels.com/rustlers_inn.html* ⤴ *20 rooms* ♿ *Some kitchenettes, some pets allowed (fee)* ⊟ *AE, D, DC, MC, V.*

### Sports & the Outdoors

FISHING   Anglers looking to cast a line in the Prineville area flock to **Centerfire Outfitters** (⊠ *126 W. 1st St., 97754* ☎ *541/447–3841*). **Go West Outfitters** (🖂 *Box 464, 97754* ☎ *541/447–4082*) leads fishing trips on a 40,000-acre private ranch and on public land.

## Redmond

❹ *40 mi east of Sisters on Hwy. 126, 15 mi northeast of Bend on U.S. 97.*

Redmond sits at the western end of Oregon's High Desert, 4 mi from the Deschutes River and within minutes of several lakes. As with Deschutes County, Redmond has experienced some of the most rapid growth in the state during the past 10 years, largely owing to a dry and mild climate and year-round downhill and cross-country skiing, fishing, hiking, mountain biking, and rock hounding. Still, this is no gentrified resort town à la Bend, as a stroll through downtown will attest. Smith Rock State Park, north of Redmond, attracts aggro rock climbers from around the world to hundreds of climbing routes and hiking trails. Wildlife is abundant in the park, which is a nesting area for birds of prey.

Picnicking and fishing are popular at **Cline Falls State Park,** a rest area commanding scenic views on the Deschutes River 5 mi west of Redmond. ⊠ *Rte. 126* ☎ *800/551–6949* ⊕ *www.prd.state.or.us* 🎫 *Free* ⊙ *Daily.*

During trout season, **Firemen's Pond** is jumping with fish. Only children and adults with disabilities are permitted to fish here. ⊠ *Lake Rd. and Sisters Ave.* ☎ *541/548–6068* 🎫 *Free* ⊙ *Daily.*

( need a break? )   Hiding just off the lobby of the New Redmond Hotel, **Redmond Coffee Works** (⊠ *521 S. 6th St.* ☎ *541/548–5964*) is a pocket-size espresso bar with light fare. After cooling your heels here, take a peek at the lobby fixtures.

A local farmer created the 4-acre **Petersen's Rock Gardens** near Bend. All of the petrified wood, agate, jasper, lava, and obsidian came from within an 85-mi radius of the garden and was used to make miniature buildings and bridges, terraces and towers. Among the structures are a micro–Statue of Liberty and five little castles up to 6 feet tall. The attraction includes a small museum and picnic tables. ⊠ *7930 S.W. 77th St., 97756* ☎ *541/382–5574* 🎫 *$3 (suggested)* ⊙ *Daily 9–5.*

★ A small, scenic viewpoint, **Peter Skene Ogden Wayside** is at the top of a dizzyingly severe 300-foot-deep river canyon 10 mi north of Redmond. ⊠ *U.S. 97 N* ☎ *541/548–7501* 🎫 *Free* ⊙ *Daily.*

Fodor'sChoice ★ Eight miles north of Redmond, **Smith Rock State Park** is world-famous for rock climbing. You might spot golden eagles, prairie falcons, mule deer, river otters, and beavers. Due to the environmental sensitivity of the region, the animal leash law is strongly enforced. ⊠ *Off U.S. 97* ☎ *541/548–7501 or 800/551–6949* ⊕ *www.prd.state.or.us* 🎫 *Day use $3 per vehicle* ⊙ *Daily.*

### Where to Stay & Eat

$ ✕ **Sully's Italian Restaurant.** The historic New Redmond Hotel building is also the site of this home-style Italian restaurant. Tuck into such classics as spaghetti and meatballs, manicotti, and eggplant parmigiana ⊠ *521 S.W. 6th St.* ☎ *541/548–5483* ▤ *MC, V* ☽ *No lunch.*

¢–$ ✕ **Mi Pueblito.** A festive blue building, seemingly airlifted from the tropics to Redmond's main drag, is the site of this Mexican restaurant, a favorite with locals. Dinner specials change nightly, taking the menu beyond the taco-burrito-quesadilla drill with south-of-the-border steaks and stews. ⊠ *404 S.W. 6th St.* ☎ *541/923–5173* ▤ *AE, D, MC, V.*

$$–$$$ ▦ **Eagle Crest Resort.** Eagle Crest is 5 mi west of Redmond, above the canyon of the Deschutes River. In this high desert area, the grounds are covered with juniper and sagebrush. The rooms are in a single building on the landscaped grounds, and some of the suites have gas fireplaces. The resort is on nearly 1,700 acres. There are 10 mi of bike trails and a 2-mi hiking trail where you can fish in the river. ⊠ *1522 Cline Falls Hwy., 97756* ☎ *541/923–2453 or 800/682–4786* 🖷 *541/923–1720* ⊕ *www. eagle-crest.com* ⇲ *100 rooms, 45 suites, 75 town houses* ⌂ *Dining room, picnic area, some kitchenettes, some microwaves, cable TV, pool, hair salon, hot tub, driving range, 4 18-hole golf courses, putting green, tennis court, hiking, horseback riding, gym, bicycles, cross-country skiing, downhill skiing, bar, children's programs (ages 3–12), playground, laundry facilities, business services, airport shuttle* ▤ *AE, DC, MC, V.*

¢–$ ▦ **New Redmond Hotel.** The classic fixtures, including a grandfather clock and an old telephone switchboard, in the lobby of this National Register hotel on Redmond's main drag, more than make up for its generic—though entirely adequate—rooms. Sully's Italian Restaurant and a small coffee bar are in the same building. ⊠ *521 S. 6th St., 97756* ☎ *541/923–7378 or 888/726–2466* 🖷 *541/923–3949* ⇲ *47 rooms* ▤ *AE, MC, V.*

¢ ▦ **Redmond Inn.** Nearby outdoor activities include horseback riding, skiing, fishing, swimming, and golfing, or, if you prefer to stay closer to home, there is a patio by the pool. Just three blocks from the center of town, this inn is convenient to both restaurants and sights. One suite includes a Jacuzzi. ⊠ *1545 U.S. 97 S, 97756* ☎ *541/548–1091 or 800/ 833–3259* ⇲ *46 rooms* ⌂ *Kitchenettes, microwaves, refrigerators, cable TV, pool, some pets allowed (fee)* ▤ *AE, D, DC, MC, V* ⦿ *CP.*

### Sports & the Outdoors

FISHING All manner of outdoor gear, for fishing and other sports, is available at **Patrick's Cent-Wise Sporting Goods** (⊠ 498 S.W. 6th St. ☎ 541/548–4422). You can also pick up maps and permits here.

GOLF Taking full advantage of the high-desert landscape outside of Redmond, **Juniper Golf Club** (⊠ 139 S.E. Sisters Ave. ☎ 541/923–8198) takes hackers through lava-rock while Cascade peaks tower above and the namesake tree perfumes the air. Greens fees run from $20 to $35.

# Ochoco National Forest

**⑤** *25 mi east of Prineville off U.S. 26.*

East of the flat, juniper-dotted countryside around Prineville the landscape changes to forested ridges covered with tall ponderosa pines and Douglas firs. Sheltered by the diminutive Ochoco Mountains and with only about a foot of rain each year, the **Ochoco National Forest**, established in 1906 by President Theodore Roosevelt, manages to lay a blanket of green across the dry, high desert of central Oregon. This arid landscape—marked by deep canyons, towering volcanic plugs, and sharp ridges—goes largely unnoticed except for the annual influx of hunters during the fall. The Ochoco, part of the old Blue Mountain Forest Reserve, is a great place for camping, hiking, biking, and fishing in relative solitude. In its three wilderness areas—Mill Creek, Bridge Creek, and Black Canyon—it's possible to see elk, wild horses, eagles, and even cougars. The **Ochoco Ranger Station** (✉ County Rd. 23 ☎ 541/416–6645) has trail maps and other information. It's open daily 7–4:30. ✉ *Ochoco National Forest Headquarters/Prineville Ranger Station, 3160 N.E. 3rd St. (U.S. 26)* ☎ *541/416–6500* ☙ *Forest year-round (some sections closed during bad weather), ranger station weekdays 7:30–4:30.*

A 43-mi scenic route, **Big Summit Prairie Loop** begins at the Ochoco Ranger Station and winds past Lookout Mountain, Round Mountain, Walton Lake, and Big Summit Prairie. The prairie abounds with trout-filled creeks and has one of the finest stands of ponderosa pines in the state; wild mustangs roam the area. The prairie can be glorious between late May and June, when wildflowers with evocative names like mules ear, wyethia, biscuit root, and yellow bells burst into bloom. ✣ *Forest Service Rd. 22 east to Forest Service Rd. 30 (which turns into Forest Service Rd. 3010) south, to Forest Service Rd. 42 heading west, which loops back to Forest Service Rd. 22.*

## Camping
Most of the area's developed campsites are open May–September. All operate on a first-come, first-served basis.

⚠ **Wildcat Campground.** On the edge of the Mill Creek Wilderness amid ponderosa pines, Wildcat is the trailhead for the Twin Pillars Trail. ♿ *Pit toilets, potable water.* ⬗ *17 sites* ✉ *Mill Creek Rd. (Forest Service Rd. 33; from Prineville head northeast on U.S. 26 for 10 mi and north on Mill Creek Rd. for 10 mi)* ⬚ *$10* ☙ *Closed Nov.–Mar., depending on weather.*

⚠ **Ochoco Forest Camp.** Elk, wild horses, and mule deer thrive at this campground adjacent to the Ochoco Ranger Station and the trailhead for the Lookout Mountain Trail. The six tent sites are along Ochoco Creek. ⬗ *6 sites* ✉ *Forest Service Rd. 2610, 25 mi east of Prineville* ⬚ *$8.*

⚠ **Walton Lake Campground.** On Walton Lake, this developed site is a great place for an afternoon swim or a trek along the nearby Round Mountain Trail. The sites fill up early on weekends and holidays. ♿ *Pit toilets, potable water.* ⬗ *30 sites* ✉ *Forest Service Rd. 22 (from Prineville head northeast on U.S. 26 for 15 mi, east on County Rd. 23 for 8 mi, and northeast on Forest Service Rd. 22 for 7 mi)* ⬚ *$8.*

## Sports & the Outdoors
BIKING  The Ochoco National Forest contains hundreds of miles of dirt roads and multiuse trails. The forest headquarters has a guide to 10 trails in the forest. Consider Cougar Trail or the more harrowing Lone Mountain Trail, both about 25 mi east of Prineville.

FISHING  Steelhead and rainbow trout pack the forest's rivers and streams, but serious fly fishers should head south of Prineville on Highway 27, which parallels Crooked River. Along the way are the bankside Bureau of Land Management campgrounds, where you can pull off and troll for fish. Walton Lake (⇨ Camping) also has fishing. Most large supermarkets sell permits, as does **Prineville Sporting Goods** (✉ 346 N. Deer St., off U.S. 26 ☎ 541/447–6883).

HIKING  Pick up maps at the Prineville or Ochoco ranger station for the trails through the 5,400-acre **Bridge Creek Wilderness** and the demanding **Black Canyon Trail** (24 mi round-trip) in the Black Canyon Wilderness. The

1½-mi **Ponderosa Loop Trail** follows an old logging road through ponderosa pines growing on hills. In early summer, wildflowers take over the open meadows. The trailhead begins at Bandit Springs Rest Area, 22 mi east of Prineville on U.S. 26. A 2½-mi, one-way trail winds through old-growth forest and mountain meadows to **Steins Pillar,** a giant lava column with panoramic views; be prepared for a workout on the trail's poorly maintained second half, and allow at least three hours for the hike. To get to the trailhead drive east 9 mi from Prineville on U.S. 26, head north (to the left) for 6½ mi on Mill Creek Road (also signed as Forest Service Road 33), and head east (to the right) on Forest Service Road 500.

ROCKHOUNDING Stones in the area include agate, obsidian, fire obsidian, petrified wood, and red and green jasper. A free brochure from forest headquarters and the informative "Rockhound's Handbook," available from the Prineville/Crook County Chamber of Commerce ( ⇨ Visitor Information), map out the best locations for prospecting. Thunder eggs can be found at **White Fir Springs** (✉ Forest Service Rd. 3350 [from Prineville head east on U.S. 26 to mile post 41, turn left, and continue for about 5 mi]).

SKIING Two loops for cross-country skiers start at Bandit Springs Rest Area, 29 mi east of Prineville on U.S. 26. One loop is designed for beginners and the other for intermediate to advanced skiers. Both traverse the area near the Ochoco Divide and have great views. Ochoco National Forest headquarters has a handout on skiing trails and can provide the required Sno-Park permits, which are also available from the **Department of Motor Vehicles** (✉ Ochoco Plaza, 1595 E. 3rd St., Suite A-3, Prineville ☎ 541/447–7855).

# Bend

**6**–**15** *58 mi south of Warm Springs, U.S. 26 to U.S. 97; 160 mi from Portland, east and south on U.S. 26 and south on U.S. 97.*

Bend, Oregon's largest city east of the Cascades, is a modern-day boomtown; in the '90s, it was the state's fastest-growing city, spurting to more than 55,000 residents (at last count) in the city, plus more in the sprawl outside its limits. The fuel for this bonanza isn't oil, gold, or timber—instead, Bend swells on the strength of its enviable climate, proximity to skiing, and its growing reputation as a playground and escape. Sadly, the growth has also propelled a soulless spread of chain stores and fast-food slingers along U.S. 20 outside of town, camouflaging Bend's attractiveness. On the other hand, stylish, highly walkable downtown Bend retains a small-city charm.

Nearby Mt. Bachelor, though hardly a giant among the Cascades at about 9,000 feet, gets snow before and keeps it after most other mountains by virtue of its location. Inland air collides with the Pacific's damp influence, creating skiing conditions immortalized in songs by local rock bands, raves in the ski press, and by excellent resort facilities. Like all other great ski hills, "the Batch" is as much a way of life as recreation for some; a strong ski-bum ethic injects Bend with a dose of hormonal postcollegiate buzz.

Alongside this outdoorsy counterculture, though, Bend has boutique shopping and upscale dining and lodging on par with anything else in the state, if not beyond. In recent years, despite Oregon's overall economic doldrums, downtown Bend has undergone a serious make-over, with flashy new restaurants and bars taking over one street corner after another.

Bend Public
Library . . . . . . .8

Century
Drive . . . . . . .10

Deschutes
Historical
Museum . . . . . .9

Downtown
Bend . . . . . . . .7

Drake Park . . . .6

High Desert
Museum . . . . .12

Lava Butte and
Lava River
Cave . . . . . . . .13

Mt. Bachelor
Ski Area . . . . .11

Newberry
National Volcanic
Monument . . .14

Pine Mountain
Observatory . .15

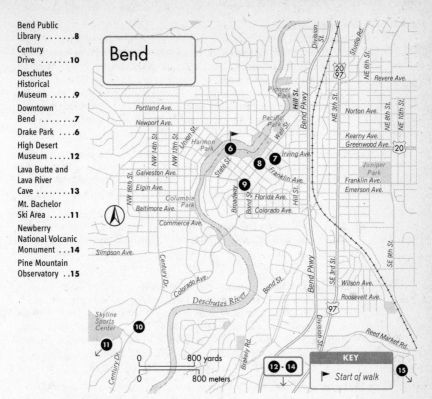

*Numbers in the text correspond to numbers in the margin and on the Bend map.*

**a good tour**

Start out by strolling through **Drake Park** 6 ▶, on the banks of the Deschutes and the Mirror Pond. Then walk a few blocks east through the city's most historic residential neighborhood to the beautiful, airy 1998 **Bend Public Library** 8. Just another block or so east, you'll find the **Deschutes Historical Museum** 9; browse there to get a sense of Bend's history. A block north on Bond Street, you'll find yourself in the bustling thick of **downtown Bend** 7, where jet-set sophistication rubs up against small-town charm. Once you've explored downtown, hop in your vehicle and head west out of town on **Century Drive** 10, a.k.a. U.S. 46. The scenic 100-mi loop leads to **Mt. Bachelor** 11. Once the Century loop brings you back to town, take Highway 97 3½ south of town to check out the **High Desert Museum** 12. The same road takes you to **Newberry National Volcanic Monument** 14, from which you can take in **Lava Butte** 13. Finally, if covering all this ground makes you yearn for a wider perspective on things, swing east from Bend on Highway 20 for the **Pine Mountain Observatory** 15, where you can take in the cosmos.

TIMING    The tour outlined here is definitely an all-day affair—completing the Century Drive loop alone, for example, should take about two hours, not counting stops at scenic points along the way. You may want to split this itinerary into two days to allow more leisurely appreciation of the High Desert Museum and other linger-worthy sights. Keep in mind that challenging winter driving conditions between October and May might prolong this or any itinerary in and around Bend.

## What to See

**⑧ Bend Public Library.** You may feel like you're in Finland when you ascend this 1998 building's main staircase—Scandinavian-style blond wood and sharp modernist architectural lines abound, and light pours through a translucent wall by sculptor Maya Radoczy. Upstairs, the library's fine collection, national and international periodicals, and dozens of public Internet terminals bask in a light-flooded, vaulted space. ⊠ *601 N.W. Wall St.* ☎ *541/388–6679* ⊕ *www.dpls.lib.or.us* ⊙ *Mon.–Thur. 10–8, Fri. 10–6, Sat. 10–5, Sun. 1–5.*

**⑩ Century Drive.** For 100 mi, this forest-highway loop beginning and ending in Bend meanders among dozens of high mountain lakes good for fishing, hiking, waterskiing, and camping. To find it take Highway 46 for the first two-thirds of the trip, and then take Highway 97 at LaPine to return to Bend.

**⑨ Deschutes Historical Museum.** A striking 1914 building constructed from locally quarried volcanic tuff has Indian artifacts, historical photos of the region, and a pioneer schoolroom. ⊠ *129 N.W. Idaho, 97701* ☎ *541/389–1813* 🎟 *Free* ⊙ *Tues.–Sat. 10–4:30.*

**Deschutes National Forest.** This 1.6-million-acre forest has 20 peaks higher than 7,000 feet, including three of Oregon's five highest mountains, more than 150 lakes, and 500 mi of streams. A pass (⇨ Sports & the Outdoors *in* Central Oregon A to Z) is required for all day and overnight use of the trailhead facilities in 13 national forests in Oregon and Washington. ⊠ *Cascades Lakes Hwy.* ☎ *541/388–2715* 🖷 *541/383–5531* ⊕ *www.fs.fed.us/r6/deschutes* 🎟 *Park pass required* ⊙ *Daily.*

**★ ⑦ Downtown Bend.** Bend's heart is an area of about six blocks, centered on Wall and Bond streets. Here you'll find boutique shops, fine restaurants, and lively nightlife establishments, as well as a few old-time pharmacies, taverns, and hardware stores keeping it real. ⊕ *www.downtownbend.com.*

**▶ ⑥ Drake Park.** Bend's first city park is also its most prominent and lovely. Eleven acres of exactingly manicured greensward and trees snake along the banks of the Deschutes just a few blocks south of downtown. Running and walking trails lead to foot bridges to the opposite bank and decorous early-century neighborhoods. ⊠ *Riverside Dr., south of downtown.*

> **need a break?**
>
> A sleekly designed coffee shop with modernist blond-wood furnishings, **Bellatazza** (⊠ 869 N.W. Wall St., Suite 101 ☎ 541/318–0606) serves morning jolts and pastries on Bend's main street. Wireless Internet access is free.

**⑫ High Desert Museum.** The High Desert—embracing Idaho, southwest Montana, Nevada and Washington, as well as Oregon—has a rich history, and it's told from several perspectives here. Intricately crafted walk-through dioramas include a stone-age Indian campsite, a pioneer wagon camp, a mine (go ahead and ring the bell in the mine shaft), and part of an Old West town (complete with a brothel). Individual stores are also meticulously re-created; walk into a telegraph office and see the equipment used to send a wire, or browse in a general store where the sounds of mah-jongg playing—Chinese-speaking men and clacking tiles—emanate from a back room. Many of the displays capture the sights and even the smells of various historical periods. The Spirit of the West exhibit shows what life was like in different states at different times of day, including a look at an Oregon Trail campsite. There are outstanding exhibits on local Native American cultures as well. A bonus is that this

FodorsChoice ★

museum is also a zoo: a "Desertarium" showcases smaller desert animals, including lizards and bats, and in an outdoor section, the spotlight is on birds of prey, including eagles, turkey vultures, and owls. Museum staff handle some of these raptors during demonstrations and there are touch exhibits where you can feel the wings and talons of various birds. Also wandering the grounds are fat porcupines, river otters, and turtles. ⊠ *59800 S. Hwy. 97, 3½ mi south of Bend* ☎ *541/382–4754* ⊕ *www.highdesert.org* ⊠ *$8.50* ☾ *Daily 9–5.*

**⑬ Lava Butte and Lava River Cave.** Lava River Cave is a 1-mi-long lava tube, 10 mi south of Bend. The Lava Butte area has several large basalt lava flows as well as the 500-foot Lava Butte cinder cone. Enter by the visitor center. ⊠ *58201 S. U.S. 97, 97707* ☎ *541/593–2421* ⊠ *$5 per vehicle* ☾ *May–Sept., daily 9–5.*

**⑪ Mt. Bachelor Ski Area.** There are five ski lodges with restaurants and bars at this ski resort 22 mi from Bend. The 9,000-foot mountain has a base at about 5,600 feet and a vertical drop of about 3,365 feet. There are lots of cross-country trails and 70 downhill runs. ⊠ *Cascade Lakes Hwy.* ☎ *541/382–2442 or 800/829–2442* ⊕ *www.mtbachelor.com* ☾ *Nov.–July, daily 8–4.*

**⑭ Newberry National Volcanic Monument.** The last time Newberry Volcano blew its top was about 13 centuries ago. Paulina Peak, up an unpaved road at the south end of the national monument, has the best view into the crater and its two lakes (Paulina and East). Lava Butte and Lava River Cave are at the north end of the monument near the visitor center. ⊠ *Visitor center: U.S. 97, 10 mi south of Bend* ☎ *541/383–5300* ⊠ *$5 per vehicle* ☾ *Memorial Day–Labor Day, daily 9:30–5; Labor Day–Memorial Day, Wed.–Sun. 9:30–5.*

**⑮ Pine Mountain Observatory.** Three reflecting telescopes, with 15-inch-, 24-inch-, and 32-inch-diameter mirrors, each in its own domed building, monitor the universe from atop 6,500-foot Pine Mountain. Take a peek, 26 mi east of Bend. ⊠ *U.S. 20, near Millican* ☎ *541/382–8331* ⊕ *www.pmo-sun.uoregon.edu* ⊠ *$3 donation requested* ☾ *May–Sept., Fri. and Sat. evenings.*

## Where to Stay & Eat

$$$–$$$$ ✕ **Meadows.** This dining room with a view of the Sunriver Resort and surrounding mountains has Pacific Northwest cuisine. This place feels like an exclusive get-away—all dark, natural wood tones and elaborate cooking—and it's priced to match. Still, for regional cuisine at its finest, it's a good choice. Entrées include fresh pastas and regional fish. ⊠ *1 Center Dr.* ☎ *541/593–3740* ⚲ *Reservations essential* ⊟ *AE, D, DC, MC, V.*

$$$ ✕ **Pine Tavern.** Opened in 1936, this is Bend's oldest restaurant. The 200-year-old, 100-foot-tall ponderosa pines growing inside are the centerpiece of the dining room that overlooks the Deschutes River. Seafood and steak are specialties here, and all the produce is locally grown. There is seating on the patio that looks onto a pond and beautifully landscaped area. A kids' menu is available. ⊠ *967 N.W. Brooks, 97701* ☎ *541/382–5581* ⊟ *AE, D, DC, MC, V* ☾ *No lunch Sun.*

$$–$$$ ✕ **The Blacksmith.** In an old, low-slung former smith's shop that looks like it was uprooted from the French Quarter, this orange-walled restaurant specializing in "new American Ranch" cuisine is unapologetically muscular: coat racks are fashioned from cast-iron horseshoes, and the menu leans toward hearty meat dishes. Entrées include the Cowboy Cobb Salad and the Cowboy Bone-In Rib Eye Steak, to hammer home the theme. ⊠ *211 N.W. Greenwood Ave.* ☎ *541/318–0588* ⚲ *Reservations essential* ⊟ *AE, D, MC, V* ☾ *Closed Mon.*

# CloseUp

## LAVA JIVE

TO UNDERSTAND THE LANDSCAPE of central Oregon, you need to know something about its geological history. The Cascades were formed thousands of years ago from the sheer force of a volcanic explosion (or, in the case of the larger mountains, from lava flow and ash buildup). In turn, they coughed up more lava, changing the course of rivers, creating lakes and caves, and leaving gaping craters. The Lava Lands Visitor Center (58201 U.S. 97, ☎ 541/593–2421; open May–mid-Oct., daily 9–5), 11 mi south of Bend on U.S. 97, lays it all out for you, explaining the molten origins of the odd formations nearby. From here you can walk or drive the 1½ mi to the 500-foot summit of Lava Butte, which commands incredible views of the Cascades. The short trail passes over hardened lava as it circles the crater of the cinder cone. Mid-June–Labor Day, a shuttle makes this trip from the center. A $5 per-person day pass or Northwest Forest Pass is required.

After an eruption, the surface of a lava flow sometimes hardens while the molten mass continues to flow underneath. Once the liquid leaves the tube, a cave is formed. Oregon's longest uncollapsed tube is the Lava River Cave (☎ 541/593–1956), about 12 mi south of Bend on U.S. 97. From mid-May to mid-September, you can explore its caverns for $3. A 2-mi (round-trip) trail leads through the cramped passages and cavernous halls;

lanterns are available for $2. If you're still curious about lava caves, head southeast on China Hat Road, which leaves U.S. 97 at the southern end of Bend. About 8 mi out, past Forest Service Road 1820, lie Arnold Ice Cave, Boyd Cave, and Wind Cave—all just waiting for that special spelunker. Bring a flashlight if you want to explore them, and wear warm clothes—temperatures hover around 40°F. The routes to the caves are unmarked due to recent vandalism.

South of the Lava River Cave lies the Lava Cast Forest, where hardened lava shows the outlines of trees that were toppled by molten flows. About 10 mi past the visitor center, Route 21 leads to the Newberry Crater, a 5-mi-wide caldera formed by powerful eruptions several thousand years ago. The crater now contains a lava flow of obsidian (black glass), a waterfall that tumbles from the rim of the crater, and two trout-filled lakes (East and Paulina). During summer, a gravel road leads up to Paulina Peak, the highest point of the volcano (almost 8,000 feet), for spectacular views of the lakes and the Cascades in the distance.

$$–$$$
Fodor'sChoice
★

✕ **Cork.** This romantic, candlelight-washed restaurant and wine bar has the feel of a much older establishment, the sort of place that's hosted countless prom dates, anniversary dinners, and convivial evening-long conversations over wine. No doubt it will. The menu consists of a tradition-minded mix of comforting standards—filet mignon, rack of pork, cioppino—awakened with subtle, almost Latin bursts of flair. A huge wine list complements the kitchen's inventive—but never gimmicky–verve. ✉ 150 N.W. Oregon Ave. ☎ 541/383–6881 ⚑ Reservations essential ☰ MC, V.

$$–$$$
Fodor'sChoice
★

✕ **Merenda.** Chef Jody Denton left San Francisco's go-go restaurant world to open this swaggering, big-city place. Her vivacious cooking draws heavily on French and Italian influences, with a reliance on seasonal and regional ingredients. You can eat tapas-style, assembling a meal from the appetizer list; order a pizza or some pasta; or simply go for a small gang of raw oysters, depending on your mood and pocketbook. An appetizer of roasted halibut cheeks aswim in a comforting, buttery sherry-spiked broth is a must-try. A salad of apple, endive, walnuts, and pungent Gorgonzola chunks is vibrant and fresh. Entrées, from meaty spare ribs to Tuscan meat loaf, tend to be hearty. Merenda claims to have the Northwest's longest list of wines by the glass. ☒ *900 N.W. Wall St.* ☎ *541/330–2304* ⌕ *Reservations essential* ▤ *AE, D, DC, MC, V.*

**$–$$$** ✕ **Ernesto's Italian Restaurant.** Authentic Italian cuisine is served in a former church building. Choose from pizzas, calzones, or pasta dishes, from spaghetti to pesto linguine to lasagne. There's a kids' menu. ☒ *1203 N.E. 3rd St.* ☎ *541/389–7274* ▤ *AE, MC, V* ☽ *No lunch.*

**$–$$$** ✕ **Roszak's Fish House.** This fish house, which opened in 1981, serves more than just fish—the menu includes other seafood entrées, plus prime rib, salads, and pasta dishes. A kids' menu is available. ☒ *1230 N.E. 3rd St., 97701* ☎ *541/382–3173* ▤ *MC, V* ☽ *Closed Sun.*

**$–$$** ✕ **Coho Grill.** Innovative Pacific Northwest dishes, geared to the season, are the hallmarks of this well-respected restaurant. Asparagus, fresh fish, and Cascade morels are on the spring menu; in the fall expect Oregon crab and fruits from the Hood River valley; and in winter try American classics like pot roast and braised lamb shanks. ☒ *61535 Fargo La., south of Bend* ☎ *541/388–3909* ▤ *AE, MC, V.*

**$–$$** ✕ **Giuseppe's Ristorante.** This downtown restaurant has home-style Italian food—homemade pastas, chicken, seafood, veal, steak, and vegetarian dishes. In the heart of downtown, it's an inexpensive alternative to some of the pricier, more nouveau restaurants cropping up around it. ☒ *932 N.W. Bond St., Downtown Bend* ☎ *541/389–8899* ▤ *AE, DC, MC, V.*

**$–$$** ✕ **Hans.** If it feels like you just stepped out of a casual downtown area into an elegant and airy dining space, you did. But Hans is as casual as it is classy. Tables are refreshingly far apart and the golden tones of the walls and light and shiny wood floor add a warmth complemented by a good wine list and creative pastas such as wild mushroom basil penne and lime cilantro chicken fettuccine. Other entrées might include halibut or salmon, roasted chicken, or pork tenderloin. The lunch menu has sandwiches and salads. Hans built his reputation as a baker, so don't slip out before sampling a German-style dessert, or, at the very least, a moist macaroon covered in chocolate. ☒ *915 N.W. Wall St.* ☎ *541/389–9700* ▤ *MC, V* ☽ *No lunch Sun.–Mon.*

**¢–$** ✕ **Alpenglow Café.** Don't walk by this nondescript breakfast and lunch spot, and if you do, locals will likely point you back to it. The mandate for freshness dictates that no can openers are permitted in the kitchen, and the yield is such delightfully hearty dishes as an overstuffed breakfast burrito, Eggs Benedict, and buttermilk pancakes. The good, strong coffee and fresh-squeezed orange juice are worthy companions to any meal. Order breakfast until closing (2 PM) or pick from tasty sandwiches and burgers. ☒ *1040 N.W. Bond Street* ☎ *541/383–7676* ▤ *MC, V* ☽ *No dinner.*

**¢–$** ✕ **Bend Brewery.** On the Deschutes River, this microbrewery has sturdy traditional ales brewed on premises and slightly upscale pub grub—think burgers, sandwiches, soups and salads. Remember, this is a working brewery, which explains the somewhat industrial look, the suds-stained brewers milling around, and the delicious aroma of hops. ☒ *1019 N.W. Brooks St.* ☎ *541/383–1599* ⌕ *Reservations not accepted* ▤ *MC, V.*

**¢–$** ✕ **Deschutes Brewery & Public House.** Try the admirable Black Butte Porter, a local ale, at this brewpub which serves upscale Pacific Northwest cuisine. Gourmet burgers and sandwiches, such as smoked salmon and a brewery-cured pastrami Reuben, dominate the menu. Vegetarians can choose the smoked vegetable sandwich or the vegetarian black bean chili. It's almost always bustling, so keep in mind that you might have to while away a short wait over a pint. Dinner specials vary daily (check the blackboard). Portions are large. ✉ *1044 N.W. Bond St., Downtown Bend* ☎ *541/382–9242* ☒ *Reservations not accepted* ▤ *MC, V.*

¢–$ ✕ **Ponte Vecchio.** Nestled among the Shops in the Old Mill District, this bright and airy spot serves more than a dozen kinds of hand-thrown pizzas, including a tasty four-cheese and pies that employ such unconventional ingredients as halibut, Thai peanut-oil sauce, or ground lamb. Panini, pastas, and salads are also available, along with beer, wine, and several well-brewed coffee drinks. ✉ *680 SW Powerhouse Drive* ☎ *541/312–9665* ▤ *MC, V.*

¢–$ ✕ **Westside Bakery and Café.** Breakfast selections—heavy on savory omelets and scrambles of many kinds—and baked goods are the draws at this kid-friendly café. The three dining rooms are chock-full of antiques and toys. The accommodating staff is known for its high tolerance of special orders, so if you don't see something you want on the menu, ask if they can whip it up. ✉ *1005 N.W. Galveston Ave., 97701* ☎ *541/382–3426* ▤ *D, MC, V* ⊘ *No dinner.*

¢ ✕ **Soba Noodle House.** Cheap bowls of ramen-noodle soup and plates of yakisoba are served in a high-ceiling cavern of a room, while vintage kung fu flicks play on TV. Barbecued pork in a tangy, scallion-studded broth with stewed greens makes for an ideal mid-day refueling stop. ✉ *945 N.W. Bond St. 97701* ☎ *541/318–1535* ▤ *No credit cards* ⊘ *Closed Sun.*

★ $$$$ 🏨 **Pine Ridge Inn.** Spacious and romantic suites with dark wood accents and modern furnishings provide a nice respite after a day of exploring Bend. Request a suite that has both a Jacuzzi tub (seven rooms do) and an outdoor deck, a pleasure for taking in deliciously icy air day or night as well as a view of the Deschutes River. If you're around in the afternoons, there's a wine tasting reception in the lobby, and mornings bring hot entrées and cereals, included in the rate. The hotel has special packages that cater to couples and spa lovers as well as anglers, golfers, and skiers. ✉ *1200 SW Century Dr., 97701* ☎ *541/389–6137 or 800/600–4095* 🖷 *541/385–5669* ⊕ *www.pineridgeinn.com* ⚑ *20 rooms* ♿ *In-room data ports, cable TV, in-room VCRs, some in-room hot tubs* ▤ *AE, D, DC, MC, V* ⫶○⫶ *BP.*

$$$$ 🏨 **Sunriver Resort.** When people refer to Bend as an "escape," this place

**Fodor'sChoice**
★ is what they're talking about. Sunriver, one of Oregon's premier outdoor resort destinations, provides a slew of facilities convenient to skiing at Mt. Bachelor; Class IV white-water rafting on the Deschutes River (which flows right through the complex); and high-desert hiking and mountain biking. Horseback-riding trails, golf courses, and extensive walking trails surround the resort. A former army base, this self-contained community has stores, restaurants, contemporary homes, condominiums, and even a private airstrip—all in a pine-scented desert landscape. You can rent condos, hotel rooms, or houses; shops rent a host of outdoorsy paraphernalia. ✉ *Box 3609, Sunriver 97707* ✛ *west of U.S. 97, 15 mi south of Bend* ☎ *541/593–1000 or 800/547–3922* 🖷 *541/593–5458* ⊕ *www.sunriver-resort.com* ⚑ *510 units* ♿ *6 restaurants, 3 18-hole golf courses, 28 tennis courts, 2 pools, hot tub, sauna, boating, fishing, bicycles, horseback riding; no smoking* ▤ *AE, D, DC, MC, V.*

$–$$$$ 🏨 **Inn of the Seventh Mountain.** This resort in the Deschutes National Forest has hosted year-round outdoor activities and relaxation for 25 years. It's on the banks of the Deschutes River, so white-water rafting and fishing are right at your doorstep in summer. On the property are a host of recreational facilities, including a 65-foot water slide, canoeing, and an outdoor ice-skating rink. Five golf courses are within 15 minutes, and Mt. Bachelor, with great downhill skiing, is only 14 mi away. The inn is child-friendly: Kids Camp 7 has activities for children ages 4 to 11. Accommodations include standard bedrooms with a queen-size bed, deluxe bedrooms with an additional Murphy bed and private deck, and studios with fireplaces and full kitchens. There are also suites and lofts with extra amenities. ✉ *18575 S.W. Century Dr., Deschutes National Forest, Bend 97702* ☎ *800/452–6810* 🖷 *541/382–3517* ⊕ *www.7thmtn. com* ⇆ *300 rooms* ♨ *3 restaurants, grocery, 2 pools, hot tub, 4 tennis courts, fishing, horseback riding, ice-skating, bar, children's programs (ages 4–11), meeting rooms* ▭ *AE, D, DC, MC, V.*

**$–$$$$** ▥ **Mt. Bachelor Village Resort.** This 170-acre compound overlooks the Deschutes. Its outdoor pool and the nearby Awbrey Glen golf course overlook soaring Cascade peaks. The River Ridge units have river views and gas fireplaces. Ski-house condos are also available. ✉ *19717 Mt. Bachelor Dr., 97702* ☎ *541/389–5900 or 800/452–9846* 🖷 *541/388– 7820* ⊕ *www.mtbachelorvillage.com* ⇆ *130 condos* ♨ *Restaurant, picnic area, some microwaves, refrigerators, in-room hot tubs, 6 tennis courts, pool, cross-country skiing, downhill skiing, laundry facilities, business services* ▭ *AE, DC, MC, V.*

**$–$$$$** ▥ **The Riverhouse.** Within earshot of the rushing Deschutes River, this hotel has large rooms with contemporary oak furniture. Many have river views—well worth the extra $10 charge. The three restaurants on premises include the fancy Crossings, a nightclub with live music, and a poolside café serving light, casual fare. ✉ *3075 N. Business 97, North Bend, 97701* ☎ *541/389–3111 or 800/547–3928* 🖷 *541/389–0870* ⊕ *www.riverhouse. com* ⇆ *220 units* ♨ *3 restaurants, bar, 2 pools, hot tub, sauna, 18-hole golf course, 2 tennis courts, gym* ▭ *AE, D, DC, MC, V.*

**$–$$$** ▥ **Lara House Bed & Breakfast Inn.** On a lot overlooking Drake Park and
**Fodor's**Choice Mirror Pond, this huge, restored 1910 Craftsman home, once a board-
★ ing house, attracts vacationing "intuitive counselors" fresh from Sedona. The rooms, all on the second floor, have seating areas and private bathrooms, and the public areas are sunny and inviting. Breakfast is included. ✉ *640 N.W. Congress St. (west 1 mi on Franklin St. from U.S. 97), Bend Historical District, 97701* ☎ *541/388–4064* ☎ *800/766–4064* ⊕ *www. larahouse.com* ⇆ *6 rooms* ♨ *Outdoor hot tub; no smoking* ▭ *D, MC, V* ⧖| *BP.*

**$–$$** ▥ **Sather House Bed & Breakfast.** The Colonial Revival Sather House, built in 1911, occupies a prominent spot in Bend's oldest residential neighborhood. The exterior, glistening white with green trim, has a wraparound veranda and overhanging eaves; period furnishings and original Douglas-fir woodwork fill the interior. Breakfast, included in the room rates and served in the formal dining room, typically consists of French toast with raspberries and almonds, or pecan pancakes; fireside teas are served in the winter, and lemonade and cookies are on the veranda in the summer. Rooms are bright with large windows and have private baths. ✉ *7 N.W. Tumalo, Bend Historical District, 97701* ☎ *541/388–1065 888/388–1065* ⊕ *www.satherhouse.com* 🖷 *541/330–0591* ⇆ *4 rooms* ♨ *No smoking* ▭ *AE, D, MC, V.*

**¢–$$** ▥ **Bend Riverside Motel.** Comfort and efficiency are the bywords at this
**Fodor's**Choice nicely landscaped property only four blocks from downtown and within
★ walking distance of shops and restaurants, including Deschutes Brewery & Public House. Every room has a balcony overlooking Pioneer Park along the river. ✉ *1565 N.W. Hill St., 97701* ☎ *541/388–4000 or 800/ 284–2363* 🖷 *541/389–2363* ✉ *bendrive@teleport.com* ⇆ *200 rooms* ♨ *Some kitchenettes, some microwaves, some refrigerators, cable TV, tennis court, indoor-outdoor pool, outdoor hot tub, laundry facilities, laundry service, business services* ▭ *AE, D, DC, MC, V.*

## Nightlife & the Arts

Bend's take on a bumping urban-modern cocktail haven, **Astrolounge** (✉ 163 N.W. Minnesota Ave. ☎ 541/389–2025) comes complete with matte-black-and-chrome industrial furnishings, a loft-style layout, and pounding hip-hop sound track. On weekend nights, Astrolounge is packed with the young, loud, and on-the-make. The bar connects to a bistro sharing the Space Age motif. The cavernous **Aviemore Arms** (✉ 1020 N.W. Wall St. ☎ 541/385–8898) pub doesn't offer much in the way of across-the-pond authenticity. It does, however, have cheap pints of Guinness ($3.50) and very friendly, competent service. Competition around the two dart boards can be fierce, while a rockin' jukebox in the rear of the sprawling space is so loud, you might think they've booked a cover band for the evening. If the cultural shift under way in Bend hasn't sunk in yet, visit **Barcelona** (✉ 920 N.W. Bond St. ☎ 541/383–8000), a slick tapas bar in the airy St. Claire's Place commercial development. With its glowing-red glass-top bar, jet-black walls, retro-Euro art, and foot-long list of specialty cocktails, Barcelona wouldn't be out of place in any major metropolitan area. This being Bend, however, you get gratitude in place of attitude from the black-clad waitstaff. Jazz duos and trios squeeze into a corner of this tiny rectangular space three or four nights a week. Oregon may be synonymous with microbrew ale and pinot noir, but until **Bendistillery Sampling Room and Martini Bar** (✉ 850 N.W. Brooks St. ☎ 541/388–6868) came along in 1995, hard stuff produced in-state usually ended up on the bottom shelves of low-end taverns. In a few short years, Bendistillery changed that, handcrafting small batches of spirits flavored with local herbs. Bend sits in the middle of one of the world's great juniper forests, so the gin is a particular treat. This slick little tasting room stirs up bracing martinis and highballs incorporating Bendistillery's products, making a perfect bar-crawl kickoff or classy nightcap. Named for the Prineville tire tycoon, **Les Schwab Amphitheater** (✉ 344 S. W. Shevlin-Hixon Dr. ☎ 541/322–0168), an open-air venue in the Old Mill District, brings national music tours to Bend.

## Sports & the Outdoors

BICYCLING  **U.S. 97** north to the Crooked River gorge and Smith Rock provides bikers with memorable scenery and a good workout. **Sunriver** has 26 mi of paved bike paths.

CANOEING  If you haven't taken a moment lately to listen to the silence of nature, a nighttime canoe ride with **Wanderlust Tours** (⌂ 143 SW Cleveland Ave. ☎ 541/389–8359 or 800/962–2862) is a palliative for the system and the soul. Owners Dave and Aleta Nissen, recognized for their dedication to ecotourism, lead trips from June to October on several of Central Oregon's smooth lakes, and depending on the season, also run other tours that include forest and volcano hikes, cave treks, and snowshoeing trips. Rates for the moonlight canoe rides are $50 per person and range from $30–$40 for most of the other trips.

GOLF  **Rivers Edge Golf Course** (✉ 400 Pro Shop Dr., North Bend ☎ 541/389–2828) is an 18-hole, par-72 course. The greens fee ranges from $52 to $66.

SKIING  Many Nordic trails—more than 165 mi of them—wind through the **Deschutes National Forest** (☎ 541/383–5300). Call for information about conditions.

**Mount Bachelor Resort** (✉ 22 mi southwest of Bend off U.S. 97 ☎ 541/382–7888 or 800/829–2442), the Northwest's largest facility, is one of the best in the United States—60% of the downhill runs are rated expert. One of the 11 lifts takes skiers all the way to the mountain's 9,065-foot summit. The vertical drop is 3,265 feet; the longest of the 70 runs is 2 mi. Facilities and services include equipment rental and repair, a ski school, ski shop, Nordic skiing, weekly races, and day care; you can enjoy restaurants, bars, and six lodges. The 36 mi of trails at the **Mount Bachelor Nordic Center,** most of them near the base of the mountain, are by and large intermediate.

### Shopping

A superb and eminently civilized bookshop, **Antiquarian of Bend** (✉ 1002 N.W. Bond St. ☎ 541/322–9788) specializes in rarities and first editions, with a particular emphasis on regional history. Check out the envelope hand-addressed by George Washington, under glass behind the front desk. Kitschy keepsakes and an eclectic selection of gifts, from African-theme coffee mugs to wind socks, crowd the riotous little **Azila Nora** (✉ 1002 N.W. Wall St. ☎ 541/389–6552). A fun, flashy little shop, **Hot Box Betty** (✉ 740 N.W. Wall St. ☎ 541/383–0050) has high fashion for women. Kenneth Cole and Diane von Furstenburg, among others, are on the racks, and old refrigerator doors guard the fitting rooms. An enthusiastic husband-and-wife team presides over **Millette's Kitchen Store** (✉ 1052 N.W. Newport Ave., Suite 103 ☎ 541/617–0312), crammed to the ceiling with fine foods. Bend was once the site of one of the world's largest sawmill operations, a sprawling industrial complex along the banks of the Deschutes. In recent years, the abandoned shells of the old factory buildings of the **Old Mill District** (✉ 545 S.W. Powerhouse Dr. ☎ 541/312–0131) have been transformed into an attractive shopping center, known as The Shops at the Old Mill District, a project honored with national environmental awards. Bend's main concentration of national chain retailers, including Gap, Banana Republic, and Victoria's Secret, can be found here, along with a multiplex movie house and the Les Schwab Amphitheater. As of this writing, an AmeriTel Inns hotel is due to open in the district. A friendly and attentive staff sells sleek modern outdoor gear and clothing at **Pandora's Backpack** (✉ 920 N.W. Bond St., Suite 101 ☎ 541/382–6694). Looking more like a stylish downtown development than a mini-mall, **St. Claire Place** (✉ 920 N.W. Bond St.) has an Aveda spa and lifestyle store, antiques shops, galleries, and the sleek Barcelona jazz club.

# Sisters

🔟 *18 mi northwest of Bend on U.S. 20.*

Sisters derived its name from a group of three Cascade peaks (Faith, Hope, and Charity) that rise to the southwest. If you enter the central Oregon high-desert area from Santiam Pass or the McKenzie River Highway, Sisters appears to be a town out of the Old West. Rustic cabins border a llama ranch on the edge of town. Western storefronts give way to galleries. A bakery occupies the former general store, and the town blacksmith's home now has a flower shop. Although its population remains under 1,000, Sisters increasingly attracts visitors as well as urban refugees who appreciate its tranquillity and charm. The Metolius River in the Riverside area near Sisters is a special find for wildflower lovers, with extensive blooms from early spring to late summer.

Three and a half miles east of Sisters, **Hinterland Ranch** has been breeding llamas and Polish Arabian horses since 1965 and has one of the largest (250) and oldest llama herds in North America. This is a working ranch where you can observe the llamas and a small number of horses. ✉ *67750 Hwy. 20 W* ✉ *Box 1839, 97759* ☎ *541/549–1215* 🖨 *541/549–5262* 🕐 *Mon.–Sat. 7:30–5.*

need a break?  In a rustic-looking former general store, **Sisters Bakery** (✉ 251 E. Cascade St. ☎ 541/549–0361) turns out high-quality pastries, coffee, and doughnuts.

## Where to Stay & Eat

¢–$$ ✕ **Bronco Billy's.** The most popular restaurant in Sisters first opened as a hotel in 1912. Broiled steaks, barbecued chicken and ribs, and Mexican dishes form the backbone of the extensive menu. The place looks like a saloon where Old West baddies might shoot it out, but the service is friendly. Outdoor dining on a covered deck is available. ⊠ 105 W. Cascade St. ☎ 541/549–7427 ⊟ AE, MC, V.

¢–$$ ✕ **Seasons.** Quiches, salads, and sandwiches are among the offerings at this small café and wine shop with a streamside picnic area in the back. ⊠ 411 E. Hood St. ☎ 541/549–8911 ⊟ MC, V ⊙ No dinner.

¢ ✕ **Depot Deli & Cafe.** A railroad theme prevails at this main-street deli.
**Fodor'sChoice** A miniature train circles above as the kitchen dishes out excellent, inexpensive sandwiches and burgers. Sit inside, bounded by the rough-
★ wood walls, or out back on the deck. ⊠ 250 W. Cascade St. ☎ 541/549–2572 ⚓ Reservations not accepted.

¢ ✕ **Harvest Basket.** Healthy snacks, sandwiches, and ready-to-go salads can be had at this organic grocery, which also shares the space with a fishmonger. It may well be the only place in the region for specialty health foods. There really isn't a place to sit down and eat on premises, so plan to picnic elsewhere. ⊠ 110 S. Spruce St. ☎ 541/549–0598.

$$–$$$ ⌂ **Black Butte Ranch.** Eight miles west of Sisters, Black Butte Ranch is a resort with gorgeous mountain views and landscaping to match, with biking and hiking paths meandering for miles around golf courses, ponds, and meadows. Ample windows in the hotel style rooms, condos, and homes, or in the Restaurant at the Lodge keep you in perpetual contact with the snowcapped mountains and pine forest that envelop the property. Horseback riding, swimming, and golf are dominant sports here, and the ranch is also convenient to Smith Rock State Park, the Deschutes River, Mt. Bachelor, and the Hoodoo Ski Bowl. ⊠ 13653 Hawks Beard, 97759 ☎ 541/595–6211 ᵬ 541/595–1299 ⊕ www.blackbutteranch.com ⇗ 126 rooms ☝ 2 restaurants, some kitchens, 2 18-hole golf courses, 23 tennis courts, 4 pools, gym, hot tub, massage, fishing, bicycles, horseback riding, cross-country skiing, snowmobiling, lounge ⊟ AE, D, DC, MC, V.

$–$$$ ⌂ **Conklin's Guest House.** You'll get a great view of the snowcapped Sisters from poolside or while having breakfast in the conservatory of this house, on 5 acres with flower gardens and ponds (for catch-and-release fishing). A short pier on the pond ends with a gazebo-covered sanctuary. The large rooms adhere to floral themes, like Columbine and Heather. ⊠ 69013 Camp Polk Rd., 97759 ☎ 541/549–0123 or 800/549–4262 ᵬ 541/549–4481 ⊕ www.conklinsguesthouse.com ⇗ 5 rooms with bath ☝ Restaurant, picnic area, some refrigerators, pool, pond, massage, laundry facilities; no kids under 11, no room phones, no room TVs, no smoking ⊟ No credit cards ⊙ BP.

$ ⌂ **Black Butte Resort Motel & RV Park.** Rooms done in a country motif are clean and have additional hide-a-beds. The grounds have several picnic areas and barbecues, and the river's a short distance away. This motel property has options for those with pets. ⊠ 25635 S.W. Forest Service Rd. 1419, 97730 ☎ 877/595–6514 or 541/595–6514 ᵬ 541/595–5971 ⊕ www.blackbutte-resort.com ⇗ 6 rooms, 29 RV sites ☝ Kitchenettes, laundry facilities ⊟ MC, V.

## Sports & the Outdoors

BICYCLING Purchase or rent cycling and skiing equipment at the well-stocked **Eurosports** (⊠ 182 E. Hood Ave. ☎ 541/549–2471) off Cascade Avenue, the main drag.

FISHING Check the white board to the left of the front door at the **Fly Fisher's Place** (⊠ 151 W. Main Ave. ☎ 541/549–3474) for a daily report of what's biting on the Metolius, Crooked, and Fall rivers.

WHITE-WATER
RAFTING

To book guided white-water raft trips in the Sisters area, call **Destination Wilderness** (⊠ 101 W. Main Ave. ☎ 541/549–1336).

## Shopping

More than a dozen central Oregon artists have a cozy showcase at the **High Desert Gallery** (⊠ 101 West Main St. ☎ 541/549–6250), a repository of affordable contemporary art that includes precious metal jewelry, clay jewelry, oil paintings, vases, and stained glass. Sisters is the site of the lavishly stocked **Lonesome Waters Books** (⊠ 221C W. Cascade Ave. ☎ 541/549–2203), one of Oregon's great independent bookstores. You can find everything from $1 paperbacks to premium first editions here.

# CENTRAL OREGON A TO Z

*To research prices, get advice from other travelers, and book travel arrangements, visit www.fodors.com.*

### AIRPORTS

Bend-Redmond Municipal Airport is served by Horizon and United Express.

🛈 Airport Information **Bend-Redmond Municipal Airport** ⊠ 2522 S.E. Jesse Butler Circle ☎ 541/548-6059. **Horizon** ☎ 800/547-9308. **United Express** ☎ 800/241-6522.

### BIKE TRAVEL

Much of central Oregon's high-desert plateau is relatively flat, easing bike travel. You don't see many people biking the region's highways, though, perhaps because major settlements tend to be far apart. However, mountain-biking trails and scenic back-road rides are plentiful throughout central Oregon. Off main highways, auto traffic is blessedly sparse. Bike rentals are widely available from the region's many outdoor outfitters. Along with ski gear, Eurosports in Sisters rents road and mountain bikes. On the Way Bike and Ski, literally on the way from Bend to Mt. Bachelor, rents equipment and road, mountain, and comfort bikes.

🛈 Rentals **Eurosports** ⊠ 182 E. Hood Ave., Sisters ☎ 541/549-2471. **On the Way Bike and Ski** ⊠ 345 S.W. Century Dr. Bend ☎ 541/322-8814 ⊕ www.on-the-way.com.

### BUS TRAVEL

Greyhound services Warm Springs, Madras, Prineville, Redmond, and Bend with one bus a day via Portland. CAC Transportation, a regional carrier, likewise runs one bus a day each way between Portland and Bend, with stops in Redmond, Madras, and Warm Springs. From Bend, you can also catch buses to other Oregon transportation hubs, including Medford, Salem, and The Dalles, but schedules are sporadic.

🛈 Depots **Greyhound Bend** ⊠ 63076 N. Hwy. 97 ☎ 800/231-2151.
🛈 Lines **CAC Transportation** ☎ 800/847-0157. **Greyhound** ☎ 800/231-2222 ⊕ www.greyhound.com.

### CAR RENTALS

National, Hertz, Avis, and Budget all have outlets at Bend-Redmond Municipal Airport. A Bend-area car dealership runs a rental service called the Carrera Collection, providing high-end luxury cars.

🛈 Agencies **Avis** ☎ 541/923-3750. **Budget** ☎ 541/923-0699. **Carrera Collection** ⊠ 1045 S.E. 3rd St., Bend ☎ 541/322-1828 ⊕ www.carreracollection.com. **Hertz** ☎ 541/923-1411. **National** ☎ 541/548-0650.

### CAR TRAVEL

U.S. 20 heads west from Idaho and east from the coastal town of Newport into central Oregon. U.S. 26 goes southeast from Portland to

Prineville, where it heads northeast into the Ochoco National Forest. U.S. 97 heads north from California and south from Washington to Bend. Highway 126 travels east from Eugene to Prineville; it connects with U.S. 20 heading south (to Bend) at Sisters. Roads throughout central Oregon are well maintained and open throughout the winter season, though it's always advisable to have tire chains in the car.

Rapid population growth in the Bend area has sparked traffic problems out of scale with the city's size. If you're trying to head out of or into town on a major highway during the morning or 5 PM rush, especially on 97 between Bend and Redmond, be advised that you may hit congestion. Parking in downtown Bend is free for the first two hours; you can park for free in the historic residential neighborhood west of downtown. Free on-street parking is plentiful in all of central Oregon's other towns and cities.

## CHILDREN IN CENTRAL OREGON
Bend's public library has an excellent children's selection on the ground floor.

🔳 **Bend Public Library** ⊠ 601 N.W. Wall St. ☎ 541/388-6679 ⊕ www.dpls.lib.or.us.

## DISABILITIES & ACCESSIBILITY
People using wheelchairs should find the downtown areas of central Oregon's major cities—Bend, Redmond, and Madras, in particular—generally navigable. Many resort destinations in the region have ADA-compliant rooms available. Central Oregon Resources for Independent Living, with its focus on helping people with disabilities do more with less outside help, would be a good place to inquire about assistance for outdoor activities. Interfaith Volunteer Caregivers, which can be contacted through Trinity Episcopal Church, provides assistance in shopping and other routine tasks to senior citizens and people with disabilities. The state's Commission for the Blind and Speech-Language & Hearing Association act as clearinghouses for resources and can answer general questions.

🔳 **Local Resources** **Central Oregon Resources for Independent Living** ⊠ 20436 Clay Pigeon Ct., Bend 97908 ☎ 541/388-8103. **Interfaith Volunteer Caregivers** ⊠ 469 N. W. Wall St., Bend ☎ 541/385-9460. **Oregon Commission for the Blind (State-wide Office)** ⊠ 535 S.E. 12th Ave., Portland 97214 ☎ 503/731-3221. **Oregon Speech-Language & Hearing Association (State-wide Office)** 🖃 Box 2042, Salem 97308 ☎ 503/370-7019.

## DISCOUNTS & DEALS
During ski season, some Bend restaurants and shops offer discounts to people with valid Mt. Bachelor ski passes. Look for the sticker decal in shop windows.

🔳 **Mt. Bachelor** ⊠ 22 mi southwest of Bend off U.S. 97 ☎ 541/382-7888 or 800/829-2442 ⊕ www.mtbachelor.com.

## EMERGENCIES
Bend's St. Charles Medical Center is central Oregon's main hospital facility, serving an area bigger than several East Coast states combined. It's the only Level II trauma center in Oregon east of the Cascades. Central Oregon Community Hospital in Redmond, Mountain View Hospital District in Madras, and Pioneer Memorial Hospital in Prineville all have emergency rooms. The major incorporated municipalities in central Oregon have police forces, supplemented by the sheriff's departments of Crook, Deschutes, and Jefferson counties. All can be reached by dialling 911.

🔳 **Hospitals** **Central Oregon Community Hospital** ⊠ 1253 N.W. Canal Blvd., Redmond 97756 ☎ 541/475-3882. **Mountain View Hospital District** ⊠ 470 N.E. A St., Madras 97741 ☎ 541/475-3882. **Pioneer Memorial Hospital** ⊠ 1201 Elm St. N, Prineville 97754

☎ 541/447-6254. **St. Charles Medical Center** ✉ 2500 N.E. Neff Rd., Bend 97701 ☎ 541/382-4321 ⊕ www.scmc.org.

🔝 Police & Sheriff's Departments **City of Bend Police Department** ☎ 541/388-5505. **City of Madras Police Department** ☎ 541/475-2424. **City of Prineville Police Department** ☎ 541/447-4168. **City of Redmond Police Department** ☎ 541/504-3400. **Warm Springs Reservation Tribal Police Department** ☎ 541/ 553-3300.

**Crook County Sheriff's Department (Prineville)** ☎ 541/447-6398. **Deschutes County Sheriff's Department (Bend)** ☎ 541/388-6655. **Deschutes County Sheriff's Department (Sisters)** ☎ 541/549-2302. **Jefferson County Sheriff's Department (Madras)** ☎ 541/475-6520.

## LODGING

Bend has numerous B&Bs, and many others are scattered around central Oregon. The state tourism office maintains a centralized reservation service at its Web site, ⊕ www.traveloregon.com. Bend Vacation Rentals lists properties ranging from 10-acre mini-ranches outside Bend to urban cottages right on the city's centerpiece, Drake Park. Sunriver Retreats rents out roomy modern houses—which can accommodate large groups—in the heart of the Sunriver recreation and resort complex.

🔝 Local Agents **Bend Vacation Rentals** ☐ Box 1393, Bend 97709 ☎ 541/385-9492 ⊕ www.bendvacationrentals.com. **Sunriver Retreats** ☐ Box 3494, Sunriver 97707 ☎ 541/593-3162 ⊕ www.sunriverretreats.com.

## MAIL & SHIPPING

Bend's central post office on Northeast 4th is open Monday–Saturday 9–5:30. Madras, Prineville, and Sisters also have post offices. Internet service is available free at the Bend Public Library. Bend's Café Internet, on Century Drive, claims to be central Oregon's only cybercafé.

🔝 Post Office **Bend Post Office** ✉ 2300 N.E. 4th St., Bend 97701 ☎ 541/318-5068. **Madras Post Office** ✉ 73 N.E. 6th St., Madras 97741. **Prineville Post Office** ✉ 115 N. E. Court St., Prineville 97754 ☎ 541/416-0649. **Sisters Post Office** ✉ 160 S. Fir St., Sisters 97759 ☎ 541/549-0412.

🔝 Internet Cafés **Bend Public Library** ✉ 601 N.W. Wall St. ☎ 541/388-6679 ⊕ www. dpls.lib.or.us. **Cafe Internet** ✉ 133 S.W. Century Dr., Suite 204, Bend 97702 ☎ 541/318-8802.

## MEDIA

As is the case elsewhere in Oregon, the Portland-based daily *Oregonian* is widely distributed and read in central Oregon. However, Bend's daily *Bulletin* gives the Big O a run for its money; it's widely respected as a solid paper with a region-wide footprint. Fast-growing Bend also has a feisty alternative weekly, *The Source*, a good place to find live music and other entertainment listings, as well as rambunctious coverage of local politics. The region's other dailies are Redmond's *Spokesman* (owned by the *Bulletin*'s parent company) and the *Madras Pioneer*. The *Nugget* is a weekly news and community newspaper published in Sisters.

RADIO & KOAB in Bend is central Oregon's public radio affiliate; it can be heard
TELEVISION at 91.3 FM. KWSO, the station operated by the Warm Springs tribe, deserves special attention as perhaps the most eclectic station in Oregon. Hip-hop hits and traditional tribal drum chants share the reservation's airwaves at 91.9 FM. Broadcast television affiliates based in the region are KFXO (Fox) and KTVZ (NBC).

## SPORTS & THE OUTDOORS

A base for fishing, rock climbing, skiing, hiking, and biking, central Oregon draws enthusiastic hordes to the area every year. Water sports are especially popular. The Deschutes River flows north from the Cascades west of Bend, gaining volume and momentum as it nears its rendezvous with the Columbia River at The Dalles. Its upper stretches, particularly those near Sunriver and Bend, are placid and suitable for leisurely canoeing. White-water rafters flock to the stretch of the Deschutes between Madras and Maupin. You need a state marine boater pass to participate. For passes and other details pertaining to the Deschutes River, contact the Bureau of Land Management in Prineville. Several businesses run white-water rafting trips on the Deschutes River near Bend.

Keep in mind that National Forest facilities in Oregon (and Washington) all require some sort of day-use fee. You can pay just once if you buy the Northwest Forest Pass, a $30-per-car tariff good for one year and in both Pacific Northwest states. You can buy the pass online at www.naturenw.org.

⊠ Bicycling **Central Oregon Trail Alliance** ⊠ 1293 N.W. Wall St., Suite 72, Bend 97701 ⊕ www.cotamtb.org.

⊠ Fishing **Oregon Department of Fish & Wildlife** ⊠ 2501 S.W. 1st Ave. ⊕ Box 59, Portland 97207 ☎ 503/872-5268 ⊕ www.dfw.state.or.us.

⊠ Hiking **US Forest Service (Deschutes & Ochoco National Forests)** ⊠ 1645 Hwy. 20 E, Bend, OR 97701 ☎541/383-5300 ⊕www.fs.fed.us/r6/centraloregon. **Western Walkers** ⊠ 61508 Fargo La., Bend 97702 ☎ 541/312-3692 ⊕ www.westernwalkers.com.

⊠ Rock Climbing **SmithRock.com** ⊠ 9988 N.E. Crooked River Dr., Terrebonne 97760 ☎ 541/923-0702 ⊕ www.smithrock.com.

⊠ Skiing **Mt. Bachelor** ⊠Cascade Lakes Hwy. ☎541/382-2442 or 800/829-2442 ⊕www.mtbachelor.com.

⊠ White-Water Rafting **Bureau of Land Management (Deschutes Wild & Scenic River Area)** ⊠ 3050 N.E. 3rd St. ⊕ Box 550, Prineville 97754 ☎ 541/416-6700 ⊕ www.nps.gov/rivers/wsr-deschutes.html. **Inn of the Seventh Mountain Whitewater Rafting** ⊠ 18575 S.W. Century Dr., Bend 97702 ☎ 541/382-8711. **Portland River Co.** ⊠ 315 S. W. Montgomery St., Portland 97201 ☎ 503/229-0551. **River Trails Deschutes** ⊕ Box 309, Maupin 97037 ☎ 541/395-2545 or 888/324-8837. **Sun Country Tours** ⊠ 531 S.W. 13th St., Bend 97702 ☎ 800/770-2161.

## TAXIS

You could probably spend six months in central Oregon without seeing a single taxi, but they do exist. You'll need to call if you want one.

⊠ Companies **Bend Cab/City Cab Company** ☎ 541/548-0919. **Central Oregon Airport Shuttle** ☎ 541/389-7469. **High Desert Taxi (Madras)** ☎ 541/475-5892. **Redmond Taxi Service** ☎ 541/541-1182.

## VISITOR INFORMATION

The best one-stop source for information is the Central Oregon Visitors Association, a thorough umbrella agency serving the entire area.

⊠ Tourist Information **Bend Chamber of Commerce** ⊠ 777 N.W. Wall Street Bend 97701 ☎ 541/382-3221 ⊕ www.bendchamber.org **Bend Visitor & Convention Bureau** ⊠ 63085 N. Hwy. 97 Bend 97701 ☎ 877/245-8484 ⊕ www.visitbend.org **Central Oregon Visitors Association** ⊠ 63085 N. Hwy. 97, Suite 104, Bend 97701 ☎ 541/389-8799 or 800/800-8334 ⊕ www.covisitors.com. **Confederated Tribes of Warm Springs** ⊠ Warm Springs 97761 ☎ 541/553-1161. **Deschutes National Forest** ⊠ 1645 Hwy. 20 E, Bend 97701 ☎ 541/383-5300. **Ochoco National Forest Headquarters and Prineville Ranger Station** ⊠ 3160 N.E. 3rd St., Prineville 07754 ☎541/416-6500. **Prineville/Crook County Chamber of Commerce** ⊠ 390 N. Fairview St., 97754 ☎ 541/447-6304 ⊕ www.prineville.org. **Sisters Chamber of Commerce** ⊠ 222 Hood Ave., 97759 ☎ 541/549-0251 ⊕ www.sisterschamber.com.

# THE WILLAMETTE VALLEY & THE WINE COUNTRY

**FODOR'S CHOICE**

Evergreen Aviation Museum, *McMinnville*

Flying M Ranch, *Yamhill*

Mattey House Bed & Breakfast, *McMinnville*

Red Agave, *southwestern fare in Eugene*

Tina's, *country French food in Dundee*

Turtles Bar & Grill, *Eugene*

Valley River Inn, *Eugene*

**HIGHLY RECOMMENDED**

RESTAURANTS   Capriccio Ristorante, *Albany*

Excelsior Café, *Eugene*

Mazatlan Mexican Restaurant, *Aloha, near Hillsboro*

Nick's Italian Cafe, *McMinnville*

HOTELS   Excelsior Inn, *Eugene*

Log Cabin Inn, *McKenzie River Highway*

SIGHTS   Amity Vineyards, *Amity*

5th Street Public Market, *Eugene*

The Oregon Garden, *Silverton*

Silver Falls State Park, *26 mi east of Salem*

Updated by
Susan
Honthumb

**DURING THE 1940S AND 1950S,** researchers at Oregon State University concluded that the Willamette Valley—the wet, temperate trough between the Coast Range to the west and the Cascade Range to the east—had an unsuitable climate for the propagation of varietal wine grapes. Evidently, they were wrong.

The faultiness of the researchers' techniques has been proven by the success of Oregon's burgeoning wine industry. More than 100 wineries dot the Willamette (pronounced "wil-*lam*-it") Valley, with the bulk of them in Yamhill County in the northern part of the state. Two dozen more wineries are scattered among the Umpqua and Rogue valleys (near Roseburg and Ashland, respectively) to the south. Their products—mainly cool-climate varietals like pinot noir, chardonnay, and Johannesberg Riesling—have won gold medals in blind tastings against the best wines of California and Europe.

## Exploring the Willamette Valley and the Wine Country

Back roads and scenic byways are the ideal venues for slowly getting to know the Willamette Valley, but if you're determined to squeeze more in, head for Interstate 5 (I–5) to zip through the valley; if you follow the coverage of this chapter, you'll be heading south on I–5—with a few dog-leg detours along the way—from Forest Grove to Drain. Likewise, if you want to take in the wine country slowly, you can either tour some of the many wineries yourself or sign up with a tour that will cover several wineries during the course of a day.

The wineries can be as central to your day as you want to make them; some, in the southern part of the Willamette Valley, are secluded and don't have environs with sights to see per se, while the northern part of the valley is closer to Portland and puts you in proximity to attractions, shops, and restaurants.

| WHAT IT COSTS | | | | |
|---|---|---|---|---|
| **$$$$** | **$$$** | **$$** | **$** | **¢** |
| RESTAURANTS over $30 | $20–$30 | $15–$20 | $10–$15 | under $10 |
| HOTELS over $180 | $140–$180 | $100–$140 | $60–$100 | under $60 |

Restaurant prices are per person for a main course at dinner. Hotel prices are for a standard double room, excluding room tax, which varies 6%–91/2% depending on location.

### Timing

A running joke in Oregon, especially in the Willamette Valley, is that native Oregonians were born with webbed toes; it rains quite a bit, especially in winter. Storms abate in late spring and early summer and begin to come again in the fall. The best time to visit is the end of May.

Be aware that the International Pinot Noir Celebration, held at McMinnville's Linfield College in late July, brings an influx of wine lovers into the area, so book lodging well in advance if you're visiting then.

## Forest Grove

▶ ❶ *24 mi west of Portland on Hwy. 8.*

Though it is named for a large grove of Oregon white oak trees situated on a knoll above the Tualatin Plains, Forest Grove is also surrounded by stands of Douglas firs and giant sequoia, including the largest giant

*Numbers in the margin correspond to points of interest on the Willamette Valley & Wine Country, Salem, and Eugene maps*

**If you have 3 days**

On day one, take a guided or self-guided winery tour, exploring the vineyards in ▦ **Forest Grove** ❶ ▶ and in **Dundee & Yamhill** ❼. Overnight in Forest Grove. On the morning of day two head south on Route 47 to see the countryside, passing through small towns like Dilley, Gaston, Cove Orchard, and ▦ **McMinnville** ❾, where you'll want to see Howard Hughes's airplane, the *Spruce Goose*. Overnight in McMinnville and head for **Salem** ⓭–㉑ in the morning, arriving early enough to tour the city for a few hours. To return to Portland, head north on I–5 for the 2½-hour drive.

**34**

**If you have 5 days**

Do the three day itinerary, lingering in the ▦ **Salem** ⓭–㉑ environs on your third day. Head to **Silverton** ⑪, whose attractions include Silver State Falls and the Oregon Gardens. Explore some vineyards around Salem or **Albany** ㉒, spending the night in Salem. On the morning of day five, head toward **Corvallis** ㉓, the site of Oregon State University as well as a national forest, a wildlife refuge, and, if you're up for it, more wineries. It's a good place to relax and unwind before heading back to Portland, which involves a small stint on Route 20 before you pick up I–5 north toward the city.

**If you have 8 days**

Follow the five-day itinerary, overnighting in ▦ **Corvallis** ㉓ and striking out on day six 5 mi west of Corvallis to sleepy Philomath. Visit the Benton County Historical Museum at what used to be Philomath College. Consider a climb on Mary's Peak, and spend the rest of the day enjoying the Siuslaw River and the Siuslaw National Forest. Backtrack toward Corvallis, catching a bit of 99 West to see the countryside and passing through the towns of Monroe and Junction City. Spend a second night in Corvallis and head toward ▦ **Eugene** ㉘–㊳ on day seven, taking in the town's attractions, parks, and buttes. You can easily overnight in Eugene and explore more of the city on your last day, or you can venture farther south to see Creswell, **Cottage Grove** ㊴, and **Drain** ㊵, the terminus of this chapter's coverage. When you're through with your travels south, head back north on the back roads of Hwy. 228 to see the Mohawk and Calapooia rivers before picking up I–5 for the drive back to Portland.

---

sequoia in the state. Originally inhabited by the Tualatin tribe, the site was settled by pioneers in 1840, and the town was incorporated in 1872. To get there, take U.S. 26 west to Highway 6 and go west to Forest Grove. For the wineries, head south from Forest Grove on Highway 47 and watch for the blue road signs between Forest Grove, Gaston, and Yamhill.

With 1,800 students, **Pacific University** is on a shady campus that provides a respite from sightseeing. It was founded in 1849, making it one of the oldest educational institutions in the western United States. Concerts and special events are held in McCready Hall in the Taylor-Meade Performing Arts Center. The school also has a College of Optometry. ✉ *2043 College Way, 97116* ☎ *503/357–6151* ⊕ *www.pacificu.edu* ⌦ *Free* ☽ *Daily.*

In the wake of a forest fire, the Oregon Department of Forestry created **Forest Grove Educational Arboretum,** a facility on 364,000 acres that addresses how the environment can be salvaged following devastating natural disasters. ⊠ *801 Gales Creek Rd., 97116-1199* ☎ *503/357–2191* ⊙ *Tours upon request.*

Just southeast of Forest Grove, **Fernhill Wetlands,** on 243 acres, is a haven for waterfowl. For a guided tour of the Fernhill Wetlands, or other wildlife areas, contact the **Tualatin Riverkeepers** (☎ 503/590–5813) ☎ *503/357– 5890 East Viewing Shelter.*

A beautiful area in the Coast Range foothills, **Scoggin Valley Park and Henry Hagg Lake** has a 15-mi-long hiking trail that surrounds the lake. Bird-watching is best in spring. Recreational activities include fishing, boating, water-skiing, and picnicking, and a 10½-mi, well-marked bicycle lane parallels the park's perimeter road. ⊠ *Scoggin Valley Rd.* ☎ *503/846–8715 or 503/359–5732* ⊕ *www.co.washington.or.us* ⊠ *$3* ⊙ *Daily dawn–dusk; facilities Mar.–Nov.*

## Wineries

Grapes have been grown at the site of **David Hill Vineyards and Winery** (⊠ 46350 N.W. David Hill Rd., Forest Grove ☎ 503/992–8545 or 877/992–8545 🖨 503/992–8586 ⊕ www.davidhillwinery.com) since 1883. Picnicking is encouraged here. It's open Tuesday–Sunday 12–5.

One of the oldest Willamette Valley wineries, **Elk Cove Vineyards** (⊠ 27751 N.W. Olson Rd., Gaston ☎ 503/985–7760 ⊕ www.elkcove.com) has 100 acres of estate vineyards and produces pinot noir, pinot gris, and Riesling. Its tasting room, open daily 10–5, is known for its views across the valley.

**Laurel Ridge Winery** (⊠ 13301 N.E. Kuehne Rd., Carlton 97111 ☎ 503/ 852–7050 🖨 503/252–7404 ⊕ www.laurelridgewines.com) prides itself on its vintage Port and has a well-regarded Sauvignon blanc. It's open daily noon–5.

With 265 acres of vineyards, **Montinore Estate** (⊠ 3663 S.W. Dilley Rd., Forest Grove ☎ 503/359–5012 ⊕ www.montinore.com) has earned acclaim from *Wine Enthusiast* for its pinot noir vintages. You're welcome to picnic in the gardens adjoining the tasting room. It's open weekends only January–May, 11–5, and June–December, daily 11–5.

Fumé blanc, chardonnay, pinot gris, and dessert wines are among the offerings at **Shafer Vineyard Cellars** (⊠ 6200 N.W Gales Creek Rd. ☎ 503/357–6604 ⊕ www.shafervineyardcellars.com), which has free wine tasting. There's a Christmas ornament shop on the property. The winery is open in January, weekends 11–5 and February–December, daily 11–5.

**Tualatin Estate Vineyards** (⊠ 10850 N.W. Seavey Rd. ☎ 503/357–5005 🖨 503/357–1702) is one of the oldest vineyards in the Willamette Valley. Semi-sparkling Muscat and pinot blanc are among its products. It's open March–December, weekends 12–5.

## Where to Stay & Eat

$–$$$  ✕ **Mothersheads.** Chef Eric Wayne makes a mean fettuccine with homemade sour cream, and if you're in the mood for something exotic, try the Forest Grove–raised buffalo. Seafood and Italian dishes round out the menu. Plush, comfy booths and a large stone fireplace lend warmth to the large dining room, which seats up to 120 people. ⊠ *1819 19th Ave.* ☎ *503/357–6623 or 877/303–0843* ⊟ *AE, D, DC, MC, V* ⊙ *Closed Mon.*

**34**

## Bicycling

It's a toss-up as to whether Oregonians bike because they're environmentally oriented, health-conscious, or just not in much of a hurry. Statistics, however, indicate that it's just an efficient means of transportation. Oregon is ranked the top state for biking; the state's department of transportation has created more than 200,000 mi of bicycle-friendly shoulders on the roadways. As you drive around Portland, Salem, Corvallis, and Eugene, you'll be especially aware of the bike paths. Some communities even have separate paths devoid of auto traffic. Bicycling organizations and shops are abundant in the region, and there are several serious bike racing groups.

Bicyclers do disappear from the roads when the rains come, but the hardy climb into their slickers and head out anyway. If you do want to try cycling in the rain, be sure your bike is equipped with rear mud guards.

One way to incorporate biking into your sightseeing is to participate in the seasonal events run by local bike clubs. Among the many good ones is Peach of a Century, sponsored by the Salem Bicycle Club; the course is marked and there are rest stops along the way.

## Wine

There are 217 wineries in Oregon, and there are more cropping up every year. Oregon is second in the nation for number of wineries, with two thirds of them in the Willamette Valley. Some wineries employ traditional techniques, aging the wine in oak barrels and corking the wine with actual cork, while others employ newer technologies, using stainless steel to store the wine and corking the wine with plastic material. Whether the methods are old-fashioned or modern, the goal is the same: to make the next batch of wine better than the last, perhaps accounting for why so many awards go to Willamette Valley vineyards.

The easiest ways to explore the Willamette Valley is to leave the work in the capable hands of a tour. EcoTours of Oregon will pick you up at your hotel and take you to four or five vineyards in Yamhill or Washington County. If you'd rather dawdle from vineyard to vineyard at your own pace, information on many of the region's wineries is provided throughout the chapter.

---

¢–$$ ✕**Poppio's.** Fresh seafood and pasta are specialties at this spot with casual family dining. Public service is another specialty here; Poppio's sets aside a certain percentage of its income to help raise money for someone in the community in need of a bone-marrow transplant. ✉ *2617 Pacific Ave.* ☎ *503/357–5242* ▬ *AE, D, DC, MC, V.*

$–$$$$ ▦ **McMenamins Grand Lodge.** On 13 acres of pastoral countryside, this converted Masonic rest home has accommodations that run from bunk-bed rooms to a three-room fireplace suite. The lodge's sturdy 1922 brick buildings also include pubs that serve several McMenamins draft beers. Rooms are furnished with period antiques such as oak night stands and porcelain sinks. For those not staying in the bunkhouse, rates include use of the European-style soaking pool, Continental breakfast during the week, and a full breakfast on weekends. Bring your food and ale to the Compass Room Theater, where feature films are screened nightly;

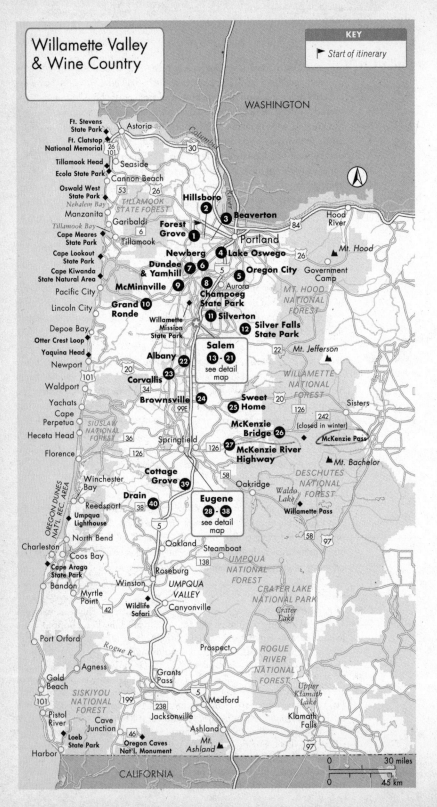

## Willamette Valley & Wine Country

**KEY**

▶ *Start of itinerary*

WASHINGTON

*Columbia River*

Ft. Stevens State Park
Ft. Clatstop National Memorial
Astoria
26 101
30
Tillamook Head
Ecola State Park
Seaside
Cannon Beach
Oswald West State Park
53
26
*Nehalem Bay*
Manzanita
**Hillsboro**
**2**
*TILLAMOOK STATE FOREST*
*Tillamook Bay*
Garibaldi
6
**3**
**Beaverton**
**Forest Grove**
**1**
Portland
Hood River
Cape Meares State Park
Tillamook
Cape Lookout State Park
**Newberg**
**4** **Lake Oswego**
84
Cape Kiwanda State Natural Area
**Dundee & Yamhill**
**7** **6**
5
**Oregon City**
**5**
26
Mt. Hood
Pacific City
**McMinnville**
**9**
**8**
Aurora
Government Camp
Lincoln City
**Grand Ronde**
**10**
**Champoeg State Park**
*MT. HOOD NATIONAL FOREST*
Depoe Bay
Willamette Mission State Park
**11** **Silverton**
Otter Crest Loop
Yaquina Head
**Albany**
**Salem**
**13 - 21**
**12** **Silver Falls State Park**
Mt. Jefferson
Newport
**22**
see detail map
22
*WILLAMETTE NATIONAL FOREST*
20
**Corvallis**
**23**
34
Waldport
Yachats
Cape Perpetua
Heceta Head
**Brownsville**
**24**
99E
**Sweet Home**
**25**
20
126
242
Sisters
(closed in winter)
*McKenzie Pass*
*SIUSLAW NATIONAL FOREST*
36
**McKenzie Bridge 26**
Florence
Springfield
126
**27**
**McKenzie River Highway**
Mt. Bachelor
126
*DESCHUTES NATIONAL FOREST*
Winchester Bay
**Cottage Grove**
**39**
58
Oakridge
Waldo Lake
*OREGON DUNES NAT'L. REC. AREA*
Reedsport
38
**Drain**
**40**
**Eugene**
**28 - 38**
see detail map
Willamette Pass
Umpqua Lighthouse
5
58
97
North Bend
Charleston
Coos Bay
Oakland
Steamboat
*UMPQUA NATIONAL FOREST*
Cape Arago State Park
Bandon
Myrtle Point
Winston
Roseburg
*UMPQUA VALLEY*
138
*CRATER LAKE NATIONAL PARK*
42
Wildlife Safari
Canyonville
*Crater Lake*
Port Orford
*Rogue R.*
Prospect
*ROGUE RIVER NATIONAL FOREST*
Agness
Gold Beach
Grants Pass
5
Medford
Upper Klamath Lake
101
*SISKIYOU NATIONAL FOREST*
199
238
Jacksonville
Ashland
Klamath Falls
Pistol River
Cave Junction
46
Loeb State Park
**Oregon Caves Nat'l. Monument**
Mt. Ashland
97
Harbor

CALIFORNIA

0        30 miles
0        45 km

kids accompanied by a guardian are permitted at the early show. ✉ *3505 Pacific Ave., 97116* ☎ *503/992–9533 or 877/992–9533* ⊕ *www. thegrandlodge.com* ↪ *77 rooms* ♨ *Spa, library, 3 bars, meeting rooms* ▤ *AE, D, DC, MC, V.*

**$** ⊡ **Oak Tree Bed & Breakfast.** Between the views of Mt. Hood and the carefully groomed rose gardens, you may not want to venture too far from this property. The Polyantha and Sunsprite rooms represent the proprietor's love for roses. If you're lucky, you might awaken to the aroma of freshly baked coffee cake and cinnamon rolls. ✉ *2300 N.W. Thatcher Rd., Forest Grove 97116* ☎ *503/357–6939* 🖷 *503/357–3297* ⊕ *www. oaktreebandb.com* ↪ *2 rooms* ♨ *Laundry facilities* ▤ *MC, V.*

## Sports & the Outdoors

BOWLING **Rainbow Lanes** (✉ 2748 19th Pl. ☎ 503/357–6321) has 16 wood lanes and a pro shop.

GOLF **Sunset Grove Golf Club** (✉ 41569 N.W. Osterman ☎ 503/357–6044) allows you to stroll through a 9-hole course while gazing at Mt. Hood. It has a small pro shop and a snack bar.

KAYAKING If you want to learn how to kayak or cross-country ski, **Adventurers Without Limits** (✉ 1341 Pacific Ave., 97116 ☎ 503/359–2568) has organized trips for these and other sports, with different excursions catering to adults, youth, and families.

## Shopping

Find antiques, jewelry, and housewares at **Collections in the Attic** (✉ 2020 Main St. ☎ 503/357–0316), built in 1875 as a general store. Medicinal herbs and spices are dispensed at **Oregon Meadow Herb Company** (✉ 238 S.E. 2nd Ave. ☎ 503/693–3540).

# Hillsboro

❷ *18 mi west of Portland on Hwy. 8.*

East Tualatin Plains was the original name for Hillsboro, but it was renamed for early settler David Hill, elected territorial governor before Oregon became a state. As trappers, Tualatin Indians, and others settled, the town began to grow and prosper and was incorporated in 1876. Over the past 20 years Hillsboro has experienced rapid growth associated with the Silicon Forest, where high-tech business found ample sprawling room. The population has grown to nearly 75,000 residents. Several of Intel's industrial campuses are in Hillsboro, as are the facilities of other leading electronics manufacturers. Businesses related to its original agricultural roots remain a significant part of Hillsboro's culture and economy. Alpaca ranches, nurseries, berry farms, nut and fruit orchards, and numerous wineries are among the area's most active agricultural businesses.

Every Saturday, from May through September, the **Hillsboro Saturday Market** sells fresh local produce—some from booths, some from the backs of trucks—as well as local arts and crafts. Live music is played throughout the day. ✉ *Main St. between 1st and 2nd Aves., and along 2nd Ave. between Main and Lincoln Sts.* ☎ *503/844–6685* ⊕ *www. tuesdaymarketplace.com* ⊙ *May–Sept., Sat. 8–1; Oct., Sat. 9–2.*

☺ The **County Museum** gives a glimpse of history through exhibits on early pioneers and the Tualatin Indians. Exhibits rotate, usually with a hands-on display geared toward children. ✉ *17677 N.W. Springville Rd.* ☎ *503/645–5353* 🎟 *$2* ⊙ *Mon.–Sat. 10–4:30.*

In 1938, Richard and Helen Rice began collecting beach agates. Over the years they developed one of the largest private mineral collections in the United States, which forms the foundation of the **Rice Northwest Museum of Rocks and Minerals.** The most popular item here is the Alma Rose Rhodochrosite, a 4-inch red crystal. The museum (in a ranch-style home) also has petrified wood from all over the world and a gallery of Northwest minerals, including specimens of rare crystallized gold. ✉ *26385 N.W. Groveland Dr., 97124* ☎ *503/647–2418* 🖷 *503/647– 5207* ⊕ *www.ricenwmuseum.org* 🎟 *$4.50* ⊙ *Wed.–Sun. 1–5.*

Part of the Tualatin River floodplain, the 710-acre **Jackson Bottom Wetlands Preserve** has several miles of trails. ✉ *2600 S.W. Hillsboro Hwy., 97123* ☎ *503/681–6424* 🖷 *503/681–6277 or 503/687–6026* ⊕ *www. jacksonbottom.org* ⊙ *Mon.–Sat. 10–4.*

Comprised of 61 acres of forest, **Rood Bridge Park** has river frontage and canoe-launching facilities, as well as a conference center. ✉ *4000 S.E. Rood Bridge Rd., From Hwy. 8 take River Rd. southeast to Rood Bridge Rd. Follow Rood Bridge Rd. south for a few blocks. Park is on east side of Rood Bridge Rd. as you cross river.*

A 13-acre grove of towering oak trees, **Shadywood Park** has a playground and a trail that winds through the park. ✉ *NE 24th Ave. and Laura St.*

## Wineries

Take in the splendid scenery of the Chehalem Mountain ridge at **Oak Knoll Winery** (✉ *29700 S.W. Burkhalter Rd.* ☎ *503/648–8198 or 800/ 625–5665* ⊕ *www.oakknollwinery.com*). For the unusual, try the native-American varietal Niagara or the Frambrosia Oregon Raspberry Wine, a special non-grape dessert wine. The winery is open weekdays 11–4 and weekends 11–5.

In the Chehalem Mountains, **Raptor Ridge** (✉ *29090 S.W. Wildhaven La.* ☎ *503/887–5595* 🖷 *503/628–6255* ⊕ *www.raptoridge.com*) produces around 2,000 cases of wine a year, using crops from several Willamette Valley wineries. Visits are by appointment only.

## Where to Stay & Eat

**$–$$** ✕ **Miller's Homestead Restaurant.** This family-style restaurant, around the corner from the Hillsboro Travelodge, serves such hearty repasts as meat loaf, pork chops, chicken-fried steak, and (on Friday and Saturday) prime rib. Pasta primavera is a local favorite. Miller's also serves breakfast all day. ✉ *640 S.E. 10th Ave., 97123* ☎ *503/640–4730* 🖷 *503/640–5108* 🖃 *AE, D, MC, V.*

**¢–$$** ✕ **Merchant of Venice Cafe.** A large hand-painted wall mural of Venice and goldish tones create warmth at this elegant but casual spot. Weekly specials might include ravioli stuffed with grilled asparagus and Taleggio cheese. ✉ *1341 N.E. Orenco Station Pkwy.* ☎ *503/640–1523* 🖷 *503/640–4603* ⊙ *Closed Sun.*

**¢–$$** ✕ **Shalimar.** Partake of wonderful breads such as the Onion Paneer Kulcha, leavened bread stuffed with onion and homemade cheese. Entrées include the stir-fried Afghani Lamb Karahi. Top off your meal with Gulab Jamon, a little round fried pastry often with pistachios and almonds. ✉ *1340 N.E. Orenco Station Pkwy.* ☎ *503/844–3838* 🖷 *503/ 648–6786* 🖃 *AE, D, DC, MC, V.*

**¢–$$** ✕ **Sports Look Restaurant.** A Gary Anthony's Portland Trailblazer jersey and assorted Oregon State University memorabilia are among the furnishings at this popular eatery connected to a bowling alley. The baby-back ribs are a favorite. ✉ *322 S.E. Washington St.* ☎ *503/693–9378* 🖃 *AE, D, MC.*

★ **¢–$** ✕ **Mazatlan Mexican Restaurant.** Though it's hidden away in a small shopping mall, this spot feels like a small village inside, with stunning murals and ceramic wall furnishings. Try the Mazatlan Dinner, a house specialty with sirloin, a chile relleno, and an enchilada, or *arroz con camarones,* prawns sautéed with vegetables. Save room for the flan or the *sopapillas* (fried dough). The kids' menu is a good value. ⊠ *20413 S. W. TV Hwy., Aloha 97006* ☎ *503/591–9536* ⊟ *AE, D, MC, V.*

$ ⌂ **Stonebrook Suites.** Stonebrook opened this property in 1999. Standing amid high-tech Silicon Forest companies, its nicely landscaped grounds and nine buildings have a residential feel. The fireplace in the lobby suggests a living room. Stonebrook prides itself on its comfortable suite accommodations with oversize bathrooms. ⊠ *6550 N.E. Brighton Dr., 97124* ☎ *503/268–6000 or 800/877–0807* ☐ *503/268–6050* ⊕ *www.stonebrooksuites.com* ⇋ *136 suites* ⚷ *In-room data ports, kitchenettes, microwaves, refrigerators, cable TV, pool, outdoor hot tub, gym, basketball, laundry service, laundry facilities* ⊟ *AE, D, DC, MC, V* ¶ *CP.*

## Sports & the Outdoors

BOWLING Sixteen wood lanes, with wood approaches, await at the **4 Seasons Bowling Center** (⊠ 322 S.E. Washington St. ☎ 503/648–3139).

FISHING Fish the well-stocked pond year-round at **Horning's Hideout** (⊠ 21277 N.W. Brunswick Canyon Rd., North Plains 97133 ☎ 503/647–2920 ⊕ www.horningshideout.com). It's on private land, so you won't need a license.

GOLF Built in 1927, **Forest Hills Golf Course** (⊠ 36260 S.W. Tongue La., Cornelius 97113 ☎ 503/357–3347) is an 18-hole course with a driving range and full-service pro shop. Fees are $15 for 9 holes, $30 for 18; carts are $10 per 9 holes. **Killarney West Golf Course** (⊠ 1270 N.W. 334th ☎ 503/648–7634) has 9 holes and a small pro shop. The largest public course is **Meriwether National Golf Course** (⊠ 5200 S.W. Rood Bridge Rd. ☎ 503/648–4143), with 27 holes, some along the Tualatin River. There's a pro shop, driving range, and restaurant. **Pumpkin Ridge Golf Course** (⊠ 12930 N.W. Old Pumpkin Ridge Rd., North Plains 97133 ☎ 503/647–4747 ☐ 503/647–2002) earned *Golf Digest*'s No. 1 ranking in 1992 for the best new public course. There are actually two courses: Ghost Creek is open for public play, and Witch Hollow is a members-only course.

## Shopping

Browse through a cornucopia of fruits and vegetables at **Fruteria La Cabana** (⊠ 451 S. 1st Ave. ☎ no phone), an indoor market where you'll get a flavor of Hillsboro's Mexican heritage. Chain stores, from Dollar Tree to natural food stores, as well as several restaurants, are in the **Hillsboro Market** (⊠ N.E. 25th Ave. and Cornell ☎ no phone). Spices in bulk, herbs, incense, and soaps are available at the **Oregon Meadow Herb Company** (⊠ 1918 Main St. ☎ 503/357–2132), which makes many of the products it sells.

# Beaverton

**❸** *7 mi west of Portland on Hwy. 8.*

Named for its location in the midst of a large network of beaver dams, Beaverton has itself become a network of residential neighborhoods, shopping areas, and business parks spanning 15 square mi. Once a small town surrounded by thriving Washington County farm fields, Beaverton today has well over 60,000 residents and is the fifth-largest community in Oregon. At 7 mi from Portland, it is considered Portland's long-expanding, affluent suburb to the west. The roots of Oregon's Silicon Forest are in Beaverton, with some of the state's largest high-tech employers contributing to the town's popularity. Among Beaverton's high-profile employers are Adidas and Nike, whose famous world-headquarters campus is regularly visited by celebrities. The town has more than 100 parks spread over 1,000 acres. There is an extensive system of hiking trails and bike paths, as well as many numerous public and private golf courses and tennis courts.

In the heart of the Silicon Forest is **Tualatin Hills Nature Park,** a real forest with creeks, ponds, fir trees, and red cedars. The 195-acre urban wilderness has, appropriately, beavers, as well as great blue herons and dozens of other bird species. There are several trails, some with boardwalks. To reach the park, take the MAX light rail to the Merlo Road station. No dogs are allowed. ⊠ *15655 S.W. Millikan Blvd., 97005* ☎ *503/644–5595* ⊕ *www.thprd.com/facilities/nature* ⊠ *Free* ☉ *Daily dawn–dusk.*

Trails, a wetland area, and a 10-acre pond stocked for fishing are at **Bethany Lake Park.** ⊠ *N.W. 185th Ave. N.W. at West Union Rd.* ☎ *503/645–6433* 🖶 *503/690–9649.*

At 22 acres, **Commonwealth Lake Park** has athletic fields, play equipment for rent, trails, wetlands, and a 3-acre fishing lake. ⊠ *S.W. Huntington Ave., S.W. Butner Rd., S.W. Foothills Dr.* ☎ *503/645–6433* 🖶 *503/690–9649.*

**Greenway Park** is on 80 acres and has playing fields, playground equipment, a wetland area, and trails, as well as a barbecue area. ⊠ *S.W. Hall Blvd. to S.W. Scholls Ferry Rd.* ☎ *503/645–6433* 🖶 *503/690–9649.*

## Wineries

Growing methods are a source of pride at **Cooper Mountain Vineyards** (⊠ 9480 S.W. Grabhorn Rd. 97007 ☎ 503/649–0027 ⊕ www.coopermountainwine.com), whose wines are made from organic grapes. The novelty of this 105-acre vineyard is that it's situated on Cooper Mountain, an extinct volcano. The vineyard is open February–December, daily 12–5, and in January by appointment.

Founded in 1970, **Ponzi Vineyards** (⊠ 14665 S.W. Winery La., Beaverton 97007 ☎ 503/628–1227 🖶 503/628–0354 ⊕ www.ponziwines. com) produces pinots and chardonnay, as well as Dolcetto and Arneis. The Ponzi family also launched the BridgePort Brewing Company in 1984 and run a wine bar and restaurant in Dundee (⇨ Dundee Bistro in Dundee). The winery is open daily from 11–5.

## Where to Stay & Eat

**$$–$$$$** ✕ **Pavilion Trattoria.** Amid the garden surroundings is fine seasonal Pacific Northwest cuisine, such as the grilled salmon served on a warm beet salad with roasted shallot vinaigrette or the apple-wood-smoked prime rib served with sweet onion rings. Early-bird suppers and a kids' menu are available, and the Sunday brunch is especially popular. ⊠ *10700 S.W. Allen Blvd., 97005* ☎ *503/626–4550* ⊟ *AE, DC, MC, V* ☉ *No lunch.*

**¢–$$$** ✕ **McCormick's Fish House & Bar.** The neighborhood feeling of this restaurant belies its association with the national chain. Try creative seasonal preparations such as macadamia-nut-crusted Alaskan halibut with mango–beurre blanc sauce or salmon baked on a cedar plank. Mounted fish are displayed on the ceiling of the rusty-brown main dining room. The restaurant is popular with local families. ⊠ *9945 S.W. Beaverton–Hillsdale Hwy.* ☎ *503/643–1322* ⊟ *AE, D, DC, MC, V* ☉ *No lunch Sun.*

**$–$$** ✕ **Sayler's Old Country Kitchen.** Home of the massive 72-ounce steak, this casual downtown restaurant also serves chicken and fish. A kids' menu is available. ✉ *4655 S.W. Griffith Dr., 97005* ☎ *503/644–1492* ▤ *AE, D, MC, V.*

¢–$$ ✕ **Thai Orchid Restaurant.** You'll be greeted and seated immediately at this modern spot, where snappy pop music plays in the background. Garlic shrimp and pad thai are the most popular dishes. ✉ ☎ *503/439–6693* 🖷 *503/439–6684* ▤ *AE, D, MC, V.*

¢–$ ✕ **Old Chicago Pasta & Pizza.** More than 130 types of beer are available at this combination sports bar–restaurant, with 10 of the on-tap brews hailing from Oregon. Creative pizzas include the zesty Thai Pie and a stuffed-spinach-artichoke pie. If you're a fan of Chicago sports teams, you'll enjoy the Sammy Sosa and Michael Jordan memorabilia, but especially original furnishings include large model planes crafted by the general manager. ✉ *17950 N.W. Evergreen Pkwy.* ☎ *503/533–4650* ▤ *AE, D, DC, MC, V.*

$ 🏨 **Phoenix Inn.** Off U.S. Highway 26, this four-story hotel has bright, clean rooms. A Continental buffet breakfast is among the amenities. ✉ *15402 N.W. Cornell Rd., 97006* ☎ *503/614–8100 or 888/944–8100* 🛏 *98 rooms* 🏷 *Microwaves, refrigerators, cable TV, indoor pool, exercise equipment, hot tub* ▤ *AE, D, DC, MC, V* ❘○❘ *CP.*

¢–$ 🏨 **Pepper Tree Motor Inn.** At this motel-style inn, built in 1979, you can park right outside your room. It's on the edge of Beaverton in a quiet residential area about 1 mi from downtown. ✉ *10720 S.W. Allen Blvd., 97005* ☎ *503/641–7477 or 800/453–6219* 🖷 *503/641–7477* ✑ *www.peppertreeinn.com* 🛏 *73 rooms* 🏷 *Microwaves, refrigerators, cable TV, in-room VCRs, pool, outdoor hot tub, laundry facilities, business services* ▤ *AE, D, DC, MC, V* ❘○❘ *CP.*

## Shopping

Fruits, vegetables, and flowers are among the bounty provided by the almost 200 growers at **Beaverton Farmers Market** (✉ S.W. Hall Blvd. between 3rd and 5th Sts., south of Farmington Rd. ☎ 503/643–5345 🖷 503/244–3927 ⊕ www.beavertonfarmersmarket.com), open from the first Wednesday of July until the end of September. The **Beaverton-Tanasbourne Town Center** (✉ 18000 N.W. Evergreen Pkwy. ☎ no phone) has Haggen Food and Pharmacy as its cornerstone, as well as a Starbuck's. Produce and live seafood are available at **Uwajimaya Asian Food Store** (✉ 10500 S.W. Beaverton–Hillsdale Hwy. ☎ 503/643–4512), a large Japanese and Asian supermarket.

# Lake Oswego

❹ *9 mi south of Portland*

Contrary to the intentions of its early founders, who built iron smelters in an effort to turn the area into "the Pittsburgh of the West," Lake Oswego is an affluent residential community immediately to the south of Portland, between the Willamette and Tualatin rivers. The Willamette Shore Trolley, operated by the Oregon Electric Railway Historical Society, carries passengers along the Willamette between downtown Lake Oswego and the Riverplace area at the south end of Portland's downtown.

Framed by an open fireplace on one end and a reflecting pond on the other, **Millennium Plaza Park** is the site of many community events as well as a Saturday farmer's market. ✉ *200 1st St., 97034* ☎ *503/675–3983* ⊗ *Mid-May–mid-Oct., Sat. 8–1.*

**Cooks Butte Park** consists of 42 acres of informal pathways and undeveloped land. ✉ *Delenka La.* ☎ *no phone.*

A circular 7-mi route around Lake Oswego, **Lake Loop** is popular with joggers, walkers, or mere gazers of scenery.

Originally built in 1887, the **Willamette Shore Trolley**—one standard and one double-decker trolley, both of museum quality—carries passengers on a 45-minute ride to Portland along a scenic 7-mi route, which you can travel one-way or round-trip; you'll take in Mt. Hood and the wooded banks of the Willamette River. In summer, there are four departures daily from Lake Oswego. Reservations are recommended. In December, there are special Lights Along the River excursions. ✉ *311 State St., 97034* ☎ *503/697–7436* ⊕ *www.trainweb.org/oerhs/wst.htm* ✏ *$9 round-trip* ⊙ *May 1–Memorial Day, weekends; Memorial Day–Labor Day, Thurs.–Sun.; Labor Day–end of Sept., Fri.–Sun.*

## Where to Stay & Eat

**$$–$$$**  ✕**Amadeus.** Reserve a table overlooking the river, select a bottle of wine from the extensive wine list—preferably an Oregon wine—and settle in for a sensuous experience. Winners are the Willapa Bay oysters, slightly panfried; the wilted spinach salad; and the pistachio-crusted salmon. ✉ *148 B Ave., 97034* ☎ *503/636–7500* 🖷 *503/636–6233* ▭ *AE, DC, MC, V.*

**$$–$$$**  ✕**Riccardo's Ristorante.** You can dine outside in the Italian courtyard or in the softly lit dining room among the real estate agents who frequent this place, charming their clients with chatter of the merits of this residential neighborhood. All the ingredients are organic and hormone-free. Try the eight-layer lasagna smothered in béchamel sauce. ✉ *16035 S.W. Boones Ferry, 97035* ☎ *503/636–4104* ▭ *AE, DC, MC, V* ⊙ *Closed Sun.*

**$–$$**  🏨**Crowne Plaza.** A complimentary van service within a 5-mi radius, upon availability, is one plus of this property with modern rooms. A bed-and-breakfast package is available. Pets up to 30 pounds are permitted in the rooms at a $10 per-day charge. ✉ *14811 S.W. Kruse Oaks Blvd., 97035* ☎ *503/624–8400* 🖷 *503/684–8324* ⊕ *www.crowneplaza.com* 📞 *161 rooms* ⚐ *Restaurant, room service, indoor-outdoor pool, exercise equipment, hot tub, bar, business services, Internet, parking, some pets allowed (fee)* ▭ *AE, D, DC, MC, V.*

**$–$$**  🏨**Lakeshore Inn.** On the lake and within walking distance of the Millennium Park, theaters, restaurants, and shopping, this property has several nifty touches like a heated lakeside pool, private decks, personal voice mail, and complimentary newspapers and pastries. Ample rooms, from a studio to two-bedroom suites, have lakeside views. Some have private patios. ✉ *210 N. State St., 97034* ☎ *503/636–9679 or 800/215–6431* 🖷 *503/636–6959* ✉ *stay@thelakeshoreinn.com* 📞 *33 rooms* ⚐ *In-room data ports, kitchens, microwaves, refrigerators, cable TV, pool, laundry service, no-smoking rooms* ▭ *AE, D, DC, MC, V* ⊙| *CP.*

**$**  🏨**Phoenix Inn—Lake Oswego.** Three miles from the Washington Square Mall, this all-minisuites motel has spacious rooms with picturesque views of Lake Oswego and a patio for relaxing. ✉ *14905 S.W. Bangy Rd., 97034* ☎ *503/624–7400 or 800/824–9992* 🖷 *503/624–7405* 📞 *62 suites* ⚐ *In-room data ports, minibars, microwaves, refrigerators, cable TV, indoor pool, exercise equipment, hot tub, laundry facilities, business services* ▭ *AE, D, DC, MC, V* ⊙| *CP.*

# Oregon City

**⑤** *6 mi southwest of Newberg on Hwy. 99 W.*

Many bits of western U.S. history converge in Oregon City. It was the first incorporated city west of the Rocky Mountains, the first capital of the Territorial government in 1848, site of the first Oregon legislative session, and site of the only federal and district court west of the Rockies in 1849, when the city of San Francisco was platted. (The plat, filed in 1850, is still in Oregon City.)

Oregon City was the destination for thousands of pioneer families, who traveled the Oregon Trail from St. Louis, Missouri, to the promised land on the western frontier. Several of Oregon's prominent early residents built homes in Oregon City on the Willamette River's east bank, where the river plunges 40 feet over a basaltic ridge at Willamette Falls. The official End of the Oregon Trail Interpretive Center in Oregon City debuted in 1993 to commemorate the 150-year anniversary of the Oregon Trail. Dozens of historic homes, churches, and other buildings have been restored and now offer tours into times past. More than 26,000 people live here today; the city is the seat of Clackamas County, one of three counties that make up the Portland metropolitan area.

Resembling three large covered wagons, the **End of the Oregon Trail Interpretive Center,** 19 mi south of Portland, is hard to miss. The history of the Oregon Trail is brought to life through theatrical shows, exhibits, and hands-on activities. Maps and guidebooks are available if you're charting a trip along the Oregon Trail from one end to the other. ✉ 1726 *Washington St., Oregon City* ☎ *503/657–9336* ⊕ *www. endoftheoregontrail.org* ✉ *Store free, show $5.50* ☉ *Store Mon.–Sat. 9–5, Sun. 10–5. Shows Memorial Day–Labor Day, Mon.–Sat. 10–4, Sun. 10:45–4; Labor Day–Memorial Day, Wed.–Sat. 10–3:30, Sun. 11–3:30.*

Waterfowl are part-time residents at the ½-acre **John Inskeep Environmental Learning Center** on the Clackamas Community College campus. The property has a trail that circles two ponds at the headwaters of Newell Creek. ✉ *19600 S. Molalla* ☎ *503/657–6958 Ext. 2351* 🖶 *503/650–6669* ⊕ *www.clackamas.cc.or.us/elc* ✉ *$2 donations accepted* ☉ *Daily dawn–dusk.*

Built in 1845, **Ermatinger House** was the first frame house built in Oregon City and the only two-story Federal-style house in the state with a flat roof. The McLoughlin Memorial Association moved the house to save it from development, and then in 1986 it was moved again to 6th and John Adams. For groups, hosts will present a Living History Tea. ✉ *6th and John Adams* ☎ *503/656–1619, 503/557–9199 tours* ✉ *$2* ☉ *Fri.–Sun. 1–4.*

An officer for a fur-trading company, Dr. John McLoughlin lost his job when he forwarded supplies to needy Oregon Trail pioneers, but his presence and deeds in the area are remembered at **McLoughlin House National Historic Site,** the mansion he moved to with his family in 1846. The site is perhaps the key historic home in the city; another, owned by the McLoughlin Memorial Association, is **Rose Farm** (✉ Holmes La. at Rilance St.). It is open March–October, daily 1–4; admission is $2. ✉ 713 *Center St.* ☎ *503/656–5146* ⊕ *www.mcloughlinhouse.org* ✉ *$4* ☉ *Feb.–Dec., Tues.–Sat. 10–4, Sun. 1–4.*

**Stevens Crawford Heritage House** celebrates the contributions of two Oregon City natives. Harley Stevens joined the Emigrant Escort Service to help protect pioneers on the Oregon Trail, and he went on to become the first telegraph operator in Oregon City. Mary Crawford was a important member of the Women's Christians Temperance Union. When the house was built in 1908, it was one of the first homes to have indoor plumbing and both gas and electric light fixtures. Special events such as tea and luncheon provide a living-history lesson as the hosts wear era-specific attire. ✉ *603 6th St., 97045* ☎ *503/655–2866* ✉ *$4* ☉ *Wed.–Fri. noon–4, weekends 1–4.*

Artifacts dating back 10,000 years are on display at the **Museum of the Oregon Territory.** One such display examines the ways different tribes of the Northwest gathered to trade with the Chinooks; another exhibit takes up the history of wedding fashion. ✉ *211 Tumwater Dr., 97045* ☎ *503/ 655–5574* 🖨 *503/655–0035* ⊗ *Weekdays 10–4, weekends noon–4.*

Along the Clackamas River and only 45 minutes from Portland, **Milo McIver State Park** is a popular rafting, canoeing, and kayaking area. An annual Civil War reenactment is staged here in April; 300 actors participate. A campground has 44 electrical and 9 primitive sites. ✉ *Rte. 213 N to Rte. 212 and Rte. 211 SE* ☎ *503/630–7150 or 800/551–6949* ⊕ *www.prd. state.or.us* 🖾 *Day use $3 per vehicle* ⊗ *Daily; some areas Mar.–Nov.*

Best known for its fruit and berry wine, **Wasson Brothers Winery**, in the hills outside Sandy, 21 mi northeast of Oregon City, enjoys a growing reputation for its grapes. Wine tasting is free. ✉ *41901 Hwy. 26, Sandy 97055* ☎ *503/668–3124* ⊕ *www.wassonbrotherswinery.com* 🖨 *503/ 668–3124* ⊗ *Daily 9–5.*

The Willamette Falls are created when the Willamette River at Oregon City spills 40 feet over a basaltic ridge. The **Willamette Falls Locks** were built in the early 1870s to move river traffic around the falls. ✉ *On Willamette River, in West Linn* ☎ *503/656–3381* ⊗ *Daily. Information Center Apr.–Oct., daily 9:30–8; Nov.–Mar., daily 7:30–6.*

### Where to Stay & Eat

¢–$$$ ✕ **Jimmy Os Pizzeria.** Large parties are drawn to this spacious spot, part family pizza joint, part community hangout. While waiting for your home-made pie, admire the drawings of Oregon City historic homes or plug some quarters into the jukebox. ✉ *1678 Beavercreek Rd., 97045* ☎ *503/655–6329* ⊟ *AE, D, MC, V.*

¢ ✕ **McMenamins Pub.** At this bustling family favorite you can order a Com-munication Breakdown Burger—Tillamook cheddar, onions, mush-rooms, and peppers—among others, including a few meatless options. Couple your burger or sandwich with a creative ale like chocolaty Black Rabbit Porter or raspberry Ruby Ale. Kid-pleasing comfort foods in-clude grilled cheese, corn dogs, and peanut butter and jelly. The pub be-comes more of a bar scene after 10 PM. ✉ *102 9th St., 97045* ☎ *503/ 655–8032* ⊟ *AE, D, MC, V.*

¢–$$$ 🏨 **Rivershore Hotel.** All rooms overlook the Willamette River and have decks with patio furniture. The property is close to shopping and restau-rants, though there's a restaurant on site; a complimentary and hot made-to-order breakfast is included in the rate. ✉ *1900 Clackamette Dr., 97045* ☎ *503/655–7141 or 800/443–7777* ⊕ *www.rivershorehotel.com* 🖨 *503/ 655–1927* 🛏 *120 rooms* ♦ *Restaurant, room service, cable TV, pool, hot tub, bar, some pets allowed (fee)* ⊟ *AE, D, DC, MC, V* 🍴 *BP.*

$ 🏨 **Tolle House Bed & Breakfast.** Though Viola Tolle has never had any-thing to do with the legendary Toll House cookies, she found that peo-ple expected the treats, which prompted her to give a cookie jar to every guest. Her complimentary breakfast might include blueberry pancakes and fresh fruit compote. One room has a rhapsody decor, another a French country flavor, and the third is a combination. Rooms will be outfitted with masculine or feminine furnishings at your request. ✉ *15921 Hunter, 97045* ☎ *503/655–4325* 🛏 *3 rooms* ⊟ *No credit cards* 🍴 *BP.*

¢–$ 🏨 **Brookside Bed and Breakfast.** The grounds of this hillside country home in Sandy are populated by chickens, ducks, geese, peacocks, goats, and llamas. There's a koi pond and perennial flower beds on the 7 acres of wooded property. The owner is an antiques dealer, and the guest rooms are furnished in different and eclectic styles. A hearty breakfast is served family-style in the dining area. ✉ *45232 S.E. Paha Loop* 🖃 *Box 1112, Sandy 97055* ☎ *503/668–4766* ⊕ *www.brooksidebandb.com* 🛏 *5 rooms* ♦ *Picnic area, laundry facilities; no a/c, no room phones, no smok-ing, no TV in some rooms* ⊟ *No credit cards* 🍴 *BP.*

## Nightlife & the Arts

The **McLoughlin Theatre** at Clackamas Community College (✉ 19600 S. Molalla Ave., 97045 ☎ 503/657–6958) showcases plays from local troupes and student productions. You'll get the blues Thursday through Saturday, plus a full menu and bar, at **Trail's End Saloon** (✉ 1320 Main St. ☎ 503/656–3031). If you'd rather not partake of the karaoke at **Wichita Bar and Grill** (✉ 19140 Molalla Ave., 97045 ☎ 503/557–0277), shoot some pool or nibble from the full menu of steak, burgers, and seafood.

## Sports & the Outdoors

Built in 1922, **Oregon City Golf Club** (✉ 20124 S. Beavercreek Rd. 97045-9554 ☎ 503/518–2846) charges $25 for 18 holes on weekends and $20 during the week. Walk-ons are permitted only during the week, and weekend tee times should be booked at least two weeks in advance. Opened in 2002, **Stone Creek Golf Club** (✉ 14603 S. Stoneridge Dr., 97045 ☎ 503/518–4653 ☎ 503/518–3299) charges $39 for 18 and $23 for 9 holes Friday–Sunday, including holidays. Weekday rates run $35 for 18 holes and $20 for 9. There are packages available that include snacks and course transportation, and there's a deli on site.

ICE-SKATING Enjoy modern facilities for open skating or work on your figure skating or stick skills at the **Sherwood Ice Arena** (✉ 20407 S.W. Borchers Dr., Sherwood 97140 ☎ 503/625–5757). If watching is more your thing, try to catch the NHL stars of tomorrow, the Portland Jr. Hawks. Admission is $6; skate rental is $2.50.

## Shopping

A retail nursery and produce market, **Dog Leg Ranch** (✉ 28300 N.E. Wilsonville Rd., 97132 ☎ 503/554–0711) entices people to stop with its eye-catching displays. It's open daily 10–6. Cindy Leffler left home to get a degree in sculpture and jewelry, and when she returned she opened **Manney B's** (✉ 211 E. 1st St. ☎ 503/554–0455). She has since moved her operation from her garage to this 1,800-square-foot space, where she crafts custom jewelry using locally cut and semi-precious stones. The shop is open Tuesday–Friday 10:30–6, Saturday 10:30–4.

# Newberg

**6** *25 mi southwest of Portland on Hwys. 99 W and 18.*

Fertile fields of the Willamette Valley surround the community of Newberg, named by the first postmaster for his Bavarian hometown, Newburgh. Many of its early settlers were Quakers from the Midwest who founded the school that has become George Fox University, an accredited four-year institution. Newberg's most famous resident, likewise a Quaker, was Herbert Hoover, the 31st president of the United States. For about five years during his adolescence, he lived with an aunt and uncle at the Hoover-Minthorn House, now a museum listed on the National Register of Historic Places. In addition to numerous well-reputed wineries, the Newberg area also offers slightly more out-of-the-ordinary entertainment, with tours of nine llama ranches and the Pacific Northwest's largest hot-air balloon company. St. Paul, a historic town with a population of about 325, is about 8 mi south of Newberg and 20 mi north of Salem. Every July, St. Paul holds a professional rodeo.

Named by *U.S. News and World Report* one of America's Best Colleges, the small **George Fox College,** founded by the Quakers in 1884, is on a 75-acre shady campus in a residential neighborhood. Centennial Tower is surrounded by a campus quad and academic buildings, the library, and the student commons. Hess Creek Canyon cuts through the campus. ✉ *414 N. Meridian* ☎ *503/538–8383 Ext. 222* ⊕ *www.georgefox. edu* 🎫 *Free* ⊘ *Daily.*

The oldest and most significant of Newberg's original structures is the **Hoover-Minthorne House,** the boyhood home of President Herbert Hoover. Built in 1881, the preserved frame house still has many of the original furnishings. Outside is the woodshed that no doubt played an important role in shaping young "Bertie" Hoover's character. ✉ *115 S. River St.* ☎ *503/538–6629* 🎫 *$2* ⊘ *Mar.–Nov., Wed.–Sun. 1–4; Dec. and Feb., weekends 1–4.*

The drive-in is a perpetual novelty, and **99W Drive-in** is a good bet for a double feature. Ted Francis built this one in 1953 and operated it until his death at 98; the business is now run by his grandson. The first film begins at dusk. Kids 6–11 get in for $3, and children 5 and under are free. ✉ *Hwy. 99 W (Portland Rd.), west of Springbrook Rd. intersection* ☎ *503/538–2738* 🎫 *$6 per person, $9 min. vehicle charge* ⊘ *Fri.–Sun.*

### Wineries

A popular producer of pinot noir, **Adelsheim Vineyard** (✉ 16800 N.E. Calkins La. ☎ 503/538–3652 📠 503/538–2248 ⊕ www. adelsheimvineyard.com) holds $10 tastings. Visitors are welcome by appointment and on Memorial Day and Thanksgiving weekends.

**Rex Hill Vineyards** (✉ 30835 N. Hwy. 99 W ☎ 503/538–0666 ⊕ www. rexhill.com), on a hill east of Newberg, produces some of the best pinot noir wines in Oregon, wines that more than hold their own against ones from California, France, and other high-profile locales. It's open daily from 11–5.

### Sports & the Outdoors

BALLOONING  If you're intrigued by what it might feel like to have the Earth gently moving toward you, ride with **Vista Balloon Adventures** (🔖 701 S.E. Sherk Pl., Sherwood 97140 ☎ 503/625–7385 or 800/622–2309 📠 503/625–3845), which has several balloons taking off daily from Sportsman Airpark in Newberg. From April through October, FAA licensed pilots take the balloons about 1,500 feet over Yamhill County's wine country. Part of the fun is that this is a hands-on experience: you and your fellow passengers assist in the inflation and deflation of the balloon. You'll have a bird's-eye view of a colorful patchwork quilt of vineyards and fields, mist blanketing treetops and the quietly winding Willamette River, and, weather permitting, you might briefly touch down on the river. You'll ultimately land in any number of places in Yamhill County depending on the winds (pilots are in constant contact with each other and the ground, and a van transports you back to the airfield). A welcome treat upon your return is a hot and hearty B&B-style brunch with libations, along with an "ascension certificate." The experience, including the set-up, flight, take-down, and meal, lasts a little over three hours (the flight is about an hour). Rates are $179 per person ($160 for a group of four or more). The question is popped during Engagement Flights ($450 per couple), and weddings (flight rates vary) with a modest size wedding party—the basket holds 6–10 passengers—have also been officiated in flight.

# Dundee & Yamhill

❼ *6 mi southwest of Newberg on Hwy. 99 W.*

William Reid traveled to Oregon from Dundee, Scotland. As he became interested in the railway business, he got support from his homeland to finance the Oregon Railway Co., Ltd. After the city was incorporated in 1895, Dundee was named after Reid's hometown in recognition of its support.

The lion's share (more than 90%) of the U.S. hazelnut crop is grown in Dundee, a haven of produce stands and tasting rooms. The 25 mi of Highway 18 between Dundee and Grande Ronde, in the Coast Range, roll through the heart of the Yamhill Valley wine country; wide shoulders and relatively light traffic earned the route a "most suitable" rating from the *Oregon Bicycling Guide*.

## Wineries

The tasting room of **Argyle Winery** (✉ 691 Hwy. 99W, Dundee 97115 ☎ 503/538–8520 ⊕ www.argylewinery.com), a producer of highly regarded sparkling wines, is in a restored Victorian farmhouse in Dundee. Hours are daily 11–5.

Merlot, chardonnay, and Gewürztraminer are among the wines emanating from **Duck Pond Cellars** (✉ 23145 Hwy. 99 W, 97115 ☎ 503/538–3199 or 800/437–3213 ⊕ www.duckpondcellars.com). Tasting is free and the tasting room also stocks goodies to buy. Picnicking in the outdoor seating area is encouraged. The winery is open November–April, daily 11–5 and May–October, daily 10–5.

**Sokol Blosser** (✉ 5000 Sokol Blosser La., 3 mi west of Dundee off Hwy. 99 W ☎ 503/864–2282 or 800/582–6668 ⊕ www.sokolblosser.com), one of Oregon's oldest and largest wineries, has a tasting room and walk-through vineyard with a self-guided tour that explains the grape varieties—pinot noir and chardonnay, among others. It's open daily 11–5.

While the winery of **Torii Mor** (✉ 18325 N.E. Fairview Dr., Dundee 97115 ☎ 503/538–2279 ⊕ www.toriimorwinery.com) is in nearby McMinnville, the tasting room and Japanese garden are in Dundee. Pinot noir is their primary product. You can visit the winery by appointment; the tasting room is open weekends noon–5, but closed in January.

**WillaKenzie Estate** (✉ 19143 N.E. Laughlin Rd., 12 mi from Newberg [head west on Hwy. 240 and north on Laughlin], Yamhill ☎ 503/662–3280 or 888/953–9463 ⊕ www.willakenzie.com) began operation of its ultramodern gravity-feed system in 1995. Its two inaugural wines, the 1995 pinot gris and pinot blanc, have enjoyed critical acclaim. It's open Memorial Day–Labor Day daily noon–5, mid-January–mid-December, weekends noon–5, and by appointment the remainder of the year.

## Where to Stay & Eat

$$$   ✕ **Tina's.** Chef–proprietors Tina and David Bergen bring a powerful one-
Fodor'sChoice   two punch to this Dundee favorite that often lures Portlanders away from
★   their own restaurant scene. The couple shares cooking duties—Tina does the baking and is often on hand to greet you—and David brings his experience as a former caterer and employee of nearby Sokol Blosser Winery to the table, ensuring that you have the right glass of wine—and there are many—to match your course. Fish and game vie for attention on the country French menu—entrees might include grilled Oregon salmon or Alaskan halibut, or a double cut pork chop, rack of lamb, or rib-eye steak. Avail yourself of any special soups, particularly if there's corn chowder in the house. A lunch menu includes soup, sandwiches, and Tina's grilled hamburger, made with free range beef. Service is as intimate and laid-back as the interior. A double fireplace divides the dining room, with heavy glass brick shrouded by bushes on the highway side, so you're not bothered by the traffic on Hwy. 99. ✉ *760 Hwy. 99W* ☎ *503/538–8880* ▭ *AE, D, MC, V.*

$–$$$  ✗ **Dundee Bistro.** Opened in 1999, this 80-seat restaurant uses Northwest organic foods such as Draper Valley chicken and local produce. Vaulted ceilings provide an open feeling inside, warmed by abundant fresh flowers and the works of local Oregon artists. The bistro is one piece of what the wine-making Ponzi family describes as the state's first "culinary center;" also part of the property are Your Northwest, a specialty food market, and the Ponzi Wine Bar, which serves Oregon wines, most prominently those from the family's winery (⇨ Ponzi Vineyards in Beaverton). ⊠ *100-A S.W. 7th St., Dundee 97115* ☎ *503/554–1650* 🖃 *AE, DC, MC, V.*

$–$$$$  🏨 **The Flying M Ranch.** Rendered in a style best described as Daniel Boone eclectic, a log lodge is the centerpiece of this 625-acre ranch, perched above the steelhead-filled Yamhill River. Choose between somewhat austere cabins (the cozy, hot-tub-equipped Honeymoon Cabin is the nicest) and riverside hotel units. In keeping with the rustic tone, there are no TVs or telephones. Book ahead for a Flying M specialty: the Steak Fry Ride, on which you climb aboard your choice of a horse or a tractor-drawn wagon and ride into the mountains for a feast of barbecued steak with all the trimmings. ⊠ *23029 N.W. Flying M Rd. (from McMinnville, off Hwy. 99 W head north on North Baker Rd.—which becomes West Side Rd.—for 5 mi, head west on Meadowlake Rd., and follow signs), Yamhill 97148* ☎ *503/662–3222* 🖶 *503/662–3202* ⊕ *www.flying-m-ranch.com* ⌕ *24 units, 7 cabins, more than 100 campsites* ⚐ *Restaurant, tennis court, fishing, basketball, hiking, horseback riding, horseshoes, bar* 🖃 *AE, D, DC, MC, V.*

**Fodor's Choice**
★

## Champoeg State Park

❽ *9 mi from Newberg, south on Hwy. 219 and east on Champoeg Rd.*

Pronounced "sham-*poo*-ee," this 615-acre state park on the south bank of the Willamette River is on the site of a Hudson's Bay Company trading post, granary, and warehouse that was built in 1813. This was the seat of the first provisional government in the Northwest. The settlement was abandoned after a catastrophic flood in 1861, then rebuilt and abandoned again after the flood of 1890. The park's wide-open spaces, groves of oak and fir, modern visitor center, museum, and historic buildings yield vivid insight into pioneer life. Tepees and wagons are also displayed here. There are 10 mi of hiking and cycle trails, and a campground has 48 electrical and 58 tent sites and 6 yurts.

Robert Newell was among the inaugural American settlers in the Willamette Valley and helped establish the town of Champoeg; a replica of his 1844 home, what is now the **Newell House Museum** (⊠ 8089 Champoeg Rd. NE, St. Paul 97137 ☎ 503/678–5537), was rebuilt inside the park grounds in 1959 and paid for by the Oregon State Society Daughters of the American Revolution. The first floor is furnished with 1860s antiques. Pioneer quilts and a collection of gowns worn by the wives of Oregon governors at inaugurations are displayed on the second floor. There's also a pioneer jail and schoolhouse. Admission is $2. It's open March through October, Friday–Sunday 1–5, Wednesday and Thursday by appointment. Also on park grounds is the historic **Pioneer Mother's Memorial Log Cabin** (⊠ 8035 Champoeg Rd. NE, St. Paul 97137 ☎ 503/633–2237), with pioneer artifacts from the Oregon Trail era. Admission is $2. It's open February–November, Monday–Saturday noon–5. ⊠ *8239 Champoeg Rd. NE, St. Paul 97137* ☎ *800/551–6949* ⌕ *$3 per vehicle* ☉ *Memorial Day–Labor Day, daily 10–6; Labor Day–Memorial Day, weekdays 8–4, weekends noon–4.*

off the
beaten
path

**OLD AURORA COLONY –** A fascinating slice of Oregon's pioneer past, the colony was the only major 19th-century communal society in the Pacific Northwest. Created by Germans in 1856, this frontier society espoused a "Love thy neighbor" philosophy, shared labor and property, and was known for its hospitality. Aurora retains many white frame houses dating from the 1860s and 1870s. Several structures have been incorporated into the Old Aurora Colony Museum (2nd and Liberty Sts. 503/678–5754, $2), which provides an overview of the colony's way of life. Follow an easy self-guided tour of the historic district, or take the guided walking tour ($3.50) given during special events. The colony is open Tuesday–Saturday 10–4, Sunday noon–4. ⌖ *About 14 mi from Champoeg State Park; take Champoeg Rd. east to Arndt Rd.; pass under I–5 and turn south onto Airport Rd., then east onto Ehlen Rd.* ⊕ *www. auroracolonymuseum.com.*

## McMinnville

⑨ *14 mi south of Newberg on Hwy. 99 W.*

The Yamhill County seat, McMinnville lies at the center of Oregon's burgeoning wine industry. There is a larger concentration of wineries in Yamhill County than in any other area of the state, and the vineyards in the McMinnville area, including some in the town of Dayton to the east, also produce the most award-winning wines. Among the varieties are chardonnay, pinot noir, and pinot gris. Most of the wineries in the area offer tours and tastings. McMinnville's downtown area, with a pleasantly disproportionate amount of bookstores and art galleries for its size, is well worth exploring; many of the historic district buildings, erected from 1890–1915, are still standing and are remarkably well-maintained.

Fodor'sChoice ★ The claim to fame of the **Evergreen Aviation Museum** is the Hughes (H-4) HK-1 Flying Boat, better known by its more sibilant nickname, the *Spruce Goose,* on permanent display here. The famous plane, which eccentric millionaire Howard Hughes flew only once—on November 2, 1947—was moved to Portland in 1992 from Long Beach, California, and eventually shipped to McMinnville in pieces; reassembly was completed on the 60th anniversary of the Pearl Harbor bombing, December 7, 2001. Supporting a maximum take-off weight of 400,000 pounds (think two Sherman tanks or 750 troops as one-time potential cargo, along with the flight crew and the weight of the equipment and fuel), the aircraft has a wingspan longer than a football field and its end zones, with the tail rising higher than an eight-story building. Statistics aside, it's something you'll just need to gawk at for a long moment. And while you won't be given the run of the flight deck, you will be permitted to walk around the immense fuselage. Hughes hated the aircraft's nickname, in part because the plane is largely composed of laminated birch; spruce is only employed in the wing spars. The craft won its perch here through a proposal submitted by the museum's founder, Captain Michael King Smith, a U.S. Air Force and Oregon Air National Guard F-15 pilot who died in an auto accident in 1995. The museum and the Captain Michael King Smith Educational Institute, chaired by Smith's father, commemorate Capt. Smith's commitment to aviation as well as the service of all military veterans. If you can take your eyes off the Spruce Goose there are also more than 45 historic planes and replicas here from the early years of flight and World War II, as well as the post war and modern eras. Among the aircraft are a Spitfire, a C-47 "Gooney Bird," a Messerschmitt Bf 109, and the sleek SR-71 Blackbird, which set both speed and high altitude records as "the world's fastest spy plane." Among the replicas are a Wright 1903—the craft the Wright brothers used for the first sustained powered flight. If you're curious to know which of these planes are still flyable, look for the telltale oil pan resting on the floor underneath the aircraft. There's a museum store and café—the Spruce Goose Café, of course—and there are ongoing educational programs and special events. ⊠ *365 N. E. Three Mile La.,* ☎ *503/434–4206* ⊕ *www.sprucegoose.org* ⊠ *$9.50* ⊙ *Daily 9–5.*

A perennial football powerhouse in NCAA Division III, **Linfield College** is an outpost of brick and ivy amid McMinnville's farmers'-market bustle. The college, founded in 1849 and the second oldest in Oregon, hosts the **International Pinot Noir Celebration** (☎ 800/775–4762) at the end of July and beginning of August. ⊠ *Linfield Ave. east of Hwy. 18* ⊕ *www.linfield.edu.*

> **need a break?** Try Tillamook Ice Cream on a waffle cone at **Serendipity Ice Cream** (⊠ 502 N.E. 3rd St. ☎ 503/474–9189), an old-fashioned ice cream parlor in the former Cook's Hotel; the building was constructed in 1886.

## Wineries

Its original tasting area was the back of a 1952 Ford pick-up. Its Gamay noir label notes that the wine gives "more enjoyment to hamburgers & fried chicken." And the winery's current architecture still includes a trailer affectionately referred to as the "mobile chateau," already on the property when winemaker Myron Redford purchased the winery in 1974. These modest and whimsical touches underscore what seems to be Redford's philosophy for **Amity Vineyards** (⊠ 18150 Amity Vineyards Road SE, Amity 97101 ☎ 503/835–2362): take your winemaking a lot more seriously than you take yourself. Resisting trends—in fact, bucking them—Redford has over the years divorced himself from methods and grapes embraced by other wineries; he got out of the chardonnay business because he felt pinot blanc better showcased the flavors of local grapes, and to bring out the taste of the fruit he uses only neutral oak or fiberglass or stainless steel tanks. Taste the pinot blanc for yourself for Redford's take on the grape, and also linger in the tasting room to sample the pinot noir and the Gewürztraminer, among other varieties. Chocolates made with Amity's pinot noir and other products are available for sale. Also drink in the impressive view of Yamhill County while you're here, and don't miss a chance to walk among the vines with Myron if he's available. Hours are daily noon–5, February–December.

In Dundee's Red Hills, **Domaine Serene** (⊠ 6555 N.E. Hilltop La., Dayton ☎ 503/864–4600 ⊕ www.domaineserene.com) is a world-class five-level winery and a well-regarded producer of Oregon pinot noir. It's open Memorial Day and Thanksgiving weekends and otherwise by appointment.

If Oregon presents the problem of so many wines, so little time, the **Oregon Wine Tasting Room and The Bellevue Market** (⊠ 19690 S.W. Hwy. 18 97128 ☎ 503/843–3787) provides a handy one-stop tasting venue, with 150 wines from 70 Oregon wineries, some of which are only open to the public twice a year. There's also a gallery and deli on the premises.

While it bottles its wine, culled with grapes from 11 vineyards, with state-of-the-art equipment, **Panther Creek Cellars** (⊠ 455 Irvine St. ☎ 503/472–8080 ⊕ www.panthercreekcellars.com) sorts the fruit by hand and ages its pinot noir in French oak barrels. Tours are by appointment only.

Older vines and Burgundian-style wines are two of the draws of **Stone Wolf Vineyards** (✉ Hwy. 99W and Farmer Rd. ☎ 503/434–9025 ⊕ www. stonewolfvineyards.com), open to visitors on Memorial Day and Thanksgiving weekends.

Like many of its fellow wineries, **Yamhill Valley Vineyards** (✉ 16250 S. W. Oldsville Rd., 5 mi from downtown McMinnville [take Hwy. 99W south to Hwy. 18 south to Oldsville Rd. and make a right] ☎ 800/825–4845 ⊕ www.yamhill.com) is dedicated to producing wines derived from pinot grapes. It's open mid-March–Memorial Day weekend, Saturday–Sunday 11–5, Memorial Day–Thanksgiving, daily 11–5. It's closed in winter.

## Where to Stay & Eat

★ **$–$$$$** ✕ **Nick's Italian Cafe.** Modestly furnished but with a voluminous wine cellar, Nick's is a favorite of area wine makers. The food is spirited and simple, reflecting the owner's northern Italian heritage. The five-course prix-fixe menu changes nightly. À la carte options are also available. ✉ *521 N.E. 3rd St.* ☎ *503/434–4471* 🖷 *503/472–0440* ⚏ *Reservations essential* ▭ *AE, DC, MC, V* ⊙ *Closed Mon. No lunch.*

**$$–$$$** ✕ **Joel Palmer House.** Joel Palmer was an Oregon pioneer, and his 1857 home in Dayton is now on the National Register of Historic Places. There are three small dining rooms, each seating about 15 people. The chef here specializes in wild mushroom dishes; a popular starter is Heidi's three-mushroom tart. Entrées include rib eye au poivre, rack of lamb, breast of duckling, and coq au vin; desserts include apricot-walnut bread pudding and crème brûlée. ✉ *600 Ferry St., Dayton 97114* ☎ *503/864–2995* 🖷 *503/864–3246* ▭ *AE, D, DC, MC, V* ⊙ *Closed Sun. and Mon. No lunch Sat.*

**$–$$$** ✕ **Old Noah's Wine Cellar & Wine Bar.** Once just a purveyor of local Oregon wine—which it still is—Old Noah's also has a full menu, specializing in salt-broiled wild chinook salmon. Overstuffed couches and large comfortable chairs provide a cozy intimacy, and local and popular musicians often perform here. A "library" of wine dates back 10–12 years. ✉ *511 E. 3rd St., 97218* ☎ *503/434–2787* ▭ *AE, D, MC, V* ⊙ *Closed Mon. No lunch.*

**¢–$$$** ✕ **Golden Valley Brew Pub.** The stained glass and recycled fir adorning this former warehouse are complemented by its enormous bar—27 feet long and 14 feet high—and crafted from solid mahogany and stained glass; it was formerly in Portland's Hoyt Hotel. In its present incarnation, the bar yields beer brewed on site; local winery oak barrels are used to age special beers, like the imperial stout. On the food side, specialties include almond halibut, ginger salmon, and hand-cut rib eye. ✉ *980 E. 4th St., 97128* ☎ *503/472–2739* ▭ *AE, D, MC, V.*

**$$** ✕ **Bistro Maison.** Soothing sunflower and mustard tones, a mosaic tile floor, comfy booths, and the music of France in the 1930s provide nice touches here. A husband-and-wife team serve a wonderful bouillabaisse, as well as coq au vin, cassoulet, and mussels with french fries. ✉ *729 N.E. 3rd St., 97128* ☎ *503/474–1888* 🖷 *503/435–2228* ⊕ *www. bistromaison.com* ▭ *D, MC, V* ⊙ *Closed Mon. and Tues.*

**$$–$$$$** ▭ **Youngberg Hill Vineyard.** This huge replica of a classic American farmhouse commands breathtaking views over mountain and valley from atop a steep hill. The 50-acre estate has 12 acres of vineyards. The spacious common areas of the house are filled with deep sofas and armchairs, and there's a wood-burning stove. The guest rooms are small to medium in size and cozy with golden oak and Victorian Cottage reproductions. There's a reasonably priced wine cellar, plus wedding facilities, if you're so inclined. ✉ *10660 Youngberg Hill Rd., 97128* ☎ *503/472–2727 or 888/657–8668* 🖷 *503/472–1313* ✐ *youngberghill@netscape.net* ⟲ 4 rooms, 3 suites ⚘ *Picnic area, hiking; no kids under 12, no room phones, no room TVs, no smoking* ☐ *MC, V* ⦿ *BP.*

**$$–$$$** ▦ **Wine Country Farm.** Built in 1908, this French-style stucco building has views of the Willamette Valley and Cascade Mountains. Rooms have an eclectic combination of antiques with a French influence. Horse-drawn buggy rides and horseback-riding tours are available, starting at $25 for half an hour. Mountain bikes, if available, are free, though the terrain is better suited to hooves than tires. After a long ride, no matter the mode, there is a masseuse available for $45 an hour. ✉ *6855 Breyman Orchards Rd., Dayton 97114* ☎ *503/864–3446 or 800/261–3446* ⊕ *www.winecountryfarm.com* ☞ *9 rooms* ⚘ *Hot tub, massage* ☐ *AE, DC, MC, V.*

**$$** ▦ **A' Tuscan Estate.** Columns frame the entryway of this white, gabled two-story 1928 inn five blocks from downtown. An original red-oak floor, Honduras-mahogany doors and cabinets, wrought-iron canopy beds, and hand-painted faux Tuscan walls make this place worthy of its title. A light breakfast is included in the rate, but you can make arrangements with the chef to prepare other meals at an additional cost. ✉ *809 N.E. Evans St., 97128* ☎ *503/434–9016 or 800/441–2214* ⊕ *www.a-tuscanestate.com* ☞ *3 rooms, 1 suite* ⚘ *Cable TV; no a/c, no room phones* ☐ *MC, V* ⦿ *CP.*

**$–$$** ▦ **Hotel Oregon.** Built in 1905, this historic facility—the former Elberton Hotel—was rescued from decay by the McMenamins chain, renovated in 1998, and reopened the following year. It's four stories of brick; rooms have tall ceilings and high windows. The hotel is outfitted in late Victorian furnishings, but its defining design element is its artwork: the hotel is whimsically decorated by McMenamins' half dozen staff artists: around every corner, even in the elevator, you'll find art—sometimes serene, often times bizarre and haunting—as well as photos and sayings scribbled on the walls. The Oregon has a first-floor pub serving three meals a day, a rooftop bar with an impressive view of Yamhill County, and a cellar wine bar, resembling a dark speakeasy, that serves only area vintages. Breakfast is included in the room rate. ✉ *310 N.E. Evans St., 97128* ☎ *503/472–8427 or 888/472–8427* ⊕ *www.mcmenamins.com* ☞ *42 rooms* ⚘ *2 bars, café, cinema, meeting rooms* ☐ *AE, D, DC, MC, V.*

**$–$$** ▦ **Mattey House Bed & Breakfast.** Built in 1982 by English immigrant Joseph
Fodor'sChoice Mattey, a local butcher, this Queen Anne Victorian mansion—on the
★ National Register of Historic Places—has several cheerful areas that define it. Downstairs is a cozy living room jammed with antiques, dual dining areas—a parlor with white wicker and a dining room with elegant furniture—and a porch with a swing. The four upstairs rooms are whimsically named after locally grown grape varieties—Riesling, chardonnay, pinot noir, and Blanc de Blanc, and are decorated in keeping with the character of those wines; the chardonnay room, for instance, has tall windows and crisp white furnishings, and pinot noir has dark wood pieces and reddish wine accents. A small balcony off the upstairs landing is perfect for sipping a glass of wine on a cool Yamhill Valley evening. Proprietors Jack and Denise will ensure you're comfortably ensconced, familiar with the local history, surrounding vineyards, and antiquing scene, and holding that glass of wine: in case you don't remember where you are, the house, on 10 acres, is bound by an orchard and its own vineyard, which the couple maintain. If you're fool enough to duck out before the fine full breakfast, which might include poached pears with raspberry sauce, frittatas, and Dutch-apple pancakes, Denise or Jack will have pastry and hot coffee available before you set off. A rule barring children under 10 is waived if you're renting the entire house. ✉ *10221 N.E. Mattey La., off Hwy. 99 W, ¼ mi south of Lafayette, 97128*

☎ *503/434–5058* ☐ *503/434–6667* ⊕ *www.matteyhouse.com* ⌻ *4 rooms ⌂ No room phones, no room TVs, no smoking* ═ *MC, V.*

## Shopping

If you have even part of a day for browsing, head to McMinnville's historic district, with an eye toward the cluster of stores on Northeast 3rd Street.

**Hopscotch** (✉ 520 N.E. 3rd St. ☎ 503/472–3702) is jam-packed with toys and books. A restored 1913 schoolhouse 5 mi north of McMinnville, the **Lafayette Schoolhouse Antique Mall** (✉ 748 Hwy. 99 W, Lafayette 97127 ☎ 503/864–2720) is the site of Oregon's largest permanent antiques show. Pottery items and Depression glass are among the offerings. Admission is free, and it's open daily 10–5. Produce, plants, and live music are plentiful at the **McMinnville Farmers' Market** (✉ Cowls St. between 2nd and 3rd Sts. ☎ 503/472–3605), open June–October, Thursday 3–8. Mary Englebreit teapots are among the items available at **SwedeMom** (✉ 321 N.E. 3rd St. ☎ 503/883–0881), open Monday–Thursday 10–6, Friday and Saturday 10–5. If scrapbooks are your thing, the store has supplies and a working room and offers classes.

# Grand Ronde

**❿** *24 mi southwest of McMinnville on Hwy. 18.*

Grand Ronde is mostly a stopping place for people en route to the coast who want to spend time at the town's Indian-operated casino. In July and August, the Confederated Tribes of Grand Ronde hold powwows; the August event draws between 12,000 to 15,000 people.

On the campus of the Confederated Tribes of Grand Ronde, the **West Valley Veterans Memorial** pays tribute to all war veterans but in particular is a marker for the 190,000 Native American veterans. Four flags surround the memorial wall: a U.S. flag, a Grand Ronde flag, an Oregon flag, and a POW-MIA flag. ✉ *9615 Grand Ronde Rd., 97347* ☎ *800/ 422–0232 or 503/879–5211* ☐ *503/879–2117* ⊕ *www.grandronde.org.*

## Where to Stay & Eat

¢–$ ✕ **Eyvette's Brookside Cafe.** This unassuming but popular spot serves 101 omelets. The most popular is the Romeo, made with bacon, sour cream, avocado, mushroom, and onion. If you're in a daring mood, try the peanut butter and jelly omelet, or perhaps the one with peanut butter and bacon. ✉ *33770 Salmon River Hwy.* ☎ *503/879–5100* ═ *AE, D, DC, MC, V* ☺ *Closed Mon. and Tues. No dinner.*

$–$$$ ✕▣ **Spirit Mountain Casino and Lodge.** Its location on Highway 18, one of the main routes from Portland to the ocean, makes this casino (owned and operated by the Confederated Tribes of the Grande Ronde Community of Oregon) a popular destination. Only 90 minutes from Portland and 45 minutes from Salem, this is the biggest casino resort in Oregon. The 183,000-square-foot casino has more than a thousand slots, as well as poker and blackjack tables, roulette, craps, Pai Gow poker, keno, bingo, and off-track betting. Big-name comedians and rock and country musicians perform in the 1,700-seat concert hall, and there's an arcade for the kids. Patrons can take advantage of complimentary shuttle service from Portland and Salem. Dining options include an all-you-can-eat buffet, a deli, and a café. Some rooms have Pacific Northwest and Native American themes, with carved wooden headboards and Pendleton Woolen Mills bedding. ✉ *27100 S.W. Hwy. 18, Grande Ronde 97396* ☎ *503/879–3764 or 888/668–7366* ☐ *503/879–3938* ⊕ *www.spirit-mountaincasino.com* ⌻ *100 rooms ⌂ 4 restaurants, lounge, room service* ═ *D, MC, V.*

# Silverton

**⑪** *14 mi northeast of Salem on I–5.*

Near the foothills of the Cascade Mountains, south of Portland and east of Salem, Silverton takes pride in the fact that it stands apart from the fast pace of urban life. Silverton remains an agricultural center, much as it was when it was established in the mid-1800s. The town is the largest producer in the world of the bearded iris. Passing these beautiful fields of flowers, which can be seen along I–5, can be quite distracting. Silverton is the gateway to Silver Falls State Park, the largest state park in Oregon.

At the **Country Museum/Restored Train Station,** photos and artifacts related to farming and logging in the Silverton area are displayed in a 1908 house and show how the community changed from 1854 forward with the advance of technology. The museum is a community effort, staffed by volunteers. ⊠ *428 S. Water St.* ☎ *503/873–4766* ☞ *$1* ⊙ *Mar.–Dec., Thurs. and Sun. 1–4.*

Produce and crafts are available at the **Farmers Market.** Plant nurseries also bring some of their stock, and local musicians perform. ⊠ *Town Square Park on corner of Main and Fiske Sts.* ⊙ *Mid-May–mid-Oct., Sat. 9–2.*

Exhibits on colonial music and tools are highlights of the **Old Aurora Colony Museum,** opened in 1966 in a building that formerly served as a barn and truck depot. ⊠ *Corner of 2nd and Liberty Sts., Aurora 97002* ☎ *503/678–5754* ⊕ *www.auroracolonymuseum.com* ☞ *$3.50.*

★ Created in the mid-'90s on a 240-acre tract of serene oak foothills, the ambitious **The Oregon Garden** is a work in progress. A dozen horticultural theme gardens showcase indigenous and introduced plants alike, ranging from kitchen herbs to an extensive collection of North American conifers. There is also a restored Frank Lloyd Wright–designed home and a preserved oak-strewn meadow, which are open for tours. Most of the gardens are wheelchair accessible. ⊠ *879 W. Main St. (1 mi south of Silverton on Sublimity Rd.), Silverton 97381* ☎ *503/ 874–6005 or 877/674–2733* ☞ *$7* ⊙ *Mar.–Oct., daily 9–6, Nov.–Feb., daily 9–3.*

## Where to Stay & Eat

**$$–$$$** ✕ **Silver Grille.** Owner and chef Jeff Nizlek uses local ingredients, ensuring that the menu changes monthly and sometimes more often. Specialties include locally raised lamb and Kobe beef and dishes prepared with Bandon cheese, Oregon truffles, and seasonal produce. There's a four-course Chef's Choice for $35, which has a vegetarian option. ⊠ *206 E. Main St.* ☎ *503/873–4035* ⊟ *AE, D, DC, MC, V* ⊙ *Closed Mon. and Tues.*

**¢–$** ✕ **Birdhouse Restaurant.** Chicken and dumplings and chicken fried steak, made from scratch, are big hits here. The apropos scenery includes wall-to-wall birdhouses and pictures of birdhouses, both of which customers can't seem to help bringing in. ⊠ *211 Oak St., 97381-1616* ☎ *503/ 873–0382* ⊟ *MC, V.*

**¢** ✕ **O'Brien's Cafe.** Antiques, which are for sale, surround you as you eat a home-cooked meal. You won't find anything fancy on the menu: a stack of buttermilk pancakes or perhaps homemade biscuits and eggs can jumpstart your day; a locally named Silver Falls omelet of ham, linguiça, and cheddar cheese is good any time; or perhaps sink your teeth into a juicy hamburger or a specialty item, chicken strips. What it lacks in unusual cuisine is countered by a beautiful view of Silver Creek. ✉ *105 S. Water St.* ☎ *503/873–7554* 🖃 *MC, V* ⊗ *No dinner, except 1st Fri. of month.*

$ 🏠 **Egg Cup Inn Bed & Breakfast.** What can you say about someone who collects egg cups? Everywhere you turn, there they are. Rooms are comfortable, and there's an arboretum on the premises. ✉ *11920 Sioux Rd. NE, 97381* ☎ *877/417–1461 or 503/873–5497* ⤺ *2 rooms* ⟁ *No-smoking rooms* 🖃 *MC, V* ⫶◎⫶ *BP.*

## Silver Falls State Park

★ ⑫   *26 mi east of Salem, Hwy. 22 to Hwy. 214.*

Hidden amid old-growth Douglas firs in the foothills of the Cascades, Silver Falls is the largest state park in Oregon (8,700 acres). South Falls, roaring over the lip of a mossy basalt bowl into a deep pool 177 feet below, is the main attraction here, but 13 other waterfalls—half of them more than 100 feet high—are accessible to hikers. The best time to visit is in the fall, when vine maples blaze with brilliant color, or early spring, when the forest floor is carpeted with trilliums and yellow violets. There are picnic facilities and a day lodge; during the winter you can cross-country ski. There are 14 cabins. ✉ *20024 Silver Falls Hwy. SE, Sublimity* ☎ *800/551–6949 or 503/873–8681* 🖃 *$3 per vehicle* ⊗ *Daily dawn–dusk.*

### Where to Stay & Eat

¢–$ ✕ **Wooden Nickel.** If you want atmosphere, this is not the place. The Wooden Nickel leans more toward being a tavern, but it's also a great family restaurant. The food's not fancy, but it's predictable. Steak, boneless pork ribs, and hamburgers are among the choices. ✉ *108 N. Center St., Sublimity* ☎ *503/769–8181* 🖃 *AE, D, MC, V.*

## Salem

⑬–㉑   *24 mi from McMinnville, south on Hwy. 99 W and east on Hwy. 22; 45 mi south of Portland on I–5.*

Salem has a rich pioneer history, but before that it was the home of the Calapooia Indians, who called it Chemeketa, which means "place of rest." Salem is said to have been renamed by missionaries. According to one story, the name is an Anglicized form of the Hebrew "shalom," or peace, while another story suggests it was named specifically for Salem, Massachusetts. Although trappers and farmers preceded them in the Willamette Valley, the Methodist missionaries had come in 1834 to minister to Native Americans, and they are credited with the founding of Salem. They also established the first academic institution west of the Rockies in 1842, now known as Willamette University.

Salem became the official capital when Oregon achieved statehood in 1859, replacing Oregon City as the capital of the Oregon Territory. Today, with a population of more than 135,000, Salem is the second largest city in Oregon and serves as the seat to Marion County as well as the home of the state fairgrounds. Because this is the state capital and county seat, government ranks as a major industry in the community, while the city's placement in the heart of the fertile Willamette Valley stimulates rich agricultural and food-processing industries. Extensive nearby farmlands are devoted to the cultivation of vegetables, berries, hops, and flowers, and at least 15 wineries are in or near Salem. The main attractions in Salem are west of I–5 in and around the Capitol Mall.

*Numbers in the text correspond to numbers in the margin and on the Salem map.*

A.C. Gilbert's
Discovery
Village ......13

Bush's
Pasture
Park ........19

Deepwood
Estate .......18

Elsinore
Theater ......14

Mission Mill
Village ......17

Mount Angel
Abbey .......21

Oregon
Capitol ......15

Willamette
Mission
State Park ....20

Willamette
University ....16

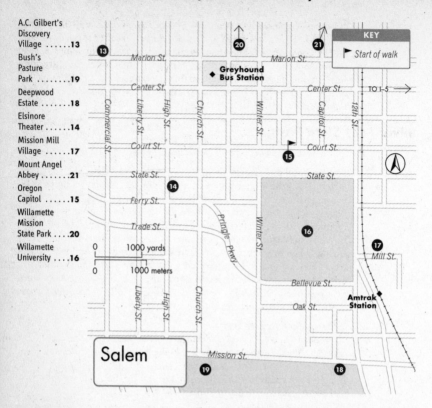

Salem

**a good walk**

Begin at Court Street and the **Oregon Capitol** ⑮ ⊩. Behind the Capitol, across State Street, is **Willamette University** ⑯. Cross over 12th Street to the **Mission Mill Village** ⑰. From there, stroll down 12th Street to **Deepwood Estate** ⑱, south of Salem's downtown district. West of here is **Bush's Pasture Park** ⑲.

TIMING    Without stopping for tours, this walk can be done in about two hours. Allot an additional half hour for a guided tour of the Capitol, two hours for a full tour of Mission Mill Village, and a half hour each for the house tours at Deepwood Estate and Bush's Pasture Park. If you're pressed for time, skip the Capitol and university and begin your tour at Mission Mill Village.

### Sights to See

⑬ **A. C. Gilbert's Discovery Village.** In a Victorian house, this museum celebrates the inventions of A. C. Gilbert, including Erector sets and American Flyer trains. The first floor and grounds are wheelchair accessible. ⊠ *116 Marion St., 97301-3437* ☎ *503/371–3631* ⊕ *www.acgilbert.org* ⌨ *$5* ⊙ *Mon.–Sat. 10–5, Sun. noon–5.*

⑲ **Bush's Pasture Park.** These 105 acres of rolling lawn and formal English gardens include the remarkably well preserved **Bush House,** an 1878 Italianate mansion at the park's far western boundary. It has 10 marble fireplaces and virtually all of its original furnishings. The house and gardens are on the National Register of Historic Places. **Bush Barn Art Center,** behind the house, exhibits the work of Northwest artists and has a sales gallery. ⊠ *600 Mission St. SE* ☎ *503/363–4714* ⊕ *www. salemart.org* ⌨ *$4* ⊙ *May–Sept., Tues.–Sun. noon–5; Oct.–Apr., Tues.–Sun. 2–5.*

**⑱ Deepwood Estate.** This fanciful 1894 Queen Anne–style house has splendid interior woodwork and original stained glass. An ornate gazebo from the 1905 Lewis and Clark expedition graces the fine gardens created in 1929 by landscape designers Elizabeth Lord and Edith Schryver. The estate is on the National Register of Historic Places. ☒ *1116 Mission St. SE* ☎ *503/363–1825* ☞ *$4* ☉ *May–Sept., Sun.–Fri. noon–4:30; Oct.–Apr., Tues.–Sat. noon–5.*

**⑭ Elsinore Theatre.** This flamboyant Tudor Gothic vaudeville house opened on May 28, 1926, with Edgar Bergen in attendance. Clark Gable (who lived in Silverton) and Gregory Peck performed on the stage. The theater was designed to look like a castle, with a false stone front, chandeliers, ironwork, and stained-glass windows. It's now a lively performing arts center with a busy schedule of bookings, and there are concerts on its Wurlitzer pipe organ. ☒ *170 High St. SE, 97301* ☎ *503/375–3574* ☎ *503/375–0284* ⊕ *www.elsinoretheatre.com.*

**⑰ Mission Mill Village.** The **Thomas Kay Woolen Mill Museum** complex (circa 1889), complete with working water wheels and millstream, looks as if the workers have just stepped away for a lunch break. Teasel gigging, napper flock bins, and the patented Furber double-acting napper are but a few of the machines and processes on display. The **Jason Lee House,** the **John D. Boon Home,** and the **Methodist Parsonage** are also part of the village. There is nothing grandiose about these early pioneer homes, the oldest frame structures in the Northwest, but they reveal a great deal about domestic life in the wilds of Oregon in the 1840s. The adjacent **Marion County Historical Society Museum** (☎ 503/364–2128) displays pioneer and Calapooia Indian artifacts. ☒ *Museum complex, 1313 Mill St. SE* ☎ *503/585–7012* ⊕ *www. missionmill.org* ☞ *$6 (includes tour)* ☉ *Daily 10–4* ☞ *Guided tours of houses and woolen mill museum leave from mill's admission booth every hr on the hr.*

**㉑ Mount Angel Abbey.** On a 300-foot-high butte, this Benedictine monastery was founded in 1882. It's the site of one of two American buildings designed by Finnish architect Alvar Aalto. A masterpiece of serene and thoughtful design, Aalto's library opened its doors in 1970 and has become a place of pilgrimage for students and aficionados of modern architecture. ✛ *18 mi from Salem, east on Hwy. 213 and north on Hwy. 214* ☎ *503/845–3030* ⊕ *www.mountangel.org* ☞ *Free.*

▶ **⑮ Oregon Capitol.** A brightly gilded bronze statue of the Oregon Pioneer stands atop the 140-foot-high Capitol dome, looking north across the Capitol Mall. Built in 1939 with blocks of gray Vermont marble, Oregon's Capitol has an elegant yet austere neoclassical feel. New east and west wings were added in 1978. Relief sculptures and deft historical murals soften the interior. Tours of the rotunda, the house and senate chambers, and the governor's office leave from the information center under the dome. ☒ *900 Court St.* ☎ *503/986–1388* ☞ *Free* ☉ *Weekdays 8–5, Sat. 9–4, Sun. noon–4. Guided tours Memorial Day–Labor Day, daily on the hr; rest of year by appointment.*

**㉒ Willamette Mission State Park.** Along pastoral lowlands by the Willamette River, this serene park holds the largest black cottonwood tree in the United States. A thick-barked behemoth by a small pond, the 265-year-old tree has upraised arms that bring to mind J.R.R. Tolkien's fictional Ents. Site of Reverend Jason Lee's 1834 pioneer mission, the park also offers quiet strolling and picnicking amid an old orchard and along the river. The Wheatland ferry, at the north end of the park, began carrying covered wagons across the Willamette in 1844, using pulleys. ✛ *Wheatland Rd., 8 mi north of Salem, I–5's Exit 263* ☎ *503/393–1172 or 800/551–6949* ⊕ *www.oregonstateparks.org* ✉ *Day use $3, or annual permit $25. Charcoal barbecue rental $25.* ⊙ *Daily 8 AM–dusk.*

**⓰ Willamette University.** Behind the Capitol, across State Street but half a world away, are the brick buildings and grounds of Willamette University, the oldest college in the West. Founded in 1842, Willamette has long been a breeding ground for aspiring politicians (former Oregon senators Mark O. Hatfield and Robert Packwood are alumni). **Hatfield Library,** built in 1986 on the banks of Mill Stream, is a handsome brick-and-glass building with a striking campanile; tall, prim **Waller Hall,** built in 1841, is one of the oldest buildings in the Pacific Northwest. ✉ *Information Desk, Putnam University Center, Mill St.* ☎ *503/370–6300* ⊙ *Weekdays 9–5.*

off the beaten path

**SCHREINER'S IRIS GARDENS –** Some call the Willamette Valley near Salem the Bulb Basket of the Nation. Irises and tulips create fields of brilliant color in near-perfect growing conditions. Schreiner's Iris Gardens, established in 1925, ships bulbs all over the world; during the short spring growing season (mid-May–early June), the 10-acre display gardens blaze with fancifully named varieties such as Hello Darkness, Well Endowed, and Ringo. ✉ *3625 Quinaby Rd. NE (north from Salem take I–5 to Exit 263, head west on Brooklake Rd., south on River Rd., and east on Quinaby)* ☎ *503/393–3232* ⊕ *www.schreinersgarden.com* ✉ *Free* ⊙ *Daily 8 AM–dusk during blooming season only.*

## Wineries

Billing itself as a "viticultural dude ranch," **Cherry Hill Vineyard** (✉ 7867 Crowley Rd., Rickreall 97371 ☎ 503/949–8805 ⊕ www.cherryhillvineyard. com) is much more than a vineyard, it's an opportunity to participate in the process. But if you don't feel like working, it's an opportunity to live the good life. Stay in one of the guest cabins and drink good pinot noir, eat good food, and admire the view of the Eola Hills.

Around since 1934, **Honeywood Winery** (✉ 1350 Hines St. SE ☎ 503/362–4111) in downtown Salem, is the oldest producing winery in the state. Pinot noir, Riesling, and chardonnay are specialties. It's open weekdays 9–5, Saturday 10–5, and Sunday 1–5.

**Redhawk Vineyard** (✉ 2995 Michigan City NW, 97304 ☎ 503/362–1596 🖷 503/362–1596 ⊕ www.redhawkwine.com) is a good example of not judging a book by its cover, as it has received awards for having the worst-looking wine label. Among the vineyard's wines are a pinot gris called Punk Floyd and a pinot noir known as Grateful Red. It's open April–November, daily noon–5.

**St. Innocent Winery** (✉ 1360 Tandem St. NE, 97303 ☎ 503/378–1526 ⊕ www.stinnocentwine.com), unlike many other wineries, elects to work with local growers rather than own and maintain its own vineyards. It's open weekends 12–5 as well as Memorial Day weekend and Thanksgiving.

## Where to Stay & Eat

$$–$$$ ✕ **Alessandro's Park Plaza.** This restaurant in downtown Salem overlooks a park with a waterfall and cooks up such dishes as pepper steak and shrimp scampi, both excellent. There is also an exclusive martini bar.

A kids' menu is available. ✉ *325 High St. SE, 97301* ☎ *503/370–9951* ⊟ *AE, D, MC, V* ⊘ *Closed Sun.*

**$–$$$** ✕ **DaVinci.** Salem politicos flock to this two-story downtown restaurant for Italian-inspired dishes cooked in a wood-burning oven. No short-cuts are taken in the preparation, so don't come if you're in a rush. But if you're in the mood to linger over seafood and fresh pasta that's made on the premises, this may be your place. The wine list is one of the most extensive in the Northwest; the staff is courteous and extremely professional. ✉ *180 High St.* ☎ *503/399–1413* ⊟ *AE, DC, MC, V* ⊘ *No lunch Sun.*

**¢–$$$** ✕ **Ram Restaurant & Brewery.** Neon signs do little to brighten the dark mahogany interiors here, but the mood is both friendly and kid-friendly. Try a Total Disorder Porter or another of the colorfully named drafts, and sink your teeth into the Willamette Burger, an entire pound of beef. ✉ *515 12th St. SE* ☎ *503/363–1904* ⊟ *AE, D, DC, MC, V.*

**¢–$** ✕ **Gerry Frank's Konditorei.** Furnished in the style of a European side-walk café, this is *the* place to go in Salem for rich desserts. Sandwiches, salads, soup, and other simple entrées are served, but most people head straight for the display cases of homemade cakes, tortes, and cheese-cakes. ✉ *310 Kearney St. SE* ☎ *503/585–7070* ⊟ *D, MC, V.*

**¢–$** ✕ **Thompson Brewery & Public House.** The intimate rooms at this pub are decked out in a funky mix of '60s rock-and-roll memorabilia and hand-painted woodwork. India Pale Ale and Terminator Stout are among the beers made in a tiny brewery enlivened by colorful origi-nal art. The food—mostly hearty sandwiches, salads, and pasta dishes—is remarkably cheap. ✉ *3575 Liberty Rd. S* ☎ *503/363–7286* ⊟ *AE, D, MC, V.*

**$** ✕▦ **A Creekside Inn, the Marquee House.** The guest rooms in this 1938 Mt. Vernon Colonial-style house are decorated with movie themes—Top-per, Auntie Mame, Blazing Saddles, and others—and there are movies and popcorn in the evening. Only nine blocks from the center of town, the house is on ½ acre of flower gardens bordering Mill Creek, a view that you can enjoy from the large porch out back. There's a two-night minimum during holidays and events at Willamette University. ✉ *333 Wyatt Ct. NE, 97301* ☎ *503/391–0837 or 800/949–0837* 🖷 *503/391–1713* ⊕ *www.marqueehouse.com* ⊲ *5 rooms* ⚹ *Picnic area, some in-room data ports; no phones in some rooms, no smoking* ⊟ *D, DC, MC, V* ⊢◯⊣ *BP.*

**¢** ▦ **Tiki Lodge.** If you don't mind a room devoid of soap or stationery, Tiki Lodge is a simple, inexpensive choice done in basic brown. If golf is your game, there's a course right around the corner. ✉ *3705 Market St., 97301* ☎ *503/581–4441* 🖷 *503/581–4442* ⊲ *50 rooms (20 with shower only)* ⚹ *Cable TV, microwaves, pool, playground, business ser-vices, some pets allowed* ⊟ *AE, D, MC, V.*

## Nightlife & the Arts

A flamboyant Tudor Gothic vaudeville house dating from 1926, the **Elsi-nore Theatre** (✉170 High St. SE ☎503/375–3574 ⊕www.elsinoretheatre.com) presents stage shows, concerts, and silent movies. The restored in-terior is worth seeing even if nothing is playing; call to arrange a tour. Clark Gable practiced for some of his auditions here.

## Sports & the Outdoors

GOLF   **Battle Creek Golf Course** (✉ 6161 Commercial St. SE ☎ 503/585–1402) is an 18-hole, par-72 course. The greens fee ranges from $23–$25; a cart costs $20. The greens fee at the 18-hole, par-72 course at the **Salem Golf Club** (✉ 2025 Golf Course Rd. ☎ 503/363–6652) is $40 ($30 twi-light); a cart costs $24.

South of Salem, the **Enchanted Forest** is the closest thing Oregon has to a major theme park. The park has several attractions in forest-like surroundings, including a Big Timber Log Ride. On it, you ride logs through flumes that pass through a lumber mill and the woods. The ride—the biggest log ride in the Northwest—has a 25-foot roller-coaster dip and a 40-foot drop at the end. Other attractions include the Ice Mountain Bobsled roller coaster, the Haunted House, English Village, Storybook Lane, the Fantasy Fountains Water Light Show, Fort Fearless, and the western town of Tofteville. The park is 7 mi south of Salem at Exit 248 off I–5. ⊠ *8462 Enchanted Way SE, Turner 97392* ☎ *503/363–3060 or 503/371–4242* ⊕ *www. enchantedforest.com* ⊠ *$7.95 (some attractions extra)* ☉ *Mar. and May–Labor Day, daily 9:30–6; Apr. and Labor Day–end of Sept., weekends, 9:30–6.*

# Albany

❷ *46 mi south of Silver Falls State Park on I–5 and Hwy. 20; 20 mi from Salem, south on I–5 and west on U.S. 20.*

To see what a quintessential Willamette Valley river town looked like before the major highways were built, explore Albany, a former wheat and produce center in the heart of the valley. It is still so rich with agricultural crops that it is known as the grass-seed capital of the world. Named by Thomas and Walter Monteith after their hometown in New York State, Albany is believed to be home to one of the largest and most varied collections of historic buildings in Oregon. Some 700 historic buildings, scattered over a 100-block area in three districts, include every major architectural style in the United States from 1850. The area is listed on the National Register of Historic Places. Eight covered bridges can also be seen on a half-hour drive from Albany. Pamphlets and maps for self-guided walking and driving tours are available from the **Albany Visitors Association** (⊠ 300 S.W. 2nd Ave. ☎ 541/928–0911 or 800/526–2256), open weekdays 9–5.

In an 1887 Italianate building in the heart of historic downtown Albany is the **Albany Regional Museum.** The Rod and Marty Tripp Reference Room has many historical documents and provides ample room to spread books out and do research projects. ⊠ *136 Lyons St. SW* ☎ *541/967–7122* ⊠ *Free* ☉ *Mon.–Sat. noon–4.*

The first frame house in Albany was Monteith House, built in 1849. Now the **Monteith House Museum,** restored and filled with period furnishings and historic photos, it is widely thought to be the most authentic restoration of a Pacific Northwest pioneer-era home. ⊠ *518 2nd Ave. SW, 97321* ☎ *800/526–2256* ⊠ *541/926–1500* ⊕ *www.albanyvisitors. com* ⊠ *Donation* ☉ *Mid-June–mid-Sept., Wed.–Sat. noon–4; mid-Sept.–mid-June, by appointment.*

## Where to Stay & Eat

¢–$$$ ✕**Buzz Saw.** Fresh seafood and prime rib are the most popular items at this riverside restaurant, along with steaks and pasta dishes. Window tables and raised booths all have a view of the river. The hottest club in town, with the same name, is right next door where a DJ keeps things moving five nights a week. There are pool tables, too. ⊠ *421 Water St., 97321* ☎ *541/928–0642* ⊠ *541/928–0644* ⊟ *AE, DC, MC, V* ☉ *No lunch.*

★ $–$$ ✕**Capriccio Ristorante.** Capriccio is *the* place for pasta in Albany. The house specialty is spinach ravioli in a cream sauce, but you might also choose from osso buco Orvieto, lemon chicken, or New York strip steak, and there's fresh fish every day. ⊠ *442 W. 1st Ave. SW, 97321*

☎ *541/924–9932* 🖶 *541/967–9454* ▤ *AE, D, DC, MC, V* ⊘ *Closed Sun. and Mon. No lunch.*

$  ✕ **Novak's Hungarian Paprikas.** The Hungarian owners of this unpretentious restaurant turn out native specialties such as *kolbasz* (homemade sausages with sweet-and-sour cabbage) and beef *szelet* (crispy batter-fried cutlets) with virtuosity. ⊠ *2306 Heritage Way SE* ☎ *541/967–9488* ▤ *MC, V* ⊘ *No lunch Sat.*

$–$$$  🏨 **Comfort Suites.** Think big when you stay here; the all-suites rooms are huge, and breakfast is quite a spread; scrambled eggs and other hot foods are served along with basic cold food items. In the afternoon, expect cookies for snacks. The hotel is less than ½ mi from I–5 and next to the Albany Municipal Airport. ⊠ *100 Opal Ct. NE, 97321* ☎ *800/517–4000 or 541/928–2053* 🖶 *541/928–2592* 🛏 *86 suites* 🍴 *Microwaves, refrigerators, cable TV, indoor pool, exercise equipment, hot tub, laundry facilities, business services* ▤ *AE, D, DC, MC* ⦿❙ *CP.*

### Shopping

Every Saturday, browse through the local produce, such as succulent strawberries, while taking in some live music at the **Albany Saturday Farmer's Market** (⊠ Water St., between Broadalbin and Ferry ☎ 541/752–1510). **Heritage Mall** (⊠ 1895 14th Ave. ☎ 541/967–8238) is a typical retail mall with a food court; grab lunch at Big Town Hero or Bob's Pizza Plus. Albany's first post office is now the site of **No Garbage Books** (⊠ 240 2nd Ave. SW, 97321 ☎ 541/926–5222), which sells used and new books.

## Corvallis

❷❸ *10 mi southwest of Albany on U.S. 20; 35 mi from Salem, south on I–5 and west on Hwy. 34.*

A compound construction of the Latin words for "heart of the valley," Corvallis is home to the Beavers and Oregon State University. But it also has more than 52,0000 residents. To some, Corvallis is a brief stopping place along the way to Salem or Portland. To others, it's a little town that gives you a chance to escape from the bigger cities. Driving the area's economy is a growing engineering and high-tech industry, including long-time Corvallis employer Hewlett Packard, a burgeoning wine industry, and more traditional local agricultural crops, such as grass and legume seeds. Corvallis offers plenty of outdoor activities as well as scenic attractions, from covered bridges to local wineries and gardens.

The **Osborn Aquatic Center** is not the site of your ordinary lap pool. There are water slides, a water channel, water cannons, and floor geysers. ⊠ *1940 N.W. Highland Dr.* ☎ *541/766–7946* 🎟 *$4.*

The pace quickens in Corvallis around the 500-acre campus of **Oregon State University,** west of the city center. Established as a land-grant institution in 1868, OSU has more than 15,000 students, many of them studying the agricultural sciences and engineering. ⊠ *15th and Jefferson Sts.* ☎ *541/737–0123* ⊕ *oregonstate.edu.*

At 75-acres, **Avery Park** includes rose and rhododendron gardens, jogging trails, and picnic shelters. ⊠ *South 15th St. and U.S. 20* ☎ *541/757–6918* 🎟 *Free* ⊘ *Weekdays.*

There are more than 20,000 pioneer and Native American artifacts on display at **Benton County Historical Museum.** There is also a cut-glass and porcelain collection, the reconstruction of a Victorian parlor, and a costume exhibit. ⊠ *1101 Main St., Philomath* ☎ *541/929–6230* 🎟 *Free* ⊘ *Tues.–Sat. 10–4:30.*

A favorite of bird-watchers, **Finley National Wildlife Refuge** has large fields of grass and grain and a wetland area that attracts Canada geese, especially the dusky Canada goose, a threatened species because of its limited breeding area. You might also spot grouse, pheasants, quail, wood ducks, and other birds, as well as numerous deer. A herd of large Roosevelt elk also calls this area home. Also within the refuge is **Fiechter House** (☎ 541/929–6230 or 541/757–7236), one of Oregon's remaining examples of Classical Revival architecture, open Sunday during the summer 10–4. ⊠ *26208 Finley Refuge Rd., 97333* ☎ *541/757–7236* 🖶 *541/757–4450* 🖼 *Free* ⏱ *Daily dawn–dusk.*

The highest point in the Coast Range, at 4,097 feet, Mary's Peak, within **Siuslaw National Forest,** offers panoramic views of the Cascades, Willamette Valley, and the rest of the Coast Range. On a clear day you can see as far as the Pacific Ocean. There are several picnicking areas, more than 10 mi of hiking trails, and a small campground. There are stands of noble fir and alpine meadows. The forest, which is 2 mi from Corvallis, includes the Oregon Dunes National Recreation Area, and the Cape Perpetua Interpretive Center. ⊠ *Rte. 34 at Hwy. 3024* ☎ *541/750–7000* ⊕ *www.fs.fed.us/r6/siuslaw* 🖼 *Free* ⏱ *Daily dawn–dusk.*

### Wineries

If you want to make your own wine, here's the place. Pick the fruit yourself at **Bald Hill Vineyard** (⊠ 1810 Bullevard, Philomath 97370 ☎ 541/ 929–4773).

**Tyee Wine Cellars** (⊠ 26335 Greenberry Rd. ☎ 541/753–8754 ⊕ www. winepressnw.com) makes pinot noir, pinot gris, pinot blanc, chardonnay, and Gewürztraminer. Admission is free. It's open April–June and September–December, weekends 12–5; July–August, Friday–Monday, 12–5.

### Where to Stay & Eat

$$$ ✕ **Michael's Landing.** In a former railroad depot overlooking the Willamette River, this restaurant is known for its large menu of steak, seafood, chicken, and pasta dishes. Try the Northwest salmon baked in a wine and butter sauce. There's a kids' menu. Sunday brunch includes omelets, quiche, and pancakes. ⊠ *603 N.W. 2nd St., 97330* ☎ *541/754–6141* 🖃 *AE, D, DC, MC, V.*

$–$$$ ✕ **The Gables.** Candlelight and linens and dark wood paneling give a touch of romance to this spot, operating since 1958. The straightforward menu includes steaks, seafood, local lamb, and prime rib. The portions are huge and satisfying. ⊠ *1121 N.W. 9th St.* ☎ *541/752–3364 or 800/815–0167* 🪑 *Reservations essential* 🖃 *AE, D, DC, MC, V* ⏱ *No lunch.*

$–$$$ ✕ **Iovino's Inc.** High ceilings convey spaciousness here, and colors accent different parts of the restaurant, whether it's the striking red on the wall, the aesthetically pleasing green, or the black in the bar area. Try the *filetto di malle alforne,* pork with a white wine sauce, or the Cornish hens stuffed with pistachio and wrapped with pancetta. There's often live music on weekends. ⊠ *126 S.W. 1st St.* ☎ *541/738–9015* 🖶 *541/738–9282* 🖃 *AE, MC, V* ⏱ *No lunch.*

$–$$ ✕ **Big River Restaurant & Bow Truss Bar.** A former Greyhound bus depot holds one of Corvallis's most popular restaurants, especially among the Willamette University crowd. The menu changes frequently but emphasizes foods from Oregon—pan-seared salmon, grilled chicken, and roasted lamb shanks. This is one of the few places in Corvallis to snag a good martini or single-malt Scotch. Live blues and jazz bands perform on Friday and Saturday evenings, and there's brunch on Sunday. ⊠ *101 N.W. Jackson St.* ☎ *541/757–0694* 🖃 *AE, MC, V* ⏱ *No lunch Sat.*

¢–$$ ✕ **Le Bistro.** The menu changes according to what fresh ingredients are available and what owner and chef Robert Merlet is in the mood to prepare. Dishes might include mustard-braised rabbit legs or *pave de porc,* a thick pork loin smothered with a mushroom sauce. Try the chocolate mousse with Grand Marnier cream. ✉ *150 S.W. Madison, 97333* ☎ *541/754–6688* ▭ *AE, D, DC, MC, V* ☉ *Closed Sun. and Mon. No lunch.*

$–$$ ▦ **Hanson Country Inn.** On a knoll overlooking the Willamette Valley, this 7,100-square-foot 1928 Dutch Colonial was once headquarters of a poultry-breeding business. Restored, it now has a massive fireplace in the living room, many sitting areas, tall windows, and a sunporch with stained-glass windows and rattan furniture. Rooms have views of either the English garden or the valley, and the largest has broad views from windows on three sides. The cottage is at the edge of the woods and has two bedrooms, a front porch, and a rear deck. ✉ *795 S.W. Hanson St., 97333* ☎ *541/752–2919* ↩ *3 suites, 1 cottage* ♿ *Picnic area, in-room data ports, cable TV, laundry service; no kids under 13, no smoking* ▭ *AE, D, DC, MC, V* ◉ *BP.*

$–$$ ▦ **Harrison House.** Maria Tomlinson runs this B&B in a 1939 Dutch Colonial–style home three blocks from the OSU campus. Chippendale, Queen Anne, and Colonial Williamsburg–era furniture fill the living and dining rooms. The three rooms on the second floor and one on the first are spacious and immaculate. Breakfast, included in the rate, might be Belgian waffles or eggs Benedict. ✉ *2310 N.W. Harrison Rd., 97330* ☎ *541/752–6248 or 800/233–6248* 🖷 *541/754–1353* ↩ *4 rooms, 2 with bath* ▭ *AE, D, DC, MC, V.*

¢–$ ▦ **Shanico Inn.** A mile from downtown Corvallis, this quiet three-story motel is close to the Oregon University campus. It's on an acre of property with a picnic area and plenty of benches. Rooms are basic but functional. ✉ *1113 N.W. 9th St., 97330* ☎ *541/754–7474 or 800/432–1233* 🖷 *541/754–2437* ⊕ *www.shanicoinn.com* ↩ *76 rooms* ♿ *Picnic area, pool, some pets allowed* ▭ *AE, D, DC, MC, V* ◉ *CP.*

## Sports & the Outdoors

GOLF **Trysting Tree Golf Club** (✉ 34028 Electric Rd. ☎ 541/752–3332) has an 18-hole, par-72 course. The greens fee is $29; a cart costs $22.

## Shopping

At the **Corvallis-Albany Farmers' Markets** (✉ 1st and Jackson Sts., on north end of Riverfront ☎ 541/752–1510), zero in on the berries and corn. The market is open from mid-April to the end of November, Saturday 9–1. If Oregon had a state shoe, it would probably be the Birkenstock, and **Footwise, Inc.** (✉ 301 S.W. Madison Ave., ☎ 800/451–1459) has a large selection of these sandals. Find knickknacks at the **Myrtlewood Mystique Gallery** (✉ 1737 Main St., Philomath 97370 ☎ 541/929–3853 or 888/249–4411). It's open Monday–Saturday 9–7, Sunday 11–7.

# Brownsville

㉔ *27 mi south of Corvallis off I–5.*

Early settler James Blakely named this area on the banks of the Calapooia River "Brownsville" after his uncle, Hugh Brown. Blakely helped lay out the town, and in 1895 the communities of North Brownsville, Amelia, and Brownsville consolidated into the city of Brownsville. This Willamette Valley town has retained much of its original character and was a character itself in the film *Stand by Me.* The **Linn County Historical Museum,** in Brownsville's 1890 railroad depot, has some noteworthy pioneer-era exhibits, including a covered wagon that arrived in

1865 after a trek along the Oregon Trail from Missouri. ⊠ *101 Park Ave.* ☏ *541/466–3390* ✉ *Free* ⊘ *Mon.–Sat. 11–4, Sun. 1–5.*

John Moyer, a carpenter turned businessman, owned a lumber mill, banks, and other businesses in the state. His house, the **Moyer House**, built in 1881, has been turned into a museum. Most of the furniture is from the 1880s. There are original murals on the ceiling and over the bay windows, artist or artists unknown. ⊠ *204 N. Main St.* ☏ *541/466–3070* ⊘ *Mon.–Sat. 11–4, Sun. 1–5.*

### Sports & the Outdoors

CROQUET If the concept of "croquet rodeo" intrigues you, head over to the **Calapooia Croquet Court** (⊠ 36176 Hwy. 228, 97327 ☏ 541/466–5589) in Pioneer Park, one of Brownsville's nicest parks.

# Sweet Home

**㉕** *About 12 mi east of Brownsville.*

Situated on the south fork of the Santiam River near the foothills of the Cascades, Sweet Home has heritage as a timber town, but that has given way to thriving recreational activities afforded by the middle and south forks of the river. Its mild climate and ample rain and sun produce one of the state's most diversified farming areas, leading the nation in the production of common and perennial ryegrass. There are also many dairy and berry farms. Keep an eye out around town for colorful murals painted by local artists.

The trials and joys of pioneer life are graphically displayed at **East Linn Museum** with artifacts, pictures, and documents from the years 1850–1940. ⊠ *746 Long St., 97386* ☏ *541/367–4580* ✉ *Donations accepted* ⊘ *Memorial Day–Labor Day, Tues.–Sat. 11–4, Sun. 1–4; Labor Day–Memorial Day, Thurs.–Sat. 11–4, Sun. 1–4; or by appointment.*

### Where to Stay & Eat

$–$$ ✕ **Mountain House Country Restaurant.** Filled with knotty pine, log beams, and a stone fireplace, this lodge is in the Willamette National Forest. You can choose among Black Angus steak, organic hamburgers, Cajun catfish, jambalaya, and other dishes, and then finish up with marion-berry cobbler. ⊠ *52855 Santiam Hwy. (Hwy. 20), 97329* ☏ *541/367–3074* ⊘ *Closed Jan.–Mar.* ⊟ *AE, MC, V.*

¢–$ ▨ **Sweet Home Inn.** Some rooms here overlook a wooded creek while others have balconies, but all are large and comfortable. The inn is near lakes and golfing. ⊠ *805 Long St., 97386* ☏ *541/367–5137* ▤ *541/367–8859* ⇆ *31 rooms* ⌂ *Some in-room hot tubs, microwaves, refrigerators, cable TV, hot tub, gym, laundry facilities* ⊟ *AE, MC, V.*

# McKenzie Bridge

**㉖** *58 mi east of Eugene on Hwy. 126.*

On the beautiful McKenzie River, the town of McKenzie Bridge is surrounded by lakes, waterfalls, covered bridges, and wilderness trails in the Cascades. Fishing, skiing, backpacking, and rafting are among the most popular activities in the area.

A 1,240-acre reservoir in the Willamette National Forest, **Blue River Dam and Lake** has miles of forested shoreline. From May through September, boats are launched from ramps at Saddle Dam and Lookout Creek. Recreational activities include fishing, swimming, water skiing, and camping at Mona Campground. ⊠ *Forest Rd. 15 in Willamette National Forest* ☎ *541/937–2131* ✉ *Free* ☉ *Daily.*

Four miles outside of McKenzie Bridge is **Cougar Dam and Lake**, the highest embankment dam ever built by the Army Corps of Engineers—452 feet above the stream bed. The resulting reservoir, on the South Fork McKenzie River, covers 1,280 acres. The public recreation areas are in the Willamette National Forest. A fish hatchery is in the vicinity. You can visit the dam year-round, but the campgrounds are open only from May to September. ⊠ *Forest Rd. 19 in Willamette National Forest* ☎ *541/937–2131* ✉ *Free* ☉ *May–Sept., daily; most areas closed rest of year.*

### Where to Eat

**$–$$$** ✕ **Holiday Farm Resort.** Heavy and hearty cooking is what you'll get in this 1876 former stagecoach stop across the street from the river. Corned-beef hash, biscuits, and steak and eggs dominate the morning menu. Barbecued beef brisket is roasted in a pit outside all day for the evening crowd. You can also order fresh salmon, halibut, or stuffed pork chops. ⊠ *54455 McKenzie River Dr., Blue River 97413* ☎ *541/822–3715* ▭ *AE, MC, V.*

### Sports & the Outdoors

WHITE-WATER RAFTING  A friendly-family business, **High Country Expeditions** (⊠ 56341 Delta Dr., 97413 ☎ 541/822–8288 or 888/461–7238) provides guided white-water rafting and fishing trips on the McKenzie and Willamette rivers, lasting from half a day to several days, for everyone from beginners to experts. In spring High Country leads 5- to 10-day white-water trips on the Owyhee River.

# McKenzie River Highway

㉗ *East of Eugene on Hwy. 126*

Highway 126, as it heads east from Eugene, is known as the McKenzie River Highway. Following the curves of the river, it passes grazing lands, fruit and nut orchards, and the small riverside hamlets of the McKenzie Valley. From the highway you can glimpse the bouncing, bubbling, blue-green McKenzie River, one of Oregon's top fishing, boating, and white-water rafting spots, against a backdrop of densely forested mountains, splashing waterfalls, and jet-black lava beds. The small town of McKenzie Bridge marks the end of the McKenzie River Highway and the beginning of the 26-mi McKenzie River National Recreation Trail, which heads north through the Willamette National Forest along portions of the Old Santiam Wagon Road.

### Where to Stay & Eat

★ **$** ✕▣ **Log Cabin Inn.** On the banks of the wild, fish-filled McKenzie River, this inn is equally appropriate for a fishing vacation or a romantic weekend getaway. Antique furniture decorates log-cabin-style buildings; each room has a river view. Six riverfront tepees share a bath. Menu standouts at the delightful restaurant include wild boar, quail, salmon, a decadent homemade beer-cheese soup, and a locally famous marionberry cobbler. ⊠ *56483 McKenzie Hwy., 97413* ☎ *541/822–3432 or 800/355–3432* 🖷 *541/822–6173* ⊕ *www.logcabinin.com* ⋺ *8 cabins, 6 tepees* ☖ *Restaurant, fishing, bar* ▭ *MC, V.*

### Sports & the Outdoors

BOATING & RAFTING  **Oregon Whitewater Adventures** (⊠ 39620 Deerhorn Rd., Springfield ☎ 541/746–5422 or 800/820–7238) operates half- to two-day rafting excursions on the river.

**off the beaten path**

**MCKENZIE PASS –** Just beyond McKenzie Bridge, Highway 242 begins a steep, 22-mi eastward climb to McKenzie Pass in the Cascade Range. The scenic highway, which passes through the Mt. Washington Wilderness Area and continues to the town of Sisters (⇨ Central Oregon), is generally closed October–June because of heavy snow. Novice motorists take note, this is not a drive for the timid: it's a challenging exercise in negotiating tight curves at quickly fluctuating speeds, often slow speeds—the skid marks on virtually every turn attest to hasty braking—so take it slow, and don't be intimidated by cars on your tail itching to take the turns more quickly.

# Eugene

**28–38** *63 mi south of Corvallis on I–5.*

Eugene was founded in 1846 when Eugene Skinner staked the first federal land-grant claim for pioneers. Back then it was called Skinner's Mudhole. Wedged between two landmark buttes—Skinner and Spencer—along the Willamette River, Eugene is the culinary, cultural, sports, and intellectual hub of the central Willamette Valley. The home of the University of Oregon is consistently given high marks for its "livability." A large student and former-student population lends Oregon's second-largest city a youthful vitality and countercultural edge. Full of parks and oriented to the outdoors, Eugene is a place where bike paths are used, pedestrians *always* have the right-of-way, and joggers are so plentiful that the city is known as the running capital of the world.

Shopping and commercial streets surround the Eugene Hilton and the Hult Center for the Performing Arts, the two most prominent downtown buildings.

*Numbers in the text correspond to numbers in the margin and on the Eugene map.*

**a good walk**

From downtown Eugene, walk north across the Willamette River on the Autzen Footbridge and stroll through **Alton Baker Park** 38 ▸. Head north to the entertaining **Science Factory** 28 science and technology museum, which is outside the park to the west of Autzen Stadium. Or follow the path that leads west along the river. Walk back across the Willamette River via the Ferry Street Bridge to Gateway Park. Stay to the left at the end of the bridge and you'll eventually hit High Street. Head south on High to the **5th Street Public Market** 29 (which, despite its name, is on 5th Avenue). The market is a great place to have lunch, as you'll want to refuel before your next stop, **Skinner Butte Park** 32. From the market take 5th Avenue west and Lincoln Street north. If you're feeling hardy, you can climb to the top of Skinner Butte for a great view. The **George E. Owen Memorial Rose Garden** 33 is west of the park. Follow the bike path west from Skinner Butte Park along the Willamette River to the garden.

**TIMING** This tour takes more than half a day unless you drive it. Plan to spend an hour or so at each stop, and add an extra hour if you visit the science center.

## What to See

▸ 38 **Alton Baker Park.** Named after the community newspaper's publisher, the Alton Baker Park is a place of many community events. Live music is performed during the summer. There's fine hiking and biking at Alton Baker, the largest of three adjoining riverside parks—Gateway and Skinner Butte are the other two—on the banks of the Willamette River. A footpath along the river runs the length of the park. Also worth seeing

Alton Baker Park . . . . . . . .**38**

Eugene Saturday Market . . . . . .**30**

5th Street Public Market . . . . . .**29**

George E. Owen Memorial Rose Garden . . . . . .**33**

Hendricks Park . . . . . . . .**36**

Hult Center for the Performing Arts . . . . . . .**31**

Lane County Historical Museum . . . . .**34**

Maude Kerns Art Center . . . .**37**

Science Factory . . . . . .**28**

Skinner Butte Park . . .**32**

University of Oregon . . . .**35**

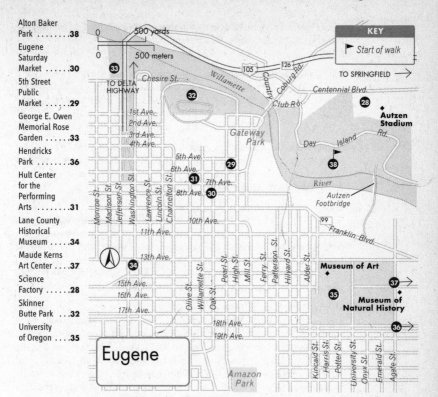

is the Whilamut Natural Area, an open space with 13 "talking stones," each with an inscription. ⊠ *Centennial Blvd. east of Ferry Street Bridge* ☎ *541/484–5307 or 541/682–2000* ⏱ *Daily 6 AM–11 PM.*

**③⓪ Eugene Saturday Market.** Every Saturday between April and November, local craftspeople, farmers, and chefs provide cheap eats and nifty arts and crafts at this outdoor market. ⊠ *8th Ave. and Oak St.* ☎ *541/686–8885* ⊕ *www.eugenesaturdaymarket.org* 🎟 *Free* ⏱ *Sat. 10–5.*

**★ ②⑨ 5th Street Public Market.** A former chicken-processing plant is the site of this popular shopping mall, filled with small crafts, art, and gifts stores. Dining includes sit-down restaurants, decadent bakeries, and the international diversity of the second-floor food esplanade. ⊠ *5th Ave. and High St.* ☎ *541/484–0383* ⏱ *Shops Sat.–Thurs. 10–6, Fri. 10–9; restaurants weekdays 7 AM–9 PM, weekends 7 AM–10 PM.*

**③③ George E. Owen Memorial Rose Garden.** Three thousand roses bloom June–September at this 9-acre garden west of Skinner Butte Park, along the Willamette River. Magnolia, cherry, and oak trees dot the grounds. ⊠ *300 N. Jefferson St.* ☎ *541/682–4824* 🎟 *Free* ⏱ *Daily 6 AM–11 PM.*

**③⑥ Hendricks Park.** This quiet park east of the University of Oregon is at its most glorious in May, when its towering rhododendrons and azaleas blossom in shades of pink, yellow, red, and purple. From the university's Franklin Boulevard gate, head south on Agate Street, east on 19th Avenue, south on Fairmont Boulevard, and east on Summit Avenue. ⊠ *Summit and Skyline Aves.*

**③① Hult Center for the Performing Arts.** This is the locus of Eugene's cultural life. Renowned for the quality of its acoustics, the center has two theaters that are home to Eugene's symphony and opera. ✉ *One Eugene Center, at 7th Ave. and Willamette St.* ☎ *541/682–5087, 541/682–5000 tickets, 541/682–5746 24-hr event recording* ⊙ *Call for hrs.*

**➌ Lane County Historical Museum.** Collections dating from the 1840s to the present are in a 14,000-square-foot building. Exhibits include period rooms, vehicles, early trades, Oregon Trail and early settlement, historic photographs, and memorabilia from the 1920s and 1930s. ✉ *740 W. 13th Ave.* ☎ *541/682–4242* ✎ *$2* ⊙ *Wed.–Fri. 10–4, Sat. noon–4.*

**➌ Maude Kerns Art Center.** The oldest church in Eugene, two blocks east of the University of Oregon, is the site of this arts facility, which exhibits contemporary fine arts and crafts. ✉ *1910 E. 15th Ave.* ☎ *541/345–1571* ✎ *Free* ⊙ *Mon.–Sat. 10–5, Sun. 1–5.*

**➋ Science Factory.** Formerly the Willamette Science and Technology Center (WISTEC) and still known to locals by its former name, Eugene's imaginative, hands-on museum assembles rotating exhibits designed for curious young minds. The adjacent **planetarium,** one of the largest in the Pacific Northwest, presents star shows and entertainment events. ✉ *2300 Leo Harris Pkwy.* ☎ *541/682–7888 museum, 541/461–8227 planetarium* ⊕ *www.sciencefactory.org* ✎ *$4* ⊙ *Fri.–Sun. noon–4.*

**➋ Skinner Butte Park.** Eugene's parks and gardens are wonderfully diverse and add to the outdoor fabric of the city. Skinner Butte Park, rising from the south bank of the Willamette River, has the greatest historic cachet, since it was here that Eugene Skinner staked the claim that put Eugene on the map. Skinner Butte Loop leads to the top of Skinner Butte, from which **Spencer Butte,** 4 mi to the south, can be seen. The two main trails to the top of Skinner Butte traverse a sometimes difficult terrain through a mixed-conifer forest. ✉ *2nd Ave. and High St.* ☎ *541/682–5521* ✎ *Free* ⊙ *Daily 10 AM–midnight.*

**➌ University of Oregon.** The true heart of Eugene lies southeast of the city center at its university. Several fine old buildings can be seen on the 250-acre campus; **Deady Hall,** built in 1876, is the oldest. More than 400 varieties of trees grace the bucolic grounds, along with outdoor sculptures that include *Pioneer* and *Pioneer Mother.* The two bronze figures by Alexander Phimster Proctor were dedicated to the men and women who settled the Oregon Territory and less than a generation later founded the university.

Eugene's two best museums are affiliated with the university. The collection of Asian art at the **University of Oregon Museum of Art** (✉ 1430 Johnson La. ☎ 541/346–3027 ⊕ www.uoma.uoregon.edu), next to the library, includes examples of Chinese imperial tomb figures, textiles, and furniture. Relics of a more localized nature are on display at the **University of Oregon Museum of Natural History** (✉ 1680 E. 15th Ave. ☎ 541/346–3024 ⊕ www.natural-history.uoregon.edu), devoted to Pacific Northwest anthropology and the natural sciences. Its highlights include the fossil collection of Thomas Condon, Oregon's first geologist, and a pair of 9,000-year-old sagebrush sandals.

On the west side of the campus, **Knight Library** (✉ Kincaid St. and E. 15th Ave. ☎ 541/346–3054) is the main building in the university's library system, which has more than 2 million volumes. It's open daily, and admission is free. *University of Oregon main entrance* ✉ *Agate St. and Franklin Blvd.* ✎ *$3 suggested donation for both museums* ⊙ *Art museum Wed. noon–8, Thurs.–Sun. noon–5; natural history museum Wed.–Fri. noon–5, weekends 11–5.*

# OREGON'S COVERED BRIDGES

OREGON HAS THE LARGEST collection of covered bridges in the western United States. At its peak, the state had more than 400 covered bridges. Most fell victim to fire, flood, or general neglect. Today 51 bridges remain, with the heaviest concentration being in the southern Willamette Valley, in the vicinity of Eugene. Lane County, with 19, has the most. Other counties with bridges include Benton, Coos, Deschutes, Douglas, Jackson, Josephine, Lincoln, Linn, Marion, Multnomah, and Polk. Linn County has nine bridges.

The covered bridges, which use truss designs to distribute the weight loads, were built from around 1916 to 1987, mostly in rural areas over creeks and narrow rivers. Wooden construction was chosen because of a lack of steel during World Wars I and II and the wide availability of timber in the state. The bridges were covered to help protect the trusses from the region's heavy rains. Covered bridges had a life span of about 80 years versus less than 10 years for uncovered varieties. Most of Oregon's bridges are a single lane wide, and today about half are open only to pedestrian traffic.

With six covered bridges, Cottage Grove in Lane County has the distinction of being known as the covered bridge capital of Oregon. Centennial Bridge is in downtown Cottage Grove next to City Hall. It was built in 1987 with recycled timber from a dismantled bridge. Also in Cottage Grove is the privately owned Chambers Railroad Bridge, the only covered railroad bridge in the state. Trains used the bridge to carry logs to a nearby lumber mill until 1943.

At 165 feet, Goodpasture Bridge over the McKenzie River in Lane County is the longest wooden span in Oregon. With its Gothic-louvered windows, it is the state's most-photographed bridge. Neal Lane Bridge in Douglas County and North Fork Yachats Bridge in coastal Lincoln County are the state's shortest, at 42 feet. All three of these bridges are open to auto traffic.

The only covered bridge near Portland is the Cedar Crossing Bridge. However, it is not an authentic covered bridge—it is not a truss-support structure and it has a concrete span. To see this bridge, built in 1982, take Foster Road east from I–205 to 134th Avenue; turn right and continue ½ mi south. South of metropolitan Portland and northeast of Salem is Gallon House. Built in 1916, this span over Abiqua Creek is Oregon's oldest covered bridge.

For more information on Oregon's covered bridges contact the Covered Bridge Society of Oregon (2495 S.W. Neill Rd., Sherwood 97120, 503/628–1906).

— By Jeff Boswell

## Wineries

Highway 126 west of Eugene curves past several wineries and the trout-filled Siuslaw River before ending in the Oregon coast town of Florence.

**King Estate Winery** (✉ 80854 Territorial Rd., 16 mi south of Veneta ☎ 541/942–9874 ⊕ www.kingestate.com) produces pinot noir, pinot gris, and chardonnay. Looming over the valley on an 820-acre estate, the modern chateau has a small tasting room and souvenir shop. It's open Memorial Day to Labor Day daily noon–5, Labor Day to Memorial Day weekends noon–5.

**LaVelle Vineyards** (✉ 89697 Scheffler Rd., north of Hwy. 126, Elmira ☎ 541/935–9406) is a quiet enclave amid a 16-acre vineyard, known for pinot vintages and sparkling wines. It's open May–September, daily noon–5; October–April, weekends noon–5.

**Secret House Vineyards Winery** (✉ 88324 Vineyard La., north of Hwy. 126, west of Veneta ☎ 541/935–3774 ⊕ www.secrethousewinery.com) is a laid-back, quintessentially Eugene operation that produces pinot noir, Riesling, and sparkling wine. Big names in music perform on a regular basis. In August, it hosts the annual Wine and Blues Festival. It's open daily 11–5.

**Silvan Ridge/Hinman Vineyards** (✉ 27012 Briggs Hill Rd., south of Hwy. 126, Eugene ☎ 541/345–1945 ⊕ www.silvanridge.com), in a Mediterranean-style stucco facility overlooking a small valley, showcases merlots and pinot noirs. Its large tasting rooms occasionally host wine-maker dinners. It's open daily noon–5.

## Where to Stay & Eat

$$$–$$$$ ✕ **Sweetwaters.** The dining room at the Valley River Inn, which overlooks the Willamette at water level, has Pacific Northwest cuisine. Try the salmon with Szechuan peppercorn crust and cranberry vinaigrette or the grilled beef fillet with Oregon blue-cheese crust. There is a bar area outside as well as a deck for open-air dining. There's a kids' menu and a Sunday brunch. ✉ 1000 Valley River Way ☎ 541/687–0123 ▭ AE, D, DC, MC, V.

$$$ ✕ **Oregon Electric Station.** The menu at this busy eatery in a renovated 1912 railroad depot, a National Historic Building, has steaks, prime rib, and seafood. You can also dine in an antique-train dining car or on the deck in the garden. There's a kids' menu. ✉ 27 E. 5th St., 97401 ☎ 541/485–4444 ▭ AE, D, MC, V ⊘ No lunch weekends.

$–$$$ ✕ **Chanterelle.** Some diners find the European cuisine at this romantic 14-table restaurant old-fashioned, but the chef, Rolf Schmidt, sees no reason to go nouvelle. He continues to prepare the region's beef, lamb, and seafood in a traditional manner. Crystal and fresh flowers fill Chanterelle, which is in an old warehouse across from the 5th Street Public Market. ✉ 207 E. 5th Ave. ☎ 541/484–4065 ▭ AE, DC, MC, V ⊘ Closed Sun. and Mon., last 2 wks in Mar., 1st wk in Apr., last 2 wks in Aug., and 1st wk in Sept. No lunch.

$–$$$ ✕ **Red Agave.** Two local women managed to establish this cozy romantic restaurant in an old building that at one point was a refuse dump, and the result is a hard-to-categorize winner that has Mexican and Latino influences. Items might include the sesame-crusted salmon with chipotle barbecue glaze, which you can consider washing down with a tamarind margarita. Flans, like much of the menu, are seasonal; try the Kahlu'a flan or the orange flan with chocolate in the middle. ✉ 454 Willamette St. ☎ 683/683–2206 ▭ DC, MC, V ⊘ No lunch.

Fodor'sChoice
★

$–$$ ✕ **Ambrosia.** Northern Italian dishes and specialty pizzas are cooked in a wood-fired oven at this popular, casual downtown restaurant. Seafood and vegetarian dishes are on the menu, and there are sidewalk tables for open-air dining. ⊠ *174 E. Broadway, 97401* ☎ *541/342–4141* ⊟ *D, MC, V* ☺ *No lunch Sun.*

**$–$$**  ✕ **Café Zenon.** You never know what you'll find on the menu here—Thai, Indian, Italian, South American, or down-home barbecue—but it's sure to be memorable and expertly prepared. Slate floors, picture windows, Parisian-style street lamps, marble-top tables, and café chairs lend this eatery the feel of a romantic, open-air bistro. The desserts are formidable—two full-time bakers produce 20 to 30 kinds daily. Look for the *zuccotto Fiorentino,* a dove-shape Italian wedding cake with rum, orange, and flavored whipped cream. ⊠ *898 Pearl St.* ☎ *541/343–3005* ⚐ *Reservations not accepted* ⊟ *MC, V.*

**¢–$$**  ✕ **Café Soriah.** The bustling crowds at this Mediterranean restaurant are here for both the convivial neighborhood atmosphere—expect every table to be filled on weekends—and the fine Greek, Italian, and Lebanese fare. Lamb, pasta, and seafood dishes dominate, with nightly pasta and grilled meat specials. Fine art decorates the walls, and summer brings crowds to its small courtyard. ⊠ *384 W. 13th Ave.* ☎ *541/342–4410* ⊟ *AE, DC, MC, V.*

★ **¢–$$**  ✕ **Excelsior Café.** Its accomplished cuisine enhances the appealing European elegance of this restaurant, bar, and bistro-style café across from the University of Oregon. The chef uses only fresh local produce, some of it grown on the premises. The menu changes according to the season, but staples include delicious salads and soups, gnocchi, grilled chicken, broiled salmon, and sandwiches. The dining room, shaded by blossoming cherry trees in the spring, has a quiet, understated feel. There's outdoor seating on the front terrace or under a grape arbor in the back. ⊠*754 E. 13th Ave.* ☎ *541/342–6963* ⊟ *AE, D, DC, MC, V.*

**¢–$$**  ✕ **Jake's Place.** If you have a sports pennant you want to part with, add it to all the others at this neighborhood spot, whose eclectic menu includes vegetarian lasagna; chicken piccata; a chicken breast sautéed with mushrooms, garlic, and capers; and a whiskey-cured prime rib. There's a good selection of wine and Northwest beer, too. ⊠ *603 W. 19th Ave.* ☎ *541/431–0513* ⊟ *MC, V* ☺ *No dinner Sun., no lunch Mon.*

**¢–$$**  ✕ **Mekala's.** The emphasis at this eatery in the Fifth Street Public Market is on healthful yet zippy Thai staples such as pad thai and curries. The owners grow their own mint and lime leaves as well as other ingredients, and they've decorated the interior with family photos and wall hangings from Thailand. ⊠ *1769 Franklin Blvd.* ☎ *541/342–4872* ⊟ *AE, MC, V.*

**¢–$$**  ✕ **Turtles Bar & Grill.** Parking around this spot is scarce and there aren't FodorsChoice enough tables, but the food is worth the obstacles. The barbecue en-★ trées, particularly the pulled-pork sandwich, are tasty, and the staff is quite friendly. ⊠ *2692 Willamette St.,* ☎ *541/465–9038* ⊟ *AE, D, DC, MC, V.*

**¢–$**  ✕ **Poppi's Anatolia.** The moussaka and *kalamarakia* (fried squid) at this home-style Greek restaurant are great; wash them down with retsina or Aegean beer. Except on Sunday nights, when the chef prepares only Greek dishes, you can also sample East Indian specialties. ⊠ *992 Willamette St.* ☎ *541/343–9661* ⊟ *MC, V* ☺ *No lunch Sun.*

**¢**  ✕ **East 19th Street Cafe.** On the outskirts of the University of Oregon campus, this is a popular spot for sandwiches and beer; offset the kick of the ragin' Cajun with a Working Man's Red. ⊠ *1485 E. 19th St.* ☎ *541/342–4025* 🖷 *541/342–7161* ⊟ *AE, D, MC, V.*

**$$$–$$$$**  ✕▥ **Valley River Inn.** At this inn on the banks of the Willamette River, FodorsChoice some rooms have an outdoor patio or balcony, some have river or pool ★ views, and concierge rooms have access to a private lounge. All rooms have hair dryers, coffeemakers, and irons. Book the fishing package and the concierge will arrange a river or ocean fishing trip; when you get back the chef will prepare your catch just for you. The inn's restaurant is the popular Sweetwaters. ✉ *1000 Valley River Way, 97401* ☎ *541/ 687–0123 or 800/543–8266* 🖷 *541/682–0289* ⊕ *www.valleyriverinn. com* ⇨ *257 rooms* ⟷ *Restaurant, pool, gym, hot tub, steam room, bicycles, bar, dry cleaning, laundry service, concierge, business services, meeting room, airport shuttle, free parking* ▭ *AE, D, DC, MC, V.*

**$–$$$** ⊡ **Campbell House.** Built in 1892 on the east side of Skinner Butte, Campbell House is one of the oldest structures in Eugene. Restored with fastidious care, the luxurious B&B is surrounded by an acre of landscaped grounds. The parlor, library, and dining rooms have their original hardwood floors and curved-glass windows. Differing architectural details, building angles, and furnishings (a mixture of century-old antiques and reproductions) lend each of the rooms a distinctive personality. One suite has a whirlpool. The room rates include a breakfast of fresh-baked pastries and other items. ✉ *252 Pearl St., 97401* ☎ *541/343–1119 or 800/264–2519* 🖷 *541/343–2258* ⊕ *www.campbellhouse.com* ⇨ *12 rooms, 6 suites* ⟷ *In-room VCRs; no-smoking room* ▭ *AE, D, MC, V.*

**$–$$$** ⊡ **Eugene Hilton.** Location, amenities, and service make this downtown hotel Eugene's most convenient and comfortable. Sliding glass doors in each of the rooms open out to the city. The top-floor restaurant, Vistas, and CJ's, the adjacent bar, have the best butte-to-butte view in Eugene. The Hilton and its extensive convention facilities adjoin Eugene's Hult Center for the Performing Arts. Downtown shopping, the Willamette River, and more than 30 restaurants are within easy walking distance. ✉ *66 E. 6th Ave., 97401* ☎ *541/342–2000 or 800/937–6660* 🖷 *541/ 342–6661* ⊕ *www.hilton.eugene.com* ⇨ *272 rooms* ⟷ *2 restaurants, indoor pool, hair salon, hot tub, gym, 2 bars, free parking, airport shuttle* ▭ *AE, D, DC, MC, V.*

★ **$–$$$** ⊡ **Excelsior Inn.** This small hotel in a former frat house manifests a quiet sophistication more commonly found in Europe than in America. Crisply detailed, with cherry-wood doors and moldings, it has rooms furnished in a refreshingly understated manner, each with a marble-and-tile bath. The rates include a delicious breakfast. The ground-level Excelsior Café is one of Eugene's best restaurants. ✉ *754 E. 13th Ave., 97401* ☎ *541/ 342–6963 or 800/321–6963* 🖷 *541/342–1417* ⊕ *www.excelsiorinn.com* ⇨ *14 rooms* ⟷ *Restaurant, café, in-room data ports, in-room VCRs, bar, no-smoking rooms, free parking* ▭ *AE, D, DC, MC, V.*

**$$** ⊡ **Campus Cottage Bed & Breakfast.** All rooms have plush comforters and overlook the sculpted European garden with its trickling fountain at the town's first B&B, only two blocks from the University of Oregon campus. ✉ *1136 E. 19th Ave., 97403* ☎ *541/342–5346 or 877/700–5346* 🖷 *541/241–0535* ⊕ *www.campuscottage.com* ⇨ *3 rooms* ⟷ *Refrigerators, cable TV; no a/c, no kids under 12, no smoking* ▭ *AE, D, DC, MC, V* ⎮◎⎮ *BP.*

**$$** ⊡ **Enchanted Country Inn Bed & Breakfast.** You are welcomed to this B&B in a forest of Douglas firs, cedars, and redwoods, with the innkeeper's homemade wines and fresh flowers in your room. Wicker furniture and hardwood floors and floral prints accent the interior of this, the closest inn to the Eugene Airport. The inn is also only 2 mi from town. The cottage has a full kitchen. ✉ *29195 Gimpl Hill Rd., 97402* ☎ *541/465–1869* 🖷 *541/465–1507* ⇨ *3 rooms, 1 cottage* ⟷ *No a/c, no room phones, no smoking* ▭ *AE, MC, V* ⎮◎⎮ *BP.*

**$$** ⊡ **Oval Door Bed and Breakfast Inn.** The wraparound porch on this 1990 house is in keeping with the 1920s neighborhood. It is near the university, the Hult Center, the Saturday Market, and restaurants. Guest rooms are named for Oregon wildflowers with decorative touches to match. A mixture of antiques, reproductions, floral prints, and an outdoor swing assure comfort. Both owners are chefs and showcase their talent at breakfast. And, yes, the house does have an oval door. ⊠ *988 Lawrence St., 97401* ☎ *541/683–3160 or 800/882–3160* 🖷 *541/485–0260* ⊕ *www.ovaldoor.com* ⋺ *4 rooms* ᗉ *In-room data ports, cable TV, hot tub; no smoking* ⊟ *AE, MC, V* ⍓ *BP.*

$ 🏠 **Country Inn Bed & Breakfast.** Four miles north of town, this 1874 homestead is truly a country inn, down to the cast-iron pot used by the inn's founders, which still hangs in the fireplace. The inn is set on 10 acres of gardens that contain more than 500 rosebushes, a gazebo, and a pond with two resident swans. The Victorian-style rooms have four-poster beds and floral comforters. ⊠ *4100 County Farm Rd., 97408* ☎ *541/345–7344 or 877/816–8757* 🖷 *541/345–0172* ⊕ *www.cibab.com* ⋺ *2 rooms* ⊟ *AE, MC, V* ⍓ *BP.*

$ 🏠 **Kjaer's House in the Woods.** On the outskirts of Eugene, this 1910 Craftsman-style B&B is a member of the Green Hotels Association (for ecologically conscious accommodations) and is 2½ mi from the University of Oregon campus. Both guest rooms have bright white bed spreads, one over an iron bedstead and one over a solid wood frame. A rosewood square grand piano, Danish plate collection, and other antiques fill the common areas. ⊠ *814 Lorane Hwy., 97405* ☎ *541/343–3234 or 800/437–4501* ⋺ *2 rooms* ᗉ *No a/c, no room phones, no room TVs* ⍓ *BP.*

## Nightlife & the Arts

The **Hult Center For the Performing Arts** (⊠ 1 Eugene Center ☎ 541/682–5733 ⊕ www.hultcenter.org), a spacious building of glass and native wood, is the locus of Eugene's cultural life. Renowned for the quality of their acoustics, the center's two theaters are home base for Eugene's symphony and opera companies. Ballets, major performers, traveling Broadway shows, and rock bands appear regularly.

Conductor Helmuth Rilling leads the internationally known **Oregon Bach Festival** (☎ 541/346–5666 or 800/457–1486 ⊕ www.bachfest.uoregon. edu) every summer. Concerts, chamber music, and social events—held mainly in Eugene at the Hult Center and the University of Oregon School of Music but also in Corvallis and Florence—are part of this 17-day event. In May and August, the **Oregon Festival of American Music** (☎ 541/687–6526 or 800/248–1615 ⊕ www.ofam.org) presents concerts at the Hult Center and parks around Eugene. **Oregon Mozart Players** (☎ 541/345–6648), the state's premier professional chamber music orchestra, plays 20 concerts a year. The **Eugene Opera** (☎ 541/682–5000 ⊕ www.eugenopera.com) produces three fully staged operas per season. The **Eugene Symphony** (☎ 541/687–9487 ⊕ www.eugenesymphony. org) performs a full season of classical, family, and pops concerts.

## Sports & the Outdoors

BASEBALL The **Eugene Emeralds** (⊠ 2077 Willamette St. ☎ 541/342–5367 ⊕ www. go-ems.com), the Northwest League (Class A) affiliate of the San Diego Padres, play at Civic Stadium.

BASKETBALL The **University of Oregon Ducks** (⊠ 1601 University St. ☎ 800/932–3668) play at MacArthur Court.

BIKING & JOGGING The **River Bank Bike Path,** originating in Alton Baker Park on the Willamette's north bank, is a level and leisurely introduction to Eugene's topography. It's one of 120 mi of trails in the area. **Prefontaine Trail,** used by area runners, travels through level fields and forests for 1½ mi. **Pedal Power** (⊠ 535 High St. ☎ 541/687–1775) downtown rents bikes.

FOOTBALL The **University of Oregon Ducks** play their home games at Autzen Stadium (⊠ 2700 Centennial Blvd. ☎ 800/932–3668).

GOLF    **Riveridge Golf Course** (✉ 3800 N. Delta Hwy. ☎ 541/345–9160) is an 18-hole, par-71 course. The greens fee is $29; a cart costs $22.

SKIING    **Willamette Pass** (✉ Hwy. 58, 69 mi southeast of Eugene ☎ 541/345–7669 or 800/444–5030), 6,666 feet high in the Cascades Range, packs an annual average snowfall of 300 inches atop 29 runs. The vertical drop is 1,563 feet. Four triple chairs and one double chair service the downhill ski areas, and 13 mi of Nordic trails lace the pass. Facilities here include a ski shop; day care; a bar and a restaurant; and Nordic and downhill rentals, repairs, and instruction.

## Shopping

Tourists coming to the Willamette Valley, especially to Eugene, can't escape without experiencing the Fifth Street Public Market in downtown Eugene. There are plenty of small crafts shops and the food mall yields many cuisines, including vegetarian, pizza, and seafood. **Smith Family Bookstore** (✉ 768 E. 13th ☎ 541/345–1651 ✉ 525 Willamette ☎ 541/343–4717) is a wonderful resource for used books. **Valley River Center** (✉ Delta Hwy. and Valley River Dr., 97401 ☎ 541/683–5511) is the largest shopping center between Portland and San Francisco. There are five department stores, including Meier & Frank and JCPenney, plus 144 specialty shops and a food court.

> off the beaten path

**WALDO LAKE –** Nestled in old-growth forest, Waldo Lake is famed as a remarkably clean and pristine body of water. The lake is accessible only after a short hike, so bring comfortable shoes. ⊹ *From Eugene take Hwy. 58 to Oakridge and continue toward Willamette Pass (follow signs north to Waldo Lake).*

# Cottage Grove

**39** *20 mi south of Eugene on I–5.*

With more than a half dozen historic "creek covers" close by, Cottage Grove's self-proclaimed title as the covered bridge capital of Oregon is well deserved. Of particular note is the Chambers Railroad Bridge, the only one of its kind west of the Mississippi River, built in 1925 to carry logs to mill. Cottage Grove's historic downtown, through which the Willamette River flows, has attracted moviemakers and light-industrial developers alike.

Formerly a mining area, **Brice Creek Trail** has been transformed into a path for hikers and bikers, though it is recommended for only intermediate and advanced riders. ⊹ *Trailhead is 25 mi southeast of Cottage Grove. From Cottage Grove, I–5's Exit 174, go right on Brice Creek Rd. No. 2470 (19 mi)* ☎ *541/942–5591* ☉ *Daily.*

A mile outside Cottage Grove in the Coast Range foothills, **Chateau Lorane Winery** produces some unusual varieties including Grignolino, Durif, pinot meunier, and Baco noir. A 25-acre lake and picnic area make this a popular spot for picnics and large events. ✉ *27415 Siuslaw River Rd., Lorane, 97451* ☎ *541/942–8028* 🖷 *541/942–5830* ⊕ *www.chateaulorane.com* ☉ *June–Sept., daily noon–5; Jan.–May and Oct.–Dec., weekends noon–5; also by appointment.*

Industrial, farm, mining, and household tools are at the **Cottage Grove Museum.** On display is a 19th-century octagonal church with its original stained-glass windows. ✉ *147 H St.* ☎ *541/942–3963* 🖾 *Free* ☉ *Mid-June–Labor Day, Wed.–Sun. 1–4; Labor Day–mid-June, weekends 1–4.*

Oregon has the largest collection of **covered bridges** in the western United States. The Willamette Valley has more than 34 of the wooden structures. There are six bridges on a loop drive outside Cottage Grove. The widest bridge in the state is off Highway 58 near Lowell. Four others are nearby. ☎ *503/986–3514* ⊕ *www.odot.state.or.us/eshtm/br.htm* ⊠ *Free* ☺ *Daily.*

Three parks at **Dorena Lake**, a reservoir built in the 1940s, offer boating, swimming, sailing, fishing, and waterskiing. Schwartz Park, downstream from the dam, and Baker Bay Park, on the south side of the lake, have campgrounds. ⊠ *Row River Rd., at Exit 174 off I–5* ☎ *541/942–1418* ⊠ *Free* ☺ *Daily.*

You can access the 15.6 mi **Row River Trail**, a scenic, flat, hiking and biking path, formerly a railroad track, by following the Row River 3 mi east of town at the Mosby Bridge. ☎ *541/942–2411.*

## Where to Stay & Eat

¢–$$$  ✕ **Cottage.** Heat from a single wood-burning stove and the sun are the only energy sources at this environmentally friendly restaurant, with healthy cooking. Entrées include seafood, steak, and chicken. There's also a wide selection of sandwiches, soups, salads, and burgers as well as a kids' menu. ⊠ *2915 Row River Rd., 97424* ☎ *541/942–3091* ▤ *MC, V* ☺ *Closed Sun.*

$  ▦ **Apple Inn Bed and Breakfast.** Just outside Cottage Grove, this modern country home has open-beam ceilings and large windows with a view of 190 acres of surrounding forest. The interior runs to country kitsch, but the guest rooms have handmade quilts, antiques, and country-style furnishings, and one has a private entrance. The hosts provide a hearty breakfast and evening snacks. ⊠ *30697 Kenady La., 97424* ☎ *541/942–2393 or 800/942–2393* 🖶 *541/767–0402* ⊕ *www.moriah.com/appleinn* ⟲ *2 rooms* ⊗ *Cable TV, outdoor hot tub; no a/c, no smoking* ▤ *D, MC, V* ⑩ *BP.*

## Shopping

**Champion Acres Nursery** (⊠ 78693 Cedar Park Rd. ☎ 541/942–7766) has 70 varieties of lavender plants. Find booths with arts, crafts, and food every Saturday at **Cottage Grove Farmers' Market** (⊠ 14th and Main St. ☎ 541/942–2230) in Coiner Park. The market season runs from May to the first weekend in November, with booths open 9–4.

# Drain

➍  *8 mi west of I–5, halfway between Roseburg and Eugene.*

Famous for its castle and covered bridge, this small timber town between Roseburg and Eugene has several Victorians and good antiques shops worth seeing. Other nearby attractions in Douglas County include Wildlife Safari and Crater Lake National Park. Drain is about 30 mi south of Eugene at the junction of Highways 99 and 38.

On the Coast Fork of the Willamette River, **Cottage Grove Lake**, a reservoir built in the 1940s, is 3 mi long. There are two parks and two campgrounds. Recreational activities include boating, swimming, waterskiing, fishing, and picnicking. The area has many birds (including bald eagles) and blacktail deer. ⊠ *75166 Cottage Grove Lake Rd., 97424* ☎ *541/942–8657 or 541/942–5631.*

Residents Charles and Anna Drain donated 60 acres of land to found the town of Drain. This Victorian, known as **Drain Castle**, was built in 1895 and is on the National Register of Historic Places. Today it serves as a school district administration office. ⊠ *500 S. Main St.* ☎ *541/836–2223.*

The only Oregon covered bridge within city limits is **Pass Creek Covered Bridge.** Built in the 1870s and rebuilt in 1925, Pass Creek bridge was moved to Drain City Park in the late 1980s. The 61-foot-long span carried cars until 1981. Today only pedestrians are welcome. ⊠ *Behind 205 W. A St.* ☎ *541/836–2417.*

### Where to Stay & Eat

¢–$   ✕ **Peggy's Restaurant.** Breakfast is served all day at this friendly diner. Entrées include chicken, steaks, seafood, and pasta. ⊠ *Exit 148 off I–5 at Rice Hill, 97135* ☎ *541/849–2841* ▤ *MC, V.*

¢–$   ✕ **Road Kill Grill.** People drive from nearby cities for the home cooking at this popular barbecue restaurant, which looks like a 1950s throwback. There are hubcaps as light fixtures and tire marks on the floor with tinsel road kill. They don't serve skunk, but they do dish up great barbecued chicken, steaks, and—their specialty—ribs. ⊠ *306 Hwy. 38, 97135* ☎ *541/836–2156* ▤ *No credit cards* ☉ *Closed Mon. No lunch.*

$$–$$$$   🏨 **Big K Guest Ranch.** A 12,000-square-foot log lodge, 4 mi south of Highway 38 and 20 mi from Drain, anchors this working ranch secluded in wooded surroundings on the Umpqua River. Fly-fishing is a staple here, as are rafting and swimming. ⊠ *20029 Hwy. 138 W, Elkton 97436* ☎ *541/584–2295 or 800/390–2445* ⎙ *541/584–2395* ⊕ *www.big-k. com* ➮ *20 cabins* ⚭ *Restaurant, hiking, horseback riding, fishing, meeting room* ▤ *AE, D, DC, MC, V.*

$   🏨 **Tuckaway Farm Inn.** In a restored 1920s farmhouse, this small bed-and-breakfast is in a quiet valley a few miles east of Drain. The rooms have private baths and are decorated with antiques. ⊠ *7179 Scotts Valley Rd., Yoncalla 97499* ☎ *541/849–3144* ⊕ *www.moriah.com/tuckaway* ➮ *3 rooms* ⚭ *Hot tub, hiking, fishing; no smoking* ▤ *MC, V* ¶◎¶ *BP.*

# THE WILLAMETTE VALLEY & THE WINE COUNTRY A TO Z

*To research prices, get advice from other travelers, and book travel arrangements, visit www.fodors.com.*

### AIR TRAVEL

You can fly into Portland's International Airport and begin your travels at the northern part of the Willamette Valley, or explore the southern end first by flying into Eugene's Mahlon Sweet Airport. The latter is served by America West, Horizon, Skywest, and United/United Express. Another option is to mix your itineraries and use both airports, as the flight from Portland to Eugene is a mere 40 minutes. There are also smaller airports scattered throughout the valley.

🛪 Airports **Albany Municipal Airport** ⊠ 525 Aviation Way SE ☎ 541/917-7676. **Chehalem Airpark** ⊠ 17770 N.E. Aviation Way, Newberg ☎ 503/537-0108 or 800/554-6359. **Corvallis Municipal Airport (COV)** ⊠ 1245 N.E. 3rd St. ☎ 541/766-6916. **Cresswell Airport** (Hobby Field) ⊠ 83501 Melton Rd., Cresswell ⊕ www.creswellairport.com. **Eugene Airport (EUG)** (Mahlon Sweet Field) ⊠ 28855 Lockheed Dr. ☎ 541/682-5430 ⊕ www.eugeneairport.com. **Hillsboro Airport** ⊠ 3565 N.E. Cornell Rd. ☎ 800/547-8411 or 503/460-4125. **Salem Air Center** (McNary Field Airport) ⊠ 3300 25th St. SE, Salem ☎ 503/364-4158 or 800/369-4698 ⊕ www.salemaircenter.com. **Twin Oaks Airport** ⊠ 12405 S.W. River Rd., Hillsboro ☎ 503/628-2817.

🛪 Carriers **America West** ☎ 800/235-9292 ⊕ www.americawest.com. **Horizon Air** ☎ 800/547-9308 ⊕ horizonair.alaskaair.com. **United/United Express** ☎ 800/241-6522 ⊕ www.ual.com.

### BIKE TRAVEL

If time is not of the essence, discover the Willamette Valley on a bike, whether it be a casual ride with friends or an organized tour. Eugene in particular is a community of bikes and pedestrian walkways, with 28 mi of off-street paths, 78 mi of on-street bicycle lanes, and 5 bicycle-pedestrian bridges spanning the Willamette River. Eugene also equips nearly every main street with a bike lane for easy commuting. Biking around the northern Willamette Valley allows you to absorb the beauty of the area and get a taste of wine country.

🚲 Rentals **Blue Heron Bicycles** ✉ 877 E. 13th, Eugene 97401-3706 ☎ 541/343-2488. **Center for Appropriate Transport** ✉ 455 W. 1st Ave. Eugene ☎ 541/344-1197 🖨 541/686-1015. **High Street Bicycles** ✉ 535 High St., Eugene 97401-2711 ☎ 541/687-1775. **South Salem Cycleworks** ✉ 4071 Liberty Rd., Salem 97302-5752 ☎ 503/399-9848.

🚲 Tours **Bicycle Adventures** 📦 Box 11219, Olympia, WA 98508 ☎ 800/443-6060 or 360/786-0989 ⊕ www.bicycleadventures.com. **Oregon Adventures** 📦 Box 148, Oakridge 97463 ☎ 541/782-2388.

## BUS TRAVEL

Between the local bus companies and the Greyhound bus system, the Willamette Valley is accessible by bus. Many of the Lane Transit District (LTD) buses will make a few stops to the outskirts of Lane County, such as to McKenzie Bridge, and buses come with bike racks so you can combine your means of transport; it's better for the environment and you can do more sightseeing by letting someone else do the driving.

🚌 Depots **Cottage Grove Bus Terminal** ✉ 1250 Gateway Blvd. ☎ 541/942-7331. **Eugene Greyhound Bus Terminal** ✉ 987 Pearl St. ☎ 541/344-6265.

🚌 Lines **Greyhound** ☎ 800/231-2222.

🚌 **Lane Transit District** ✉ 1080 Willamette ☎ 541/687-5555 ⊕ www.ltd.org. **Salem Area Mass Transit District** ✉ 555 Court St. NE, Suite 5230 ☎ 503/588-2424 🖨 503/566-3933 ⊕ www.cherriots.org.

## CAR RENTALS

Avis, Budget, Hertz, and Enterprise all have branches at the Mahlon Sweet Airport. Other options are Eugene Van & Car Rental and Rent-A-Wreck in Springfield. If you're looking to tool up to the vineyards in style, there's Centennial BMW Car Rentals.

🚗 Agencies **Avis** ☎ 541/688-9053. **Budget** ☎ 541/463-0422. **Centennial BMW Car Rentals** ✉ 1790 W. 7th St. ☎ 541/342-1763. **Enterprise** ☎ 541/689-7563. **Eugene Van & Car Rental** ✉ 380 Goodpasture Island Rd. ☎ 541/342-6161 Ext. 2 ⊕ www.elmcars. com. **Hertz** ☎ 541/688-9333 or 800/654-3131. **Rent-A-Wreck** ✉ 1863 Laura Springfield ☎ 541/747-1275 or 800/655-4573.

## CAR TRAVEL

I–5 runs north–south the length of the Willamette. Many Willamette Valley attractions lie not too far east or west of I–5. Highway 22 travels west from the Willamette National Forest through Salem to the coast. Highway 99 travels parallel to I–5 through much of the Willamette Valley. Highway 34 leaves I–5 south of Albany and heads west, past Corvallis and into the Coast Range, where it follows the Alsea River. Highway 126 heads east from Eugene toward the Willamette National Forest; it travels west from town to the coast.

## CHILDREN IN THE WILLAMETTE VALLEY & THE WINE COUNTRY

The Eugene Public Library is a fantastic place to bring kids on a rainy day. Science Factory will provide ample entertainment for busy fingers. For recreation, you might also try Putter's Miniature Golf, with wonderful pizza and other foods, or, right next door, Strike City bowling.

🎡 **Eugene Public Library** ✉ 100 W. 10th. Ave. ☎ 541/682-5450 ⊕ www.ci.eugene. or.us/library. **Putters Miniature Golf** ✉ 1156 Hwy. 99 N ☎ 541/688-8901. **Science Factory** ✉ 2300 Leo Harris Pkwy., Eugene ☎ 541/682-7888 ⊕ www.sciencefactory. org. **Strike City** ✉ 1170 Hwy. 99 N ☎ 541/688-8900.

## DISABILITIES & ACCESSIBILITY

Travelers with disabilities will find that for the most part, Eugene, Salem, and Corvallis are easy to get around. All buses in Eugene use lifts for wheelchairs. Senior & Disabled Services can give you a rundown on wheelchair-accessible properties in Lane County. Eugene is headquarters of Mobility International, which troubleshoots accessibility issues worldwide. 🔲 Local Resources **Mobility International** ☎ 541/343-1284 tel. and TTY ⊕ www.miusa.org. **Senior & Disabled Services** ⊕ www.sdslane.org ☎ 800/441-4038, 541/682-4567 TTY.

## EMERGENCIES

🔲 Doctors & Dentists **Tuality Healthcare Physician Referral** ✉ 335 S.E. 8th Ave., Hillsboro ☎ 503/681-1750.

🔲 Emergency Services **American Red Cross** ✉ 862 Bethel Dr., Eugene 97402 ☎ 541/344-5244 🖷 541/345-4806 ⊕ www.oregonpacific.redcross.org. **Oregon State Police** ✉ 255 Capitol St. NE, 400 Public Service Bldg., Salem 97310 ☎ 503/378-3720 or 503/378-3725 🖷 503/378-8282 ⊕ www.osp.state.or.us. **Salvation Army** ✉ 1785 N.E. Sandy Blvd., Portland 97232 ☎ 503/234-0825 🖷 503/239-1211 ⊕ www.tsacascade.org.

🔲 Hospitals **Albany General Hospital** ✉ 1046 6th Ave. SW, Albany 97321 ☎ 541/812-4000 ⊕ samhealth.org. **Good Samaritan Regional Medical Center** ✉ 3600 N.W. Samaritan Dr., Corvallis 97330 ☎ 541/768-5111 🖷 541/768-5124 ⊕ www.samhealth.org. **Sacred Heart Medical Center** ✉1255 Hilyard St., Eugene 97440 ☎541/686-7300 ⊕www.peacehealth.org.

## LODGING

BED-AND-
BREAKFASTS

There are quite a few bed-and-breakfasts in the Willamette Valley. In the spring and summer, advance reservations are essential, especially during festival days and spring track season. The Convention & Visitors Association of Lane County Oregon and Planet Eugene have B & B listings. 🔲 Reservations Services **Convention & Visitors Association of Lane County Oregon** ✉ 115 W. 8th St., Suite 190, Eugene 97401 ☎ 541/484-5307 or 800/547-5445 🖷 541/343-6335 ⊕ www.visitlanecounty.org. **Planet Eugene** ⊕ www.planeteugene.com.

## MAIL & SHIPPING

Eugene has several post offices. For Internet access, the public library system is the most reliable resource, though there are Internet cafés in Eugene and other towns. 🔲 Post Offices **Eugene Main Office Carriers** ✉ 50 W. 5th St., Eugene 97401 ☎ 541/341-3649. **Gateway Retail Unit** ✉ 3148 Gateway St., Eugene 97401 ☎ 541/341-3649. **River Road Station** ✉ 255 River Ave., Eugene 97404 ☎ 541/341-3669. **University Station** ✉ 1222 E. 13th Ave., Eugene 97403 ☎ 541/341-3692. **Westside Eugene** ✉ 950 Tyinn St., Eugene 97402 ☎ 541/341-3694.

🔲 Internet Cafés **Sip N' Surf Cybercafé** ✉ 99 W. 10th St., Suite 119, Eugene 97401 ☎ 541/343-9607 ⊕ www.sipnsurf.com. **The Web Zone** ✉ 296 E. 5th Ave., Suite 102, Eugene 97401 ☎ 541/434-0442.

## MEDIA

There are many dailies and weeklies throughout the Willamette Valley & Wine Country, though the most prominent papers are the *Eugene Register-Guard* and the *Statesman Journal* in Salem.

## SPORTS & THE OUTDOORS

Oregon is more of a participant-sport state than one for spectators, though watching a Class A baseball game is a good reminder of why people love baseball: fans huddle on cozy little fields, watching players who have a glimmer in their eye of making it to the big leagues. 🔲 Baseball **Eugene Emeralds** ✉ 2077 Willamette St., Eugene 97405 ☎ 541/342-5367 🖷 541/342-6089 ⊕ www.go-ems.com. **Salem-Keizer Volcanoes** ✉ 6700 Field of Dreams Way NE, Keizer 97307 ☎ 503/390-2225 ⊕ www.volcanoesbaseball.com.

### TAXIS

While you might find a cab roving the outskirts of an airport or bus station, you'll generally have to call one, even in Eugene. Fares ought to be posted, and a tip of 20% of the fare is recommended.

▶ Companies **Jerry's Taxicab Co** ✉ 570 Lawrence St., Suite 103, Eugene ☎ 541/688-8761. **Vip Limo & Taxi** ✉ 1940 W. 12th Ave., Eugene ☎ 541/484-0920.

### TOURS

Eugene Tours LLC allows you to create your own tour or go with a prepared tour. Off the Beaten Path will take you around the valley and its environs. For a bike tour, try Oregon Adventures.

▶ **Eugene Tours LLC** ✐ Box 2321, Eugene 97402-0073 ☎ 541/579-8266 🖷 541/344-0525 ⊕ www.eugenetours.com. **Northwest Gold Tours** ✉ 13195 S.W. Oakwood St., Beaverton 97005 ☎ 503/672-9985 or 888/401-TOUR 🖷 503/672-7565. **Off the Beaten Path** ✉ Junction City ☎ 541/998-2450. **Oregon Adventures** ✐ Box 148, Oakridge 97463 ☎ 541/782-2388 ⊕ www.oregon-adventures.com.

### TRAIN TRAVEL

Traveling the Willamette Valley by train is quick and easy. Amtrak has stops from Portland to Cottage Grove.

▶ **Amtrak** ☎ 800/872-7245 ⊕ www.amtrak.com.
▶ Stations **Albany Station** ✉ 110 W. 10th St., Albany 97321 ☎ 541/928-0885. **Eugene-Springfield** ✉ 433 Willamette St., Eugene 97401. **Salem Station** ✉ 500 13th St. SE, Salem 97301 ☎ 503/588-1551.

### VISITOR INFORMATION

▶ Tourist Information **Beaverton Chamber of Commerce** ✉ 4800 S.W. Griffith Dr., Suite 100, 97005 ☎ 503/644-0123 🖷 503/526-0349 ⊕ www.beaverton.org. **Brownsville Chamber of Commerce** ✐ Box 278, 97327 ☎ 541/466-5311 🖷 541/466-5312. **Corvallis Convention and Visitors Bureau** ✉ 420 N.W. 2nd St., 97330 ☎ 541/757-1544 or 800/334-8118 ⊕ www.visitcorvallis.com. **Cottage Grove Chamber of Commerce** ✉ 700 E. Gibbs, Suite C, 97424 ☎ 541/942-2411 🖷 541/431-7044 ⊕ www.cgchamber.com. **Eugene Convention & Visitors Bureau** ✉ 115 W. 8th St., Suite 190, 97440 ☎ 541/484-5307 or 800/547-5445 ⊕ www.visitlanecounty.org. **Forest Grove Chamber of Commerce** ✉ 2417 Pacific Ave., 97116 ☎ 503/357-3006 🖷 503/357-2367 ⊕ www.fgchamber.org. **Greater Hillsboro Area Chamber of Commerce** ✉ 334 S.E. 5th Ave., 97123 ☎ 503/648-1102 🖷 503/681-0535 ⊕ www.hilchamber.org. **Lake Oswego Chamber of Commerce and Visitor's Center** ✉ 242 B St., 97034 ⊕ www.lake-oswego.com. **Lane County Convention and Visitors Association** ✉ 115 W. 8th Ave., Suite 190, Eugene, 97401 ☎ 541/343-6335 or 800/547-5445 ⊕ www.visitlanecounty.org. **McMinnville Chamber of Commerce** ✉ 417 N.W. Adams St., 97128 ☎ 503/472-6196 ⊕ www.mcminnville.org. **Newberg Area Chamber of Commerce** ✉ 115 N. Washington St., 97132 ☎ 503/538-2014 🖷 503/538-2463 ⊕ www.newberg.org. **North Plains Area Chamber of Commerce** ✐ Box 152, North Plains 97133 ☎ 503/647-2207 🖷 503/647-2838 ⊕ www.northplains.org. **Oregon City Chamber of Commerce** ✉ 1810 Washington St., 97045 ☎ 503/656-1619 or 800/424-3002 🖷 503/656-2274. **Philomath Area Chamber of Commerce** ✐ Box 606, Philomath 97370 ☎ 541/929-2454 🖷 541/929-4420 ⊕ www.philomathchamber.org. **Salem Convention & Visitors Center** ✉ 1313 Mill St. SE, 97301 ☎ 503/581-4325 or 800/874-7012 ⊕ www.scva.org. **Sweet Home Chamber of Commerce** ✉ 1575 Main St., 97386 ☎ 541/367-6186 ⊕ www.sweethomechamber.org. **Yamhill County Wineries Association** ✐ Box 25162, Portland 97298 ☎ 503/646-2985. **Yamhill Valley Visitors Association** ✉ 417 N.W. Adams, 97128 ☎ 503/883-7770 🖷 503/472-6198 ⊕ www.oregonwinecountry.org.

# SOUTHERN OREGON

**6**

## FODOR'S CHOICE

Black Sheep, *Ashland pub*

Crater Lake Lodge, *Crater Lake National Park*

Crater Lake National Park, *off Route 62*

Jacksonville Cemetery, *Jacksonville*

Out N' About, *tree-house hotel near Oregon Caves*

The Steamboat Inn, *Steamboat*

Under the Greenwood Tree, *Medford B & B*

Valley of the Rogue State Park, *Grants Pass*

## HIGHLY RECOMMENDED

RESTAURANTS    Chateaulin, *Ashland*

Hong Kong Bar, *Ashland*

HOTELS    Ashland Creek Inn, *Ashland*

Jacksonville Inn, *Jacksonville*

Mt. Ashland Inn, *Ashland*

SIGHTS    Abacela Vineyards and Winery, *Roseburg*

Rim Drive, *Crater Lake National Park*

Wildlife Safari, *Winston*

Wizard Island, *Crater Lake National Park*

Updated by
Zach Dundas

**APPROACHED FROM THE NORTH, SOUTHERN OREGON BEGINS** where the verdant lowlands of the Willamette Valley give way to a complex collision of mountains, rivers, and ravines. The intricate geography of the "Land of Umpqua," as the area around Roseburg is somewhat romantically known, signals that this is territory very distinct from neighboring regions to the north, east, and west. Wild rivers—the Rogue and the Umpqua are legendary for fishing and boating—and twisting mountain roads venture through the landscape that saw Oregon's most violent Indian wars and became the territory of a self-reliant breed. Don't-Tread-on-Me southern Oregonians see themselves as markedly different from fellow citizens of the Pacific Wonderland. In fact, several early-20th-century attempts to secede from Oregon and proclaim a "state of Jefferson" survive in local folklore and culture—the region's beloved public radio affiliate, for instance, is Jefferson Public Radio.

Some locals refer to this sun-kissed, sometimes blistering-hot landscape as the Mediterranean; others call it Oregon's banana belt. It's a climate built for slow-paced pursuits and a leisurely outlook on life. Folks like to chat down here, and the big cultural draws are Ashland's Oregon Shakespeare Festival and Jacksonville's open-air, picnic-friendly Britt Festivals concert series.

The centerpiece of the region is actually at the region's eastern edge: Crater Lake, created by the violent eruption of Mt. Mazama, is the deepest lake in the United States. Its dark blue clarity is mesmerizing on sunny days but equally stunning in winter, when its rim is covered with snow.

## Exploring Southern Oregon

Many of southern Oregon's prime attractions cluster along the north–south axis of Interstate 5. Roseburg and the complex geography of the Umpqua River form one compact sub-region. Medford, Jacksonville, and Ashland, along the state's southern border, are so close together that you can give them all a cursory inspection during a day's drive. Klamath Falls lies inland, in the midst of one of North America's greatest, and most endangered, wetlands. Crater Lake is north of Klamath Falls, east of Roseburg and northeast of Medford.

Public transportation in the region is uneven, though Medford has a respectable bus system serving Jacksonville and Ashland, and commercial flights serve Rogue Valley International near Medford. Klamath Falls is the only major town in southern Oregon served by passenger rail. Driving is your best bet for a thorough canvass of the region. To reach Crater Lake from either Medford or Klamath Falls, take Highway 62. If you're coming from Central Oregon or the Willamette Valley, Highway 138 by way of Highway 97 is the way to go. Keep in mind that wintery weather may affect driving conditions profoundly any time between October and May, particularly around Crater Lake.

### About the Restaurants

In general, southern Oregon restaurants are more old-fashioned than counterparts in Portland, Eugene, or the resort-focused Bend area. Ashland's hordes of Shakespeare lovers revere the time-tested French cooking of Chateaulin, for example, though trendier alternatives abound in a hopping dining scene.

### About the Hotels

In the streets of Jacksonville and Ashland, one could quickly come to believe B&Bs have taken over the universe. In Medford, Roseberg, and Klamath Falls, more conventional options dominate, often offering bargain accommodations within easy drives of Ashland's Shakespearean delights or Crater Lake. A number of rustic fishing lodges serve anglers around Roseburg. Two rehabbed classics—Crater Lake Lodge and the Beaux Arts tower of Ashland Springs Hotel—deserve special attention from those with a yen for sleeping amid local history. The Oregon Shakespeare Festival, the Britt Festivals, and the pull of other cultural and outdoors activities bring a riptide of summer tourists to the area; if you're visiting the region—particularly Ashland and Jacksonville—between June and September, book accommodations early.

| WHAT IT COSTS | | | | | |
|---|---|---|---|---|---|
| | $$$$ | $$$ | $$ | $ | ¢ |
| RESTAURANTS | over $30 | $20–$30 | $15–$20 | $10–$15 | under $10 |
| HOTELS | over $180 | $140–$180 | $100–$140 | $60–$100 | under $60 |

Restaurant prices are per person for a main course at dinner. Hotel prices are for a standard double room, excluding room tax, which varies 6%–9 1/2% depending on location.

### Timing

Most of southern Oregon is accessible and desirable year-round. In winter, skiing at Mt. Ashland, hard by the California border, attracts snow addicts, who can also bask in the comparatively mild climate of the banana belt's foothills. If you're keen to visit Crater Lake, however, winter may not be the best time; much of park is snow-packed between mid-October and mid-July, and though the park doesn't close, many of its amenities do. Hardy souls camp and cross-country ski in the frozen backcountry.

# Crater Lake National Park

► ❶ *Route 62, 75 mi northeast of I–5 and 30 mi northwest of U.S. 97; Route*
Fodor'sChoice *138, 87 mi east of I–5 and 15 mi west of U.S. 97.*
★

The pure, untrammeled blue of Crater Lake defies easy description but never fails to astound at first sight. The 21-square-mi lake was created 7,700 years ago after the eruption of Mt. Mazama. Rain and snowmelt filled the caldera, creating a sapphire lake so clear that sunlight penetrates to 400 feet (the lake is 1,943 feet deep). Crater is the clearest and deepest lake in the United States, and the world's seventh deepest. Aside from the breathtaking sight of the lake, the 183,224-acre park is a geologic marvel: the aftermath of geologic activity is everywhere, including huge cinder cones, pumice deserts, and old lava flows.

Prospectors discovered the lake in 1853. Pioneer photographer Peter Britt (for whom the Britt Festivals in Jacksonville are named) brought this natural wonder to national attention in the 1870s and '80s. After years of campaigning by pioneer–activist–journalist–jack-of-all-trades William Gladstone Steel, Crater Lake became Oregon's only national park, in 1902. Steel first heard of the lake when he was a Kansas farm boy in 1870. After a visit in 1885, he dedicated his life to preserving it, overcoming opposition from ranchers and timber interests.

All park and visitor facilities at Crater Lake are within a few miles of each other at Mazama Village near Route 62, at Steel Information Center, and at Rim Village and Crater Lake Lodge. Except for a few picnic areas and overlooks, the rest of the park is completely undeveloped. Entrance to the park costs $10 per vehicle; the pass is good for seven days.

*Numbers in the margin correspond to points of interest on the southern Oregon map*

**6**

### If you have 3 days

On the morning of your first day, head directly for 🏛 **Crater Lake National Park ①** ▶. If you're visiting sometime between early July and mid-October, when the park isn't choked with snow, you'll be able to cruise the 33-mi Rim Drive Loop around the glistening lake. Book one of the several daily boat trips to Wizard Island, and pack a picnic lunch. Overnight in Crater Lake. On day two, cruise southwest on Highway 62, stopping to check out some of the wild Rogue River scenery along the way to **Medford ③** and its environs. From downtown Medford, it's a short 5-mi westerly trip to 🏛 **Jacksonville ④**, the well-preserved gold-rush town: spend the afternoon exploring vintage streets and the wooded hills above town, including the historic pioneer cemetery. Choose from one of Jacksonville's many restaurants for dinner and overnight there or back in Medford. On day three, set course south on I–5 for 🏛 **Ashland ⑤** and enjoy its excellent shopping, walking, and people-watching. Picnic in Lithia Park, and snag early dinner reservations and tickets to one of the Oregon Shakespeare Festival's productions, if in-season. Overnight in Ashland, possibly in one of its lovely B&Bs.

### If you have 5 days

Follow the suggested three-day itinerary above, and after breakfast in **Ashland ⑤** on day four, head for Cave Junction in the Siskiyou Mountains' remote Illinois River valley. **Oregon Caves National Monument ⑦**, "the Marble Halls of Oregon," is worth an afternoon's underground exploration via one of the hourly guided tours. If there's time left over, check out the charming historic downtown in 🏛 **Grants Pass ⑥**, overnighting there or in the environs of the Oregon Caves. On day five, head north to **Roseburg ⑧** and the surrounding "Land of Umpqua," the scores of mountain valleys through which the north and south branches of the Umpqua tumble. Hike to one of the area's dozens of waterfalls or into the North Umpqua's Wild & Scenic reserve, which draws fly-fishermen from every corner of the globe. Finish the day with a glass of wine at one of the area's many vineyards, most of which are open daily for free tastings.

### If you have 7 days

Thoroughly explore 🏛 **Crater Lake National Park ①**, perhaps going beyond the standard Rim Drive tour and hiking some of the 90 mi of backcountry trails. Overnight in Crater Lake, and on day two, head southeast on Highway 62 for 🏛 **Klamath Falls. ②**. Spend a day in one of the falls' half-dozen wildlife refuges, glorying in what remains of the so-called Western Everglades. If the time is right, you may see hundreds of bald eagles; even if you don't glimpse the national symbol, there will be plenty of birding to do. Wander downtown Klamath Falls, stopping in at the eccentric Flavell Museum to examine the private collection of Western and Native American artifacts. Overnight in Klamath Falls. On day three, take Highway 140 west and travel the triangle formed by 🏛 **Medford ③**, 🏛 **Jacksonville ④**, and 🏛 **Ashland ⑤**, spending the balance of the day soaking up Jacksonville's Wild West charm and overnighting there. Use days four and five to enjoy Ashland's streets and cultural zing. Spend both nights in Ashland, or consider staying over in Medford, especially if Ashland lodgings are brimming over with Shakespeare fans. On days six and seven, follow the course suggested at the end of the five-day itinerary above, exploring the ⊞ **Oregon Caves National Monument** ❼, ⊞ **Grants Pass** ❻ and the Umpqua country around ⊞ **Roseburg** ❽; all three points have places to stay.

---

Virtually everyone who comes to the park makes the 33-mi circle of the crater on Rim Drive, which is open roughly mid-July to mid-October. The road is narrow, winding, and hilly, so to take in the scenery it's imperative that you pull off at some of the 30 overlooks. Begin your circumnavigation of the crater's rim by heading northeast on Rim Drive, allowing an hour to stop at a few overlooks—be sure to check out the Phantom Ship rock formation in the lake below. As you continue around the lake, stop at the Watchman for a short but steep hike to this peak above the rim, which affords not only a splendid view of the lake but a broad vista of the surrounding southern Cascades. Wind up your visit at Crater Lake Lodge—allowing some time to wander through the lobby.

Technically, the park is open 24 hours a day year-round; however, snow and freezing temperatures close the park and most of its roadways from mid-October through mid-July. The rest of the year, snow closes all park roadways and entrances except Highway 62 and the access road to Rim Village from Mazama Village. Rim Drive is typically closed because of heavy snowfall from mid-October to mid-July, and icy conditions can be encountered any month of the year, particularly in early morning. Crater Lake receives more snowfall—an annual average of 44 feet—than any other national park except for Mt. Rainier. High season for the park is July and August. September and early October—which can have delightful weather—bring much smaller crowds. The road is kept open to the rim in winter, except during severe weather.

The park's elk and deer are reclusive but can sometimes be seen at dusk and dawn feeding at forest's edge. Birds are more commonly seen in the summer in the pine and fir forests below the lake.

The highest road-access overlook on the Crater Lake rim, **Cloudcap Overlook** has a westward view across the lake to Wizard Island and an eastward view of Mt. Scott, the volcanic cone that is the park's highest point, 2 mi from the overlook. ⊠ *2 mi off Rim Dr., 13 mi northeast of Steel Information Center.*

Fodor'sChoice ★   First built in 1915, the muscular log-and-stone **Crater Lake Lodge** is considered one of the country's most glorious national-park lodges. Lake views from the lodge perched right on the caldera rim are sensational. The original lodgepole pine pillars and beams and stone fireplaces and abutments remain. Its grand lobby has leather furniture, Pendleton wool throws, and rustic trimmings such as mounted animals. The lodge porch, which overlooks the lake, offers an unmatched view. ⊠ *Rim Village east of Rim visitor center.*

In summer, a campground, motor inn, amphitheater, gas station, post office, and small store are open at **Mazama Village.** ⊠ *Mazama Village Rd. near Annie Spring entrance station* ☎ *541/830–8700* ⊕ *www.nps. gov/crla* ☼ *June–Sept., daily 8–6.*

Ascending from the banks of Sand and Wheeler creeks, the unearthly spires of eroded ash at **Pinnacles Overlook** resemble the peaks of fairytale castles. Once upon a time, the road continued east to a former entrance. A path now replaces the old road and follows the rim of Sand Creek (and more views of pinnacles) to where the entrance arch still stands. ⊠ *5 mi northeast of Steel Information Center.*

Off Rim Drive, the 7-mi southeast drive of **Pinnacles Road** scoots along Sand Creek Canyon, with its exotic volcanic landscape, and ends up at the Pinnacles, a canyon full of spires and hoodoos composed of hardened ash deposits. ⊠ *Rim Dr., 9 mi east of Steel Information Center.*

★ A 33-mi loop around the lake, **Rim Drive** is the main scenic route, affording views of the lake and its cliffs from every conceivable angle. The drive alone takes up to two hours. Frequent stops at viewpoints and short hikes can stretch this to half a day. Rim Drive is typically closed because of heavy snowfall from mid-October to mid-July. Along Rim Drive are many scenic turnouts and picnic areas. Two of the best spots are on the north side of the lake, between Llao Rock and Cleetwood Cove, where the cliffs are nearly vertical. ⊠ *Rim Drive leads from Annie Springs entrance station to Rim Village, where drive circles around the rim; it's about 4½ mi from entrance station to Rim Village. From north entrance at Route 230, it's 10 mi on North Crater Lake access road to where it joins Rim Drive.*

In summer you can obtain park information from the **Rim Visitor Center**, take a ranger-led tour, or stop into the nearby Sinnott Memorial, with a small museum and a 900-foot view down to the lake's surface. In winter snowshoe walks are offered on weekends and holidays. The Rim Village Gift Store and Cafeteria are the only services open in winter. Backcountry campers and hikers must obtain a free wilderness permit here or at the Steel Information Center. ⊠ *Rim Dr. on south side of lake, 7 mi north of Annie Spring entrance station* ☎ *541/594–3100* ⊕ *www.nps.gov/crla* ☉ *July–Sept., daily 9:30–5:30; June, daily 9:30–5.*

Part of the park headquarters, **Steel Information Center** has rest rooms and a first aid station. There's a small post office and shop that sells books, maps, and postcards. In the auditorium, an ongoing 18-minute film, *The Crater Lake Story,* describes Crater Lake's formation. Backcountry campers and hikers must obtain a free wilderness permit here or at the Rim Visitor Center. ⊠ *Rim Dr., 4 mi north of Annie Spring entrance station* ☎ *541/594–3100* ⊕ *www.nps.gov/crla* ☉ *Early Apr.–early Nov., daily 9–5; Early Nov.–early Apr., daily 10–4.*

It's a moderate ¼-mi hike through wildflowers and dry meadow to **Sun Notch,** an overlook of Crater Lake and the spooky little island known as Phantom Ship. Mind the steep edges. ⊠ *E. Rim Dr., 4 mi northeast of Steel Information Center.*

★ To get to **Wizard Island** you've got to hike down Cleetwood Cove Trail (and back up upon your return) and board the tour boat for a 1¾-hour ride. Plan to picnic. ⊠ *Cleetwood Cove Trail, Wizard Island dock* ☎ *541/594–3000* ☉ *Late June–mid-Sept., daily.*

## Where to Stay & Eat

$–$$$ ✕ **Dining Room at Crater Lake Lodge.** Virtually the only place where you can dine well once you're in the park, this spot serves ambitious fare in decidedly upscale surroundings. The room itself is magnificent, with a large stone fireplace and views out over the clear blue waters of Crater Lake. The evening menu usually includes fresh Pacific Northwest seafood, a pasta dish, pork medallions, and steak Oscar. The wines are from Oregon and Washington. Breakfast runs from standard two-eggs-with-bacon plates to specialty omelets and a salmon scramble. ⊠ *Crater Lake Lodge, Rim Village* ☎ *541/594–2255* ⚓ *Reservations essential* ▭ MC, V ☉ *Closed mid-Oct.–mid-May.*

$ ✕ **Watchman Restaurant.** Within Crater Lake Lodge, this casual alternative to the Dining Room also affords a view of the lake, but there's no menu—it's an all-you-can-eat buffet, with salads, soups, potato bar, taco bar, and entrées like salmon, Salisbury steak, and chicken. ⊠ *Crater Lake Lodge, Rim Village* ☏ *541/594–2255* ▭ *MC, V* ✆ *Closed mid-Sept.–mid-May. No lunch.*

¢ ✕ **Llao Rock Cafeteria.** It's family-style dining at this barn-like cafeteria, where hamburgers and sandwiches constitute the bulk of the menu. ⊠ *Rim Dr. on south side of lake, 4½ mi north from Annie Spring entrance station* ☏ *541/594–2255* ▭ *MC, V.*

$$–$$$ 🏛 **Crater Lake Lodge.** The period feel of this 1915 lodge on the caldera's rim survived a much-needed mid-'90s renovation. Lodgepole pine columns, gleaming wood floors, and stone fireplaces grace the common areas, and modern couches and chairs blend in perfectly. The lodge has only two telephones, in the lobby area. ⊠ *1211 Ave. C, White City 97503* ☏ *541/830–8700* ☐ *541/830–8514* ⊕ *www.crater-lake.com* ➽ *71 rooms* ♻ *Restaurant; no room phones, no room TVs, no-smoking rooms* ▭ *MC, V* ✆ *Closed mid-Oct.–mid-May.*

$ 🏛 **Mazama Village Motor Inn.** This 40-room Forest Service complex south of the lake provides basic accommodations in 10 A-frame buildings. ⊠ *Box 128, Crater Lake, Rim Village 97604* ☏ *541/830–8700* ☐ *541/830–8514* ➽ *40 rooms* ♻ *Laundry facilities* ▭ *MC, V.*

$ ◬ **Lost Creek Campground.** The small, remote sites here are usually available on a daily basis. In July and August arrive early to secure a spot. Lost Creek is for tent campers only; RVs must stay at Mazama. ♻ *Flush toilets, drinking water, fire grates* ➽ *16 sites* ⊠ *Grayback Dr. and Pinnacles Rd.* ☏ *541/594–3000* ▱ *$10* ◈ *Reservations not accepted* ✆ *Open July–mid-Sept.*

$ ◬ **Mazama Campground.** All the sites here, along with 900 more in the surrounding national forests, are available on a first-come, first-served basis. Facilities include flush toilets, potable water, and showers. ♻ *Laundry* ➽ *198 sites* ⊠ *Mazama Village near Annie Springs entrance station* ☏ *541/594–2255* ▱ *$13* ✆ *Open mid-June–mid-Oct.*

## Sports & the Outdoors

No off-road driving or bicycling is permitted in the park because of the fragile alpine and volcanic soils. No private craft are allowed on the lake, no bicycle or boat rentals are available, and hiking and rock climbing are strictly prohibited within the caldera.

BIRD-WATCHING Clark's nutcracker and Steller's and gray jays are found throughout the park, and ravens strut and croak near almost all rim viewpoints. Keen observers on the lake rim are likely to spot raptors such as eagles, hawks, and falcons soaring in the updrafts. Songbirds are most often seen in the lower-elevation woods below the caldera rim.

HIKING **Annie Creek Canyon Trail** (⊠ Mazama Campground, Mazama Village Rd., near Annie Spring entrance station) is strenuous but still easy compared to some of the steep rim hikes, such as that of the Cleetwood Trail. The 2-mi loop threads through Annie Creek Canyon, giving views of the narrow cleft scarred by volcanism. This is a good spot to look for flowers and deer.

A 1-mi creekside loop in the upper part of Munson Valley, **Castle Crest Wildflower Trail** (⊠ across street from Steel Information Center parking lot, Rim Dr.) is one of the park's flatter and less demanding hikes, with only some uneven ground of which to be mindful. In July the wildflowers are in full bloom.

## Fishing the Umpqua

The North Umpqua River near Roseburg, like the Rogue to the south, is a designated Wild and Scenic River. It is also renowned for fly-fishing. Its annual runs of sea-going salmon and steelhead inspire awe even among seen-it-all veteran anglers. Almost all of the 33.8-mi Wild and Scenic area is reserved for fly-fishing only, though the area's profusion of waterfalls and hiking trails offer plenty of diversion even for those who haven't the faintest idea what to do with a wooly bugger (a type of fly-fishing lure). If you are stalking gilled prey, remember that native steelhead must be released on capture; hatchery steelhead, distinguished by a clipped fin, can be kept. The Northwest Forest Pass (☎ 800/270–7504) is the prime ticket to public land in Oregon and Washington and is needed to access much of the Umpqua drainage. Passes are $30 per year or $5 for the day. The U.S. Forest Service (☎ 541/496–3532) offers a daily fishing report on Umpqua conditions.

## Lesser-Stomped Wineries

When it comes to Oregon wine, the pinot noirs of the Willamette Valley hog the limelight. That leaves an oenophile much to discover in the Umpqua, Rogue, and Applegate appellations. The area's hot and dry weather allows vintners to experiment with grapes never seen in the valley's wetter climes. Varietals from Italy, Spain, and Portugal bolster the area's claim to be Oregon's "Mediterranean." Southern Oregon's wineries, both fewer in number and less crowded than those in the state's more established appellations, also retain a feeling of being uncharted territory for the purple-tongued pilgrim.

## Taming the Rogue

To white-water enthusiasts, southern Oregon is synonymous with the Wild Rogue. In 1968, Congress designated a suitably unruly stretch of the Rogue River a Wild and Scenic sanctuary, and the area's rapids and waterfalls have lured thrill-seeking boaters ever since. Between May 15 and October 15, trip permits, at a cost of $10 per person, per trip, are required. As access is limited, it's a good idea to reserve dates early with the Bureau of Land Management, or book a guided trip with one of the region's licensed outfitters. The BLM doesn't charge trip fees during the off-season but asks adventurers to register at the Smullin Visitor Center (☎ 541/479–3735). Keep in mind that no commercial trips of any kind are allowed in the off-season, so you're on your own. The Hellgate Recreation Area, at the mouth of the Applegate River, is outside the Wild and Scenic district, with campgrounds and boat-launch facilities accessing 27 mi of serious white water.

---

**Cleetwood Cove Trail** (✉ Cleetwood Cove trailhead, north Rim Dr., 11 mi north of Rim Village) is a 1-mi strenuous hike that descends 700 ft down nearly vertical cliffs along the lake to the boat dock. Allow 1½ hours.

Between Steel Information Center and the Castle Crest Wildflower Trail, take the road down Munson Valley to reach the parking area for **Godfrey Glen Trail** (✉ 2 mi off Rim Dr., 2²⁄₁₀ mi south of Steel Information Center), a 2-mi loop. It'll take you through an excellent example of what geologists term a hanging valley—the place where one valley

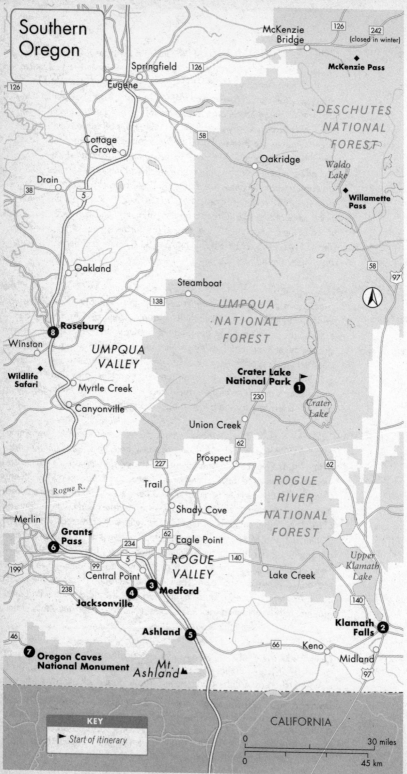

Southern
Oregon

McKenzie
Bridge

126

242
(closed in winter)

♦ McKenzie Pass

Springfield

126

Eugene

126

DESCHUTES

NATIONAL

FOREST

58

Cottage
Grove

Oakridge

Waldo
Lake

Drain

38

5

♦ Willamette
Pass

Oakland

58

97

Steamboat

UMPQUA

138

NATIONAL

8 Roseburg

FOREST

Winston

UMPQUA
VALLEY

♦ Wildlife
Safari

Crater Lake
National Park

Myrtle Creek

1

Canyonville

230

Crater
Lake

Union Creek

Rogue R.

62

Prospect

227

ROGUE

Trail

RIVER

Shady Cove

NATIONAL

Merlin

62

Eagle Point

FOREST

Grants
Pass

6

234

140

Upper
Klamath
Lake

199

5

ROGUE

Central Point

VALLEY

Lake Creek

238

3

140

Jacksonville

4

Medford

Klamath
Falls

46

Ashland

5

2

7 Oregon Caves

National Monument

66

Keno

Midland

Mt.
Ashland ▲

97

KEY

► Start of itinerary

CALIFORNIA

0            30 miles

0            45 km

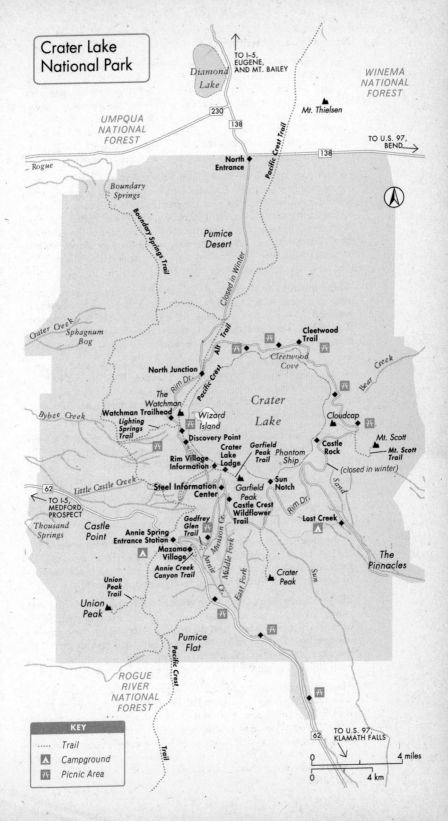

# Crater Lake National Park

**Diamond Lake**

TO I-5, EUGENE, AND MT. BAILEY

**WINEMA NATIONAL FOREST**

*Mt. Thielsen*

**UMPQUA NATIONAL FOREST**

230

138

*Rogue*

**North Entrance**

138

TO U.S. 97, BEND

*Boundary Springs*

*Pumice Desert*

*Pacific Crest Trail*

*Boundary Springs Trail*

*Crater Creek*

*Sphagnum Bog*

*Closed in Winter*

*Alt. Trail*

**Cleetwood Trail**

*Cleetwood Cove*

**North Junction**

*Pacific Crest*

*Rim Dr.*

*Crater Lake*

*Bear Creek*

*The Watchman*

**Watchman Trailhead**

*Lighting Springs Trail*

**Discovery Point**

▲ *Wizard Island*

*Bybee Creek*

**Cloudcap**

*Mt. Scott*

**Crater Lake Lodge**

*Garfield Peak Trail*

*Phantom Ship*

**Castle Rock**

*Mt. Scott Trail*

*(closed in winter)*

**Rim Village Information**

**Steel Information Center**

*Garfield Peak*

**Sun Notch**

*Castle Crest Wildflower Trail*

*Rim Dr.*

*Sand*

62

TO I-5, MEDFORD, PROSPECT

*Little Castle Creek*

**Lost Creek**

*Thousand Springs*

*Castle Point*

**Godfrey Glen Trail**

**Annie Spring Entrance Station**

*Munson Cr.*

**Mazama Village**

*Annie Creek Canyon Trail*

*Middle Fork*

*Annie Cr.*

*East Fork*

*Crater Peak*

*Sun*

**The Pinnacles**

*Union Peak Trail*

**Union Peak**

*Pumice Flat*

*Pacific Crest*

**ROGUE RIVER NATIONAL FOREST**

62

TO U.S. 97, KLAMATH FALLS

*Trail*

**KEY**

⋯⋯ *Trail*

△ *Campground*

🏕 *Picnic Area*

0 — 4 miles

0 — 4 km

hangs over a lower valley, with a cliff and a waterfall between them. Deer are frequently seen here, and the flowers are plentiful.

The 2½-mi **Mt. Scott Trail** (✉ 14 mi east of Steel Information Center, across E. Rim Dr. from road to Cloudcap Overlook) takes you to the park's highest point, the top of Mt. Scott, at 8,929 feet. It will take the average hiker 90 minutes to make the steep uphill trek and about 45 minutes to get down. The trail starts at an elevation of about 7,450 feet, so the climb is not extreme but does get steep in spots. The view of the lake is wonderful, and views to the east and south of the broad Klamath Basin are equally spectacular. Mt. Scott is the oldest volcanic cone of Mt. Mazama.

You can join up with the **Pacific Crest Trail** (✉ Pacific Crest Trail parking lot, north access road 2 mi north of Rim Dr., 8 mi south of park's north entrance station), which extends from Mexico to Canada and winds through the park for more than 30 mi. For this prime backcountry experience of the park, catch the trail about a mile east of the north entrance road, where it shadows the road along the west rim of the lake for about 6 mi, then descends down Dutton Creek to the Mazama Village area. An on-line brochure offers further details.

While numerous overlooks along Rim Drive provide car-bound visitors many perspectives on Crater Lake, the best short hike reaches the **Watchman Trail** (✉ Watchman Overlook, 3⅔ mi northwest of Rim Village on W. Rim Dr.). Though it's less than a mile each way, the trail climbs more than 400 feet—not counting the steps up to the actual lookout.

PICNIC AREAS  Abuzz in summer with songbirds, squirrels, chipmunks, and other forest denizens, the small canyon in which **Godfrey Glen Trail** (✉ Rim Dr., 1 mi east of Annie Spring entrance station) is nestled has a south-facing, protected location. The half-dozen picnic tables are in a small meadow; there are a few fire grills and a pit toilet.

Perhaps a half dozen picnic-area turnouts encircle the lake on **Rim Drive.** All have good views, but they can get very windy. Most have pit toilets, and a few have fire grills. There is no running water at any of them.

**Rim Village** (✉ Rim Dr. on south side of lake, 7 mi north of Annie Spring entrance station) is the only park picnic area with running water. The tables are set behind the visitor center, and most have some view of the lake below. There are also flush toilets inside the visitor center.

In the upper reaches of Sun Creek, the four picnic tables at **Vidae Falls** (✉ Rim Dr., 2½ mi east of Steel Information Center, between turnoffs for Crater Peak and Lost Creek) enjoy the sound of the small but closeby falls across the road. There is a vault toilet and a couple of fire grills.

The park's best picnic venue is on **Wizard Island**; to avail yourself of this experience you've got to pack a picnic lunch and book yourself on one of the early-morning boat tour departures, reserving space on an afternoon return. There are no formal picnic areas and just pit toilets, but there are plenty of sunny, protected spots where you can have a quiet meal and appreciate the astounding scene around you.

SKIING  There are no maintained ski trails in the park, although some are marked with blue diamonds or snow poles. Most cross-country skiers park at Rim Village and follow a portion of West Rim Drive as best they can toward Wizard Island Overlook (4 mi). The road is plowed to Rim Village, but it may be closed temporarily by severe storms. Snow tires and chains are essential. The park's on-line brochure (available at ⊕ www. nps.gov/crla/brochures/skiing.htm) lists additional trails and their length and difficulty.

SNOWMOBILING  Snowmobiling is allowed only on the 9-mi stretch of the north entrance road up to its junction with Rim Drive. Some adventurous cross-country skiers ride snowmobiles to the remote north rim to ski that area or the large, flat Pumice Desert.

SWIMMING  Swimming is allowed in the lake, but it's not usually advised. Made up entirely of snowmelt, Crater Lake is very cold—about 45°F to 62°F during summer. When swimming takes place it's in a lagoon on Wizard Island or at Cleetwood Cove, but even then it's only appealing when the air temperature rises above 80°F. On the other hand, how many people can say they've taken a dip in the deepest lake in the United States?

TOURS  The most extensively used guided tours in Crater Lake are **boat tours** (⊠ Cleetwood Cove Trail, off north Rim Dr., 10 mi from Rim Village ☎ 541/594–3000 ⊠ $21 ⊙ July–mid-Sept., daily), aboard launches that carry 49 passengers on a one-hour, 45-minute tour accompanied by a ranger. The boats circle the lake and make a brief stop at Wizard Island, where you can get off if you like. The first of seven tours leaves the dock at 10 AM; the last departs at 4 PM. After Labor Day, the schedule is reduced. To get to the dock you must hike down Cleetwood Cove Trail, a 1-mi walk that drops 700 feet. Rest rooms are available at the top and bottom of the Cleetwood Trail.

Naturalists and park rangers discuss topics ranging from volcanic activity to the legend of Sasquatch at **evening campfire programs** (⊠ Mazama Campground amphitheater, Mazama Village near Annie Spring entrance station ☎ 541/594–3000 ⊙ July–Sept., daily at dusk).

Park rangers lead **interpretive walks** (⊠ Crater Lake Lodge, 565 Rim Village Dr., east of Rim visitor center ☎ 541/594–3090 ⊙ July–Sept., daily) and natural history discussions.

During a 10- to 15-minute **introduction to Crater Lake,** learn about the lake's origins (⊠ Sinnott Memorial Overlook, Rim visitor center, Rim Dr. on south side of lake, 4½ mi north of Annie Spring entrance station ☎ 541/594–3090 ⊙ July–Sept., daily).

During the **Junior Ranger Program** (☎ 541/594–3090), youngsters can learn from a ranger about volcanoes, Crater Lake, and the unique environment of the southern Cascades. Junior Ranger booklets and badges are available at Steel Information Center and Rim visitor center.

## Shopping

**Camper's Service Store** (⊠ Mazama Village Rd., near Annie Spring entrance station ☎ 541/594–2255) is the park's only store, but it carries food supplies and such camping necessities as stove fuel, firewood, and lantern mantels. Also available are coin-operated laundry and showers. It's open daily June 8–8, July–September 7 AM–10 PM, and October 8–8. The shop at **Diamond Lake Resort** (⊠ Rte. 138, 25 mi north of Crater Lake ☎ 541/793–3333 or 800/733–7593) has basic food supplies and fishing tackle. It's open daily May–October 7–10 and November–April 8–6. **Rim Village Gift Store** (⊠ Rim Dr. on south side of lake, 4½ mi north of Annie Spring entrance station ☎ 541/594–2255 Ext. 3623) has Northwest and volcano-theme mementos, books, postcards, and T-shirts. It's open daily May–October 8–8 and November–April 8–6.

# Klamath Falls

❷ *60 mi south of Crater Lake National Park on U.S. 97.*

Often overlooked by visitors to the region, the Klamath Falls area is one of the most beautiful parts of Oregon. The city of Klamath Falls stands at an elevation of 4,100 feet, on the southern shore of Upper Klamath Lake. The highest elevation in Klamath County is the peak of Mt. Scott, at 8,926 feet. The Klamath Basin, with its six national wildlife refuges, hosts the largest wintering concentration of bald eagles in the contiguous United States. Each February nature enthusiasts from around the world flock to Klamath Falls for the Bald Eagle Conference, the nation's oldest birding festival. There are more than 82 lakes and streams in Klamath County, including Upper Klamath Lake, which covers 133 square mi.

Many species of migratory birds congregate in the Klamath Basin, including the largest concentration of migratory waterfowl on the continent. The Nature Conservancy has called the basin a western Everglades because it is the largest wetland area west of the Mississippi. Humans have significantly damaged the ecosystem through farming and development. More than 25% of vertebrate species in the area are now endangered or threatened. Where 30 years ago about 6 million birds used the area every year, today that number is down to 2 to 3 million. Environmental organizations are working to reverse some of the damage. In 2000 and 2001, severe droughts led to bitter, borderline-violent fights over water use among Native Americans, farmers, environmentalists, and federal officials; it's worth keeping in mind that feelings inflamed by the issue linger.

A frontier military post was established in 1863 at the site of what is now **Fort Klamath Museum and Park** to protect pioneers from Indian attack. In 1973, 8 acres of the original post, including the original buildings, were dedicated as Klamath County Park. In 2001 the museum's main log-cabin building burned to the ground, taking some larger exhibits with it. The bulk of the museum's collection survived, however, and is now in a replica of the fort's original guard post. Actors in period military duds lead interpretive tours of the grounds. ✛ *44 mi north of Klamath Falls on Hwy. 62* ☎ *541/381–2230* ✉ *Donation requested* ☉ *Late May–Sept., Wed.–Mon. 10–6.*

Almost 1 million waterfowl use the **Lower Klamath National Wildlife Refuge** during fall migration. In summer white pelicans, cormorants, herons, egrets, terns, white-faced ibis, grebes, and gulls congregate here. But the area's star is the bald eagle: the largest concentration of bald eagles in the lower 48 U.S. states, an estimated 1,000, winters here. ✉ *8 mi south of Klamath Falls on U.S. 97* ☎ *530/667–2231.*

The anthropology, history, geology, and wildlife of the Klamath Basin are explained at **Klamath County Museum,** with special attention given to the hardships faced by early white settlers. ✉ *1451 Main St., 97601* ☎ *541/883–4208* ✉ *$3* ☉ *Tues.–Sat. 9–5.*

On 9 acres along the Williamson River, **Kla-Mo-Ya Casino,** 22 mi north of Klamath Falls, has 300 slot machines, poker, blackjack, and a buffet restaurant. The casino is owned by the Klamath, Modoc, and Yahooskin tribes. ✉ *22 mi north of Klamath Falls on Hwy. 97 at Crater Lake Junction, Chiloquin 97417* ☎ *888/552–6692.*

Thirty miles north of Klamath Falls, **Collier Memorial State Park and Logging Museum** sits on land given to the State of Oregon by the locally born Collier brothers in honor of their parents. A historic log-cabin exhibit and antique logging equipment dating to the 1880s are among the displays. The park also has picnic areas and a campground. ✉ *46000 Hwy. 97, Chiloquin 97624* ☎ *541/783–2471* ⊕ *www.collierloggingmuseum. org* ✉ *Free* ☉ *May–Oct., daily 8–8; Nov.–Apr., daily 8–4.*

More than 100,000 Native American artifacts, the works of 300 major contemporary Western artists, and the largest miniature-gun collection in the world are on display at **Favell Museum of Western Art and Native American Artifacts** in a building made from local volcanic rock. ⊠ *125 W. Main St., 97601* ☎ *541/882–9996* ⌑ *$4* ☉ *Tues.–Sat. 9:30–5:30.*

Three miles north of Fort Klamath, **Jackson F. Kimball State Park** is at the headwaters of the Wood River, which has good fishing. A campground with 10 primitive sites is next to a spring-fed lagoon. ⊠ *U.S. 97* ☎ *541/ 783–2471 or 800/551–6949* ⊕ *www.prd.state.or.us* ⌑ *Day use $3 per vehicle* ☉ *Mid-Apr.–Oct., daily.*

The 800-seat **Ross Ragland Theater** hosts the 30-year-old Linkville Players theater group, as well as traveling and local plays and musical performances. ⊠ *218 N. 7th St., 97601* ☎ *541/884–0651.*

The history of the region is the focus of a guided tour and exhibits at **Senator George Baldwin Hotel Museum**, a former hotel that the turn-of-the-20th-century politico Baldwin ran and where President Theodore Roosevelt once stayed. Some of the photographs on display were part of Senator Baldwin's daughter Maud's own collection. In summer you can take a replica street trolley from here to the Klamath County Museum. ⊠ *31 Main St., 97601* ☎ *541/883–4207 or 541/883–4208* ⊕ *www.co.klamath.or.us* ⌑ *$4* ☉ *June–Sept., Tues.–Sat. 10–4.*

Twelve miles north of Klamath Falls, **Winema National Forest** covers 1.1 million acres on the eastern slopes of the Cascades. It borders Crater Lake National Park. Hiking, camping, fishing, and boating are popular. In winter snowmobiling and cross-country skiing are available. ⊠ *U.S. 97* ☎ *541/883–6714* ⊕ *www.fs.fed.us/r6/winema* ⌑ *Day use $3 per vehicle* ☉ *Daily; campgrounds and picnic areas Memorial Day–Labor Day.*

## Where to Stay & Eat

$$–$$$  ✕ **Chez Nous.** The dark-wood dining room in this 1920 house suggests more formal pleasures but encourages dining in a relaxed mood. A thoughtful French chef prepares duck in orange sauce, Chateaubriand, veal dishes, and the house specialty, rack of lamb. Fresh strawberry shortcake often appears on the menu, and there's a good wine list. ⊠ *3927 S. 6th St., 97603* ☎ *541/883–8719* 🖷 *541/883–3996* ▭ *AE, MC, V* ☉ *Closed Sun. and Mon. No lunch.*

¢–$$$  ✕ **Satellite Restaurant.** Most of this airport restaurant's business comes not from travelers but from neighborhood residents. Tuck into prime rib, a char-broiled burger, or a plate of pasta as you watch planes take off. ⊠ *3000 Airport Way, Suite 200, 97603* ☎ *541/882–5509* ▭ *D, MC, V.*

¢–$  ✕ **Mia & Pia's Pizzeria and Brewhouse.** Sit on the garden patio among the fountains or in the huge 200-seat dining room and sample the house brews from the off-site brewery. The large menu has pizza but also includes burgers, soups, salads, and chicken dishes. ⊠ *3545 Summers La., 97603* ☎ *541/884–4880* ▭ *D, MC, V.*

$$–$$$$  🏠 **Running Y Ranch Resort.** Golfers rave about the Arnold Palmer–designed course here, which wends its way through a juniper-and-ponderosa–shaded canyon overlooking Upper Klamath Lake. The resort consists of a main lodge and several town house complexes, with hiking, biking, horseback riding, sailing, fishing, and wildlife watching the prime activities. Rooms in the lodge are spacious and modern, if undistinguished; the two- to three-bedroom town houses have a plethora of amenities. ⊠ *5115 Running Y Rd., 5 mi north of Klamath Falls, 97601* ☎ *541/850–5500 or 888/850–0275* 🖷 *541/850–5593* ⊕ *www.runningy.com* 🛏 *83 rooms* ⌖ *18-hole golf course, 4 tennis courts, hiking, horseback riding, laundry service, meeting rooms* ▭ *AE, D, DC, MC, V.*

¢–$  ⌘ **Cimarron Motor Inn.** The largest lodging facility in Klamath Falls, the Cimarron offers a standard selection of room configurations, with a few kitchenette units available. It's near restaurants and shopping. ⊠ *3060 S. 6th St., 97603* ☎ *541/882–4601 or 800/742–2648* 🖷 *541/882–6690* ⛃ *163 rooms* ⌂ *Microwaves, refrigerators, cable TV, pool, business services, some pets allowed (fee)* ⊟ *AE, D, DC, MC, V* ⦿ *CP.*

¢  ⌘ **Maverick Motel.** This friendly, quiet, clean, and inexpensive motel, built in 1964, is a good value. The kidney-shape swimming pool is a mid-'60s motel classic. The Maverick is downtown, and you can walk to restaurants and antiques shops. ⊠ *1220 Main St., 97601* ☎ *541/882–6688 or 800/404–6690* 🖷 *541/885–4095* ⛃ *49 rooms* ⌂ *Cable TV, pool* ⊟ *AE, D, DC, MC, V* ⦿ *CP.*

### Sports & the Outdoors

The **Klamath Basin Audubon Society** (⊠ Box 354, Klamath Falls 97601 ☎ 541/884–0666 or 800/445–6728) has information on birds and other wildlife in the Klamath Falls Basin. For information on national wildlife refuges in the Klamath Falls area, contact the **Klamath Basin National Wildlife Refuge Complex** (⊠ Rte. 1 ✆ Box 74, Tulelake, CA 96134 ☎ 530/667–2231 ⊕ www.klamathnwr.org). **Meridian Sail Center** (⊠ 531 S. 8th St. ☎ 541/884–5869) rents boats and schedules charters.

# Medford

❸ *88 mi south of Roseburg on I–5.*

Although Medford has only about 60,000 residents, the community is the professional, retail trade, and service center for eight counties in southern Oregon and northern California. As such, it offers more professional and cultural venues than might be expected for a city of its size. The town has four major shopping centers and the fruit marketing company Harry and David. Lodging and dining tend to be much cheaper in Medford than in nearby (and easily accessible) Ashland and Jacksonville. Near two major rivers and more than 30 lakes and streams, Medford is 71 mi southwest of Crater Lake and 80 mi southwest of the Oregon Caves, so it makes a good starting place for tours of both places.

An 1872 water-powered flour grist mill, **Butte Creek Mill** is listed in the National Historic Register and still produces whole-grain food products, which you can buy at the country store here. There's also a modest display of antiques. ⊠ *402 Royal Ave. N, Eagle Point* ☎ *541/826–3531* ⊕ *www.buttecreekmill.com* ▤ *Free* ⊙ *Mon.–Sat. 9–5.*

The late Hollywood star Ginger Rogers retired to this area, and the restored vaudeville house **Craterian Ginger Rogers Theater** presents concerts, ballets, theatrical works, and touring shows like the Vienna Boys Choir and Brazil Night. ⊠ *23 S. Central Ave., 97501* ☎ *541/779–3000* 🖷 *541/779–8175* ⊕ *www.craterian.org.*

need a break?
Next door to the Craterian Theater, **Sonny's Downtown Cafe** (⊠ 210 E. Main St. ☎ 541/245–1616 ⊙ closed weekends, no dinner) is a friendly deli with inexpensive sandwiches, cinnamon rolls, and coffee.

Jackson County's natural history and collections of the Roxy Ann Gem and Mineral Society are on display at **Crater Rock Museum.** ⊠ *2002 Scenic Ave., Central Point* ☎ *541/664–6081* ▤ *Free* ⊙ *Tues.–Sat. 10–4.*

Thirty-four miles from Medford, **Joseph H. Stewart State Park** overlooks Lost Creek Reservoir, where you can rent canoes. There are 8 mi of hiking trails. The campground has 151 electrical and 50 tent sites. ⊠ *Hwy. 62* ☎ *541/560–3334 or 800/551–6949* ▤ *Free* ⊙ *Mar.–Nov., daily.*

Covering 630,000 acres, **Rogue River National Forest** has fishing, swimming, hiking, and skiing. Motorized vehicles and equipment—even bicycles—are prohibited in the 113,000-acre Sky Lakes Wilderness, south of Crater Lake National Park. Its highest point is the 9,495-foot Mt. McLoughlin. Summers here are warm and dry, while winters are bitterly cold, with lots of snow. ⊠ *I–5 to Exit 39, Hwy. 62 to Rte. 140* ☎ *541/858–2200* ⊕ *www.fs.fed.us/r6/rogue* ☞ *Free for most of forest; some of trailheads have fees. Call for details* ⊙ *Daily.*

The focus at **Southern Oregon History Center** is on the Rogue Valley's past, with a research library augmenting rotating exhibits on pioneer history. ⊠ *106 N. Central Ave.* ☎ *541/773–6536* ⊕ *www.sohs.org* ☞ *Free* ⊙ *Weekdays 9–5, Sat. 1–5.*

A popular spot for weddings and picnics, **Tou Velle State Park** is a day-use park with beautiful hiking trails that wind through a wildlife viewing area. ⊠ *Off I–5 to Table Rock Rd.* ☎ *541/582–1118 or 800/551–6949* ⊕ *www.prd.state.or.us* ☞ *Day use $3 per vehicle* ⊙ *Daily.*

## Where to Stay & Eat

$-$$ ✕ **Samovar Restaurant.** Vintage Russian advertisements from the early 20th century line the walls of this candlelit downtown place next to a bank. The restaurant serves vegetarian borscht, stuffed cabbage, *pelmeni* (Russian ravioli), and other traditional Russian specialties. ⊠ *101 E. Main St., 97501* ☎ *541/733–4967* ⊟ *MC, V* ⊙ *Closed Sun. and Mon.*

¢-$ ✕ **Tasty Thai.** Food is served family-style to lunching businesspeople and families who share the small, booth-filled dining room with two non-fruit-bearing banana trees. Try yellow chicken curry or the classic pad thai. ⊠ *725 S. Central Ave., 97501* ☎ *541/779–1148* ⊟ *MC, V* ⊙ *Closed Sun.*

¢-$ ✕ **Vinny's Italian Kitchen.** You watch Vinny cook his family's Ischia Island recipes in the open kitchen of this place where the walls are covered with family photos. Try the La Vigna pasta with artichokes, broccoli, chicken, and olives. ⊠ *970 N. Phoenix Rd., 97504* ☎ *541/618–8669* ⊟ *AE, MC, V* ⊙ *Closed Mon.*

¢ ✕ **C. K. Tiffins.** Healthy food is the focus of this downtown place. It serves poached eggs at breakfast, along with waffles, pancakes, and baked goods made fresh every morning on site. Try the popular chicken sesame salad or vegetarian lasagna at lunch; red meat is not served. The restaurant is on the site of a former early-20th-century men's clothier and displays the work of local artists. ⊠ *226 E. Main St., 97501* ☎ *541/779–0480* ⊟ *AE, D, MC, V* ⊙ *No dinner.*

$$-$$$ 🛏 **Under the Greenwood Tree.** Regulars at this B&B between Medford
Fodor'sChoice and Ashland find themselves hard-pressed to decide what they like
★ most: the luxurious and romantic rooms, the stunning 10-acre farm, or the breakfasts cooked by the owner, a Cordon Bleu–trained chef. Gigantic old oaks hung with hammocks shade the inn, a 130-year-old farmhouse exuding genteel charm. There's a manicured 2-acre lawn and a creaky three-story barn for exploring; an outbuilding holds the buckboard wagon that brought the property's original homesteaders westward on the Oregon Trail. The interior is decorated in Renaissance splendor and all rooms have private baths. Afternoon tea is served. ⊠ *3045 Bellinger La. (head west from I–5's Exit 27 on Barnett Rd., south briefly on Hwy. 99, west on Stewart Ave., south briefly on Hull Rd., and west on Bellinger), 97501* ☎ *541/776–0000, 800/766–8099* ⊕ *www. greenwoodtree.com* ⇄ *5 rooms* ⊟ *MC, V.*

$-$$ 🛏 **Rogue River Guest House.** The wide front porch of the 1890s farmhouse 12 mi north of town looks out to fir, catalpa, and holly trees. This is one of the few bed-and-breakfasts that welcomes children, and business travelers will find a small office at their disposal. One room overlooks the

Rogue from a private deck, while a two-room suite is available for larger traveling parties. ✉ *41 Rogue River Hwy., Gold Hill 97525* ☎ *541/855–4485 or 877/764–8322* ➫ *3 rooms* ♻ *Some cable TV, business services, some pets allowed; no room phones* ◻ *No credit cards* ⦿◻ *BP.*

$ ⊡ **Reston Hotel.** This is a business hotel with 10,000 square feet of meeting, exhibit, and banquet space. The rooms are comfortable and spacious. It is only ½ mi to local shopping and restaurants. ✉ *2300 Crater Lake Hwy., 97504* ☎ *541/779–3141 or 800/779–7829* 🖷 *541/779–2623* ⊕ *www.restonhotel.com* ➫ *165 rooms* ♻ *Bar, cable TV, indoor pool, business services, airport shuttle, some pets allowed (fee)* ◻ *AE, D, DC, MC, V.*

$ ⊡ **Windmill Inn.** Rooms at this pleasant inn are plush and comfortable. Complimentary hot beverage, juice, muffin, and newspaper are delivered to your door in the morning. The hotel is within walking distance of downtown shops and parks. ✉ *1950 Biddle Rd., 97504* ☎ *541/779–0050 or 800/547–4747* ⊕ *www.windmillinns.com* ➫ *123 rooms* ♻ *Cable TV, pool, hot tub, bicycles, library, business services, airport shuttle, some pets allowed* ◻ *AE, D, DC, MC, V* ⦿◻ *CP.*

## Sports & the Outdoors

GOLF **Cedar Links Golf Club** (✉ 3155 Cedar Links Dr. ☎ 541/773–4373 or 800/853–2754), an 18-hole, par-70 public golf course, charges a $24–$26 greens fee, plus $10 per rider for an optional cart.

JET-BOAT **Hellgate Jetboat Excursions** (✉ 966 S.E. 6th, Grants Pass ☎ 800/648–4874) EXCURSIONS operates jet-boat trips down the Rogue River's Hellgate Canyon May–September.

## Shopping

**Bartlett Street Book Store** (✉ 16 S. Bartlett St. ☎ 541/772–8049) makes a delightfully cool break from the scorching weather Medford gets on summer days. The low-lit labyrinth of high-quality used books includes tremendous collections of art, history, and regional books, with plenty of first editions, drawing a fervent clientele. **Harry and David/Jackson & Perkins** (✉ 2500 S. Pacific Hwy. ☎ 800/547–3033 or 800/872–7673) are two of the largest mail-order companies in the world: Harry and David for fruit and gift packs, Jackson & Perkins for roses. The Harry and David Country Store in the complex is a retail outlet for its products, most of which are grown in the nearby Bear Creek Orchards. The rose gardens at Jackson & Perkins are quite extensive.

Italian immigrants founded the **Rogue Valley Creamery** (✉ 311 N. Front St., Central Point ☎ 541/665–1155) in 1935, aiming to re-create the high-quality cheese making of their homeland. Today, the folksy business in the agricultural suburb of Central Point finds itself, ironically, on the cutting-edge—the techniques used to produce its pungent blue cheeses and flavored cheddars anticipated the current "artisanal cheese" vogue by about 65 years. Stop in at the unprepossessing factory store to sample the goods a few feet from where they're made. An antiques hunter can score big-time at **Timeless Treasures** (✉ 406 W. Main St. ☎ 541/779–7800), a friendly and well-stocked shop full of furniture, vintage (and pristine) 1930s advertising posters from the region's fruit industry, and an amusing collection of old-time bric-a-brac.

# Jacksonville

❹ *5 mi west of Medford on Hwy. 238.*

A glimpse down Jacksonville's Wild West main drag, California Street, may inspire a brief flicker of panic: you forgot your six-shooter and have no idea how far behind the sheriff's posse may be. This perfectly preserved town founded in the frenzy of the 1851 gold rush has served as the backdrop to several western flicks. It's easy to see why. (J-Ville, as locals rather jauntily refer to it, is one of only eight towns anointed to the National Register of Historic Places lock, stock, and barrel.) These days, living-history exhibits offering a glimpse of pioneer life and the world-renowned Britt Festivals of classical, jazz and pop music are the draw, rather than gold. Trails winding up from the town's center lead to the Festival amphitheater, 150-year-old gardens, exotic madrona groves, and an intriguing pioneer cemetery.

For free maps and guides to Jacksonville's many historic structures, stop by the **Jacksonville Visitors Information Center** (⊠ 185 N. Oregon St. ☎ 541/899–8118).

History comes alive as actors dressed in costumes of the period portray the Beekman family at **Beekman House,** an 1875 house with original furnishings. The Beekman Bank, established in 1863, is also open to the public. ⊠ *352 E. California St.* ☎ *541/773–6536* ✉ *$2* ☉ *Memorial Day–Labor Day, daily 1–5.*

In the 1920 Jackson County Jail, the **Children's Museum** has hands-on exhibits of pioneer life and a collection of antique toys. There's an Indian tepee and an old-fashioned store in which to play. A special display highlights local resident Pinto Colvig, the original Bozo the Clown, who co-composed "Who's Afraid of the Big Bad Wolf" and was the voice of a Munchkin, Goofy, both Sleepy and Grumpy, and many other animated film characters. The adjacent **Jacksonville Museum,** inside the old Jackson County Courthouse, has intriguing gold-rush-era artifacts. The "Jacksonville! Boomtown to Home Town" exhibit lays out the area's history. ⊠ *206 N. 5th St., 97530* ☎ *541/773–6536* 🖶 *541/776–7994* ⊕ *www.sohs.org* ✉ *$3, $7 pass for both museums* ☉ *Wed.–Sat. 10–5, Sun. noon–5.*

Perched on a bench in the scenic Applegate Valley, **Valley View Vineyard** enjoys one of the best settings in all Oregon. The valley's especially sunny, warm climate produces rich chardonnay, merlot, and cabernet sauvignon vintages. First founded in the 1850s by pioneer Peter Britt, the vineyard was reestablished in 1972. A restored pole barn houses the winery and tasting room. Valley View also operates a tasting room and gift shop (⊠ 125 W. California St. ☎ 541/899–1001) in Jacksonville. ⊠ *1000 Upper Applegate Rd., 10 mi southwest of Jacksonville* ☎ *541/899–8468 or 800/781–9463* ⊕ *www.valleyviewwinery.com* ☉ *Daily 11–5.*

Native Americans avoided the **Oregon Vortex Location of the House of Mystery,** referring to it as "forbidden ground." Birds and other wildlife appear to avoid it as well. In fact, tennis balls really do seem to roll uphill here, and brooms do stand on end in this 1-acre spherical area. It opened as a tourist attraction around 1930. ⊠ *4303 Sardine Creek Rd., Gold Hill 97525* ☎ *541/855–1543* ⊕ *www.oregonvortex.com* ✉ *$8* ☉ *Mar.–May, Sept., and Oct., daily 9–5 (last tour at 4:15); June–Aug., daily 9–6 (last tour at 5:15).*

FodorsChoice ★ A trip up the winding road—or, better yet, a hike via the old cart-track marked "Catholic access"—leads to the **Jacksonville Cemetery,** resting place of the clans (the Britts, the Beekmans, and the Orths) that built Jacksonville. You'll also get a fascinating, if sometimes unattractive, view of the social dynamics of the Old West: older graves (the cemetery is still in use) are strictly segregated, Irish Catholics from Jews from Protestants. A somber granite plinth erected in the late '90s marks the Pauper's Field, where those who found themselves on the losing end of gold rush economics entered eternity anonymously. The cemetery closes at sundown. ⊠ *Oregon St. (follow posted direction signs from downtown).*

## Where to Stay & Eat

$$–$$$ ✕ **Jacksonville Inn.** The Continental fare and 600-label wine cellar at this dining room in a gold-rush-era bed-and-breakfast are among the best in southern Oregon. Book well in advance, particularly between late June and August, during the Britt Festival. Try the fresh razor clams and veal dishes. There are tables on the patio for dining alfresco. Breakfast and a Sunday brunch, which tends to highlight seasonal and regional fruits, are also offered. ⊠ *175 E. California St.* ☎ *541/899–1900* ⚲ *Reservations essential* ⊟ *AE, D, DC, MC, V* ⊘ *No lunch Mon.*

$$–$$$ ✕ **McCully House.** This small bed-and-breakfast occupies the oldest house in Oregon, which is now an inn. Its three charming little rooms have antiquey, neo-Victorian themes to match. A ground-floor restaurant serves high-quality meat-and-potatoes fare with a faint Mediterranean zing, with one window-lined dining room overlooking a lush little garden. A lower-cost "blue plate" menu supplements the dinner selection. ⊠ *240 E. California St.* ☎ *541/899–1942* ⊕ *www.mccullyhouseinn.com* ⚲ *Reservations essential* ⊟ *AE, MC, V* ⊘ *No lunch.*

$$ ✕ **Gogi's Restaurant.** Locally famous chef William Prahl's philosophy that the continents can be united through our taste buds is manifest in the international menu of seasonally varied dishes, including traditionally prepared rack of lamb, Asian hoisin-glazed prawns, and hazelnut salmon croquettes. The dining room, at the foot of the Britt Gardens, has white tablecloths, warm yellow walls, and rich, dark-wood tables and bar. ⊠ *235 W. Main St., 97530* ☎ *541/899–8699* ⊟ *D, MC, V* ⊘ *Closed Mon. No lunch.*

$–$$ ✕ **Bella Union.** At this unpretentious restaurant in an 1870s saloon, the emphasis is on sophisticated pub food. Fresh fish—familiar species and more exotic ones like Hawaiian opah and mako shark—is flown in daily, and the pasta is handmade on the premises. Pizzas, salads, and sandwiches round out the menu. ⊠ *170 California St.* ☎ *541/899–1770* ⊟ *AE, D, MC, V.*

★ $–$$$$ ✕⌷ **Jacksonville Inn.** The spotless period antiques and the host of well-chosen amenities at this 1861-vintage inn evoke what the Wild West might have been had Martha Stewart been in charge. In addition to the main building, the inn includes three larger and more luxurious cottages with fireplaces and saunas. The room rates include a full breakfast. One of the eight rooms in the main inn is named in honor of ubiquitous Jacksonville founding father Peter Britt, while another, the Blanchet Room, honors one of the area's earliest Catholic priests. Both have meticulous pioneer-period furnishings. The inn's Continental restaurant is among the best places to eat in the region. ⊠ *175 E. California St., 97530* ☎ *541/899–1900 or 800/321–9344* ⚲ *541/899–1373* ⊕ *www.jacksonvilleinn.com* ⇝ *8 rooms, 3 cottages* ⚭ *Restaurant, refrigerators* ⊟ *AE, D, DC, MC, V.*

$–$$ ✕⌷ **The McCully House Inn.** One of Jacksonville's six original homes, a gleaming white Gothic Revival mansion built in 1860, McCully House sits in the midst of a fragrant rose garden. The period-decorated rooms, one with a fireplace and all of them filled with antiques, are on the second floor and have private baths. One upstairs bedroom is furnished with the original bedstead that was shipped around Cape Horn. The room rates include a full breakfast. ⊠ *240 E. California St., 97530* ☎ *541/899–1942 or 800/367–1942* ⚲ *541/899–1560* ⇝ *3 rooms* ⚭ *Restaurant* ⊟ *AE, MC, V.*

$$$ ⌷ **Hannah House.** You can hear the Britt Music Festival concerts from the front porch of this 1868 house across from the festival grounds. One

suite has its own wine cellar, one has a screened balcony, and every suite is filled with antiques and has a full kitchen. ✉ *285 S. 1st St., 97530* ☎ *800/373–9775* ⬚ *4 suites* ⬚ *Kitchens* ⊟ *D, MC, V.*

$$–$$$ ⬚ **Applegate River Lodge.** Each room is different in this lodge 12 mi west of town. One has century-old barn wood and gold-mining tools, and one has an old wagon wheel, saddle, and chaps. Every room has a deck overlooking the Applegate River and Pioneer Bridge. ✉ *15100 Hwy. 238* ☎ *541/846–6690* ⬚ *7 rooms* ⬚ *Restaurant, in-room hot tubs; no room phones, no room TVs* ⊟ *D, MC, V* ⊓⊙⊢ *CP.*

$$–$$$ ⬚ **Orth House B&B.** Built in 1880, this brick Italianate villa is on a quiet street above Jacksonville's center and a block from the Britt Festivals amphitheater. Furnished with an eclectic collection of antiques and locally made quilts, the two rooms and one suite are colorful and warm. Bathrooms have deep claw-foot tubs. ✉ *105 W. Main St., 97530* ☎ *541/899–8665 or 800/700–7301* ⊕ *www.orthbnb.com* ⬚ *2 rooms, 1 suite* ⊟ *D, MC, V.*

$–$$$ ⬚ **Stage Lodge.** In the heart of historic Jacksonville and close to the Britt Festival, this bed-and-breakfast is plush and modern, with fireplaces in the rooms. It's Jacksonville's only motor inn. ✉ *830 N. 5th St., 97530* ☎ *541/899–3953 or 800/253–8254* ⊕ *www.stagelodge.com* ⬚ *27 rooms, 2 suites* ⬚ *Microwaves, some refrigerators, cable TV, some pets allowed (fee)* ⊟ *AE, D, DC, MC, V* ⊓⊙⊢ *CP.*

$$ ⬚ **Touvelle House.** This intimate bed-and-breakfast in a restored 1916 Craftsman is filled with antiques. It is only two blocks from the center of Jacksonville and four blocks from the site of the Britt Music Festival. Built by one of Jacksonville's early leading families, the Touvelle House now hosts historic-themed parties through a deal with the local theater company. ✉ *455 N. Oregon St., 97530* ☎ *541/899–8938, 800/846–8422 reservations* ⬚ *541/899–3992* ⊕ *www.wave.net/upg/touvelle* ⬚ *3 rooms, 2 suites* ⬚ *Picnic area, in-room data ports, pool, hot tub, business services; no kids under 12* ⊟ *AE, D, DC, MC, V* ⊓⊙⊢ *BP.*

$–$$ ⬚ **Combest House.** This downtown home a block from Main Street and a short walk to the Britt Festival grounds was first built by homesteaders in 1862 and named for onetime owner Valentine Combest, who mined the property. There are two guest suites, one with two bedrooms and a shared bathroom, the other with one bedroom and a kitchenette. The rooms have different layouts, but share a rustic look heavy on old-fashioned quilts. ✉ *160 W. C St., 97530* ☎ *541/899–7537* ⬚ *2 suites* ⬚ *Cable TV* ⊟ *MC, V.*

$–$$ ⬚ **Reims Country House.** This antebellum Victorian inn two blocks from downtown is on the National Register of Historic Places. You can relax in the perennial flower garden, on the wide front porch, or in your antiques-filled room. There's a TV in the common area. ✉ *540 E. California St., 97530* ☎ *541/899–2848 or 800/846–8422* ⬚ *6 rooms* ⬚ *No room phones* ⊟ *AE, MC, V* ⊓⊙⊢ *BP.*

## Nightlife & the Arts

Every summer some of the finest musicians in the world gather for the **Britt Festivals** (☎ 541/773–6077 or 800/882–7488), outdoor concerts and theater presentations lasting from mid-June to early September. Folk, country, pop, and classical performances are staged in an outdoor amphitheater on the estate of 19th-century photographer and painter Peter Britt. Tickets must be obtained well in advance for most performances, and those who wish the best spaces on the lawn near the stage should show up early.

## Shopping

In Jacksonville's prospector heyday, **Terra Firma** (✉ 135 W. California St. ☎ 541/899–1097) likely would have been known as a place that sold "notions." An eclectic and eccentric mix of gifts, books, toys, and games is available.

# Ashland

**⑤** *20 mi from Jacksonville, east on Hwy. 238 and southeast on I–5.*

As you walk Ashland's twisting hillside streets, it seems like every house is a restored Victorian operating as an upscale B&B, though that's not quite all that there is to this town: the Oregon Shakespeare Festival attracts about a quarter of a million theater lovers to the Rogue Valley every year, from mid-February to early November (though tourists don't start showing up en masse until June or so). That influx means Ashland is more geared toward the arts, more eccentric, and more expensive than its size might suggest. The mix of well-heeled theater tourists, bohemian students from southern Oregon University, and dramatic show folk imbues the town with some one-of-a-kind cultural frissons. The stage isn't the only show in town—skiing at Mt. Ashland and the town's reputation as a secluded getaway keep things hopping year-round.

☞ At the Oregon Shakespeare Festival's **Exhibit Center** in the festival complex, theater fans can try on costumes and see displays that outline the history of the festival. A fascinating guided backstage tour includes peeks at production shops and the Angus Bowmer Theatre, and a walk to the very heavens above the Elizabethan Theatre's stage. ⊠ *S. Pioneer and Main Sts.* ☎ *541/482–4331* 🖷 *541/482–8045* ✉ *Backstage tour $11 early June–early Oct., $8.25 Feb.–early June and mid–late Oct. (under 5 not admitted); exhibit center $2* ☉ *Tues.–Sun. 10–11:45.*

The Elizabethan Theatre overlooks **Lithia Park**, a 99-acre jewel that is Ashland's physical and psychological anchor. Whether thronged with colorful hippie folk and picnickers on a summer evening or buzzing with joggers and dog walkers in the morning, Lithia is a well-used, well-loved, and well-tended spot. An old-fashioned band shell, a duck pond, a children's playground, nature trails, and Ashland Creek make this a perfect spot for a pretheater picnic. On summer weekend mornings, the park plays host to a '60s-ish artisans' market. Each June the festival opens its outdoor season by hosting the Feast of Will in the park, with music, dancing, bagpipes, and food. Tickets (about $16) are available through the festival box office.

The **Schneider Museum of Art**, at the edge of the southern Oregon University campus, includes a spruce, light-filled gallery devoted to special exhibits by Oregon, West Coast, and international artists. Hallways and galleries throughout the rest of the 66,000-square-foot complex display many works by both students and faculty. ⊠ *250 Siskiyou Blvd.* ☎ *541/552–6245* ⊕ *www.sou.edu/sma* ☉ *Tues.–Sat. 10–4; extended hrs 1st Fri. of month.*

**Mt. Ashland Ski Area.** This winter sports playground in the Siskiyou Mountains is halfway between San Francisco and Portland. The ski runs get more than 300 inches of snow each year. There are 23 trails in addition to chute skiing in a glacial cirque called the bowl. The 6,350-foot mountain has a vertical drop of 1,150 feet. ⊠ *Exit 6 off I–5 (access road to top)* ☎ *541/482–2754 snow conditions, 541/482–2897* ⊕ *www.mtashland.com* ☉ *Nov.–Apr., daily 9–4.*

## Where to Stay & Eat

The Oregon Shakespeare Festival has stimulated one of the most extensive networks of B&Bs in the country—more than 50 in all. High season for Ashland-area bed-and-breakfasts is between June and October.

# THE PLAY'S THE THING

I N 1935, a vision seized a young professor at an obscure teaching college in an equally obscure southern Oregon town. Seven decades later, that town is one of the most famous theater centers in the world and arguably the greatest venue for William Shakespeare's plays outside the Bard's homeland. Ashland's **Oregon Shakespeare Festival**, from mid-February to early November, has snowballed into a cultural juggernaut, selling an astounding 400,000 tickets a year to its 11-show season and attracting about 100,000 visitors to this urbane mini-city in the Siskiyou foothills.

It's fair to say Angus L. Bowmer didn't foresee such a frenzy on the Depression day when he noticed that a decaying hulk of civic architecture smack in Ashland's center looked a bit like an Elizabethan theater.

In the late 19th and early 20th century, the Chatauqua Movement, named for the upstate New York lake where it began, aimed to bring high culture to small-town America. The classic Chatauqua was a moveable feast of literature, music, debate, performance and pure socializing, usually in a rustic grange hall or big-top tent. The democratic effort won loyal followings (Teddy Roosevelt called it "the most American thing in America"), and some ambitious towns erected permanent venues. Ashland built its 1917 domed Chatauqua pavilion right downtown, hard by Lithia Park, the city's centerpiece. Problem was, Chatauqua expired about the time radio took over America. By the early '30s, wrecking crews had claimed Ashland's grand dome, leaving behind crumbling concrete walls. Enter Angus, stage left.

Invariably described as "enthusiastic" (and one can only imagine), Bowmer insisted the tumble-down structure was a civic treasure in disguise. Depression-era economic recovery funds helped pay for a stage and renovations in the old Chatauqua complex, and the city fathers rather reluctantly appropriated $400 to aid the young prof's cause. Over Fourth of July weekend in 1935, Bowmer produced Twelfth Night and Merchant of Venice.

Worried such high-brow fare wouldn't hold much interest, the city booked day-time boxing matches (a very Elizabethan touch) to supplement the plays. As it happened, the Bard outdrew the pugilists, and the experiment wasn't repeated.

High-profile radio appearances helped the newly minted Oregon Shakespeare Festival make its reputation before World War II forced a six-year hiatus. After the war, Bowmer's little brainstorm simply boomed. Attendance topped 50,000 by 1963, then tripled within eight years. A 1983 Tony Award served to cement the festival's reputation within the national theater community, though the public didn't need telling.

Today, OSF operates in three theaters: the (much-improved) outdoor Elizabethan Theater; the marquee Angus Bowmer theater; and the New Theater, which tends to stage slightly more experimental work. A typical OSF season includes pomp-and-circumstance Shakespeare under the stars in the Elizabethan, as well as inventive reimaginings of the Bard's work and plays by cutting-edge modern playwrights. (A recent season, for example, saw the world premiere of a highly political two-play cycle by British writer David Edgar, in addition to tried-and-true Romeo and Juliet.)

It is no exaggeration to say the festival has made Ashland what it is—a widely revered culture center and one of the most beguiling small towns in the country. The flood of visitors feeds its network of B&Bs and top-flight dining scene, while the presence of one of the country's biggest repertory theater companies has spawned all manner of fringe culture. The city has reaped quite a return on that $400 initial investment. One hopes citizens take a private moment to sing Angus Bowmer's praises at least once a year.

— By Zach Dundas

Expect to pay $90–$150 per night, which includes breakfast for two; during the off-season the rates are between $60 and $100. The **Ashland B&B Network** (☎ 800/944–0329 ⊕ www.abbnet.com) provides referrals to local inns. The **Southern Oregon Reservations** (☎ 541/488–1011 or 800/547–8052 ⊕ www.sorc.com) clearinghouse handles both hotel rooms and theater packages.

**$$$** ✕ **Chata.** In a cozy roadside cottage, this restaurant serves excellent Polish dishes; try the cabbage rolls. In addition to seating for about 100 in the restaurant, there are six tables in the flower-filled grapevined arbor patio. ⊠ 1212 S. Pacific Hwy., 97520 ☎ 541/535–8949 ▤ MC, V.

**$$–$$$** ✕ **Beasey's on the Creek.** While Beasey's claim that it serves "Texas Mediterranean" fare is a head scratcher, just think beef: this is the place to tackle a classic steak platter, sip an Old Fashioned, and listen to Sinatra before decamping to the theater. The cooking here is rock-ribbed and 100% all-American. The interior is rather plain, but the service is friendly. ⊠ 51 Water St., Ashland ☎ 541/488–5009 ⚲ Reservations essential ▤ MC, V.

★ **$$–$$$** ✕ **Hong Kong Bar.** Hidden on the third floor of a Main Street building and accessed by elevator, this wood-panel, atmospheric Asian restaurant and lounge feels a little like a Shanghai speakeasy circa 1935. In the restaurant, Chinese flavors dominate a menu based on a three-course dinner, with the lemon halibut with fresh ginger perhaps the most distinctive entrée. Despite its discreet location, the bar draws an enthusiastic drinking crowd in the post-theater hours. ⊠ 24 North Main ☎ 541/488–5511. ▤ MC, V ☉ Closed Mon.

**$$–$$$** ✕ **Tabu.** Pat South's sultry restaurant brings the tapas and Nuevo Latino crazes to Ashland. Dine on several of many spicy small plates (the lamb chops are particularly great) or more traditional Spanish-inflected entrées. The downstairs bar is full of pillow-strewn couches, inviting a long linger over cocktails. ⊠ 76 N. Pioneer St. ☎ 541/482–3900 ⚲ Reservations essential. ▤ MC, V.

**$–$$$** ✕ **Black Sheep.** In an 1879 downtown building, this pub is what many
**Fodor's Choice** quasi-British bars want to be but aren't. Cluttered tables, gold stars on
★ the black ceiling, and an authentic red phone booth lend it cultural credibility, while a rock sound track and funky servers chase away any hint of stodginess. The obligatory traditional fish-and-chips match up with creative dishes like venison with gin and juniper-berry sauce. The bread pudding is not to be missed. ⊠ 51 N. Main St., 97520 ☎ 541/482–6414 ▤ MC, V.

★ **$–$$$** ✕ **Chateaulin.** One of southern Oregon's most romantic restaurants is in an ivy-covered storefront a block from the Oregon Shakespeare Festival exhibit center, where it dispenses French food, local wine, and impeccable service with equal facility. This might be Ashland's most iconic restaurant, the fixed point in a hopping dining scene, where Shakespeare pilgrims return religiously year after year. The bar is the center of the post-theater social scene. Try the pan-roasted rack of lamb with a white-wine demi-glace sauce of roasted garlic, fresh basil, black olives, and sun-dried tomatoes, accompanied by a bottle of Ken Wright Cellars Pinot Noir. ⊠ 50 E. Main St. ☎ 541/482–2264 ⚲ Reservations essential ▤ AE, D, MC, V ☉ Closed Mon. No lunch.

**$–$$$** ✕ **Lela's Bakery & Cafe.** This cheerful back-street bistro packs 'em in with reasonably priced lunches and dinners with a contemporary French accent. The Hungarian mushroom soup is a cut above most versions of this often-bland dish. ⊠ 258 A St., Suite 3, ☎ 541/482–1702 ⚲ Reservations essential ▤ MC, V ☉ Closed Mon.

**$–$$$** ✕ **Winchester Country Inn.** The menu is small but imaginative at the restaurant inside this inn built in 1886. High-window dining rooms, set among manicured gardens, radiate a feeling of casual elegance. Menu items are seasonal but sometimes include an ambrosial roast duck in a sauce of caramel, brandy, and fresh fruit; the homemade scones, crab Benedict, and duck hash with orange hollandaise, served for Sunday brunch, are equally memorable. The restaurant is closed on Monday between November and May. ⊠ *35 S. 2nd St.* ☎ *541/488–1113 or 800/ 972–4991* 🖷 *541/488–4604* 🖃 *AE, D, MC, V* ⊗ *No lunch.*

**$–$$** ✕ **Arbor House.** The Arbor House, in the nearby town of Talent, has a varied international menu that includes jambalaya, curries, braised lamb, and charbroiled steaks. Local people in the know come here often for the seafood and the excellent service. ⊠ *103 W. Wagner St., Talent 97540* ☎ *541/535–6817* 🖃 *No credit cards* ⊗ *Closed Sun.–Mon. (except for Sun. brunch). No lunch.*

**$–$$** ✕ **Ashland Bakery and Café.** This popular café is famous for its vegetarian fare. The bakery turns out artisan breads, pastries, cakes, and box lunches. Given its central location—on the Plaza, around the corner from the Shakespeare Festival grounds—the café is where many Ashlanders and visitors get their morning caffeine jolt. Breakfast is also served. ⊠ *38 E. Main St., 97520* ☎ *541/482–2117* 🖃 *MC, V* ⊗ *Closed Tues. No dinner Mon.*

**¢–$** ✕ **Gepetto's.** Kids seem to love this unpretentious eatery. The friendly and fast-moving staff serves pasta dishes and delicious and unusual sandwiches, salads, and soups. Try the fresh-grilled marinated turkey served on crispy cheese bread. Breakfast, which might include anything from bacon and eggs to tofu sausage, is also available. ⊠ *345 E. Main St.* ☎ *541/482–1138* 🖃 *MC, V.*

**¢–$** ✕ **Il Giardino.** An orange Vespa parked in the front entrance sets the casually chic tone at this Italian-run restaurant. The dozen or so pasta dishes are based on traditional recipes but incorporate local ingredients; the remainder of the menu is divided between meat and fresh fish. ⊠ *5 Granite St.* ☎ *541/488–0816* 🖃 *MC, V.*

**¢–$** ✕ **Thai Pepper.** Spicy Thai-style curries and stir-fries are the specialties at this restaurant above Ashland Creek. With an interior filled with local art, rattan, linen, and crystal, the restaurant feels like a French café in downtown Bangkok. Try the coconut prawns or the Thai beef-salad appetizers, followed by the house curry. ⊠ *84 N. Main St.* ☎ *541/482– 8058* 🖃 *AE, DC, MC, V* ⊗ *No lunch Sat.–Thurs.*

**¢** ✕ **Morning Glory.** Breakfast reaches new heights at this distinctive café across the street from southern Oregon University. In a blue Craftsman-style bungalow, the café has eclectic furnishings, and an attractive patio space bounded by arbors, that complement the food—omelets bursting with fillings such as mushrooms, apple-wood-smoked bacon, toasted walnuts, and fontina cheese; gingerbread waffles; and sourdough blueberry pancakes. ⊠ *1149 Siskiyou Blvd.* ☎ *541/488–8636* 🖃 *MC, V.*

★ **$$$–$$$$** ▣ **Mt. Ashland Inn.** Close to the summit ski area on Mt. Ashland, 15 mi south of Ashland, this 5,500-square-foot lodge, hand-built of cedar logs, has magnificent views of Mt. Shasta and the rest of the Siskiyou Mountains; the Pacific Crest Trail runs through the parking lot. A large stone fireplace, antiques, hand-stitched quilts, and natural wood provide welcoming warmth. The room rates include a three-course breakfast that's wonderfully prepared and gracefully served, and the owners plan bike trips and provide snowshoes for guests. ⊠ *550 Mt. Ashland Rd., 97520, (take Exit 6 from I–5 and follow signs west toward ski area to beyond Mile Post 5)* 🖷🖷 *541/482–8707* ☎ *800/830–8707* 🖘 *5 rooms* ⌂ *Outdoor hot tub, sauna, hiking, mountain bikes, cross-country skiing* 🖃 *D, MC, V.*

**$$$–$$$$** ▣ **Peerless Hotel & Restaurant.** Sensational, rich shades of burgundy and green and opulent fabrics distinguish the furnishings at this deluxe small inn. Converted from a two-story brick boarding house built in 1900, the guest house provides spacious quarters, luxuries such as two-person showers or side-by-side claw-foot tubs, and such amenities as in-room cable music systems. A garden courtyard leads to the adjoining restaurant, which serves hearty fish, meat, and pasta dishes. Breakfast is included with the room rate. ⊠ *243 4th St., 97520* ☎ *541/488–1082 or 800/460–8758* ⊕ *www.peerlesshotel.com* ⤴ *9 suites* 🖃 *AE, DC, MC, V* ⍥ *BP.*

★ **$$–$$$$** ⊡ **Ashland Creek Inn.** Every one of the seven plush suites in this converted mill has a geographic theme—if it's Tuesday, this must be Normandy, while Moroccan and New Mexican motifs prevail next door. Each sitting room–bedroom combo has its own entrance and a deck just inches from burbling Ashland Creek. Privacy, space, high-concept elegance, and dynamite breakfast served in an understated central dining room make this well-run place an alternative to up-close-and-personal traditional B&Bs. Downtown shopping, Lithia Park, and the theaters are within an easy walk. ⊠ *70 Water St.,* ☎ *541/482–3315* 🖷 *541/482–1092* ⊕ *www.ashlandcreekinn.com* ⤴ *7 suites* ♨ *Kitchens; no smoking* 🖃 *MC, V* ⍥ *BP.*

**$$–$$$$** ⊡ **Ashland Springs Hotel.** This cream-and-white 1925 building towers over Ashland's downtown—indeed, the nine-story spire, in which Beaux Art, Gothic, and Arts and Crafts styles mingle, was once the tallest building between San Francisco and Portland. Remodeled to a high pitch of elegance, this swanky place recalls an era when staying in a hotel really meant something. Tea is served on Sunday afternoons on the mezzanine overlooking the airy lobby. Guests must provide their own white linen suits and F. Scott Fitzgerald novels. ⊠ *212 E. Main St.,* ☎ *541/488–1700* 🖷 *541/488–1701* ⊕ *www.ashlandspringshotel.com* ⤴ *70 rooms* ♨ *In-room data ports, Internet* 🖃 *AE, D, DC, MC, V.*

**$$–$$$$** ⊡ **Country Willows Bed and Breakfast Inn.** Built in 1896, this country inn is set against a hillside on 5 acres of farmland, surrounded by the Siskiyou and Cascade mountains. It is 2 mi from downtown Ashland. Rooms with private patios are available. There's a TV in the common area. ⊠ *1313 Clay St., 97520* ☎ *541/488–1590 or 800/945–5697* 🖷 *541/488–1611* ⊕ *www.willowsinn.com* ⤴ *9 rooms (3 with shower only), 4 suites* ♨ *In-room data ports, microwaves, some refrigerators, pool, hot tub, business services; no kids under 12, no smoking, no TV in some rooms* 🖃 *AE, D, MC, V* ⍥ *BP.*

**$$–$$$$** ⊡ **Lithia Springs Inn.** A hot spring on the 8-acre property supplies water for the whirlpool baths in all but five of the rooms in this sprawling 1993 Cape Cod–style inn. Gardens, ponds, and meandering paths surround the inn. Amusing trompe l'oeil touches enliven the interior; there's a TV in the common area. There's a 3-night minimum on summer weekends. ⊠ *2165 W. Jackson Rd., 97520* ☎ *541/482–7128 or 800/482–7128* 🖷 *541/488–1645* ⊕ *www.ashlandinn.com* ⤴ *5 rooms, 6 suites, 12 cottages* ♨ *Some minibars, some refrigerators; no kids under 12, no room phones, no smoking* 🖃 *AE, D, MC, V* ⍥ *BP.*

**$$–$$$** ⊡ **Arden Forest Inn.** On a quiet street only four blocks from the three Oregon Shakespeare Festival theaters, this early-20th-century cross-gabled farmhouse has bold colors, light pine furnishings, a collection of fantasy art, and a library of current novels. A garden, lawn, and shade trees are a casual and comfortable complement to the interior. Two rooms and the common areas are wheelchair-accessible. ⊠ *261 W. Hersey St., 97520* ☎ *541/488–1496 or 800/460–3912* ⊕ *www.afinn.com* ⤴ *4 rooms, 1 suite* ♨ *In-room data ports, pool; no kids under 10, no smoking* 🖃 *MC, V* ⍥ *BP.*

**$$–$$$** ⊡ **McCall House.** A National Historic Landmark, this small inn is a former residence of a Civil War veteran and mayor of Ashland. It's one block from the theaters. The restored Victorian paint job—an explosion of yellow and green—makes this an unmistakable downtown landmark. Guests with a military mind-set can stay in the General Sherman room. ⊠ *153 Oak St., 97520* ☎ *541/482–9296 or 800/808–9749* ⌨ *541/482–2125* ⊕ *www.mccallhouse.com* ⌨ *10 rooms* ⌂ *No kids under 12, no smoking* ☱ *MC, V* ⦿⦿⦿ *BP.*

**$$–$$$** ☷ **Morical House.** Fine woodwork and stained-glass windows highlight this restored farmhouse built in 1882. This "garden inn" touts its "metropolitan luxury" and indeed has a much more modern feel than most chintz-choked B&Bs. Colors tend toward a muted, pan-Asian palette of ivories and earth tones. Three newer rooms are in a detached carriage house. ⊠ *668 N. Main St., 97520* ☎ *541/482–2254 or 800/ 208–0960* ⌨ *541/482–1775* ⊕ *www.garden-inn.com* ⌨ *7 rooms* ⌂ *Picnic area, in-room data ports, some in-room hot tubs, microwaves, refrigerators, business services; no kids under 12, no smoking* ☱ *AE, D, MC, V* ⦿⦿⦿ *BP.*

**$$–$$$** ☷ **Winchester Inn.** The restored Victorian main house of this multi-building inn, built in 1886 and on the National Historic Register, once served as the area's first hospital. A gazebo highlights the surrounding tiered English tea garden; a 2003 renovation added a glassed-in English-style conservatory. The inn is two blocks south of the Oregon Shakespeare Festival theaters. ⊠ *35 S. 2nd St., 97520* ☎ *541/488–1113 or 800/972– 4991* ⌨ *541/488–4604* ⊕ *www.winchesterinn.com* ⌨ *19 rooms, 8 suites* ⌂ *Restaurant, some in-room hot tubs, cross-country skiing, downhill skiing; no smoking, no TV in some rooms* ☱ *AE, D, MC, V* ⦿⦿⦿ *BP.*

**$–$$$** ☷ **Best Western Bard's Inn.** Original local art hangs on the walls of this property close to the theaters. The rooms, decorated with oak and knottypine furniture, are small but have Rogue Valley views. ⊠ *132 N. Main St., 97520* ☎ *541/482–0049 or 800/528–1234* ⌨ *541/488–3259* ⌨ *91 units* ⌂ *Refrigerators, pool, outdoor hot tub* ☱ *AE, D, DC, MC, V.*

**$–$$$** ☷ **Iris Inn.** This charming and efficient B&B makes its home in a 1905 Victorian a block off Main Street. The staff is a great source of information about local and regional events. Rooms are decorated in a comfortable country style. ⊠ *59 Manzanita St.* ☎ *541/488–2286* ⌨ *541/ 488–3709* ⊕ *www.irisinnbb.com* ⌨ *5 rooms* ⦿⦿⦿ *BP.*

## Nightlife & the Arts

From mid-February to early November, more than 100,000 Bard-loving fans descend on Ashland for the **Oregon Shakespeare Festival** (⊠ 15 S. Pioneer St., 97520 ☎ 541/482–4331 ⌨ 541/482–8045 ⊕ www. osfashland.org), presented in three theaters. Its accomplished repertory company mounts some of the finest Shakespearean productions you're likely to see on this side of Stratford-upon-Avon—plus works by Ibsen, Williams, and contemporary playwrights. Between June and October, plays are staged in the 1,200-seat Elizabethan Theatre, an atmospheric re-creation of the Fortune Theatre in London, the 600-seat Angus Bowmer Theatre, a state-of-the-art facility typically used for five different productions in a single season, and the 350-seat New Theater, which tends to host productions of new or experimental work. The festival generally operates close to capacity, so it's important to book ahead.

Ashland's after-theater crowd (including many of the actors) congregates in the wood-and-brick-lined bar at **Chateaulin** (⊠ 50 E. Main St. ☎ 541/ 482–2264).

**Q's Music Hall** (⊠ 140 Lithia Way ☎ 541/488–4880), a rock and jazz club that's literally down a back alley, books local and touring acts aimed at Ashland's sizeable youth culture.

### Sports & the Outdoors

The **Adventure Center** (⊠40 N. Main St., Ashland 97520 ☎541/488–2819 or 800/444–2819) books outdoor expeditions in the Ashland region, including white-water raft trips, fishing outings, and bike excursions.

SKIING **Mt. Ashland** (⊠ Mt. Ashland Access Rd., 18 mi southwest of downtown Ashland; follow signs 9 mi from I–5's Exit 6 ☎ 541/482–2897 or 888/747–5496), a cone-shape, 7,523-foot Siskiyou peak, has some of the steepest runs in the state. Two triple and two double chairlifts accommodate a vertical drop of 1,150 feet; the longest of the 22 runs is 1 mi. Facilities include rentals, repairs, instruction, a ski shop, a restaurant, and a bar.

### Shopping

Since Ashland owes a great deal of its considerable good fortune to the power of the written word, it's no surprise to find an uncommonly strong crop of locally owned bookstores. **Bloomsbury Books** (⊠ 290 E. Main St. ☎ 541/488–0029) is the most prominent, with its Main Street location and late hours (it's open until 10 most nights) serving as a beacon for Ashland book lovers. Standouts include strong selections of local and regional history and, naturally, drama and theater books. **Chateaulin Wine Shoppe** (⊠ 52 E. Main St. ☎ 541/488–9463), next door to the acclaimed restaurant of the same name, sells high-quality regional wines and foodstuffs. A light and airy apothecary and home store, **Maizey's** (⊠ 90 N. Pioneer St. ☎ 541/482–6771) has many handmade, locally produced products. The vast, brick-walled **Paddington Station** (⊠ 125 E. Main St. ☎ 541/482–1343) calls itself Ashland's Eclectic Emporium and has a bumper selection of off-kilter trinkets to prove it.

# Grants Pass

❻ *30 mi northwest of Medford on I–5.*

"It's the Climate!" So says a confident neon sign of 1950s vintage presiding over the downtown of Josephine County's seat. Grants Pass bills itself as Oregon's white-water capital. The Rogue River, preserved by Congress in 1968 as a National Wild and Scenic River, runs right through town. Downtown Grants Pass is a National Historic District, a stately little enclave of 19th-century brick storefronts housing folksy businesses harking back to the 1950s. It's all that white water, however, that compels most visitors—and not a few moviemakers. If the river alone doesn't serve up enough natural drama, the sheer rock walls of nearby Hellgate Canyon rise 250 feet.

A city museum, **Grants Pass Museum of Art** in Riverside Park, displays classic and contemporary art, including the works of local artists. Sculpture and painting dominate, and the focus is on American and regional work. A first-Friday art night is a community rallying point. ⊠ 229 S. W. G St. ☎ 541/479–3290 ☜ Free ☉ Tues.–Sat. noon–4.

You'll see some of Oregon's most magnificent scenery on a tour of Hellgate Canyon, via **Hellgate Jetboat Excursions,** which depart from the Riverside Inn. The 36-mi round-trip from Grants Pass through Hellgate Canyon takes 2 hours. There is also a 5½-hour, 75-mi round-trip from Grants Pass to Grave Creek with a stop for a meal on an open-air deck (cost of meal not included). ⊠ 966 S.W. 6th ☎ 541/479–7204 or 800/648–4874 ⊕ www.hellgate.com ☜ 2-hr trip $27; 5½-hr trip $50; brunch cruises $40; lunch excursion $35; supper cruises $43; special rates for children ☉ May–Sept., daily; brunch cruises May–Sept., weekends 9:15; supper cruises May–Sept., weekends 4:15 (3:15 in Sept.).

In the Klamath Mountains and the Coast Range of southwestern Oregon, the 1.1-million-acre **Siskiyou National Forest** contains the 35-mi-long Wild and Scenic section of the Rogue River, which races through the Wild Rogue Wilderness Area, and the Illinois and Chetco Wild and Scenic Rivers, which run through the 180,000-acre Kalmiopsis Wilderness Area. Activities include white-water rafting, camping, and hiking, but many hiking areas require trail-park passes. There are 25 campgrounds. ⊠ *Off U.S. 199* ☎ *541/471–6516* ⊕ *www.fs.fed.us/r6/siskiyou* ⊠ *Park pass required* ☉ *Daily.*

Fodor's Choice ★ **Valley of the Rogue State Park** has a 1¼-mi hiking trail that follows the Rogue River bank. A campground along 3 mi of shoreline has 97 full hookups, 49 electrical and 21 tent sites, and 6 yurts. There are picnic tables, walking trails, playgrounds, and rest rooms. ⊠ *Exit 45B off I–5* ☎ *541/582–1118 or 800/551–6949* ⊕ *www.prd.state.or.us* ⊠ *Day use $3 per vehicle* ☉ *Daily.*

## Where to Stay & Eat

$$$–$$$$ ✕ **Morrison's Rogue River Lodge.** On the Rogue River, this rafting and fishing resort serves country-style cuisine with a twist—the apple-walnut torte dessert has attracted the notice of national food magazines. Priority seating is given to those staying at the lodge. Supper is an all-inclusive four-course meal. ⊠ *8500 Galice Rd., Merlin 97532* ☎ *541/476–3825* ⌂ *Reservations essential* ☰ *D, MC, V* ☉ *Closed Nov.–Apr. No lunch.*

$–$$$ ✕ **Yankee Pot Roast.** The restaurant in this restored 1905 house is as well known for its biscuits as it is for its eponymous beef dish, but it also serves fresh halibut, salmon, roast chicken, meat loaf, and steak. True to the traditions of Yankee pot-roast restaurants everywhere, this incarnation is casual and family-friendly. ⊠ *720 N.W. 6th St., 97526* ☎ *541/476–0551* ☰ *MC, V* ☉ *Closed Tues. No lunch.*

¢–$$ ✕ **The Brewery.** No beer has been brewed in this 1886 building since Prohibition, but the name sounds good anyway. You can order Australian lobster tails (at the market price, more expensive than most of the entrées), steak, Caribbean jerk catfish, and other surf-and-turf dishes from the extensive menu. Dine under exposed beams between the original brick walls, which surround three dining rooms filled with booths and oak tables. Brunch is served on Sunday. ⊠ *509 S.W. G St., 97526* ☎ *541/479–9850* ☰ *AE, D, DC, MC, V* ☉ *No lunch Mon. or Sat.*

¢–$$ ✕ **Hamilton River House.** Familiar dishes receive special attention here: brick-oven pizza, salmon ravioli, baby-back ribs, rotisserie chicken, Caesar salad with blackened salmon, seafood fettuccine, and steaks and fresh seafood. A deck overlooks the river, and all tables, some elevated, have a river view. There are jazz and blues on weekends and a popular live jam on Wednesday night. ⊠ *1936 Rogue River Hwy., 97527* ☎ *541/479–3938* ☰ *AE, D, MC, V.*

¢–$$ ✕ **Matsukaze.** Matsukaze means "breeze through the pines" in Japanese, and the surroundings are enhanced with woodwork, rice-paper lanterns, and wood-slat lamps. Chicken teriyaki, tempura, and beef cooked on a grill at the table are the most popular items, but you can also have sushi, sukiyaki, mahimahi, and the special spicy barbecued chicken. There are some Korean dishes, too, and, because of the owners' background, the menu has something of a Hawaiian flair. ⊠ *1675 N.E. 7th St., 97526* ☎ *541/479–2961* 🖷 *541/479–2961* ☰ *D, MC, V* ☉ *Closed Sun.*

¢–$ ✕ **Royal Barge Thai Cuisine.** As you enter the Royal Barge, you're greeted by a life-size statue of a Thai girl in traditional costume, a fixture in many restaurants in Thailand. Pictures of the country enhance the mood. Many dinners are served family-style, and there are curries, vegetarian dishes with brown rice, and barbecued chicken with Thai spices and seasonings. End your meal, as most diners do, with the homemade coconut ice cream. ⊠ *120 S.W. H St., 97526* ☎ *541/474–6942* ☰ *AE, D, DC, MC, V* ⊗ *Closed Sun.*

¢–$ ✕ **Sunshine Natural Foods.** In the downtown business district, near parks, shops, and galleries, this very popular lunch spot has an impressive buffet, along with sandwiches. Those in the know come for the curry bow-tie pasta. ⊠ *128 S.W. H St., 97526* ☎ *541/474–5044* ⚱ *Reservations not accepted* ☰ *MC, V* ⊗ *No dinner.*

¢ ✕ **Big Daddy's.** Cherry-red bar stools, Formica tables, and a black-and-white-check floor welcome you to this back-to-the-'50s diner, which prides itself on shakes and burgers. ⊠ *956 Rogue River Hwy., 97527* ☎ *541/ 479–8667* ☰ *MC, V.*

¢ ✕ **Grants Pass Pharmacy.** A classic, out-of-time soda fountain is besieged by cheesy souvenirs—ignore the ceramic dolls and concentrate on the root beer floats. Grants Pass may be the only town in America where teenagers still race into the soda fountain hollering "Gimme a phosphate!" These multi-flavored little coolers are 75¢. Solid sandwiches come for $5 or less, though an odd ordering routine requires you to order food and drink at separate counters. ⊠ *414 S.W. 6th St.* ☎ *541/476–4262* ⊗ *Closed Sun.* ☰ *MC, V.*

$–$$$$ ▦ **Riverside Inn Resort and Conference Center.** On the Rogue River, this large resort covers three city blocks. The rooms are cozy and decorated with fabrics highlighting Pacific Northwest themes. Almost all rooms overlook the river. Hellgate Jetboat Excursions depart from a nearby dock May–September. ⊠ *971 S.E. 6th St., 97526* ☎ *541/476–6873 or 800/334–4567* 🖷 *541/474–9848* ⊕ *www.riverside-inn.com* ⤴ *162 rooms* ⚭ *Restaurant, some in-room hot tubs, cable TV, 2 pools, hot tub, bar, business services, some pets allowed (fee)* ☰ *AE, D, DC, MC, V.*

$–$$$$ ▦ **Weasku.** Among tall pine trees in the heart of the Rogue Wilderness, this rustic inn built in 1924 has nine suites with fireplaces and private decks overlooking the Rogue River. There is also an A-frame cabin and two spacious suites with dining areas, fireplaces, and private decks. The lodge, which is filled with antiques, also has five second-floor standard rooms; the cabin and suites are priced differently than the rooms. ⊠ *5560 Rogue River Hwy., 97527* ☎ *541/471–8000, 800/493–2758 for reservations* 🖷 *541/471–7038* ⊕ *www.weasku.com* ⤴ *5 rooms, 11 suites in lodge, 1 cabin* ⚭ *Picnic area, some in-room hot tubs, cable TV, business services; no kids under 12, no smoking* ☰ *AE, D, DC, MC, V* ❚⊙❚ *CP.*

$$–$$$ ▦ **Morrison's Rogue River Lodge.** Twelve miles west of Grants Pass on a peaceful bend in the Rogue River, guests of Morrison's tend to favor the nearby rafting and fishing. The rooms have fireplaces, private decks, and covered parking. A luxurious lawn fronts the rustic-style lodge. ⊠ *8500 Galice Rd., Merlin 97532* ☎ *541/476–3825 or 800/826–1963* 🖷 *541/ 476–4953* ⊕ *www.morrisonslodge.com* ⤴ *4 rooms in lodge, 9 cottages* ⚭ *Restaurant, picnic area, refrigerators, in-room VCRs, pool, tennis courts, business services* ☰ *D, MC, V* ⊗ *Closed mid-Nov.–Apr.*

$–$$$ ▦ **Flery Manor.** On 7 acres of mountainside, this secluded inn has cozy, elegant rooms filled with antique furniture and fresh flowers. Some of the rooms have fireplaces. Robes are provided. Coffee or tea is delivered to your door before breakfast. ⊠ *2000 Jumpoff Joe Creek Rd., 97526* ☎ *541/476–3591* 🖷 *541/471–2303* ⊕ *www.flerymanor.com* ⤴ *4 rooms* ⚭ *Picnic area, business services; no kids under 10, no room TVs, no smoking* ☰ *MC, V* ❚⊙❚ *BP.*

$–$$ ▦ **Doubletree Ranch.** The four cabins on this 160-acre 1891 homestead with almost a mile of private Rogue River frontage are filled with furniture that has been on the ranch for four generations. You can enjoy the peace and quiet and mountain or river view from the deck of your cabin 11 mi northwest of town. ⊠ *6000 Abegg Rd., Merlin 97532* ☎ *541/*

476–0120 ♺ *4 cabins* ♿ *Kitchenettes, hiking, fishing; no room phones, no room TVs* 🖵 *MC, V* ⊙ *Closed Oct.–May.*

¢–$ 🏠 **Ivy House.** In the Historic District, this 1908 English Arts and Crafts-style brick home was originally a restaurant and tea room. The restored interior is unfussy, but the guest rooms have eider down quilts and antiques, and there are two sitting rooms. From the porch, you can enjoy the rose bushes, which were planted in 1908. Restaurants, theaters, galleries, and the river are all within walking distance. The charming English owner observes a fine old tradition: you can have morning tea and biscuits in bed before your full English breakfast. There's a TV in the common area. ✉ *139 S. W. I St., 97526* ☎ *541/474–7363* 🖷 *541/474–7363* ✉ *ivyhousebb@msn.com* ♺ *5 rooms* ♿ *No smoking* 🖵 *D, MC, V* 🍽 *BP.*

¢ 🏠 **Crest Motel.** Across the street from a store where everything is a dollar is this tiny roadside motor lodge with standard rooms. This might just be the best deal in town. ✉ *1203 N.E. 6th St., 97526* ☎ *541/479–0720* ♺ *10 rooms* ♿ *Cable TV* 🖵 *AE, MC, V.*

## Sports & the Outdoors

WHITE-WATER **Ferron's Fun Trips** (📪 Box 585, Merlin 97532 ☎ 541/474–2201 or 800/
RAFTING 404–2201) leads many kinds of excursions into the Rogue country, from half-day lunch outings to two-day wildlife adventures. Gear is also available for rental. **Rogue Wilderness, Inc.** (📪 Box 1110, Merlin 97532 ☎ 800/336–1647) is a full-service outfitter, leading multi-day rafting and fishing trips into the Rogue's Wild and Scenic area. Some packages include a stay at a rustic lodge accessible only via the river.

## Shopping

Pick up newspapers, magazines, paperbacks, and snacks at **Blind George's Newsstand** (✉ 117 S.W. G St. ☎ 541/476–3463), a 1922 vintage downtown shop. **Wild West** (✉ 214 N.E. 6th St. ☎ 541/955–8000), an "old-fashioned mercantile," has regionally themed souvenirs and Old West toys for tots.

# Oregon Caves National Monument

❼ *90 mi from Jacksonville, west on Hwy. 238, south on U.S. 199, and east on Hwy. 46.*

The town of Cave Junction is the turnoff point for the Oregon Caves National Monument. The "Marble Halls of Oregon," high in the verdant Siskiyou Mountains, have enchanted visitors since local hunter Elijah Davidson chased a bear into them in 1874. Huge stalagmites and stalactites, the Ghost Room, Paradise Lost, and the River Styx are part of a ½-mi subterranean tour that lasts about 75 minutes. The tour includes more than 200 stairs and is not recommended for anyone who experiences difficulty in walking or has respiratory or coronary problems. Children over six must be at least 42 inches tall and pass a safety and ability test, because they cannot be carried. ✉ *Hwy. 46, 20 mi southeast of Cave Junction* ☎ 541/592–3400 💵 *$7* ⊙ *May–mid-June, daily 9–5; mid-June–Sept., daily 9–7; Oct.–Apr., daily 8:30–4.*

In the pine-oak foothills of Siskiyou Mountain, **Foris Vineyards,** where coastal and inland climates mingle, has earned a reputation for richly flavored varietal wines such as pinot noir, merlot, and cabernet sauvignon. ✉ *654 Kendall Rd.* ☎ *800/843–6747* ⊕ *www.foriswine.com* ⊙ *Daily 11–5.*

Documenting area Native American and pioneer history, **Kerbyville Museum** is centered in an 1871 home on the National Register of Historic Places. You can investigate your pioneer and mining ancestors in the research library and see exhibits of taxidermy and antique dolls, as well as local Native American artifacts. ⊠ *24195 Redwood Hwy., 97531* ☎ *541/592–5252* ▨ *$3* ⊙ *Mid-May–mid-Sept., Mon.–Sat. 10–5, Sun. noon–5; mid-Sept.–mid-May, by appointment only.*

### Where to Stay & Eat

¢ ✕ **Wild River Pizza Company & Brewery.** Cool your heels at the communal redwood picnic tables in this pizza parlor on the north end of town. If you aren't in the mood for pizza, choose from fish-and-chips, chicken dishes, and sandwiches. There is also an all-you-can-eat buffet, and the restaurant's own seasonal brews are on tap. ⊠ *249 N. Redwood Hwy., 97523* ☎ *541/592–3556* ▭ *D, MC, V.*

$ ✕▥ **Oregon Caves Lodge.** If you're looking for a quiet retreat in an unusual place, consider this lodge on the grounds of the national monument. Virtually unchanged since it was built in 1934, it has a rustic authenticity. Rooms, all with their original furnishings, have canyon or waterfall views. The dining room serves the best regional fare in the vicinity. ⊠ *20000 Caves Hwy., Cave Junction 97523* ☎ *541/592–3400* ▤ *541/592–6654* ⇱ *22 rooms, 3 suites* ⌂ *Restaurant, coffee shop, hiking* ☞ *No smoking* ▭ *MC, V.*

$–$$$ ▥ **Out N' About.** You sleep among the leaves in the tree houses of this
FodorsChoice extraordinary resort—the highest is 37 feet from the ground. One has
★ an antique, claw-foot bath; another has separate kids' quarters connected to the main room by a swinging bridge. There is also an earthbound cabin with a view of the old-growth forest. There is a two-night minimum stay Memorial Day–Labor Day. ⊠ *300 Page Creek Rd.,* ☎ *541/592–2208* ⊕ *www.treehouses.com* ⇱ *10 tree houses* ⌂ *Some kitchenettes, horseback riding; no a/c, no room phones, no room TVs* ▭ *AE, D, MC, V* ▯ *CP.*

¢–$ ▥ **Country Hills Resort.** A motel, cabins, camping in tents, and RV parking are all available at this resort 12 mi from the Oregon Caves. A golf course is nearby. Cabins include full kitchen facilities. The resort sits on more than 20 acres of forest land. ⊠ *7901 Caves Hwy., 97523* ☎ *541/592–3406 or 800/997–8464* ⊘ *mike@crater-lake.com* ⇱ *11 rooms* ⌂ *Some kitchenettes, laundry facilities, some pets allowed* ▭ *AE, D, MC, V* ▯ *CP.*

# Roseburg

❽ *73 mi south of Eugene on I–5.*

Fishermen the world over hold the name Roseburg sacred. The timber town on the Umpqua River attracts anglers in search of a dozen popular fish species including bass, brown and brook trout, and chinook, coho and sockeye salmon. The native steelhead, which makes its run to the sea in the summer, is king of them all.

The seat of Douglas County is the old-economy Northwest in a nutshell—with 3 million acres of commercial forest land and the largest stand of old-growth timber in the world close at hand, the timber business dominates local enterprise, and knocks suffered in recent years hit Roseburg particularly hard. Suffice it to say the spotted owl is not a popular beast here, and environmental politics remain a tough sell.

The north and south branches of the Umpqua River meet up north of Roseburg. The roads that run parallel to this river give spectacular views of the falls, and the North Umpqua route also provides access to trails, hot springs, and the Winchester fish ladder. White-water rafting, riverside hiking, horseback riding, mountain biking, snowmobiling, and skiing are available in the area.

Sixty miles due west of the northern gateway to Crater Lake National Park and in the Hundred Valleys of the Umpqua, Roseburg produces innovative, well-regarded wines. Wineries are sprouting up throughout the mild, gorgeous farm country around town, mostly within easy reach of I–5.

One of the best county museums in the state, **Douglas County Museum** surveys 8,000 years of human activity in the region. Its fossil collection is worth a stop. ⊠ *123 Museum Dr.* ☎ *541/957–7007* ⊕ *www.co.douglas. or.us/museum* ✑ *$3.50* ⊙ *Weekdays 9–5, Sat. 10–5, Sun. noon–5.*

★ ☾ Come face to face with free-roaming animals at the 600-acre **Wildlife Safari,** a drive-through wildlife park. There's also a petting zoo, a miniature train, and elephant rides. The admission price includes two drive-throughs in the same day. From I–5 take Exit 119, follow Highway 42 west 3 mi to Lookingglass Road, and take a right on Safari Road. ⑦ *Box 1600, Winston 97496* ☎ *541/679–6761* ⊕ *www.wildlifesafari. org* ✑ *$17.50* ⊙ *Daily 9–5.*

## Wineries

★ **Abacela Vineyards and Winery** (⊠ 12500 Lookingglass Rd., Roseburg [from I–5's Exit 119, head into Winston, take a right on Hwy. 42, a right on Brockway Rd., and a left on Lookingglass Rd.] ☎ 541/679–6642 ⊕ www.abacela.com) derives its name from an archaic Spanish word meaning "to plant grapevines," and that's exactly what this winery's husband-wife team did not so very long ago. Abacela released its first wine in 1999, and quickly established itself as an innovator in the region. Hot-blooded Spanish Tempranillo is this place's pride and joy, though inky malbec and torrid Sangiovese also highlight a repertoire heavy on Mediterranean varietals. Admission is free. Hours are 11–5 daily.

**Girardet Wine Cellars** (⊠ 895 Reston Rd., Tenmile [from I–5's Exit 119 head south on Hwy. 99 to town of Winston, west on Hwy. 42, and north on Reston] ☎ 541/679–7252) has won gold medals for its Baco Noir and other wines—its pinot noir and rare Maréchal Foch are two standouts. Admission is free. Hours are 11–5 daily.

**Henry Estate Winery** (⊠ 687 Hubbard Creek Rd., Umpqua [from I–5's Exit 136 head west ¼ mi on Hwy. 138 and take 1st left onto Fort McKay Rd.—on some maps the Sutherlin–Umpqua Rd. or County Rd. 9—which runs into Hubbard Creek] ☎ 541/459–5120 or 800/782–2686 ⊕ www.henryestate.com), north of Roseburg along the Umpqua River, produces pinot noir, chardonnay, Gewürztraminer, and Riesling wines. The vineyard's flower garden is perfect for summer picnics. The winery is open daily 11–5. Admission is free.

**La Garza Cellars** (⊠ 491 S.W. Winery La., Roseburg [head southwest from I–5's Exit 119 to Winery La. and turn left] ☎ 541/679–9654 ⊕ www.winesnw.com/lagarzacellars.htm), known for cabernet sauvignon and chardonnay, has a covered deck for picnics and a shop selling many regional wines. Admission is free. The winery is open daily 11–5; a restaurant, La Garza Gourmet, is open during the summer Wednesday–Sunday 11–4.

**Melrose Vineyards** (⊠ 885 Melqua Rd., Roseburg [from I–5's Exit 125, head northwest on Garden Valley Rd., take a left on Melrose Rd., and go right on Melqua Rd.] ☎ 541/672–6080), founded in 1996 on the bench of the South Umpqua, already enjoys a formidable reputation in the wine media. A sampling of the establishment's smoky, oaky pinot noir or rare hybrid Baco Noir (dubbed Big Red, with good reason) makes clear why. A renovated century-old barn serves as Melrose's tasting room, commanding a sweeping view of vineyards and riverbank. Admission is free. Hours are 11–5 daily.

## Where to Stay & Eat

$–$$$ ✕ **Tolly's.** You can go formal or informal at this restaurant in Oakland, 18 mi north of Roseburg. Have an old-fashioned soda or malt downstairs in the Victorian ice cream parlor, or head upstairs to the oak- and antiques-filled dining room for expertly prepared beef, chicken, seafood, and lamb. Try the grilled salmon or the grilled flank steak marinated and served with fiery chipotle chilies. ✉ *115 Locust St., (take I–5's Exit 138 and follow the road north from the exit for 4 mi, cross the railroad tracks, and turn west on Locust)* ☎ *541/459–3796* ▭ *AE, D, MC, V* ⊙ *Closed Mon.*

¢–$$ ✕ **Casey's Family Dining.** Do they serve breakfast? "Honey, we always serve breakfast." Got it? This classic small-town diner—in a busy highwayside spot that doesn't feel exactly like Mayberry—dishes up massive omelets and crispy hash browns, along with other hearty items for lunch and dinner. ✉ *326 N.W. Garden Valley Blvd.,* ☎ *541/672–1512* *Reservations not accepted* ▭ *AE, D, MC, V.*

$–$$$ Fodor's Choice ★ ✕ **The Steamboat Inn.** Every fall a Who's Who of the world's top fly fishermen converges here, high in the Cascades above the emerald North Umpqua River, in search of the 20-pound steelhead that haunt these waters; guide services are available, as are equipment rentals and sales. Others come simply to relax in the reading nooks or on the broad decks of the riverside guest cabins. Another renowned attraction is the nightly Fisherman's Dinner, a multi-course feast served around a massive 50-year-old sugar-pine dinner table. Lodging choices include riverside cabins, forest bungalows, and riverside suites; the bungalows and suites have kitchens. Make reservations well in advance, especially for a stay between July and October, the prime fishing months. ✉ *42705 N. Umpqua Hwy. (38 mi east of Roseburg on Hwy. 138, near Steamboat Creek), Steamboat 97447* ☎ *541/498–2230* 📠 *541/498–2411* 🌐 *www.thesteamboatinn.com* *8 cabins, 5 bungalows, 2 suites* *Restaurant, library, meeting room; no smoking* ▭ *MC, V* ⊙ *Closed Jan. and Feb.*

$ ✕ **Seven Feathers Hotel and Casino Resort.** South of Roseburg, about halfway between Medford and Eugene, is a hotel and a casino owned by the Cow Creek Tribe. It has 500 slots, blackjack, roulette, poker, craps, keno, and bingo. Big-name entertainers perform in the showroom, and for the kids, there's an arcade and an ice cream parlor. There's a 32-space RV park on the premises. ✉ *146 Chief Miwaleta La., Canyonville 97417* ☎ *541/839–1111 or 800/548–8461* 📠 *541/839–4500* 🌐 *www.sevenfeathers.com* *154 rooms* *2 restaurants, lounge, in-room data ports, indoor pool, hot tub, steam room, gym, concierge* ▭ *AE, MC, V* *CP.*

$ **Windmill Inn.** Rooms at this pleasant inn are plush and comfortable. Complimentary hot beverage, juice, muffin, and newspaper are delivered to your door in the morning. ✉ *1450 Mulholland Dr., 97470* ☎ *541/673–0901 or 800/547–4747* 🌐 *www.windmillinns.com* *128 rooms* *Restaurant, in-room data ports, cable TV, pool, hot tub, exercise equipment, bar, laundry facilities, business services, airport shuttle, free parking, some pets allowed* ▭ *AE, D, DC, MC, V* *CP.*

off the beaten path

**ROGUE RIVER VIEWS –** Nature lovers who want to see the Rogue Rive at its loveliest can take a side trip to the Avenue of the Boulders, Mill Creek Falls, and Barr Creek Falls, off Highway 62, near Prospect. Here the wild waters of the upper Rogue foam through volcanic boulders and the dense greenery of the Rogue River National Forest.

# SOUTHERN OREGON A TO Z

*To research prices, get advice from other travelers, and book travel arrangements, visit www.fodors.com.*

### AIRPORTS

Horizon and United Express serve the Rogue Valley International-Medford Airport (MFR) in Medford.

🛈 Airport Information **Rogue Valley International-Medford Airport (MFR)** ☎ 541/772-8068.

### BIKE TRAVEL

Not many people travel by bike via major highways between southern Oregon's larger towns, but the region's endless country roads—paved and unpaved, flat and otherwise—attract a legion of skinny-tire and mountain-bike enthusiasts. Ashland is nicely set up for two-wheeled exploration, with dedicated bike paths and lanes throughout its streets. For more information on backcountry biking, contact the Southern Oregon Mountain Bike Association.

🛈 Rentals & Information **Siskiyou Cyclery** ✉ 1729 Siskiyou Blvd., Ashland ☎ 541/482-1997. **Southern Oregon Mountain Bike Association** ☎ 541/552-0427.

### BUS TRAVEL

A half-dozen Greyhound buses a day connect Portland, Salem and other northern points on the I–5 corridor to Medford, southern Oregon's transportation hub. Direct Greyhound service from some other parts of the state can be harder to come by, though you can reach Medford from almost every major Oregon town by some combination of regional carriers. Most bus service to other southern Oregon cities from outside the region goes through Medford. Greyhound serves Klamath Falls and environs via Bend.

The Rogue Valley Transportation District is the area's major public transportation provider. RVTD provides a number of bus routes within Medford itself, service from Medford to Ashland every half-hour between 7 AM and 6:30 PM, and nine buses a day from Medford to Jacksonville.

🛈 Bus Information **Greyhound** ☎ 800/231-2222 ⊕ www.greyhound.com. **Rogue Valley Transportation District** ☎ 541/779-5821 ⊕ www.rvtd.org.

### CAR RENTALS

Car rental, like other transportation services in the region, is centered in Medford. Hertz, Avis, National and Budget all maintain offices at Rogue Valley International-Medford Airport. Enterprise's local outlet is outside the airport grounds.

🛈 Agencies **Avis** ☎ 541/773-3003. **Budget** ☎ 541/773-7023. **Enterprise** ☎ 541/772-1200. **Hertz** ☎ 541/773-4293. **National** ☎ 541/779-4863.

### CAR TRAVEL

I–5 runs north–south the length of the Umpqua and Rogue River valleys, linking Roseburg, Grants Pass, Medford, and Ashland. Many regional attractions lie not too far east or west of I–5. Jacksonville is a short drive due west from Medford. Highway 138 winds along the Umpqua River, east of Roseburg to the back door of Crater Lake National Park. Highway 140 passes through Klamath Falls.

### CHILDREN IN SOUTHERN OREGON

Wildlife Safari, the park full of exotic beasts near Roseburg, is arguably southern Oregon's premier attraction for the younger set. Older kids with an interest in history or the Wild West will probably like Jacksonville, with its historic cemetery and main street straight out of prospector days. The behind-the-scenes tour offered by the Oregon Shakespeare Festival in Ashland may interest kids too young to sit through even the bloodiest production of *Macbeth*; however, OSF does cater to many school groups, so consult with festival personnel regarding particular plays' suitability for children. Jackson County Library Services runs an excellent network of branch libraries throughout the region. If all else fails, there's always the Oregon Vortex and its kooky phenomena.

🔒 **Jacksonville Chamber of Commerce** ✆ Box 33, Jacksonville 97530 ☎ 541/899–8118. **Jackson County Library Services** ✉ 413 W. Main St., Medford 97501 ☎ 541/774–8689 ⊕ www.jcls.org. **Oregon Shakespeare Festival** ✉ 15 S. Pioneer St., Ashland 97520 ☎ 541/482–4331. **Oregon Vortex** ✉ 4303 Sardine Creek L Fork Rd., Gold Hill 97525 ☎ 541/ 855–1543. **Wildlife Safari** ✆ Box 1600, Winston ☎ 800/355–4848.

## DISABILITIES & ACCESSIBILITY
Travelers with disabilities should generally find major attractions in southern Oregon in line with the latest legal accessibility requirements and social expectations. The Oregon Shakespeare Festival employs an access coordinator's office to facilitate theater-going by the hearing- and sight-impaired and people using wheelchairs (☎ 541/482–2111 Ext. 425). Crater Lake has historically not been easily accessible to travelers using wheelchairs, but the National Park Service's strategic plan for the park calls for significant accessibility improvements. Jacksonville's Britt Festival grounds, on a hillside above the town, are wheelchair-accessible.

🔒 **Local Resources** **The ARC of Jackson County** ✉ 121 N. Central Ave., Medford ☎ 541/779–4520. **Deaf Services of southern Oregon** ☎ 541/664–5765. **Handicapped Awareness Support League** ✉ 1252 Redwood Ave., Grants Pass ☎ 541/479–4275. **Oregon Shakespeare Festival** ☎ 541/482–2111 Ext. 425.

## EMERGENCIES
Emergency services in all major localities, including Crater Lake National Park, can be reached by dialing 911.

🔒 **Emergency Rooms** **Ashland Community Hospital** ✉ 280 Maple St., Ashland ☎ 541/482–2441. **Merle West Medical Center** ✉ 2865 Daggett, Klamath Falls ☎ 541/ 882–6311. **Providence Medford Medical Center** ✉ 1111 Crater Lake Ave., Medford ☎ 541/732–5000. **Rogue Valley Medical Center** ✉ 2825 E. Barnell Rd., Medford ☎ 541/608–4900.

## LODGING
B&Bs are simply everywhere in southern Oregon. For many visitors to such high-traffic destinations as Ashland and Jacksonville, B&B lodging is synonymous with visiting the region. Even in more remote locations, the idea of a country inn offering highly personalized service is alive and well.

It is a good idea to book well in advance if you'd like to stay in a southern Oregon B&B between May and October, when high-season rates apply and space can be hard to come by. Almost all establishments offer less expensive off-season rates. The Southern Oregon Reservation Center provides numerous lodging and entertainment packages, including rental cottages and houses. The southern Oregon Lodging Directory is an on-line compendium of hostelries and vacation rental properties.

🔒 **Lodging Services** **Ashland B&B Network** ☎ 800/944–0329 ⊕ www.abbnet.com. **southern Oregon Lodging Directory** ⊕ www.southernoregon.com. **Southern Oregon Reservation Center** ✆ Box 477, Ashland 97520 ☎ 800/547–8052 ⊕ www.sorc.com.

## MEDIA
As is the case throughout the state, the *Oregonian* maintains a hefty presence in southern Oregon, though the Portland-based metro daily must

share top billing in the region with the *San Francisco Chronicle*. Ashland's *Daily Tidings,* like the community it serves, reflects a decidedly more liberal political stance than most other papers in the region. Medford's *Mail-Tribune* generally steers a more moderate course, though its letters column is as free-wheeling as the region's libertarian political traditions would lead one to expect. Roseburg's *News-Review* and Klamath Falls' *Herald and News* offer good coverage of their little cities' surprisingly raucous political scenes.

RADIO & TELEVISION  While commercial radio in southern Oregon is no less homogenous than elsewhere in the United States, the region has a treasure in **Jefferson Public Radio.** Named in honor of the sovereign state southern Oregon and northern California almost (but never quite) became, JPR covers a huge territory, with the largest public-radio translator network in the country. The network's three services—two FM stations mixing classical music and news and eclectic pop and acoustic with news, respectively, and an all-news AM format—can be heard from Roseburg to Redding, California. See ⊕ www.jeffnet.org for more information.

### SPORTS & THE OUTDOORS

Water, water, water—that's the key to outdoor recreation in southern Oregon. The section of the North Umpqua near Roseburg designated Wild and Scenic is an international fly-fishing hot spot. A dozen species run this pristine stretch of mountain water, with native steelhead the most prized (though you have to release them once you catch them).

If you visit Crater Lake you'll likely find yourself on the 33-mi Rim Drive, but consider hiking one of the 90 mi of trail around the lake and into the park's pristine backcountry. A permit is required for all overnight trips; much of the park is covered in snow between October and May. The park office maintains updated trail information.

The Wild and Scenic section of the Rogue River froths with some of Oregon's finest white water. Access is limited during the summer months, so reserve a spot early or book a trip through a licensed outfitter. The Bureau of Land Management handles traveler registration at its Smullin Center.

🖪 Hiking **Crater Lake Park Office** ☎ 541/594-3100.

🖪 White-Water Rafting **Smullin Center** ☎ 541/479-3735.

### TOURS

Southern Oregon Nature Excursions offers many tours of the region with a wilderness focus, ranging from standardized half-day and full-day tours to customized expeditions.

🖪 Tour Information **Southern Oregon Nature Excursions** ✉ 2320 Talent Ave., Talent 97540 ☎ 541/601-5761 or 877/868-7245 ⊕ www.oregonnature.com.

### TRAIN TRAVEL

Amtrak's Coast Starlight line, which links Los Angeles and Seattle, is the only passenger rail service to reach any part of southern Oregon, and the only city it serves is Klamath Falls; the route arrives at Klamath Falls Station once a day northbound, once a day southbound.

🖪 Amtrak ⊕ www. amtrak.com. **Klamath Falls Station (KFS)** ✉ 1600 Oak St., Klamath Falls ☎ 800/USA-RAIL.

### TRANSPORTATION AROUND SOUTHERN OREGON

For southern Oregon's true flavor, you'll probably want a car to explore country back roads, trek to wineries, and take advantage of the compact clusters of attractions around centers like Roseburg, Medford, and Klamath Falls. Most mass transit options revolve around Medford, with the region's only major airport and the base of its most extensive bus system, which also serves Ashland and Jacksonville.

**VISITOR INFORMATION**
Ashland Chamber of Commerce and Visitors Information Center (⊠ 110 E. Main St., 97520 ☎ 541/482–3486 ⊕ www.ashlandchamber.org). Grants Pass Visitors & Convention Bureau (⊠ 1501 N.E. 6th St., 97526 ☎ 541/476–7717 or 800/547–5927 ⊕ www.visitgrantspass.org). Illinois Valley Chamber of Commerce (Cave Junction and Oregon Caves National Monument) (⊟ Box 312, Cave Junction 97523 ☎ 541/592–3326 ⊕ www.cavejunction.com). Jacksonville Chamber of Commerce (⊟ Box 33, 97530 ☎ 541/899–8118 ⊕ www.jacksonvilleoregon.org). Klamath County Chamber of Commerce (⊠ 507 Main St., 97601 ☎ 541/884–5193 or 877/552–6284 ⊕ www.klamath.org). Medford Visitors & Convention Bureau (⊠ 101 E. 8th St., 97501 ☎ 800/469–6307 or 541/779–4847 ⊕ www.visitmedford.org). Roseburg Visitors & Convention Bureau (⊠ 410 S.E. Spruce St., 97470 ☎ 541/672–9731 or 800/444–9584 ⊕ www.visitroseburg.com). Southern Oregon Visitors Association (⊠ 332 W. 6th St., Medford 97501 ☎ 541/779–4691 ⊕ www.sova.org).

# EASTERN OREGON

## FODOR'S CHOICE

Foley Station, *contemporary food in La Grande*

Hells Canyon, *30 mi northeast of Joseph*

John Day Fossil Beds National Monument, *John Day*

Parker House, *Pendleton B&B*

Pine Valley Lodge, *Halfway*

Raphael's, *adventurous Pendleton cuisine*

Summit Grill and Alpine Patio, *Joseph*

Underground, *old west tour in Pendleton*

Union Hotel, *Union*

## HIGHLY RECOMMENDED

RESTAURANTS Eagle's Nest, *Lakeview*

Frazier's, *Diamond*

Phone Company, *Baker City*

Terminal Gravity Brew Pub, *Enterprise*

The Outpost Pizza, Pub, and Grill, *John Day*

HOTELS Fish House Inn Bed and Breakfast and RV Park, *Dayville*

Geiser Grand Hotel, *Baker City*

Hotel Diamond, *Diamond*

Stang Manor Bed and Breakfast, *La Grande*

SIGHTS Echo, *old west town south of Hermiston*

Hart Mountain National Antelope Refuge, *northeast of Lakeview*

Kam Wah Chung & Co. Museum, *John Day*

National Historic Oregon Trail Interpretive Center, *Baker City*

Wallowa Lake Tramway, *Joseph*

Updated by
Sarah Kennedy

**TRAVEL EAST FROM THE DALLES, BEND,** or any of the foothill communities blossoming in the shade of the Cascades, and a very different side of Oregon makes its appearance. The air is drier, clearer, and often pungent with the smell of juniper. The vast landscape of sharply folded hills, wheat fields, and mountains shimmering in the distance evokes the Old West. There is a lonely grandeur in eastern Oregon, a plain-spoken, independent spirit that can startle, surprise, and entrance.

Much of eastern Oregon consists of national forest and wilderness, and the people who live here lead very down-to-earth lives. This is a world of ranches and rodeos, pickup trucks and country-western music. Some of the most important moments in Oregon's history took place in the towns of northeastern Oregon. The Oregon Trail passed through this corner of the state, winding through the Grande Ronde Valley between the Wallowa and Blue mountain ranges. The discovery of gold in the region in the 1860s sparked a second invasion of settlers and eventually led to the displacement of the Native American Nez Perce and Paiute tribes. Pendleton, La Grande, and Baker City were all beneficiaries of the gold fever that swept through the area. Signs of even earlier times survive, from the John Day Fossil Beds with its fragments of saber-toothed tigers, giant pigs, and three-toed horses to Native American writings and artifacts hidden within canyon walls in Malheur County's Leslie Gulch.

## Exploring Eastern Oregon

Eastern Oregon extends the length of the state, from Washington to Nevada, east of the Cascades. Exploring such a huge area is no small endeavor, and you should be prepared to drive long distances and to see few signs of civilization in between many of your destinations. The most heavily touristed areas of the region are in the northeastern corner of the state and include Pendleton, Hells Canyon National Recreation Area, and Wallowa Lake. You will find information about these areas in the beginning of the chapter, followed by the other major attraction in the region, the John Day Fossil Beds, in the center of eastern Oregon between the Malheur and Umatilla national forests. The least-populated and least-traveled areas are in the southeast, south of John Day, but this area also has some of the state's most serene and fascinating landscapes and wildlife. There's information about this area, including the communities of Lakeview, Frenchglen, and Diamond, at the end of the chapter. To explore most areas in eastern Oregon, you must have a car. Look carefully at maps to determine which routes to travel; there are two-lane paved roads in most areas in the region, but a few destinations mentioned in this book are accessible only on unpaved roads. Any state road map will indicate which routes these are, so pay close attention so you can allow enough time for potentially slow going in some areas.

### About the Restaurants

Eastern Oregon is cowboy country, and nowhere is this more evident that in the region's many restaurants; with hundreds of miles of ranch land surrounding most towns and cities in the area, it is no surprise that burgers, steak, and prime rib dominate most menus. No matter where you go, you can count on some really tasty beef. Most cities also have a smattering of decent Mexican and Chinese restaurants, but don't expect any of the creative contemporary creations that pervade the big-city dining scene. Vegetarians, beware: the pickings will be slim, but every restaurant always has at least one vegetarian option, though it may simply be called "vegetable dish."

Numbers in the text correspond to numbers in the margin and on the Eastern Oregon map.

**If you have 3 days**

In three days your best bet is to focus on the region's northeastern corner, where towns with several popular sights are not that far apart—by eastern Oregon standards. Spend your first morning exploring the city of **Pendleton** ❸ ➤, taking the Underground Tour and visiting the Woolen Mills. In the afternoon, drive at your leisure through some of the surrounding areas, and wind your way to 🏨 **La Grande** ❹ to spend the night. On day two, drive to **Joseph** ❻, walk around town, and then set off on Routes 82 and 39 to explore the beautiful area surrounding the Wallowa Mountains, Wallowa Lake, and Hells Canyon. If you're there May–October, drive through the Wallowa-Whitman National Forest and Hells Canyon along Route 39, and overnight in 🏨 **Halfway** ❽; the rest of the year, when a portion of the road is closed, retrace your route on I–82 and I–84 to overnight in 🏨 **Baker City** ❾. On your third day, set off from Baker City and drive through the forest on Route 7, and then head out to explore the John Day Fossil Beds on Routes 26 and 19. Depending on your next destination, spend the night in 🏨 **John Day** ⓫, Dayville (9 mi east of **Sheep Rock** ⓬), or **Mitchell** ⓭, or keep heading west back toward Portland.

**If you have 5 days**

Spend your entire first day in and around 🏨 **Pendleton** ❸ ➤ and spend the night. On your second morning, take a leisurely drive toward **La Grande** ❹, winding your way south through Battle Mountain and Lehman Hot Springs or north through the Umatilla Wilderness and Elgin. Keep heading east on I–82, spending the night in 🏨 **Joseph** ❻. On day three, quit Joseph for the Wallowa Mountains, Wallowa Lake, and Hells Canyon. As in the three-day itinerary, head through Wallowa-Whitman National Forest and Hells Canyon in summer when the road is open, overnighting in 🏨 **Halfway** ❽, or, in the off-season, head back west and south to 🏨 **Baker City** ❾. On day four, visit the National Historic Oregon Trail Interpretive Center, and walk around Baker City before driving west on Route 7 through the Malheur National Forest. Spend the night in 🏨 **John Day** ⓫ or Dayville, and on day five, devote yourself to the John Day Fossil Beds, checking out all three of the monument's "units" at **Sheep Rock** ⓬, **Painted Hills** ⓮, and **Clarno** ⓯.

**If you have 8 days**

The first several days of your tour will closely resemble the five-day itinerary above, with a few modifications to allow you more time in some areas. Spend your first day in and around 🏨 **Pendleton** ❸ ➤, and on the second day take a scenic drive to **La Grande** ❹ by heading south on Route 395 through Battle Mountain State Park and northeast on Route 244. Keep heading east; spend the next two nights in 🏨 **Joseph** ❻ and soak up the charming town and its environs, including Hells Canyon, Wallowa Lake, and the Wallowa Mountains. On day four, drive back along Route 82 and I–84 to 🏨 **Baker City** ❾, or, in good weather, drive the scenic road that passes through the forest and Hells Canyon. Spend your fourth night in Baker City or 🏨 **Halfway** ❽. On day five explore Baker City and the National Historic Oregon Trail Interpretive Center, and spend the night in 🏨 **Mitchell** ⓭; rise early and spend all of day six exploring the John Day Fossil Beds. Overnight in 🏨 **John Day** ⓫,

34

and on day seven, head south on Routes 395 and 205, passing through the Malheur National Forest, **Burns** ⑯, and the **Malheur National Wildlife Refuge** ⑰. Spend the night at one of the historic inns in the tiny secluded towns of **Frenchglen** ⑲ or **Diamond** ⑱. On day eight, drive south on Route 205 and west on Route 140, and spend your last night in **Lakeview** ⑳.

## About the Hotels

Like most other areas of the country, eastern Oregon has its share of chain hotels and motels that are generally lacking in character; they often pop up on unappealing strips of highway alongside other hotels, gas stations, and chain restaurants. Best Westerns, Super 8s, Days Inns, and the like are prevalent in such towns as Pendleton, La Grande, Baker City, Ontario, and Lakeview. You can assume that any of these places will have clean and spacious rooms, cable TVs, free parking, and an accommodating staff. Every establishment listed in this chapter offers at least this degree of comfort, but generally, hotels in the ¢ price range offer little more, with basic, unadorned rooms and few additional amenities. For travelers who desire something a little more interesting, eastern Oregon also has many B & Bs, small historic hotels, and cabin rentals in the midst of natural wonders such as the Wallowa Mountains. A handful of towns such as Frenchglen, Diamond, and Halfway are completely untouched by corporate America and have reasonably priced lodgings.

| WHAT IT COSTS | | | | | |
|---|---|---|---|---|---|
| | $$$$ | $$$ | $$ | $ | ¢ |
| RESTAURANTS | over $30 | $20–$30 | $15–$20 | $10–$15 | under $10 |
| HOTELS | over $180 | $140–$180 | $100–$140 | $60–$100 | under $60 |

Restaurant prices are per person for a main course at dinner. Hotel prices are for a standard double room, excluding room tax, which varies 6%–9 1/2% depending on location.

## Timing

Many parts of eastern Oregon get large amounts of snowfall in the winter, and a few of the roads at the highest elevations are impassable as late in the season as May. Most notably, the scenic Route 39 between Halfway and Joseph through the Wallowa-Whitman National Forest and Hells Canyon is generally open only from May until October. Due to the weather, therefore, most travelers flock to eastern Oregon in the summer months. The national wilderness areas attract many hikers and backpackers, and Wallowa Lake is a popular spot for summer water sports. Along with summer come higher hotel rates and steeper competition for available rooms; between June and September, book your lodging at least several weeks in advance. Winter, on the other hand, draws a smaller enthusiastic crowd of skiers, snowboarders, and snowmobilers to the ski areas at North Powder and Anthony Lakes and to the all-terrain trails in the Umatilla and Wallowa-Whitman national forests.

# Umatilla

❶ *185 mi east of Portland on I–84 and Rte. 730; 36 mi northwest of Pendleton.*

Umatilla is at the confluence of the Umatilla and Columbia rivers. It was founded in the mid-1800s as a trade and shipping center during the gold rush, and today it is a center for fishing activities. Just east of Umatilla,

Hat Rock State Park contains the unusual geological formation from which it gets its name. Farther upstream, McNary Dam generates extensive hydroelectric power and impounds a lake that extends from Umatilla to Richland, Washington, some 70 mi away.

On the south shore of Lake Wallula, **Hat Rock State Park** was the first major landmark that Lewis and Clark passed on their expedition down the Columbia. The rock itself stands tall amid rolling sagebrush hills and looks down upon the lake, which is a popular spot for jet skiing, swimming, boating, and fishing for walleye and sturgeon. In addition to water sports, the park provides scenic picnic spots and gorgeous views of the stark, desert-like landscape. Be aware, however, that it abuts an upscale lakeside housing development that's visible from some of the park, making it a little difficult to pretend you're in the days of Lewis and Clark. ⊠ *U.S. 730, 9 mi. east of Umatilla* ☎ *800/551–6949* ⊕ *www. prd.state.or.us* ☞ *Free* ☉ *Mid-Mar.–Oct., daily.*

On the Columbia River, the hydroelectric dam at **McNary Lock and Dam,** completed in 1954, impounds a lake that extends 70 mi upstream from Umatilla to Richland, Washington. Today the area surrounding the dam includes the McNary Wildlife Nature Area, two small parks and picnic areas, an elaborate visitor center with an exhibit and information about Pacific salmon, and a trail that follows the Columbia River bank for 3 mi to Hat Rock State Park. Above the dam, McNary Beach Park's picnic area overlooks a large swim beach, while Hat Rock Scenic Corridor also leads to Hat Rock State Park. ⊠ *U.S. 730* ☎ *541/922–4388* ☞ *Free* ☉ *Daily; marinas June–Sept., daily.*

With a marina, a boat-launch, a small swimming area, and an RV campground with 26 full hookups, the unadorned **Umatilla Marina Park** provides great access to the Columbia, but if you're planning a relaxing afternoon of picnicking or lounging on land, go to Hat Rock State Park or one of the parks at McNary Dam. There's little in the way of scenery or greenery here. ⊠ *3rd Ave. on Columbia River* ☎ *541/922–3939* ☞ *Day use free; full hookups $20, tent sites $12* ☉ *Marina daily 7–7.*

Stretching from west of Boardman to Irrigon, the 23,555-acre **Umatilla National Wildlife Refuge** includes marsh, woodland, and wetland habitats that make it vital to migrating waterfowl and bald eagles, in addition to myriad species of resident wildlife. Although there are numerous routes to access portions of the refuge, the best and easiest way to view wildlife in ponds and wetlands is to drive along the McCormick Auto Route, accessible from Paterson Ferry Road, off Route 730, 9 mi west of Umatilla. ⊠*Stretches from Boardman, 20 mi west of Umatilla, to Irrigon, 9 mi west of Umatilla, north of I–84 along Columbia River* ☎ *503/922–3232* ⊕ *www.fws.gov* ☞ *Free* ☉ *Daily dawn–dusk on designated roadways only.*

## Where to Stay & Eat

$–$$ ✕ **Desert River Inn.** With large booths and pastel walls, this casual and family-friendly spot—widely regarded as the best restaurant in either Umatilla or Hermiston—has no pretention of urban chic, but the large menu of prime rib, fresh pasta, and seafood, as well as the vegetarian entrées (a rare find in eastern Oregon), is bound to tempt most palates. A stop here is a satisfying finish to a day of exploring, boating, or golfing at the course next to the inn. ⊠ *705 Willamette Ave., 97882* ☎ *541/992–1000 or 877/922–1500* ☐ *AE, D, DC, MC, V.*

$ ☐ **Desert River Inn.** The largest and, by far, the most well-equipped hotel in Umatilla, the Desert River Inn acts as the centerpiece of the town, with its restaurant, golf course, and banquet rooms making it far more than a place to spend the night. The rooms are large and comfortable, even if the furnishings—brown shag carpet offset by blue bedspreads and curtains—are a bit dated. Some rooms have kitchenettes. ✉ *705 Willamette Ave., 97882* ☎ *541/922–1000 or 877/922–1500* 🖷 *541/922–1200* 🛏 *66 rooms* ⚲ *Restaurant, room service, in-room data ports, some kitchenettes, microwaves, refrigerators, cable TV, 18-hole golf course, pool, gym, outdoor hot tub, horseshoes, bar, meeting rooms, free parking, some pets allowed (fee)* ☰ *AE, D, DC, MC, V* ⫶◯⫶ *CP.*

¢–$ 🖀 **Tillicum Inn.** If you need to stay in Umatilla proper, this is a reliable and inexpensive choice, with friendly owners. Rooms are unglamorous, but most have microwaves and refrigerators, and for an extra fee, you can get a room with an adjoining full kitchen. ✉ *1481 6th St., 97882* ☎ *541/922–3236* 🖷 *541/922–5889* 🛏 *40 rooms* ⚲ *Pool* ☰ *AE, D, DC, MC, V.*

### Sports & the Outdoors

GOLF  The **Umatilla Golf Course** (✉ 705 Willamette Ave. ☎ 541/922–3006), adjoining the Desert River Inn, is a public 18-hole, par-70 course.

# Hermiston

❷  *188 mi east of Portland on I–84, 28 mi northwest of Pendleton.*

Although its population is just over 10,000 residents, Hermiston is the urban service center for nearly three times that many people in the expansive and productive agricultural industry that surrounds it. Irrigated farmlands and ranch lands produce livestock and crops, including alfalfa, potatoes, corn, wheat, and the watermelons for which Hermiston is best known. The town was named for Robert Louis Stevenson's unfinished novel, *The Weir of Hermiston.* Hermiston contains more than 75 acres of city parks, with the Columbia River 6 mi to the north and the Umatilla River and Blue Mountains nearby.

The railroad came to Hermiston in 1883, and some of the original tracks are still at **Maxwell Siding Railroad Display,** an outdoor exhibit of railroad cars and memorabilia. There is a 1910 rotary snowplow, a 1913 diner from the Oregon Short Line, a 1912 passenger car, a 1949 steam-powered snowplow (the last of its kind used in the United States), and two cabooses; if you like, you can arrange to get married in one of them. There are some unusual automobiles too, including a rare 1922 Buda. ✉ *200 W. Highland Ave., across from Hermiston High School, 97838* ☎ *541/567–8532 or 541/567–3759* 🖾 *Donation* ⊙ *Sat. and by appointment.*

★  Ten miles south of Hermiston, off I–84, the tiny town of **Echo,** site of Fort Henrietta, sits at the intersection of the Oregon Trail and the transcontinental railroad that arrived in 1881. With only a handful of streets comprising the center of town, a short walking tour will take about an hour. You'll pass several buildings erected in the town's heyday—in the late 19th and early 20th centuries—and you'll see the Chinese House/ON&R Railroad Museum, originally a bunkhouse for Chinese railroad crews, which now has railroad artifacts. From Echo, head back to Hermiston or along the scenic old Highway 30 to Pendleton (21 mi). ⊕ *1 mi south of I–84 at Exit 188.*

> **need a break?**  After exploring historic Echo, grab a cup of coffee or an ice cream cone at **Little River Cafe** (✉ 231 W. Main St., Echo ☎ 541/376–8573).

### Where to Stay & Eat

$–$$$  ✕ **Hale's Restaurant and Lounge.** With rodeo artifacts on the walls, country music playing, a menu bound in soft brown leather, and dark red

## Animal Channels

**34**

Along with other vast spaces throughout the Northwest, eastern Oregon has become a haven for birds and mammals—including yellow-headed blackbirds, cliff swallows, egrets, herons, bighorn sheep, pronghorn antelope, and coyotes. Several wildlife refuges, most notably the Malheur National Wildlife Refuge, but also the Hart Mountain National Antelope Refuge, the Umatilla Wildlife Refuge, and the Cold Springs National Wildlife Refuge, afford travelers great views of animal life. To get the best tour of the refuges, and to avoid scaring wildlife, it is recommended that you stay in your car, where you can move quietly through these natural habitats without creating a disturbance. There are generally a few designated hiking trails as well, but to protect the delicate environment and yourself, don't ever stray from designated routes—on foot or in your car—even for a peek. For a close look at the birds bring binoculars or a telephoto lens. You can't really miss the larger animals if they come into view, and if you stick around long enough, you'll probably find them—or they you. For travel in the larger refuges, be sure that your gas tank is full and that you have plenty of drinking water.

## Follow the Oregon Trail

Most places in northeastern Oregon have at least one or two historical landmarks devoted to the Oregon Trail. This route, followed by hundreds of thousands of pioneers who trekked 2,000 mi by covered wagon to the West Coast in the mid-19th century, passes near Ontario, Baker City, La Grande, and Pendleton, before heading farther west toward Portland. Many places, such as Farewell Bend State Park near Ontario, have informational kiosks explaining the significance of a given spot, and other areas, such as the National Oregon Trail Interpretive Center near Baker City, devote an entire museum to exploring the challenging experience that led to the main waves of settlement in the state. At some spots, you can still see the ruts left by wagon wheels on particularly well-traveled sections of the trail. It would be difficult to spend more than a day or two in northeastern Oregon without being struck by the significance of this mass migration.

## Why Cowboys Come to the City

In case you need a reminder that eastern Oregon is Old West ranching land, just listen for the buzz of anticipation when rodeo time is coming around in any town, large or small. The Pendleton Round-Up is by far the largest and most hyped-up rodeo in the region. You can tour the Round-Up Hall of Fame year-round to try to find out what the locals are talking about, but you'll never really understand unless you are in town in the middle of September, when the generally laid-back city is overrun by cowboys and cowgirls flooding in from hundreds of miles away. The Round-Up might be the biggest, but it is by no means the only rodeo that lures cowboys into the cities: the Baker County Fair and Panhandle Rodeo in Halfway on Labor Day Weekend, the Farm City Pro Rodeo in Hermiston in early August, and Chief Joseph Days in Joseph in late July are but a few of the others in the area.

leather booths, Hale's manages to create a classy, upscale feel with an old West rodeo flair. A Hermiston institution since 1906, Hale's is a dependable choice for prime rib, steak, and pork chops. Open from 10 AM daily, it also serves a breakfast menu all day, including huge omelets and steak and eggs. ⊠ *174 E. Main St.* ☎ *541/567–7975* ⊟ *AE, D, DC, MC, V.*

¢–$  ✕ **La Finca.** About a mile west of Main Street, La Finca's piñatas, banners, and colorfully painted booths and walls draw crowds. It feels (and costs) more upscale than your neighborhood burrito joint, and its full-color glossy menu describes enchiladas, tostadas, and margaritas that are difficult to resist. ⊠ *315 S.W. 11th St.* ☎ *541/567–7499* ⊟ *AE, D, DC, MC, V.*

¢–$  ✕ **Roy and Venita's.** It feels like a mix between an old-fashioned diner and a grandmother's kitchen in here, and the menu of meat loaf, steak, sandwiches, and all-day breakfast reinforces this first impression. Open from 5 AM through dinner daily, this small restaurant attracts loyal locals, who come in for good old-fashioned food and good, friendly service. ⊠ *508 E. Main St.* ☎ *514/567–5223* ⊟ *MC, V.*

$–$$  ▨ **Oxford Suites.** Perhaps Hermiston's most luxurious hotel, this all-suites facility has lovely, spacious rooms in two buildings, all with large sitting areas with work desks and sofas. In addition to a complimentary breakfast buffet, an evening reception with free food and drinks is held daily in the lounge area. ⊠ *1050 N. 1st St., 97838* ☎ *514/564–8000 or 888/545–7848* 🖶 *514/564–0633* ⊕ *www.oxfordsuites.com* ⇲ *127 suites* ⚐ *Dining room, in-room data ports, microwaves, refrigerators, cable TV with VCRs, indoor pool, gym, spa, shop, laundry facilities, business services, meeting rooms, free parking, no-smoking rooms* ⊟ *AE, D, DC; MC, V* ⦿l *BP.*

$  ▨ **Oak Tree Inn.** Comfortable and well equipped, this hotel is directly behind Safeway Supermarket, minutes from Main Street. The newest addition to Hermiston's fleet of hotels, it has lovely rooms and useful amenities inside a surprisingly plain and understated exterior. Microwaves and refrigerators are available upon request. ⊠ *1110 S.E. 4th St., 97838* ☎ *503/567–2330 or 800/537–8483* ⇲ *62 rooms* ⚐ *In-room data ports, cable TV, gym, hot tub, spa, laundry facilities, free parking; no smoking* ⊟ *AE, D, DC, MC, V.*

¢–$  ▨ **Oxford Inn.** The more modest counterpart to the Oxford Suites down the street, the inn is in an older building that shows its age with slightly dated furnishings and worn-down corridors, but its well-cared-for guest rooms ensure a comfortable stay. Some rooms have full kitchens. ⊠ *655 N. 1st St., 97838* ☎ *541/567–7777 or 888/729–7848* 🖶 *541/567–3085* ⇲ *90 rooms* ⚐ *Restaurant, cable TV, microwaves, refrigerators, laundry facilities, business services, some pets allowed (fee), no-smoking rooms* ⊟ *AE, D, DC, MC, V* ⦿l *CP.*

## Sports & the Outdoors

RODEO  The **Farm City Pro Rodeo** (⊠ 495 E. Main St. ☎ 541/564–8500) is held for several days in August each year, in conjunction with the Umatilla County Fair.

## Shopping

**RoeMark's Men's and Western Wear** (⊠ 201 E. Main St. ☎ 541/567–3831) has everything a good western man could ever want or need to wear, from a huge collection of cowboy boots and cowboy hats to durable shirts, pants, and outerwear for work and for play. The **Village Antiques and Gifts** (⊠ 920 S.E. 4th St. ☎ 541/567–0272) is part antiques store, part country gift shop, part natural food store, and part vitamin center. Do not miss a chance to wander the three floors of this cute old house, where each small room complicates the fascinating collage of things to buy and see.

# Pendleton

▶ ❸ *211 mi east of Portland, 129 mi east of The Dalles on I–84.*

At the foot of the Blue Mountains amid vast wheat fields and cattle ranches, Pendleton is a quintessential western town with a rip-snorting history. The herds of wild horses that once thundered across this rolling landscape were at the center of the area's early Native American cultures. Later, Pendleton became an important pioneer junction and home to a sizable Chinese community. Lacking a sheriff until 1912, Pendleton was a raw and wild frontier town filled with cowboys, cattle rustlers, saloons, and bordellos. The many century-old homes still standing vary in style from simple farmhouses to stately Queen Annes.

Given its raucous past, Pendleton, the largest city in eastern Oregon (population almost 17,000), looks unusually sedate. But all that changes in September when the **Pendleton Round-Up** (⇨ Sports & the Outdoors) draws thousands for a rodeo and related events. Motels fill up, schools close down, and everybody goes hog-wild for a few days.

Perhaps Pendleton's main source of name-recognition in the country today comes from the Pendleton Woolen Mills, home of the trademark wool plaid shirts and colorful woolen Indian blankets that are sold nationwide. Pendleton also produces a full line of men's and women's clothing, and although Pendleton headquarters has moved to Portland, the Pendleton mill is still operating and is available to tour.

The collection at the **Round-Up Hall of Fame Museum** spans the rodeo's history since 1910 with photographs—including some great ones of Rodeo Queens and the Happy Canyon Princesses (all Native American)—as well as saddles, guns, costumes, and even a stuffed championship bronco named War Paint. ⊠ *Round-Up Grounds, 1205 S.W. Court Ave., near S.W. 12th St.* ☎ *541/278–0815* ⊡ *Free* ☉ *May–Oct., daily 10–4; other times, call for appointment.*

**Fodor'sChoice** ★ The **Underground,** a 90-minute vividly guided tour, yields clues about life in Pendleton more than a century ago, when the town held 32 saloons and 18 brothels. The first half of the tour heads into a subterranean labyrinth that hid gambling rooms, an opium den, and other illegal businesses. Chinese laborers lived in a chilly jumble of underground rooms. The second half focuses on the life of Madame Stella Darby, the town's best-known madam, and includes a visit to her bordello. Tours operate year-round and leave throughout the day. Call for information; reservations are strongly recommended. ⊠ *37 S.W. Emigrant Ave.* ☎ *541/276–0730 or 800/226–6398* ⊕ *www. pendletonundergroundtours.com* ⊡ *$10.*

**need a break?** A popular little laid-back spot across from the Underground Tours, the **Cookie Tree** (⊠ 39 S.W. Emigrant Ave. ☎ 514/278–0343) is good for a quick breakfast, sandwich, pastry, or fresh bread.

Displays and photographs at the **Umatilla County Historical Society Museum** outline Pendleton's story. The town's old railway depot houses the museum. ⊠ *108 S.W. Frazer Ave.* ☎ *541/276–0012* ⊡ *$2* ☉ *Tues.–Sat. 10–4.*

The **Pendleton Chamber of Commerce** (⊠ 501 S. Main St. ☎ 541/276–7411 or 800/547–8911 ⊕ www.pendleton-oregon.org ☉ weekdays 8–5), has information about the town and surrounding area, including the Umatilla National Forest and the Blue Mountains.

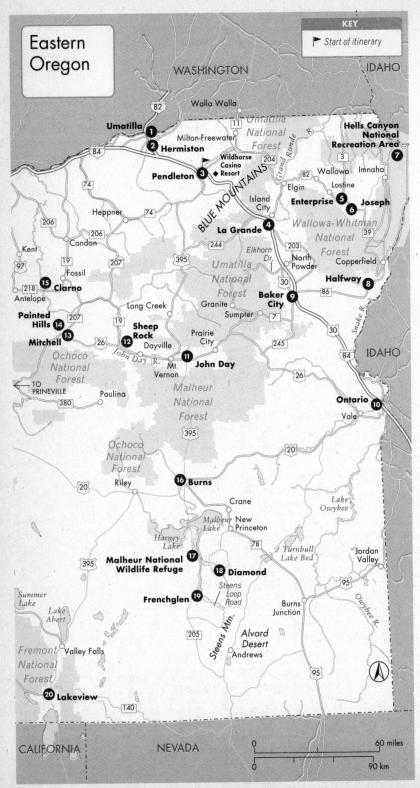

Eastern
Oregon

KEY

▶ *Start of itinerary*

WASHINGTON

IDAHO

82

Walla Walla

Umatilla ①

Milton-Freewater

② Hermiston

11

Umatilla
National
Forest

204

Hells Canyon
National
Recreation Area ⑦

3

84

Pendleton ③

Wildhorse
Casino
Resort

Wallowa

Imnaha

74

Island
City

Elgin

82

Lostine

Enterprise ⑤

Joseph

Heppner

74

206

La Grande ④

Wallowa-Whitman

⑥

Condon

206

244

Elkhorn
Dr.

203

North
Powder

National

39

Kent

207

395

Umatilla
National
Forest

30

Copperfield

97

19

Fossil

Halfway ⑧

218

⑮ Clarno

Long Creek

Granite

Baker
City ⑨

86

Antelope

Painted
Hills ⑭

207

19

Sheep
Rock ⑫

Sumpter

7

30

IDAHO

Mitchell ⑬

26

Dayville

Prairie
City

245

Ochoco
National
Forest

John Day R.

Mt.
Vernon

⑪ John Day

26

84

← TO
PRINEVILLE

Paulina

Malheur
National
Forest

Ontario ⑩

380

Vale

395

Ochoco
National
Forest

20

20

Riley

⑯ Burns

Lake
Owyhee

Crane

Malheur
Lake

New
Princeton

Harney
Lake

78

Turnbull
Lake Bed

Jordan
Valley

Summer
Lake

395

Malheur National
Wildlife Refuge

⑰

⑱ Diamond

Steens
Loop
Road

95

Owyhee R.

Lake
Abert

Frenchglen ⑲

Burns
Junction

205

Steens Mtn.

Alvord
Desert

95

Fremont
National
Forest

Valley Falls

Andrews

⑳ Lakeview

140

CALIFORNIA

NEVADA

0                    60 miles

0                    90 km

The **Pendleton Woolen Mills** produce superb Indian blankets and Pendleton shirts and sportswear. In days past the clothing of choice for cowboys, the western and Indian–inspired threads have gained popularity among urbanites for their colors, warmth, and durability. A free tour that lasts about 20 minutes describes the weaving process from start to finish. The mill's retail store stocks blankets and men's and women's clothing; there are good bargains on factory seconds. ⊠ *1307 S.E. Court Pl.* ☎ *541/276–6911 or 800/568–3156* ⊙ *Mon.–Sat. 8–5, Sun. 11–3; tours weekdays at 9, 11, 1:30, and 3.*

The Confederated Tribes of the Umatilla Reservation, composed of the Umatilla, Cayuse, and Walla Walla Tribes, combined to form a single tribal government in 1949, nearly a hundred years after the groups collectively ceded several million acres of land to the U.S. government. Today, the 172,000-acre **Umatilla Indian Reservation,** bordered by Pendleton to the west and the Umatilla National Forest to the east, has about 2,000 tribal members. One of the major economic ventures undertaken by the tribe is the Wildhorse Casino Resort and the Tamastslikt Cultural Institute, found 6 mi east of Pendleton, near the Reservation's westernmost edge. ⊠ *Bounded by I–84, Rte. 11 (to Athena), and the Umatilla National Forest. There is also a smaller section south of I–84. Governing bodies found in Mission, about 6 mi east of Pendleton.*

The **Tamastslikt Cultural Institute** at the Wildhorse Casino Resort opened in 1998. The 45,000-square-foot building has exhibits depicting history from the perspective of the Cayuse, Umatilla, and Walla Walla tribes. An art gallery showcases art of local and regional tribal artists. There's also a museum gift shop, a theater, and a café. The institute is operated by the Confederated Tribes of the Umatilla Indian Reservation. Tamastslikt means "interpret" in the Walla Walla native language. ⊠ *72789 Hwy. 331, north of I–84 at Exit 216, 97801* ☎ *541/966–9748 or 800/654–9453* ⊕ *www.tamastslikt.com* ⊠ *$6* ⊙ *Daily 9–5.*

Near the summit of the Blue Mountains, **Emigrant Springs State Heritage Area,** a park in an old-growth forest, is the site of a popular pioneer stopover along the Oregon Trail. The park has picnic areas, hiking trails, historical information, and gathering spaces for special events. At the campground, in addition to 18 full hookups and 33 tent sites, you will find six charming rustic cabins and two totem cabins. There also is a six-site horse camp. ⊠ *Off I–84 at Exit 234* ☎ *541/983–2277 or 800/551–6949* ⊕ *www.prd.state.or.us* ⊠ *Day use free* ⊙ *Mar.–Nov., daily.*

Seven miles south of Pendleton, the 1,836-acre **McKay Creek National Wildlife Refuge,** next to McKay Reservoir, provides a home for waterfowl and plant life. You can drive along gravel roads for several miles through the enchantingly stark expanse of wild grass and sage. ⊠ *Along U.S. 395, 7 mi south of Pendleton* ⊠ *Free* ⊙ *Mar.–Sept., daily dawn–dusk.*

Near the summit of Battle Mountain, **Battle Mountain Scenic Corridor** is a state park with gorgeous views and picnic facilities at the edge of the Umatilla National Forest. The park makes for a good place to relax and eat lunch (as long as it's not snowing), but the real treat is getting here. The drive from Pendleton winds through hills of farmland as it ascends into the mountains and, near the top, affords jaw-dropping views of the green mountains and valleys around each turn. Beware of difficult road conditions through the winter and much of the spring, and remember that the park is bound to be much colder than temperate Pendleton. ⊠ *U.S. 395, 9 mi north of Ukiah; about 40 mi south of Pendleton* ☎ *800/551–6949* ⊕ *www.prd.state.or.us* ⊠ *Free.*

The North Fork of the John Day River and Camas Creek, which flow through **Ukiah-Dale Forest State Park,** have excellent trout, steelhead, and salmon fishing. Three miles southwest of Ukiah, this park is quite a hike from Pendleton, but if you want to camp in the Umatilla National Forest, or are heading as far as Ukiah on a day of scenic driving, be sure to check it out. A campground has 27 primitive sites. ⊠ *U.S. 395, about 50 mi south of Pendleton* ☎ *541/983–2277 or 800/551–6949* ⊕ *www. prd.state.or.us* ☞ *Free* ☉ *Mid-Apr.–Nov., daily.*

The 1.4-million-acre **Umatilla National Forest** has three wilderness areas, as well as the Blue Mountain Scenic Byway and 22 campgrounds. In the Blue Mountains of northeastern Oregon and southeastern Washington, the diverse forest land is found both east and south of Pendleton and extends south almost as far as John Day, where it borders the Malheur National Forest. To the east, it is bordered by the Wallowa-Whitman National Forest. Major thoroughfares, including I–84, U.S. 395, and Routes 204 and 244, pass through portions of the forest. In the summer months, the Blue Mountain Scenic Byway provides a beautiful way to travel to Baker City from Ukiah or points farther west. A ski area in the Umatilla National Forest, **Spout Springs** (⊠ Summit of Hwy. 204 at Tollgate, Milepost 22 ☎ 541/566–0327 ☉ Thurs. 5 PM–9 PM, Fri. 1 PM–9 PM, Sat. 9–9, Sun. 9–4) has an elevation of 4,950 feet at the base, 5,550 feet at the top, and a vertical drop of 550 feet. There are 11 runs and 21 km of Nordic trails. ☎ *541/278–3716* ☉ *Some areas only in summer; call to confirm accessibility.*

## Where to Stay & Eat

$–$$$

Fodor's Choice
★

✕ **Raphael's.** Chef Raphael Hoffman serves traditional steaks, seafood, and fettuccine dishes, but she also specializes in adventurous seasonal cuisine—venison, elk, rattlesnake, blackened Cajun alligator, and Indian salmon topped with huckleberries. This may be the only place in eastern Oregon to get a huckleberry daiquiri. Native American artwork figures prominently among the interior furnishings, and a garden out back is perfect for alfresco dining. ⊠ *233 S.E. 4th St.* ☎ *541/276–8500* ▭ *AE, D, DC, MC, V* ☉ *Closed Sun. and Mon. No lunch.*

¢–$$ ✕ **Cimmiyotti's.** Eat here just to enjoy the Old West–style chandeliers and flocked wallpaper. Well-prepared steaks and Italian food are the main fare. ⊠ *137 S. Main St.* ☎ *541/276–4314* ▭ *AE, DC, MC, V* ☉ *Closed Sun. No lunch.*

¢–$$ ✕ **Crabby's Underground Saloon.** Like so many other restaurants in northeast Oregon, Crabby's specializes in steak, prime rib, and burgers. Unlike many other places, however, it is in a basement tavern, has entertainment nightly, and has a great late-night menu of cheap eats. ⊠ *220 S.W. 1st St.* ☎ *503/276–8118* ▭ *AE, D, DC, MC, V.*

¢–$ ✕ **Rainbow Cafe.** Even if you don't eat here—but it is worth your while to do so—you owe it to yourself to step through the swinging door and into the past: the Rainbow is a glimpse of how the West was fun. Take a seat at the counter surrounded by locals eating fried-egg sandwiches, tall stacks of hotcakes, and fried chicken. Be aware that this is very much a bar—plenty smoky, and not ideal for kids. ⊠ *209 S. Main St.* ☎ *541/ 276–4120* ▭ *No credit cards.*

¢ ✕ **Great Pacific Wine and Coffee Company.** Open until 8 PM, this downtown café serves a fine latte as well as bagels, muffins, and deli sandwiches; dozens of beers and wines are also available. ⊠ *403 S. Main St.* ☎ *541/276–1350* ▭ *AE, MC, V* ☉ *Closed Sun.*

¢ ✕ **Main St. Diner.** Pictures of Elvis and old movie posters fill the walls of this small, flashy retro diner. The black-and-white tile floors and teal vinyl booths might seem a little too self-consciously hip in a larger city, but here in Pendleton, it just feels earnestly fun and friendly. Stop in for an inexpensive breakfast of bacon and eggs, or a basic burger for lunch. ⊠ *349 S. Main St.* ☎ *541/278–1952* ▤ *MC, V* ⊘ *No dinner.*

**$–$$** ⌂ **Oxford Suites.** Just west of downtown Pendleton and only half a mile from the Round-Up grounds, this all-suites facility is one of the more luxurious offerings in the Pendleton area. In addition to a full breakfast buffet, an evening reception with drinks and hors d'oeuvres is included free. Each guest suite includes a work desk and sitting area. ⊠ *2400 S.W. Court Pl., 97801* ☎ *541/276–6000 or 877/545–7848* ▤ *541/278–8556* ⊕ *www.oxfordsuites.com* ➫ *87 suites* ♿ *In-room data ports, microwaves, refrigerators, cable TV with VCRs, indoor pool, gym, hot tub, shop, laundry facilities, business services, meeting rooms, free parking, no-smoking rooms* ▤ *AE, D, DC, MC, V* ¡◯¡ *BP.*

**$** ⌂ **A Place Apart Bed and Breakfast.** This gorgeous Colonial Revival home on the eastern edge of downtown Pendleton used to be one of the most extravagant homes in the neighborhood, and it remains a beautifully maintained remnant of the past. No detail is forsaken here: original brass hardware and antiques fill the common spaces and guest rooms. With only two guest rooms, it is an intimate place to enjoy your vacation, and one you should reserve well in advance, especially during the summer. A delicious breakfast is served daily. ⊠ *711 S.E. Byers Ave., 97801,* ☎ *541/276–0573 or 888/441–8932* ⊕ *www.aplace-apart.com* ➫ *2 rooms with shared bath* ♿ *No kids, no smoking* ▤ *MC, V* ¡◯¡ *BP.*

**$** ⌂ **Parker House.** Virtually unchanged since it was built in 1917, this handsome pink stucco home in Pendleton's North Hill neighborhood is a very grand reminder that the Old West had its share of wealth and worldly sophistication. A hybrid blend of French neoclassical and Italianate styles, Parker House is a rarity among B&Bs: it still has its original Chinese wallpaper, custom fittings, and woodwork, which is nothing less than astonishing. The rooms, furnished with period furniture, are quiet and comfortable. Four of the rooms share one bathroom, but once you see it you'll understand why the owner has chosen to preserve everything as it was rather than adding modern "improvements." Breakfasts are delicious and filling and might include eggs Benedict with smoked salmon or pecan-and-cranberry-stuffed French toast. ⊠ *311 N. Main St., 97801* ☎ *541/276–8581 or 800/700–8581* ➫ *5 rooms, 1 with bath* ▤ *AE, MC, V* ¡◯¡ *BP.*

Fodor'sChoice
★

**$** ⌂ **Wildhorse Casino Resort.** Owned and operated by the Cayuse, Umatilla, and Walla Walla tribes, this gaming resort is about 6 mi east of downtown Pendleton, making it Oregon's easternmost casino. Gamblers can hunker down at 400 slot machines, poker, blackjack tables, keno, bingo, and off-track betting, while golfers can play the 18-hole championship golf course (greens fee range $21–$26, carts $22). The entertainment highlight of the year is the July 4–6 Pow-Wow, which draws up to 1,000 Native American dancers. The motel-style rooms, many of which have whirlpools, are large and comfortable, if not particularly luxurious. There's a buffet restaurant and snack bar, as well as a 100-space RV park. ⊠ *72777 Hwy. 331 (head north from I–84's Exit 216), 97801* ☎ *541/276–0355 or 800/654–9453* ▤ *541/276–0297* ⊕ *www.wildhorseresort.org* ➫ *100 rooms* ♿ *2 restaurants, indoor pool, gym, hot tub, sauna, steam room, lounge* ▤ *AE, D, DC, MC, V* ¡◯¡ *CP.*

**¢–$** ⌂ **Working Girls Hotel.** In downtown Pendleton, this 1890s building served at different times as a boardinghouse and a bordello—hence its name—before it was restored and opened as a hotel in 1991. Today, it is owned and operated by the Underground Tours. The rooms, with 18-foot-high ceilings and exposed-brick walls, are individually furnished with antiques dating from the early 1900s to the 1950s, and a full kitchen and dining room are available to guests. ⊠ *17 S.W. Emigrant Ave., 97801* ☎ *541/276–0730 or 800/226–6398* 🖶 *541/276–0665* ⬩ *4 rooms share 1 bath, 1 suite* ⚬ *No kids, no smoking* ⊟ D, MC, V.

¢ ▦ **Tapadera Inn.** Convenient to shopping and restaurants, this motel-style inn has some of the cheaper, albeit more spartan, rooms in Pendleton. Stetson's House of Prime adjoins the motel. ⊠ *105 S.E. Court Ave., 97801* ☎ *541/276–3231 or 800/722–8277* 🖶 *541/276–0754* ⬩ *47 rooms* ⚬ *Restaurant, refrigerators, cable TV, bar, some pets allowed (fee)* ⊟ AE, D, DC, MC, V.

⚠ **Emigrant Springs State Heritage Area.** At this historic site, which was part of the Oregon Trail, campers can stay in covered wagons or rustic cabins with heat and electricity, pitch a tent, or hook up an RV. The full-service facility has exhibits, a nature trail, a horse camp, and a free day-use area. ⚬ *Flush toilets, drinking water, showers.* ⬩ *32 tent sites, 18 full hookups, 2 covered camper wagons, 6 rustic cabins, 2 totem cabins, 6-site horse camp.* ⊠ *I–84 (Exit 234 W), 26 mi east of Pendleton* ☎ *541/983–2277, 800/452–5687 reservations only* ⬩ *Covered wagons $25, cabins (sleep 4) $25–$37, RV sites $16, tent sites $8–$13* ☉ *Open Apr.–late Oct.; limited access rest of year.*

## Nightlife & the Arts

In the 1916 Carnegie Library, **Pendleton Center for the Arts** (⊠ 214 N. Main St., 97801 ☎ 541/278–9201) has undergone an elaborate renovation. The beautiful facility has several free rotating exhibits each year, in addition to a crafts gallery, performance space, and several art studios and classrooms where community classes and summer art camps are held.

## Sports & the Outdoors

FISHING Oregon's largest full-service fly shop east of the Cascades, **Blue Mountain Anglers and Fly Shop** (⊠ 1847 Westgate ☎ 800/825–1548) also has a fishing school and information about angling in the area; the focus here is on fishing in the Umatilla River for steelhead, trout, and salmon.

GOLF **Milton-Freewater Golf Course** (⊠ off Hwy. 11, 32 mi northeast of Pendleton ☎ 541/938–7284) is a public, 18-hole course near the town of Milton-Freewater, south of the Washington border. The greens free is $6–$14.

RODEO The Blue Mountains may be the area's largest attraction, but the **Pendleton Round-Up** is certainly the biggest; more than 50,000 people roll into town for this overwhelming event, one of the oldest and most prominent rodeos in the United States. Held on the second full week of September, it attracts rodeo performers and fans for four days of rodeo events, wild-horse races, barbecues, parades, and milking contests. Vendors line the length of Court Avenue and Main Street, selling beadwork and western-style curios while country bands twang in the background. Tickets for the events—which include the Happy Canyon Pageant and Dance—cost between $6 and $12; make your reservations far in advance. ⊠ *Rodeo Grounds and ticket office: 1205 S.W. Court Ave., at S.W. 12th St.* ⬩ *Box 609, Pendleton 97801* ☎ *541/276–2553 or 800/457–6336.*

## Shopping

Claiming to be "Pendleton's Favorite Store," **Clough's on Main** (⊠ 216 S. Main St. ☎ 541/276–2227) has plenty of women's clothing, jewelry, gifts, leather goods and handcrafted wood products worth browsing, as long as you can endure the strong scents emanating from the adjoining nail and hair salon. The **Collector's Gallery** (⊠ 223 S.E. Court Ave. ☎ 541/276–6697) is a large, disorganized antiques store where you get the feeling there are always more fun treasures to be unearthed around the next corner. On-site craftspeople fashion hand-tooled saddles that are considered the best in the world at **Hamley & Co. Western Store & Custom Saddlery** (✉ 30 S.E. Court Ave. ☎ 541/276–2321), which carries authentic cowboy and cowgirl gear and quality leather products. The only store in town that sells the women's line of Pendleton fashions is **Murphy House** (✉ 1112 S.E. Emigrant Ave. ☎ 541/276–7020). Inside the Center for the Arts, **Pendleton Foundation Craft Gallery** (✉ 214 N. Main St. ☎ 541/278–9201) sells the original artwork and crafts pieces of approximately 40 local artists. **Picket Fences** (✉ 239 S.E. Court Ave. ☎ 541/276–9515) is a charming country store with home and garden gifts, as wells as some antiques.

## La Grande

❹ *56 mi southeast of Pendleton on I–84 at Rte. 82.*

La Grande started life in the late 1800s as a farming community. It grew slowly while most towns along the Blue Mountains were booming or busting in the violent throes of gold-fueled stampedes. When the railroad companies were deciding where to lay their tracks through the valley, a clever local farmer donated 150 acres to ensure that the iron horse would run through La Grande. With the power of steam fueling a new boom, the town quickly outgrew its neighbors, claimed the title of county seat from fading Union City, and now, with its population of 12,000, sits at the urban center of the valley. La Grande is also the site of the only four-year college in the region, Eastern Oregon State College. The town is a convenient stop if you're heading to the nearby Wallowa Mountains.

Stop by the **La Grande Visitor Center** for information and brochures. ✉ *102 Elm St.* ☎ *541/963–8588 or 800/848–9969* ⊕ *www.visitlagrande.com.*

The **Wallowa Mountains** form a rugged U-shape fortress between Hells Canyon on the Idaho border and the Blue Mountains, west of the Grande Ronde Valley. Sometimes called the American Alps or Little Switzerland, the granite peaks in this range are between 5,000 and 9,000 feet in height. Dotted with crystalline alpine lakes and meadows, rushing rivers, and thickly forested valleys that fall between the mountain ridges, the Wallowas have a grandeur that can take your breath away. Bighorn sheep, elk, deer, and mountain goats populate the entire area. Nearly all the trails in the Wallowa Mountains are at least partially contained within the Eagle Cap Wilderness. The offices and visitor center for the mountains are in Enterprise. ⊕ *From La Grande, Routes 82, 203, and 237 will all lead to parts of the Wallowa Mountains.*

> **need a break?**
>
> Don't visit **Joe and Sugar's** (✉ 1119 Adams Ave. ☎ 514/975–5282) if you want to remain an anonymous tourist; you can't avoid being chatted up by the funny, friendly, and helpful owner of this sweet-smelling café and coffee shop. If you make it past the cookies and pastries that greet you at the front counter without filling up, you can look forward to some truly delicious homemade soup.

The 358,441-acre **Eagle Cap Wilderness**, the largest in Oregon, encompasses most of the Wallowa range and has 534 mi of trails for hardcore backpackers and horseback riders. Most of the popular trailheads are along the wilderness' northern edge, most accessible from Enterprise or Joseph, but you also can find several trailheads 20 to 30 mi southeast of La Grande along Route 203. For wilderness information, contact the Wallowa Mountains Visitor Center in Enterprise. To park at most trailheads, you must purchase a Northwest Forest Pass: $5 per day, $30 per year; to hike into the wilderness, you also must get a free permit that will alert rangers of your plans. Some areas of the wilderness are accessible year-round, while the high-elevation areas are accessible only for a few months in the summer. ✉ *East of La Grande, via Rte. 82 and Rte. 203.*

Several miles southeast of La Grande, **Union's National Historic District** is a Victorian-era town that is working to restore many of its historic buildings along the several-block stretch of Main Street. In addition to the charming buildings lining Main Street, the main attractions are the **Union Hotel** (✉ 326 N. Main St. ☎ 541/562–6135 ⊕ www.theunionhotel.com), a beautifully restored hotel with a restaurant and parlor, and the **Union County Museum** (✉ 333 S. Main St. ☎ 541/562–6003 ☉ May–mid-Oct., Mon.–Sat. 10–4, Sun. 1–4, or by appointment), which has the Cowboy Heritage Collection. ✉ *11 mi southeast of La Grande via Rte. 203.*

## Where to Stay & Eat

¢–$$$

FodorsChoice
★

✕ **Foley Station.** Widely regarded as one of La Grande's finest places to eat, this local favorite has an open kitchen, exposed-brick walls, comfortable booths, and lovely outdoor seating. The rotating menu incorporates Northwest ingredients in innovative creations such as lamb chops grilled with fire-roasted Fuji apples and Jack Daniels jus, and Italian crespelle (like a crepe) with spinach, mushrooms, tomato, and cheese saffron risotto. At lunch look for anything from rock-shrimp gemellini to gyros, fish-and-chips, and burgers, and at breakfast choose from seven varieties of waffles (including lemon poppy seed and Cuban banana) or go all out for a frittata with scallops, bacon, asparagus, and smoked Gouda. ✉ *1011 Adams Ave.* ☎ *541/963–7473* ▤ *MC, V* ☉ *Closed Mon. and Tues. No dinner Sun. or Wed.*

¢–$$$

✕ **Ten Depot St.** In a stylish historic brick building that has a VFW upstairs, Ten Depot St. has everything from burgers to beautifully prepared steak and seafood dishes. With dark wood throughout accented by plum tablecloths and teal plates and napkins, it's an elegant place to dine. Start off your evening with a drink at the adjoining bar. ✉ *10 Depot St.* ☎ *514/963–8766* ▤ *AE, D, DC, MC, V* ☉ *Closed Sun. No lunch.*

¢–$$

✕ **Smokehouse Restaurant.** Outside of La Grande's historic downtown, the Smokehouse is on a less scenic portion of East Adams Avenue than many other restaurants but is a good, simple place to find large portions of steak, seafood, and sandwiches. All-day breakfast includes eggs and pancake dishes. ✉ *2208 E. Adams Ave.* ☎ *541/963–9692* ▤ *D, MC, V.*

¢

✕ **Highway 30 Coffee Co.** Sandwiches, soups, coffee drinks, and pastries are all on tap at this small but lively coffeehouse. There are several tables downstairs, but the place's real character is upstairs in the loft: a comfy couch and a few small tables provide a retreat for reading and relaxing. ✉ *1302 Adams Ave.* ☎ *541/963–6821* ☉ *Closed Sun. No dinner.*

★ $–$$

▨ **Stang Manor Bed and Breakfast.** Get a feel for the luxury of a bygone era at this 10,000-square-foot Georgian Revival mansion built in 1926 by a timber baron. The elegant and beautifully maintained guest rooms in this house, which has remained unmodified except for its wall coverings, include the Maid's Room, with seven doors and a balcony overlooking the rose garden, and the Fireplace Suite, with a queen canopy bed and sitting room with a fireplace. Breakfast is a lavish multicourse affair served in the formal dining room by the charming and witty hosts. ✉ *1612 Walnut St., 97850* ☎ *541/963–2400* 🖷 *888/286–9463* ⊕ *www.stangmanor.com* ⇌ *3 rooms, 1 suite* ▤ *MC, V.*

¢–$

▨ **Best Value Sandman Inn.** This affordable hotel is not in the most scenic part of town, but it is just a short drive from historic downtown, restaurants, and shopping. Rooms are spacious and comfortable. A Continental breakfast is included in the room rate. ✉ *2410 East R. Ave., 97850* ☎ *541/*

963–3707 or 888/315–2378 🖨 541/962–0224 ⇌ 63 rooms ♨ Cable TV, indoor pool, hot tub, laundry facilities, free parking, no-smoking rooms ⊟ AE, D, DC, MC, V ⭑○❙ CP.

**¢–$**    🏨 **Union Hotel.** The lavish Union Hotel first opened in 1921 and, after
**Fodor'sChoice** a period of disrepair late in the century, was renovated and reopened in
★    1996, providing the historic town of Union with a gorgeous and reasonably priced hotel. It's also a handy place if you're exploring the historic towns in the area or are just looking for a place to sleep between jaunts into the great outdoors. The accommodations run from spacious and romantic suites to far smaller and simpler bedrooms. The Northwest Room has antique timbers, a kitchenette, and Jacuzzi; the Davis Brothers Room has a walk-in wood-panel shower and western decor; and the Southwest Room has live cacti and handcrafted log furniture. ⊠ 326 N. Main St., Union 97883 ☎ 541/562–6135 or 888/441–8928 ⊕ www.theunionhotel.com ⇌ 13 rooms ♨ Restaurant, lounge, shop; no room phones, no room TVs ⊟ MC, V.

### Sports & the Outdoors

BICYCLING   **Cycle Sports** (⊠ 112 Depot St. ☎ 541/962–7441) can answer all your cycling and snowboarding needs. Cyclists should check in with La Grande's Chamber of Commerce, which actively touts the region's paths. Two short trails leave from **Spring Creek** (⊠ about 16 mi west of La Grande). Eight pairs of great gray owls—the largest concentration of the species in the world—live along the routes. To reach the trailhead from La Grande, take I–84 west 13 mi to the Spring Creek exit and head south on Spring Creek Road/Forest Service Road 21 for 3 mi. The area surrounding **Lehman Hot Springs** (⊠ about 30 mi southwest of La Grande on Rte. 244 ☎ 541/427–3015) is great for mountain biking and horseback riding as well as snowmobiling and ATV-ing.

FISHING &  **Little Creek Outfitters/Hells Canyon Whitewater** (⊠ 1505 L. Ave. ☎ 541/
RAFTING  963–7878) guides fly anglers through the John Day River, the Grande Ronde River, and the Snake River and leads white-water trips along the Snake River in Hells Canyon.

### Shopping

**Marie Josephine** (⊠ 111 Depot St. ☎ 541/663–0933) has a collection of work by local artists, unique Northwest gifts and furnishings, and clothing for men, women, and children. **Sunflower Books** (⊠ 1114 Washington St.) uses all the space on the first floor of a cozy little house, with shelves of books in every nook and cranny and tea, coffee, and tea cakes for sale while you browse.

en route   Heading north from La Grande, Highway 82 passes through the small towns of Elgin and Minam before looping south toward Wallowa, Lostine, Enterprise, and Joseph en route to Wallowa Lake, where it dead-ends. Packed with RVs and cars during the summer, the road sprouts diners, motels, and plenty of antiques shops in every town it passes. If you have only limited time for browsing, save it for Joseph.

# Enterprise

❺  *6 mi north of Joseph on Rte. 82.*

The seat of Oregon's northeasternmost county, Enterprise is surrounded by some of the region's most rugged natural beauty and is a locus for rugged outdoor activities in winter and summer. To the west lie the Eagle Cap Wilderness, the alpine Wallowa Mountains, and pristine Wallowa Lake, and to the east is the Hells Canyon National Recreation Area.

For information about the Eagle Cap Wilderness, stop in at the **Wallowa Mountains Visitors Center** outside Enterprise. It has videos of the area, pamphlets, and topographical maps. ⊠ *Hwy. 82, 1 mi west of Enterprise* ☎ *541/426–5546* ☉ *Memorial Day–Labor Day, Mon.–Sat. 8–5; Labor Day–Memorial Day, weekdays 8–5.*

**Wallowa County Chamber of Commerce** (⊠ 936 W. North St. ☎ 541/426–4622 or 800/585–4121) has valuable information about the whole county, including lodging, dining, and sightseeing in Joseph, Enterprise, and around Wallowa Lake and Hells Canyon.

At the **Wallowa Valley Ranger District** headquarters (⊠ 88401 Hwy. 82 ☎ 541/426–4978) you can find detailed information about the Wallowa-Whitman National Forest and its recreational possibilities.

## Where to Stay & Eat

★ ¢–$ ✕ **Terminal Gravity Brew Pub.** Beer connoisseurs from across the state, and just about all the locals, rave about the India Pale Ale at this tiny microbrewery in a yellow house on the outskirts of downtown, but with kids and dogs lounging on the front porch and in the small upstairs dining room, it is clear that it's not just about the booze in this friendly local hangout. The menu is short and simple, with creative sandwiches and burgers. There's a rotating selection of the brews on tap. ⊠ *803 School St.* ☎ *541/426–0158* ▭ *No credit cards* ☉ *No lunch. Closed Mon. and Tues. Limited hrs in winter (call ahead).*

¢ ✕ **Cloud 9 Bakery.** Doughnuts and cakes are the ticket at this charming café, which is open for breakfast and lunch. Although much of the business is to-go, there are a few comfortable tables inside, if you'd like to stay there and savor a pastry and a cup of coffee. ⊠ *105 S.E. 1st* ☎ *541/426–3790* ▭ *MC, V* ☉ *No dinner.*

$ ▦ **Ponderosa Motel.** The charmingly rustic exterior of this cabin-like motel is mirrored by the interior: picture frames, end tables, and dressers are all made of a knotty light wood that adds a fun western flair to the large, spacious, and modern rooms. With the same owners as at the Wilderness Inn, the Ponderosa Motel reveals a similar attention to detail and comfort and is the slightly more upscale of the two inns. ⊠ *102 E. Greenwood, 97828* ☎ *541/426–3186* ⇩ *33 rooms* ⟐ *Microwaves, refrigerators, cable TV, free parking, some pets allowed (fee), no-smoking rooms* ▭ *AE, D, DC, MC, V.*

¢–$ ▦ **Cherokee Mingo Motel.** About 16 mi west of Enterprise, the tiny town of Wallowa has a main street, a couple of restaurants, and a few stores, as well as this small and friendly motel. Each room has a different theme, ranging from celestial bodies to sea life. Bedspreads, borders, and shower curtains all share a colorful pattern that gives each large room a unique flair; the furnishings aren't subtle, but they're fun, and the rooms stand out from the run-of-the-mill units to be found in other motels in the same price range. If you are headed into the Wallowa-Whitman National Forest, or are just seeking to avoid some of the summertime crowds in Enterprise and Joseph, consider spending a night at this little outpost of civilization. ⊠ *102 N. Alder, Wallowa 97885* ☎ *541/886–2021* ⇩ *11 rooms* ⟐ *Refrigerators, cable TV* ▭ *D, MC, V.*

¢–$ ▦ **Wilderness Inn.** Right in the center of town, the Wilderness Inn is within walking distance of restaurants and the courthouse and an easy drive from Wallowa Lake and other area attractions. In the wake of a recent face-lift, the inn has surprisingly spacious, comfortable, and spotless rooms with tables and desks. This motel is truly a step above many other independent roadside motels with similarly low prices. Many rooms include refrigerators and microwaves. ⊠ *301 W. North St., 97828* ☎ *541/426–4535 or 800/965–1205* 🖶 *541/426–0128* ⇩ *28 rooms, 1 suite*

♨ *Cable TV, sauna, free parking, some pets allowed (fee), no-smoking rooms* ▤ *AE, D, DC, MC, V.*

### Sports & the Outdoors

CAMPING  Pick up gear and supplies for camping, backpacking, and fishing at **Wallowa Outdoors** (✉ 110 S. River St., 97828 ☎ 541/426–3493). You can also get information on fishing and river conditions.

GOLF  **Alpine Meadows Golf Course** (☎ 541/426–3246) is the county's only 18-hole course.

# Joseph

**❻**  *80 mi east of La Grande on Hwy. 82.*

The area around Wallowa Lake was the traditional home of the Nez Perce Indians—the town of Joseph is named for Chief Joseph, their famous leader. The peaks of the Wallowa Mountains, snow-covered until July, tower 5,000 feet above the town and Wallowa Lake, which are the regional tourist hubs.

✋  The **David and Lee Manuel Museum** has a superb collection of Nez Perce clothing and artifacts. The museum, which also has pioneer wagons, is one of the town's leading bronze foundries, with 14,000 square feet of facilities in separate buildings. There are also a children's museum and an exhibit of bronze sculptures. ✉ *400 N. Main St.* ☎ *541/432–7235* ▨*$6* ☉ *June–Oct., daily 8–5; Nov.–May, Mon.–Sat. 10–4; tours at 10:15 and 2:15.*

> **need a break?**
>
> Across from the David and Lee Manuel Museum, **Magnoni's Market Place** (✉ 403 N. Main St. ☎ 541/432–3663) has an Italian restaurant with pasta and salads, plus an espresso café, a beauty salon, and gift shops.

To tour the **Valley Bronze of Oregon** foundry facility, head to its showroom, the **Valley Bronze Gallery** (☎ 541/432–7445 ✉ 18 S. Main St.), which displays the bronze sculptures of many artists whose works are cast at the foundry, in addition to the work of other artists from around the world. The gallery is open Monday–Saturday 10–5, Sunday noon–5. The foundry itself is a ¼ mi away, and your tour guide will lead you there after you have gathered at the showroom. ✉ *307 W. Alder St.* ☎ *541/432–7551* ⊕ *www.valleybronze.com* ▨ *$5* ☉ *Two tours daily; call for times.*

The **Wallowa County Museum** in Joseph has a small but poignant collection of artifacts and photographs chronicling the Nez Perce Wars, a series of battles against the U.S. Army that took place in the late 1870s. The building, originally built as a bank in 1888, was robbed in 1896, an event that is reenacted with full pageantry every Wednesday at 1 PM in the summer, complete with music, dancing girls, gunshots, and yelping. ✉ *110 S. Main St.* ☎ *541/432–6095* ▨ *Free* ☉ *Memorial Day–Sept., daily 10–5.*

From Joseph, Highway 82 continues south and ends at sparkling, blue-green **Wallowa Lake** (✉ Wallowa Lake Hwy.), the highest body of water in eastern Oregon (elevation 5,000 feet). Call the **Joseph Chamber of Commerce** (✉ 102 E. 1st St., 97846 ☎ 541/32–1015) for information about Wallowa Lake and its facilities.

Six miles south of Joseph, **Wallowa Lake State Recreation Park** is a campground surrounded on three sides by 9,000-foot-tall snowcapped mountains. It also serves as a gateway to Hells Canyon. It has 121 full hookups,

89 tent sites, and 2 yurts. Popular activities include fishing and boating as well as hiking on wilderness trails, horseback riding, and canoeing. There are also bumper boats and miniature golf. You can ride a tramway to the top of one of the mountains. ⊠ *Rte. 82* ☎ *541/432–4185 or 800/ 551–6949* ⊕ *www.prd.state.or.us* ☜ *Day use $3 per vehicle* ☉ *Daily.*

★ The **Wallowa Lake Tramway,** the steepest gondola in North America, rises to the top of 8,150-foot Mt. Howard in 15 minutes. Vistas of mountain peaks, forest, and Wallowa Lake far below will dazzle you on the way up and at the summit. Two and a half miles of hiking trails await you at the top, and you can enjoy lunch at the Summit Grill and Alpine Patio before descending to Earth. ⊠ *59919 Wallowa Lake Hwy.* ☎ *541/432–5331* ☜ *$14.95* ☉ *May, June, and Sept., daily 10–4; July and Aug., daily 10–5.*

## Where to Stay & Eat

¢–$  ✕ **Embers Brewhouse.** The inside dining room of this wood-frame bungalow-like brewhouse is quite small, but a huge wooden deck and patio provide ample seating outside for the crowds on summer evenings. In addition to the region's standard burger fare, Embers serves pizzas and calzones as well as its finely brewed beer. ⊠ *204 N. Main* ☎ *541/432– 2739* ⊟ *MC, V.*

¢–$  ✕ **Magnoni's Market Place.** Upstairs at Magnoni's, enjoy an all-you-can-eat buffet of pastas, salads, and homemade breads, or do as as the locals do and focus on the lasagna and seafood fettuccine. The restaurant is open on three sides, and tables have bright umbrellas under the roof. Downstairs there's a gift shop and an even more casual café serving espresso and lattes as well as the full menu from upstairs. ⊠ *403 N. Main St., 97846* ☎ *541/432–3663* 🖷 *541/432–3663* ⊟ *AE, D, MC, V.*

¢–$  ✕ **Outlaw Restaurant and Saloon.** In keeping with most other eastern Oregon restaurants, Outlaw serves great burgers and steaks; top them off with ice cream at the adjoining ice cream café. High ceilings and bright natural light lend this restaurant a refreshing and relaxing air, and in the good weather, you can sit outside on the patio in front. ⊠ *108 N. Main St.* ☎ *541/432–4321* ⊟ *MC, V.*

¢–$  ✕ **Stubborn Mule Saloon and Steakhouse.** With a dark red and green barn-like exterior behind large wooden columns, this restaurant and bar really does feel like an old saloon from the outside. Inside is a small no-frills dining room, where you seat yourself at simple wooden tables, and an adjoining tavern where locals drink beer and play pool. The family-friendly restaurant makes great burgers (nothing smaller than a half-pound), sandwiches, and steak, and there are plenty of beers on tap. ⊠ *104 S. Main St.* ☎ *541/432–6853* ⊟ *MC, V* ☉ *Closed Mon.*

¢  ✕ **Summit Grill and Alpine Patio.** At an altitude of 8,200 feet on Mt. Howard, this is the Northwest's highest restaurant, reached by a 15-minute ride on the Wallowa Lake Tramway. The menu is limited to burgers, sandwiches, burritos, salads, chili, soups, and Oregon beers and wines, but the view of four bordering states is striking. ⊠ *59919 Wallowa Lake Hwy.* ☎ *541/432–5331* 🖷 *541/432–1300* ⊟ *No credit cards* ☉ *Open Memorial Day–Labor Day, daily 10–4.*

**Fodor'sChoice**
★

$–$$$$  ✕▥ **Wallowa Lake Lodge.** At this friendly 1920s lodge, handmade replicas of the structure's original furniture fill a large common area with a massive fireplace. The lodge's rooms are simple yet appealing; the grandest have balconies facing the lake. The cabins, all with fireplaces and some with lake views, are small, old-fashioned havens of knotty pine. The on-site restaurant serves standard American fare for breakfast, lunch, and dinner. ⊠ *60060 Wallowa Lake Hwy., Wallowa Lake 97846* ☎ *541/432–9821* 🖷 *541/432–4885* ⊕ *www.wallowalake.com* ↘ *22 rooms, 8 cabins* ⚐ *Restaurant; no smoking, no room phones, no room TVs* ⊟ *D, MC, V* ☉ *Lodge closed weekdays in winter.*

**$–$$$** 🏠 **Eagle Cap Chalets.** With cabins, motel-style "chalet" rooms, "condos," and RV sites ($22), this elaborate facility probably has something to suit most travelers. The chalet rooms have refrigerators and microwaves, and the condos, available with either one or two bedrooms, have a living room, full kitchen, and fireplace. The log cabins run from studios to two-bedroom apartments, most with full kitchens and fireplaces. All the lodgings are on landscaped grounds in this wooded wilderness area at the mouth of Wallowa Lake. On-site luxuries include an indoor pool, espresso bar, and miniature golf course. ✉ *59879 Wallowa Lake Hwy., 97846* ☎ *541/432–4704 or 541/432–8800* 📠 *541/432–3010* 🌐 *www. eaglecapchalets.com* 🛏 *21 chalet rooms, 5 condos, 9 cabins, 58 RV sites* ⚐ *Coffee shop, picnic area, some microwaves, some refrigerators, cable TV, miniature golf, indoor pool, hot tub, meeting rooms, no-smoking rooms* ⊟ *AE, D, MC, V.*

**$–$$$** 🏠 **Flying Arrow Resort.** One- to four-bedroom fully equipped cabins with sundecks are available at this resort ½ mi south of Wallowa Lake. These cabins are particularly intended to act as homes-away-from-home during vacation time, and in keeping with this philosophy, there is no daily housekeeping service (although fresh linens are available upon request). In the peak of the summer, a five-night minimum stay is required and in the late spring and early fall it's three nights. ✉ *59782 Wallowa Lake Hwy., 97846* ☎ *541/432–2951* 🌐 *www.flyingarrowresort.net* 🛏 *18 cabins* ⚐ *Picnic area, kitchens, cable TV, pool, hot tub, free parking* ⊟ *D, MC, V* ☽ *Half of cabins closed Nov.–Feb.*

**$–$$** 🏠 **Collett's Cabins and Fine Arts.** Collett's cabins are 6 mi from Joseph via Highway 82, a 10-minute walk from Wallowa Lake and a short, rural stroll to the Wallowa Lake Lodge and the Wallowa Lake Tramway. Surrounded by ponderosa, firs, spruce, and lots of deer, the cabins range from studios to two-bedroom units, some with gas fireplaces. The owners are artists, and the cabins are filled with original artwork. A small gallery and shop display more of their work. ✉ *84681 Ponderosa La., 97846* ☎ *541/432–2391* 📠 *541/432–2391* 🌐 *www.collettscabins.com* 🛏 *2 suites, 8 cabins* ⚐ *Picnic area, some kitchens, some kitchenettes, some microwaves, some refrigerators, cable TV, shop, some pets allowed (fee); no a/c, no room phones, no smoking* ⊟ *D, MC, V.*

**¢** 🏠 **Indian Lodge.** This small motel, which belonged to actor Walter Brennan in the 1950s, has the least-expensive rooms in the area, making it a great jumping-off place for folks who just need a place to rest their heads before heading off to Wallowa Lake or Hells Canyon. With a fantastic location on Main Street in Joseph, 1 mi from Wallowa Lake, and with spacious and comfortable rooms, it is truly a fantastic find for such low prices. ✉ *201 S. Main St.* ☎ *541/432–2651 or 888/286–5484* 📠 *541/432–4949* 🛏 *16 rooms* ⚐ *Cable TV, refrigerators, some pets allowed (fee)* ⊟ *D, MC, V.*

## Sports & the Outdoors

Rainbow trout, kokanee, and mackinaw are among the species of fish in 300-foot-deep, 4½-mi-long Wallowa Lake. You can picnic on the water at several moored docks.

HIKING **BackCountry Outfitters** (✉ Box 137, 97846 ☎ 541/426–5908 or 800/966–8080) leads pack trips into the Eagle Cap Wilderness and Hells Canyon.

HORSEBACK **Eagle Cap Wilderness Pack Station** (✉ 59761 Wallowa Lake Hwy. ☎ 541/
RIDING 432–4145 or 800/681–6222), at the south end of Wallowa Lake, conducts guided rides and leads summer pack trips into the Eagle Cap Wilderness.

RAFTING & **Cooley River Expeditions** (✉ Box 1068, 97846 ☎ 541/432–0461 or 888/
BOATING 468–5998) leads white-water rafting and kayaking trips on the Deschutes, Grande Ronde, and John Day rivers. **Hells Canyon Adventures** (✉ 4200

Hells Canyon Dam Rd., Oxbow ☎ 541/785–3352 or 800/422–3568 ⊕ www.hellscanyonadventure.com) runs white-water rafting and jet-boat trips on the Snake River through Hells Canyon. **Wallowa Lake Marina Inc.** (✉ Wallowa Lake, south end ☎ 541/432–9115), open May to September, rents paddleboats, motorboats, rowboats, and canoes by the hour or by the day.

## Shopping

Handicraft and antiques shops line Main Street; galleries exhibit the works of area artists and bronze castings from local metal foundries.

**Anton's Home and Hearth** (✉ 12 S. Main St. ☎ 541/432–2690) is a lovely country store, with gifts and home furnishings, candles, and soap. **Art Angle** (✉ 1 S. Main St. ☎ 541/432–1155) has fine prints and collectibles. **Kelly's Gallery on Main** (✉ 103 N. Main St. ☎541/432–3116) displays and sells some of the area's finest original bronze sculpture. The **Mangy Moose General Mercantile** (✉ 103 E. 1st St. ☎ 541/432–4730) has fun antiques and collectibles, as well as woodwork, bronze work, candy, and gifts, in a large wood cabin off Main Street.

en route | The **Wallowa Mountain Loop** is a relatively easy way to take in the natural splendor of the Eagle Cap Wilderness and reach Baker City without backtracking to La Grande. The 3½-hour trip from Joseph to Baker City, designated the Hells Canyon Scenic Byway, winds through the national forest and part of Hells Canyon Recreation Area, passing over forested mountains, creeks, and rivers. Before you travel the loop, check with the Joseph Chamber of Commerce about road conditions; in winter always carry chains. *⊹ From Joseph take Little Sheep Creek Hwy. east for 8 mi, turn south onto Forest Service Rd. 39, and continue until it meets Hwy. 86, which winds past town of Halfway to Baker City.*

# Hells Canyon

❼ *30 mi northeast of Joseph on Wallowa Mountain Loop.*

Fodor'sChoice
★

This remote place along the **Snake River** is the deepest river-carved gorge in North America (7,900 feet), with many rare and endangered animal species. There are three different routes from which to view and experience the canyon, though only one is accessible year-round.

Most travelers take a scenic peek from the overlook on the 45-mi **Wallowa Mountain Loop,** which follows Route 39 from east of Halfway on Route 86 to east of Joseph on Route 350. At the junction of Route 39 and Forest Road 3965, take the 6-mi round-trip loop to the 5,400-foot-high rim at Hells Canyon Overlook. This is the easiest way to get a glimpse of the canyon, but be aware that Route 39 is open only during the summer and early fall months. During the late fall, winter, and spring, the best way to experience Hells Canyon is to follow a slightly more out-of-the-way route along the **Snake River Segment** of the Wallowa Mountain Loop. Following Highway 86 north from Copperfield, the 60-mi round-trip route winds along the edge of Hells Canyon Reservoir, crosses the Snake River to Hells Canyon Dam on the border of Oregon and Idaho, and continues on to the Hells Canyon National Recreation Site, with a visitor center and hiking trails. The canyon is 10 mi wide in places. The trip is a memorable one, but be certain you have a full tank before starting out, as there are no gas stations anywhere along the route. If you are starting from Joseph, you also have the option of heading to the **Hat Point Overlook.** From Joseph, take Route 350 northeast to Imnaha, a tiny town along the Imnaha River. From there Forest Road 4240 leads southeast to Route 315, which in turn heads northeast up a steep gravel road to the overlook. This route is also open only during the summer. Be sure to have plenty of gas, as well as water for yourself and your car.

The **Hells Canyon National Recreation Area** is the site of one of the largest elk herds in the United States, plus 422 other species, including bald eagles, bighorn sheep, mule deer, white-tailed deer, black bears, bobcats, cougars, beavers, otters, and rattlesnakes. The peregrine falcon has also been reintroduced here. Part of the area was designated as Hells Canyon Wilderness, in parts of Oregon and Idaho, with the establishment of the Hells Canyon National Recreation Area in 1975. Additional acres were added as part of the Oregon Wilderness Act of 1984. There are now 219,006 acres and about 360 mi of trails in the wilderness area, and the trails are closed to all mechanized travel. If you want to visit the wilderness it must be on foot or horseback. Environmental groups have proposed the creation of Hells Canyon National Park to better manage the area's critical habitat. A wildlife-viewing guide is available from the Idaho Department of Fish and Game. ⊠ *88401 Hwy. 82, Enterprise, OR 97828* ☎ *541/426–4978* ⌕ *Idaho Department of Fish and Game, Box 25, Boise, ID 83707.*

The **Wild and Scenic Snake River Corridor** consists of 67½ mi of river federally designated as part of the National Wild and Scenic Rivers System. Extending ¼ mi back from the high-water mark on each shore, the corridor is available for managed public use. Since the corridor itself is not designated wilderness and wilderness area regulations do not apply, there are developed campsites and man-made structures here, and some motorized equipment is allowed. In season, both powerboaters and rafters must make reservations and obtain permits for access to the river corridor. ☎ *509/758–1957 float reservations, 509/758–0270 powerboat reservations* ⊙ *Daily Memorial Day–early Sept.*

## Camping

⚠ **Imnaha River.** Hells Canyon National Scenic Byway runs through the Imnaha corridor, a critical habitat for the chinook salmon and bull trout. Access to the camping areas is via dirt and gravel roads that are generally not suitable for passenger cars. Some of the areas have toilets, RV hookups, picnic areas, swimming, and boat launches. Forest Road 46, or the Wellamotkin Drive area, has two developed campsites along the rim area within timbered groves north and west of Enterprise, permitting spectacular views of Hells Canyon. The Hat Point area begins at the Imnaha River and ends at Hat Point Lookout. Duck Lake and Twin Lakes campgrounds are in an alpine zone near the lakes for which they are named. ⌕ *Wallowa-Whitman National Forest, Box 907, Baker City 97814* ☎ *541/523–4476.*

# Halfway

**8** *63 mi south of Joseph on Wallowa Mountain Loop.*

Halfway, the closest town to Hells Canyon, originally got its name because it was midway between the town of Pine and the gold mines of Cornucopia, but in 2000, the official name of the town was changed to half.com, as a promotional venture between the town and a Philadelphia start-up Internet company. Halfway changed its name in exchange for cash, computers, and a little notoriety that residents hoped would draw some tourism. Don't worry: everyone still calls it Halfway, and its quiet, laid-back character reveals none of this kitschy ad-campaign. On the southern flanks of the Wallowas, it's a straightforward, unpretentious community with a Main Street and a quiet rural flavor.

## Where to Stay & Eat

**$–$$$**  ✕⊡ **Pine Valley Lodge.** From the outside, this building on Main Street
**Fodor's**Choice  is styled like many others built in eastern Oregon during the timber boom
★  of the late 1920s. Inside, the common area is artfully cluttered with a
mixture of antique fishing gear, Native American artifacts, and paint-
ings. Guest rooms, available in the main lodge, the Blue Dog house next
door, and the Love Shack, have antiques and western memorabilia, as
well as original artwork by the inn's owner, Babette Beatty, a cook who
prepares a full breakfast for guests each morning. Her restaurant, the
Halfway Supper Club, used to be open to the public but now serves as
a private dining room for guests; Babette will prepare dinner upon re-
quest. ⊠ *163 N. Main St., 97834* ☎ *541/742–2027* ⊕ *www.pvlodge.
com* ➮ *6 rooms, plus Love Shack* ♿ *Dining room, coffee shop, meet-
ing room, free parking, some pets allowed (fee); no room phones, no
room TVs, no smoking* ⊟ *No credit cards* ⦿⦿ *BP.*

**$**  ⊡ **Clear Creek Farm Bed and Breakfast.** Amid 160 acres of orchards, woods,
and fields on the southeastern flank of the Wallowa Mountains, this 1880s
Craftsman-style farmhouse is a simple but comfortable rural retreat. The
main house has four rooms. Two bunkhouses with ceilings but no win-
dows are available May–October. Lakeview, with a balcony overlook-
ing a small pond, is the better of the two. Breakfast, served in an outdoor
kitchen in warm weather, includes eggs, buffalo sausage, Dutch babies
(sweet, fluffy omelets), and homegrown raspberries and peaches in sea-
son. You can choose between paying a standard rate, which includes
breakfast, and taking the Ranch Privileges Plan, in which, for $30 more,
you get three meals a day, free use of bicycles, fishing, and several tour
options. ⊠ *4821 Clear Creek Rd., off Fish Lake Rd., 5½ mi north of
Halfway, 97834* ☎ *541/742–2238 or 800/742–4992* ⧆ *541/742–5175*
➮ *5 rooms in lodge, two 2-room bunkhouses share 3 baths* ♿ *Out-
door hot tub, laundry facilities, some pets allowed* ⊟ *MC, V.*

## Sports & the Outdoors

CAMPING  **Hells Canyon Outdoor Supply** (⊠ Pine Creek, 2 mi southwest of Oxbow
on Hwy. 86 ☎ 800/785–3358), is the home office of Hells Canyon Shut-
tle and sells outdoor supplies, water, and some groceries. **Wallowa Lla-
mas** (⊠ Rte. 1 ⬡ Box 84, 97834 ☎ 541/742–4930) conducts guided tours
into the Eagle Cap Wilderness. The llamas, which walk alongside the hik-
ers, carry most of the gear necessary for a comfortable backpacking trip
and are even-tempered and calm enough to be easily led by those with
no previous experience, including children. The company provides tents,
eating utensils, and all meals on three- to seven-day pack trips.

RAFTING  **Canyon Outfitters** (⬡ Box 893, 97834 ☎ 541/742–7238 or 877/742–
7270) leads rafting, fishing, and camping trips into Hells Canyon.

# Baker City

❾  *53 mi west of Halfway on Hwy. 86, 44 mi south of La Grande on U.S.
30 off I–84.*

You'd never guess that quiet Baker City, positioned between the Wal-
lowa Mountains and the Elkhorn Range of the Blue Mountains, was
once bigger than Spokane and Boise. During the gold-rush era in the
late 19th century, the town profited from the money that poured in from
nearby mining towns. With the end of the gold rush, the city transformed
itself into the logging and ranching town it is today. Remnants of its
opulence are still visible in the many restored Victorian houses and down-
town shops, but all this history seems minor when you consider the re-
gion's fascinating geography.

Oregon Trail pioneers first glimpsed the Oregon Territory from the Baker Valley. History buffs will be particularly interested in Baker City, now the location for the National Historic Oregon Trail Interpretive Center. At the same time, outdoor enthusiasts will appreciate the nearby venues for fishing, hunting, waterskiing, canoeing, hiking, cycling, and skiing. Baker City has received national recognition for its historic restoration efforts and success in attracting visitors to its out-of-the-mainstream location near the Eagle Cap and Wallowa Mountains.

The **Baker County Visitors and Convention Bureau** (⊠ 490 Campbell St. ☎ 541/523–3356 or 800/523–1235 ⊕ www.visitbaker.com) operates a small pioneer museum and has information on area attractions.

The **Oregon Trail Regional Museum** may seem rather staid after a turn through the National Historic Oregon Trail Interpretive Center, but the museum has an enormous butterfly collection and one of the most impressive rock collections in the West, including thunder eggs, glowing phosphorescent rocks, and a 950-pound hunk of quartz. A back room has a covered wagon, an old firefighting wagon, and pioneer tools. ⊠ *2480 Grove St., at Campbell St.* ☎ *541/523–9308* ☞ *$3.50* ☉ *Late Mar.–Oct., daily 9–5; off-season by appointment.*

A small gold display just inside the entrance to **U.S. Bank** (⊠ Washington and Main Sts.) contains the 80.4-ounce Armstrong Nugget, found in 1913.

★ The **National Historic Oregon Trail Interpretive Center,** 5 mi east of Baker City, does a superb job of re-creating pioneer life in the mid-1800s. From 1841 to 1861 about 300,000 people made the 2,000-mi journey from western Missouri to the Columbia River and the Oregon coast, looking for agricultural land in the West. A simulated section of the Oregon Trail will give you a feel for camp life, the toll the trip took on marriages and families, and the settlers' impact on Native Americans; an indoor theater presents movies and plays. A 4-mi round-trip trail winds from the center to the actual ruts left by the wagons. ⊠ *Hwy. 86 E, east of I–84* ☎ *541/523–1843* ☞ *$5* ☉ *Apr.–Oct., daily 9–6; Nov.–Mar., daily 9–4.*

In the tiny town of Haines, several miles north of Baker City, **Eastern Oregon Museum,** which almost resembles an antique store or flea market at first glance, has 10,000 household, farming, mining, and pioneer artifacts. On the grounds is the old Union Pacific depot, built in the 1880s and given to the museum when the railroad discontinued stops at Haines in 1962. ⊠ *610 3rd St., 4 blocks from Hwy. 30, Haines 97833* ☎ *541/ 856–3233* ☞ *Donations accepted* ☉ *Mid-Apr.–mid-Oct., daily 9–5, or by appointment off-season.*

In the Wallowa-Whitman National Forest, **Anthony Lakes Ski Area** has a vertical drop of 900 feet and a top elevation of 8,000 feet. There are 21 trails, two lifts, and a 13-km cross-country route. Snowboards are permitted. ⊠ *Exit 285 off I–84 to Anthony Lakes Rd., 19 mi west of North Powder* ☎ *800/856–3277* ☞ *Lift tickets $28* ☉ *Nov.–Apr., Thurs.–Sun. 9–4.*

The scenic 106-mi loop of **Elkhorn Drive** winds from Baker City through the Elkhorn Range of the Blue Mountains. Only white-bark pine can survive on the range's sharp ridges and peaks, which top 8,000 feet; spruce, larch, Douglas fir, and ponderosa pine thrive on the lower slopes. The route is well marked; start on Highway 7 west of Baker City, turn onto County Road 24 toward Sumpter, pass Granite on Forest Service Road 73, and then return to Baker City along U.S. 30.

The original track of the **Sumpter Valley Railway** was scrapped in 1947. With an all-volunteer work force, the railroad has rebuilt more than 7 mi of track on the original right-of-way. Today it operates along a 5.1-mi route in Sumpter. Trains leave from the McEwen and Sumpter stations; call for departure information. ⊠ *On Hwy. 7, 22 mi west of Baker City* ☎ *800/523–1235* ⊕ *www.svry.com* ≊ *$9* ☉ *Memorial Day–Sept., weekends and holidays.*

The smell of juniper fills the air at the high-desert **Unity Lake State Park,** 26 mi southwest of Baker City on U.S. 245. The Burnt River runs through the park where Unity Dam created the small lake. There is a boat ramp, 35 electrical campsites, and two tepees. ⊠ *U.S. 245 at U.S. 26* ☎ *541/932–4453 or 800/551–6949* ⊕ *www.prd.state.or.us* ≊ *Free* ☉ *Apr.–Oct., daily* ≊ *Hookups $12–$17, tepees $29.*

**Wallowa-Whitman National Forest.** The 2.3-million-acre forest, found both east and west of Baker City, ranges in elevation from 875 feet in the Hells Canyon Wilderness to 9,845 feet in the Eagle Cap Wilderness. There are two other wilderness areas: Monument Rock and North Fork John Day. ⊠ *Roads leading into and through the forest accessible via Rtes. 7 and 237, west of Baker City, as well as Rtes. 86 and 203 on east side* ☎ *541/523–6391* ⊕ *www.fs.fed.us/r6/w-w/index.htm* ≊ *Free* ☉ *Daily.*

### Where to Stay & Eat

★ **$–$$** ✕ **Phone Company.** In the Victorian historic district, this suitably named restaurant operates out of an old Bell Telephone building. Staples are steak, chicken, salads, pasta, and seafood, especially salmon. The real specialty, though, is chicken *mamou,* a Cajun pasta dish with a spicy tomato sauce named after the small town in southeastern Louisiana from which it supposedly originated. You can order it mild, medium, hot, or nuclear. ⊠ *1926 1st St., 97814* ☎ *541/523–7997* ⊟ *MC, V* ☉ *Closed Sun. No lunch Sat.*

¢–$$ ✕ **Barley Brown's Brew Pub.** In the historic 1940 home of Gwilliam Brothers Bakery, this restaurant and brewpub prides itself not only on its handcrafted ales but also on its loyalty to local, sustainable agriculture, most notably in its relationship with Oregon Country Beef, a co-operative of family ranches producing free-range beef. Enjoy burgers and steak while sitting in a cozy wooden booth, sipping on a house-made brew. ⊠ *2190 Main St.* ☎ *541/523–4266* ⊟ *AE, D, DC, MC, V* ☉ *Closed Sun. No lunch.*

¢–$ ✕ **Baker City Cafe–Pizza à Fetta.** The pizzas here are made from hand-thrown dough; the pesto and three-tomato pies are particularly good. The menu also has pasta, salads, and espresso. The clam chowder is especially worthy. ⊠ *1915 Washington Ave., 1 block from Main St.* ☎ *541/523–6099* ⊟ *MC, V* ☉ *Closed weekends.*

¢–$ ✕ **Oregon Trail Restaurant.** Green leather booths and a lunch counter give this casual family restaurant an old-fashioned feel, and the menu, heavy on steak and burgers, feels about the same. Next door to the motel of the same name, the Oregon Trail opens every morning at 6 and serves hearty breakfasts such as ham or steak and eggs, and plenty of potatoes. ⊠ *211 Bridge St.* ☎ *541/523–5844* ⊟ *AE, D, DC, MC, V.*

¢ ✕ **Charley's Ice Cream Parlor.** A black-and-white checkered floor, vinyl chairs, and a soda-fountain counter give you the distinct feeling that you've stepped back in time when you enter this ice cream parlor. Hot dogs, chili, and other comfort foods dominate the lunch menu. It's open until 9 during the week but closes at 7 on Saturday and 6 on Sunday. ⊠ *2101 Main St.* ☎ *541/523–5550* ⊟ *No credit cards.*

¢ ✕ **Front St. Cafe and Coffee Co.** Sit at one of the swiveling vinyl stools at the old soda-fountain counter or at one of the picnic tables that fill the

# GHOST TOWNS OF EASTERN OREGON

**D**USTY, WINDSWEPT STREETS *and ramshackle clapboard buildings occupy many ghost towns in eastern Oregon. Each settlement has its own story and is open for exploring year-round—plus, they're convenient to reach, given that many are within an hour's drive of Baker City. Here you can immerse yourself in pioneer times.*

*Along Route 7 heading east from Baker City, the closest ghost town is Auburn, established on Blue Canyon Creek in 1862. Supposedly the site of the first gold rush in eastern Oregon, the town quickly declined after prospectors moved on to other gold finds in the mid-1860s.*

*One of the best-known ghost towns is Sumpter, established in 1862 by settlers who intended to farm the rich countryside. Gold prospectors took over after gold was discovered nearby, and mining, dredging, and logging soon became major industries. The land and riverbanks became eroded, ruining any farming potential, and many settlers moved on after the early 1900s. Newer buildings, a museum, and rail depot were later added to attract tourists, who often outnumber the town's meager population of under 200.*

*Northeast of Sumpter is Bourne, a town originally called Cracker, which was later renamed after Senator Johnathon Bourne. There's just one long main street, framed by cliffs that prevented the town from growing any direction but sideways. Although a flood in 1937 washed away most of the residences, many of the original buildings—including the 1895 post office—still remain.*

*Whitney was the main depot station on the 80-mi, narrow-gauge Sumpter Valley Railroad. At its peak, the town housed 14 rail crews, as well as 75 people who worked at the sawmill to supply lumber for the gold-mining camps. When the mill burned down in 1918, settlers left to find other prospects. Many of the original buildings remain, including several cabins, a farmhouse, and the mill.*

*South of The Dalles, Shaniko is one of the West's most attractive ghost towns, complete with all the original buildings but with added tourist facilities. Built in 1898, the settlement began as a simple rail depot for moving wool from the surrounding sheep ranches to the processing facilities in The Dalles. You can take a walking tour past the old sheep pastures, a barn full of antique cars, a water tower, the schoolhouse, and the chapel—where more than 300 weddings are performed each summer.*

rest of the café to enjoy a basic breakfast of eggs and hash browns, French toast or pancakes, or just a cup of joe. There is something to look at in every direction at this fun and friendly place; vintage advertisements, lunch boxes, and food tins crowd the brick walls and the shelves behind the counter. ⊠ *1840 Main St.* ☎ *541/523–0223* ▭ *MC, V* ☯ *No dinner.*

★ **$–$$$$** ✕▥ **Geiser Grand Hotel.** Considered for many years the finest hotel between Portland and Salt Lake City, the Geiser Grand was built in 1889 during the height of the gold rush. The Italian Renaissance Revival gem reopened in 1997 after a meticulous restoration. The rooms, filled with period furnishings, have 18-foot ceilings, enormous windows (many overlooking the nearby mountains), and large bathrooms. The striking Palm Court, with a suspended stained-glass ceiling, dominates the first floor. The hotel's Swan dining room, serving steaks, prime rib, fresh fish, and pasta dishes, is Baker City's finest restaurant. ⊠ *1996 Main St., 97814* ☎ *541/523–1889 or 888/434–7374* 🖷 *541/523–1800* ⊕ *www.geisergrand.com* ⇐ *30 rooms* ⟁ *Restaurant, room service, cable TV with VCRs and movies, hair salon, bar, library, laundry service, dry cleaning, meeting rooms, free parking, some pets allowed (fee), no-smoking floors* ▭ *AE, D, MC, V.*

¢–$ ▥ **Always Welcome Inn.** The owners of this hillside inn overlooking the Elkhorn Mountains pride themselves on keeping the large, soundproofed rooms spotlessly clean. And if you need a refrigerator or microwave, they'll happily bring one to your room. ⊠ *175 Campbell St., 97814* ☎ *541/523–3431 or 800/307–5206* ⇐ *24 rooms* ⟁ *In-room data ports, cable TV, meeting room; no smoking* ▭ *D, MC, V* ⦿ *CP.*

¢–$ ▥ **Rodeway Inn.** The rooms at this former Quality Inn are spacious, and all have small sitting areas. With a red thatched roof, Santa Fe–style pink adobe exterior, exposed-wood beams, and lanterns hanging over the outdoor walkways, the exterior of the motel is remarkably attractive and festive. Some rooms have refrigerators. ⊠ *810 Campbell St., 97814* ☎ *541/523–2242* ⇐ *52 rooms* ⟁ *Cable TV, free parking, some pets allowed (fee), no-smoking rooms* ▭ *AE, D, DC, MC, V.*

¢ ▥ **Bridge Street Inn.** Right off of Main Street, Bridge Street Inn is one of the least-expensive motels in town and in a much better location than some of the others in the same price range. With rooms that are clean and reliable, it is an excellent option if you're short on funds. Some rooms have microwaves and refrigerators, and a Continental breakfast is included. ⊠ *134 Bridge St., 97814* ☎ *541/523–6571 or 800/932–9220* 🖷 *541/523–9424* ⊕ *www.bridgestreetinn.com* ⇐ *40 rooms* ⟁ *Cable TV, some pets allowed (fee), no-smoking rooms* ▭ *MC, V* ⦿ *CP.*

¢ ▥ **Eldorado Inn.** This small motel has clean rooms and low rates and prides itself on its friendly service and Spanish-style architecture. ⊠ *695 E. Campbell St., 97814* ☎ *541/523–6494 or 800/537–5756* 🖷 *541/523–6494* ⇐ *56 rooms* ⟁ *Cable TV with VCRs, indoor pool, hot tub, some pets allowed (fee)* ▭ *AE, D, DC, MC, V.*

¢ ▥ **Oregon Trail Motel.** The Oregon Trail is two blocks from Main Street, near shops and restaurants. With many in-room amenities, this motel offers slightly more luxury than others in the same price range. ⊠ *211 Bridge St., 97814* ☎ *541/523–5844 or 800/628–3982* 🖷 *541/523–6593* ⇐ *54 rooms* ⟁ *Restaurant, in-room data ports, microwaves, refrigerators, cable TV, pool, sauna, laundry facilities, free parking, some pets allowed (fee), no-smoking rooms* ▭ *AE, D, DC, MC, V.*

⛺ **Anthony Lake.** The premier camping spots near Baker City are the three campgrounds at Anthony Lake. These sites, which usually fill up early during summer weekends, are available on a first-come, first-served basis. ⊠ *Anthony Lakes Hwy., 20 mi west of North Powder off I–84, from Baker City take U.S. 30 (when it splits off from I–84) north*

*10 mi to the Haines exit, turn west on County Rd. 1146, and follow the Elkhorn Drive Scenic Byway signs about 24 mi to the lake ☎ 541/523–4476 ⬩ 37 campsites ✉ $3–$5 ⊙ Open late June–Sept.*

## Sports & the Outdoors

AUTO RACING  **Thunder Mountain Speedway** (✉ 9 mi east of Baker City on I–84 ☎ 541/523–2358) was built in the late 1990s and is a popular place to watch professional car racing.

GOLF  **Baker Municipal Golf Course** (✉ 2801 Indiana Ave. ☎ 541/523–2358) is a public, 18-hole course.

# Ontario

⑩ *70 mi southeast of Baker City on I–84.*

At the far eastern edge of Oregon, less than 5 mi from the Idaho border, Ontario is the largest town in the state's second-largest county, Malheur. Its 10,000 residents make up more than one-third of the county's population. For the adventurous visitor, the Ontario area offers an abundance of outdoor recreation.

Ontario's multi-ethnic heritage is on display at the **Four Rivers Cultural Center and Museum.** Learn about the populations of Northern Paiute Indians, Japanese-Americans, Mexican-Americans, and people from the Basque country. Most interesting and moving is a reconstructed barracks from a Japanese-American WWII internment camp. A 645-seat theater presents music, drama, and other events, from local productions to the Oregon Symphony. ✉ 676 S.W. 5th Ave., 97914 ☎ 541/889–8191 *or* 888/211–1222 ⊟ 541/889–7628 ⊕ www.4rcc.com ✉ Museum $4 ⊙ Mon.–Sat. 10–5.

On the Snake River's Brownlee Reservoir, **Farewell Bend State Park** includes historic markers and displays describing the relevance of this point on the Oregon Trail, where pioneers bid adieu to their route along the Snake River and headed inland. Recreational activities on the lake include fishing, waterskiing, swimming, and boating. A campground has 101 electrical and 30 tent sites, 4 tepees, 2 cabins, and 2 covered wagons. ✉ Day use $3. Hookups $17, tent sites $15, cabins $37. ✉ Exit 353 off I–84 ☎ 541/869–2365 or 800/551–6949, 800/452–5687 reservations only ⊕ www.prd.state.or.us ⊙ Daily; only 10 sites open in winter.

Boat, fish, swim, or picnic at **Ontario State Park,** on the west bank of the Snake River. ✉ Exit 374 off I–84 ☎ 541/869–2365 ✉ Free ⊙ Daily.

Twenty-eight miles south of Ontario, **Lake Owyhee State Park** has picture-perfect views of the surrounding mountains. It is next to a 53-mi-long reservoir formed by the Owyhee Dam. The area has bighorn sheep, pronghorn antelope, golden eagles, coyotes, mule deer, wild horses, and a few cougars. A campground has 31 electrical, 8 tent sites, and 2 teepees. ✉ Off Rte. 201 ☎ 800/551–6949 ⊕ www.prd.state.or.us ✉ Day use $3 per vehicle. Hookups $12–$16, tent sites $10–$14 ⊙ Mar.–Nov., daily.

## Where to Stay & Eat

$–$$$  ✕ **Nichols Steak House.** Paintings by local artists and antiques cover the walls of this steak house in nearby Fruitland, Idaho. It is known for prime rib and 22-ounce T-bone steak suppers. ✉ 411 S.W. 3rd St., Fruitland, ID 83619 ☎ 208/452–3030 ⊟ D, MC, V ⊙ Closed Mon. No lunch Sat.

¢–$  ✕ **DJ's.** Chicken-fried steak is served for breakfast, lunch, and dinner at this place, which provides room service for the Holiday Motel next door. You can order a burger, steak, chicken potpie, or one of the popular breakfast cinnamon rolls at a table or at the coffee bar. ✉ *625 E. Idaho Ave., 97914* ☎ *541/889–4386* ▭ *D, MC, V.*

¢–$ ✕ **Fiesta Guadalajara.** Tuck into all the traditional favorites—burritos, enchiladas, quesadillas, and chalupas—from a high-back, lacquered wooden chair amid the brightly colored murals and south-of-the-border artifacts that fill this downtown eatery. ✉ *336 S. Oregon St., 97914* ☎ *541/889–8064* ▭ *AE, D, MC, V.*

¢ ✕ **Mongolian Express.** You choose the size of your bowl and the ingredients that go in it, then watch the cooks stir-fry your individual meal over a big round grill in the middle of the restaurant. This no-frills family-style restaurant is a local favorite. ✉ *1182 S.W. 4th Ave., 97914* ☎ *541/889–0448* ▭ *AE, D, DC, MC, V.*

¢–$ ▨ **Carlile Motel.** Most of the rooms in this mom-and-pop motor lodge five blocks from downtown have kitchenettes, and some have full kitchens with stoves. With everything from standard rooms with one double bed to multi-room family suites with three beds and two bedrooms, the friendly owners here seem prepared for the needs of everyone from business travelers to large families. ✉ *589 N. Oregon St., 97914* ☎ *541/889–8658* ⮑ *18 rooms* ⚬ *Some kitchens, some kitchenettes, cable TV, some pets allowed (fee); no smoking* ▭ *AE, D, DC, MC, V.*

¢–$ ▨ **Sears & Roebuck Bed & Breakfast.** This 1900 Sears & Roebuck mail-order Victorian is the closest B&B to Ontario, 17 mi west of town in nearby Vale. The two-story inn has a wide front porch with a bird-cleaning room, dog kennels, and horse stables and hosts many pheasant hunters. The rooms are ornately furnished in period pieces, including brass and four-poster beds. ✉ *484 N. 10th St., Vale 97918* ☎ *541/473–9636* ⮑ *5 rooms* ⚬ *No room phones* ▭ *AE, DC, MC, V* ⦿ *BP.*

¢ ▨ **Colonial Motor Inn.** This motel overlooking the Necanicum River is 1 mi from Ontario Center, within walking distance of the mall, and surrounded by several other motels and hotels off I–84. Very clean and simple, the Colonial Motor Inn is a reliable choice. The Continental breakfast is a simple one: juice, coffee, and doughnuts. ✉ *1395 Tapadera Ave., 97914* ☎ *541/889–9615 or 800/727–5014* ⮑ *78 rooms* ⚬ *Cable TV, indoor pool, hot tub, no-smoking rooms* ▭ *AE, D, MC, V* ⦿ *CP.*

¢ ▨ **Holiday Motel.** The basic budget accommodations here are convenient to restaurants and fishing and one block west of I–84. Rooms are attractively decorated in dark greens and pinks, with armchairs and work desks. D.J.'s restaurant is next door. ✉ *615 E. Idaho Ave., 97914* ☎ *541/889–9188* ⊟ *541/889–4303* ⮑ *72 rooms* ⚬ *Restaurant, room service, cable TV, pool, some pets allowed, no-smoking rooms* ▭ *AE, D, DC, MC, V.*

# John Day

**⑪** *80 mi west of Baker City on U.S. 26.*

More than $26 million in gold was mined in the John Day area. The town was founded shortly after gold was discovered there in 1862. Yet John Day is better known to contemporaries for the plentiful outdoor recreation it offers and for the nearby John Day Fossil Beds. The town is also a central location for trips to the Malheur National Wildlife Refuge and the towns of Burns, Frenchglen, and Diamond to the south.

As you drive west through the dry, shimmering heat of the John Day Valley on U.S. 26, it may be hard to imagine this area as a humid subtropical forest filled with lumbering 50-ton brontosauruses and 50-foot-long crocodiles. But so it was, and the eroded hills and sharp, barren-looking ridges contain the richest concentration of prehistoric plant and animal fossils in the world.

# THE LESSER-KNOWN GOLD RUSH

N THE MID-19TH CENTURY, the Oregon Trail was packed not only with pioneering families looking to settle in the new land of opportunity west of the Rockies but also with men of all ages eager to make their fortune in the wave of the gold rush. Most well known, of course, is the California Gold Rush of 1849, which drained Oregon of many of its able-bodied workers as they descended upon northern California in the hope of getting rich quick. Perhaps even more influential in Oregon's history, however, is the gold rush in eastern Oregon. The gold prospecting that began here in the 1860s and continued into the 20th century had far-reaching effects on the settlement of the state, its economic prosperity, and the lives of its non-white populations.

Gold was discovered near Canyon City in 1862 and led to the birth of both John Day and Canyon City, which had more than 10,000 residents combined during the height of the action. During subsequent years, prospectors struck the precious metal in several areas of the region, and boomtowns including Auburn, Sumpter, Elkhorn, and Mitchell popped up to accommodate the influx of people settling in the area. In the years that followed, more than $26 million of gold was mined in the John Day–Canyon City area. Nearby, Baker City was profiting from the money coming from small mining towns and was, for a time, bigger than Spokane and Boise. The 80.4-ounce Armstrong Nugget, found in 1913, is still on display in Baker City at the U.S. Bank.

These short boom periods did not benefit all who lived in and moved to the vicinity. One of the darkest sides of the story comes in the history of the Nez Perce Indians, whose federal reservation land was reduced after white gold prospectors sent out a rallying cry attempting to remove the reservation lands from any areas including gold fields. In 1863, the Nez Perce reservation was cut in size to one-tenth of the land originally set aside, redesignated in a treaty highly contested by many Nez Perce leaders.

The eastern Oregon gold rush was also accompanied by an influx of Chinese immigrants to the region, who worked in the gold mines and settled in communities including John Day and Baker City. In 1879, the census recorded that 2,468 Chinese miners were at work in the mines of eastern Oregon, compared with only 960 whites. The work was often excruciating, and the Chinese were often ostracized within these small mining towns; the history of the Chinese experience in the region is explored at the Kam Wah Chung & Co. Museum in John Day.

Today the legacy of this dynamic period in eastern Oregon's history is seen in places like the Geiser Grand Hotel in Baker City, a remnant of an era of great wealth and renown in a city that has evolved into a modest town with a strong sense of history. Perhaps an even greater reminder of the days of a booming gold economy, however, are the ghost towns that remained after the gold strikes petered out. You can walk through a dusty settlement with no more than a few houses, and imagine it in the late 19th century, when hundreds or thousands of workers called it home and hoped that they would leave with a fortune.

— By Sarah Kennedy

Two miles south of John Day, Canyon City is a small town that feels like it hasn't changed much since the Old West days. Memorabilia from the gold rush is on display at the small **Grant County Historical Museum** there, along with Native American artifacts and antique musical instruments. ✉ *101 S. Canyon City Blvd. (2 mi south of John Day), Canyon City* ☎ *541/575-0362* 💲 *$4* ⊙ *Mid-May–Sept., Mon.–Sat. 9–4:30.*

★ The **Kam Wah Chung & Co. Museum** was a trading post on The Dalles Military Road in 1866 and 1867. It later served as a general store, a Chinese labor exchange for the area's mines, a Chinese doctor's shop, and an opium den. The museum contains a completely stocked Chinese pharmacy, items that would have been sold at the general store, and re-created living quarters. Adjacent to the City Park, the museum is an extraordinary testament to the early Chinese community in Oregon. ✉ *Ing-Hay Way off Canton St., adjacent to City Park* ☎ *541/575-0028* 💲 *$3* ⊙ *May–Oct., Mon.–Thurs. 9–noon and 1–5, weekends 1–5.*

Fodor'sChoice The geological formations that compose the **John Day Fossil Beds National**
★ **Monument** cover hundreds of square miles and preserve a diverse record of plant and animal life spanning more than 40 million years of the Age of Mammals. The national monument itself is divided into three "units"— Sheep Rock, Painted Hills, and Clarno ( ⇨ Sheep Rock, Painted Hills, and Clarno sections)—each of which looks vastly different and tells a different part of the story of Oregon's prehistory. Each unit has picnic areas, rest rooms, visitor information, and hiking trails. The main visitor center is in the Sheep Rock Unit, though bear in mind that it's almost 40 mi northwest of John Day; and Painted Hills and Clarno are about 70 and 115 mi northwest of John Day, respectively. ☎ *541/987-2333* 💲 *Free.*

### Where to Stay & Eat

¢–$$ ✕ **The Grubsteak Mining Co.** Breakfasts of bacon and eggs, potatoes, and silver-dollar pancakes are served until 4 PM daily in the simple, casual dining room of this neighborhood joint. For lunch and dinner, try the excellent burgers, steaks, and seafood. Locals can be found at all hours in the adjoining bar at the back of the house, where you can choose from the full menu, shoot a game of pool, and drink a few beers. ✉ *149 E. Main St.* ☎ *541/575-1970* 🖃 *MC, V.*

★ ¢–$$ ✕ **The Outpost Pizza, Pub, and Grill.** Having moved in 2003 to a new building a few doors down from its old one, the Outpost is now in one of the sleekest spaces in town, in a large building with a log-cabin exterior, a vast entry lobby, and a bright, spacious, high-ceiling dining room. They serve creative pizzas and have a lengthy menu of standard entrées including burgers, steak, seafood, salads, and quesadillas. Breakfast is also available. ✉ *155 W. Main St.* ☎ *541/575-0250* 🖃 *MC, V.*

¢–$ 🏨 **Dreamers Lodge.** The outside of this hotel is quite dated and unglamorous, but the rooms themselves are a definite step up from the exterior, with comfortable armchairs as well as some appliances in all the rooms. For simple accommodations, they are well equipped and reliable. In addition, there are two apartment-style suites. ✉ *144 N. Canyon Blvd.* ☎ *541/575-0526 or 800/654-2849* 🖷 *541/575-2733* 🛏 *25 rooms* ⚒ *Microwaves, refrigerators, cable TV, some pets allowed (fee)* 🖃 *AE, D, DC, MC, V.*

¢ 🏨 **John Day Sunset Inn.** The modest and inexpensive Sunset Inn is a simple no-frills motor lodge near the center of town. It is within walking distance of most John Day attractions and restaurants. ✉ *390 W. Main St., 97845* ☎ *541/575-1462 or 800/452-4899* 🖷 *541/575-1471* 🛏 *44 rooms* ⚒ *Refrigerators, cable TV, pool, hot tub, some pets allowed (fee), no-smoking rooms* 🖃 *AE, D, DC, MC, V.*

# Sheep Rock

**12** *40 mi from John Day, west 38 mi on U.S. 26 and north 2 mi on Hwy. 19.*

The visitor center at this unit of the John Day Fossil Beds serves as a small museum dedicated to the fossil beds, with fossils on display, in-depth informational panels, handouts, and an orientation movie. Two miles north of the visitor center on Highway 19 is the impressive **Blue Basin**, a badlands canyon with sinuous blue-green spires. Winding through this basin is the ½-mi **Island in Time Trail**, where trailside exhibits explain the area's 28-million-year-old fossils. The 3-mi **Blue Basin Overlook Trail** loops around the rim of the canyon, yielding some splendid views. ⊠ *Visitor center on Hwy. 19, north of the junction with U.S. 26* ☎ *541/987–2333* ⊙ *Memorial Day–Labor Day, daily 9–6; Mar.–Memorial Day and Labor Day–late Nov., daily 9–5; late Nov–Feb., weekdays 9–5.*

## Where to Stay

★ ¢–$ ⊞ **Fish House Inn Bed and Breakfast and RV Park.** One of the only places to stay near the Sheep Rock fossil beds is found 9 mi east in the small town of Dayville. The piscatory touches at this lovely B&B includes fishing gear, nets, and framed prints of fish. The main house, built in 1908, has three bedrooms upstairs that share an outdoor deck and a separate entrance, and behind it is a cottage with a large bedroom and suite. The friendly hosts serve a huge country breakfast (on the lawn in good weather). Low-fat and vegetarian options are available as well. While you're in town, stop by the Dayville Mercantile, a century-old general store on U.S. 26. With one café, a bar, and a gas station, Dayville can fill most of your traveling needs and has the only services in the area. ⊠ *110 Franklin St., Dayville 97825* ☎ *541/987–2124 or 888/286–3474* ⇨ *5 rooms, 2 with shared bath* ⊟ *MC, V* ⦿ *BP.*

## Shopping

If you spend the night in Dayville, be sure to stop by **Dayville Antiques & Hardware** (⊠ Hwy. 26, on main street coming into town ☎ 541/987–2143), with an overwhelmingly huge and impressive collection of antique tools and hardware supplies. Both the interior and the huge lawn in front and alongside the house are packed with fascinating goodies.

# Mitchell

**13** *37 mi east of Sheep Rock.*

Mitchell, an authentic homey desert town that has managed to avoid all corporate invasion, truly feels like a slice of the Old West. While you're passing through town for food or fuel, you will have the strange thrill of observing the town's main "attraction": a black bear named Henry that is kept in a cage next to the town's gas station. Henry's owner will occasionally play and wrestle with the bear, who luckily seems to be in remarkably good spirits despite its unusual captivity. Mitchell is the closest town to the Painted Hills unit of the John Day Fossil Beds, about 9 mi away. From Mitchell, U.S. 26 continues southwest for 48 mi through the Ochoco National Forest to Prineville.

## Where to Stay & Eat

¢–$ ✕ **Bridgecreek Cafe.** A friendly glow envelops this sunny roadside café serving old standards: pancakes for breakfast, sandwiches for lunch, burgers and fried chicken with all the fixings for dinner. ⊠ *218 U.S. 26* ☎ *541/462–3434* ⊟ *No credit cards.*

¢  ✕ **Little Pine Cafe.** Orange vinyl chairs and an orange tile floor set the mood for this casual, down-to-earth café, which serves biscuits and gravy all day, and burgers, deli sandwiches, and some good old-fashioned milk shakes during lunch. A small collection of jewelry, gifts, and Native American art is for sale. ✉ *100 E. Main St.* ☎ *541/462–3733* ⊙ *Closed Tues.–Thurs. No dinner.*

¢–$  ▦ **Sky Hook Motel.** This carefully tended inn surrounded by flower and vegetable gardens is a welcome haven after a day's hike in the fossil beds. The owners are friendly and the rooms, two with kitchens, are homey and comfortably furnished. ✉ *101 U.S. 26, 97750* ☎ *541/462–3569* ⊸ *6 rooms* ⚲ *No room phones* ▭ *MC, V.*

## Painted Hills

⑭  *9 mi from Mitchell; head west on U.S. 26 and follow signs north.*

The fossils at Painted Hills, another unit of the John Day Fossil Beds National Monument, date back about 33 million years and reveal a climate that had become noticeably drier than that of Sheep Rock's era. The eroded buff-color hills reveal striking red and green striations created by minerals in the clay. Come at dusk or just after it rains, when the colors are most vivid. Take the steep ¾-mi **Carroll Rim Trail** for a commanding view of the hills or sneak a peek from the parking lot at the trailhead, about 2 mi beyond the picnic area. The unit is open daily and admission is free.

## Clarno

⑮  *67 mi from Mitchell, north 25 mi on Hwy. 207, north 21 mi on Hwy. 19 (to Fossil), and west 20 mi on Hwy. 218.*

The 48-million-year-old fossil beds in this small section have yielded the oldest remains in the John Day Fossil Beds National Monument. The drive to the beds traverses forests of ponderosa pines and sparsely populated valleys along the John Day River before turning through a landscape filled with spires and outcroppings that attest to the region's volcanic past. A short trail that runs between the two parking lots contains fossilized evidence of an ancient subtropical forest. Another trail climbs ¼ mi from the second parking lot to the base of the **Palisades**, a series of abrupt, irregular cliffs created by ancient volcanic mud flows. The unit is open daily and admission is free.

## Burns

⑯  *76 mi south of the town of John Day on U.S. 395.*

Named after poet Robert Burns, this town was the unofficial capital of the 19th-century cattle empires that staked claims to these southeastern Oregon high-plateau grasslands. Today Burns is a working-class town with only about 3,000 residents, surrounded by the 10,185 square mi of sagebrush, rimrock, and grassy plains that compose Harney County, the ninth-largest county in the United States. As the only place in the county with basic tourist amenities, Burns serves as a convenient stopover for many travelers, but its usefulness as a source of modern conveniences comes hand in hand with the sense that its Old West flavor has been largely lost, unlike in many of the region's smaller outposts. Think of it not as your final destination but as a jumping-off point for exploring the real poetry of the Malheur National Wildlife Refuge, Steens Mountain, and the Alvord Desert. Outdoor recreation at this gateway to the Steens Mountains includes fishing, backpacking, camping, boating, and hiking.

The Harney County Chamber of Commerce and the Bureau of Land Management office in Hines ( ⇨ Visitor Information *in* Eastern Oregon A to Z) are good places to obtain information about the area.

You can cut through the 1.4-million-acre **Malheur National Forest** in the Blue Mountains as you drive from John Day to Burns on U.S. 395. It has alpine lakes, meadows, creeks, and grasslands. Black bears, bighorn sheep, elk, and wolverines inhabit thickly wooded stands of pine, fir, and cedar. Near Burns the trees dwindle in number and the landscape changes from mountainous forest to open areas covered with sagebrush and dotted with junipers. ⊠ *Between U.S. 26 and U.S. 20, accessible via U.S. 395* 🕮 *Information from Bureau of Land Management Office in John Day at 541/575–3000* ▱ *Free* ☉ *Daily.*

On the site of a former brewery, the **Harney County Historical Museum** keeps a photo collection documenting the area's history. There's also a display of handmade quilts and a turn-of-the-20th-century kitchen exhibit. ⊠ *18 W. D St., 97720* 🕮 *541/573–5618* ▱ *$4* ☉ *Apr.–Sept., Tues.–Sat. 9–5.*

> **need a break?**
> Sip an espresso and browse through cards, gifts, and books at the **Book Parlor** (⊠ 181 N. Broadway 🕮 541/573–2665), in the center of town.

## Where to Stay & Eat

$–$$$$  ✕ **Pine Room Cafe.** Paintings of Harney County scenery cover the walls of this old-fashioned but classy restaurant, which serves the finest food in Burns. The menu has steaks and seafood, and house specialties include chicken liver bordelaise and stuffed prawns. All dinners come with soup, salad, potatoes, and bread. ⊠ *543 W. Monroe St.* 🕮 *541/573–6631* ▱ *AE, D, DC, MC, V* ☉ *Closed Sun. and Mon. No lunch.*

¢–$  ✕ **El Toreo.** In the spacious, unembellished dining room of this family-owned restaurant, you can get large portions of Mexican staples: enchiladas, tacos, tostadas, tamales, chili rellenos, and chimichangas. But most folks come here for fajitas. ⊠ *293 N. Broadway, 97720* 🕮 *541/573–1829* ▱ *MC, V.*

¢–$  ✕ **Hilander Restaurant.** In 1997 the wood-panel Hilander began serving basic Chinese food in addition to its usual American dishes. Daily specials might include pork chops with apple sauce or roast beef with brown gravy, but spicy Szechuan chicken, curry beef, and several foo yungs and chow meins dominate the menu. ⊠ *195 N. Broadway* 🕮 *541/573–2111* ▱ *MC, V* ☉ *Closed Mon.*

¢–$  🖭 **Best Inn.** On a fairly busy strip, this basic and comfortable hotel is just a short drive from the walkable downtown area. Second-floor rooms have small balconies, while first-floor rooms have entrances both to the outside and to an interior corridor. A small Continental breakfast is served daily. ⊠ *999 Oregon Ave., 97720* 🕮 *541/573–1700* 🖷 *541/573–2331* ▱ *38 rooms* ᘀ *In-room data ports, cable TV, refrigerators, indoor pool, hot tub, laundry facilities, some pets allowed (fee), no-smoking rooms* ▱ *AE, D, DC, MC, V* ⦾⃝ *CP.*

¢  🖭 **Bontemps Motel.** The Bontemps is a throwback to the days when motels had personalities. The small rooms, which surround a courtyard in the center of the property, incorporate an eclectic mix of new and aging furnishings—a far cry from of the standard, streamlined approach of many chain motels. Don't expect any glamorous vintage luxury, however; the accommodations are very modest, and it feels like an inexpensive motel with reliable but basic rooms. Four rooms have kitchenettes. ⊠ *74 Monroe St., 97220* 🕮 *541/573–2037 or 800/229–1394* 🖷 *541/*

# OREGON TRAIL, 1853

**W**EDNESDAY, JUNE 1. *It has been raining all day long and we have been traveling in it so as to be able to keep ahead of the large droves. The men and boys are all soaking wet and look sad and comfortless. (The little ones and myself are shut up in the wagons from the rain. Still it will find its way in and many things are wet; and take us all together we are a poor looking set, and all this for Oregon. I am thinking while I write, "Oh, Oregon, you must be a wonderful country." Came 18 miles today.)*

Wednesday, June 15. *Passed Independence Rock this afternoon, and crossed Sweetwater River on a bridge. Paid 3 dollars a wagon and swam the stock across. The river is very high and swift.*

Wednesday, July 27. *Another fine cow died this afternoon. Came 15 miles today, and have camped at the boiling springs, a great curiosity. They bubble up out of the earth boiling hot. I have only to pour water on to my tea and it is made.*

Monday, August 1. *This evening another of our best milk cows died. Cattle are dying off very fast all along this road. We are hardly ever out of sight of dead cattle on this side of the Snake River. This cow was well and fat an hour before she died. Cut the second cheese today.*

Monday, August 8. *We have to make a drive of 22 miles, without water today. Have our cans filled to drink. Here we left unknowingly our Lucy behind, not a soul had missed her until we had gone some miles, when we stopped a while to rest the cattle; just then another train drove up behind us with Lucy. She was terribly frightened and so were some more of us when we found out what a narrow escape she had run. The little ones have curled down and gone to sleep without supper. Wind high, and it is cold enough for a great coat and mittens.*

Friday, August 19. *Quite cold this morning, water frozen in the buckets. Traveled 13 miles over very bad roads without water. After looking in vain for water, we were about to give up as it was near night, when husband came across a company of friendly Cayuse Indians about to camp, who showed him where to find water. The men and boys have driven the cattle down to water and I am waiting for water to get supper. This forenoon we bought a few potatoes from an Indian, which will be a treat for our supper.*

Thursday, September 1. *We have encamped not far from the Columbia River. Made a nice dinner of fried salmon. Quite a number of Indians were camped around us, for the purpose of selling salmon to the emigrants.*

Thursday, September 8. *There is very little chance to turn out of this road, on account of timber and fallen trees, for these mountains are a dense forest of pines, fir, white cedar or redwood (the handsomest timber in the world must be here in these Cascade Mountains). Many of the trees are 300 feet high and so dense to almost exclude the light of heaven. We have camped on a little stream called Sandy.*

Tuesday, September 13. *Here we are in Oregon making our camp in an ugly bottom, with no home, except our wagons and tent. It is drizzling and the weather looks dark and gloomy.*

Friday, September 17. *In camp yet. Still raining. Noon—It has cleared off and we are all ready for a start again, for some place we don't know where.*

*A few days later my eighth child was born. After this we picked up and ferried across the Columbia River, utilizing skiff, canoes and flatboat to get across, taking three days to complete. Here husband traded two hoke of oxen for half section of land with one-half acre planted to potatoes and a small log cabin and lean-to with no windows. This is the journey's end.*

— Diary of Amelia Knight, 1853

573–2577 📞 15 units ♿ Some kitchenettes, microwaves, refrigerators, cable TV 🖃 MC, V.

### Sports & the Outdoors

GOLF **Valley Golf Club** (✉ 345 Burns–Hines Hwy. ☎ 541/573–6251) has a challenging 9-hole, par-36 course open to the public; the clubhouse facilities are reserved for members. The greens fee is $20; a cart costs $20.

ROCKHOUNDING Rockhounding enthusiasts flock to Harney County to collect fossils, jasper, obsidian, agates, and thunder eggs. The Stinkingwater Mountains, 30 mi east of Burns, contain petrified wood and gemstones. Warm Spring Reservoir, east of the mountains, is a good source for agates. At Charlie Creek, west of Burns, and at Radar, to the north, black, banded, and brown obsidians can be found. It is illegal to remove arrowheads and other artifacts from public lands. Check with the **Harney County Chamber of Commerce** (✉ 75 E. Washington St. ☎ 541/573–2636) for more information on rockhounding.

## Malheur National Wildlife Refuge

⑰ *32 mi southeast of Burns on Hwy. 205.*

Highway 205 slices south from Burns through one of the most unusual desert environments in the West. The squat, snow-covered summit of Steens Mountain is the only landmark in this area of alkali playas, buttes, scrubby meadows, and, most surprising of all, marshy lakes. The **Malheur National Wildlife Refuge,** bounded on the north by Malheur and Harney lakes, covers 193,000 acres. It's arid and scorchingly hot in the summer, but in the spring and early summer more than 320 species of migrating birds descend on the refuge's wetlands for their annual nesting and mating rituals. Following an ancient migratory flyway, they've been coming here for nearly a million years. The species include sandhill cranes, snowy white egrets, trumpeter swans, numerous hawks, golden and bald eagles, and white-faced ibis. The number of birdwatchers who turn up for this annual display sometimes rivals the number of birds.

The 30-mi Central Patrol Road, which runs through the heart of the refuge, is your best bet for viewing birds. But first stop at the **Malheur National Wildlife Refuge Headquarters,** where you can pick up leaflets and a free map. The staff will tell you where you're most likely to see the refuge's winged inhabitants. The refuge is a short way from local petroglyphs (ask at the headquarters); a remarkable pioneer structure called the **Round Barn** (head east from the headquarters on Narrows–Princeton Road for 9 mi; road turns to gravel and then runs into Diamond Highway, a paved road that leads south 12 mi to the barn); and **Diamond Craters,** a series of volcanic domes, craters, and lava tubes (continue south from the barn 6 mi on Diamond Highway). *Malheur National Wildlife Refuge Headquarters ✉ 32 mi southeast of Burns on Hwy. 205 (follow signs 26 mi south of Burns) ☎ 541/493–2612 🖼 Free ☉ Park daily dawn–dusk; headquarters Mon.–Thurs. 7–4:30, Fri. 7–3:30, also 8–3 weekends mid-Mar.–Oct.*

## Diamond

⑱ *54 mi from Burns, south on Hwy. 205 and east on Diamond–Grand Camp Rd.*

Diamond claimed a population of two year-round residents in 2003, and you could probably do the census yourself as you take in the undisturbed cluster of a few houses and the lone Hotel Diamond in the midst of the vast scenery and wildlife found near the Malheur National Wildlife Refuge. During its heyday at the turn of the 20th century, Diamond had a population of about 50, including the McCoy family ranchers, who continue to run the town's hotel today.

Not far from town is the **Kiger Mustang Lookout,** a wild-horse viewing area run by the Bureau of Land Management. With their dun-color coats, zebra stripes on knees and hocks, and hooked ear tips, the Kiger mustangs are perhaps one of the purest herds of wild Spanish mustangs in the world today. Once thought to be the descendants of Barb horses brought by the Spanish to North America in the 16th century, the Kiger horses remain the most sought-after for adoption throughout the country. The viewing area is accessible to high-clearance vehicles only and is passable only in dry weather. The road to it descends from Happy Valley Road 6 mi north of Diamond. ⚓ *11 mi from Happy Valley Rd.* ☎ *541/573–4400* ✆ *Free* ☉ *Dry season (generally May–Oct.) dawn–dusk.*

### Where to Stay & Eat

★ ¢–$ ✕ **Frazier's.** Adjoining and owned by the Hotel Diamond, Frazier's is a small pub-style restaurant in a renovated icehouse, the oldest building in Diamond. Burgers, steaks, salads, and sandwiches are served for lunch and dinner. Aside from the reservations-only dinners served in the hotel, this is the only place in town to buy a meal. And as the Bureau of Land Management firefighters can tell you, it's also the only place for many miles to play a game of pool. The unmarked restaurant is found around the back of the Hotel Diamond and often looks like it might not be open, but head on through the doors for some friendly service. ✉ *At Hotel Diamond, 10 Main St.* ☎ *541/493–1898* ▤ *MC, V.*

★ $ 🏠 **Hotel Diamond.** A hundred years ago the Hotel Diamond served the local population of ranchers, Basque sheepherders, and cowhands. Now it caters to the birders, naturalists, and high-desert lovers who flock to the Malheur refuge. The air-conditioned rooms are clean, comfortable, and pleasantly furnished with an eclectic mix of furniture including wicker chairs, old wooden desks, and four-poster beds. Family-style meals are served both to hotel guests and to the general public at 6:30 PM, by reservation only. The hotel, owned and operated by the fifth-generation ranch family who formerly ran the now defunct McCoy Creek Inn, is also the only place in town to buy gas or groceries. ✉ *10 Main St., 10 mi east of Hwy. 205, 97722* ☎ *541/493–1898* ⇌ *8 rooms, 5 with shared bath* ♨ *Restaurant, dining room, no-smoking room* ▤ *MC, V* ⅋ *CP.*

## Frenchglen

⑲ *61 mi south of Burns on Hwy. 205.*

Frenchglen, the tiny town near the base of Steens Mountain, has no more than a handful of residents and in the off-season offers no basic services to travelers. Don't go expecting groceries and fuel; instead, prepare yourself for a small outpost of civilization that is refreshingly untrammeled by the mundane conveniences of the 21st century.

Frenchglen is the gateway to **Steens Mountain.** Amid the flat landscape of eastern Oregon, the mountain is hard to miss, but the sight of its 9,700-foot summit is more remarkable from the east, where its sheer face rises from the flat basin of the desolate Alvord Desert, which stretches into Idaho and Nevada. On the western side, Steens Mountain slopes gently upward over a space of about 20 mi and is less astonishing. Steens is not your average mountain—it's a huge fault block created when the ancient lava that covered this area fractured. Except for groves of aspen, juniper, and a few mountain mahogany, Steens is almost entirely devoid of trees and resembles alpine tundra. But starting in June, the wildflower displays are nothing short of breathtaking, as are the views: on Steens you'll encounter some of the grandest scenery in the West.

The mountain is a great spot for hiking over untrammeled and unpopulated ground, but you can also see it by car (preferably one with four-wheel drive) on the rough but passable 52-mi **Steens Loop Road,** open mid-July–October. You need to take reasonable precautions; storms can whip up out of the blue, creating hazardous conditions.

On the drive up you might spot golden eagles, bighorn sheep, and deer. The view out over **Kiger Gorge,** on the southeastern rim of the mountain, includes a dramatic U-shape path carved out by a glacier. A few miles farther along the loop road, the equally stunning **East Rim viewpoint** is more than 5,000 feet above the valley floor. The view on a clear day takes in Alvord Desert. ⊕ *Northern entrance to Steens Loop Rd. leaves Hwy. 205 at south end of Frenchglen and returns to Hwy. 205 about 9 mi south of Frenchglen.*

**Frenchglen Mercantile,** Frenchglen's only store, is packed with intriguing high-quality western merchandise, including Stetson hats, horsehair belts, antique housewares and horse bits, fossilized shark's teeth, silver and turquoise Native American jewelry, Navajo rugs, books, postcards, and maps. Cold drinks, film, sunscreen, good coffee, snacks, and canned goods are also for sale. The store is only open in the summer, and the dates may change each year; if you are counting on finding something there, be sure to call ahead to ensure it's open. ⊠ *Hwy. 205* ☎ *541/493–2738.*

## Where to Stay & Eat

¢–$$ ✗**Buckaroo Room.** In a region where the food is basic, this tiny restaurant adjoining the Frenchglen Mercantile serves sophisticated fare. The rustic but carefully furnished dining room has a sloping ceiling, rough-hewn timber walls, deer heads, period memorabilia, and kerosene lamps. Sandwiches only are served for lunch. Dinner entrées are few but expertly prepared: Basque chicken coated with olive oil and marinated in herbs and Greek wine, a succulent filet mignon, pasta, and (a rarity in meat-and-potato land) a vegetarian dish. There's a good selection of beer and wine, and the only full bar for miles around. It's closed fall through spring, and sometimes into early summer; call ahead to be on the safe side. ⊠ *Hwy. 205* ☎ *541/493–2738* ⌂ *Reservations essential* ☰ *AE, D, MC, V.*

¢–$$ ⊡ **Steens Mountain Resort.** Bordering the Malheur National Wildlife Refuge and overlooking vast prairie and mountain land, the Steens Mountain Resort has many lodging options for anyone who wants to fall asleep under the stars and wake up to an undisturbed Oregon sunrise. Small modular cabins and log cabins, RV sites, tent space, and a fully equipped "homestead" are all available. A small selection of groceries, beer, wine, and guidebooks are available for sale in the office. All the two-room cabins come with a fully equipped kitchen, but you must bring your own bedding. The homestead sleeps four adults and has two bathrooms, a kitchen, living room, and laundry facilities. ⊠ *North Loop Rd., 2 mi from Frenchglen, 97736* ☎ *541/493–2415 or 800/542–3765* ☐ *541/493–2484* ⌂ *No room phones, no room TVs* ☰ *AE, D, MC, V.*

$ ⊡ **Frenchglen Hotel.** Past the large front porch of this simple white wooden house built in 1920 is a warm and comfortable inn filled with a community of people who appreciate the peaceful retreat that Frenchglen and the state-owned Frenchglen Hotel can provide. Every evening a family-style dinner (reservations essential) is served to guests and the public at the long wooden tables in the combination lobby-dining room; breakfast and lunch are also served. The small bedrooms, upstairs off a single hallway, share two bathrooms. ✉ *Hwy. 205, 97736* 🏚 *541/ 493–2825* 🛏 *8 rooms* ⚶ *Restaurant; no room phones, no room TVs, no smoking* 🍴 *D, MC, V* ⊘ *Closed mid-Nov.–mid-Mar.*

⚶ **Page Springs.** A profusion of birds greets you as you set up camp at this idyllic oasis—easily the best campsite in the desert—next to the Blitzen River. ⚶ *Pit toilets, potable water* 🛏 *3 campsites* ✛ *4 mi east of Frenchglen on N. Steens Loop Rd.* ☎ *541-573-4400* ⚹ *Campsites $4* ⊘ *Open Apr.–Oct.*

| off the beaten path | **ALVORD DESERT** – With the eastern face of Steens Mountain in the background, the Alvord Desert conjures up western-movie scenes of parched cowboys riding through the desert—though today you're more likely to see wind sailors scooting across these hard-packed alkali flats and glider pilots using the basin as a runway. But once the wind jockeys and flyboys go home, this desert is deserted. Snowmelt from Steens Mountain can turn it into a shallow lake until as late as mid-July. ✛ *From Frenchglen take Hwy. 205 south for about 33 mi until road ends at T-junction near town of Fields; go left (north) to Alvord Desert and the tiny settlement of Andrews.* |
|---|---|

# Lakeview

⑳ *144 mi southwest of Burns on U.S. 395.*

At 4,800 feet, Lakeview is the highest town in Oregon. It is surrounded by such natural wonders as Old Perpetual Geyser (in Hunter's Hot Springs), which erupts every 90 seconds, consistently shooting 60 feet in the air. There's also Abert Rim, about 20 mi to the north of town, the best known of the numerous earthquake and volcano remnants. This earth fault is more than 2,000 feet deep and 30 mi long. The Lakeview area is considered one of the state's best for hang gliding, rockhounding, fishing, and enjoying winter sports.

It's possible to camp, picnic, boat, ski, or swim at **Drews Reservoir,** in the high desert of the Fremont National Forest. ✉ *1300 S. G St., 97630* ☎ *541/947–2151* ⊕ *www.fs.fed.us/r6/fremont* ⚹ *Free* ⊘ *Daily.*

The 1.2-million-acre **Fremont National Forest** is 2 mi north of Lakeview and supports small populations of cougars, bobcats, and black bears, as well as the bald eagle and the peregrine falcon. There are 600 mi of streams and many lakes and reservoirs scattered throughout the forest. Anglers will find that the largemouth bass, yellow perch, black and white crappie, bullhead, and trout are plentiful. The winter recreation season, which runs from December through March, provides downhill and cross-country skiing, snowmobiling, snowshoeing, and ice fishing. In summer there's backpacking and camping. ✉ *Rte. 140* ☎ *541/947–2151* ⊕ *www.fs.fed.us/r6/fremont* ⚹ *Free* ⊘ *Daily.*

Established in 1936 as a home for remaining antelope herds, the 270,000-★ acre **Hart Mountain National Antelope Refuge,** surrounding Hart Mountain, provides a haven for the fastest land animal in North America, as well as more than 300 other species, including myriad birds, bighorn sheep, and coyotes. Camping, biking, horseback riding, and fishing are all permitted in designated areas, and hiking is encouraged throughout the refuge. ✛ *Northeast of Lakeview; take Rte. 140 east 28 mi to Adel, north 18 mi to Plush, and east to refuge headquarters* ☎ *541/947–3315* ⊕ *www.fws.gov* ⚹ *Free* ⊘ *Daily.*

One mile north of Lakeview, on the grounds of Hunter's Hot Springs Resort, **Old Perpetual** is the only active geyser in the Far West. Although the immediately surrounding area is not particularly scenic, it is worth stopping by on your way into town to witness the geyser, which spouts every 90 seconds. ⊠ *U.S. 395, 1 mi north of town, 97630.*

People have lived in **Paisley**, 48 mi north of Lakeview, for as long as 10,000 years. Evidence of its earlier inhabitants has been found in caves and rock paintings in the region. Over the years, the Northern Paiute, Modac, and Klamath Indians settled here. Today Paisley itself is a tiny cowboy town with a general store and a restaurant. ⊠ *Rte. 31, 97636.*

Run by the Oregon chapter of the Daughters of the American Revolution, **Schminck Memorial Museum** has glassware, china, books, tools, toys, and dolls from pioneer Lake County families. ⊠ *128 S. E St.* ☎ *541/ 947-3134* ☞ *$2* ⊘ *Feb.–Nov., Tues.–Sat. 1–5; also by appointment.*

Next door to the Schminck Memorial Museum, the **Lake County Museum** is in a 1926 building and displays local artifacts. ⊠ *118 S. E St.* ☎ *541/ 947-2220* ⊘ *June–Sept., Tues.–Sat. 1–4:30; Oct.–Dec., Mar., and Apr. Thurs.–Sat. 1–4:30.*

## Where to Stay & Eat

★ ¢-$$ ✕**Eagle's Nest.** Some of the finest food in the area is served here, including excellent steak, shrimp, and chicken dishes. If you're not up for a full entrée at dinner, which comes with soup, salad, potatoes, bread, and sorbet, try Eagle's Nest's other claim to fame: the Essie Cobb chicken salad, named after the Lakeview-born "inventor" of the Cobb salad. Breakfast is also served daily. ⊠ *117 N. E St.* ☎ *541/947–4824* ⊟ *AE, D, DC, MC, V.*

¢ ✕**Burger Queen.** A far cry from the "King" of fast food, this "Queen" is independently and locally owned. As in its franchised counterparts, you order at the counter and eat in a brightly lit, streamlined dining room, but here you can chat with the friendly owners and count on a first-rate burger, hot dog, steak sandwich, or deli sandwich. ⊠ *109 S. F St.* ☎ *541/947–3677.*

¢ ✕**Green Mountain Deli & Bakery.** You can find some truly delicious homemade doughnuts in this modest, understated establishment, which also serves tasty, inexpensive breakfast sandwiches and deli sandwiches, grinders, and soup for lunch. ⊠ *512 Center St.* ☎ *541/947–4497* ⊘ *No dinner.*

¢ ✕**Jumpin Java Espresso and More.** The menu is short at this small café, which looks like a simple coffee shop but offers an appealing bunch of inexpensive breakfast items including spicy breakfast burritos and waffles, and soups and burgers for lunch. It doubles as a cybercafé, with high-speed Internet available. ⊠ *16 N. F St.* ☎ *541/947–4855* ⊘ *No dinner.*

¢-$ ▥ **Best Value Inn and Suites–Lakeview Lodge Motel.** Close to downtown, this basic motel has friendly owners, large rooms with ample seating, and several spacious suites. ⊠ *301 N. G St., 97630* ☎ *541/947–2181* ☐ *541/947–2572* ⊕ *www.bestvalueinn.com* ⇗ *40 rooms* ⊘ *Cable TV, microwaves, refrigerators, exercise equipment, hot tub, sauna, some pets allowed (fee)* ⊟ *AE, D, DC, MC, V.*

¢ ▥ **Interstate 8 Motel.** This motel on the edge of downtown Lakeview has the least expensive and simplest rooms in town. They are clean and comfortable, with small seating areas and refrigerators in all the rooms, and are a good value. A small Continental breakfast is served in the lobby. ⊠ *354 N. K St., 97630* ☎ *541/947–3341* ☐ *541/947–4288* ⇗ *32 rooms* ⊘ *Cable TV, refrigerators, laundry facilities, some pets allowed (fee), no-smoking rooms* ⊟ *AE, D, DC, MC, V.*

### Sports & the Outdoors

Lakeview is known as the hang gliding capital of the west, and many launch spots can be found in the Fremont National Forest.

HORSEBACK **Coop's Guiding and Packing** (📪 Box 682, 97630 ☎ 541/947–4533)
RIDING leads horseback trail rides and pack trips, among other excursions.

SKIING & **Warner Mountain Ski Area** (✉ 10 mi northwest of Lakeview ☎ 541/947–
SNOWBOARDING 5001) is a local skiing and snowboarding destination with lift tickets for $20.

# EASTERN OREGON A TO Z

*To research prices, get advice from other travelers, and book travel ar-
rangements, visit www.fodors.com.*

### AIRPORTS

The only passenger airport in eastern Oregon is the Eastern Oregon Regional Airport in Pendleton, which is served primarily by Horizon Air, flying only to Portland, and Pasco, Washington. Depending on your destination, however, you may find it more convenient to fly into one of the airports in western Idaho. Lewiston-Nez Perce County Regional Airport is 88 mi north of Enterprise along the Washington-Idaho border and is served by Horizon Air, flying to Boise, Portland, and Seattle; the Boise Airport, by far the largest in the region, is only 60 mi east of Ontario and is served by all major airlines, flying to most major cities in the country.

🖈 Airport Information **Boise Airport (BOI)** ✉ 3201 Airport Way ☎ 208/383–3110. **Eastern Oregon Regional Airport (PDT)** ✉ 2016 Airport Rd., Pendleton ☎ 541/276-7754. **Horizon Air** ☎ 800/547-9308. **Lewiston-Nez Perce County Regional Airport (LWS)** ✉ 406 Burrell Ave., Lewiston ID ☎ 800/547-9308.

### BIKE TRAVEL

In the more remote parts of eastern Oregon, you often go for 50 mi or so without seeing any signs of civilization. Keep this in mind if you plan on doing any major cycling in the region: the roads are excellent for long-distance cycling, but it is no small undertaking. Be sure to carry plenty of water, a patch kit, a bike pump, and tools for small repairs. In general, the region can be very hilly (or mountainous); the southeastern corner of the state and the area along the Wallowa River in the north tend to be somewhat flatter.

Mountain biking is a popular way to explore some of the region's wilderness. Particularly good trails are in Fremont National Forest and around Hells Canyon. Mountain-bike rentals are available in many towns, including Joseph, La Grande, and Pendleton. Don't attempt to traverse rough off-road terrain on a road bike or a touring bike.

A bicycling map of Oregon is distributed by the Oregon Department of Transportation and is available at many visitor centers. Additionally, La Grande/Union County publishes a bike-route packet with several routes that is available at the La Grande Visitors Center ( ⇨ Visitor Information).

### BUS TRAVEL

The vast majority of travelers in eastern Oregon get around by car, but with a little planning, you'll discover that many of the cities in the region can be reached by Greyhound bus or by a smaller, regional bus line. The major Greyhound route in the area travels along I–84, passing through Pendleton, La Grande, Baker City (whose depot is only open 7–9:30 AM and 5–8 PM), and Ontario, with the Wallowa Valley Stage Lines operating a secondary route once daily, every day except Sunday, between

La Grande and Joseph along Route 82. A north–south Greyhound route runs between Bend and Klamath Falls. One offshoot of this route, run by the People Mover bus line, goes just once a day, on weekends only, between Bend to John Day along U.S. 26. Another line, run by Red Ball Stage Lines, runs twice daily between Klamath Falls and Lakeview.

While you can get to many cities and towns by bus, bear in mind that once you get there you won't usually have public transportation available for getting around, and not all cities have car-rental outlets. Also, most area bus routes operate only once or twice a day, and some don't run on weekends; be sure to check schedules ahead of time.

◪ Lines **Greyhound** ☎ 800/231-2222. **People Mover** ☎ 541/575-2370. **Red Ball Stage Lines** ☎ 541/269-7183. **Wallowa Valley Stage Lines** ☎ 541/569-2284.
◪ Depots **Baker City Station** ✉ at Baker Truck Corral, 515 Campbell St. ☎ 541/523-5011. **Hermiston Station** ✉ 650 S. U.S. 395 ☎ 541/564-6170. **La Grande Station** ✉ 2108 Cove Ave. ☎ 541/963-5165. **Ontario Station** ✉ at Pilot Travel Center, 653 E. Idaho Ave. ☎ 541/823-2567. **Pendleton Station** ✉ at Virginia Conrad, 320 SW Ct. ☎ 541/276-1511.

## CAR RENTALS

With the only area airport in Pendleton, it makes sense that the most readily available car rentals in the region are found there as well. Outside of Pendleton, Hermiston, and Baker City, there are virtually no major car-rental chains with locations in eastern Oregon. However, several cities have an independent car-rental agency, and in some towns, a dealership or repair shop doubles as a rental facility. Rather than deal with the hassle of arriving via bus or train in a small town in eastern Oregon and then trying to rent a car, save yourself some time and headaches by renting a car at a larger city farther west and driving east from there.

◪ Agencies **Budget** ✉ 2016 Airport Rd. Pendleton ☎ 541/996-6113. **Enterprise** ✉ 80406 Hwy. 395 at Swain Motors, Hermiston ☎ 541/564-8870. **Hertz** ✉ 2016 Airport Rd., Pendleton ☎ 541/276-3183. **Jerry Smith Auto Wholesale Round-Up Rent-a-Car** ✉ 309 S.W. Emigrant, Pendleton ☎ 541/276-1498. **Legacy Ford-Lincoln-Mercury** ✉ 2906 Island Ave., La Grande ☎ 541/963-2161. **Practical Rent A Car** ✉ 800 Campbell St. Baker City ☎ 541/523-6292. **Rent-a-Wreck** ✉ 1890 N. 1st St., Hermiston ☎ 541/667-8079. **Sunray Auto Rentals** ✉ 3850 Hwy. 201, Ontario ☎ 541/889-5531.

## CAR TRAVEL

I–84 runs east along the Columbia River and dips down to Pendleton, La Grande, and Baker City. U.S. 26 heads east from Prineville through the Ochoco National Forest, passing the three units of the John Day Fossil Beds. U.S. 20 travels southeast from Bend in central Oregon to Burns. U.S. 20 and U.S. 26 both head west into Oregon from Idaho.

To reach Joseph take Highway 82 east from La Grande. Highway 86 loops down from Joseph to Baker City. From Baker City, Highway 7 heading west connects to U.S. 26 and leads to John Day. U.S. 395 runs south from John Day to Burns. Highway 205 heads south from Burns through the Malheur National Wildlife Refuge to Frenchglen, Steens Mountain, and the Alvord Desert (all accessed by local roads). In all these areas, equip yourself with chains for winter driving.

## CHILDREN IN EASTERN OREGON

While you won't find water parks or petting zoos in eastern Oregon, the natural surroundings more than compensate for a lack of kid-specific attractions. At state parks and recreation areas throughout the region, picnic areas abound, and many have swimming areas. If you don't mind taking long drives with the family, the Malheur National Wildlife Refuge might give your children their first look at a coyote or pronghorn antelope. And although the John Day Fossil Beds don't have any dinosaur bones, they have fossils from other large prehistoric mammals that will likely thrill any budding paleontologists.

## DISABILITIES & ACCESSIBILITY

Travelers with disabilities will find that the vast majority of hotels in eastern Oregon have at least a few wheelchair-accessible rooms, although bed-and-breakfasts and some other historic inns do not. As for the regional sights and attractions, people using wheelchairs may find it a mixed bag: much of the area's beauty is best experienced by driving through it, and several places such as the John Day Fossil Beds have some trails that are navigable by wheelchairs. On the other hand, another major component of travel in eastern Oregon includes exploring mountainous terrain, wilderness, and scenic rivers, and some of these areas can only be reached on foot or horseback. Still, between scenic drives and stunning overlook points, most areas can at least be sampled, making it a viable and worthwhile destination for travelers with disabilities.

## EMERGENCIES

With several national forests in the region that are extremely susceptible to wildfires, fire safety is a topic that eastern Oregon takes very seriously. You will notice signs in all the national wildlife areas indicating the "fire danger" level for that particular time of the year. Be careful never to dispose of burning material in forest areas, including cigarette butts. Each national forest has a fire management office; report any signs of fire, or call 911.

🗲 Forest Fire Management **Malheur National Forest Fire Management** ✉ 431 Patterson Bridge Rd., John Day ☎ 541/575–1321. **Lakeview Interagency Fire Center (Fremont National Forest)** ✉ 1000 S. 9th St., Lakeview ☎ 541/947–6315.

## MEDIA

The *Oregonian* is widely available throughout the region if you want the big picture. Papers with local news and features include the daily *East Oregonian* from Pendleton and the *Argus Observer* from Ontario; the *La Grande Observer,* published weekdays; the *Baker City Herald,* published weekdays; and the twice-weekly *Hermiston Herald.* Weeklies include the *Wallowa County Chieftain,* the *Blue Mountain Eagle* from John Day, and the *Lake County Examiner.*

Radio in eastern Oregon is dominated by country music and Christian rock. You can always tune into National Public Radio at 89.9 FM and Northwest Public Radio at 89.1 FM.

## TOURS

Eagle Cap Fishing Guides operates guided fishing trips on the Grande Ronde, Wallowa, and Imnaha rivers. The company's customized tours ($80–$325) in air-conditioned vans explore the wildlife, wildflowers, and geology of Hells Canyon and the Eagle Cap Wilderness. A trip by raft or jet boat on the Snake River is an exciting and unforgettable way to see Hells Canyon. Hells Canyon Adventures operates jet-boat and other trips of varying lengths.

🗲 **Eagle Cap Fishing Guides** ✉ 110 S. River St., Enterprise 97828 ☎ 541/426–3493 or 541/432–9685. **Hells Canyon Adventures** ✉ Box 159, Oxbow 97840 ☎ 800/422–3568.

## TRAIN TRAVEL

A major Amtrak route runs close to I–84, passing through Hermiston, Pendleton, La Grande, Baker City, and Ontario. Throughout the state, a few secondary routes known as the Thruway System connect more rural Oregon communities to the national Amtrak system: in eastern Oregon, the Oregon Cross-State Route is operated by Porter Stage Lines and runs between Bend and Ontario, passing through Burns and Vale.

Much like bus travel in the region, train travel can get you to many destinations but requires you to have a means of getting around once you are there. Particularly in the cities reached by the Oregon Cross-State Route, there is little in the way of car-rental facilities, and no local public transportation.

## Transportation around Eastern Oregon
Much of the joy of traveling in eastern Oregon is in the beautiful driving found between cities and towns. If you are traveling in your own car, you have the freedom to stop whenever you want, take little excursions off the beaten path, or stay off major routes completely, traveling along small roads through lush scenery and small cowboy towns. For this reason, if your goal is to truly experience the region, you really must have a car at your disposal. Due to the shortage of airports and car-rental agencies in the area, you probably will find it easiest to fly into Portland or Boise, rent a car there, and take your time driving into the heart of the region. Eastern Oregon is not an area to be explored on a whirlwind tour, so give yourself some time and enjoy the open roads. Bus and train travel is only really practical if you have reason to go to a single town or city to stay for there for a few days without wanting to explore the region in greater depth.

### VISITOR INFORMATION
Visitor centers and chambers of commerce are always eager to furnish you with information on area attractions, dining, lodging, and shopping. They are generally open from 9 to 5 during the week, sometimes with slightly reduced hours on the weekends and in the off-season. In addition, eastern Oregon has several visitor centers and ranger stations geared toward the forests, wildlife areas, and recreation areas in the region.

Tourist Information **Baker County Visitors and Convention Bureau** ⊠ 490 Campbell St., Baker City 97814 ☎ 541/523-3356 or 800/523-1235 ⊕ www.visitbaker.com. **Bureau of Land Management** ⊠ Hwy. 20 W, Burns 97220 ☎ 541/573-5241. **Harney County Chamber of Commerce** ⊠ 18 W. D St., Burns 97720 ☎ 541/573-2636 ⊕ www.harneycounty.com. **La Grande Chamber of Commerce** ⊠ 1912 4th St., Suite 200, La Grande 97850 ☎ 541/963-8588 or 800/848-9969 ⊕ www.visitlagrande.com. **La Grande Visitors Center** ⊠ 102 Elm St. ☎ 541/963-8588 or 800/848-9969 ⊕ www.visitlagrande.com. **Pendleton Chamber of Commerce** ⊠ 501 S. Main St., 97801 ☎ 541/276-7411 or 800/547-8911 ⊕ www.pendleton-oregon.org.

# UNDERSTANDING OREGON

OREGON COUNTRY

PACIFIC NORTHWEST FIELD GUIDE

BOOKS & MOVIES

# OREGON COUNTRY

**N**O MATTER WHAT you're looking for in a vacation, few states offer more than Oregon. Within a 90-minute drive from Portland or Eugene you can lose yourself in the recreational landscape of your choice: uncrowded ocean beaches, snow-silvered mountain wilderness, or a monolith-studded desert that has served as the backdrop for many a Hollywood western. In the Willamette Valley wine country, scores of tasting rooms offer up the fruit of the vine. Food lovers find that Oregon produces some of the nation's best fruits, vegetables, and seafood, all of which can be enjoyed in fine restaurants throughout the state. Plenty of attractions keep the kids busy, too, from the Enchanted Forest near Salem to the exceptional Oregon Coast Aquarium in Newport. And shoppers, take note—there's no sales tax in Oregon.

Evidence of Oregon's earliest Native American inhabitants is tantalizingly rare, but what does exist suggests that tribes of nomadic hunter-gatherers lived in the region many centuries before the first white explorers and settlers arrived. In eastern Oregon, a pair of 9,000-year-old sagebrush sandals (now in the Oregon Museum of Natural History in Eugene) and nets woven from reeds have been discovered; on the coast, ancient shell middens indicate that even the earliest Oregonians feasted on seafood.

Although historians now suspect Sir Francis Drake secretly visited the Oregon coast in 1579, the first officially recorded visit came much later. In 1792, Robert Gray, an American trading captain, followed a trail of debris and muddy water inland and came upon the Columbia River. Shortly thereafter, British Army lieutenant William Broughton was dispatched to investigate Gray's find, and he sailed as far upriver as the rapids-choked mouth of the Columbia River Gorge. Within a few years, a thriving seaborne fur trade had sprung up, with American and British entrepreneurs exchanging baubles, cloth, tools, weapons, and liquor with the native peoples for high-quality beaver and sea-otter pelts.

In 1805, American explorers Meriwether Lewis and William Clark reached the site of present-day Astoria after their epic overland journey, spurring an influx of white pioneers—mostly fur trappers and traders sent by John Jacob Astor's Pacific Fur Company in 1811 to do business and claim the land for the United States. The English disputed American claims to the territory on the basis of Broughton's earlier exploration, and after the War of 1812 began, they negotiated the purchase of Astoria from Astor's company. It wasn't until 1846, with the signing of the Oregon Treaty, that the British formally renounced their claims in the region.

Oregon Country, as it was called, grew tremendously between 1841 and 1860 as more than 50,000 settlers from the eastern United States made the journey westward over the plains in their covered wagons. There is a story, never confirmed, that early pioneers arriving at a crossroads of the Oregon Trail found a pile of gold quartz or pyrite pointing the way south to California. The way north was marked by a hand-lettered sign: TO OREGON, and Oregonians like to think that the more literate of the pioneers found their way here, while the fortune hunters continued south. As settlers capitalized on gold-rush San Francisco's need for provisions and other supplies, Oregon reaped its own riches, and the lawless frontier gradually acquired a semblance of civilization. Most white pioneers settled in the Willamette Valley, where the bulk of Oregon's 3.4 million residents still live. The territory's residents voted down the idea of statehood three times, but in 1859, Oregon became the 33rd U.S. state.

The state still attracts many newcomers every year, and it's no wonder, since it has so much to offer. Not only do Oregonians take full advantage of the outdoors, making them some of the hardest-playing Americans, but they have also been called the hardest-working Americans. Much of rural Oregon's economy is still dependent on timber (the state is America's largest producer of softwood), agriculture (hazelnuts, fruit, berries, wine, seed crops, livestock, and dairy products), and fishing. A major high-tech center known as the Silicon Forest, producing high-speed computer hardware and sophisticated instruments, has taken root west of Portland in the Tualatin Valley, side by side with the wine industry. Today, high-tech products such as computer chips are Oregon's top export.

In the meantime, tourism grows in importance every year as visitors from all over the world discover the scenic and recreational treasures that so thrill Oregonians themselves. You'll feel more than welcome here, but when you visit, expect a little ribbing if locals catch you mispronouncing the state's name: it's "*Ore*-eh-gun," not "Ore-uh-*gone*."

# PACIFIC NORTHWEST FIELD GUIDE

## Ecological Communities

**Alpine zone.** Thrashed by winter storms of hurricane strength and snowbound until June or July, the alpine zone of the Cascade Mountains is a place where summer is brief but glorious. At timberline, where the larches and high-country firs give way to open meadows, there are lilies, columbines, Indian paintbrush, penstemons, and bluebells blanketing the ground in a vivid tapestry. Marmots whistle, bumblebees poke into blossoms, and hawks and eagles soar in the thermal currents. By the end of August, the seedheads dry, shrubs such as huckleberry begin to turn crimson and purple, and bull elk racks reach their height and lose their velvet. By the time the elks bugle in late September the first storms are swirling in the North Pacific and the entire ecosystem begins a nine-month hibernation under snow that can pile 20 feet deep. It's one of the harshest, and most beautiful, environments on earth.

**Pacific shore.** South-flowing currents of cold water bring remarkable uniformity to the Pacific Coast climate and habitat. From Eureka, California to Vancouver Island there's a near-uniform ecosystem consisting of spruce, cedar, and hemlock trees; and salal, salmonberry, and thimbleberry undergrowth. The shore itself is a long stretch of rocky headlands and sea stacks interspersed with gray-sand and pebble beaches, especially along the wilderness coast of Olympic National Park. Oregon's coast has the most sand dunes. Harbor seals and California sea lions are common, especially in estuaries, harbors, and river mouths, where they find and eat salmon. The intertidal zone exposed at low tide holds a colorful array of anemones, starfish, mussels, and barnacles, and is a delight for visitors of all ages to explore—taking care not to damage the fragile creatures therein.

**Temperate rain forest.** The maritime rain forests of the Pacific Northwest depend in large part on the fierce winter rainstorms that drop more than 100 inches of rain on the rain forest valleys of the Olympic Peninsula and the west slopes of the Cascades. In summer, long days at this northerly latitude provide plenty of energy for growth (even if filtered through clouds), and the mild coastal climate adds a long growing season. The region is, in effect, a cool greenhouse. Summer temperatures hover around 70°F; winter temperatures rarely drop below 20°F. As a result, temperate rain forests contain more biotic matter (plant and animal material), by weight than any other habitat on Earth. The trees are redwood, Douglas fir, western red cedar, western hemlock, big-leaf maple, and red alder. The understory is a jungle of shrubs that thrive in low light, such as salmonberry, skunk cabbage, and devil's club; slightly drier locales hold huckleberries. Symbiotic hangers-on (literally) in the rain forest range from the mosses of the lower canopy to the rarely seen flying squirrels that spend almost their whole lives without touching ground. Although the above-ground forest seems lush and rich, the soil in the Northwest's temperate rain forest is quite rocky and shallow. Volcanic in origin, it is leached by the constant winter rain; biologists have discovered that most of the forest's essential nitrogen supply is produced by mosses and lichens that grow in the canopy.

## Fauna

**Bald eagle.** The Northwest is one of the strongholds where America's national symbol survived its mid-20th-century brush with extinction. With a wingspan of up to 8 feet, the bald eagle is as large as any North American bird except the condor. It likes to roost in cottonwoods, but will usually nest in conifers such as Douglas fir, and it's most often seen near water. This eagle thrives on the salmon and waterfowl of the Pacific coast. Some lowland populations are year-round residents, while others migrate as far north as Alaska. The bald eagle does not develop its distinctive white head and tail until maturity at five years. Its late winter mid-air courting dance is sensational.

**Rufous hummingbird.** A flash of carmine, a sharp chittering cry, and a steep dive— these are the hallmarks of the West Coast hummingbird. Aggressive enough that it has been known to "dive-bomb" people near a food source (such as a feeder), the rufous spends winter in California and summer (April–September) as far north as the Alaska panhandle, nourishing itself with flower nectar and small insects.

**Steller's jay.** The midnight-blue cap (head and shoulders) of this West Coast bird distinguishes it from the blue jay of the Rockies. While it is not shy, it isn't inclined to steal food like the gray jay familiar to most who have camped in the West.

**Pacific salmon.** Four species of salmon are born in and return to Northwest rivers— Chinook (king), the largest at up to 60 pounds; coho (silver), the most widely sought by anglers; pinks; and chum. Most rivers and streams in the national parks are the scene of salmon runs; the best viewing sites are in Olympic National Park. Salmon remain in freshwater until they are about a year old, migrating then to the ocean to feed and grow, and returning to spawn in the fresh waters of their birth after two years. A separate species, steelhead, is considered a trout, and is the only one that sometimes spawns more than once. All Pacific salmon are descended from rainbow trout.

**Sunflower starfish.** These distinctive orange stars, found in tide pools and sometimes above water at low tide, grow quite large, adding arms with age. Some specimens may have 16 arms and spread 2 feet. Starfish feed on oysters and clams, prying open the shells to get at the meat inside.

**Black bear.** *Ursus americanus,* one of the most common animals in the Northwest forests, thrives on the region's spring greens and summertime berries. The black bear grows up to 6 feet long and 600 pounds, but is usually smaller. It can be cinnamon-colored, but is not as large as a brown bear (grizzly). You may see the black bear along roadsides, especially in early summer. *Never* approach or feed a bear.

**Black-tailed deer.** A subspecies of the common Western mule deer, the black-tail is slightly smaller but no less numerous. It is most often seen at the forest edge at dusk and dawn. Mature bucks have racks 1–4 feet long.

**Gray whale.** Once on the verge of extinction, the California gray whale population is back to relatively healthy numbers, thanks to federal protection laws. The midsize baleen (bottom-feeding) whale grows to almost 50 feet and migrates along the Pacific coast to the Gulf of Alaska in spring, returning in fall. Often seen within a couple miles of shore in March and April, the gray whale can be recognized by its spout. Unlike the humpback and the orca, it rarely breaches.

**Marmot.** You know you're in the high country when you hear the distinctive, piercing whistle of the marmot, a denizen of rocky slopes near and above timberline. The hoary marmot of the Pacific Northwest is a chunky animal, about 2 feet long. The Olympic marmot, found only on its namesake peninsula, is a separate species. Marmot, especially the tail, was a favorite prospector delicacy.

**Roosevelt elk.** The Pacific coast variety of elk is slightly shorter, stockier, and more inclined to browse—eat small plants and brush, as well as grass—than the more numerous Rocky Mountain elk. The imminent disappearance of this magnificent creature prompted Theodore Roosevelt to declare its Olympic Mountains habitat a national monument in 1909, thus the elk's name. Mature bulls reach 5 feet at the shoulder and their mating calls, or bugles, resound from the high ridges in September and October.

**Seals and sea lions.** The harbor seal and California sea lion, close cousins, both prowl the waters of the Pacific coast. The sea lion is larger, usually 6–7 feet in length; the seal grows to 4–5 feet. Difficult to distinguish in the water, especially at a distance, the two species differ chiefly in that the seal does not have ears, and the sea lion has a longer snout. Both feed on fish. Sea lions consume so much salmon in some areas that they are considered a pest by fishermen. The raucous barking of sea lions on buoys, docks, and rock perches can carry a mile or more and is one of the most common sounds of the Pacific coast.

## Flora

**Glacier lily.** Look for the low-growing, pendant yellow trumpets of this lily at the edges of receding snowbanks in the highlands of North Cascades, Mount Rainier, and Olympic national parks.

**Tiger lily.** The vivid, cheery, orange-red trumpets of this native Northwest lily attracted hybridizers, and today it's one of the ancestors of some common garden lilies. Look for its 2-foot stems at the forest edge in the mid- and upper elevations of the Cascades.

**Devil's club.** Long, sharp thorns mark the stems of this shrub, which is common in the boggy ground of rain-forest valleys. It grows 6–10 feet tall, with huge leaves to gather what little light penetrates to the forest floor.

**Huckleberry.** Both red and dark-blue forms of the huckleberry, a relative of the blueberry, are found in and around the temperate rain forests of the Northwest. The bushes grow 2–8 feet in height, often in the understory of old-growth forest. If you're looking for bears, the place to find them is a huckleberry patch in August.

**Poison oak.** Similar to poison ivy, the three-lobed leaves of this shrub are distinctive—and memorable to anyone who has experienced the itchy, blistering rash that contact with them causes. Found in drier locales along the Pacific coast, poison oak turns a most attractive crimson-auburn in late summer and fall.

**Salmonberry.** The pink blossoms of salmonberries announce the arrival of spring along the Pacific coast from Mendocino to Alaska, drawing rufous hummingbirds north. Orange and reddish berries follow in June. Salmonberry thickets grow in rain-forest valleys wherever light penetrates, reaching 8 feet in height and an impenetrable thickness.

**Big-leaf maple.** The sizeable leaves that mark the Northwest's largest deciduous tree are sometimes more than a foot across (usually on saplings). Common to lowland valleys such as the Hoh, Queets, and Quinault in Olympic National Park, big-leaf maples can grow to 100 feet, with trunks up to 5 feet in diameter.

**Black cottonwood.** Tall and straight unlike its plains cousin, the Pacific coast cottonwood lines almost every river from Northern California to the Yukon. It can reach heights of 80 feet; only the mature tree develops the black, furrowed bark that gives the cottonwood its name. The branches, lined with heart-shaped leaves, are a favorite perch for bald eagles and ospreys. Some inland tribes used the wood for canoes.

**Douglas fir.** Craggy, deeply lobed reddish bark marks the maritime Northwest's most famous tree. Although it grows throughout the West (and can adapt to dry landscapes) Douglas fir reaches its greatest heights on the west slopes of the Cascades and Olympics, where it can grow to 300 feet high and 11 feet in diameter. It and ponderosa pine are America's two most significant timber species. Old-growth Douglas fir lumber, now very expensive, is so hard that nails cannot be driven into it.

**Red alder.** The reddish inner bark of this ubiquitous lowland tree gives it its name. A relative of aspen, alder grows in dense thickets along stream-courses from northern California to southeast Alaska; its wood was traditionally used by coastal Native Americans to roast salmon, and is now used for furniture.

**Redwood.** Redwoods are the tallest and most admired of the West Coast's giant trees. The dark-amber bark, graceful spire shape, and incredible size and age of the trees lend redwood groves a cathedral-like air unmatched in any other forest. Redwoods grow only in the coastal ranges from Big Sur to southern Oregon, and are highly dependent on moisture from the intense winter rains and the summer morning coastal fog.

**Sitka spruce.** The near-shore forest of the Northwest is composed mainly of this dense-canopied tree that can reach 10 feet in diameter. Its light wood was once used for airplane frames (the reason that the Boeing Company started up in Seattle) and is now valued for musical instruments such as guitars and pianos.

**Vine maple.** The slender, whiplike stems of this small tree make it seem like a shrub. Found at the edge of clearings in Douglas fir groves, vine maple is unremarkable 10 months of the year. Late August through early October, however, its leaves turn incandescent shades of crimson, maroon, and burgundy, making it the most conspicuous rain forest tree in autumn.

**Western red cedar.** There's almost no end to the uses coastal Natives made of cedar—the bark yielded clothing, rope, fish-nets and baskets; the wood made planks for housing; entire trunks were carved into canoes. The huge, pyramidal base of the red cedar helps to hold the tree fast in the wet ground it prefers. The tops of old red cedars are almost always snapped off by storms, and the side branches that spring up create the "candelabra" appearance. Red cedars can reach 20 feet in diameter and surpass 1,000 years in age. Highly valued for decking and roofing material, most available old-growth cedar has been cut, and second-growth wood is not nearly as rot-resistant.

## Geology and Terrain

Two huge forces shaped the Northwest landscape—glaciation, both local and during ice ages; and the tectonic dynamism of the Pacific Rim, whose earthquakes and volcanic eruptions are almost constant events on the geologic time scale. Most of the Pacific coast is relatively young, its volcanoes less than a million years old. The Cascade Range is also just a teenager in geological time.

**Caldera.** Although it is the largest and deepest example, the bowl-shaped depression in which Crater Lake lies is only one of many along the Pacific Rim. Created when volcanoes blow their tops, small caldera remnants lie atop Mount Rainier and Mount Baker, and a bigger one remains on Mount St. Helens, where its side blew out in 1980.

**Glacial valley.** The steep-sided, tunnel-shape valleys that wrinkle the Cascades are the result of glacial carving that occurred during the most recent ice ages 15,000 and 35,000 years ago. Excellent examples are the Stehekin Valley in the Lake Chelan National Recreation Area, the Carbon River Valley on the northwest side of Mount Rainier National Park, and the Elwha Valley on the north side of Olympic National Park.

**Glaciers.** Heavy snow compacted by centuries of accumulation forms the distinctive blue, dense ice of a glacier. Incremental movement, usually inches a year, is what distinguishes a glacier from a snowfield; most of the glaciers in the continental United States are in Washington and Oregon, and most are receding due to global warming.

**Sea stacks.** Perched offshore, from San Francisco to Vancouver, Canada, sea stacks are rock headlands and pinnacles. They are composed of basalt and other volcanic material and have been separated from the mainland by the Pacific's erosive force. Some West Coast sea stacks rise more than 100 feet above the surf, and with breakers surging onto and around them, they are highly photogenic. Some of the best are found from Eureka, CA to Port Orford, OR; and from Queets to Neah Bay, WA. Sea caves and arches are rarer.

**Volcanoes.** The volcanoes of the West Coast—including Mount Rainier, Crater Lake, Mount Hood, and Mount Baker—are not, as commonly believed, dormant. Instead, most are described as "episodically active," as Mount St. Helens was in 1980. Most of the Northwest's volcanoes are much younger than a million years old. The mountains themselves are composed of basalt and pumice.

# BOOKS & MOVIES

## Books

The magical, mystical Pacific Northwest has inspired countless writers, whose works have pondered the region's landscape and history. Twenty writers closely connected with the Pacific Northwest discuss it in Nicholas O'Connell's *At the Field's End.*

The imaginative novels of Tom Robbins offer a sometimes surreal take on the Northwest. Annie Dillard's first novel, *The Living,* is an evocative account of life in the Pacific Northwest at the end of the 19th century. A few of the bittersweet short stories of Raymond Carver are set in the region as well. Other writers for whom Oregon has been a muse include the novelist and historical writer Norman MacLean and the science-fiction author Ursula Le Guin. The *Journals of Lewis and Clark* make for interesting reading as you follow in the 19th-century explorers' path. Ken Kesey's novel *Sometimes a Great Notion* is about a troubled Oregon logging dynasty. Andrew Vachss' *Pain Management,* one of several popular novels starring a vigilante named Burke, takes place in Portland and other parts of the Pacific Northwest.

For a historical take on the coastal region read *The Interwoven Lives of George Vancouver, Archibald Menzies, Joseph Whidbey, and Peter Puget: Exploring the Pacific Northwest,* by John Michael Naish.

John T. Gaertner's *North Bank Road: The Spokane, Portland and Seattle Railway* outlines the impact that railroads had on the Northwest. The book is one of several titles on the subject published by Washington State University Press, whose other titles include *The Way We Ate: Pacific Northwest Cooking 1843–1900.*

Cherry Hartman's *The Well-Heeled Murders* is a police mystery set in Portland. In photographs and poetry the book explores Portland, from the warehouse district to Nob Hill and up into Forest Park. The book portrays the gentrification of the city in the early 1990s.

## Movies

The Oregon desert has supplied the backdrop for numerous westerns—as early as 1915, when the silent film *Where Cowboy Is King* was shot in and around Pendleton.

Loretta Young and Robert Mitchum star as the title characters in *Rachel and the Stranger* (1948), a fine western, some footage for which was shot in the Eugene area. Baker City appears in the western–musical comedy *Paint Your Wagon* (1969), starring Lee Marvin, Clint Eastwood, and Jean Seberg. The film version of *Sometimes a Great Notion* (1970) was shot all along the central coast of Oregon. Director Bob Rafelson's *Five Easy Pieces* (1970) includes scenes shot in Oregon.

The Deschutes National Forest and the Rogue River were among the Oregon backdrops for the John Wayne western *Rooster Cogburn* (1975). Many of the frat-house antics in *National Lampoon's Animal House* (1978) were shot in the Eugene area. Much of Robert Towne's directorial debut, *Personal Best* (1982), about the relationship between two women training for the Olympic Games, was also filmed in and around Eugene.

Gus Van Sant has set all or part of several films in Portland, including his gritty debut, *Mala Noche* (1986), about a gay man who falls for an illegal alien from Mexico; *Drugstore Cowboy* (1988), about junkies who rob drugstores to pay for their drugs; and *My Own Private Idaho* (1991), in which River Phoenix and Keanu Reeves play a pair of hustlers (Reeves is the son of the Portland mayor in the film). The stern-wheeler *Portland,* on display at the Oregon Maritime Center & Museum in Portland, was used as a location for the western *Maverick* (1994). Harbor scenes for the navy diver drama *Men of Honor* (2000), with Robert De Niro and Cuba Gooding Jr., were filmed in the Old Town/Chinatown area of Portland as well as North Plains and Rainier.

Other films with scenes shot in Oregon include *Free Willy* (1993) and the 1995 *Free Willy 2* (a third installment, *Free Willy 3*, was filmed elsewhere in 1997). The anti-captivity theme of the movies had basis in reality: the films' star, Keiko the killer whale, was airlifted from Mexico City in 1996 to a temporary home at the Oregon Coast Aquarium in Newport; he was moved to Icelandic waters in 1998; Keiko died in December 2003 at the age of 27.

Madonna lives on a Portland houseboat in the campy *Body of Evidence* (1993). Richard Dreyfuss plays a Portland high school music teacher in *Mr. Holland's Opus* (1995). Jim Jarmusch's *Dead Man* (1996) was also filmed in the state.

Some scenes from *The Postman* (1997), with Kevin Costner as a post-apocalyptic mail carrier, were filmed in central Oregon. Parts of *Zero Effect* (1998), a comedy-thriller starring Ben Stiller and Ryan O'Neal, were filmed in Portland and at Crown Point State Park in the Columbia River Gorge.

Gresham and Portland were the backdrop for some scenes in the Steven Spielberg film *A.I. Artificial Intelligence (2001)*. Also in 2001, the robbery yarn *Bandits* was filmed partly in California and throughout Oregon, including Oregon City, Portland, Salem, and Silverton. Parts of the 2002 thriller *The Ring* were filmed in Astoria and Newport.

# INDEX

## A

A. C. Gilbert's Discovery Village, 224
Abacela Vineyards and Winery, 279
Adelsheim Vineyard, 214
Albany, 228–229
Albany Regional Museum, 228
Alder House II, 24
Alsea Bay Bridge Interpretive Center, 36–37
Alton Baker Park, 234–235
Alvord Desert, 324
American Advertising Museum, 71, 72
Amity Vineyards, 218
Anderson House Museum, 152
Ankeny Square, 73
Annual Spring Rose Show, 68
Anthony Lakes Ski Area, 309
Argyle Winery, 215
Arlene Schnitzer Concert Hall, 70, 116–117
Artists Repertory Theatre, 117
Ashland, F28, 268, 270–274
Ashland Creek, 268
Ashland Creek Inn ⊡, 272
Astoria, F29, 5–6, 9–11
Astoria Column, 5
Astoria Riverfront Trolly, 6
Auto racing, 120, 313
Avery Park, 229
Ayer-Shea House, 74, 75
Azalea Park, 54

## B

Baker City, 308–310, 312–313
Bald Hill Winery, 230
Ballet, 116
Ballooning, 214
Bandon, 48–50
Bandon Beach State Park, 48
Bandon Historical Society Museum, 48
Bars and lounges, 111–112
Baseball, 121, 241
Basketball, 121, 241
Battle Mountain Scenic Corridor, 295
Bayfront, 30
Beaches, 54, 7, 14–17, 19, 30, 31, 35, 48, 52–53
Beacon Rock, F31, 146
Beaverton, 207–209
Bed and breakfast, 268, 270
Bend, 184–193
Bend Public Library, 185, 186
Bend Riverside Motel ⊡, F27, 191
Benson Hotel ⊡, 102
Benton County Historical Museum, 229
Bethany Lake Park, 208

Beverly Beach State Park, 31, 35
Bicycling
Central Oregon, 183, 192, 194
Columbia River Gorge & Oregon Cascades, 151, 163
Eastern Oregon, 301
Portland, 65, 118
Willamette Valley/Wine Country, 203, 241
Big Cliff Dam, 159
Big Summit Prairie Loop, 183
Bird-watching, 254
Bistro, The ✕, 15
Black Sheep ✕, F28, 270
Blue Basin, 317
Blue Heron Bistro ✕, 47
Blue Heron French Cheese Company, 20
Blue Lake Regional Park, 120
Blue River Dam and Lake, 232–233
Boating
Columbia River Gorge and Oregon Cascades, 145
Eastern Oregon, 305–306
jet-boat excursions, 53, 264, 274
Oregon Coast, 35, 37, 43, 53
riverboat tours, 145
Willamette Valley/Wine Country, 233, 262, 264
Bonneville Dam, 145
Bonneville Fish Hatchery, 145
Bowling, 205, 207
Bowman Museum, 180
Brandy Peak Distillery, 54–55
Breitenbush Hot Springs Retreat and Conference Center, 161
Brew pubs, brew theaters, and microbreweries, 65, 91, 112–113
Brice Creek Trail, 242
Bridge of the Gods, 146
Bronze founderies, 303
Brookings, 54–55
Brownsville, 231–232
Bullards Beach State Park, 48
Burns, 318–319, 321
Bush Barn Art Center, 224
Bush House, 224
Bush's Pasture Park, 224
Butte Creek Mill, 262

## C

Cabins Creekside at Welches ⊡, 158
Camp Sherman, 164–165
Campbell Townhouses, 74, 75
Camping
Central Oregon, 183
Columbia River Gorge & Oregon Cascades, 160, 162, 163

Eastern Oregon, 298, 303, 307, 308, 312–313
Oregon Coast, 19, 34, 37, 43, 50
Southern Oregon, 254
Cannon Beach, 14–17
Canoeing, 192
Canyon Life Museum, 159
Cape Arago Lighthouse, 46
Cape Arago State Park, 46
Cape Blanco Lighthouse, 50
Cape Blanco State Park, 50–51
Cape Foulweather, 29
Cape Kiwanda State Natural Area, 22
Cape Lookout State Park, 22
Cape Meares Lighthouse, 22
Cape Meares State Park, 22
Cape Perpetua F31, 40
Cape Sebastian State Park, 52
Capriccio Ristorante ✕, 228–229
Carl G. Washburne Memorial, 42
Cascade Locks, 145–146
Cascade Dining Room ✕, 154
Cascade Room at Dolce Skamania Lodge ✕, F28, 146
Casinos, 24, 260
Cave Junction, 277
Caves, 40, 277–278
Celilo Park, 152
Central Library, 63, 64
Century Drive, 185, 186
Chamber music, 115
Champoeg State Park, 216–217
Chapman and Lownsdale squares, 64
Charleston, 46
Chateau Lorane Winery, 242
Chateaulin ✕, 270
Cheese-making plant, 20
Cherry Hill Vineyard, 226
Chetco River, 54
Chetco River Inn ⊡, 55
Chetco Valley Historical Museum, 54
Children, attractions for
Central Oregon, 172, 186–187
Columbia River Gorge and Oregon Cascades, 149, 157
Eastern Oregon, 303
Oregon Coast, 5, 6, 20, 30–31, 32, 35, 40, 41, 43, 44, 54
Portland, 72, 77, 79, 80, 82–83, 120
Southern Oregon, 265, 268, 279
Willamette Valley/Wine Country, 205, 236
Children's Museum (Jacksonville), 265

Children's Museum (Portland), 77
Chinatown, 71–72, 90, 92
Chinatown Gate, 71, 72
Chinese history museum, 316
Chinook Winds (casino), 24
Churches, 63, 64
Cinco de Mayo Festival, 65, 67
City Hall, 64
Clarno, 318
Classical Chinese Garden, F30, 71, 73
Classical music, 115
Clear Creek Distillery, 74, 75
Cleawox Lake, 41
Cline Falls State Park, 181
Coffeehouses and teahouses, 113
Collier Memorial State Park and Logging Museum, 260
Columbia Gorge (ship), 145
Columbia Gorge Discovery Center–Wasco County Historical Museum, 152
Columbia Gorge Interpretive Center, 146
Columbia Gorge - Mount Hood Loop, 134
Columbia Gorge Sailpark, 148
Columbia River Maritime Museum, F29, 5
Comedy club, 113
Commonwealth Lake Park, 208
Cook Butte Park, 209
Cooper Mountain Vineyards, 208
Coos Bay, 45–47
Coos County Historical Society Museum, 45
Coquille Lighthouse, 48
Coquille River Museum, 48
Cork ✕, F28, 188
Corvallis, 229–231
Cottage Grove, 242–243
Cottage Grove Lake, 243
Cottage Grove Museum, 242
Cougar Dam and Lake, 233
County Museum (Hillsboro), 205
County Museum/Restored Train Station, 222
Couvron ✕, 87
Cove Palisades State Park, F31, 178
Covered bridges. 237, 243, 244
Coxcomb Hill, 5
Crabbing, 7, 37
Crater Lake Lodge ☒, F26, 252, 254
Crater Lake National Park, F29–F30, 250, 252–255, 257–259
Crater Rock Museum, 262
Craterian Ginger Rogers Theatre, 262
Credit card abbreviations, F45

Crook County Courthouse, 180
Crooked River, 180
Crown Pointe State Park, 140
Crystal Springs Rhododendron Garden, 80
Curry County Historical Museum, 52

**D**

D River, 24
Dabney State Park, 141
Dalles, The, 151–153
Dalles Dam and Reservoir, 152
Dancing, 113
Darlingtona Botanical Wayside, 41
David and Lee Manuel Museum, 303
David Hill Vineyards and Winery, 202
Day Building, 74, 75
Dean Creek Elk Viewing Area, 44
Deepwood Estates, 224, 225
Delores Winningstad Theater, 70
Depoe Bay, 27–29
Depot Deli & Café, The ✕, F28–F29, 194
Deschutes Historical Museum, 185, 186
Deschutes National Forest, 186
Detroit, 159–160, 162
Detroit Dam, 159
Devil's Churn State Park, 39
Devil's Elbow State Park, 40
Devil's Lake State Park, 24
Devil's Punchbowl State Natural Area, 29, 31
Diamond, 321–322
Diamond Craters, 321
Dining Room at Salishan ✕, 26
Distillery, 74, 74
Dog racing, 121
Dolce Skamania Lodge ☒, F26, 147
Domaine Serene (winery), 218
Dorena Lake, 243
Douglas County Museum, 279
Downton Bend, 185, 186
Drag racing, 179
Drain, 243–244
Drain Castle, 243
Drake Park, 185, 186
Drews Reservoir, 324
Drift Creek Wilderness, 37
Duck Pond Cellars, 215
Dundee, 214–216
Dune buggies, 43

**E**

Eagle Cap Wilderness, 299–300
Eagle's Nest ✕, 325
East Linn Museum, 232

Eastern Oregon Museum, 309
Echo, 290
Ecola State Park, 14
Elk, 44
Elk Cove Vineyards, 202
Elkhorn Drive, 309
Elsinore Theatre, 225, 227
Emigrant Springs State Heritage Area, 295, 298
Enchanted Forest, 228
End of the Oregon Trail Interpretive Center, 211
Enterprise, 301–303
Ermatinger House, 211
Eugene, F26, F28, 234–236, 238–242
Eugene Saturday Market, 235
Evergreen Aviation Museum, F29, 217–218
Excelsior Café ✕, 239
Excelsior Inn ☒, 240

**F**

Face Rock Wayside, 49
Farewell Bend State Park, 313
Favell Museum of Western Art and native American Artifacts, 261
Fernhill Wetlands, 202
Festivals and seasonal events
Portland, 68, 114, 115
Southern Oregon, 267, 268, 269, 273
Willamette Valley/Wine Country, 241, 267, 268, 269, 273
5th Avenue Suites Hotel ☒, 103
5th Street Public Market, 234, 235
Film, 116
Finley National Wildlife Refuge, 230
Fireman's Pond, 181
First Congregational Church, 63, 64
Fish House Inn Bed and Breakfast and RV Park ☒, 317
Fishing
Central Oregon, 181, 182, 183, 194
Eastern Oregon, 298, 301
fish hatchery, 145
Oregon Coast, 18, 44, 52, 54
Portland, 118–119
Southern Oregon, 255
Willamette Valley/Wine Country, 207
Flavel House, 5
Fleet Week, 68
Flerchinger Vineyards, 149
Florence, 41–43
Flying M Ranch ☒, F26, 216
Fodor's Choice, F26–F31
Fogarty Creek State Park, 28
Foley Station ✕, F28, 300
Football, 241

Forest Discovery Center Museum, 77
Forest Grove, 200–203, 205
Forest Grove Educational Arboretum, 202
Forest Park, 77
Foris Vineyards, 277
Fort Clatsop National Memorial, F29, 5
Fort Dalles Museum, 152
Fort Klamath Museum and Park, 260
Fort Stevens, 6
Fountains, 67, 71, 73–74
Four Rivers Cultural Center and Museum, 313
Frazier's ✕, 322
*Free Willy* (movie), 30
Fremont National Forest, 324
Frenchglen, 322–324
Frenchglen Mercantile, 323

**G**

Gardens
*Oregon Coast,* 41, 51
*Portland,* F30, 71, 73, 77, 79, 80
*Willamette Valley/Wine Country,* 222, 226, 234, 235
Garibaldi, 18
Gay and lesbian clubs, 114
Geiser Grand Hotel ▦, 312
Genoa ✕, 96
George E. Owen Memorial Rose Garden, 234, 235
George Fox College, 213–214
George Huesner House, 75
Ghost towns, 311
Giant Spruce Trail, 40
Girardet Wine Cellars, 279
Glazed Terra-Cotta National Historic District, 64
Gleneden Beach, 26–27
Glenn Creek, 48
Gold Beach, F26, 52–53
Gold rush, 315
Golden and Silver Falls State Park, 48
Goldendale area, Washington, 165–166
Goldendale Observatory State Park and Interpretive Center, 166
Golf
*Central Oregon,* 182, 192
*Columbia River Gorge & Oregon Cascades,* 151, 158
*Eastern Oregon,* 290, 298, 303, 313, 321
*Oregon Coast,* 21, 26, 27, 43, 47, 50, 53
*Portland,* 119–120
*Southern Oregon,* 264
*Willamette Valley/Wine Country,* 205, 207, 213, 227, 231, 242
Government Camp, 155–157
Governor Hotel ▦, 102

Governor Tom McCall Waterfront Park, 63, 65, 67
Grand Floral Parade, 68
Grand Ronde, 221
Grants Pass, 274–277
Grants Pass Museum of Art, 274
Greenway Park, 208
Gresham, 138, 140
Gresham History Museum, 138
Grotto, The, 80, 82

**H**

Halfway, 307–308
Harney County Historical Museum, 319
Harris Beach State Park, 54
Harris Ranch Trail, 37
Hart Mountain National Antelope Refuge, 324
Hat Rock State Park, 289
Hatfield Library, 226
Hatfield Marine Science Center, 30–31
Hawthorne District, 79, 80
Haystack Rock, 14, 22
Heathman Hotel ▦, F26, 103
Heathman, The ✕, 86
Heceta Head, 40–41
Heceta Head Lighthouse, 40
Heceta House, 40
Hells Canyon, F30, 306–307
Hells Canyon National Recreation Area, 307
Hendricks Park, 235
Henry Estate Winery, 279
Heritage Museum, 6
Hermiston, 290, 292
*Hero* (ship), 43
Higgins ✕, F28, 86
High Desert Museum, F29, 185, 186–187
Hiking, 183–184, 254–255, 258, 305
Hillsboro, 205–207
Hillsboro Saturday Market, 205
Hinterland Ranch, 193
Historic Columbia River Highway, 140
Homes
*historic,* 214, 224, 225
*manor,* 77, 79
*Victorian,* 5, 74, 75–76
Honeyman Memorial State Park, 41
Honeywood Winery, 226
Hong Kong Bar ✕, 270
Hood River, 148–151
Hood River Valley fruit, 139, 148
Hood River Vineyards, 149
Hoover, Herbert, 214
Hoover-Minthorne House, 214
Horse racing, 121
Horseback riding, 16, 41, 147, 305

Horsethief Lake State Park, 165–166
Hot Point Overlook, 306
Hotel Diamond ▦, 322
Hotels, F26–F27, F43, F44–F45. ⇨ *Also under specific areas*
*price categories,* F43, 2, 4, 102, 137, 172, 200, 250, 288
Hoyt Arboretum, 77
Hult Center for the Performing Arts, 235–236, 241
Humbug Mountain State Park, 51
Hutson Museum, 148

**I**

Ice hockey, 121
Ice skating, 120, 213
Imago Theatre, 117
Imnaha River, 307
Indian Beach, 14
Inn £ Northrup Station ▦, 108
International Pinot Noir Celebration, 218
International Rose Test Garden, 68, 77, 79
Ira Keller Fountain, 67

**J**

Jackson Bottom Wetlands Preserve, 206
Jackson F. Kimball State Park, 261
Jacksonville, 264–268
Jacksonville Cemetery, F29, 265–266
Jacksonville Inn ▦, 266
Jacksonville Museum, 265
Japanese Garden, F30, 77, 79
Japanese-American Historical Plaza, 71, 72
Jason Lee House, 225
Jean Vollum Natural Capital Center, 71, 72
Jefferson County Museum, 178
Jogging, 241
John D. Boon Home, 225
John Day, 314, 316
John Day Fossil Beds National Monument, F30, 316
John Inskeep Environmental Learning Center, 211
Joseph, 303–306
Joseph Bergman House, 75
Joseph H. Stewart State Park, 262
Josephson's, 6, 10
Justice Center, 64, 67

**K**

Kah-Nee-Ta Resort and Casino, 174
Kam Wah Chung & Co. Museum, 316

Kayaking, *10, 19, 50, 205*
KC's Espresso & Deli ✕, *160*
Keiko (whale), *30*
Keller Auditorium, *63, 67, 117*
Kerbyville Museum, *277–278*
Kiger Gorge, *323*
Kiger Mustang Lookout, *322*
King Estate Winery, *238*
Kiteboarding, *139*
Klamath Basin Audubon
   Society, *262*
Klamath Basin National
   Wildlife Refuge, *262*
Klamath County Museum, *260*
Klamath Falls, *259–262*
Kla-Mo-Ya Casino, *260*
Knight Library, *236*
KOIN Center, *63, 67*

**L**

La Garza Cellars, *279*
La Grande, *299–301*
La Serre ✕, *F28, 38*
Ladybug Theater, *82*
Lake County Museum, *325*
Lakecliff Bed & Breakfast ⌂,
   *150*
Lakeview, *324–326*
Lane County Historical
   Museum, *236*
Lara House Bed & Breakfast
   Inn ⌂, *F27, 191*
Lake Oswego, *209–210*
Lake Owyhee State Park, *313*
Latimer Quilt and Textile
   Center, *20*
Laurel Ridge Winery, *202*
Laurelhurst Park, *80*
Lava Butte and Lava River
   Cave, *185, 187*
LaVelle Vineyards, *238*
Lewis & Clark College, *71*
Lighthouses
   *Oregon Coast, 22, 29, 32, 36,
   40, 44, 46, 48, 50*
Lincoln City, *23–26*
Lincoln County Historical
   Society Museums, *31*
Linfield College, *218*
Linn County Historical
   Museum, *231–232*
Lion and the Rose ⌂, *F27,
   106*
Lithia Park, *268*
Llamas, *308*
Loeb State Park, *54*
Log Cabin Inn ⌂, *233*
Lost Lake, *149*
Lower Klamath National
   Wildlife Refuge, *260*

**M**

MacMaster House ⌂, *108*
Main City Park (Gresham),
   *138*
Malheur National Forest, *319*
Malheur National Wildlife
   Refuge, *321*

Manzanita, *18*
Marine Discovery Tours, *31*
Marine Gardens, *29*
Mariner Square, *31*
Marion County Historical
   Society Museum, *225*
Mark O. Hatfield U.S.
   Courthouse, *63, 67*
Mary Smith House, *75*
Maryhill Museum of Art, *165*
Mattey House Bed & Breakfast
   ⌂, *F27, 220–221*
Maude Kerns Art Center, *236*
Maxwell Siding Railroad
   Display, *290*
Mayer State Park, *152*
Mazatlan Mexican Restaurant
   ✕, *206–207*
McKay Creek National Wildlife
   Refuge, *295*
McKenzie Bridge, *232–233*
McKenzie Pass, *234*
McKenzie River, *233*
McKenzie River Highway, *233*
McKenzie River National
   Recreation Trail, *233*
McLoughlin House National
   Historic Site, *211*
McMenamins Edgefield ⌂,
   *F27, 141*
McMenamins Kennedy School
   ⌂, *107*
McMinnville, *F27, 217–221*
McNary Lock and Dam, *289*
Meal plan abbreviations, *F7,
   F43*
Medford, *F27, 262–264*
Melrose Vineyards, *279–280*
Memorial Coliseum, *117*
Merenda ✕, *F28, 188–189*
Metal foundries, *303*
Methodist Parsonage, *225*
Metolius Recreation Area,
   *F30, 162–164*
Metolius River Resort ⌂,
   *F26, 164–165*
Millennium Plaza Park, *209*
Mills End Park, *70*
Milo McIver State Park, *212*
Mission Mill Village, *224, 225*
Mitchell, *317–318*
Monastery, *225*
Montage ✕, *F28, 95*
Monteith House Museum, *228*
Montinore Estate (vineyards),
   *202*
Monuments, *185, 187,
   277–278, 316*
Mount Angel Abbey, *225*
Mount Ashland Inn ⌂, *271*
Mount Ashland Ski Area, *268*
Mount Bachelor Ski Area, *185,
   187, 192–193*
Mount Hood, *F26, 153–155*
Mount Hood National Forest,
   *154*
Mount Hood Scenic Railroad
   and Dinner Train, *148–149*

Mount Tabor Park, *79, 80*
Moyer House, *232*
Mugg Estuarine Park, *23*
Multnomah Falls, *143*
Multnomah Falls Lodge ✕,
   *F28, 143*
Museum of the Oregon
   Territory, *211–212*
Museum of Warm Springs,
   *F29, 172*
Museums, *F29*
   *Central Oregon, 172, 178, 180,
   185, 186*
   *Columbia River Gorge and
   Oregon Cascades, 138, 148,
   149, 152, 159, 165*
   *Eastern Oregon, 293, 300, 303,
   309, 313, 316, 325*
   *Oregon Coast, 6, 20, 31, 42,
   45, 48, 52, 54*
   *Portland, 63, 67, 69, 71, 72,
   73, 77, 79, 82–83*
   *Southern Oregon, 260, 261,
   262, 265, 268, 274,
   277–278, 279*
   *Willamette Valley/Wine
   Country, 205, 206 211–212,
   216, 222, 225, 228, 229,
   231–232, 236, 242*
Music, *114–115*

**N**

Nathan Loeb House, *75*
National Historic Oregon Trail
   Interpretive Center, *309*
National parks
   *Southern Oregon, F29–F30,
   250, 252–255, 257–259*
Nature Conservancy Cascade
   Head Trail, *22–23*
Naval Air Station Museum, *20*
Neahkahnie Mountain, *14, 16*
Nehalem Bay Winery, *18*
Neptune State Park, *37*
Newberg, *213–214*
Newberry Volcanic National
   Monument, *185, 187*
Newell House Museum, *216*
Newmark Theater, *70*
Newport, *30–36*
Newport Belle Bed & Breakfast
   ⌂, *F26, 33*
Nicholas' Restaurant, *97*
Nick's Italian Cafe ✕, *219*
NikeTown, *64, 67*
North Bend, *45*
North Clackomas Aquatic
   Park, *80, 82*
Northwest Alpacas Ranch, *82*
Nude sunbathing, *120*
Nye Beach, *30*

**O**

Oak Knoll Winery, *206*
Oaks Amusement Park, *80, 82*
Ochoco National Forest,
   *182–184*

Ochoco Viewpoint, *180*
Old Aurora Colony, *217*
Old Aurora Colony Museum, *222*
Old Church, *63, 69*
Old Perpetual, *324–325*
Old St. Peter's Landmark, *152*
Ona Beach State Park, *31*
Oneonta Gorge, *143*
Ontario, *313–314*
Ontario State Park, *313*
Opera, *115, 241*
Oregon Ballet Theatre, *116*
Oregon Capitol, *224, 225*
Oregon Caves National Monument, *277–278*
Oregon Children's Theatre, *117*
Oregon City, *210–213*
Oregon Coast Aquarium, *30*
Oregon Dunes National Recreation Area, *41, 44*
Oregon Garden, *222*
Oregon History Center, *63, 69*
Oregon Islands National Wildlife Refuge, *46*
Oregon Maritime Center and Museum, *71, 72*
Oregon Museum of Science and Industry, *79, 82–83*
Oregon Puppet Theater, *117*
Oregon Shakespeare Festival, *268, 269, 273*
Oregon State University, *229*
Oregon Symphony, *115*
Oregon Trail, *211, 151, 291, 309, 320*
Oregon Trail Regional Museum, *309*
Oregon Vortex Location of the House of Mystery, *265*
Oregon Wine Tasting Room and the Bellevue Market, *218*
Oregon Zoo, *77, 79*
Oregon's International Museum of Carousel Art, *149*
Osborn Aquatic Center, *229*
Oswald West State Park, *17–18*
Otter Crest Loop, *29*
Out N' About ⚑, *F27, 278*
Outpost Pizza, Pub, and Grill, The ✕, *316*

**P**

Pacific City, *22–23*
Pacific Crest Trail, *146, 154*
Pacific University, *201*
Painted Hills, *318*
Paisley, *325*
Paley's Place ✕, *F28, 93*
Palisades, *318*
Pambiche ✕, *96*
Panini Bakery ✕, *F29, 33*
Panther Creek Cellars, *218–219*

Parker House ⚑, *F27, 297*
**Parks**
*Central Oregon, 186*
*Gresham, 138*
*national parks, F29–F30, F45–F46, 250, 252–255,257–259*
*Oregon Coast, 27, 54*
*Portland, 65, 67, 70, 77, 79, 80*
*Southern Oregon, 260, 268*
*Willamette Valley/Wine Country, 202, 206, 208, 209, 229, 234–235, 236*
**Pass Creek Covered Bridge**, *244*
Pendleton, *293, 295–299*
Pendleton Round-Up, *291, 293, 298*
Pendleton Woolen Mills, *295*
*Peter Iredale* (ship), *6*
Peter Skene Ogden Wayside, *181*
Petersen's Rock Gardens, *181*
Pettygrove House, *74, 76*
PGE Park, *117*
Phone Company ✕, *310*
Piety Knob, *162*
Pine Mountain Observatory, *185, 187*
Pine Ridge Inn ⚑, *190*
Pine Valley Lodge ⚑, *F27, 308*
Pioneer Courthouse, *69*
Pioneer Courthouse Square, *63, 69*
Pioneer Mother's memorial Log Cabin, *216*
Pioneer Museum, *20*
Pittock Mansion, *77, 79*
Planetarium, *236*
Police Museum, *67*
Ponzi Vineyards, *208*
Port Orford, *51*
Portland Art Museum, *63, 69*
Portland Arts Festival, *68*
Portland Audubon Society, *77*
Portland Baroque Orchestra, *115*
Portland Building, *64, 69–70*
Portland Center for the Performing Arts, *63, 70, 117*
Portland Center Stage, *117*
Portland Classical Chinese Garden, *F30, 71, 73*
Portland Institute for Contemporary Art, *71, 73*
Portland International Airport, *109, 111*
Portland Opera, *115*
Portland Saturday Market, *F30, 71, 73, 121*
Portland State University, *63, 70*
Portland's White House ⚑, *105–106*
Powell's City of Books, *F30, 71, 73*

Prehistoric Gardens, *51*
**Price categories**
*hotels, F43, 2, 4, 102, 137, 172, 200, 250, 288*
*restaurants, F40, 2, 4, 83, 137, 172, 200, 250, 288*
Prineville, *179–181*
Prineville Reservoir State Park, *180*

**R**

Rafting
*Central Oregon, 179, 195*
*Eastern Oregon, 301, 305–306, 308*
*Southern Oregon, 277*
*Willamette Valley/Wine Country, 233*
Railroads, *148–149*
Raphael's ✕, *F28, 296*
Raptor Ridge (winery), *206*
Red Agave ✕, *F28, 238*
Redhawk Vineyard, *226*
Redmond, *181-182*
Reedsport, *43–44*
Research reserve, *46–47*
**Restaurants**, *F27–F29, F40.*
⇨ *Also under specific areas*
*price categories, F40, 2, 4, 83, 137, 172, 200, 250, 288*
Rex Hill Vineyards, *214*
Rice Northwest Museum of Rocks and Minerals, *206*
Richardson's Recreational Ranch, *178*
Rim Drive (Crater Lake National Park), *253*
Ripley's Believe It or Not, *31*
Robert Straub State Park, *22*
Rockaway Beach, *19*
Rockhounding, *184, 321*
Rodeo, *292, 293, 298*
Rogue River, *52, 255, 280*
Rogue River National Forest, *263*
Rood Bridge Park, *206*
Rooster Rock State Park, *141*
Rose Farm, *211*
Rose Festival, *68*
Rose Festival Airshow, *68*
Rose Garden Arena, *117*
Roseburg, *278-280*
Roseland Theater, *117*
Ross Ragland Theater, *261*
Round Barn, *321*
Round-Up Hall of Fame Museum, *293*
Row River Trail, *243*

**S**

Saddle Mountain State Park, *12*
St. Innocent Winery, *226*
Salem, *223–228*
Salishan, *26*

Salmon Street Fountain, 63, 67
Samuel H. Boardman State Park, 53
Sauvie Island, 120
Schminck Memorial Museum, 325
Schneider Museum of Art, 268
Schreiner's Iris Gardens, 226
Science Factory, 234, 236
Scoggin Valley Park and Henry Hagg Lake, 202
Sea Gulch, 31
Sea Lion Caves, 40
Seaside, 11–14
Seaside Aquarium, 12
Secret House Vineyards, 238
Sellwood District, 80, 83
Senator George Baldwin Hotel Museum, 261
Shadywood Park, 206
Shafer Vineyard Cellars, 202
Shanghai Tunnels, 110
Sheep Rock, 317
Shopping
Central Oregon, 179, 193
Columbia River Gorge & Oregon Cascades, 140, 141, 143, 148, 151, 153, 158
Eastern Oregon, 292, 298–299, 301, 306, 317
Oregon Coast, 10–11, 14, 17, 26, 27, 29, 35, 39, 43, 50
Portland, 121–126
Southern Oregon, 259, 264, 267–268, 274
Willamette Valley/Wine Country, 205, 207, 213, 221, 229, 231, 242, 243
Shore Acres State Park, 46
Siltcoos River Canoe Trail, F30, 42
Silvan Ridge/Hinman Vineyards, 238
Silver Falls State Park, 48, 223
Silverton, 222–223
Siskiyou National Forest, 275
Sisters, 193–195
Siuslaw National Forest, 230
Siuslaw Pioneer Museum, 42
Skidmore Fountain, 71, 73–74
Skiing
Central Oregon, 184, 187, 192–193
Columbia River Gorge and Oregon Cascade, 155, 156–157, 164
Eastern Oregon, 309
Portland, 120
Southern Oregon, 258, 268, 274
Willamette Valley/Wine Country, 242
Skinner Butte Park, 234, 236
Smith Rock State Park, F31, 181
Snake River, 306, 307

Snowmobiling, 259
Sokol Blosser (winery), 215
South Beach State Park, 32
South Slough National Estuarine Research Reserve, 46–47
Southern Oregon History Center, 263
Spencer Butte, 236
Spout Springs, 296
Spouting Horn, 28
Sprague Community Theater, 48–49
Spruce Goose (flying boat), 217
Stang Manor Bed and Breakfast ⌸, 300
Stark Raving Theatre, 117
Starlight Parade, 68
State of Oregon Sports Hall of Fame, 63, 70
State parks
Central Oregon, 178, 180, 181
Columbia River Gorge and Oregon Cascades, 140, 141, 152, 165–166
Eastern Oregon, 289, 296, 310, 313
Oregon Coast, 12, 14, 17–18, 22, 24, 28, 31, 32, 37, 39, 40, 41, 44, 46, 47, 48, 50–51, 52, 53, 54, 55
Southern Oregon, 260, 261, 262, 263, 275
Willamette Valley/Wine Country, 212, 216–217, 223, 225–226
Steamboat Inn, The ⌸, F2, 280
Steens Mountain, 322–323
Stephanie Inn ⌸, 15
Stevens Crawford Heritage House, 211
Stevenson, Washington, 146–148
Stone Wolf Vineyards, 219
Strawberry Hill State Park, 39
Summer sports, 157
Summit Grill and Alpine Patio ✕, F29, 304
Sumpter Valley Railway, 310
Sunriver Resort ⌸, F26, 190
Sunset Bay State Park, 46, 47
Surfing, 14, 16, 35
Suttle Lake Resort and Marina ⌸, 163
Sweet Home, 232
Swimming and sunbathing, 120, 259
Symbols, F7

**T**

Tamastslikt Cultural Institute, 295
Temple Beth Israel, 74, 76
Tennis, 120
Terminal Gravity Brew Pub ✕, 302

Terry Schrunk Plaza, 64, 70
Theater, 24, 34–35, 48–49, 70, 82, 117, 140, 213, 225, 227, 261, 262
Theatre West, 24
Thomas Kay Woolen Mill Museum, 225
Three Capes Loop, 21–22
Three Doors Down, 96–97
Tillamook, 19–21
Tillamook Bay, 18
Tillamook County Creamery, 20
Tillamook Head, 14
Tillamook Naval Air Station Museum, 20
Tillamook Rock Light Station, 14
Timberline Lodge ⌸, F26, 154–155
Timberline Lodge Ski Area, 155
Tina's ✕, F27, 215
Torii Mor (winery), 215
Tou Velle State Park, 263
Trevett-Nunn House, 74, 76
Trolley cars, 63, 67
Troutdale, 140–141, 143
Tualatin Estate Vineyards, 202
Tualatin Hills Nature Park, 208
Tu Tu' Tun Lodge ⌸, F26, 53
Turtles Bar & Grill ✕, F28, 239
Tyree Wine Cellars, 230

**U**

U.S. Bank, 309
Ukiah-Dale Forest State Park, 296
Umatilla, 288–290
Umatilla County Historical Society Museum, 293
Umatilla Indian Reservation, 295
Umatilla Marina Park, 289
Umatilla National Forest, 296
Umatilla National Wildlife Refuge, 289
Umpqua Discovery Center, 43
Umpqua Lighthouse Park, 44
Umpqua River Lighthouse, 44
Under the Greenwood Tree ⌸, F27, 263
Underground, The, F29, 293
Undersea Gardens, 31
Union County Museum, 300
Union Hotel ⌸, F27, 300, 301
Union Station, 71, 74
Unity Lake State Park, 310
University of Oregon, 236
University of Oregon Museum of Art, 236
University of Oregon Museum of Natural History, 236
Uppertown Firefighters Museum, 6

USS *Blueback* (submarine), 82

USS *Rasher* (submarine), 5

**V**

Valley Bronze of Oregon, 303
Valley of the Rogue State Park, F30, 275
Valley River Inn 🔲 , F26, 239–240
Valley View Vineyard, 265
Vista House, 140–141

**W**

Waldo Lake, 242
Waldport, 36–37
Waller Hall, 226
Wallowa County Museum, 303
Wallowa Lake, 303
Wallowa Lake State Recreation Park, 303–304
Wallowa Lake Tramway, 304
Wallowa Mountain Loop, 306
Wallowa Mountains, 299.
Wallowa-Whitman National Forest, 310
Warm Springs, 172, 174–175
Wasco County Courthouse, 152
Wasson Brothers Winery, 212
Water sports, 26, 151, 162
Waterfalls, 48, 139, 143, 212, 223

Wax Works, 31
Web sites, F50
Welches, 157–158
West Coast Game Park, 49
West Valley Veterans Memorial, 221
*Westward Ho!* Sternwheeler, 42
Whales, 28, 29, 30, 31, 40
Whispering Spruce Trail, 40
Wild and Scenic Snake River Corridor, 307
Wildlife refuges, 46, 120, 260, 262, 289, 295, 321, 324
Wildlife Safari, 279
Willakenzie Estate, 215
Willamette Falls Locks, 212
Willamette Mission State Park, 225–226
Willamette Shore Trolley, 210
Willamette University, 224, 226
William M. Tugman State Park, 44
Winchester Bay's Salmon Harbor, 44
Windsurfing, 139, 152
Winema National Forest, 261
Wineries
  *Columbia River Gorge & Oregon Cascades, 149*
  *Oregon Coast, 18*

*Southern Oregon, 255, 265, 277, 279–280*
*Willamette Valley/Wine Country, 200, 202, 203, 206, 208, 212, 214, 215, 218–219, 226, 230, 238, 242*
*wine tasting, 279*
Winston, 279
Wizard Island, 253
World Champion Cypress Tree, 54
World Trade Center, 63, 70

**Y**

Yachats, F28, 37–39
Yachats Ocean Road State Recreation Area, 38
Yamhill, F26, 214–216
Yamhill National Historic District, 63, 70
Yamhill Valley Vineyards, 219
Yaquina Bay Bridge, 30
Yaquina Bay Lighthouse, 29
Yaquina Bay State Park, 32
Yaquina Head, 29
Yaquina Head Lighthouse, 32
Yaquina Head Natural Outstanding Area, F31, 32

**Z**

Zigzag, 157–158
Zoo, 77, 79

# NOTES

# NOTES

# NOTES

# NOTES

# FODOR'S KEY TO THE GUIDES

America's guidebook leader publishes guides for every kind of traveler.
Check out our many series and find your perfect match.

### FODOR'S GOLD GUIDES

America's favorite travel-guide series offers the most detailed insider reviews of hotels, restaurants, and attractions in all price ranges, plus great background information, smart tips, and useful maps.

### COMPASS AMERICAN GUIDES

Stunning guides from top local writers and photographers, with gorgeous photos, literary excerpts, and colorful anecdotes. A must-have for culture mavens, history buffs, and new residents.

### FODOR'S CITYPACKS

Concise city coverage in a guide plus a foldout map. The right choice for urban travelers who want everything under one cover.

### FODOR'S EXPLORING GUIDES

Hundreds of color photos bring your destination to life. Lively stories lend insight into the culture, history, and people.

### FODOR'S TRAVEL HISTORIC AMERICA

For travelers who want to experience history firsthand, this series gives in-depth coverage of historic sights, plus nearby restaurants and hotels. Themes include the Thirteen Colonies, the Old West, and the Lewis and Clark Trail.

### FODOR'S POCKET GUIDES

For travelers who need only the essentials. The best of Fodor's in pocket-size packages for just $9.95.

### FODOR'S FLASHMAPS

Every resident's map guide, with dozens of easy-to-follow maps of public transit, restaurants, shopping, museums, and more.

### FODOR'S CITYGUIDES

Sourcebooks for living in the city: thousands of in-the-know listings for restaurants, shops, sports, nightlife, and other city resources.

### FODOR'S AROUND THE CITY WITH KIDS

Up to 68 great ideas for family days, recommended by resident parents. Perfect for exploring in your own backyard or on the road.

### FODOR'S HOW TO GUIDES

Get tips from the pros on planning the perfect trip. Learn how to pack, fly hassle-free, plan a honeymoon or cruise, stay healthy on the road, and travel with your baby.

### FODOR'S LANGUAGES FOR TRAVELERS

Practice the local language before you hit the road. Available in phrase books, cassette sets, and CD sets.

### KAREN BROWN'S GUIDES

Engaging guides—many with easy-to-follow inn-to-inn itineraries—to the most charming inns and B&Bs in the U.S.A. and Europe.

### BAEDEKER'S GUIDES

Comprehensive guides, trusted since 1829, packed with A–Z reviews and star ratings.

### OTHER GREAT TITLES FROM FODOR'S

Baseball Vacations, The Complete Guide to the National Parks, Family Vacations, Golf Digest's Places to Play, Great American Drives of the East, Great American Drives of the West, Great American Vacations, Healthy Escapes, National Parks of the West, Skiing USA.